Arthur Quiller-Couch

The Cornish Magazine

Volume I.

Arthur Quiller-Couch

The Cornish Magazine
Volume I.

ISBN/EAN: 9783741132292

Manufactured in Europe, USA, Canada, Australia, Japa

Cover: Foto ©Andreas Hilbeck / pixelio.de

Manufactured and distributed by brebook publishing software (www.brebook.com)

Arthur Quiller-Couch

The Cornish Magazine

THE

CORNISH MAGAZINE

Edited by

A. T. QUILLER-COUCH

('Q.')

Vol. I.

JULY to DECEMBER 1898

Truro
JOSEPH POLLARD
London: SERVICE & PATON, 5 Henrietta Street

PILCHARDS
(From the picture by C. NAPIER HEMY, A.R.A.)

THE CORNISH MAGAZINE

JULY 1898

TRURO CATHEDRAL

I. ITS HISTORY

THAT Cornwall of our day has once more its own bishopric; that the union of the old diocese with the Devonian See at Crediton in 1027, transferred to Exeter by Edward the Confessor in 1046, has after 800 years been severed, is due to the enthusiasm, patience, and perseverance of a few earnest men. The labours of Archdeacon Hobhouse, Prebendary Tatham, and Mr. Edmund Carlyon of St. Austell, the far-seeing policy of Bishop Phillpotts, the generous co-operation of Bishop Temple, and the splendid munificence of Lady Rolle, made what was once regarded with some contempt as the dream of a few ecclesiastical pedants a practical reality. That in a remote peninsula of England, in a county greatly impoverished by mining depression, and depleted largely by emigration, a really noble cathedral should have been planned and to a considerable extent built, richly furnished, and partially endowed, is due mainly to the lofty conception, sanguine initiative, and zealous action of the first bishop of the revived Cornish bishopric, Edward White Benson. The choice of Truro as the See city made, in his mind, the building of a cathedral almost a necessity. The noble church of St. Germans, once apparently the See of a Cornish bishop, Burhwold, in 1018, lay too far away at the eastern extremity of the diocese. The large and dignified church of St. Petroc at Bodmin, though never in any exact sense a cathedral, was, perhaps, at times used as such during the days of the West-Saxon bishops of Cornwall, and would not have been unworthy of the honour of being selected as the mother-church of the newly formed diocese. But when the question was finally settled in favour of Truro, and the old parish church of that town dignified with the title of cathedral, the newly consecrated Bishop, very soon after his enthronement within its walls, gave his mind to the scheme of erecting a building that should take its place alongside the ancient mother-churches of the land, and be not altogether unworthy of comparison with them. Bishop Benson was consecrated on St. Mark's Day, April 25, 1877, and at his first diocesan conference, in October of the same year, a committee was appointed to consider the project of a cathedral at Truro. In April 1878 a county meeting was held under the presidency of the Lord Lieutenant, the Earl of Mount Edgcumbe, who has been from the first a generous contributor, and a most courteous and businesslike Chairman of the Building Committee. He was supported by a number of zealous laymen and clergymen of Cornwall, many of whom survive, who devoted not only considerable sums of money, but many hours taken out of busy lives, to carry out the great scheme of building the cathedral. To some the enlargement of St. Mary's Church or the erection of an entirely new building of very modest proportions, not much beyond those of a large parish church, appeared sufficient for the needs of Cornwall. But Dr. Benson pleaded for a real cathedral, embodying in visible shape the great ideals which he had learned to value when Chancellor of Lincoln, and which he expressed at length in his admirable work, 'The Cathedral.' Finally, this idea won the day; most happily, as all those think who rejoice over the erection in the nineteenth century of the first cathedral of the Church of England founded and built not only since the Reformation, but for some centuries previously.

The site of the new cathedral was determined mainly by the fact that St. Mary's Church was named as the cathedral church in the Act of Parliament constituting the See. By some an entirely new building on some lofty spot in the outskirts of the city, visible far and wide, was suggested. Against this, among other difficulties, was objected the creation of a new ecclesiastical centre in addition to the already numerous parish churches of Truro. It was, indeed, thought inexpedient by many to plant a splendid architectural pile low down in the city, with little space round it, with houses and clustering shops to it. But, on the other hand, the desirability of identifying the cathedral with the old ecclesiastical centre of Truro, of linking it with the many associations and historic memories of a most ancient municipality and parish, prevailed. On the whole, this cannot be regretted. The narrow streets and lanes by which the cathedral is approached remind those who visit it of many an old French town with its ancient minster hemmed in by humble dwellings in the heart of the population, close by its market, townhall, and other daily resorts of the inhabitants. What was wanted was not a show-place for visitors with a pleasant, trim environment, but a mother-church and working ecclesiastical centre. The agreeable 'amenities' (as a Scotch gardener would say) of a cathedral close with the peaceful retirement of a deanery and its garden, quiet canonical residences and the like, are necessarily wanting under existing circumstances, or at least indefinitely postponed. But, on the other hand, it is a real advantage that Truro Cathedral is not altogether new. It has incorporated into itself a substantial portion of the old parish church, and retains much of the ancient associations of the past; it stands in the old 'High Cross,' and is reached through the old 'Church Lane.' Underneath its crypt and nave lie the buried remains of many a citizen and worthy of olden times: their monuments are preserved and their history not altogether forgotten. Those who worship in the old parish aisle, and even in the new cathedral, are kneeling on the ground consecrated by at least six centuries of prayer and praise.

The old church contained some interesting monuments, among them a

Photo by   *Argall, Truro*
OLD ST. MARY'S CHURCH

fine Renaissance tomb to John Robarts and his wife, of the year 1614. This had been fairly well preserved, but had suffered from the figures being periodically 'black-leaded,' as the most effective way of cleaning them according to the notions of the officials of the last century. There was also a group of memorials to the Vivian family, including the first Lord Vivian, better known in history as Sir Hussey Vivian, cavalry commander at Waterloo. A former rector named Phippen, or Fitzpen, who suffered for his principles in the days of the Commonwealth, is commemorated by a brass, and his brother by a tombstone relating his marvellous escape from captivity on board a Turkish galley, which he succeeded in capturing by aid of his fellow-prisoners and bringing into a Spanish port as a prize worth 6,000*l*. Some fragments of stained glass coeval with the building which was erected in 1518, on a site where two earlier churches had successively stood—a fine specimen of the carved wagon-roof so usual in Cornwall, long hidden by a plaster ceiling, a sweet-toned organ once belonging to one of the royal chapels, a quaint inlaid wooden pulpit, and some later stained windows of unequal merit—make up the principal details of what was a typical Cornish parish church. They have been carefully retained, the principal monuments, after judicious and conservative repair, being placed in the north transept of the cathedral.

In the autumn of 1880 the old church was, with the exception of the south aisle, pulled down. The north side of the building and the western tower were not of sufficient age, beauty, or interest, to secure them from demolition; but the portion that has been preserved, with its external carving similar to that which can be seen at St. Austell, St. Mary Magdalene, Launceston, and elsewhere, not only gives an element of antiquity to the new building, but has proved, under the skilful treatment of Mr. Pearson, an occasion for adding special architectural beauty to the internal arrangements of the aisles. After the choice of the site had been decided, and the architect, Mr. J. L. Pearson, R.A., selected, in August 1878, preparations were made for laying the foundations of the building. This took place on May 20, 1880, and was a day much to be remembered by Cornish Churchmen. The Duke of Cornwall, Albert Edward, Prince of Wales, the Princess of Wales, and their two young sons, Albert Victor and George, attended the ceremony. Two foundation stones were laid by the Prince with full masonic ceremonies, one at the north-east corner of the choir and another in the nave. The grand officers of England and the provincial officers of Cornwall assisted. Among those present were Sir F. Truscott, Lord Mayor of London, a son of Truro Lord Falmouth, and a vast concourse of men and women of all ranks and stations. The Bishops of Exeter (Dr. Temple) and of Madagascar (Dr. Kestell-Cornish, a native of Kenwyn) stood by the Bishop of the diocese, his honorary canons and a great body of the clergy; while a choir, gathered from various parts of Cornwall, chanted the Psalms and Hymns.

From that day forward the work proceeded steadily. A large sum, 10,000*l*., had to be expended in the purchase of the site and the adjacent property, and the foundations were necessarily deeply laid and costly. But Cornish men and women were generous and energetic, and funds were not slow in coming in. The parishioners of St. Mary's had gathered between 3,000*l*. and 4,000*l*. for the restoration of their parish church, and readily consented to the money being applied to the common building fund. The rector, who was also patron, Canon Fox Harvey, now Vicar of Probus, generously placed the advowson of the rectory in the hands of the Bishop, and thus materially aided the ecclesiastical changes rendered necessary. In 1883 Dr. Benson was translated to the Primacy, and his removal might well have been regarded as a serious check to the fulfilment of his great scheme. But it was not so. The Committee had hitherto limited their hopes of building to the completion of the choir only, including the union of the old south aisle of the parish church. The departure of Bishop Benson was made the occasion of commemorating his six years' episcopate by the erection of the south transept, which will go down to posterity as the 'Benson Transept.' It has been still further identified with his name by the gift of the tracery of the rose window by the masters and scholars of Wellington College, of which he was the first headmaster, by the bequest of his episcopal staff, recently placed in a niche therein, and by a brass commemorating deceased members of his family. The building of the south transept led to the undertaking of the

Photo by   *Ellery, Truro*
THE CHOIR, TRURO CATHEDRAL

erection of the north transept, of the first stage of the central tower, the lower portion of two bays of the nave, and of the clock tower. In addition to these features, the Baptistery (by some considered the gem of the whole building) was built as a memorial to Henry Martyn, a son of Truro, the distinguished senior wrangler, devoted missionary, and learned linguist, who died in Armenia in 1812. Canon Phillpotts, of Porthgwidden, generously gave the beautiful south porch, by some critics considered too ornate for the severity of the style of architecture adopted for the cathedral, but justified as serving to harmonise the more florid portion of the old perpendicular south aisle with the new early English building. Advantage was taken of the slope of the ground to build a crypt under the lofty choir. The space thus gained has been admirably utilised for providing a chapter room, and vestries for the bishop, the canons, and the choir. The principal features of the building are its adequate height, its fine groined roof, and the absence of a too exact and mechanical symmetry in its parts and details. A great variety of mouldings, inequality of span of arches, and other designed departures from uniformity, relieve the building from a hard and dull monotony. Cornish materials have been largely used in the building. The walls are externally of the hard grey St. Mabe granite, internally of St. Stephen's china-claystone, a species of soft granite. The dressings are of Bath stone, but the detached shafts of grey Polyphant from East Cornwall. The Lizard has supplied serpentine of various shades of colour for a considerable part of the steps to the choir and baptistery, as well as of the shafts of the arcading of the latter-named portion of the building. Cornish copper has been employed for the roofing of the spire of the clock tower; and, had not the cost been too great, would have been used for the other roofs as well. It is acknowledged on all sides that the architect has succeeded in his efforts to build a real cathedral; that not only from an artistic point of view has he produced a beautiful specimen of Gothic architecture of the purest style, but that his creation has a peculiar power to impress those who enter it with feelings of reverence as well as admiration.

Great statesmen like Mr. Gladstone and Mr. W. H. Smith, who visited the cathedral about eight years ago, bishops from all parts of the world, eminent Nonconformist leaders, Roman Catholic dignitaries, and thousands of other visitors, have borne their testimony to the beauty and dignity of the building even in its present unfinished state.

In 1884 the second Bishop of Truro, Dr. G. H. Wilkinson, formerly Vicar of St. Peter's, Eaton Square, set on foot a movement only second in importance to that of his predecessor. This was the raising of a fund to provide suitable ornaments and furniture for the new cathedral. By a happy inspiration, he called into existence the 'Association of Cornish Women,' who in an incredibly short time raised 16,000*l.* to provide internal fittings. The twelve rural deaneries were thoroughly organised under the leadership of Mrs. Arthur Tremayne, of Carclew, and each undertook to provide some important feature or ornament, as the stalls, reredos, organ, stained glass, marble pavement, and the like. The result was that few cathedrals can vie with Truro for the costly and artistic altar-plate, richly worked frontals, and other splendid ornaments possessed by it. The throne was the gift of clergymen ordained by Bishop Phillpotts, the costly and elaborately carved reredos by 'faithful men and women' of the Deanery of Powder. Chairs were provided by the energy and self-denial of a pious Cornishwoman of Truro, the font by the Sunday-school children of the diocese. The design of every ornament was carefully superintended by the architect, and all incongruity thereby avoided.

The erection of the choir and other portions of the building already completed required more than seven years, and on November 3, 1887, these were consecrated with great pomp and ceremony. The Prince of Wales once more came to his Duchy to take part in the ceremonies, and the building was thronged with about 2,700 persons. These were by no means all or mostly of the classes usually called 'privileged,' for special care was taken that working people, fishermen, and miners should be represented, and the humbler and poorer contributors towards the building and its ornaments occupied prominent seats as well as the more wealthy and highly placed persons of the county. The consecration ceremonies were conducted by the Bishop of the Diocese, Dr. G. H. Wilkinson, and the sermon was preached by the late Archbishop of Canterbury, who had the great satisfaction of seeing his ideal to some extent realised. Twenty other Bishops of England, Scotland, and the Colonies, including Bishop Harold Browne, of Winchester, formerly Vicar of Kenwyn, a vast number of clergy, a choir supplemented by representatives of many cathedral establishments, contributed to form a most impressive procession and a very solemn service. At the afternoon service the preacher was the present Archbishop of Canterbury, then Bishop of London, who, as Bishop of Exeter, had taken a leading part in the foundation of the Truro Bishopric. During the octave of the consecration, 2,300 members of choirs from all the Rural Deaneries of Cornwall, together with a large number of Church workers, came daily to take part in a great musical service. Altogether some 10,000 persons were present.

Each day some eminent preachers, among whom were Canon Mason, the first Diocesan Missioner of Cornwall, Bishop Wilberforce, of Newcastle, Canons Scott Holland and Gore, addressed these assemblies of Cornish Church people, miners, fishermen, agricultural labourers, from all parts of the Duchy; and there is not a village in Cornwall where, then or since, some of the men, women, lads, and girls have not seen their mother-church in all its beauty and learned to be proud of it. Annual gatherings of choirs, Sunday-school teachers, Temperance Societies, G. F. S. members and associates, assemble within its walls, and prove that it is to them something more than a mere ecclesiastical or architectural show-place. On these occasions surprising efforts are made by the more distant parishes to send up their representatives to the cathedral city. If choristers or Church workers from the rugged cliffs by Tintagel and the North coast, or the Land's End, or from the moorland parishes between Bodmin and Launceston, or the porths and coves of the Lizard district and South coast, or on the borderland of the Tamar banks, desire to take their place along with the miners of Redruth and Camborne, and the townsfolk of Falmouth and Penzance, in some great Church gathering, it involves often rising with the sun and returning home after midnight tired out with a long day's journey, but cheered and brightened by a great act of common worship and a joyous sense of fellowship. The cathedral, in fact, has in ten years become a real centre and rallying point for Cornish Church people. They have learned to realise more than ever their unity and strength, and the memories of old Cornish Churchmen have helped this. As they walk about its aisles they cannot fail to see that it is their own cathedral. They remember that the second Bishop of Truro has in his possession a book containing 23,000 of their names as contributors to the building and its contents, and that, though there were indeed some large and splendid gifts, yet the cathedral was built by the many, not the few. An inscription on a monument or on stained glass recalls to them that this deanery or that parish gave a screen or a window, a marble pavement or a canon's stall; that a Robartes, a Pole Carew, a Fortescue, a Bolitho, a Willyams, is here or there commemorated; that famous Cornishmen like John Couch Adams, of Laneast, the astronomer, or Henry Martyn the missionary, or Hussey Vivian the soldier, have their renown recorded within its walls. Indeed, the Cathedral already promises to become a kind of Westminster for the worthies of Cornwall of all times. Those who first planned it had some thought of this in their minds.

It was a statesmanlike stroke of policy, though the matter may appear trifling, to give historic and local associations to the Honorary Canons of the Cathedral, and link them with the names of ancient Saints. Ecclesiastical Commissioners and other officials seldom rise above the prosaic level of entitling cathedral stalls as 'Canonry number one,' 'number two,' &c. Bishop Benson added a touch of poetry and quaintness to his cathedral by affixing to the stalls the names of St. Piran, St. German, St. Germoc, and others. This example has since been followed at Wakefield and Newcastle, where the heroes of the ancient Northern Church are now commemorated on the Canons' seats. Dr. Benson also very rightly pressed for certain alterations in the proposed figures on the altar screens in the Sanctuary, by which are now recorded the names of the early Cornish bishops and missionaries, as Kenstec, St. Petroc, St. Buriena, and others. Moreover, in the elaborately planned scheme of subjects for the stained-glass windows illustrating the sacred history of the world under the Old and New Testaments and the fortunes of the Christian Church of all centuries, notable Cornish Saints and worthies are given a prominent position. Some of them, like St. Constantine, St. Winnow, and others, are already to be seen in the lancet windows of the Baptistery.

But perhaps the surest indication of the hold that the cathedral has upon the affections of Cornish people (and that includes not merely members of the Church of England) is that great sacrifices have been made not only to build but to maintain and continue it. To endow the bishopric 30,000*l*., in addition to the munificent donation by Lady Rolle of 40,000*l*., was collected. To build and furnish the present portion of the cathedral 118,000*l*. more was raised.

Very little endowment for the canons and officials, organist, choir, care of fabric, exists. Through the foresight of Bishop Phillpotts a fifth Exeter canonry, worth 1,000*l*. a year, was reserved at the time when under the Cathedral Act of 1840 almost all cathedral establishments were restricted to four residentiary stalls, and this endowment was afterwards transferred to Truro, and provides a modest income for two residentiary canons of 400*l*. a year each and 200*l*. for the maintenance of the fabric and services. The noble bequest of Miss Pedler, of Liskeard, of 15,000*l*., and smaller sums left by Miss Field and others, enable the choir and services to be maintained in part, but it would be impossible to sustain all the heavy expenses of the care of the fabric and of Divine Service if it were not for the generous help given by the diocese

TRURO CATHEDRAL, AS IT IS

generally. For ten years since the consecration of the cathedral, through the agency of the 'Cathedral Union' about 500*l*. a year, made up by subscriptions, donations, and collections in church, has been collected throughout Cornwall for the expenses of the mother-church. This is no insignificant token of the value placed upon the cathedral and its services by the Church people of the Duchy.

Perhaps the interest felt in the cathedral throughout the diocese is to some extent kept alive by the frequent visits of members of the Chapter to the outlying rural as well as the urban parishes. When Dr. Benson compiled the statutes for his new foundation, taking those of Lincoln for his model, he carefully laid down the principle that the officers of the cathedral had obligations to the diocese as well as to the central church. And so it happens that not only the Bishop, who is also Dean, is, as a matter of course, constantly moving about the diocese, but the other members of the residentiary and general Chapters, by visits, sermons, lectures, meetings, to say nothing of the parochial missions, retreats, quiet days conducted by the Canon Missioner and his assistants, carry, as it were, the cathedral into the diocese, and prove that its Chapter is not altogether an otiose and stagnant body living luxuriously in a cathedral close.

It may be said that in Truro Cathedral something of an experiment has been and is being attempted—namely, how to utilise the old-world institution of a cathedral for the modern needs of the Church. It is not to be supposed that so new and so slenderly equipped a capitular establishment as that of Truro can undertake to solve all or many of the difficult problems involved in this experiment. Time and enlarged endowments are required to deal successfully with them. But there are some signs at home and abroad that a little has been already achieved to encourage other dioceses in more wealthy parts of the country to follow where Dr. Benson led the way. In more than one of the other newly founded English bishoprics efforts after the revival of capitular and cathedral life are being made. In the United States and in the colonies Churchmen have looked to Truro for models of statutes, organisation, and services; and if in a small city in a sparsely populated county, with a people largely alienated in past years from the Church of England, it has been proved in any degree that a revived cathedral is not an anachronism, a mediæval toy or a costly mistake, no unimportant end has been gained by the founders and benefactors of Truro Cathedral.

The following words from Dr. Benson's sermon at the consecration service are worthy of remembrance: 'This beautiful work of God among us to-day—the first such founded and built these eight long centuries, founded and built for centuries to come, which has received so much love and grown to many as dear as if it were a living thing, and been prayed for daily, and in the realised fellowship of "Quiet Days," not for what it is, but for what it is to be, a pledge of growing unity, a seed of unity to come—have not blessings and answers to prayers been so abundant (we ask who know), ever since it began, that the most anxious and laborious cannot speak of even this early seedtime as a time of tears, as a time of anything but joy and vigour and visible growing; and still are we not sure that its harvests will in their season be hundredfold of the seed sown?'

But now, as visitors gaze at its truncated tower, the rough west wall, the half-built column standing on the site of the nave, the question is often asked, 'Will Truro Cathedral remain a fragment, like the glorious choir of Beauvais,

OLD ST. MARY'S AISLE

or wait like Cologne for centuries before it is finished, and its great architect's plans completely realised? The strenuous efforts of the last twenty-one years might seem, as is often said, sufficient for our time, and the completion of the whole design be left to a future generation. This was the case over and over again with our ancient cathedrals; why not so with Truro? There is much to be said for such a view, though it must not be forgotten that if the building of particular cathedrals and minsters was slow in the days of the Plantagenets, yet many were undertaken, if not completed, in an age when England was thinly populated, distracted by foreign and civil wars, infinitely poorer in material wealth than she is now, with no world-wide trade, colonies, and empire. It might fairly be brought as a reproach to the Church of England that, with so many wealthy sons and daughters, she failed, in this great century of progress and advancement in riches and power, to add even one cathedral to the many she has inherited from the 'ages of faith.' There is also a legitimate demand, frequently made, that the choral services of the cathedral should be held, not merely, as now, on Sundays and Festivals, but daily, as in almost all other cathedrals. To supply this defect requires a very considerable sum that can only be obtained by freewill offerings. And yet there are not wanting certain indications that the Cornish Cathedral will not have to wait so very long for its extension or completion.

During the nearly nine years that had passed from its consecration up to October 1896, more than 13,000*l.* had been given for the continuation of the building. This sum included the noble gift of 5,000*l*. by Canon Wise, and 1,500*l*., part of Miss Pedler's large bequest. When its founder, Archbishop Benson, was called away so suddenly in October 1896, a great meeting in London, summoned to commemorate his life and work, indicated the completion of at least part of Truro Cathedral as his most fitting monument, after some special memorial had been provided for at Canterbury. This meeting, though its immediate financial results were not as large as many hoped, stirred up, invited, and compelled Cornish Churchmen to a fresh effort. A hearty response has been made, and up to the present time 27,000*l*. in all has been given or promised. The old organisation of 'The Women of Cornwall' has been revived, and is working once more with zeal and energy. To finish the whole of the architect's plans, including towers and spires, chapter house, and cloister, would involve an outlay of more than 70,000*l*. But if the nave were undertaken, with only that part of the western front and towers necessary for the stability of the structure, about 36,000*l*. would suffice. With 27,000*l*. already secured, the balance of 9,000*l*. does not seem too heavy an amount to raise within the next four or five years.

AUG. B. DONALDSON.

II. ITS FUTURE

You ask me to give you my view of the completion of our cathedral. If this is of any value it must stand, not on my opinion or wish, but on the facts that are before us. The future is sown in the past. Let us see then the result of the past that is already doing its work among us.

When I entered Cornwall seven years ago I expected to find that the restoration of the parish churches had been neglected in favour of the cathedral building. But I find that the opposite has been the case, and the effort of raising our mother church has not spent itself till it included almost every church in the diocese.

The same result has followed the beauty of the cathedral service. It has lifted the standard of worship from the Tamar to the Isles of Scilly.

It is likely therefore that the completion of the cathedral will complete the great work which its beginning began.

The very act of building becomes a building up of the character of the county; the energy it inspires, the brotherhood of men which grows under combined effort, the interest of a man's life represented by something outside himself and above the world, the work of beauty daily rising into fuller beauty before our eyes, the sacrifice which is called out in each who gives as much as he can. These things make character and adorn what is already made. The biography of our great cathedrals reveals the age of their builders as a greater age than that of their heirs; the greatness of this greater age may be ours.

And yet our children will rise up and call us blessed, they will understand us better by our works than by our words, and appreciate us more truly by our chief public buildings than by our literature, gifted as it is; for it only took one man to produce the "Idylls of the King," but it will take a county and its friends to raise our cathedral.

And then only in a finished minster will our organ pour forth all its glory, and the Church of Cornwall enter there to lift their hearts with the voice of holy music.

Not till then can we invite the several regiments of the soldiers of Christ to kneel side by side before the King.

The Sunday-school teachers of the whole diocese offering their Sunday toil to the Heavenly Father of their children; or the Communicants of Cornwall kneeling as one man in their Communion of Saints; or the representative mothers of this Celtic race in the sisterhood of their cares and hopes, gaining a blessing on their homes in their mother church.

For the cathedral is not for Truro, but for Cornwall. For Truro it is

TRURO CATHEDRAL

already sufficient. It is to express and to ripen the unity of Cornwall, its one-and-all-ness, its bearing the burdens of others, and rejoicing in each other's weal, the common gladness in each race well run, and in each battle of life well won.

For the larger church gives a larger heart and a greater soul to those who truly use it.

Therefore I am asking my fellow Cornishmen to rise and build, and to finish the work they have so grandly begun.

JOHN TRURON.

CORNUBIENSIBUS ADOPTIVUS

O generous hearts, brave spirits of the West,
   Clear-sighted, open brow and open hand,
   Wise, wistful, laughter-loving, fearless band,
So swift to clasp the stranger to your breast,
So faithful to remember; ye are blest,
   Who 'twixt the bleak moor and the blowing sand,
   Live hardly, love your frugal mother-land,
Can toil, and, rarer gift of Heaven, can rest!

So ordered He, who made you shrewd and brave,
   And bade your myriad streamlets blithely run,
     And knit the marble promontories, and nursed
     A sacred race, and bade them know the first
Kiss of the stately landward-marching wave,
   And latest flash of the ocean-dipping sun.

                        ARTHUR CHRISTOPHER BENSON.

THE MYSTERY OF JOSEPH LAQUEDEM

A Jew, unfortunately slain on the sands of Sheba Cove, in the parish of Ruan Lanihale, August 15, 1810: or so much of it as is hereby related by the Rev. Endymion Trist, B.D., then vicar of that parish, in a letter to a friend, and now for the first time made public.

My dear Friend,—You are right, to be sure, in supposing that I know more than my neighbours in Ruan Lanihale concerning the unfortunate young man, Joseph Laquedem, and more than I care to divulge; in particular concerning his tragical relations with the girl Julia Constantine, or July, as she was commonly called. The vulgar knowledge amounts to little more than this —that Laquedem, a young Hebrew of extraordinary commercial gifts, first came to our parish in 1807 and settled here as managing secretary of a privateering company at Porthlooe; that by his aptitude and daring in this and the illicit trade he amassed a respectable fortune, and at length opened a private bank at Porthlooe and issued his own notes; that on August 15, 1810, a forced 'run' which, against his custom, he was personally supervising, miscarried, and he met his death by a carbine-shot on the sands of Sheba Cove; and, lastly, that his body was taken up and conveyed away by the girl Julia Constantine, under the fire of the preventive men.

The story has even in our time received what I may call some fireside embellishments; but these are the facts, and the parish knows little beyond them. I (as you conjecture) know a great deal more; and yet there is a sense in which I know nothing more. You and I, my old friend, have come to an age when men do not care to juggle with the mysteries of another world, but knowing that the time is near when all accounts must be rendered, desire to take stock honestly of what they believe and what they do not. And here lies my difficulty. On the one hand I would not make public an experience which, however honestly set down, might mislead others, and especially the young, into rash and mischievous speculations. On the other, I doubt if it be right to keep total silence and withhold from devout and initiated minds any glimpse of truth, or possible truth, vouchsafed to me. As the Greek said, 'Plenty are the thyrsus-bearers, but few the illuminate;' and among these few I may surely count my old friend. Therefore I am going to compromise, and will tell you all I know, but on the single condition that you do not make it public.

It was in January 1807—the year of the abominable business of Tilsit— that my churchwarden, the late Mr. Ephraim Pollard, and I, in cleaning the south wall of Lanihale Church for a fresh coat of whitewash, discovered the frescoes and charcoal drawings, as well as the brass plaque of which I sent you a tracing; and I think not above a fortnight later that, on your suggestion,

I set to work to decipher and copy out the old churchwardens' accounts. On the Monday after Easter, at about nine o'clock P.M., I was seated in the Vicarage parlour, busy transcribing, with a couple of candles before me, when my housekeeper Frances came in with a visiting-card, and the news that a stranger desired to speak with me. I took the card and read 'Mr. Joseph Laquedem.'

'Show the gentleman in,' said I.

Now the fact is, I had just then a few guineas in my chest, and you know what a price gold fetched in 1807. I dare say that for twelve months together the most of my parishioners never set eyes on a piece, and any that came along quickly found its way to the Jews. People said that Government was buying up gold, through the Jews, to send to the armies. I know not the degree of truth in this, but I had some five and twenty guineas to dispose of, and had been put into correspondence with a Mr. Isaac Laquedem, a Jew residing by Plymouth Dock, whom I understood to be offering 25s. 6d. per guinea, or a trifle above the price then current.

I was fingering the card when the door opened again and admitted a young man in a caped overcoat and tall boots bemired high above the ankles. He halted on the threshold and bowed.

'Mr. ——?'

'Joseph Laquedem,' said he in a pleasant voice.

'I guess your errand,' said I, 'though it was a Mr. Isaac Laquedem whom I expected. Your father, perhaps?'

He bowed again, and I left the room to fetch my bag of guineas. 'You have had a dirty ride,' I began on my return.

'I have walked,' he answered, lifting a muddy boot. 'I beg you to pardon these.'

'What, from Torpoint Ferry? And in this weather? My faith, sir, you must be a famous pedestrian!'

He made no reply to this, but bent over the guineas, fingering them, holding them up to the candlelight, testing their edges with his thumbnail, and finally poising them one by one on the tip of his forefinger.

'I have a pair of scales,' suggested I.

'Thank you, I too have a pair in my pocket. But I do not need them. The guineas are good weight, all but this one, which is possibly a couple of grains short.'

'Surely you cannot rely on your hand to tell you that?'

His eyebrows went up as he felt in his pocket and produced a small velvet-lined case containing a pair of scales. He was a decidedly handsome young man, with dark intelligent eyes and a slightly scornful—or shall I say ironical?—smile. I took particular note of the steadiness of his hand as he adjusted the scales and weighed my guinea.

'To be precise,' he announced, '1·898, or practically one and nine-tenths short.'

'I should have thought,' said I, fairly astounded, 'a lifetime too little for acquiring such delicacy of sense!'

THE MYSTERY OF JOSEPH LAQUEDEM 17

He seemed to ponder. 'I dare say you are right, sir,' he answered, and was silent again until the business of payment was concluded. While folding the receipt he added, 'I am a connoisseur of coins, sir, and not of their weight alone.'

'Antique, as well as modern?'

'Certainly.'

'In that case,' said I, 'you may be able to tell me something about this:' and going to my bureau I took out the brass plaque which Mr. Pollard had detached from the planks of the church wall. 'To be sure, it scarcely comes within the province of numismatics.'

He took the plaque. His brows contracted, and presently he laid it on the table, drew my chair towards him in an absent-minded fashion, and, sitting down, rested his brow on his open palms. I can recall the attitude plainly, and his bent head, and the rain still glistening in the waves of his black hair.

'Where did you find this?' he asked, but without looking up.

I told him. 'The engraving upon it is singular. I thought that possibly——'

'Oh, that,' said he, 'is simplicity itself. An eagle displayed, with two heads, the legs resting on two gates, a crescent between, an imperial crown surmounting—these are the arms of the Greek Empire, the two gates are Rome and Constantinople. The question is, how it came where you found it. It was covered with plaster, you say, and the plaster whitewashed? Did you discover anything near it?'

Upon this I told him of the frescoes and charcoal drawings, and roughly described them.

His fingers began to drum upon the table.

'Have you any documents which might tell us when the wall was first plastered?'

'The parish accounts go back to 1594—here they are: the Registers to 1663 only. I keep them in the vestry. I can find no mention of plastering, but the entries of expenditure on whitewashing occur periodically, the first under the year 1633.' I turned the old pages and pointed to the entry '*Ite*' *paide to George mason for a dayes work about the churche after the Jew had been, and white wassche* i^s vj^d.'

'A Jew? But a Jew had no business in England in those days. I wonder how and why he came.' My visitor took the old volume and ran his finger down the leaf, then up, then turned back a page. 'Perhaps this may explain it,' said he. '*Ite*' *deliuēd Mr. Beuill to make puīsion for the companie of a fforeste barke y^t came ashoare* iii^s iv^d.' He broke off, with a finger on the entry, and rose. 'Pray forgive me, sir; I had taken your chair.'

'Don't mention it,' said I. 'Indeed I was about to suggest that you draw it to the fire while Frances brings in some supper.'

To be short, although he protested he must push on to the inn at Porthlooe, I persuaded him to stay the night; not so much, I confess, from desire of his company, as in the hope that if I took him to see the frescoes next morning he might help me to elucidate their history.

VOL. I. C

I remember now that during supper and afterwards my guest allowed me more than my share of the conversation. He made an admirable listener, quick, courteous, adaptable, yet with something in reserve (you may call it a facile tolerance, if you will) which ended by irritating me. Young men should be eager, fervid, *sublimis cupidusque*, as I was before my beard grew stiff. But this young man had the air of a spectator at a play, composing himself to be amused. There was too much wisdom in him and too little emotion. We did not, of course, touch upon any religious question—indeed, of his own opinions on any subject he disclosed extraordinarily little: and yet as I reached my bedroom that night I told myself that here, behind a mask of good manners, was one of those perniciously modern young men who have run through all beliefs by the age of twenty, and settled down to a polite but weary atheism.

I fancy that under the shadow of this suspicion my own manner may have been cold to him next morning. Almost immediately after breakfast we set out for the church. The day was sunny and warm; the atmosphere brilliant after the night's rain. The hedges exhaled a scent of spring. And, as we entered the churchyard, I saw the girl Julia Constantine seated in her favourite angle between the porch and the south wall, threading a chain of daisies.

'What an amazingly handsome girl!' my guest exclaimed.

'Why, yes,' said I, 'she has her good looks, poor soul!'

'Why "poor soul"?'

'She is an imbecile, or nearly so,' said I, fitting the key in the lock.

We entered the church. And here let me say that, although I furnished you at the time of their discovery with a description of the frescoes and the ruder drawings which overlay them, you can scarcely imagine the grotesque and astonishing *coup d'œil* presented by the two series. To begin with the frescoes, or original series. One, as you know, represented the Crucifixion. The head of the Saviour bore a large crown of gilded thorns, and from the wound in His left side flowed a continuous stream of red gouts of blood, extraordinarily intense in colour (and intensity of colour is no common quality in fresco-painting). At the foot of the cross stood a Roman soldier, with two female figures in dark-coloured drapery a little to the right, and in the background a man clad in a loose dark upper coat, which reached a little below the knees.

The same man reappeared in the second picture, alone, but carrying a tall staff or hunting spear, and advancing up a road, at the top of which stood a circular building with an arched doorway and, within the doorway, the head of a lion. The jaws of this beast were open and depicted with the same intense red as the Saviour's blood.

Close beside this, but further to the east, was a large ship under sail which from her slanting position appeared to be mounting over a long swell of sea. This vessel had four masts; the two foremost furnished with yards and square sails, the others with lateen-shaped sails, after the Greek fashion; her sides were decorated with six gaily painted bands or streaks, each separately charged with devices—a red saltire on a green ground, a white crescent on a blue, and so forth; and each masthead bore a crown with a flag or streamer fluttering beneath.

Of the frescoes these alone were perfect, but fragments of others were scattered over the wall, and in particular I must mention a group of detached human limbs lying near the ship—a group rendered conspicuous by an isolated right hand and arm drawn on a larger scale than the rest. A gilded circlet adorned the arm, which was flexed at the elbow, the hand horizontally placed, the forefinger extended towards the west in the direction of the picture of the Crucifixion, and the thumb shut within the palm beneath the other three fingers.

So much for the frescoes. A thin coat of plaster had been laid over them to receive the second series, which consisted of the most disgusting and fantastic images, traced in black. One of these drawings represented Satan himself— an erect figure, with hairy paws clasped in a supplicating posture, thick black horns, and eyes which (for additional horror) the artist had painted red and edged with a circle of white. At his feet crawled the hindermost limb of a peculiarly loathsome monster with claws stuck in the soil. Close by a nun was figured, sitting in a pensive attitude, her cheek resting on the back of her hand, and her elbow supported by a hideous dwarf, and at some distance a small house, or prison, with barred windows and a small doorway crossed with heavy bolts.

As I said, this upper series had been but partially scraped away, and as my guest and I stood at a little distance, I leave you to imagine, if you can, the incongruous tableau; the Prince of Darkness almost touching the mourners beside the cross; the sorrowful nun and grinning dwarf side by side with a ship in full sail, which again seemed to be forcing her way into a square and forbidding prison, &c.

Mr. Laquedem conned all this for some while in silence, holding his chin with finger and thumb.

'And it was here you discovered the plaque?' he asked at length.

I pointed to the exact spot.

'H'm!' he mused, 'and that ship must be Greek or Levantine by its rig. Compare the crowns on her masts, too, with that on the plaque . . .' He stepped to the wall and peered into the frescoes. 'Now this hand and arm——'

'They belong to me,' said a voice immediately behind me, and turning, I saw that the poor girl had followed us into the church.

The young Jew had turned also. 'What do you mean by that?' he asked sharply.

'She means nothing,' I began, and made as if to tap my forehead significantly.

'Yes, I do mean something,' she persisted. 'They belong to me. I remember——'

'What do you remember?'

Her expression, which for a moment had been thoughtful, wavered and changed into a vague foolish smile. 'I can't tell . . . something . . . it was sand, I think . . .'

'Who is she?' asked Mr. Laquedem.

'Her name is Julia Constantine. Her parents are dead; an aunt looks after her—a sister of her mother's.'

He turned and appeared to be studying the frescoes. 'Julia Constantine —an odd name,' he muttered. 'Do you know anything of her parentage?'

'Nothing except that her father was a labourer at Sheba, the manor-farm. The family has belonged to this parish for generations. I believe July is the last of them.'

He faced round upon her again. '*Sand*, did you say? That's a strange thing to remember. How does *sand* come into your mind? Think, now.'

She cast down her eyes; her fingers plucked at the daisy-chain. After a while she shook her head. 'I can't think,' she answered, glancing up timidly and pitifully.

'Surely we are wasting time,' I suggested. To tell the truth I disapproved of his worrying the poor girl.

He took the daisy-chain from her, looking at me the while with something between a 'by-your-leave' and a challenge. A smile played about the corners of his mouth.

'Let us waste a little more.' He held up the chain before her and began to sway it gently to and fro. 'Look at it, please, and stretch out your arm; look steadily. Now your name is Julia Constantine, and you say that the arm on the wall belongs to you. Why?'

'Because . . . if you please, sir, because of the mark.'

'What mark?'

'The mark on my arm.'

This answer seemed to discompose as well as to surprise him. He snatched at her wrist and rolled back her sleeve, somewhat roughly, as I thought. 'Look here, sir!' he exclaimed, pointing to a thin red line encircling the flesh of the girl's upper arm, and from that to the arm and armlet in the fresco.

'She has been copying it,' said I, 'with a string or ribbon, which no doubt she tied too tightly.'

'You are mistaken, sir; this is a birthmark. You have had it always?' he asked the girl.

She nodded. Her eyes were fixed on his face with the gaze of one at the same time startled and fascinated; and for the moment he too seemed to be startled. But his smile came back as he picked up the daisy-chain and began once more to sway it to and fro before her.

'And when that arm belonged to you, there was sand around you—eh! Tell us, how did the sand come there?'

She was silent, staring at the pendulum-swing of the chain. 'Tell us,' he repeated in a low coaxing tone.

And in a tone just as low she began, 'There was sand . . . red sand . . . it was below me . . . and something above . . . something like a great tent.' She faltered, paused and went on, 'There were thousands of people. . . .' She stopped.

'Yes, yes—there were thousands of people on the sand——'

'No, they were not on the sand. There were only two on the sand . . . the rest were around . . . under the tent . . . my arm was out . . . just like this. . . .'

The young man put a hand to his forehead. 'Good Lord!' I heard him say, 'the amphitheatre!'

'Come, sir,' I interrupted, 'I think we have had enough of this jugglery.' But the girl's voice went on steadily as if repeating a lesson:—

'And then you came—'

'*I!*' His voice rang sharply, and I saw a horror dawn in his eyes, and grow. 'I!'

'And then you came,' she repeated, and broke off, her mind suddenly at fault. Automatically he began to sway the daisy-chain afresh. 'We were on board a ship . . . a funny ship . . . with a great high stern. . . .'

'Is this the same story?' he asked, lowering his voice almost to a whisper; and I could hear his breath going and coming.

'I don't know . . . one minute I see clear, and then it all gets mixed up again . . . we were up there, stretched on deck, near the tiller . . . another ship was chasing us . . . the men began to row, with long sweeps. . . .'

'But the sand,' he insisted, 'is the sand there?'

'The sand? . . . Yes, I see the sand again . . . we are standing upon it . . . we and the crew . . . the sea is close behind us . . . some men have hold of me . . . they are trying to pull me away from you. . . . Ah!——'

And I declare to you that with a sob the poor girl dropped on her knees, there in the aisle, and clasped the young man about the ankles, bowing her forehead upon the insteps of his high boots. As for him, I cannot hope to describe his face to you. There was something more in it than wonder— something more than dismay, even—at the success of his unhallowed experiment. It was as though, having prepared himself light-heartedly to witness a play, he was seized and terrified to find himself the principal actor. I never saw ghastlier fear on human cheeks.

'For God's sake, sir,' I cried, stamping my foot, 'relax your cursed spells! Relax them and leave us! This is a house of prayer.'

He put a hand under the girl's chin, and, raising her face, made a pass or two, still with the daisy-chain in his hand. She looked about her, shivered and stood erect. 'Where am I?' she asked. 'Did I fall? What are you doing with my chain?' She had relapsed into her habitual childishness of look and speech.

I hurried them from the church, resolutely locked the door, and marched up the path without deigning a glance at the young man. But I had not gone fifty yards when he came running after.

'I entreat you, sir, to pardon me. I should have stopped the experiment before. But I was startled—thrown off my balance. I am telling you the truth, sir!'

'Very likely,' said I. 'The like has happened to other rash meddlers before you.'

'I declare to you I had no thought——' he began. But I interrupted him:

'"No thought," indeed! I bring you here to resolve me, if you can, a curious puzzle in archæology, and you fall to playing devil's pranks upon a half-witted child. "No thought!"—I believe you, sir.'

'And yet,' he muttered, 'it is an amazing business : the sand—the *velarium* —the outstretched arm and hand—*pollice compresso*—the exact gesture of the gladiatorial shows——'

'Are you telling me, pray, of gladiatorial shows under the Eastern Empire?' I demanded scornfully.

'Certainly not: and that,' he mused, 'only makes it the more amazing.'

'Now, look here,' said I, halting in the middle of the road, 'I'll hear no more of it. Here is my gate, and there lies the highroad, on to Porthlooe or back to Plymouth, as you please. I wish you good morning, sir; and if it be any consolation to you, you have spoiled my digestion for a week.'

I am bound to say the young man took his dismissal with grace. He halted then and there and raised his hat; stood for a moment pondering; and, turning on his heel, walked quickly off towards Porthlooe.

It must have been a week before I learnt casually that he had obtained employment there as secretary to a small company owning the *Lord Nelson* and the *Hand-in-hand* privateers. His success, as you know, was rapid; and naturally in a gossipping parish I heard about it—a little here, a little there —in all a great deal. He had bought the *Providence* schooner; he had acted as freighter for Minards' men in their last run with the *Morning Star*; he had slipped over to Cork and brought home a Porthlooe prize illegally detained there; he was in London, fighting a salvage case in the Admiralty Court; and so forth. Within twelve months he was accountant of every 'trading' company in Porthlooe, and agent for receiving the moneys due to the Guernsey merchants. And in 1809, as you know, he opened his bank and issued notes, those from $1l.$ to $5l.$ payable at his own establishment, and those for larger sums at the house of Christopher Smith, alderman of London. A year later he acquired two of the best farms in the parish, Tresawl and Killifreeth, and held the fee simple of the harbour and quays.

During the first two years of his prosperity I saw little of the man. We passed each other from time to time in the street of Porthlooe, and he accosted me with a politeness to which, though distrusting him, I felt bound to respond. But he never offered conversation, and our next interview was wholly of my seeking.

One evening towards the close of his second year at Porthlooe, and about the date of his purchase of the *Providence* schooner, l happened to be walking homewards from a visit to a sick parishioner, when at Cove Bottom, by the miller's footbridge, I passed two figures—a man and a woman standing there and conversing in the dusk. I could not help recognising them; and halfway up the hill I came to a sudden resolution and turned back.

'Mr. Laquedem,' said I, approaching them, 'I put it to you, as a man of education and decent feeling, is this quite honourable?'

'I believe, sir,' he answered courteously enough, 'I can convince you that it is. But clearly this is neither the time nor the place.'

'You must excuse me,' I went on, 'but I have known Julia since she was a child.'

To this he made an extraordinary answer. 'No longer?' he asked; and added, with a change of tone, 'Had you not forbidden me the vicarage, sir, I might have something to say to you.'

'If it concern the girl's spiritual welfare—or yours—I shall be happy to hear it.'

'In that case,' said he, 'I will do myself the pleasure of calling upon you —shall we say to-morrow evening?'

He was as good as his word. At nine o'clock next evening—about the hour of his first arrival—Frances ushered him into my parlour. The similarity of circumstance may have suggested to me to draw the comparison; at any rate I observed then for the first time that rapid ageing of his features which afterwards became a matter of common remark. The face was no longer that of the young man who had entered my parlour two years before; already some streaks of grey showed in his black locks, and he seemed even to move wearily.

'I fear you are unwell,' said I, offering a chair.

'I have reason to believe,' he answered, 'that I am dying.' And then, as I uttered some expression of dismay and concern, he cut me short. 'Oh, there will be no hurry about it! I mean, perhaps, no more than that all men carry about with them the seeds of their mortality—so why not I?. But I came to talk of Julia Constantine, not of myself.'

'You may guess, Mr. Laquedem, that as her vicar, and having known her and her affliction all my life, I take something of a fatherly interest in the girl.'

'And having known her so long, do you not begin to observe some change in her, of late?'

'Why, to be sure,' said I, 'she seems brighter.'

He nodded. '*I* have done that; or rather, love has done it.'

'Be careful, sir!' I cried. 'Be careful of what you are going to tell me! If you have intended or wrought any harm to that girl, I tell you solemnly——'

But he held up a hand. 'Ah, sir, be charitable! I tell you solemnly our love is not of *that* kind. We who have loved, and lost, and sought each other, and loved again through centuries, have outlearned that rougher passion. When she was a princess of Rome and I a Christian Jew led forth to the lions——'

I stood up, grasping the back of my chair and staring. At last I knew. This young man was stark mad.

He read my conviction at once. 'I think, sir,' he went on, changing his tone, 'the learned antiquary to whom, as you told me, you were sending your tracing of the plaque, has by this time replied with some information about it.'

Relieved at this change of subject, I answered quietly (while considering how best to get him out of the house), 'My friend tells me that a similar design is found in Landulph Church, on the tomb of Theodore Paleologus, who died in 1636.'

'Precisely; of Theodore Paleologus, descendant of the Constantines.'

I began to grasp his insane meaning. 'The race, so far as we know, is extinct,' said I.

'The race of the Constantines,' said he slowly and composedly, 'is never extinct; and while it lasts, the soul of Julia Constantine will come to birth again and know the soul of the Jew, until——'

I waited.

'——Until their love lifts the curse, and the Jew can die.'

'This is mere madness,' said I, my tongue blurting it out at length.

'I expected you to say no less. Now look you, sir—in a few minutes I leave you, I walk home and spend an hour or two before bedtime in adding figures, balancing accounts; to-morrow I rise and go about my daily business cheerfully, methodically, always successfully. I am the long-headed man, making money because I know how to make it, respected by all, with no trace of madness in me. You, if you meet me to-morrow, shall recognise none. Just now you are forced to believe me mad. Believe it then; but listen while I tell you this:—When Rome was, I was; when Constantinople was, I was. I was that Jew rescued from the lions. It was I who sailed from the Bosphorus in that ship, with Julia beside me; I from whom the Moorish pirates tore her, on the beach beside Tetuan; I who, centuries after, drew those obscene figures on the wall of your church—the devil, the nun, and the barred convent—when Julia, another Julia but the same soul, was denied to me and forced into a nunnery. For the frescoes, too, tell *my* history. *I* was that figure in the dark habit, standing a little back from the cross. Tell me, sir, did you never hear of Joseph Kartophilus, Pilate's porter?'

I saw that I must humour him. 'I have heard his legend,' said I;[1] 'and have understood that in time he became a Christian.'

He smiled wearily. 'He has travelled through many creeds; but he has never travelled beyond Love. And if that love can be purified of all passion such as you suspect, he has not travelled beyond forgiveness. Many times I have known her who shall save me in the end; and now in the end I have found her and shall be able, at length, to die; have found her, and with her all my dead loves, in the body of a girl whom you call half-witted—and shall be able, at length, to die.'

And with this he bent over the table, and, resting his face on his arms, sobbed aloud. I let him sob there for a while, and then touched his shoulder gently.

He raised his head. 'Ah,' said he, in a voice which answered the gentleness of my touch, 'you remind me!' And with that he deliberately slipped his coat off his left arm and, rolling up the shirt sleeve, bared the arm almost to the shoulder. 'I want you close,' he added with half a smile; for I have to confess that during the process I had backed a couple of paces towards the door. He took up a candle, and held it while I bent and examined the thin red line which ran like a circlet around the flesh of the upper arm just below the apex of the deltoid muscle. When I looked up I met his eyes challenging mine across the flame.

---

[1] The legend is that as Christ left the judgment hall on His way to Calvary, Kartophilus smote Him, saying, 'Man, go quicker!' and was answered, 'I indeed go quickly; but thou shalt tarry till 1 come again.'

'Mr. Laquedem,' I said, 'my conviction is that you are possessed and are being misled by a grievous hallucination. At the same time I am not fool enough to deny that the union of flesh and spirit, so passing mysterious in everyday life (when we pause to think of it), may easily hold mysteries deeper yet. The Church Catholic, whose servant I am, has never to my knowledge denied this; yet has providentially made a rule of St. Paul's advice to the Colossians against intruding into those things which she hath not seen. In the matter of this extraordinary belief of yours I can give you no such comfort as one honest man should offer to another: for I do not share it. But in the more practical matter of your conduct towards July Constantine, it may help you to know that I have accepted your word and propose henceforward to trust you as a gentleman.'

'I thank you, sir,' he said, as he slipped on his coat. 'May I have your hand on that?'

'With pleasure,' I answered, and, having shaken hands, conducted him to the door.

From that day the affection between Joseph Laquedem and July Constantine, and their frequent companionship, were open and avowed. Scandal there was, to be sure; but as it blazed up like straw, so it died down. Even the women feared to sharpen their tongues openly on Laquedem, who by this time held the purse of the district, and to offend whom might mean an empty skivet on Saturday night. July, to be sure, was more tempting game; and one day her lover found her in the centre of a knot of women fringed by a dozen children with open mouths and ears. He stepped forward. 'Ladies,' said he, 'the difficulty which vexes you cannot, I feel sure, be altogether good for your small sons and daughters. Let me put an end to it.' He bent forward and reverently took July's hand. 'My dear, it appears that the depth of my respect for you will not be credited by these ladies unless I offer you marriage. And as I am proud of it, so forgive me if I put it beyond their doubt. Will you marry me?' July, blushing scarlet, covered her face with her hands, but shook her head. There was no mistaking the gesture: all the women saw it. 'Condole with me, ladies!' said Laquedem, lifting his hat and including them in an ironical bow; and placing July's arm in his, escorted her away.

I need not follow the history of their intimacy, of which I saw, indeed, no more than my neighbours. On two points all accounts of it agree: the rapid ageing of the man during this period and the improvement in the poor girl's intellect. Some profess to have remarked an equally vehement heightening of her beauty; but, as my recollection serves me, she had always been a handsome maid; and I set down the transfiguration—if such it was—entirely to the dawn and growth of her reason. To this I can add a curious scrap of evidence. I was walking along the cliff track, one afternoon, between Porthlooe and Lanihale churchtown, when, a few yards ahead, I heard a man's voice declaiming in monotone some sentences which I could not catch; and rounding the corner, came upon Laquedem and July. She was seated on a rock; and he, on a patch of turf at her feet, held open a small volume which he laid face downwards as he rose to greet me. I glanced at the back of the book and saw it was a volume of Euripides. I made no comment, however, on this small discovery; and whether he had indeed taught the girl some Greek, or whether she merely listened for the sake of hearing his voice, I am unable to say.

Let me come then to the last scene, of which I was one among many spectators.

On the morning of August 15, 1810, and just about daybreak, I was awakened by the sound of horses' hoofs coming down the road beyond the vicarage gate. My ear told me at once that they were many riders and moving at a trot; and a minute later the jingle of metal gave me an inkling of the truth. I hurried to the window and pulled up the blind. Day was breaking on a grey drizzle of fog which drove up from seaward, and through this drizzle I caught sight of the last five or six scarlet plumes of a troop of dragoons jogging down the hill past my bank of escalonias.

Now our parish had stood for some weeks in apprehension of a visit from these gentry. The riding-officer, Mr. Luke, had threatened us with them more than once. I knew, moreover, that a run of goods was contemplated: and without questions of mine—it did not become a parish priest in those days to know too much—it had reached my ears that Laquedem was himself in Roscoff bargaining for the freight. But we had all learnt confidence in him by this time—his increasing bodily weakness never seemed to affect his cleverness and resource—and no doubt occurred to me that he would contrive to checkmate this new move of the riding-officer's. Nevertheless, and partly I dare say out of curiosity, to have a good look at the soldiers, I slipped on my clothes and hurried downstairs and across the garden.

My hand was on the gate when I heard footsteps, and July Constantine came running down the hill, her red cloak flapping and her hair powdered with mist.

'Hullo!' said I, 'nothing wrong, I hope?'

She turned a white, distraught face to me in the dawn.

'Yes, yes! All is wrong! I saw the soldiers coming—I heard them a mile away, and sent up the rocket from the church-tower. But the lugger stood in—they *must* have seen!—she stood in, and is right under Sheba Point now—and he——'

I whistled. 'This is serious. Let us run out towards the point; we—you, I mean—may be in time to warn them yet.'

So we set off running together. The morning breeze had a cold edge on it, but already the sun had begun to assert itself and wrestle with the bank of sea-fog. While we hurried along the cliffs the shoreward fringe of it was ripped and rolled back like a tent-cloth, and through the rent I saw a broad patch of the cove below; the sands (for the tide was at low ebb) shining like silver; the dragoons with their greatcoats thrown back from their scarlet breasts and their accoutrements flashing against the level rays. Seaward, the lugger loomed through the weather; but there was a crowd of men and black boats —half a score of them—by the water's edge, and it was clear to me at once that a forced run had been at least attempted.

I had pulled up, panting, on the verge of the cliff, when July caught me by the arm.

'*The sand!*'

She pointed; and well I remember the gesture—the very gesture of the hand in the fresco—the forefinger extended, the thumb shut within the palm. '*The sand . . .* he told me . . . it would come. . . .'

Her eyes were wide and fixed. She spoke, not excitedly at all, but rather as one musing, much as she had answered Laquedem on the morning when he waved the daisy-chain before her.

I heard an order shouted, high up the beach, and the dragoons came charging down across the sand. There was a scuffle close by the water's edge; then, as the soldiers broke through the mob of free-traders and wheeled their horses round, fetlock deep in the tide, I saw a figure break from the crowd and run, but presently check himself and walk composedly towards the cliff up which climbed the footpath leading to Porthlooe. And above the hubbub of oaths and shouting, I heard a voice crying distinctly, ' Run, man! 'Tis after thee they are! *Man, go faster!*'

Even then, had he gained the cliff-track, he might have escaped; for up there no horseman could follow. But as a trooper came galloping in pursuit, he turned deliberately. There was no defiance in his attitude; of that I am sure. What followed must have been mere blundering ferocity. I saw a jet of smoke, heard the sharp crack of a firearm, and Joseph Laquedem flung up his arms and pitched forward at full length on the sand.

The report woke the girl as with the stab of a knife. Her cry—it pierces through my dreams at times—rang back with the echoes from the rocks, and before they ceased she was halfway down the cliffside, springing as surely as a goat, and, where she found no foothold, clutching the grass, the rooted samphires and sea pinks, and sliding. While my head swam with the sight of it, she was running across the sands, was kneeling beside the body, had risen, and was staggering under the weight of it down to the water's edge.

'Stop her!' shouted Luke, the riding-officer. 'We must have the man! Dead or alive, we must have'n!'

She gained the nearest boat, the free-traders forming up around her, and hustling the dragoons. It was old Solomon Tweedy's boat, and he, prudent man, had taken advantage of the skirmish to ease her off, so that a push would set her afloat. He asserts that as July came up to him she never uttered a word, but the look on her face said ' Push me off,' and though he was at that moment meditating his own escape, he obeyed and pushed the boat off ' like a mazed man.' I may add that he spent three months in Bodmin Gaol for it.

She dropped with her burden against the stern sheets, but leapt up instantly and had the oars between the thole-pins almost as the boat floated. She pulled a dozen strokes, and hoisted the mainsail, pulled a hundred or so, sprang forward and ran up the jib. All this while the preventive men were straining to get off two boats in pursuit; but, as you may guess, the free-traders did nothing to help and a great deal to impede. And first the crews tumbled in too hurriedly, and had to climb out again (looking very foolish) and push afresh, and then one of the boats had mysteriously lost her plug and sank in half a fathom of water. July had gained a good hundred yards' offing before the pursuit began in earnest, and this meant a good deal. Once clear of the point the small cutter could defy their rowing and reach away to the eastward with the wind just behind her beam. The riding-officer saw this, and ordered his men to fire. They assert, and we must believe, that their object was merely to disable the boat by cutting up her canvas.

Their first desultory volley did little or no damage. I stood there, high on the cliff, and watched the boat, making a spy-glass of my hands. She had fetched in close under the point, and gone about on the port tack—the next would clear—when the first shot struck her, cutting a hole through her jib, and I expected the wind to rip the sail up immediately, but it stood. The breeze being dead on-shore, the little boat heeled towards us, her mainsail hiding the steerswoman.

It was a minute later, perhaps, that I began to suspect that July was hit, for she allowed the jib to shake and seemed to be running right up into the wind. The stern swung round and I strained my eyes to catch a glimpse of her. At that moment a third volley rattled out, a bullet shore through the peak halliards, and the mainsail came down with a run. It was all over.

The preventive men cheered and pulled with a will. I saw them run alongside, clamber into the cutter, and lift the fallen sail.

And that was all. There was no one on board, alive or dead. Whilst the canvas hid her, in the swift two minutes between the boat's putting about and her running up into the wind, July Constantine must have lifted her lover's body overboard and followed it to the bottom of the sea. There is no other explanation; and of the bond that knit these two together there is, when I ask myself candidly, no explanation at all, unless I give more credence than I have any wish to give to the wild tale which Joseph Laquedem told me. I have told you the facts, my friend, and leave them to your judgment.

A. T. Quiller-Couch.

MADAME FANNY MOODY AT HOME

A TALK WITH THE CORNISH NIGHTINGALE

THE nightingale does not sing in Cornwall. 'Of singing Birds,' wrote Carew in his *Survey*, 'they haue Lynnets, Goldfinches, Ruddockes, *Canarie* birds, Blacke-birds, Thrushes, and diuers others; but of Nightingals few, or none at all;' and he goes on to suggest that there may be 'some naturall antipathie betweene them and the soyle.' Or perhaps they are afraid of being caught and put into a pasty. But the best and most patriotic explanation has been given in these words—'They 'm jilles!'

At any rate the Duchy now boasts a nightingale of its own of whom it believes the bird may well be jealous: a songstress whose voice thrills all hearers, but speaks particularly to the hearts of her countrymen, possibly because her own heart feels most keenly when she sings to them. The favourite heroine of many operas, the popular prima donna of scores of platforms, Madame Fanny Moody is before all things a Cornishwoman, and the title she wears most proudly is that of the Cornish Nightingale.

It is only necessary to spend a short half-hour with this gifted woman, to learn how much she is wrapped up in the country of her birth. She is as Cornish to-day in tastes, in sympathies, in association, and in her love of the West Country as she was in her girlhood, which she spent at Redruth; and there can be no greater treat to her than to sit and talk of friends and kinsmen in the delectable Duchy, and to revive memories of bygone times when she was one of a happy musical family there, and when the voice which has since won for her such world-wide fame was often heard in the cause of local charity.

Madame Fanny Moody, or, as she now is, Mrs. Charles Manners, is not often to be found in London, although she and her husband have established themselves in a cozy house in the neighbourhood of Portman Square; for their many engagements take them all over the three kingdoms, and sometimes much further afield. Thus it was fortunate for me when I secured both husband and wife for a good long afternoon's talk and the promise that we should not be interrupted by any one; 'not even a prospective tenor or a future contralto,' I urge upon Mr. Manners, who is very much occupied with the organising of the Moody-Manners Opera Company. I have some little time to wait before my host and hostess join me, and I divide the interim between keeping a watchful eye on 'Paddy,' a favourite dog of Madame's, whom I know by repute to be sometimes averse to strangers, although I believe generally those of the sterner

Photo by   *J. Moody, Redruth*

sex come in for his chief displeasure, and making a tour of the drawing-room, on the walls of which there are endless tokens of the appreciation the owners are held in. On the piano stands a full-length portrait of the late Sir Augustus Harris and near it one of the late Carl Rosa, the two impresarios to whom the world owes the introduction of the popular prima donna. Madame Marie Roze smiles on her sister artiste from a frame on a table near at hand. There are dozens of representations of Madame Moody and of Mr. Manners in their favourite parts, and framed testimonials from choral societies, companies, and associations. By this time my hostess has joined me, and we immediately plunge into conversation about the life and the successes of the 'Nightingale.'

'I believe you are a member of a large family, madame?'

'We were thirteen, and I think we were nearly all born musical; but then, you know, that is not an uncommon thing to say of a Cornish family, for every one is musical down there; even the girls in the mines sing at their dismal work, and sing well too. Perhaps in one respect we were somewhat unique, for out of thirteen we have provided the musical world with two sopranos, two contraltos, and two professional musicians. My eldest sister is well known as a pianist and teacher of singing; whilst the youngest one, Hilda, is just now singing in the new piece which has replaced *The Geisha* at Daly's Theatre. "The Miniature Madame Moody," they call her in the provinces. My eldest brother has a good baritone voice, so we may justly claim to be a musical family.'

'And you have still further added to your connection with the profession by your marriage, madame?'

Photo by   *J. Moody, Redruth*

'Yes. My husband is, of course, well known in the operatic and concert worlds as Charles Manners. He is really a son of the late Colonel J. C. Mansergh, late Royal Horse Artillery, and J.P. for Cork and Tipperary. He was intended for the army, but fortunately he renounced the idea of soldiering for singing. He was, as I think you know, for many years principal bass in the Carl Rosa Opera Company and at the Royal Italian Opera.'

'How soon did you begin your musical career?'

'Well, I think in my cradle,' is the laughing answer. 'They say, you know, that I hummed tunes before I was able to speak. I was ten, I think, when I sang at local amateur concerts, and then when I was sixteen Mrs. Basset, of Tehidy, undertook my musical education. My father was not a wealthy man, and we were such a large family that it would have been impossible to devote much money to one of us, therefore I feel I owe everything to Mrs. Basset's generosity. I went to London, and I had three years' good training under that incomparable teacher, Madame Sainton Dolby. My teaching was to fit me for oratorio work, for up to the end of the time I was with Madame Dolby I had no idea of doing anything operatic. I had been brought up with somewhat strict Presbyterian notions, which rendered the idea of stage life rather distasteful than otherwise to me. One day, however, my great friend Lady

Photo by   Elliott and Fry
MADAME FANNY MOODY AS MARGUERITE

Morell Mackenzie wrote and told me that Carl Rosa wished to meet me. I went and I sang for him, with the result that he offered me a three years' engagement; and he told me I might choose my own *rôle* for my first appearance. I thought I should like it to be Michaela in *Carmen*, and wrote and told him so, and then I was put out of conceit of this idea by friends who urged upon me the impossibility of making a successful *début* with another soprano on the stage. I wrote again and said that I would rather try Mignon. Then some other counsellor suggested Marguerite, and off went a third note to

Carl Rosa, who very wisely wrote and said, when I had "quite come to a decision it would be time enough to arrange matters." Finally I made my *début* on the London stage as Michaela. Previous to this I had appeared in Liverpool as Arline in *The Bohemian Girl*. I had three years with the Carl Rosa Company, singing the principal parts in *Mignon, The Bohemian Girl, Faust, Maritana*, and many others; but I think then, as it has ever been, Mignon was my favourite part, and next to that I place Marguérite. I always look back with great pleasure to my Carl Rosa days; I played good parts, I had a good salary, and I made delightful friendships, and then last, but not least, I met my husband whilst a member of the company. By the way, it is a strange coincidence that we both joined the Carl Rosa Company on the same day.'

'What was the extent of your *répertoire* during the three years you toured with Carl Rosa?'

'I think it was a fairly comprehensive one. I learnt about fifty operas and about forty oratorios, and, of course, of fugitive songs I have a great number, including some purely Cornish ones such as "Shall Trelawney die?" Lady Trelawney gave me a copy of this just before we sailed for South Africa in the December of 1896, as she said that the thousands of Cornishmen in Johannesburg would love to hear their famous county song.'

'I want to hear all about your South African visit. It must have been a great pleasure to you.'

'You shall hear about it; but first I must tell you of earlier experiences. The first presentation I had was in 1887, when the Edinburgh students gave me an illuminated address, together with a poetical parody on the famous song in *The Bohemian Girl*—the 'Old Girl,' as we always call it. It ran this way:

> 'When other lips shall praises shower,
> And every hand applauds,
> Oh! sometimes think upon the flower
> Once offered by the gods.
>
> 'And when your fame in noonday blaze
> Upon the world shall burst,
> Remember those whose heartfelt praise
> Foretold it from the first.

The next year they gave me a lovely diamond bracelet. They are very enthusiastic, these students, and more than once they have taken the horses out of the carriage and dragged us back to our hotel. One year Mr. Manners and I were both singing at the Students' Union in Edinburgh. The hall was simply crammed, and the late Professor Blackie came on to the platform and asked me to sing Scotch songs as encores, which of course I did, and the audience encored all the encores. At the end of the concert the Council of the University presented us with two huge bouquets, which long before we reached the hotel were reduced to mere stumps, as all the flowers were distributed as mementoes. Then I had to appear at my window in the hotel and sing "Auld Lang Syne," and as that failed to make them think of the lateness of the hour, and of the attractions of their own homes, I added "Home, sweet

Home," and even a speech, and to this they responded with "For She's a jolly good Fellow." This sort of thing went on in almost all parts of the country, for we were a newly married couple in those days, and the public seemed bent upon congratulating us wherever they possibly could. After we left the Carl Rosa Company we formed a concert party under Mr. Manners's management, with Signor Mascheroni as conductor. We gave costume recitals of opera, sometimes filling up the whole of the programme in this way; at others only half of it, the rest being reserved for ballads.'

'This must necessitate your travelling a great deal?'

'It certainly does, but I am never in such good voice as when singing five nights a week, month after month; and we shall have even more going about when we start the Moody-Manners Opera Company next September. By the way, I think I should tell you that last Christmas Day was the first we ever spent at home, that is since our marriage, and that was only owing to my being ill.'

'Where do you propose to make your first appearance as the Moody-Manners Company?'

'At Longton in Staffordshire, and then we take Manchester, Oldham, Wigan, and other Lancashire towns, and we hope to get down to Plymouth after Christmas. We shall be seventy in number.'

'I suppose you always look forward to the tours which take you down to the West of England?'

'Yes, indeed we do, and our Cornish tour is the only one we undertake on our own responsibility. We are always sure of success there. Everywhere we meet with the most enthusiastic receptions, and friends seem to crop up at every corner. I often say that in all my travels I never come across any place to equal dear old Cornwall. Each time I come down I see the same friendly faces, the same familiar spots, and I just long to be able to stay and sing for the pleasure of my friends.'

'And your husband, what does he say to all the ovations you receive there?'

'Oh, he is quite pleased that it should be so; indeed, he says it seems as if everyone claims acquaintance with me when in Redruth through my father, who, I think I told you, is a photographer there. My husband was stopped in the street by a man who said, "How do you do, Mr. Manners, and how is Madame Fanny?"'

'"Do you know Madame Fanny?" replied my husband.'

'"Well, I did before you ever saw her."'

'"Did her father photograph you then?"'

'"Well, no, but I once went up in a balloon in a field over there, and her father was in that field when I went up."'

'I understand that it was the Cornish residents who gave you such a reception on the Rand.'

'Yes, it was, for a great number of natives of Cornwall are living there, especially in Johannesburg. You must see the beautiful tiara they gave me, and this album of photographs of the principal donors that accompanied it.

When we arrived at the Park station a perfect mob of people appeared to be awaiting us. They gave a hearty cheer when they saw me, and they also presented me with an illuminated address of welcome. Amongst the people there were many I had known in my Redruth days, or who had at least known some member of my family. Indeed, it seemed as though every Rand man who had hailed from the rocky moorland, every Jack from Camborne or Redruth, every fisherman from Mount's Bay, and every reefman who claims the Duchy as his native heath, made it his business to be on the platform that morning. After the presentation of the address and hearty congratulations from "one and all," Captain Tonkin, of the Cornish Association of South Africa, announced that the Committee of Reception had arranged for a Cornish night at the Theatre Royal, when I was to sing, and said he hoped that they would roll up "one and all," and give Madame Moody a real Cornish welcome. Then we got into the carriage that was waiting for us, and the horses were unyoked and replaced by a score or so of Cornishmen, who dragged us to the Grand National Hotel, and this, mind you, in the noontide heat of a South African day.'

Photo by Gordon & Smith, Cape Town
MADAME FANNY MOODY

'I think you sang for your many Cornish admirers from the balcony of the hotel?'

'I did on the Saturday night, and long before the hour fixed for the impromptu concert every corner which commanded a view of the hotel was filled, and, to quote the words of a local paper, there was "an assemblage of enthusiastic but none too exuberant Cornishmen; for a few minutes this congregation of robust Romeos waited for their Juliet to appear upon the balcony. It was a beautiful starry night, and the star of the evening was not long in presenting herself to their view." I sang "Home, sweet Home," and then they dispersed. We had a most successful week at the Theatre Royal, doing *Philemon and Baucis*, *Faust*, *Maritana*, and other operas, and finishing with a Cornish concert in the Masonic Hall. It was on this occasion that they gave me the beautiful tiara, and my husband a handsome diamond stud. I sang the good old Cornish ditty, "Tre, Pol, and Pen," and I joined Miss Balfour and my husband in "Crows in a Cornfield." The programme was indeed especially arranged for the evening, many of the songs we gave being dear to the hearts of Cornishmen, and perhaps all the more welcome for the waste of waters which divided us from the land of their nativity. My husband sang "One and All," and the audience joined lustily in the chorus, and then he added the following verse :

> '" Old Cornwall can boast of her daughters, too,
>   They're happy and gay and free.
> There may be as good in other lands,
>   But better there cannot be.
> So in that land I found my bride,
>   And thus I think you'll see
> I've proved my taste to sing with pride,
>   A Cornish girl for me." '

' Do you ever feel nervous, Madame Moody ? '

' I do, and sometimes I feel most so in the *rôles* I know best; but I think it is all a question of health, although mind you, I agree in the idea that no one who possesses the artistic temperament to even a certain degree can be quite free from such variations of it as feeling nervous or the reverse. In order to be quite successful, more especially on the operatic stage, a singer must have magnetism. I remember the first time I sang in Carl Rosa's Company, he asked me just before the performance began if I felt nervous, and on my saying no, for I really did not recognise my own sentiments at the time, he said he was sorry, as no great artist ever achieved that position without feeling so.'

' Do the people you are acting with affect your impersonation much ? '

' Yes, I am sure they do, but I prefer acting with the merest strangers ; if the part contains any love-making I should be too self-conscious if I had to do this with my husband, and I believe that it is the music which enables one to do such parts with fervour. To me the man whom I address as my lover is nothing more or less than a cabbage. Of course, I know that actresses feel differently from singers on this point. I must tell you that I learnt my dramatic art from one of the best of teachers, Mrs. Brutone. Sometimes people ask me if I find it difficult to sing and dance at the same time ; it is *more* than difficult, it almost renders me breathless.'

Photo by   *Gordon & Smith, Cape Town*
MR. CHARLES MANNERS

'As I am afraid I shall do if I keep you talking any longer.'

'Oh, there are a great many more things I should like to have told you, but I know that space is precious, and to my own cost I feel that time is flying.'

Regretfully I take leave of my host and hostess, whom I feel to be sterling artistes, delightful companions, and as great an ornament in their own home, as happy types of husband and wife, as they certainly are as hero and heroine on stage or platform.

LAURA ALEX. SMITH.

THE TIARA

THE DUCHY'S HARVEST

OF our four or five fish families of considerable commercial importance, none can take precedence of the herrings. The salmon and the more delicate of the flat fishes are available to only the comparatively few. The cod family, it is true, furnishes every class of consumer with food, both fresh and smoked. But in the herring, sprat and pilchard we have three fish—a little enterprise among the too conservative fishermen might add a fourth in the anchovy— that can be eaten either fresh, dried, or preserved in oil. And the most interesting and valuable, at any rate in the south country, is *Clupea pilchardus*, the pilchard of our west Cornish coast, the sardine of the French, the 'sardella' of the Italian fishermen. Of the identity of pilchard and sardine there is no longer any reasonable doubt, though until comparatively recently some confusion existed, even in well informed quarters, and there were not wanting intelligent writers who attributed to the word 'sardine' a meaning not its own. Generally speaking, it may be treated as merely the French for pilchard, though the modern innovation of preserving Deal sprats by a similar process and offering them for sale under the same name has invested it with a commercial significance, denoting sundry small fish of the herring tribe tinned in oil.

With the fresh pilchard Englishmen are, unless they know Cornwall, unfamiliar, as the fish rarely finds its way in numbers into any nets east of the Duchy. A curious error, by the way, which is perhaps worth recording here, existed among the Bournemouth longshoremen—fishermen proper there are none nearer than Poole—until the present writer managed with some trouble to correct it. The name pilchard was there applied, as recently as a couple of years back, to the scad, or horse mackerel, thousands of which are netted on that part of the Hampshire coast every summer, while not a few are taken with hook and line from the pier and from boats.

Though unknown, however, with any regularity east of at any rate Devon, and not much further north than the Bristol Channel, the pilchard, *alias* sardine, is sufficiently abundant on the west coast of France, particularly in the neighbourhood of Brest. In the Mediterranean, too, though the fisheries are less extensive and the canning industry practically unknown, sardines are plentiful, and they form, for instance, together with anchovies, the bulk of the food given to the fish in the famous Naples Aquarium. As bait, moreover, they are in general use in those parts, and the writer has used them in this way when angling on the coasts of Italy and Sicily, as also, as recently as

April in the present year, in the Straits of Gibraltar. So much, briefly, for the pilchard's distribution in European waters.

In point of size and appearance, and compared with its relations, the pilchard is somewhat smaller than a herring—though the average size varies, as in most fish, in different seas—and rather larger than a sprat, while it is at once distinguished from these by the larger scales along its sides, as well as by conspicuous markings on the gill covers. Moreover, its dorsal fin commences closer to the tip of the snout than to the root of the tail, whereas in the herring it starts midway, and in the sprat its starting point is nearer the tail. The last-named fish, again, has a sharp serrated edge to the belly.

With regard to the exact spawning time of the pilchard, there appears to be considerable difference of opinion, and as pilchards containing ripe spawn are rarely taken in quantity in the nets, the practical fishermen are unable to throw any light on the question. The balance of evidence, so far as it can safely be sifted, seems to be in favour of two spawnings between Midsummer and October, but the period doubtless varies in different latitudes. The eggs float, as indeed do those of everyone of our commercial fish, with the single remarkable exception of the herring, the spawn of which adheres to the stones and weeds on the sea bed, and is in consequence exposed to the direct disturbing influence of the trawl. It has been suggested that the ripe pilchards keep at some distance from the land, which, if it is the case, explains at once their scarcity in the nets, the latter being rarely shot far from shore.

This brings us to the consideration of the pilchard's migrations, the most economically important by far of the various episodes in its life history. As in the case of the allied herring, the general tendency at present is to regard these concerted movements as of only limited range, and there seems every reason, relying on the evidence of practical observers such as he, to agree with Mr. Matthias Dunn, of Mevagissey, that the pilchards remain in the Channel throughout the year, though, as already suggested, a very inconsiderable journey in the offing might easily take them beyond the ken of the netsmen, whose luggers, unless after mackerel, mostly hug the coast.

These migrations, whatever their extent, are in all probability nothing more than the very pressing search for food, and it seems that a deal of unnecessary mystery has been allowed to cloud the issue. Their periodic desertion, for example, of one stretch of our coast for another—whereby, indeed, Mevagissey at one time sprang up as the centre of an important industry—need indicate nothing more than the result of the discovery on their part of new and prolific grounds for the hunting of the larval crabs on which they feed. When, disturbed by either the trawlers or more natural causes, these tiny creatures take up new quarters, it is not difficult to imagine the hungry pilchards following suit, which will, without mystery, explain the falling off of recent years in many of the once apparently inexhaustible fisheries of the Biscay coast, the sardines having, on the other hand, appeared in their millions off parts of the Portuguese and African coasts but ill equipped with nets and fleets for the reception of the visitors.

Of some antiquity are the pilchard fisheries of Cornwall—indeed Couch claims for the sean-fishery Phœnician introduction. The historic aspect of the industry has, however, received its share of attention so often, that it may well be overlooked here. Pilchards are taken by one of two methods, the sean or the drift-net. The sean consists of a moving wall of small-meshed netting, kept in position by cork buoys along its upper edge and by leaden weights below. As it is designed to capture fishes that move close to the surface, the upper or buoyed edge must be flush with the surface of the water. In like manner, the leaded edge must hug the ground to prevent the escape of the fish below. Obviously, then, the sean can only be used in water of less than its own depth—about ninety-six feet—and it is in fact used only in the shallows. The principle of the sean is the enclosing of a particular shoal of passing fish, and the position and movements of these, indistinguishable from sea level, are fortunately observed without difficulty from the lofty cliffs so characteristic of the Cornish coast. On the highest points, watchers, or 'huers,' are accordingly placed; men who get fixed monthly wage, as well as a small percentage of every catch they are instrumental in compassing. As soon as the 'huers' have signalled, with a kind of military code peculiar to the profession, the presence of pilchards in the shoal water, the roomy sean-boats, manned by seven men, are got in readiness, and the nets are cleverly worked round the shoals, smaller boats being in attendance with stop-nets, which are shot at right angles to the larger sean in order to cut off the flight of the alarmed fish. In order to prevent the profitless disturbance of such precious shoals as enter the bay, there is a wise regulation fixing a minimum length of about three hundred yards for each sean, which has a corresponding depth of some thirty yards and a mesh which is rather under the inch square. The mesh of the drift-net is, as we shall presently see, much larger—an inch square at least—but its object is to allow of the fish strangling themselves, each in a mesh, whereas the sean has to enclose dense shoals of living fish and retain them unhurt.

As soon as the wall of netting has encircled the fish, the ends are drawn together, round as much of the shoal as the net can reasonably be expected to retain, and the fish are scooped out with a tuck-net worked inside the others, either immediately or when the tide is sufficiently low. The crews employed, then, in actually capturing the shoal are limited, but in hauling the sean ashore and getting the harvest as quickly as possible from the net, a large number of extra hands are requisitioned, the women often turning out as well. The days of the sean are numbered. Already it is being laid by at many ports where, until recently, its use was general, and not one has been out at Mevagissey for some years now.

As already mentioned, the principle of the drift-net differs materially from that involved in the working of the sean. While the latter method is a more or less straightforward attack on the shoal, a rapid flanking movement encircling the bewildered pilchards ere they have time to outmanœuvre their assailants, we have in the drift-net a deadly ambuscade, a death trap, laid only in the darkness of night, into which the unseeing fish must find their own way. The limitation of the sean is that it can be used only in shallow water; that of the drift-net is that it is effective only on dark nights, even the moonlight, or excessive phosphorescence of the water, being at times sufficient to spoil the fishermen's game.

Like the sean, the drift-net is a wall of netting, but, unlike it, it need not by any means reach the bottom of the sea, since, with a mesh of over an inch, it is capable of holding imprisoned by the gills every fish that unwittingly strikes it. In consequence of the uselessness of this net by daylight, the luggers, each of them from thirty to forty-five feet long—forty-two feet is the rule—and carrying two or three men and a lad, and fully two-thirds of a mile of netting, do not put out from port much before sunset, somewhat earlier or later in the afternoon according to the tide, also taking into consideration the particular grounds it is intended to work. They rarely fish far from land, not more than ten or fifteen miles out, but occasionally they have to go some distance along the coast before they strike likely conditions. More often, however, they fish in their own bays, shoot the nets by eight o'clock, haul at eleven or thereabouts, and are back in the harbour a little after midnight.

The huers would, of course, be of no use in determining the whereabouts and movements of deep-water fish, and the commodore of the driving fleet must therefore rely for his guidance on more natural indications, foremost among them the signs of feeding gannets and porpoises. When the shoal, or rather the activity of its natural enemies, is seen, the nets are shot, each boat riding at the head of its net and, with the help of what little 'air' there is at the time, keeping it taut and clear of the rest. As the darkness increases, the shoals, deceived maybe by a welcome ripple on the surface, strike the nets. Then follows the hauling, a particularly attractive spectacle when there is phosphorescence or, as the men call it, 'briming' on the waters, though, as already mentioned, the catches are not on such occasions heavy, owing, no doubt, to the betraying luminosity that reveals the snare to its intended victims. Most of the pilchards are dead ere released from the meshes, but at times there are a number, probably enmeshed just before the hauling, still struggling on the decks.

Quickly the nets are got aboard, and they are cleared of the fish as they come in over the gunwale, the fleet returning to its moorings in the pool shortly afterwards. The sales of the night's harvest are effected long before dawn in such cases, and already before breakfast time the jowders are on their way inland, and have sold fresh pilchards at many a wayside farm. The price fetched by the fish, as also the catch per boat, is naturally subject to much variation. The boats draw anything in the night's lottery, from a blank to a hundred thousand fish, and the price, regulated by the usual conditions of sale, may be anything from twelve shillings a thousand down to five. The greater portion of the Mevagissey take is daily bought by Mr. Dunn for the sardine factory on the quay. Whether British sardines will ever supplant those of French make has yet to be seen, but it is fair to surmise that this desirable consummation will not at any rate be in way of achievement until Cornish fishermen use a smaller mesh to their nets, and take pains to intercept, in sean or drift-net, the small yearling fish. Mr. Dunn assigns as an interesting reason of the greater prevalence of small fish in the French nets, the pains taken in those parts to feed them on cod's roe, on which as much as sixty thousand pounds sterling has, he says, been spent in some years, the feeding beginning in March. At the same time, Mr. Dunn admits the abundance of these small pilchards on our own coasts in the autumn. As it is, these, like the anchovy, are woefully neglected in British seas, and the preference is rightly given to the more delicate small French fish. With young and tender pilchards of a year's growth in place of the more sinewy and bony veterans at present tinned in our factories, there is no reason why British sardines should not in the near future be something more than a name, or why the bulk of our pilchards should continue to find their way to the Spanish and Italian markets.

F. G. AFLALO.

MAN'S DAYS

A sudden wakin', a sudden weepin' ;
A li'l suckin', a li'l sleepin' ;
A cheel's full joys an' a cheel's short sorrows,
Wi' a power o' faith in gert to-morrows.

Young blood red hot an' the love o' a maid ;
Wan glorious day as'll never fade ;
Some shadows, some sunshine, some triumphs, some tears,
Wi' a gatherin' weight o' the flyin' years.

Then auld man's talk o' the days behind 'e ;
Your darter's youngest darter to mind 'e ;
A li'l dreamin', a li'l dyin',
A li'l lew corner o' airth to lie in.

EDEN PHILLPOTTS.

THE GOLDEN HARBOUR

In a little wind-beaten hamlet on the Land's End peninsula there dwelt towards the end of the last century a couple of lean, withered grandsires who were regarded by the villagers with singular curiosity as being men of strange experiences and of a sadness equally rare.

Long ago, when both were youngsters in their teens, the two friends, out one night for a frolic, had borrowed a boat belonging to a crabber in the cove and had taken a trip vaguely 'out to sea :' determined for once to taste the luxury of adventure, even if they were never to know the flavour of it again.

They had taken with them a bottle of wine, a loaf of bread, and some fruit, which they had purchased out of their savings of the last month or two, and thus fortified against the weariness of the brief spring night, they had rowed out stealthily into the open and there set sail and stole westward with the breeze.

The moon hung in the sky like a globe of frosted silver, an incessant stream of thin white clouds ever drifting airily across its disc, and what with the fresh breeze sighing against the sail and whining or whispering softly across the grey undulations, the fascination of their position held them like a song.

The weirdness and mystery of the unfathomable wastes around, the suggestiveness of the alien world hanging high above them, and of the steady, persistent march of the clouds, coming out of infinity to pass and disappear, and, more alluring still, the inscrutable secrets of the future—its promises, its seductive daydreams, its unfathomable possibilities—all these combined to fill the brains of the two adventurers with an airy drift of fancies as elusive as it was sweet, till it seemed as though the unknown and the unfamiliar were drawing near to them, were as close as the glint of moonlight on the wave ridges just ahead.

They had long felt in their blood the craving for adventure, the desire to outstep the commonplaces of life, and to taste for themselves the flavour of romance, and all the vague, untranslatable wonderment of their hopes filled and thrilled them now with a zest that was irresistible.

To be here on the sea in the remote and quiet midnight was in itself an experience that smacked choicely on their palates, and their thoughts began to freshen and to widen in response.

Presently they opened the bottle and took a generous draught of wine, and then, lolling on the seat in the shadow of the sail, they regaled themselves lightheartedly with the fruit and a crust of bread.

Meanwhile the boat went ever gliding westward towards the unknown future and its unknown lands, of which they had already begun vivaciously to dream, till it seemed to them, so remote was the hungry world of effort, that the perfumes of a distant Araby began already to sweeten the air.

By-and-by, however, they were oppressed by a sense of drowsiness. A delicious relaxation of thought stole over them, and one proposed to the other that they should take a nap in turns: 'for a few minutes only, just sufficient to freshen them up.'

So the youngest fell asleep in the shadow of the sail, and the other sat beside him with the tiller in his grasp.

The glitter on the water made the watcher's eyes tired, and he dropped his lids once or twice—merely for a second or two.

Then he opened them with a start—once more closed them drowsily—and finally sank down against his comrade fast asleep.

Whether their slumbers were brief or lengthy they were neither of them able to say. When they woke they found the boat was still speeding onward, and still the great wan moon looked down on them wistfully, while the homeless night wind whined across the swell. So once more they had recourse to the wine in the locker, and let the boat speed westward while they dallied with their thoughts.

How far and how long they thus glided onward—ever moving deeper into the vast blue distance, down which the moon had already begun to drop—neither of the adventurers was able to decide. Presently, however, they perceived dimly ahead of them the grey and shadowy outlines of an island, like a dark boss set in the silver round of sea.

Thitherward the adventurers accordingly steered their course, and as they gradually drew nearer to the unknown island, they were aware of a troop of naked seamaidens gambolling around the boat in the most playful manner, some even climbing up and clinging to the gunwale, while their hair streamed over their wet pink shoulders, and their eyes laughed temptingly and caressingly at the twain.

Then one of the seamaidens clambered lightly into the boat, and, seating herself beside them in the shadow of the sail, she began to sing softly to the enchanted voyagers, accompanying herself on a tiny golden harp.

Such singing the twain had never heard before. Not even the poignant sweetness, the thrilling passion of the nightingale, could rival its exquisite cadences, with their wonderful depth and range; and the rare, alluring magic of it was sweeter than love itself. It soothed, it lifted to rapture, it was voluptuous—what was it not? The two adventurers, as they sat and listened to it, were as men who were married to bliss: desiring nothing, remembering nothing, conscious only of pure content.

But presently, and all too soon, the music dwindled and narrowed its notes, till it seemed to merge in the drowsy monotone of the mighty sea itself.

Past them, now, the grim Phantom Ship of the sea seemed to steal like a bulk of faint grey shadow, the wan, thin moonbeams shining through her sails and striking through the insubstantial ribs of her hull like spokes of light escaping from a lantern; above the crests of the waves, touched with weird phosphorescence, peered the dead-white faces of long-drowned sailors; and in the shallow furrows between the grey undulations uncouth sea monsters, with glimmering eyes, swam and gibbered, and passed away like dreams.

Still nearer to the boat the seamaidens swam and gambolled, but among them now huge whales rolled and spouted, and sinister-looking sharks, with crafty eyes, moved like purple shadows through the clear blue water, their great fins waving like gigantic arms. Occasionally, too, naked tritons rose above the swell, blowing faint distant music from grotesquely twisted shells, from which long green sea-tangles swayed and floated. And although it was moonlight—if moonlight, indeed, it were—dainty little sea-swallows and lavender-pinioned kittiwakes sailed airily to and fro, piping quaintly as they wheeled.

At last, in through the shallows the boat glided buoyantly, the crowd of sea creatures drifted behind and disappeared, and, as the brown sail idly flapped against the mast, the maiden with the harp beckoned graciously to the voyagers, and out they stepped on the firm yellow sand.

When would wonders ever cease in this enchanted voyage of theirs!

Here were booths and crowds of merrymakers, dancing girls and humorous clowns, a very wilderness of shows and delightful entertainments, and the scene alive with jollity, turn where they would. Here were shops whose rich display pictures had never equalled; and buildings whose stately grandeur outrivalled even an artist's dreams. And everywhere was the dewy witchery of morning: the deep and jocund happiness of May. In the leafy thickets the nightingales sang rapturously, their seductive strains thrilling with the very ecstasy of love; and brilliant-petalled flowers blossomed lavishly everywhere, making splashes of gorgeous colour among the herbs and feathery grass.

The high green roof with its chequered light and shadow, the mosaic of things beautiful on the soft green floor, the delicate stirring everywhere of innumerable forms of life, these were but so many notes in the orchestra of nature, all blending and merging exquisitely in the harmony of the whole. And in that whole the thread of melody in the hearts of the voyagers was by no means one of the least alluring for their thoughts.

Everywhere was youth, buoyant and unhampered. Youth with its infinite witchery of promise: youth with its equally infinite hopes. Grey hairs, failures, the bitterness of defeat—not a hint of these was visible, turn where one would. It was the morning of the year in the woodlands and in the meadows: it was the morning of the year in the narrower field of life.

Through this wonderland the two friends moved delightedly; while ever at their side kept their companion from the sea, clothed only, yet clothed sufficiently, in the glory of her hair. And all about them sounded melodies dulcet and most ravishing; and the woods were full of perfumes; and the blood was sweet in their veins.

And, oh! how generously kind to them everyone was! Their hands were loaded with gifts of the most goodly description, and they were feasted royally in the open booths with their hangings of coloured silks, and the musicians played sweetly to them, and the air was soft around them always, and their hearts were empty of sorrow and their souls were filled with peace.

How long they lingered here the voyagers never knew; and why they left its Golden Harbour was a greater mystery still.

But one evening—if it were ever evening in this land of joy and sunshine—they found themselves again embarking sorrowfully in their boat that lay rocking in the shallows with the seagulls wheeling above its sail.

And presently they were drifting dolefully across a sea as grey as steel; the maiden sitting beside the mast, harping to them, oh, how sorrowfully! and the boom and crash of breakers sounding menacingly at their backs.

By-and-by they were aware that the dawn was brightening round them, and that the dim and ghostly heavens were pulsing slowly back to blue.

But as the first dazzling sun-rays streamed across the waves—touching, as with blood, the long undulations—the maiden rose from her seat with a low and grievous cry. Sweeping up the gifts they had deposited on the seat beside her, she seized them in both her hands and plunged wailingly into the sea.

The voyagers stared aghast to see their treasures vanish thus—their heaps of gold and pearls, their silks and precious merchandise—and, more than all, to see the dainty companion of their adventures sink beneath the waters and irrevocably disappear.

Steadily and inexorably the light broadened around them, till the mystery and infinitude of the dawn had vanished utterly; and, as they looked out sombrely on the weary leagues of water, they were aware that they were again speeding back to the common day.

Then despair seized hold on them, and they began to lament and wring their hands; till presently, like men who were drunken through much sorrow, they lay down on the footboards helplessly—hopeless, and waiting for death.

Hours must have passed, during which they must have become insensible. When they woke to life again they were on the deck of a little collier, whose crew stood clustered around gaping at them wonderingly, yet with something like a touch of mockery in their regard.

It was the wine that did it all, the rescuers persisted in saying. It was merely a drunken dream, this island and these adventures of theirs; neither more nor less than that—had not all of them known the like?

Vainly did the two voyagers endeavour to argue with them; these men of the cabin and the forecastle were not to be convinced. The seamaidens and the island—it was all a drunken dream!

And when they returned to their native village, the tale followed them even there. Their adventures in the Golden Harbour, and the treasures that would have proved their story—they were all a freak of fancy, they were all a drunken dream!

But the two adventurers knew better, and were not lightly to be put down.

Often did they relate to unbelieving ears the tale of their marvellous voyage and of the Golden Harbour at the end of it, and hotly did they argue for the truth of all they told.

But this was in the vigorous morning of life.

As they grew older, the two friends were content to argue less; it sufficed them to remember, and to feed their hearts on this.

In secret, however, they earnestly would talk together of their experiences; of the wonders they had seen—the allurements and the many mysteries—and of that rare and exquisite haven in which it was always May. And sturdily did they resolve that, before death should seal their eyelids, they would set out again for that harbour of many hopes, once more to taste its pleasures and there peacefully to end their days.

But the world is tame and prosaic, and its tasks are very hard. To the dreamer and the man of memories it holds out only an empty platter. 'Would you eat my food?' it grumbles; and then menaces, 'Do my tasks!'

And besides, there were the seductions and the temptations close at their elbows. There were maidens they would like to be kind to; there were experiences they would like to taste. And when the passionate thoughts of lovers presently began to whisper to them, they delayed until ' to-morrow ' that more distant quest that could wait.

And now the years strode up to them sombre and menacing; each with its draught that dulls and lethargises, and each with its ties that bind faster even than steel. And as the magic net of life entangled them more and more, the two friends, helpless amid the perplexity of its meshes, half-wondered whether memory were given merely for a torment, and hope only that a man might taste the bitterness of despair.

But, through it all, their thoughts yearned persistently towards the island, and often did they talk of it as they sat at their doorsteps of an evening, when the swifts were flying high against the faint pink afterglow, and, lower down among the shadows, the bats flitted furtively—ungainly and uncanny, like their own abortive hopes.

Once—but this was when the heyday of life was over—they did, indeed, set off for the island; having heartened themselves to the height of this adventure through dwelling on the gathering shadows of their lives.

But the sea ahead of them seemed now strangely lonely and inhospitable, full of unknown terrors and of infinite perplexities, and the warm and fruitful land, the familiar things they were leaving, drew them back with a clinging urgency they were powerless to withstand.

Presently they fell to fishing for their wives; and when the fish were piled-up silverly at their feet, they turned and sailed back to the village with their harvest; protesting to each other, with suspicious iteration, that, for a voyage like this they meditated, the present was unpropitious, but that 'one day' they would prepare for it and would deliberately carry it through.

As the years rolled on, the position of the two friends became picturesquely unique. Young men full of the unrest of their prime—flushed with the quickened pulse, the dancing life-blood of the morning—would come to listen hungrily to the tale of the marvellous island, and to revel in the idea that presently, to them also, would be granted visions as goodly and adventures equally rare. Then there came over-tired women, worn with child-bearing and wifely troubles, whom it rested (so they said) to hear of a life so happy—a life in a land where Care had never set her foot. And young girls, tremulously throbbing with their hopes, stole near occasionally to listen furtively to the talk, that they might feed their hearts with dreams of the beauty and the mystery, and might yearn and sigh in secret for a happiness so complete. And old men, hopelessly worsted in the strife, depressed and full of inarticulate bitterness, came again and again to listen to the story ; if haply they might believe it—if only for an hour.

So the two friends ripened slowly for the sickle ; men of glamour for their neighbours, tragic failures for themselves.

At last one evening, through the jessamine-scented dusk, to the little thatched cottage of one of the friends came Death, and, tapping at the window-pane, imperiously beckoned him forth.

As his old companion held his wasted hand tenderly, the dying man whispered, 'I can see it now, William ! I shall be there waiting for you. I can hear the music—*hark* !' And with that his eyelids quivered and his spirit passed out to Death.

The solitary survivor, now fallen into decrepitude, seemed to his neighbours to weaken in mind even more pitifully than he weakened in body. He would sit for hours silent in the afternoon sunshine, silent and full of a sadness which they could none of them comprehend.

Was he beginning at last to realise the inevitable tragedy of life's illusions, the profound irony that forms the ground-note to its most seductive music, the subtle poison of experience with which it ultimately murders hope ?

And the Golden Harbour that in youth he had visited in his boat of dreams, did he realise *now* that it was more distant from him even than heaven ; that, though he lived for a hundred years, he would see it never again ?

He spoke of many things to his neighbours as he sat at his doorstep in the evenings, but of the distant Golden Harbour he no longer uttered a word.

At last one afternoon when the folks of the hamlet were away haymaking, and the air was full of the far-off music of their voices, the old man, stick in hand, rose from his bench and slowly and painfully hobbled down the empty street.

And on their return through the hush and the paling gold of the afterglow, the haymakers found that he was nowhere to be seen.

Then one of his grandsons—himself a husband and a father—remembering the old man's babble of the Golden Harbour, hurried down to the beach with his children trooping at his heels.

And there, in a boat which the ebbing tide had left stranded, they found the old man lying with his face to the sunset, but with his lips closed smilingly in the quiet sleep of death.

J. H. PEARCE.

When that I view my Country o'er:
Of goodly things the plenteous store:
The Sea and Fish that swim therein,
And underground the Copper and Tin:
Let all the World say what it can,
Still I hold by the Cornishman,
And that one more especially
That first found out the Cornish Pastie.

When the Tinner to Bal takes a touchpipe for crowse
He cannot have Hot-meat sent from his house:
Yet hath no stomach for victuals cold,
So a Pasty he takes in a Napkin rolled:
And though he leave it for half the day,
Within his Hogan Bag warm 'twill stay.
So I wish him joy whoever he be
That first found out the Cornish Pastie.

And when the Fisher a-fishing goes,
Though rough winds redden his ears and nose,
Little he careth how hard it blow,
So his Pasty lie safe in the locker below.
For though the lugger should ship a sea
Within its crust still dry 'twould be.
So I wish him joy whoever he be
That first found out the Cornish Pastie.

When lasses and lads to Country go
To bring in the May with a halantow:
The men choose the field-path (longer by miles)
To help the maidens over the stiles.

Belike then a Basket may fall to the ground:
Yet if it hold Pasties they still are sound.
So I wish him joy whoever he be
That first found out the Cornish Pastie.

When of dancing the Maidens have had their fill:
Although their swains would be dancing still:
Is not Nick's Pasty the sweeter yet
For being shared with his sweetheart Bet?
And does not Jan's the better taste,
For that his Jenifer made the paste?
So I wish him joy whoever he be
That first found out the Cornish Pastie.

For a Hearty Man's dinner 'tis ample fare,
With naught too little nor none to spare:
And here again it deserveth praise
That when it has vanished its virtue stays:
For it gives sweet ease to the scullery quean,
Who hath nor platters nor knives to clean.
So I wish him joy whoever he be
That first found out the Cornish Pastie.

Now in the World since it first began,
What other dish has been made by man,
Both Knife and Fork: both Plate and Table,
Meat and Bread and Vegetable?
So one and all come drink to his health:
May he live merry in peace and wealth!
And give him a cheer with three times three
That first found out the Cornish Pastie!

R. MORTON NANCE.

MARGARET GODOLPHIN

TWO NOBLE DAMES

MARGARET GODOLPHIN—GRACE GRENVILE

In the wide domain of history there are many garden plots. Some blaze at us down the centuries with flaming tulips and carnations: we look at them with admiration, but they leave no mark upon our minds. And some are heavy scented with the clinging odours of luscious shrubs, too sweet and subtle for the common use of all mankind, while some are stiff with formalism that repels us. Others again are buried in deep gloom, or choked with poisonous weeds. But here and there is one so fresh and sweet and sunny that it can be likened to nothing but an old vicarage garden such as one may see here and there upon the coast, where on some spring evening the scent of wallflowers growing thickly mingles with the salt odours of the flowing tide.

Such, and so fragrant, is the garden plot which Margaret Godolphin tended during her short life, and of which old John Evelyn, who loved her with a love such as his austere old heart bestowed on few objects in this naughty world, has left us a description very apt to catch our sympathy even to-day, by the deep feeling which breaks out continually from its somewhat formal paragraphs of eulogy. Indeed it is not often that an old moralist, sick with disgust at the antics of a Court which he sees growing daily more corrupt, finds a pure flower growing in the midst of rottenness, a woman who walked straight and fearless when all around her had lost their way, a soul which clung to a simple clue when her fellow courtiers were misled by levity and cleverness, and yet, with all this rarity of aim, this singularity of strength, a woman by no means austere or reserved, but beautiful and witty, charming in conversation, sympathetic in her actions, speaking ill of none, devoid of jealousies, sweet and courteous in temper. Such are few women of whom records have descended to us, but such was Margaret Godolphin; and can one wonder that John Evelyn, who was no more insensible than the rest of us to the attraction of a pretty woman, but who had checked and mortified his human inclinations because in his generation he saw not how to indulge them, remaining clean, felt his heart leap towards a maid of honour who outshone the rest in beauty, who held her own in any conversation, yet was purity itself in all her thoughts and actions?

Daughter of a brave and trusted Royalist colonel, and of a mother so honourable and sagacious that in the few years over which her widowed life extended she not only paid off the debts bequeathed to her (as to many another lonely woman by a husband who grudged nothing to the king), but also built up a competence for three daughters, Margaret inherited rare excellencies of character, of which indeed she had sore need. For she had scarce reached her twelfth year when Anne Hyde, Duchess of York, begged her of her mother as a maid of honour, and she came to Court, a pretty, unprotected child, cast among a gang of profligates who had cut out 'faith' from their vocabulary, and only spoke of 'honour' at the gaming table or on the duelling ground. Of her fellow maids of honour Pepys gives us inimitable glimpses. 'What mad freaks,' he cries, ' the Mayds of Honour at Court have : that Mrs. Jennings, one of the Dutchesse's Maids, the other day dressed herself like an orange wench, and went up and down and cried oranges, till falling down, or by some accident, her fine shoes were discerned, and she put to a great deal of shame, such as these tricks being ordinary, and worse among them, whereby few will venture upon them for wives.' Poor, pretty Margaret, coupled with so riotous a crew, and with how few protectors! 'Be sure never to talk to the King!' she notes among the good resolutions in her journal, betraying in that private record her conviction that in the anointed person of his Majesty there lurked a danger greater than all others. No wandering heroine of romance ever walked among greater perils, and none ever passed more scatheless through them. For the child had conceived a plan of life when other children of her age were dreaming of their toys, and she had set her whole thoughts towards Heaven, all her steadfastness and energy towards salvation, long years before John Evelyn met her.

But many a day went by ere Evelyn, sick and blinded by the steaming iniquities of Whitehall, could see her as she was. To him Mrs. Blagge—for she was not married then—was no different from any other lady of the Court; he noted that she was 'a very agreeable lady,' but scoffed at his wife's assurances that a charming manner covered aims and practices which were as rigid and sincere as his own. He had sounded so many souls at Court, and found so few which were not tainted. He had no heart for further search. 'To believe there were many saints in that Country,' he said long afterwards,

'I was not much inclined;' and had it not been that the compulsion of some affairs drove him once more to Court, he might well have lived and died in ignorance of the beauty of that character whose fragrance he cherished so ardently when at last he recognised it.

Reluctantly, and yielding only to the enforcement of good manners, which made it impossible for him to ignore at Court a lady who had visited at his house in the country, Evelyn called on Mrs. Blagge. 'I fancied her,' he says, 'some airy thing, that had more Witt than Discretion.' He went expecting levity, and found the atmosphere of a temple. It was a day of solemn devotion with Margaret. She said little, looked very humble; and the stern moralist came away doubting whether he had not misjudged her. The doubt became conviction. Evelyn began to frequent her rooms willingly and even eagerly; and on her part, Margaret, who was hungry for a wise friend and a discreet adviser, encouraged him to do so, telling him at last that 'if I were not weary of her, and would be so charitable, she should take it kindly that I came often to her.'

Not long afterwards it happened that he found her more thoughtful than ordinary. 'I asked her what made her look so solemnly. She told me she had never a friend in the world. Noe, said I, that's impossible; I believe nobody has more; for all that know you must love you, and those that love you are continually your friends.' And thereupon he ventured to speak of one who was more than a friend, namely Godolphin, who afterwards became her husband. But Margaret put aside that subject, repeating that she wanted a friend; 'in that name, she said, is a great deale more than I can express: a faithfull friend, whome I might trust with all that I have, and God knows that is but little. . . . Madam, said I, doe you speak this to me, as if I were capable of serving you in anything considerable? I believe you the person in the world (replyed she) who would make such a friend as I wish for, if I had meritt enough to deserve it. . . . Madam, said I, to be called your friend were the most desirable in the world. . . . Pray leave your complimenting (said she smileing) and be my friend then, and looke upon me henceforth as your Child. To this purpose was her obligeing reply; and, there standing pen and ink upon the table, in which I had been drawing something upon a paper like an Alter, she writt these words: "Be this the Symboll of Inviolable Friendshipp,' Mary Blagge, 16th October, 1672," and underneath, "For my brother E. . . ," —and soe delivered it to me with a smile.'

Nothing that Margaret did or said was undertaken lightly; and not even the memorable exposition of the obligations of friendship which Evelyn immediately gave her caused her hesitation. 'You are to write to me,' said her new friend, 'when I am absent; mention me in all your prayers to God, to admonish me of all my failings, to visitt me in sickness, to take care of me when I am in distress, and never to forsake me, change or lessen your particular esteeme, till I prove inconstant or perfidious, and noe man's friend.' So this rare friendship was knotted tightly between the girl maid of honour and the dour old Puritan who might have been her father. 'I may grow old or forgettful,' Margaret wrote to him, 'and melancholy or stupid, and in that case

will no more answer for myself than for a stranger; butt, whilst I am myself
and a Christian, I will be yours;' and Evelyn on his side looked on her 'as my
child indeed.'

It is not difficult to understand how Margaret must have hungered for the
friendship of a strong, wise, fatherly adviser. But in one way, which she may
perhaps have hardly seen for herself, Evelyn's robust and rugged sense was
invaluable to her. It is clear that she was in some danger of setting down
her human instincts as so many sins, or at least temptations; and of subsiding
into a devotee. Her religion was at times a source of terror to her. It was
he who taught her that it should be always joyful. She left the Court, that
she might be the freer for good works, and in this her friend upheld her; but
when the beauty of an unmarried life threatened to obtain sovereignty over
her, and she was hovering on the verge of perpetual celibacy, he threw all the
weight of his influence and friendship against her fancy for seclusion, and in
favour of Godolphin, that true lover who had waited for her nine years already,
and would have none but her, if he died unwedded. 'Marry, in God's name,'
said he, 'since my advice you ask: itt is finally what I think you ought to
resolve on.' And so strengthened and encouraged, Margaret linked her saintly
life with the head of that great family of Godolphin which is one of the noble
memories of Cornwall.

This was that Sidney Godolphin who rose in after days to the rank of
Lord High Treasurer, and on whom men look back in these times as a slow,
frugal, cautious, patient minister, who went out of office poorer than he entered
it, and by simple qualities did his country greater service than the brilliant
intellects around him. Evelyn tells us nothing of his character; but we can
guess what Margaret loved in him, and we can believe that she was right. For the
things worth doing in the world need for the most part no brilliancy of intellect,
nor are they done by very clever people. They require only slow and simple
gifts, patience, honesty, tenacity, a deliberate, clear way of looking for the
fact—rare qualities at Charles II's Court, but those in which Godolphin
excelled, and those precisely which Margaret would value most. Such was
the origin of their long attachment, the substance of their short life together,
and the foundation of that long faith which kept the wife's place vacant in her
husband's home during six-and-thirty years of continuous honour, fame, and
sorrow. He had found his true companion, and when he lost her he knew that
in the world there was no other.

Thus in this marriage Margaret was as free to be herself as if she were
still single, and she bent her strength towards doing good. 'She would enquire
out the poor and miserable,' Evelyn tells us, ' even in Hospitals, humble cells,
and cottages, whither I have sometimes accompanied her, as far as the very
skirts and obscure places of the Towne. . . . How many naked poore creatures
she covered!' She was too generous to the poor to be otherwise than frugal
on herself. 'I will never play this half year,' she notes, 'butt at 3 penny
omber, and then with one att halves. I will not, I doe not vow, but I will not
do it.' And the money which she would not squander on play found its way
infallibly to the poor, to visit whom she would walk out alone and on foot and

fasting, when (says Evelyn) 'it was hardly fit to send a servant out.' With all this, she was a pretty mimic, and would often give rein to her sense of humour. She was especially delightful in mimicking a French friar, whom she had heard preaching on the profession of a nun, and whose fantastic speech and gestures she could copy to the life.

Thus the pretty house in Scotland Yard where the Godolphins lived was the happiest of homes. It lacked but one charm, the patter of children's feet, and the ring of little voices. Margaret's motherly instinct sought an outlet upon an orphan child which she adopted; but a more natural joy was in store for her, and on September 3, 1678, Evelyn coming to pay his customary visit in the forenoon was admitted, after an hour's anxious waiting, to see a new-born child in its mother's arms, and to receive her injunction to give thanks to God for His infinite mercy to her. But even while Evelyn went away with a joyful and a grateful heart, the shadow was drifting up dark and heavy. Four days passed, and then, as Evelyn came out of church, a hasty note from Godolphin was given him. A fever had seized Margaret, and she lay desperately ill, raving frequently, and much distressed by the weather, which was inordinately hot. All that night Evelyn hurried to and fro in search of skilful doctors, who were found with difficulty. When morning came, all hope was gone; and nothing remained but for him to walk with his friend up to the very gate of death, which he did, holding her hand in his until that strong fellowship could give her no comfort any more.

'If I might,' she wrote in her last loving message to her husband, penned some days before her illness, with a prevision that the time for saying such things was at hand, 'if I might, I would beg that my body might lye where I have had such a minde to goe myselfe, att Godolphyn, among your friends. I believe, if I were carried by sea, the expense would not be very great; but I don't insist on that place, if you think it not reasonable; lay me where you please.' But Godolphin's only pleasure was to lay her where she wished; and so the dust of one of the truest and noblest women known in our history was carried to the old house in the valley underneath the twin hills, Godolphin and Tregonning, and rests now in Breage church, perhaps not wholly forgotten, even though the mansion which should have been her home is dropping into decay, its pleasaunce overgrown, its courtyard grassy, its rafters falling in the great hall, and in its only habitable portion a desolating aspect of middle-class comfort at sight of which the imagination, seeking to reconstruct the dignified old life of the Godolphins, stops baffled and perplexed. How different from the grand solitude, and perfect repair, of that other great mansion at Trerice, whose vast and noble rooms seem still tenanted by the majestic figure of John Arundel! Have we no nobler use in our Duchy to which these houses could be put? What a wide and easy gateway each one of them might be to the past history of Cornwall, its deeds and its old associations!

But, for the most part, as each ancient family dwindles and decays, its house, however famous, begins to perish also. So it has happened to Trefusis; and such has been the fate of that which above all others we should have wished intact, because it was the grandest of them all. I speak of Stowe, the home of the second noble lady whose name, dear and honoured in all Cornwall still, stands at the head of these pages. In strict order of time I should have set her first; but the place of honour in an article is at the end, and I wished the last impression on the minds of those who read this tribute to be the memory of Grace, Lady Grenvile, that true wife who must surely, despite her sorrows, be counted among the happiest women whom we know; for if she suffered years of widowhood, she lived also through nearly a whole generation of domestic peace, for the most part, doubtless, quite untroubled by any anticipation of the terrors and the sorrows which were gathering over England. To us who look back on the early days of Charles I., knowing what torrents of noble blood were poured out before those fatal dissensions were composed, the whole period seems full of warning signs, such as must have taught the nation what was coming on it. But the portents were little noticed by the multitude then, just as we may be neglecting signs of other dangers now; and even in the days when Sir Beville, her noble husband, then plain Mr. Grenvile, was acting with his close friend, John Eliot, in stubborn opposition to the Court, it is probable that Mrs. Grenvile's anxieties never went the length of fearing that a time might come when the tenantry would be called up fully armed, or when her husband would lead them in a desperate pitched battle on the very confines of his own estate.

We know  nothing of Grace Grenvile before her marriage, save

GRACE GRENVILE

that she was daughter of Sir G. Smythe of Exeter, and, by her mother's side, of Cornish descent as noble as her husband's; and indeed, so scanty are the family memorials of the days in which she lived, that it is only by occasional sidelights that we can see a woman rare enough to be called 'sister' by John Eliot, who was bound to her by no tie of blood. We may be sure that grave and lofty patriot did not bestow terms of such affection lightly on any whom he met; and she whom he chose to call sister in those troublous times must have owned some qualities very nobly feminine, such as could solace and encourage and restore even that strong spirit to press forward on the path which led through the Tower and the grave to imperishable honour. Some trusty account of the intercourse of John Eliot with Grace Grenvile would be a precious document indeed; but it is lost beyond repair, and we are left to guess and wonder.

Such glimpses as we have of the home life of Beville and Grace Grenvile are so simple and so happy that we may very well surmise what drew the affection of the weary politician so strongly to the quiet country lady who longed to have her husband always with her. 'My dearest,' her husband wrote from London, 'I am exceedingly glad to heare from you, but doe desire you not to be so passionat for my absence. I vow you cannot more desire to have me at home than I desire to be there.' And then he proceeds, like a man whose heart was always in his home, to give her directions for the masons ' to goe on as fast as they can about the stable, that if it be possible, the walls may be up and finished against my coming down,' with a dozen such commissions, which it was doubtless her pleasure to fulfil. On his part, too, good Mr. Grenvile was not to let the Parliament business occupy all his thoughts during his weary absences in London. His memory was charged with many trifles to which he gave his mind cheerfully enough, as the following letter witnesses : ' My dearest,—I have received yours by Mr. Browning, and Dick's; I cannot expresse my joye for all your healthes, but shall pray for the continuance. Your Beds are a-making; and some Turkey worke for stooles and chaires I have seene, but not bargained for; it is verrie deare, but if money hould out, I will have them. I have lighted upon a prety commodetie of Damaske and Diaper, and am told it is so cheape as I shall not meete with it soe ordinarily, therefore I ventured a little money in it. . . . I do now send it to the carriers, but forbeare cutting of it till I come Downe, y^t we may consider together.'

It was the happiest of lives. 'Charge Postlett and Hooper,' wrote Sir Beville, 'that they keepe out the Piggs and all other things out of my new nursery, and the other orchard too. Let them use any meanes to keepe them safe, for my trees will all be spoild if they com in, wch I would not for a world.' Many of us who know Beville and Grace Grenvile only by reputation as set upon an eminence of fame and sorrow a little higher than our human sympathies, will feel a sudden kindness for the good man anxious about his apple trees.

'Sweet Mr. Grenvile, . . . I am in no better health of mind or body than when we parted; but God keepe you well, however I am, y^t will never be other than

'Y^r faithfull wife
'GRACE GRENVILE.

So wrote this simple lady; and added in a postscript, ' If you please to bestowe a plaine black Gownd of any cheape stufe on me I will thank you and some black shoes.' Were many wives so modest even in the country in those old quiet days?

There are many such passages in the still existing letters of Grace Grenvile, all revealing the woman as she was in life, firm, sagacious, and intensely loving towards her husband and her children. I feel some hesitation in dilating on these intimate self-revelations, precious as they were to the eyes for which they were written, but intended for no other. Yet we who honour the men and women who have lived before us are entitled, in all reverence and tenderness, to see so much of the secret chambers of their lives as may enable us to understand their characters; and I take from the book, before I close it, one more letter, written to Sir Beville when he had followed the King upon his Scotch expedition, riding at the head of a regiment raised on his own estate.

'O my Dearest,

'I have receavd yours dated the 15 of May from Newcastle bringing me the glad tidings of y^r recovery before I heard of your sickness, wch I praise God for, and shall long to heare the same of Dick, whose sicknes being so foolishly gotten, I feare may prove dangerous, and must confesse till I heare againe shall remayne in much doubt. I am both sorry and ashamed he should erre so much to his own prejudice, having had so many warnings, but I shall and doe beseech God to restore him, and blesse him with judgment and grace to serve God truly and obey your precepts. I must beseech you though at this distance that you will pardon ordinary errors in him. . . . Many times I am in doubt that his sicknes was more than y^r letter expressed, and that you might prepare me for worse news. God grant my feares be vaine; and, deare Mr. Grenvile, pardon my infirmity in doubting the worst, if there be no cause. . . .'

There is evidence enough among the existing letters of both wife and husband that the scapegrace Dick, their eldest son, wrung their hearts sorely many times before he died. This was by no means the first occasion on which his mother had pleaded that at least his 'ordinary errors' might be forgiven him; and doubtless she did not plead in vain. But other troubles and anxieties were thickening about the Grenvile household, and the shadow of griefs more poignant than those caused by the erring Dick was rising fast across Grace Grenvile's path. Her husband brought back knighthood from his Scotch expedition; but the distinction counted little with a woman to whom her husband's safety was more than any honours he could bring. England grew stormier from day to day; and even those truehearted men in whom there was no faction began to see that the time for moderation had gone by, that the sword was going to be drawn, and they must resolve under whose banner they would fight. Sir Beville's choice had long been made. There has been much marvel among those who have written of his actions that a man who had supported John Eliot, and opposed the Court, should in his riper age be a valiant soldier of the King. I know not why any mystery should be seen in the conduct of one willing to oppose the policy of heady ministers, yet prepared to sacrifice life and fortune when the safety of the Crown itself was menaced. The distinction may be sound or unsound, but it is clear, and has in all ages been counted good enough to die for. In great and stirring times men fall into line on one side or the other because they approve some broad and simple principle. It was loyalty, not sympathy with every action of the Crown, which brought Sir Beville under the King's banner; and it was loyalty which brought the best and bravest flocking out of every hall and manor house from Jacobstow to Buryan, Bassetts and

Godolphins, Trelawneys, Arundels, Trevanions, Kendals, and a hundred more names of gallant gentleman making up the muster-roll of that Cornish army which broke the enemy like water and spent itself so nobly at Bradock Downs, at Stamford Hill, at Lansdown, and at Bristol.

Of all the women who stayed at home and wept in Cornwall during those great days, there was none who had set more happiness on the cast of battle than Grace Grenvile; nor was there any to whom the terrors of war came home more nearly. For having watched the muster of the tenantry at Stowe all armed, having seen them ride away, headed not only by Sir Beville, but by their son John—he who afterwards held out in Scilly for the King—and followed by the burly giant, Anthony Payne, whose towering height and vast strength were worth ten men in a mêlée, she had but a few months to wait before a great army of Parliament troops marched near Stowe, and took up their position on Stamford Hill, some eight miles west. She knew that the Cornish army, headed by Hopton and her husband, were marching from Launceston to attack this strong position; and on the next day from early morning till dusk she must have heard the sound of battle rolling along the coast, till at last when night fell her long agony was turned to joy by the news of a total victory won by the Cornish against amazing odds. It is said that Sir Beville himself rode home that night—the meeting of husband and wife must have been a scene comparable only to that drawn by the tenderest of Latin poets, who tells us how another husband came home suddenly from the wars, and found his wife Lucretia spinning among her maidens, and watched her weeping out of love and fear for him, and sprang forward to let her see that he was safe. 'Pone metum, venio.' Such must have been the meeting of Grace Grenvile with Sir Beville; followed quickly by what was probably their last parting, for it was in May that Stamford's horse was driven headlong out of Cornwall; and ere July was out Sir Beville lay stark and dead on the slope of Lansdown Hill, while his own troops, gasping, bleeding, and sore laboured, gained the top and held it.

'Maddam,' wrote Sir John Trelawney, 'hee is gone on his journey but a little before us; wee must march after when it shall please God.' It was four years before Grace Grenvile heard and answered to the marching bugle—years of anxiety as well as sorrow; for the cause of the King began to fail in Cornwall, and there were evil days for those who would fain have held it up. But in June 1647 the signal came for release; the true wife marched after her husband, and we may well believe he lingered on his way until she caught him up.

A. H. NORWAY.

A STRONG MAN

MY week at Portrewan was a week of blustering gales. From south-east to south-west they shifted, and round to the north and back again, bringing rain and hail and sea fog, with now and then some hours of dazzling sunshine. But with all their changes their force never abated. The little village, set snugly in a cleft in England's southernmost walls, was in a state of suspended animation. All the winter's work was done, boats repaired, gear mended, nets barked, fifteen hundred new crab-pots piled ready in the lofts; there was nothing left to do but await the wind's pleasure.

A spell of stillness was on the place. The sea roared without, the wind whistled high overhead, sometimes—but that was seldom—finding its way down the valley or round the headland, and sweeping the street bare of litter and odour. And in the midst of hurry and welter Portrewan reposed, silent and idle. Up the valley Nature was at work, heedless of her servant's rebellious bluster. The elms stood up in a mist of delicate ruddy purple, the blackthorn hedges were wreathed in their snow, green blades and disks had burst from every chink in the grey stone hedges; the shameless rooks, to whom domestic privacy is unknown, were squabbling and fighting round their naked, high-swinging nests; the smaller birds were going more discreetly about the great business of the year; and in every sheltered spot Spring had written her name full and clear in violets, and set her primrose seal beside it. 'Twas no time to be sitting and waiting, but to sit and wait was Portrewan's lot.

The bread-winning half of Portrewan took the delay calmly and philosophically, as is its nature; only it found it expedient to escape from the domestic circle as early as might be, and to range itself in a lounging row against the door of the lifeboat house, there to remain, motionless and mostly silent, from morn to eve, through rain and shine, in womanless peace. For the tongues of wives grow sharp when nothing is doing, and the sight of a great hulking chap sprawling about the kitchen day after day, while the little pile of sovereigns in the top drawer upstairs grows less and less, is apt to prove too much for the feminine temper, be it ever so sweet and reasonable.

One soon got to know the little world of Portrewan by heart—at least in its idle aspect. One day resembled another as a pea its neighbour in the cod. Day broke, clear or overcast, but always heralded by the raucous matins of the gulls, circling and shouting at an incredible height above the cove. Then, as soon as the sun was up—sometimes before—a shambling step outside my window told me that the village natural had begun his tireless, day-long ramble. He never sat down, he seldom stood still for a minute, he never quitted the confines of the village, but as long as light remained in the sky he wandered up and down, peering into houses and cellars, greeting every passer-by with an uncouth chuckle, and incessantly talking, talking to himself. Portrewan opines that in his poor silly brain there lurks a dim notion that on his vigilance the town's peace and safety depend. Somebody once dubbed him 'Policeman Billy,' and the nickname stuck.

Later, between six and seven, came the sound of doors unlatching, and the swish of brooms on floors of stone and wood. The housewives of Portrewan are notable women all, and cleanliness is a passion with them. Seas may be rough or seas may be calm, but dust will ever gather, and no lie-abed can hope to wage successful war against it.

Then thin threads of smoke arose from twenty chimneys. The women-folk, their skirts tucked up, came to the doors, taking stock of the weather and shouting shrill greetings to one another, but postponing gossip till the idler hours. Then, precisely at eight o'clock, each house disgorged with difficulty a small boy or girl, yawning, sleepy-eyed, white jug in hand, on the way to fetch the breakfast milk from the farm on the hill. Still no sign of man, except Policeman Billy and the coastguardsman, hurrying down break-fastward from his look-out on the cliffs. Next, the return of the milk carriers, no longer dragging weary limbs, but shouting, leaping, running down the steep hill, to the imminent peril of the precious fluid. 'Twas a point of honour with them to vie with one another in courting the risk of a spill and the 'tight cobbing' which would inevitably follow.

The smoke increased in volume. Breakfast was toward. Half an hour, and the street suddenly filled with children, and for five minutes Portrewan was lively with shrill voices and twinkling legs, till the mothers rushed out with scolding exhortations and swept them up the hill to school. Then a pause. Then a man, hands in pockets. Another man, and another, and another, all converging towards the lifeboat house, where they met without salutation, silently squared their shoulders against the doors, and by inveterate habit turned their eyes seawards. More men. Shoulder space against the lifeboat house was at a premium. The row of immobile humanity extended along the wall of the adjacent fish cellar, and an overflow hooked itself on the sides of an old boat on the other side of the street. Then for two hours nothing but an occasional woman or dog moved through the village.

Towards midday came the only bustling time, when the outer world invaded Portrewan in the shape of three, four, or even five tradesmen with their carts. The rival butchers arrived from opposite directions, passed half-way, exchanged cutting sarcasms on the age and quality of each other's commodities, and drew up at opposite ends of the street. The greengrocer, who loved to do things in style, came rattling down the hill at a rate that shook the apples out among the taties and upset the rhubarb into the basket of broc'lo. Perhaps the bootmaker drove over from the market town in his smart little gig, or the Johnny-come-fortnight in his lumbering van full of calicoes and gown-stuffs. Then the women issued forth, and voices were loud for a season. But the men stirred not, till a glance at the chimney tops warned them that the dinner hour was near.

And the afternoon was like the morning, without its interruptions, till the children straggled home from school, and silence fled from Portrewan, only to return with returning night.

So the days passed and the wind blew, till the week was up, and I left Portrewan to its idle waiting, carrying away a vivid picture of white walls and brown thatch, of handsome bearded statues, and comely keen-faced women, and rosy children, the loveliest ever seen, but knowing scarcely anything, save by imperfect divination, of the inner life of the place. For I was a foreigner, and to foreigners Portrewan folk are silent and reserved beyond the wont even of Cornishmen. Unlike the rooks that share their valley, they do not care to wash their dirty linen in public. When the stranger approaches the dispute is hushed and the joke bottled for future consumption. Gentlemen all, they offer no rebuff to civil advances from a visitor; they are quite ready to exchange small talk about the weather and the fishing; you may even, with patience, extract from them a yarn or two about storm and wreck; but they never lose sight of the fact that between the Cornishman and the foreigner a great gulf is fixed, not to be bridged in a week or a year or a lifetime. So of Portrewan I can make no story—only a picture of still life. One figure alone moves and lives in my memory, and that in rather a curious, striking way; but it is a figure that does not properly belong to Portrewan at all; and it was not until I had left the village on my way back to shops and railways that a casual encounter brought it striding out of the painted canvas into life.

The fourth morning of my visit was fine. The wind had gone to the eastward in the night, and swept the sky bare of cloud and mist. Abundant sunlight poured down on the village; the white walls of the cottages dazzled the eyes; the rocks in the cove shone many-coloured, rising out of a many-coloured sea. Disinclined for either company or complete solitude, I went down to the cove, and found a seat on a piece of timber a little way apart from the silent assembly of sea-gazers. It was still early in the day, and for a full hour nothing happened to disturb the idle, blissful monotony. The children were at school; the women were afield, hanging linen to bleach on the gorse and blackthorn bushes. The lazy influence of the place was overpowering. In the general stillness, whatever moved suddenly took a supreme, exaggerated interest. The progress down the street of a little black dog, sniffing and foraging with the lively scrutiny of his kind, was followed by twenty pairs of eyes, as a great event. I watched the gulls soaring overhead, balancing themselves like rope-dancers with imperceptible wing-dips on the tense invisible cord of rushing air, until luminous specks danced in my eyes. The rhythmic thunder of the tide on the beach grew more and more insistent, beating like a great slow pulse within the ears, conquering thought, reducing the brain to the same delicious apathy that ruled the body.

At eleven o'clock the spell was broken by the rattle of carts. First came the butcher from Henliston, and not far behind him his rival from St. Mellyn. A fisherman from Porthcool, where boats run big and fish are caught in all weathers, led a jibbing pony down the hill, crying the freshness of his mackerel as he went. The dashing greengrocer from Lanwiddock swooped down, scattering chickens and dogs like foam on either side, and pulled up with magnificent abruptness. Women poured into the street; a babel of bargaining voices arose, and continued for a long half-hour. Then horses were whipped up, and one by one the invaders departed. The world had done with Portrewan for the day.

Not quite. Half an hour later, when the last relic of excitement had disappeared within doors on the heels of the last woman, I was gazing idly up the street when I saw yet another equipage appear round the corner. A very small, very cautious donkey came very slowly down the hill, stopping and firmly bracing its feet together at every step. It drew behind it a miniature cart—little more than a barrow. On the cart were piled a few wicker baskets and a loose heap of greenstuff. And on the off-shaft, leaning backwards and nodding his head drowsily against the baskets, sat the ablest-bodied man I ever set eyes on. He was rather stout, though not very; he was not more than ordinarily tall, though taller than he seemed; but his shoulders were broad even to deformity, the muscles of his arms bulged immense under the sleeves of his jumper, the jumper was stretched to rending point across a Herculean chest. His head, which seemed disproportionately small on those shoulders, was covered with closely curling black hair, slightly grizzled at the temples. His face, red, good-natured, coarse, was clean shaven or what passes for clean shaven at Portrewan in the middle of the week. His eyes were small, sleepy, cunning; his lips full, sensuous, humorous. And down the hill he jolted towards me, his feet scraping the road, one arm hanging relaxed with open hand, the other hand loosely holding the reins, but leaving the diminutive donkey to the unfettered exercise of its own judgment.

Having picked its way cautiously down the slope, the donkey stopped short of its own accord on the level, sank its head, bent one knee, and lapsed into patient meditation. It was half a minute before the man stirred a limb; then he rolled off the shaft, stretched himself, lounged to the back of the cart, picked an apple out of a basket, and began to munch it, leaning against the cart-wheel.

It was then that I noticed an unwonted stir among the bronzed buttresses of the lifeboat house. Two or three were actually standing upright and unsupported, several were exchanging remarks, and all had their eyes fixed on the man with the donkey cart. So far as I could construe their looks, it was no unfamiliar sight they were feasting on. Wonder was not in their gaze, nor the unwinking critical stare to which every stranger in Portrewan must submit. But there was admiration, if I mistook not, and gloating pride, and something of the intent rapt interest with which farmers round a show-pen follow every movement of a prize ox.

Then one of the men—it was George Corin, coxswain of the lifeboat—detached himself from the wall and rolled towards me. To all appearance he was ignorant of my presence; his eyes were fixed on the sea, his gait was the gait of a man starting on an aimless stroll; but for all that I knew he was going to speak to me, and I wondered what could have conquered his shy taciturnity and led him to come and accost the foreigner without invitation or encouragement. He did not come straight up to me, but went to a windlass close by and leaned his chest against the handle-bar. Still he took no notice of me, but I knew the ways of Portrewan, and waited expectantly, watching the stranger, who had finished his apple and thrust his hands in his pockets.

Presently Mr. Corin, his eyes still on the sea, jerked a casual thumb in the direction of the donkey cart, and remarked to the waves:

'Big chap, edn' 'a?'

I thought he was the biggest chap I had ever seen.

'Ess,' said Corin. 'Edn' many bigger chaps out o' Cornwall. Nor in Cornwall, nuther,' he added, after a pause, apparently to consider whether he could venture the further assertion without belittling his native land.

I thought it very unlikely.

'Though there's a sight o' big chaps in Cornwall,' said Corin.

I agreed.

Corin turned his eyes on me for the first time, and sidled up closer.

'Could 'ee give a guess, now, as to who that chap might be?' he asked.

I hadn't a notion.

'That's Theophilus Pennywarn,' said Corin in an impressive whisper.

Was it indeed?

Corin regarded me with an aggrieved expression. 'Don't believe you ever heerd tell of en,' he said.

To tell the truth, I hadn't.

Corin proceeded to crush me. 'Theophilus Pennywarn, that held the belt two year runnin'.'

'What belt?' I asked, and sank for ever in Corin's estimation. For a moment he seemed inclined to waste no more words on me. Then he relented.

'Champion belt—Cornwall an' Devon. For wrestlin',' he explained pityingly.

My endeavour to express intense interest and astonishment passed muster.

'There edn' a man in Portrewan that Theophilus Pennywarn couldn' pick up with one hand,' said Corin. 'An' Portrewan men are as big as most, 'a b'lieve.'

I admitted this ungrudgingly. Corin regarded me with some favour, and continued.

'Ess. Two year runnin' Theophilus held the belt. Throwed Jacob Treskilly an' big Ben Rutter over to Bodmin, an' the pick of the Devon men overplush. Not one of 'em looked to 'ave a chanst wi' Theophilus. An' two year runnin' he held the belt.'

I wanted to know who beat him the third year. Corin boiled over.

'Beat en? Beat Theophilus Pennywarn? There wadn' a man alife could do et. What's more, though he's twenty year aulder than he was then, there edn' a man alife could do et now. Beat Theophilus? No, no; nobody bet en, then nor sence. He guv the belt up of his own self—what you d' call resigned et.'

I asked why.

'Chap dursn't use his stren'th,' said Corin impressively.

Again I asked why.

'Look!' exclaimed Corin, dramatically pointing to the subject of his discourse. 'There's a pair of arms to be liftin' broc'lo heads an' measurin' out gallons o' potates an' bushels of apples. Sellin' greens—edn' that a mean trade for the strongest man in Cornwall? All that power an' all them shoulders wastin' theirselves on cabbage an' rhubarb—edn' that a mellincully sight for 'ee? But he don't dare do more, an' there's danger fur 'n in that. "How?" you say, an' I'll tell 'ee.

'The year after Theophilus won the belt, wan o' these Devon chaps sent him a challenge. I don't mind the name o' the chap; 'don't matter, nuther, for 'a wadn' no account at all, an' Theophilus throwed en every time. 'Twould take a stronger man than ever come out o' Devon to throw Theophilus, or any other Cornishman, in a fair match. "Fair," I d' say, for they're trickish; they've bet us afore now, but 'twas all through trickishness. We edn' allers up to their artfulness, but stren'th to stren'th they edn' nothin' in the sight o' we. Well, Theophilus went up to Plymouth an' bet the Devon chap, and sent a tallygram home-along to St. Mellyn to say so. St. Mellyn's Theophilus's locality, where he was reared to. Well, St. Mellyn chaps were mazed wi' joy an' thanksgivin', as you may suppose. They knawed he'd win, barrin' trickishness; but they wadn' none the less thankful to get the news; an', says they, "we'll gie Theophilus a feast when 'a do come back." An' so they ded—sent a grand carriage to meet en, an' druv en round the town, hollerin' an' singin'; an' then they tuk en to Ebenezer school-room an' guv en a rare good come-out. An' when they'd done, they drank his health, an' cheered en till their uzzles ached.

'Then Theophilus got up, lookin' brave an' solemn about somethin'; an'— "Naibours," says he, "here stand I, Theophilus Pennywarn, in the midst o' glory an' thanksgivin'. An' what's the state o' my feelin's in the midst o' glory an' thanksgivin'? Dust an' ashes is my feelin's," says he. An' you might ha' knocked 'em all down with a feather. "Naibours," says Theophilus, "glory's holler trade arter all; an' as for thanksgivin', 'tes nothin' but a bladder; wan teeny pin 'll do fur 'n. An' I've got the pin handy," says he. Then he stopped an' looked round 'pon 'em all. "Men o' St. Mellyn," says he, "I've fought my laast fight an' wrestled my laast throw. You mus' fit an' sarch for another champion," says he.

'Well, there was a rare auld to-do at that, you may be sure. First they went gaspin' wan upon another like a heap o' fish fresh catched. Then 'twas— "How, Theophilus?" an', "Wha's mane, Theophilus?" an', "Art mazed, Theophilus?" till they were all hollerin' 'pon 'm to wance.

'Theophilus, he put up his hand. "Naibours," says he, "listen to my murnful tale." An' then he tauld 'em how, when the wrestlin' was auver, he felt a queer sort o' pain in his innards, like as ef 'twas a hand squeezin' the heart of en. 'A dedn' pay no 'tention to en at first, but et got worse an' worse till he couldn' stand, set nor go. "What's up wi' 'ee, Theophilus?" says he to hisself. "Better fit you go see for a doctor." An' so 'a ded, an' found wan not fur off, a reg'lar quality doctor—brass plate, bells, an' speakin'-tubes all complete. "Doctor," said Theophilus, "my heart do ache." "Who's the maid?" says doctor. "No maid," says Theophilus, "'tes indigestion 'a b'lieve; gie me some strong trade, will 'ee?" Well, doctor out with his tally-scope an' tuk an observation on Theophilus's chest. "Hullo!" says he, brave an' solemn. "Tell 'ee what 'a es," says he, "you'd best be careful, soase. Your heart's diseased," says he, "an' there edn' no doctor's trade in the world that'll cure 'ee. Edn' no danger, so's you do keep quiet. But you mus'n' exert yourself. Keep out o' fights an' wrestlin' matches, an' don't go liftin' no heavy weights, an' you may be an auld man 'fore die. You're a strong man," says doctor. "Beware o' your stren'th. If you d' make use of en, sooner or later you drop, an' so I warn 'ee. An' my fee's five shellen," says he, hauldin' out his hand. "But I've just won the belt!" hollered Theophilus. "I mus'n' give en up without a fight, or me an' Cornwall 'll be disgraced." "Don't 'ee get egzited, an' don't 'ee holler," says the doctor; "edn' nothin' more dangerous. An' wrestle another throw arter what I've tauld 'ee, and 'a'll be suicide; an' I'll see fur 'n that you don't get Christian burial—mind that. An' my fee's five shellen," says he, hauldin' out his hand agin. So Theophilus paid en an' come away.

'That's what Theophilus tauld the men o' St. Mellyn at the feast they'd made fur 'n; an' all their joy was turned into murnin' when they heerd en, you may be sure. An' sence that day Theophilus hasn' dared use his stren'th, fightin' or workin'. He fit an' bought a donkey an' cart, an' started sellin' taties and greens, bein' the lightest ockypation 'a could think for; an' he's done nothin' but sell taties an' greens ever sence.'

With these words Corin relapsed abruptly into silence. I gazed with a new interest at the fallen hero. He was still in the same attitude, leaning lazily against the cart, with his hands in his pockets and his eyes half closed. Nobody had come to buy of him since he entered the village, nor had he made the slightest effort to dispose of his goods. I remarked as much to my companion.

'Well, you see,' said he, 'Theophilus is an independent sort o' chap; he don't come here nor nowheres else reg'lar, only when he've a mind to. An' gen'rally, when 'a do come, Lanwiddock chap, who's a bustler an' no mistake, has been before him, an' there edn' much business left for Theophilus. But *he* don't care; you may buy off of en or not, as you plaise; he waan't put hisself out for you or nobody. Edn' proud, nuther: allers ready for a chat an' a glass—p'ticklerly a glass.'

I suppose I smiled at this, and Corin realised that he had been guilty of an indiscretion in exposing a fellow-countryman's frailty to the stranger; for suddenly his communicative mood dried up, and he grunted and moved off. Then I had occasion to go up to my lodgings, and when I returned later on, Theophilus, donkey and cart, had disappeared.

I saw no more of him during my brief stay; but he occupied my thoughts a good deal. The real pathos of his story was so apparent through the grotesqueness of its setting. Corin was right; it was piteous to see a man endowed with such superabundant strength, and barred by a death penalty from exerting it. No gift of nature is so welcome to man; none yields such fierce intoxicating delight in the use; and the use was forbidden him for life. One could imagine the fret and chafe of dammed-up energy, the wild recurrent temptation to whistle prudence down the wind and do one deed worthy of his power and fame. One pictured him, the Bible on his knees, pondering over the story of Samson and his heroic end. One sketched a story, still more heroic than Samson's, in which the end came in a blaze of supreme, self-sacrificial effort, not with Samson's revengeful motive, but to save some life—a child's, say, or an old woman's—from deadly peril. One realised his feelings as he left the doctor's presence, crushed and bowed under the fatal sentence. And with what loathing, what impotent revolt, he must regard the petty occupation to which he was doomed! A steam-hammer is sometimes made to crack a nut, by way of show; imagine a steam-hammer endowed with sentience and the pride of life, and set to crack nuts perpetually!

It is true that now and again, as I pursued my imaginary analysis of a brave soul at odds with fate, a disturbing image intruded itself of a lazy careless vagabond leaning against a cart-wheel, munching apples and drowsing in the sun; and I was conscious of a certain incongruity. Yet if I knew anything of the Cornish folk, with their intense appreciation of the joy of life, their passionate aversion from all that threatens to spoil that joy, I was sure that the man must feel as I imagined him to feel. A known danger he would face with a light heart, and cheerfully shoulder any burden incident to the common lot of man; but how could a man of the Twilight Race live without morbid broodings under such bizarre conditions, with the spectre of sudden death ever lurking near, dogging his footsteps wherever he went? He must have his dark hours sometimes, though not a line on his face betrayed them.

My time was up. The day of departure was fine, and I decided to go on foot, entrusting my luggage to the ramshackle omnibus that crawls twice a week from Portrewan to the market town. Five miles from Portrewan I came to the Cross Roads Inn, a solitary little alehouse. Before the door stood Theophilus Pennywarn's diminutive donkey and cart, and, as luck would have it, just as I passed, Theophilus himself lounged out. Presently I heard the patter of the donkey's feet and the rattle of the cart-wheels coming up the road behind me. They caught me up, and Theophilus and I exchanged greetings. His face was rather flushed, and he exhaled a rich aroma of beer.

We were just at the foot of a little hill. The donkey slackened its pace to a walk, and as we trudged up side by side we fell into conversation. Theophilus was very communicative, not to say garrulous, under the benign influence of beer. In three minutes we were great friends. Presently my chance came, and I dropped a casual remark about wrestling. Theophilus turned his face full on me, and his eyes twinkled.

'You're right,' he said; 'wrestlin' edn' what 'a was in my young days.'

I made a complimentary allusion to his early prowess. Theophilus fetched a sigh, but his eyes still twinkled.

'Aw ess!' he said; 'those days are over. They make me sad to think upon. You've heard my murnful tale, s'pose?'

I had. I venture to offer condolences. Theophilus checked a beery laugh with another portentous sigh.

'Turr'ble, edn'.'a?' he said with excellent dolefulness. 'There edn' many 'ud keep up their sperits in my place, are there now? Why, they d' often come to me an' say, "Theophilus, how are you so cheerful? Dostn' mind that the shadder o' death is hangin' over 'ee all the while? Dostn' feel shame for the mean trade you're fo'ced to work at?" That's how they d' talk. But I say to them, "Look, soase," I say, "we've all got our burdens in this here sinful world; ess, 'tes our doom to carry the water of affliction, some in jugs an' some in barr'ls. 'Tes a reg'lar osgate wi' me; but don't 'ee fret; my shoulders are brave an' broad." That's what I d' say to 'em. Nobody ever heerd *me* hollerin'. I edn' that sort. Maybe I d' get the doldrums now an' agin, same's as other folk, an' more reason, p'raps, but I edn' one to show et.'

Now I began to understand Theophilus, and to respect and admire him as he surely deserved for his attitude of brave simple dignity under the frowns of Fortune. I endeavoured to express my admiration in becoming terms.

'Thank 'ee, sir,' he said, and again his eyes twinkled; 'tes kind for 'ee to say so.' Then, quite suddenly, he fell into a silence which lasted, broken only by one or two mysterious chuckles, until we reached the top of the hill. Here the road branched and our ways separated. I said goodbye, expressing my pleasure at having made his acquaintance, and my regret that I should probably never see him again. And so we parted.

But I had not gone ten paces when Theophilus called me back.

'Asking your pardon,' he said, 'but ded I understand 'ee to say you were leavin' these parts?'

I explained that I was going to London.

'For good? Edn' 'ee comin' back to these parts no more?'

I said it was very unlikely.

Theophilus looked at me steadily.

'How shouldn' I?' he said, half to himself. 'I've kept et to myself all these years; but a joke edn' no joke without you tell en to somebody. So I will.'

He looked cautiously round, took my hand by the wrist, and laid it against his mighty chest, right over his heart.

'Feel that,' he whispered. '*Sound as a bell!*'

'What!' I exclaimed. 'Do you mean to say——?'

'Never wadn' nothin' the matter wed 'n,' said Theophilus, and burst into a roar of laughter.

'And the doctor at Plymouth?'

'*I* never went to no doctor in all my life,' he chuckled. 'Men like me cdn' got no 'casion for doctors.'

'Then why on earth——?' I stammered.

'Look!' said Theophilus. 'I'll tell 'ee.' He turned up his sleeve and displayed a hairy arm, on which the muscles stood out in great lumps. 'That's the strongest arm in Cornwall this day,' he said. 'Somethin' to be proud for, edn' 'a? So you d' think. What a grand thing, you say, to be as strong as any three men! With an arm like that, you say, there edn' nothin' a man could look for but what he'll get en. Glory! Honour! Dominion! Power!' and at each sounding word he dealt the arm a vicious smack. 'That's what you d' say. An' what do *I* say, that the arm do belong to? I say, stren'th like mine's a curse to a quiet, easy-goin' chap like me—nothin' but a curse. Look! Before I went to Plymouth that time, I worked over to Pennymore at the quarries; an' ef I did one man's work there I did four, an' all along o' my stren'th. Ef there should be a g'eat big stone to shift, that nobody else couldn' move, 'twas allers the same—" Liv en to Theophilus; *he*'ll see fur 'n." Ef a cart should get oversot, 'twas—"Liv en be, you chaps. Where's Theophilus? *He*'ll putt en to rights." An' when I'd finished up my work 'twas just as bad. I might be for a quiet dust before the fire; but no! Maybe Aunt Maria Jago's nevvy an' nace were home on a visit. In they come. " This 'ere's Theophilus," says Aunt Maria; " ded 'ee ever be'old such a tremenyous chap? Would 'ee mind bendin' the poker, Theophilus, for my nevvy an nace to see?" Or maybe I should stroll down to the cove, an' the men were haulin' up the boats. Then 'twas—" Lend a hand, Theophilus, thou g'eat bussa!"—an' sure's I set a finger 'pon the windlass, all the rest 'ud give auver, an' stand round gaspin' an glazin' to see me haul en up by my own self. An' 'twas allers the same, all the while, wherever I went. I med as well ha' been born a horse to wance, for all the thanks or profit I got out o' my stren'th. An' me a quiet chap that likes to take things easy! So at last— 'twas in the train comin' home from Plymouth that time—I said to myself, " Theophilus," said I, " better fit you break your arm to wance; then you'll have a bit o' peace maybe." Well, 'course, I dedn' want to go so fur 's that, azackly; but I started thinkin' an' schemin', an' soon I hit 'pon a way. You d' knaw what 'a was. They swallered my yarn as ef 'twas a dish o' crame, an' they a passel o' cats, an' I haven' had no trouble from that day to this. Why, you wouldn' believe, but ef they see me goin' to use my stren'th, liftin' or pullin', they'll come stavin' up with—" 'Ere, Theophilus, liv that to me; I'll see fur 'n "—for fear they should see me drop before their eyes. Edn' often I have to load my li'll cart myself, I can tell 'ee; allers somebody ready an' proud to lend a hand to poor auld Theophilus. Aw, 'tes grand! Many's the laugh I've had!'

He laughed now, the reprobate! his mighty shoulders shaking, the tears standing in his cunning little eyes. And I had to laugh too, in spite of my vexation at the memory of the sympathy I had wasted on the lazy vagabond. Sheer laziness—there was nothing else the matter with him. And for twenty years the impostor had lolled on a throne, receiving tribute, sniffing incense. It was scandalous, but what could I do but laugh?

CHARLES LEE.

HOW TO DEVELOP CORNWALL AS A HOLIDAY RESORT

OPINIONS OF EMINENT CORNISHMEN AND OTHERS

Sir Joseph Fayrer, Bart. I am glad to find that you propose to bring more prominently to notice the advantages and amenities of Cornwall as a place of resort both for amusement and health. It appears to me that people have never sufficiently known and appreciated how well the South of England is calculated to achieve these objects. My own experience of Cornwall is derived from residence at Falmouth during the winter. I have, therefore, not the personal experience which enables me to speak of it as a summer resort, but for the autumn and winter months and the early spring it has many recommendations. The chief desideratum in a climate is, for so many, that it should be equable, sheltered from prevailing winds, and sunshiny. All these qualities much of Cornwall possesses to a great degree, and yet it seems to be hardly known that these conditions exist in our island. It is hard to say why this ignorance should prevail as it seems to do. The peculiar advantages of this part of England have been pointed out in early times by Dr. Paris, Sir James Clarke, Sir E. Sieveking, and latterly by Dr. Dickinson, who has written a most able and interesting paper describing the advantages of Cornwall.

But Cornwall is not only a place where invalids or the delicate may find those physical advantages which are so essential to them; it has many others which commend it to the ordinary visitor or those who may be seeking change of air and scene, or rest from the toil and labour of their daily life. Why so many of those with such needs, and who are interested in the physical conditions of the country as well as its historical associations, should go to the extreme north of our island or, it may be, across the water, can only be accounted for, I think, by the prevailing ignorance as to the advantages of the south in all these respects, which I trust your magazine will help to dispel.

The means of mental relaxation and recuperation of physical lassitude, the result of long work and confinement in London or any other great centre of thought and labour, exist eminently in this most beautiful part of our island. The scenery is charming; the objects of antiquarian and historical interest are numerous; there are the usual opportunities, I believe, of shooting and hunting—though perhaps not so much as in other parts of England. But, at all events, sea-fishing is hardly to be excelled, and the places on the sea-coast where this most invigorating of all occupations can be followed are numerous, whilst the scenery of the shore and the inland creeks is replete with beauty and charm. I cannot tell how it is that the knowledge of all this seems to be so limited. It is therefore desirable that Cornwall should be more widely known than it is at present, for it would assuredly give a pleasant variety to the travels of those who are seeking change, either on the ground of health or amusement.

Sir Joseph Pease, Bart., M.P. My experience of the county is considerable, and I have never had any difficulty in making it a very pleasant summer resort without any further development.

Sir Edwin Durning-Lawrence, Bart., M.P. For a popular holiday resort the first requisite is accessibility. I have myself endeavoured at various times to urge upon the Chairman of the Great Western Railway and others that in great measure the prosperity of the county of Cornwall will depend not, as of old, upon its copper, its tin, and its fish, but upon its natural physical advantages of climate and scenery; upon its glorious sea and its marvellous coastline, which presents for the choice of the traveller a southern, a northern, or a western aspect. I have also pressed the question upon the present Postmaster-General, and suggested that Cornwall required, and ought to receive, special favour from the Post-Office, as it is in the far west and not leading to other counties and districts. I am aware that the railway company has no right to spend the shareholders' money to promote the prosperity of any place except in so far as the prospects of such place will surely afford full compensating advantages to the shareholders by the eventual extension of a profitable traffic; but it seems almost a demonstrable certainty that a profitable passenger and goods traffic will follow fuller accommodation and more extended railway and other communication.

Next after accessibility is that public attention should be awakened to the variety and beauty of the Cornish scenery. In a word, to use a popular phrase, that Cornwall should be *discovered*. Now, what has mainly induced me to reply to your communication is the thought that it is possible that your own effort to establish your Magazine may assist in the discovery of Cornwall and its general recognition as a health resort second to none in any part of England or on the continent of Europe. Among popular caterers for public patronage the universal maxim is 'Advertise! advertise!! advertise!!!'—for advertisement is the soul of business. Now I do not know that Cornwall can put up sky-signs and revolving lights in every town of the kingdom bearing the legend 'Cornwall's the place to spend a happy month in;' but I think if an effort were made it might be possible to bring the claims and advantages of Cornwall considerably more under the public eye than has hitherto been the case.

Well, next after accessibility and fame, when you have caught your hare or made sure of so doing, suitable accommodation must be provided for the visitors at our call. This is to a certain, even to a considerable, extent being provided by the erection of suitable hotels in various parts of the county. But something more than this and different from this is also required. There must be a courteous readiness on the part of the inhabitants to surrender a portion of their own home comforts for the benefit of the newcomers. It will take time and experience fully to perform this very necessary task wisely and well, but the first thing to do is to awaken in the county the absolute necessity of attempts being generally—I had almost said universally—made in this direction. In saying this much I must add that there must be a true report spread that a trip to Cornwall will not prove too costly, but that visitors may rely on finding what they require without incurring a ruinous expense.

Other matters, such as suitable amusements; way-leaves to visitors only, if you will, for certain months; and various other advantages and privileges might be referred to, but I think that I have said sufficient, and need not further occupy your space on the present occasion.

Sir Richard Tangye
Summer skies, cool breezes, hospitable people, and delightful scenery—what more can the heart of man desire when 'on touring bent'? And all can be found on every hand, but particularly on the north coast of dear old Cornwall.

Mr. Edward Hain
Considering that Nature has been so lavish of her gifts in dealing with Cornwall, it is strange that Art should have done so little to supplement those natural advantages and turn them to pleasurable and profitable account. A county so rich in romantic scenery and legendary lore deserves a wide and generous appreciation, and it may be worth while to consider in what respects the county offers most scope for development as a health resort and recreation ground for the people of our large cities and towns.

The old Cornish motto—'Fish, Tin and Copper'—has become almost obsolete; and with the decline of our mining industry and the poverty of our fisheries, it is imperative for the county to encourage by every means in its power the development of this new source of income and possible wealth. To do this it is not sufficient to rely merely on the admitted charm and beauty of our coast scenery, or the health-giving properties of the Atlantic breezes which sweep our shores. Nature must be assisted and added to as far as possible, and that without injury to her many and varied attractions.

In these days the question of improved sanitation has been placed in the front rank as a matter of the highest importance, and any place which aspires to recognition as a health resort must make up its mind to all such necessary reforms, even if they entail an apparently large expenditure of public money. It is astonishing in these enlightened days to observe that many of our small public authorities entirely fail to realise that money spent in this direction is money well spent and the truest economy in the long run. Sanitation as near perfection as possible, with a pure and abundant water supply, are essential conditions to the development of a health resort. Our county Sanitary Committee might well add to the usefulness of their work by the appointment of a county Medical Officer of Health—an officer fully qualified and experienced on questions of sanitation, who would periodically visit all parts of the county, consult with the local Medical Officers of Health, and, being removed from the influences of a private practice, report impartially to the County Council. I believe this would be a step in the right direction.

Then in the matter of train service from London there is much to be desired. Eight and a half hours from Paddington to Penzance is considered a somewhat formidable journey. It is eighty miles further to Edinburgh, and the journey is accomplished in six and a half hours. Of course the Northern lines have not the same difficulties of gradient and curve to contend with as the Great Western Railway, and we must gladly recognise the rapid strides being made in Cornwall by the Great Western Company, who are spending vast sums in doubling the line and in rebuilding bridges and stations with a view to improving and increasing the facilities for travel. It is said that when the link lines from Devizes to Westbury, and from Castle Cary to Langport are completed, the Cornish trains will run over the new route from Reading to Taunton, avoiding the longer journey *via* Bristol, and, by running from Paddington to Exeter without a stop, save about forty minutes in time, which, with a more rapid service through Cornwall, will probably shorten the journey from Paddington to Penzance to not exceeding seven hours. The Great Western directors are evidently alive to the possibilities of Cornwall as a holiday resort.

In order to attract people of wealth and position who do not mind any cost so long as their requirements are provided for in an adequate manner, hotel accommodation of absolutely the highest class is necessary, and in this direction much is being done by local capital and enterprise in many parts of the county.

In my next and concluding suggestion for the development of Cornwall as a holiday resort I shall probably tread upon more debatable ground. I frequently hear from people who have travelled extensively in all parts of the world remarks to the following effect:—

'Yes, we admit to the full the beauty of your coast scenery, which has a certain charm of its own scarcely equalled elsewhere, and we acknowledge the many advantages of the Cornish climate, but one cannot live on scenery alone, and, to be perfectly candid, we find after the first few days that it becomes exceedingly dull. Why cannot you do something to enliven your towns? At the Continental holiday resorts people are never at a loss—the fashionable promenade to the strains of the fine military bands, the open-air cafés and concerts and entertainments of various kinds, all give an air of brightness and colour and animation to the scene, which is wanting in Cornwall, and until you do something of the kind you will never attract the class of people you want.'

I fear that from the visitors' point of view there is much truth in this contention. The gifted authoress of 'An Unsentimental Journey through Cornwall' was evidently influenced by the dulness of many of the places she visited. I should gather from her remarks that she reached St. Ives some time after dark and left it before daylight next morning, putting up at a second-rate hotel. The shops were closed, and there were no public lamps alight, because the almanac said there was, or ought to have been, a moon, and her only source of information was a talkative old gentleman who regretted he could not spare any more of his time as he was 'on his way to chapel.' He probably meant well, but the result was unfortunate, as anyone who reads the 'Unsentimental Journey' may discover. Yet there are very many who think the quaint old town, with the graceful sweep of its beautiful bay, likened to that of Naples, the birthplace and inspiration of a score of pictures which adorn the walls of this year's Academy, worthy of more appreciative notice.

I have memories of the broad 'Rambla' at Barcelona, where of an evening the whole city promenades under the trees and the scene is animated and beautiful; of the promenade along the sea-front at Palermo; of the similar promenade at Odessa overlooking the harbour, where one may listen to the music of the fine Russian military bands; and, brightest scene of all, the Quay at Smyrna, where until long after midnight, under an Eastern sky, people of every race and shade of colour and variety of costume throng and crowd each other in bewildering movement.

It will be objected that such scenes are quite impossible in Cornwall, or indeed in England, because we have no large and wealthy municipalities or autocratic Governments to spend as they will for the pleasure of their citizens; that such scenes are only possible under Southern or Eastern skies, where the genius of the people, combined with their surroundings, lends itself to picturesque grouping and to the colour and movement of an out-of-door life. This, of course, is to a certain extent true; but the success attending the out-of-door entertainments at Earl's Court and other places in London in recent years proves that our people are only waiting for the opportunity for such recreation and rational amusement to be offered to them to enjoy it to the full.

Whether our Municipal and District Councils will agree to the necessary expenditure for the provision of these attractions, or whether the Puritan spirit (still so strong in Cornwall) will allow it to be done, is perhaps open to question; but if it be at all possible to move in the direction I have indicated, then I am confident the county of Cornwall will occupy that very first rank as a holiday resort to which she is justly entitled by her undoubted natural attractions.

(*We propose to continue this discussion next month*)

RECENTLY DISCOVERED CROSSES

Since the publication, in 1896, of Mr. Arthur G. Langdon's work on 'Old Cornish Crosses,' greater interest has in most cases have passed unnoted. The consequence is that at any rate four crosses can be added to Mr. Langdon's

CROSS AT TRENYTHON

been developed in Cornwall respecting these relics of bygone ages, and 'finds' are now recorded which previously would list. One, now set up in the grounds of the Bishop of Truro at Trenython, was found by Mr. Wilfred Gott at the bottom of a dried-up pond. It is only a fragment of a four-holed cross, but, as the illustration shows, must once have been of exceptional beauty. The height of this fragment is 38 inches, and the thickness of the stone is 8 inches. We do not know any exactly similar specimen in the county.

The Manor of Halligan, in Crowan, was once held by a family of that name, and afterwards by the Kemyell family, from whom it passed to the St. Aubyns by the marriage of Elizabeth Kemyell to Geoffrey St. Aubyn, in the time of Richard II.[1] On October 26, 1399, Geoffrey St. Aubyn, his wife Elizabeth, and their children were granted a licence to have an oratory in connection with their mansion,[2] which was doubtless erected in the field known still as the Chapel Field, adjoining the house, and of which the present strongly moulded and segmental-headed window of the kitchen in the farmhouse very possibly once formed part. Just outside the corner of this Chapel Field, and towards the house, a cross was found several years ago by Mr. Eva, the present tenant. At the time of its being observed by Mr. Rundle, in 1897, it served as a stand for a flower-pot; but the tenant, Mr. Eva, on having his attention drawn to the character of the stone, at once promised to place it where it could be protected from further injury. He

THE HALLIGAN CROSS

remembers a similar stone on the farm, which, he believes, has been built into a hedge, and for which he is 'keeping his eye open.' The Halligan Cross is almost identical with the one at Pendarves, described and figured by Mr. Langdon on p. 244 of his work. The diameter of the head is 1 foot 8 inches; that of the incised circle, which is concentric with the head, 1 foot 3 inches. There is, however, no bead on the edge of the head, and the inner circle is not so wide as on the Pendarves

[1] Lyson's *Magna Britannia*.
[2] Bishop Stafford's *Register*, i. 31b.

specimen. The cross is plain at the back, where the stone has either been much mutilated, or, as is more probable, was never worked at all. The greatest thickness is 8 inches. The shaft, down which ran the wide incised line, of which a portion is shown in the illustration, was apparently about 7 inches wide.

But by far the most interesting cross found in the county of late years is one that was brought to light, in 1896, by Mr. Joseph Holman, a working-man member of the Camborne Students' Association. Just outside Camborne are the remains removed to its present position in the cemetery of Camborne Church. During its removal a second cross was found beneath it!

On that side of the first cross which lay uppermost is a good wheel cross, but the edges of it have been unfortunately trimmed to make it fit into its place. The side limbs of the cross are each 5 inches in length, the top limb being 4 inches, and the bottom limb apparently of the same length, but too injured to admit of exact measurement. Two incised lines run to the foot of the stone, the

CRANE CROSS AS DISCOVERED

of the old manor-house of Crane, one of the arched doorways of which still stands in a cottage that occupies part of the site. In front of this cottage is a well, one side of which was formed of a cross, as shown in the illustration. Mr. Holman was examining the ironwork when his foot slipped and knocked off some of the growth of weed that hid the cross. He at once cleaned the stone and, with pardonable pride, announced his discovery to his fellow-students. The consent of the landowner, Mr. Basset, of Tebidy, having been obtained, the cross was space between them forming a shaft 4 inches across. This face has been much injured by the boring of holes for the irons of the 'plump,' which have been more than once shifted. From this mutilation the under surface largely escaped, and that side of the cross is of great beauty. Here, too, the head carries a wheel cross deeply cut, the limbs expanding from $2\frac{1}{2}$ inches at the centre to $3\frac{1}{2}$ inches where they join the outer band. Remains of bold ridges are seen at each side of the shaft, and fragments of projections still show at the neck. Down the centre of

CRANE CROSS AS RE-ERECTED

SECOND CROSS

this face runs an incised line, to the right of which the surface is ornamented with a bold zigzag surmounting two interlaced circles, and below them there is a plaited design. To the left of the groove is a figure, apparently male, standing on a shield, beneath which are interlaced circles and plaited work similar to those on the right. The base on which the cross is now mounted is the stone the stocks were formerly fastened to.

The cross found in Crane well below the one just described appears to have been unfinished because of flaws in the granite. The better side of the two is shown in the illustration. The stone is 2 feet 2 inches high and 1 foot 3½ inches across. This also has been afforded room in the churchyard.

There are no less than six other crosses in Camborne, all noted in Langdon's work.

CORNISH DIAMONDS

'What's the difference between poetry and blank verse?' inquired William of Blind Dick. 'Why,' answered Blind Dick, 'ef you say

> He went up mill-dam
> And falled down slam,

that's poetry. Ef you say

> He went up mill-dam
> And falled down wop,

that's blank verse. Knaw now, do 'ee?'

A miner whose mother had daily made for him a pasty for 'croust,' married a cook who had been in the service of a wealthy family. On going to the mine after his marriage he took with him a pasty of his wife's making. 'How did you like the pasty?' asked she when he returned in the evening. 'Ee waden no good,' replied the miner. 'Time I got down to the fifty fathom ee was sent to lembs. The wans mother made wuden braek ef em falled to the bottom. They *was* pasties.'

A man who was returning to his home late at night, after an absence of two or three years, missed his way in crossing some mine 'burrows.' Stumbling over a rope, he fell, but managed to grab what he discovered was the collar of a mine shaft. This he clung to with all his strength, feeling that if he let go he would either break his neck in the shaft or be drowned in the water that filled the mine. When he was nearly worn out by fatigue and fear, his hoarse cries were heard by a miner on his way to 'bal.' 'Pull me up, mate—pull me up,' eagerly shouted he; to which the miner replied, 'Get down, thee great buffle-'ead—the shaft was filled up two year agone;' and, looking round in the dim light of early morning, the man saw that the rubbish reached to within a few inches of his feet.

'Gwain to larn your boy the fiddle, are 'ee?'
'Iss.'
'He wain't never play the fiddle toall.'
''Ow shouldn't aw?'
''Cos his head's too big.'
'Go on with 'ee. The bigger head he's got, the more tunes he'll hold.'

'I sha'n't name no names,' said Uncle Billy, 'but Jack Tremenheere's the man.'

Captain Joe Vivian and Captain Dick Tredinnick, two trusty mine captains, fell into a dispute as to their skill with the plough, and the argument ended in bets being made. A match was arranged and the sticklers appointed. On the day each one did his turn with the plough, and afterwards the umpires gave their decision. 'We've a seed the ploughan, an' Cappen Joe Vivian's ploughan was the worst we ever seed; but we're gwain to give he the prize, 'cos Cappen Dick Tredinnick's ploughan wadn't no ploughan toall.'

The gallants of Fowey were once the lords of the Channel, and no ship sailed in or out without their leave. The King of France complained to the King of England that his subjects could not sail in safety because of these pirates of Fowey, and the King of England sent a message to the gallants of Fowey that they must not attack the Frenchmen because 'I am at peace with my brother of France.' And the gallants of Fowey sent back this message to the King of England: 'That may be, but we are at war with the King of France.'

WISH 'EE WELL!

The ensign's dipped; the captain takes the wheel.
  'So long!' the pilot waves, and 'Wish 'ee well!'
—Go little craft, and with a home-made keel,
'Mid loftier ships, but with a heart as leal,
  Learn of blue waters, and the long sea swell!

Through the spring days we built and tackled thee,
  Tested thy timbers, saw thy rigging sound,
Bent sail, and now put forth unto the sea
Where those leviathans, the critics, be;
  And other monsters, diversely profound.

Some bronz'd Phœnician with his pigmy freight
  Haply thy herald was, who drave of yore
Deep-laden from Bolerium by the Strait
Of Gades, and beside his city's gate
  Chaffered in ingots cast of Cornish ore.

So be thou fortunate as thou art bold;
  Fare, little craft, and make the world thy friend
And, it may be—when all thy journey's told,
With anchor dropped, and tattered canvas rolled,
  And some good won for Cornwall in the end,—

Thou wilt recall, as best, a lonely beach,
  And a few exiles, to the barter come,
Who recognised the old West-country speech,
And touched thee, reverent, whispering each to each—
  'She comes from far—from very far—from home.'

EDITOR'S WORD

By issuing this first number of THE CORNISH MAGAZINE *we have ventured to challenge the sagacity of several respectable prophets. They have prudence on their side : we have youth. They confidently predict that no tribal magazine (as they put it) can hold its own. We dare to hope that one can. And our aim, in brief, is to prove that it can, by finding out the way.*

We freely admit that this, our first effort, is a tentative one. And if anyone should chance to see the way more clearly than we do, we shall be heartily obliged to him for indicating it. We have worked hard and in some haste to produce this first number, and are well aware that it is capable of improvement. We are going to pursue after that improvement.

Our aim is to produce a Magazine which shall cost sixpence, and be worth more than sixpence to anybody, and considerably more than sixpence to any Cornishman; to fill it with sound and readable information, honest fiction, good illustrations ; to satisfy the judges at home and carry to our kinsmen abroad a word of home and an assurance that their home remembers them ; finally, to do some good for Cornwall, or at least earn the respect due to a brave attempt.

This is our aim, and the rest the public and our countrymen must judge. But they can help too. They can help with suggestions, they can help with that silent but effective good-will which is the best encouragement for such a venture as ours. And here we must thank the many who have already lent a hand. We are speaking, not of money, but of other help. Whatever happens, these unselfish and practical expressions of kindness will be a great part of our repayment. They prove that our motto is no dead form of words, but a living rule of conduct. Long may it live to inspire us !

THE HEALTH OF THE BRIDE
(From the picture by STANHOPE A. FORBES, A.R.A.)

A Newlyn Retrospect.

AM asked to write a few reminiscences of Newlyn and its group of artists.

In wondering whether some notes by one of these painters may prove entertaining to Cornish readers, I find my chief encouragement in recalling the countless evidences of kindly interest in our welfare which I have myself witnessed since I have lived and worked in Newlyn.

It would seem unnecessary to explain to any patriotic Cornishman the charm of his native county, to show wherein lies the fascination which it possesses for the artist; but the question is so often asked, What tie binds them to this district? that I will invite the questioner to ramble with me along the cliff and through the narrow streets of which Newlyn is composed, whilst I point out its features and tell the story of our connection with the place.

Let us meet on the little bridge at the entrance to the village, the bridge which I remember so well first crossing some fifteen years ago. I had come from France, where I had been studying, and wandering down into Cornwall, came one spring morning along that dusty road by which Newlyn is approached from Penzance. Little did I think that the cluster of grey-roofed houses which I saw before me against the hill side would be my home for so many years.

What lodestone of artistic metal the place contains I know not, but its effects were strongly felt, in the studios of Paris and Antwerp particularly, by a number of young English painters studying there, who just about then, by some common impulse, seemed drawn towards this corner of their native land.

We cannot claim to have been the discoverers of this artistic Klondyke, and indeed found already settled here many old acquaintances, fellow-students of the Quartier Latin and elsewhere.

It is difficult to say who was the original settler, for painters seem always to have known of the attractions of the place; but about the time I am speaking of the tide set strongly in to Mount's Bay, and it is curious to think of the number of painters, many of whom have attained distinction, who visited this coast about then.

There are plenty of names amongst them which are still, and I hope will long be, associated with Newlyn, and the beauty of this fair district, which charmed us from the first, has not lost its power and holds us still.

I like to recall those early days in the history of the colony, when, starting our careers full of enthusiasm and hope, so many of us came together and formed fast friendships, when the comradeship which still exists was solidly founded.

But here is the village before us, a busy little port, so different to that which I can remember when first it met my eye. In place of those two fine piers which now stretch out and form such an excellent harbour for the fishing fleet, only that little weather-beaten structure out yonder existed, capable at the most of giving shelter to a schooner or perhaps one or two fishing boats.

The brown-sailed luggers would in those days lie at their moorings out in the bay, or in rough weather seek the shelter of Penzance harbour. Yet though scarcely so large and important, the little port was active and picturesque, and the commerce of the place, carried on under more primitive conditions, was none the less attractive to an artist's eye.

From the first I was fascinated by those wet sands, with their groups of figures reflected on the shiny surface, which the auctioneer's bell would gather around him for the barter of his wares.

If you look back now towards Penzance you will see, stretching out far into the bay, the sands at low tide. It was there that I elected to paint my first Newlyn picture, and out on that exposed beach, for many a month, struggled over a large canvas. I blush to recall what my models must have suffered posing for these early works of mine, and am only consoled by so often meeting healthy strapping lasses, or bronzed-faced young fishermen, whom I can remember as children shivering on the beach or roasting in the August sun whilst a young and over-zealous painter, forgetting all but his work, wrestled with the difficulties of light and shade.

Yes, those were the days of unflinching realism, of the cult of Bastien Lepage. It was part of our artistic creed to paint our pictures directly from Nature, and not merely to rely upon sketches and studies which we could afterwards amplify in the comfort of a studio.

It is a debatable practice, and this is no place to argue such technicalities, but I mention it because, being strongly held by many of us, it imparted a noticeable feature to the village. Artists are common enough objects by the seaside; but it was scarcely so usual to see the painter not merely engaged upon a small sketch or panel, but with a large canvas securely fastened to some convenient boulder, absorbed in the very work with which he hoped to win fame in the ensuing spring; perhaps even the model posing in full view of the entire populace, the portrait being executed with a publicity calculated to unnerve even our practised brother artist of the pavement.

A NEWLYN STUDIO.
By J. D. Mackenzie

These singular goings on of the new-comers at first provoked much comment from the inhabitants, but by degrees they grew familiar with such strange doings, and scarce heeded the work which progressed before their eyes.

Even the small folk grew tired of gazing, and at that dread moment when the school doors opened and let loose upon their chosen victims the arch tormentors of our race, a few moments of misery would ensue, and the harassed painter, with a sigh of relief, would find himself alone, once more free to continue his labours undisturbed.

Nothing, too, could exceed the good nature with which the village folk came to regard behaviour which might well have been thought intrusive on the part of any others than the members of our craft.

Painters have an easy way of walking into other people's houses, calmly causing their occupants no little inconvenience. It is this habit of theirs which perhaps causes them to congregate in places where their oddities are known and their motives understood. I can remember with a shudder my experiences in Holland, where, speaking no word of Dutch, I have sometimes endeavoured to explain to the bewildered natives that I had no burglarious intentions, but merely followed a peaceful if somewhat eccentric calling. When one considers the interest aroused by our proceedings, it speaks well for the good nature of the village folk that I can scarcely ever remember asking permission to set up my easel without it being freely accorded.

With such favouring conditions it may be guessed that the place soon became a veritable artists' paradise, free from the drawbacks and hindrances that so commonly beset us. Let us on through the village, glancing as we go at the harbour, with its busy life so full of interest, for the mackerel fishery is in full swing, and alongside the quay are moored the laden boats; looking down upon them is a motley crowd of fishermen and fishwives, salesmen and onlookers. Down that little lane formerly stood an old foundry, in which were cast or forged the capstans and other iron gear belonging to the fishing fleet, an interesting old place which has now unfortunately ceased to exist.

Here, too, is the village post office, and around it those quaint old houses which served Walter Langley for the background of his dramatic picture, ' Among the Missing,' and which with many another picturesque corner will be preserved long after the progress of civilisation, as I suppose we must politely term the hideous invasion of the modern builder, has swept them away.

Following a narrow winding lane, we come down upon a beach which separates the two distinct villages of which Newlyn is composed—viz. Street-an-nowan and Newlyn town. This has always been a favourite haunt of the artists, and here we shall surely find one or two camped out, though not so many perhaps as in former years, for glass houses and studios have sprung up, and with advancing years we have grown bashful and shy of being overlooked.

From here we obtain what is perhaps the most characteristic view of Newlyn. Alas! again many an old house, which made the irregular line along that uneven cliff still more interesting, has been pulled down and its place filled by some terribly commonplace modern structure, devoid of character

THE WITCH
By Mrs. Stanhope Forbes

and charm. One cannot help foreseeing a time soon approaching when the unfortunate painters must needs forsake their native land, and seek refuge in countries where age and beauty are thought worthy of respect.

However, let us be thankful that the new piers which we see so well from here are as thoroughly satisfactory to the eye as they are fitted for the work for which they were constructed. Severe and simple, they are yet pleasing to look upon, and have added to the beauty of the harbour rather than in any way marring it. At the end of one of them is a small lighthouse, which I can never contemplate without certain uneasy sensations. For off that pier head day after day for months I painted in a crazy old fishing boat, which lay at anchor there, and with unsteady hand endeavoured to dodge the motion of the waves.

Leaving the beach we ascend into Newlyn proper, and soon find ourselves in what might be termed the Melbury Road of this town. It boasts of the characteristic name of Trewarveth

THE CHILD ENTHRONED
By T. C. Gotch

Street, which means, I believe, the street of the hill. Fortunately we are ascending, for it is a perilous journey to make one's way down its ill-paved surface.

That old thatched cottage, with a window in its roof, is scarcely a remarkable edifice, but Newlyn painters point to it with pride as the little studio in which Frank Bramley painted his 'Hopeless Dawn.'

It stands at the corner of a little lane which some wag has christened the 'Rue des Beaux Arts,' a name which, painted in large letters on a board, serves to mystify the villagers greatly.

Just beyond here you can see a black gate, and alongside it a threatening notice warning parents that the direst penalties of the law await any unhappy urchin who strays within these portals.

Be reassured: the Newlyn painters whose sanctuary this is are upon most excellent terms with the small fry of the village, and merely wish to have peace and quiet reigning round them when at work. Indeed, it is fortunate for us that the relations of the artist to the villagers have always been so cordial and satisfactory. A well-known portrait painter is said to have observed that he counted as many enemies as he had painted portraits.

Luckily this feeling does not exist here, else were the lot of some of us an unenviable one. Scores of the village folk, young and old, men, women and children, have sat to us and bear no malice—indeed, take pride in successes in which they rightly feel they have their part. And truly to the models is due no small amount of the success the place has had. I am afraid painters are generally accredited with far too vivid and powerful imaginations; and at the risk of destroying an illusion flattering to their powers, I must confess that the co-operation of the model is indispensable, and without such aid our flights of fancy are sorely curbed. From the first little difficulty was found in this direction. The people intelligently grasped the idea that there was nothing derogatory to their dignity in being painted—indeed, saw and felt the implied compliment.

And what better material could artists have wished for? A fine-knit race of men and women, engaged in a healthy and picturesque occupation, and one which by its nature gives the painter his opportunity, when storms and tempests arise, to secure the necessary sittings; swarms of children, many of them charmingly pretty; no wonder that enough material has been found to keep us engaged these many years.

Of almost equal importance, too, is the costume worn, if dress as it is understood in England can be thus designated. Perhaps the attire of a fisherman comes as near deserving the name as anything we can show (in this country), for it is distinctive and characteristic of his calling. I can remember occasional lapses, which made one fear that this too was passing away with other old-fashioned and paintable things, and one awful moment when a hideous fashion in hats set in—a hard, black abomination in place of the usual soft sailorlike headgear or quaint old sou'-wester. But on the whole fishermen in their working dress, clad in jerseys or white duck frocks, and wearing their great sea-going boots, are far from being as unpicturesque as the male portion of our race seem to delight in making themselves. The women, too, have a charming instinct of dress; but at the risk of offending them I must confess to admiring the neat blouses and cotton aprons of everyday wear rather than the grandeur and finery of their Sunday toilettes. They might, however, retaliate by reminding me that after all I met with some of my best success when, painting a wedding party, I had perforce to do justice to a style of costume which I now have the ingratitude to decry.

Against the dress of the little ones there is not a word to be said. Always neat and tidy, the mothers, with excellent taste, choose for great occasions either white or pale colours, which seen in the sunshine, massed together in those charming processions the Cornish galas, have an altogether delightful effect.

But we have lingered long enough at the gate of the meadow, as this field is called which we now enter, to find a whole encampment of studios clustered together on a slope overlooking the bay. At first we had been contented with improvising our workshops out of discarded net lofts, or any other available structure—indeed, I fear we must at times have acted the part of the cuckoo and evicted their rightful occupants—but by degrees the more conventional studio has sprung into existence, and these were amongst the first of them. They were originally founded by one of the best friends the artists have had, Mr. Arthur Bateman, a gentleman who came to live and paint at Newlyn in the early days of the colony, and who, out of a strong feeling of comradeship and a desire to help his friends by facilitating their work, purchased this field and dedicated it to the service of artists and of art. And truly it has served us well, for in turn each of these buildings has been tenanted by one or other of our best known painters, and this spot has been the birthplace of many a picture which has won fame for the School.

Let us knock at the door of this large studio by the gate and see if its owner be disengaged, when we may persuade him to show us some of those beautiful and careful studies he has made for his well-known pictures, enabling us to realise how much thought, how much hard work, it has taken to achieve a result all have admired. Here he has painted several of those notable works which a visit to Florence and an intense appreciation of Italian art have inspired. Before leaving we will ask him to let us have a peep at the lovely draperies he has collected, and induce him to unfold for our inspection his precious antique brocades.

Further on in that higher studio we shall find much to interest us, for there a wanderer has come to rest after years of travel, and has brought home sketches and studies from all lands, and of all people; a unique and splendid collection. We might spend days ransacking the treasures of these portfolios, but another friend has beckoned us from his point of 'vantage and awaits us above. After climbing a steep ladder we inspect and admire many charming notes and impressions, and listen to an admirable exposition of their author's views. Then to my own studio, the glass house of which commands so fine a view of the bay. And yet at times I have had to forego this, for driven out of my favourite foundry by smoke and grit, forced to abandon my cherished principles, I once built myself a smithy in this same glass house, and herein forged an anchor with brushes and paint.

But to-day the view is uninterrupted. Down below us one painter seems to have abandoned work, and heedless of the sarcasm of a brother artist is occupied in tying up a flower. Think not that he neglects his craft, for this is a future model, and when its blooms expand he will sally forth and render its charm immortal. In yonder glass house, amidst a heap of what would seem to the uninitiated the veriest rubbish, we can catch a glimpse of a painter hard at work. But that old crab-pot, those fishing nets, and other gear are in reality valuable properties, and have often figured in the pictures of our friend, who, unconscious of our gaze, continues his labour. Over there is one of the veterans of the colony, a pioneer of the School and one of its most faithful adherents, whilst leaning against the door of the most recent of these buildings we see the athletic form of a distinguished water-colourist. Strange sights have been seen in that meadow, and a few years ago a visitor might have been astonished to see a group of Elizabethan gentlemen in doublets and hose chatting pleasantly with swarthy blacksmiths, whilst a little maiden in mediæval attire would lean over the steps and gossip with these gentry of another age. For it is the hour of the models' repose, and for a short period they have escaped from the hot studio to stretch their limbs and breathe the air.

Other models there are, too, that know their way to this field.

I remember one poor old horse who used to trudge through the gates of this meadow day after day, without a soul to lead him, and quietly amble up to the spot where he had learnt it was his fate to stand. Up yonder grew the hollyhocks which Bramley loved to paint, and which he uses with such charming effect in 'After Fifty Years,' and along that border whole groves of evening primrose night after night unfold their blossoms to appreciative eyes.

As we leave one cannot repress a slight feeling of regret at the recollection of those pleasant days when the field was gay with crowds of visitors who had flocked thither for our yearly private view. It was, I think, Percy Craft who with me a good many years ago first introduced to Newlyn this fashion, and by degrees the custom grew until almost everyone adopted it, and the numbers of

AFTER FIFTY YEARS
By Frank Bramley

our visitors swelled from a handful of personal friends to that large crowd that each year filled the meadow, strolling from studio to studio, gazing at the pictures and getting a glimpse of our workshops and our ways.

But when fate in the person of Mr. Passmore Edwards decreed that we should possess an art gallery, it became inevitable that the pictures could no longer be exhibited in this novel manner, and seeing the many advantages which the possession of a properly constructed exhibition room has conferred upon us, it were ungenerous to cavil at so small a matter.

It was a kind and generous thought of the giver to bestow this admirable little gallery upon us, and not the less gratifying for being so entirely spontaneous and unsought for. The success it has met with so far, not only from the support which the public of West Cornwall has given it, but also from the valuable assistance of many eminent artists who have lent us interesting works, augurs well for its future prosperity.

We have seen the building just before entering the village. Its exterior, with four walls bare of windows by the necessities of its construction, scarcely afforded much opportunity to its architect, but those panels of beaten copper on the façade are worth noticing. They are a product of the place, one of the latest developments of Newlyn art.

In the narrowest part of the little lane we stumbled along on our way through the village, there hangs a curiously fashioned sign, indicating that here an industrial class is held. A terrible din assails your ears, and, curious to find what occasions it, you enter a courtyard, and, climbing a steep ladder into an old net loft, find a room full of lads all busy hammering away at curiously shaped pieces of brass or copper. Originally started by that good friend of Newlyn, Mr. Bolitho, with the co-operation of the artists, and chief amongst them Messrs. Gotch and Percy Craft, the idea was to find employment for the spare moments of fisher-lads, and certainly a more admirable safety valve for their superfluous energy could not have been devised.

But it has served another and very different purpose, and has been the means of giving his opportunity to an artist of rare and very individual talent. Mr. J. D. Mackenzie has displayed a perfect wealth of imagination in executing a whole series of designs for the multitude of objects which the class and his able lieutenant Philip Hodder have wrought in repoussé work; and so the name of Newlyn has become linked with an art other than that of painting pictures. To have introduced the best qualities of design into some of the commonest objects of our daily use—surely this is an achievement to be proud of, and probably no work the colony has done will tend more to the true mission of the artist, which is to foster and encourage the love of beauty and grace.

But to resume our ramble. All around us now are the houses in which at one time or another most of us have found a home. Newlyn is not very fortunately situated in this respect, for good lodgings are not plentiful, and at times the demand exceeds the supply. Built at a time when an invasion of painters was not foreseen, the village possesses few houses which can do more than accommodate the fishermen and their families who inhabit them;

and this difficulty of procuring rooms has somewhat tended to check our expansion. We have sometimes seen with regret comrades depart, won over by the greater facilities which neighbouring colonies can offer.

Still there are comfortable and pleasant quarters to be found by searching, in which we have lived happily enough. Here is one old house endeared to many of us by the recollection of the old days when we lived there side by side. In its garden stands a wooden studio which I saw constructed, and afterwards shared with Percy Craft and at times with Chevallier Tayler. In it I painted a wedding feast, which was the forerunner of my own. Pleasant times to look back upon, though the picture was not carried through without infinite painstaking labour, or finished without much misgiving and doubt of its reception. Yet when the other day I saw it hanging in the fine gallery which Sir Henry Tate has given to the nation, I could only remember the good luck it brought me, the happy fortune I owe to its success.

Further on is a charming house, under whose hospitable roof a genial host and hostess have done so much to promote and encourage that feeling of good fellowship which has always existed amongst us—the home of Mr. and Mrs. Gotch. Indeed, this quarter of Newlyn is the very centre of the social life of the colony. Amongst the pleasantest of our recollections are the visits of those foreign painters, many of whom have made lengthy sojourns here, won by the charm of this fair English county, by the wild grandeur of its rugged coast, or by the softer beauty of its valleys and woodland glades. And the presence of those strangers, who, foreign only by race, are of our close kith and kin in the near relationship of art, is of an importance beyond measure, for the value to artists of an interchange of views and ideas with their foreign brethren cannot be over-estimated. Cornwall has, indeed, been fortunate in attracting the artists of other lands. I remember finding in a house at St. Ives where I was calling, four painters of four different nationalities. In that town Zorn, the well-known Swedish artist, painted his first oil picture, which now hangs in the Luxembourg, and for it his palette was set by an equally celebrated American painter who at that time resided there.

Indeed, so many of our transatlantic cousins have visited us, that who can tell to what extent we may not claim to have fostered those cordial relations which we are told now exist between the two nations?

Newlyn, too, has not failed to find favour in the eyes of foreigners; and painters of distinction, our own fellow countrymen, whom we can scarcely claim as members of our little coterie, have from time to time paid us transitory visits.

On one occasion having heard of the arrival of a famous draughtsman, I called at the studio which I was told he had just taken. The first thing that caught my eye on the familiar walls was a huge and admirable caricature of my own face and figure. Quite unabashed its author rose to greet me, and this was my first introduction to Phil May.

Great is the rivalry between the adjacent colonies when some more than usually interesting stranger finds his way down, and fierce fights are waged over the possession of his person and his paints.

THE LAST BLESSING
By R. Chevallier Tayler

But except for this nothing could be more cordial than the relations between the art settlements in Cornwall, which, found so close together, are yet so distinct in character and diverse in their aim. It is curious how a few miles can affect the style of a body of workers. Men working together and constantly observing each other's methods must unconsciously affect one another, but though this may have its drawbacks, I am equally convinced as to its benefits, for ours is an art in which mutual aid and counsel are invaluable, and none know this better than those who are fortunate enough to have a helpmate upon whose judgment they can rely.

But we have still much to see, so resume our wanderings and, prying into the little passages and courts which abound in Newlyn, obtain a glimpse of a fisherman's home life and ways. We shall find many another studio tucked away in odd corners, queer old ramshackle places, many of them exceedingly serviceable and admirably suggestive.

Leaving the village now, for a glance at the country around, we might follow the course of a charming little brook up the rich coombe or valley down which it trickles. It is difficult to think that this can be the same river that only a few years ago came roaring down this quiet valley, through the heart of the village, wreaking destruction and havoc around on the day of the memorable flood. Now we pass a church where Newlyn marriages take place, for there are few Benedicts left amongst us, and another Newlyn school exists of which the little scholars are fast growing up, the future hope of the colony, the present sunshine of our homes.

We have still to climb that terrible hill that leads up into the higher land above to see the favourite haunts of our landscape painters. Wandering inland we may perhaps be overtaken by some of them spinning past, with canvas and brushes strapped to their bicycles, hurrying to their daily task; perhaps out on the moors, or in the heart of some quiet wood, catch sight of those little wooden shanties, excellent movable studios, which some have lately adopted.

Passing through this little hamlet I can point out a smithy, in the smoke and grime of which, working for months, I managed to carry to completion a large picture; and further on by the roadside a spot where one day I was forced to snatch up a seven-foot canvas, and, leaping a hedge, fly before a herd of advancing cattle.

But pictures bear a charmed life, and, as a friend of mine is fond of remarking, only the painter himself can hurt them. Once in an unlucky moment I left one leaning against a wall at a safe angle, as I had many a time left it before, but being nearly finished, for better security I asked a small boy to watch it in my absence. Imagine my feelings on returning, to find that my guardian—a stout-built chubby little fellow—had discovered a novel form of canvas chair, and was comfortably seated on the picture. I am told that a well-known colour merchant in London still quotes this experience of mine, with proper pride in the quality of the canvas which he manufactures.

Before turning homewards we might prolong our walk through the lovely valley of Lamorna, until we reach a group of farm buildings by the side of the road, where we stop to admire the very latest achievement of two distinguished artists, a sign hanging on the wall of a cottage, indicating by a most charming painting that refreshments can here be obtained for wearied cyclists.

And now we have seen Newlyn, and something of the lives of its painters, and have had a peep behind the scenes. Meanwhile each year the curtain at Burlington House rises upon the little dramas and comedies we have fashioned, and our puppets act their parts and earn their meed of praise or blame. It is not perhaps for me to take part in this, but as the actor is permitted to visit the theatre, and join in the plaudits which greet his friends, so I may be allowed to express the pride I feel in the successes of these my comrades and associates. For indeed the applause has not been stinted, and the Newlyn School can surely not complain of want of recognition.

It counts many successes, and those pleasant occasions when we have met together to celebrate some honour won, some distinction gained, have been frequent in our annals. True it has not escaped criticism, nor failed to find detractors, yet doubtless has been the better for this wholesome discipline. We have outlived the obloquy of the square touch, and survived unkind references to the camera—indeed, I am sure that many of us have vastly profited by these comments on our defects, else what is the use of criticism, and how vain the labour of those who so unselfishly devote their lives to pointing out our limitations!

We have at times been charged with a tendency to a grey and sombre tone, to a love of gloomy and depressing motives. I am glad that this sketch of mine, this little picture of Newlyn life, cannot incur such censure, for it shows a singularly happy and fortunate community, and the sun which we are told is wanting in our pictures has not failed to shine upon our lives. I know not whether I have made clear the reasons of our affection for this adopted home of ours, and shown something of the nature of our attachment to it. To me it seems simple enough and easily understood, resting much on the memories of happy bygone days passed together working side by side in common aim.

STANHOPE A. FORBES.

LYONESSE

The listless tides arise and fall,
  With murmur of their old distress,
O'er shadowy tower and knightly hall
    Of ancient Lyonesse.

Far down within the changing deep,
  That splendid realm unchanging lies,
Where many a lord and lady sleep
    Neath scutcheon'd canopies.

A land of fair romance long lost—
  Enchanted held in perfect rest,
All lapp'd in golden light, and cross'd
    With tincture of the west.

The happy youth, with lute in hand,
  Sings to the maiden in her bower,
And banners hang above the land
    From many a silent tower.

And knights are there in armour dight,
  And white-haired minstrels sit serene,
And there is one, that Land's delight—
    A solitary Queen.

She dreams of love and olden wars,
  Her maidens lying at her feet,
A moon amid a heaven of stars
    In loveliness complete.

James Dryden Hosken.

A BACHELOR'S DIARY

I

EVERYONE who went down the single narrow street which made up the village of Tregantock made a point of looking in at the doorway of Joseph Mayne's shop, to receive the pleasant greeting he kept for all who passed. Many had been in the habit of doing so for close on thirty years, for it was almost that time since he had taken over the business from Josiah Cundy, a tradesman of old standing, who had died almost immediately after disappearing from his wonted place in the shop.

There were lovers of old times in Tregantock who found Joe Mayne's shop-window one of the pleasantest objects of contemplation within the bounds of the village. The sea lay beyond the houses to the south of the street; the moorland began on the other side of the hedges of the gardens which sloped up beyond those which stood on the north of it. Neither of these had changed greatly, but Joe's window gave an even more comforting assurance of stability in a world confused with many motions. Allowing for trifling inexactnesses of recollection, it remained precisely what it had been on the day when Josiah Cundy retired from the public view, and Joe Mayne took his place before the world.

No one would have sworn that the grandfather's clock which stood in a corner was the one Josiah had always owned, but no one was prepared to assert that it was not. It bore on its face the name of a famous maker up to Tallywarn, and everyone knew that he had ceased from his labours half a century before. His grave in the churchyard there was much visited by pious folk on summer evenings after service, and old-fashioned people who possessed clocks of his making were wont to exhibit them to visitors, pointing out his name upon the face, and quoting the lines inscribed on his tombstone.

There were a couple of candle-sticks, a cream jug, and one or two other objects, in Sheffield plate. No one had ever been induced to make an offer for them, since the copper showed through the silver in places, and made it evident that they were not silvered—as good plate so obviously should be—on a basis of white metal, which looks sufficiently well even when the silver is worn off here and there.

There were a few watches, most of them having greyish silver faces and gold hands. These and a miscellaneous array of springs and other odds and ends came near to complete the outfit of the window. An electroplated cruet-stand with china bottles, a pair of fish carvers (bought from a prize-winner in local athletics), and a plated toast rack, seemed entirely out of place, and were huddled away in a corner, where a big hanging clock rendered them insignificant.

Inside the shop Joe Mayne sat with magnifying glass screwed into his eye and attended to the watches and clocks of his neighbours. Here and there a few ornate modern 'timepieces' were scattered about the shelves, where they would surely remain until some devoted Sunday-school teacher was about to get married and had to receive a wedding present. There were also spoons and forks in packets, watch-keys, chains of steel and silver, a few brooches of antique fashion, and a couple of dozen pairs of earrings on cards. Dressy people still wore earrings in Tregantock.

Joe had always plenty to occupy him if opportunities for conversation were lacking. But he supplied a felt want in the village, inasmuch as he knew all that had ever befallen anyone who lived within a radius of two or three miles, and was always ready to place his knowledge at the disposal of his friends if they should come to him with a piece of news that needed discussion. 'No, my dear,' he would say on such occasions, ' there's no need for 'ee to run away. If you do want to tell Willie Sampson you can bring 'en in here: there's chairs for all, I believe, and them that can't find them must sit 'pon the counter. I must work to live, I suppose, but I'm going to live. So, if you've got anything to tell, bring Willie Sampson in here, and let's know what everyone do think.' Then he would lay aside work and take up the pipe which he was wont to fill in the morning and finish after he had done with supper.

He was not too much troubled with customers, and most of these were his familiars. If any such should enter in the midst of a discussion he would raise his finger and speak warningly. ' Sit down, George, my son. You aren't in no hurry, I suppose. James Hendra here is telling us a nice little story, and if you do listen you'll know so much as we do. When 'tis over we'll attend to your business ; but, I tell 'ee, if 'tis to make that ol' watch of yours keep good time 'tedn' in the power of man to do it. 'Tis worn out, and I told 'ee so before.'

The customer always waited. Sometimes the interloper was a woman, and in such cases the story was interrupted while she was attended to ; but whenever propriety admitted even the women were asked to remain, and it thus happened that Joe was in high repute among the more critical sex, most of its members having admired at one time or another the magnificent way in which he conducted and controlled a discussion. They wondered especially that he had never got married, and they told him so. In the end he wondered almost as strongly as they did, but he had his explanations. ' Well, my dear, there's never no accounting for things of that sort. I aren't going to say that I haven' cast eyes on maidens that was good to see, in the old days when I was young : I aren't going to say that I couldn' have had some of them if I had been in the mind to ask. But I never done it. I suppose 'tis in the family. I know my Father always intended for me to have another mother. He courted her for three years, on and off, but I suppose he didn' make hisself clear, for she went and married another man. She came into a fortune afterwards, too. Father was always fond of Mother, but he could never forget that. However, 'tis all done with now. I do love the sight of a pretty maiden to this day, but I shall live and die a bachelor.'

There came a time when the matter which brought the public to the shop was an affair of Joe's. A distant and much respected relative died suddenly, and Joe attended the funeral. To his enormous surprise he found that the dead man had left a sum of no less than 500*l*., 'to my respected cousin and old friend, Joseph Mayne, of Tregantock.' He gave out the news, as in duty bound, and that evening half the village visited the shop to discuss with him the subject of what he should do with the money. He listened with patience, but it was not for some days that he announced his intentions, and when he did so it was once more agreed among the women-folk that his good nature ought to have made some woman insist upon his marrying her ages ago, so that it should not be wasted, as the virtues of a single man necessarily are.

Thomasin Tregenna was one of the prettiest girls in the village, and one of the poorest. She had been born after the death of her father, who had been drowned at sea, and her mother had died two days after her birth. An aunt, Martha Tregenna, had taken charge of her and brought her up. She had used her little garden to the utmost, spending long hours in it daily and selling its produce at the best prices to people who knew and respected her. Often she had risen early to pick blackberries or mushrooms, and, coming back to a frugal breakfast, had gone forth to do a hard day's needlework. More than once she might have married well, but she had promised her brother's wife to look after the child, and for the child's sake she had remained single. She was forty now, and an affliction of the eyes had made her all but blind. People pitied her greatly, because of the sacrifices she had made, and some of the women remembered that Joe Mayne had at one time seemed to be fond of her. Thomasin was engaged to be married, but she also was to be pitied. Despite her constant gaiety, her delight in all that was bright and beautiful, she also had a sense of duty, and now she was doing for the older woman all that had been done for her in the olden days. Her lover was content to wait, it was said, and he was passionately fond of her; but lovers are proverbially impatient, and, though everyone praised Thomasin for her devotion to duty, there were some who looked upon her sadly when she had gone gaily by, wondering if her life also was to have no other end than that of the performance of arduous tasks.

Joe's announcement of his intention was awaited with the utmost impatience.

'I been thinkin',' he said at last, 'and now I can tell 'ee what I'm going to do. I can't hardly fancy this shop is like it ought to be.'

'What's wrong with the shop?' asked some one. 'I never heard no complaints of it.'

'No,' answered Joe. 'I don't suppose you did: what I do undertake is done so well as it can be done, here or elsewhere. But how is it so many people do go to Trenear when they are in need of watches and rings and things? The shop edn' what it ought to be, and I haven' been a credit to

Tregantock like I might have been. I'm going to use my little capital and make differences that all can see.'

'What are 'ee thinkin' to do?' asked some one.

'I'm going to have the place cleaned and painted, and I shall turn out the old rubbish from the drawers, and send for travellers and get a fine stock. There's lots of money in Tregantock waiting to be spent, and I can't see why it should go to Trenear.'

''Twill be some work for 'ee if you're going to be all the time selling things. When will 'ee do the repairs? Will 'ee take an apprentice?'

'No,' said Joe. 'I was apprentice myself back along a bit, and I aren't going to be troubled like my poor master was. I shall have a little maid to fit meat for me and keep the house to rights, and when she edn' doing anything else, she can 'tend the shop. 'Twill be liberty for me.'

'Have 'ee thought 'pon who you're going to have?'

'When you've got a plan like this in your head,' said Joe, 'you can't fix up everything in a minute. There's lots of things I aren't certain of yet. I can't hardly say whether I sha'n't sell bicycles and a little clome. And I haven't made up my mind yet about the maid I'm going to have to help me. I must think upon it for a bit o' while, and when I'm decided you will know as well as any body else.'

This announcement was tantamount to an invitation of suggestions, which were immediately forthcoming in plenty. Joe Mayne listened patiently, commending with admirable impartiality all those whose suggestions seemed to be in any wise praiseworthy. But at the end of the discussion he contented himself with the statement that these new plans of his must needs be many days before they could come to maturity, and that for the present there were many points on which he preferred to keep an open mind. It was almost a week later that the village learned the conclusion to which he had come. Tamsin Tregenna was to help him and was to get 7s. a week and meals in return for her services. Joe was to make ready his own breakfast, and the girl was to be at liberty to go as soon as she liked after five o'clock. The arrangement was universally approved. 'She's a good girl, and he won't be hard on her, nor she cheat him.' No surprise was expressed when it became known that Joe had extended Tamsin's privileges, permitting her to delay her coming on the day of Trenear market until she had had time to go in, as she had done regularly since blindness came on her aunt, to dispose of such saleable commodities as the garden produced. Her sweetheart had promised to see that these should not be fewer than of old, and, indeed, Miss Tregenna was sti'l able to do some work among the growing things she loved.

II

THE shop was cleaned and painted, and the new stock—which included several bicycles—began to arrive. Joe was heavily in arrears with his repairs, for he had hardly considered the size of the shop in ordering these replenishments. Tamsin came, and her master almost regretted his change of life when she proclaimed that the house was not fit to live in, and began to make it clean. Still, she sang pleasingly while she was at her work, and looked most charming with her sleeves turned up, and her hair hidden under a handkerchief to keep it from the dust. Also, she prepared him such meals as he had hardly tasted since he left his mother's house. He was not altogether discontented.

At the end of the first day Tamsin left punctually at five. 'I shall stop later to-morrow,' she said, 'but I didn' know how dirty the house was, and I promised her I'd be home in good time.'

Arrived at home, where Miss Tregenna had made ready the tea, Tamsin became eloquent.

''Tis a good job he had that five hundred pound,' she said. 'I suppose 'twas that that made 'en decide to have some one in to look after the house, and he didn' make up his mind before 'twas time. I never saw such a place for dirt.'

'I suppose he've got nice things enough, too?' asked Miss Tregenna.

'Couldn' be better for looks nor comfort if they was only kept as they should be. He've a passel of fine things of one sort and another. If only some woman had married him, she'd be fine and proud of him.'

'Perhaps he never thought to ask anybody,' said Miss Tregenna, with a sigh.

'I suppose that's it,' assented Tamsin. 'But 'tis a pity. He's like a great child about the house. 'Twould have been a wonderful thing for him if he had married just such a woman as you are twenty years ago.'

Miss Tregenna laughed a little bitterly, letting her hands drop, with the knitting that engaged them, upon her lap. ''Twould ha' done him a passel o' good to have an old blind woman feeling her way round his house.'

Tamsin became angry. 'You aren't allowed to say that. Any man would have been happier if he had your love. You aren't so blind now but what you can make work easy for me, and I could cry sometimes to think that you've hurted your eyes sitting up o' nights and working for me. I won't hear you say it again, and you know it.'

Joe Mayne was quite looking forward to her arrival in the morning, and one of his first questions, after he had greeted her, was an inquiry after Miss Tregenna. ''Tis a sad thing to think she haven' got the use of her eyes,' he said. 'She used to be wonderful lively when she was a girl.' He sighed and turned to his work. At the end of the day he spoke again: 'Goin', are 'ee? Well, run up and pick a few roses for your aunt. She used to be brave and fond of them some few years ago, and I suppose she can smell them even if she can't see them.' He was passionately fond of his roses, and hated to have the blooms picked. It was therefore necessary that he should add, 'Mind you do pick a good handful. They aren't no use to me.'

Tamsin's training had been such as to render her extremely handy about the house. After these earliest disturbances Joe rejoiced publicly at having had the wisdom to choose her, for she did a hundred things daily to enhance his comfort, and he had to be continually on the alert lest by chance he should fail in gratitude. People noticed that he seemed to have grown older in manner, but few of them were wise enough to observe that this change was simply the result of the gently paternal way in which he regarded Tamsin. Perhaps their blindness was due to the fact that Tamsin's attitude in regard to him was quite monumentally maternal.

'Mr. Mayne,' she said one day, opening the door at the back of the shop, 'I do want for you to do me a favour.'

'Speak it,' said Joe, ' and if 'tis in my power you may call it done.'

'Oh,' said Tamsin, laughing, ' 'tis no great thing, after all. Do you know what clothes you've got?'

Joe looked at her, completely puzzled. 'What is the maid talking about now?' he asked, regarding the stock.

'I mean,' said Tamsin, laughing again, ' I can't fancy you do know whether you've got four suits, or ten, or only the one you've got on. I'm sure you don't know if the moth is in them. 'Tis the same with socks, and things. And I do want for you to let me turn out your chest of drawers and the old oak chest, and put everything in order.'

Joe was manifestly relieved. 'My dear,' he said, ' you can go where you mind to, and do what you please. I never knew the meaning of comfort until you took charge of me. You're like a mother to me.'

There were sounds of great activity overhead, but he hardly noticed them. The shop was full, and one of the usual discussions was at its height, when Tamsin reappeared at the door. 'Mr. Mayne——' She began to apologise.

'All right, Tamsin,' he said. 'If you do want me I'll be with 'ee in a minute.' Just at that moment a somewhat critical point had arisen, and before he could leave the assembly it was necessary that he should put them in the way of arriving at a proper conclusion. When this had been done he apologised for a moment's withdrawal. 'I've never been so well looked after in all my days,' he said. 'I used to think my mother was a wonderful woman, but that little maid is all the time discovering something new that must be attended to at once; and she's always right, though I may have gone for twenty years without finding out.'

On entering the room—half-kitchen, half-parlour—at the back of the shop, a brown-paper parcel lay upon the table, and it was manifestly about this that Tamsin wished to speak. Joe Mayne regarded her with dismay.

'I was sure you didn' know what clothes you had,' she said. 'This is a new suit, and never opened, if I aren't mistaken.'

'I tried it on once,' said Joe, guiltily.

Tamsin immediately began to undo the parcel, and Joe watched. One after the other she lifted the garments up and let them fall open. The parcel had held a perfectly preserved suit of dark-blue broadcloth, and she faced him indignantly. 'You've never worn it,' she said. 'I can see by the cut of it you've had it for several years. I suppose you don't remember how long you've had it, or what you paid for it? I suppose you had forgotten all about it?'

'No,' said Joe, shamefacedly. 'I always knew I had it somewhere.'

'How long have you had it?' continued Tamsin. 'I suppose you've been saving it up against the time you was married?'

Joe quailed. 'I've had it more than twenty years,' he said. 'But you wouldn' think well of me if I was to tell you why I got it, and why I've never worn it since.'

'I couldn' think you more foolish than I shall until I know what made 'ee put by a lovely suit like that without ever wearing it. 'Tis gone old-fashioned now. I wouldn' say you could have it made fit to wear now, even if you was to go to the best tailor in Trenear, though the cloth is good enough for the biggest gentleman in the land.'

'I'm afraid 'tis just as useless as if 'twas clean worn out,' said Joe. 'The fact is, Tamsin, I had a mind to ask a little maid to marry me one Whitsuntide, and I was going to wear that suit. But I never asked her, and I never wore the suit.'

'Did she marry some one else?' asked Tamsin impatiently.

'No,' said Joe.

'Then how didn' 'ee ask her?'

Joe looked at her piteously. 'My dear maid, you've got some tongue for questions, but I can't answer 'ee that. 'Tis a thing I've asked myself ever since the day I put the coat away. All I can say is, I didn' do it.'

Tamsin's look had changed. 'Did she die?' she asked solemnly.

'No,' said Joe, 'she is not dead.'

Then he retreated into the shop. ''Tis only a small thing,' he said. 'The little maid found an old coat and thought I ought to give it to the poor. If Artie Gundry is so well looked after when she is his wife as I have been lately he'll be a happy man. . . . Well, neighbours, where are 'ee got to now?'

But he did not enter into the discussion with all his usual heartiness.

III

THE rest of the story may be told quite briefly. When once the house had been reduced to order Tamsin found that she had hardly enough work to give her the full occupation she craved. She began to suggest that her master, as a man of means, ought to allow himself an occasional holiday, and, in order that the business might not suffer through his adopting her advice, she desired to be told the whereabouts of the articles most commonly in demand, and their prices.

Once or twice there were busy days when Joe Mayne found it exceedingly convenient to have her assistance in the shop, and when at last he was called to another funeral and knew he would need to be absent most of the day he left her in sole charge, and went upon his journey with mind at ease.

Tamsin had little to do until the afternoon, and the customers who appeared happened in all cases to pay cash. But in the afternoon they sent down from the Big House for some small article that was needed in a hurry, and the coachman who brought the order explained that the debt was to be booked. When he had gone Tamsin went to the desk and chose a pen. She discovered that the ink was merely so much mud, and went out and cleansed the pot. She filled it, and was just upon the point of making the entry on a right-hand page when she chanced to see her own name written on the other side amid the business notes. Curiosity prevailed upon her and she read:

Mrs. Curgenven. *Cleaning her husband's watch*, 2s. Mrs. Treloar, *clock, new hand*, 3d. Joe Wright, *steel chain*, 6d. *Tamsin still a blessing. Made up mind to go to Mr. Lanyon's funeral.* George Symons, *piercing coins for chain*, 2d. . . .

Tamsin would hardly have been human if she had not turned back, and by a woman's instinct she was led to begin a systematic investigation at about the place where she had entered into Joe Mayne's life. She had to search for awhile, but at last she came to what for her was the beginning of things :

May 23*rd.* Mrs. Bassett, — — —; John Smith, — — —; *Cousin James's funeral : some crowd there. Heard of my good fortune. The Lord is good : never expected no such thing. Told Mrs. Curtis I would never hear of her paying her account, she being a widow.* George Laity, — — —; James Cundy — — —; *et cetera.*

She turned over the page and read again. There were the usual entries of small debts, but only one sentence need be extracted :

May 24*th. Everyone seeming wonderfully pleased.*

A page or two more was turned, and then she came on another sentence, interpolated in the same way in the midst of matters of no interest :

May 29*th. Made up my mind to do bigger things. Thought upon having a little maid to keep the house nicer than it have been, and fit meat for me. I can afford a bit of comfort now.*

There was another interval, and she found nothing that interested her personally, though it was evident that this volume had always been the diary of a lonely man. After a while she came upon an entry that made her even more curious than she had been hitherto :

June 3*rd. Made up my mind to get Mary Tregenna's little niece. If she's like her aunt I shall do better than I deserve.*

Two days later there was this addition :

June 5*th. Mary's niece came. Tamsin by name. A dear little maid, and fitted me the prettiest meal I've eaten in Tregantock. But I knew one that was more than her equal long ago. Told her to pick some roses and take them home to Mary. She stripped the* Catherine Mermet *in the greenhouse.*

Tamsin found this latest entry altogether to her liking, and when she read about the *Catherine Mermet* she laughed aloud, and then looked up, fearful lest some importunate customer should be coming to disturb her peace. She remembered how she had taken Joe's roses to her aunt; and that she had picked a splendid bunch because the home garden was of necessity filled rather with vegetables and fruit trees than with flowers.

'Mr. Mayne told me to pick these for you,' she had said. 'He told me to take so many as I had a mind to : said they were no use to him.'

Her aunt had flushed delightedly and buried her face in the closely massed blooms. Then she had spoken reprovingly. ''Twas wonderful kind of him to say so, for he used to be wonderful fond of roses. I'm afraid you stripped his little garden. You must be sure and give him my best thanks when you do go in in the morning. 'Tis kind of him to think of an old woman like me, that's nearly blind.'

Thinking of this Tamsin smiled again, and went on reading:

June 10th. Some fuss about the house, but 'tis like a new place, and I never had better meals, nor any that were so cheap.

June 12th. Tamsin away to Trenear market. A whisht dinner.

She laughed again here, remembering that upon her return he had confessed to her what he confided to his diary. She rejoiced that she had thought on that day of bringing some little delicacy from Trenear for his tea. She read on :

June 24th. Tamsin going on wonderful. How can a man stop single when he's young enough to marry?

Other entries followed which might well have made her odiously conceited. Then there came this long record, which seemed to have been written in a moment of agitation :

July 9th. Tamsin couldn't find anything to do, so she asked if I knew how many suits of clothes and pairs of socks I had. Said I couldn't tell. She said she'd be bound the moth was in the most of them, and set forth to see. She found the blue suit and asked why I had never worn it. Nearly told her everything, and if I hadn't stopped in time she would have guessed it all, being wonderful clever.

Thomasin had read thus far when a customer entered. At Joe Mayne's nobody ever wanted to do business quickly : the girl took sixpence and wasted half an hour. Then other customers came to occupy her time, and the shop was not empty again until it was high time for the master to return. When at last she was free again she wrote on a big sheet of paper in a good large hand

'*LOOK IN THE DAY-BOOK.*'

She then went to the desk and made an entry on the page which still failed to record the debt she should have booked : ' How don't you tell her if you are still so fond of her ? Even the blind can't see what has never been shown to them. And thank you kindly.—THOMASIN.'

She took her watch at the doorway, glancing back at the glazed door that opened into the house, as if to make sure of her retreat. After a long time Joe Mayne appeared in the distance. She pinned her paper in a prominent position and disappeared into the house, being vastly more frightened than she would ever have admitted to herself.

She heard him enter the shop. Then he stopped—he was reading her notice. He moved again and she knew he had gone to the day-book. Her heart beat with unwonted and uncomfortable rapidity. She waited in a passion of attention during the long pause which followed. At last he moved. She heard a sound as of a man brushing his clothes carefully. Then Joe left the shop, and she had time to get to one of the front windows and see him disappearing down the street in the direction of her aunt's house.

He was late in returning, and the shop was kept open until long past the usual hour. When he returned, a happier man than he had ever been before, he found that she had already donned her hat and jacket.

'You'll find your supper ready in the sitting-room. May I go now?' she said as she slipped swiftly past him.

'Bless the maid,' said Joe, so fervently that he seemed to be masquerading in his decent funeral clothes.

H. D. LOWRY.

SIR HENRY IRVING'S CHILDHOOD

THE GREAT ACTOR'S REMINISCENCES OF CORNWALL

OF the influence of environment upon the moulding of character in childhood, you shall hold your own theory and none may say you nay. For there are men with heads of wood who have been brought up in surroundings that might put soul into a wood-louse. And there have been Cockneys who have risen from squalid courts to teach new thoughts of beauty. Between the two extremes lies the great world of the commonplace; and it is safer to assume that whether you be genius, blockhead, or the average person depends more upon a fortuitous combination of hereditary characteristics than upon acquired impressions. In other words, genius will out, though it live in Cornwall or Cockneytown, and the ordinary mind can never be galvanised into the extraordinary.

To say so much is not to deny that genius develops more quickly in favouring circumstances. Otherwise Cornwall could claim no share in the making of John Henry Brodribb into Sir Henry Irving, first and foremost actor of his age. It is truth that a childhood spent in the county gave bent to his inborn talent, and quickened his 'arrival.'

No one recognises this more than Sir Henry himself. 'My impressions of Cornwall,' he said to me, 'are to this day vivid and convincing. At this distance of time—it may be because of it—faces, incidents and happenings stand out very clearly. But I have lost the half-tones, the subtle lights and shades of my early life. Perhaps they might modify my present mental attitude. I do not know. I have the belief that the things which last in the recollection are the lasting things, the enduring things, and that in the vista of years the trivial and insignificant get blotted out. Yet I don't think I shall uphold the statement when I tell you that at this moment, roving back over the past, I recall equally well my aunt reading the Bible, a joke we children once played on an old Granny, my uncle Penberthy in a rare passion, and—the comic waddling of a lame duck across the roadway, falling over itself in haste to reach the evening meal! I don't think I can justify the lame duck as a chief event in my youth. It is evidently one of the trivialities which get permanently photographed on the memory. To say more would be to become metaphysical.'

The story has been often told of Irving's early life in Cornwall, and it need only be summarised here. John Henry Brodribb was born on February 6, 1838, at Keinton, near Glastonbury. He left Keinton when he was about four years

Photo by]   *[Window & Grove*
SIR HENRY IRVING

old, in the early forties, and did not return until the eighties, when he revived his youthful impressions. Irving's father had married a Miss Behenna, one of six sisters belonging to an old Cornish family. Another of these, Sarah Behenna, married Captain Isaac Penberthy, who settled down as captain of mines in Halsetown, near St. Ives, after a successful experience of mining in Mexico. To Halsetown, when Mr. and Mrs. Brodribb were removing to the metropolis, did the mother take the four-year-old son, leaving him in charge of her sister.

'I have a permanent mental view of them all and of the place and the neighbours,' said Sir Henry. ' My uncle was a big man, bearded, broad in the shoulders, perhaps a bit rough, and possessing the Celtic temper. He was a man born to command and to be loved. I can hardly describe to you how dominating was his personality, and yet how lovable. I remember that my aunt, my cousins, and myself went to meet him coming home from the mines every evening, that his greeting was boisterously affectionate, and that we knew no better task than to win his approval. I find this the more remarkable when I remember my aunt Penberthy. It was the

CAPTAIN ISAAC PENBERTHY'S HOUSE AT HALSETOWN

SIR HENRY IRVING'S CHILDHOOD

MRS. PENBERTHY, SIR HENRY IRVING'S AUNT

union of two strong individualities. She was a woman of severe simplicity in dress—the straight lines of her gowns are before me now--and deeply religious in character. It was the time of the great religious revival in Cornwall. My aunt was a teetotaller and a Methodist, and her whole life was coloured by her convictions. Perhaps the stern asceticism of the daily routine imposed by my aunt may have jarred upon us youngsters; but it was tempered by strong affections. At any rate, the angles have worn off that recollection. My aunt inspired both respect and affection among us, and I have no doubt the discipline imposed upon us was good and healthful.'

You are to know the character of this part of the Duchy before you can appreciate the influences which fostered the genius of the actor. 'I recall Halsetown,' he said, in reply to a leading question, 'as a village nestling between sloping hills, bare and desolate, disfigured by great heaps of slack from the mines, and with the Knill monument standing prominent as a landmark to the east. It was a wild and weird place, fascinating in its own peculiar beauty, and taking a more definite shape in my youthful imagination by reason of the fancies and legends of the people. The stories attaching to rock and well and hill were unending; every man and woman had folk-lore to tell us youngsters. We took to them naturally—they seemed to fit in wisely with the solitudes, the expanses, the superstitious character of the Cornish people, and never

CAPTAIN JOHN PENBERTHY, SIR HENRY'S PLAYMATE AT HALSETOWN

clashed in our minds with the Scriptural teachings which were our daily portion at home. These legends and fairy stories have remained with me but vaguely —I was too young—but I remember the "guise dancing," when the villagers went about in masks, entering houses and frightening the children. We imitated this once, in breaking in on old Granny Dixon's sleep, fashioned out in horns and tails, and trying to frighten her into repentance for telling us stories of hell-fire and brimstone. The attempt,' he added with a smile, ' was not too successful.'

Of his aunt Penberthy Sir Henry Irving told a good story which Joseph Hatton published in the 'Idler' some years back. It will well bear the retelling here, as illustrating the character of the woman. Mrs. Penberthy once came to town, and the actor took her to see the Baroness Burdett-Coutts.

'Oh yes,' she said, when the usual inquiry was made, ' I am very well indeed; and on these long journeys I carry with me a small flask of brandy, and take a little; the travelling fatigues me, and I find the brandy gives me life. It is the elixir vitæ '!

Sir Henry's own comment on the incident is the fitting one.

'Fine, was it not?' he said. ' Here is a woman strong enough all her life to be teetotal, yet sensible enough to take a little alcohol as a medicine.'

Then there is another anecdote already recorded by Mr. Hatton, and of which I reminded Sir Henry. 'It is quite right and I recall it well,' was his response. ' I told it to Hatton to show how these two strong natures, one strong and cheerfully stern—if I can use the expression—and the other strong and passionate, could yet live together in perfect concord. Nothing could disturb my aunt's appreciation of the sterling qualities of her husband. She was away from home one afternoon when he strode into the house and surprised us youngsters playing in the kitchen by starting to smash up the furniture. He was in a great rage about something, I forget what, and he broke the chairs across his knees as if they were matchwood, threw over the tables, and made havoc generally. We had scuttled into shelter like startled rabbits and trembled at the destruction, wondering if our turn would come next. But having smashed up everything portable he went out again, and we could see his big figure striding along

Photo by] *[Window & Grove*
AS 'THE VICAR' IN 'OLIVIA'

Photo by]   *[London Stereoscopic Company*
AS 'MATTHIAS' IN 'THE BELLS'

the road to the mine, with arms waving.

'It was not in the scope of our youthful minds,' Sir Henry continued, smiling introspectively, ' to guess what my aunt's attitude would be to this extraordinary outbreak. We wondered and waited, fearing trouble. But none came. When the time arrived to meet him in the evening, my aunt gathered her brood together and out we set. There was no difference in our greetings, and we all returned in the best of humours. At the threshold of the kitchen—it was our living-room, by the way, and looked cosy enough with its ingle-nook and old oak beams embellished with rows of hams—my uncle stopped to laugh. You might have heard it for miles. It was the hearty guffaw of a giant. You know what the laughter was about. Aunt Penberthy had gathered together the wreckage of the furniture and hung it on the walls as if it composed a collection of precious works of art. A woman of less character would have found ample justification for angry recriminations; my aunt was strong enough to treat the affair as a joke. I shall not easily forget our childish wonderment and subsequent admiration at this turning of the tables, or the table legs. We were a very happy family that night.'

The life at Halsetown was well calculated to develop a sense of the poetic and dramatic aspect of life in young Irving. At home there were the Scriptural teachings and readings daily, and a Puritan simplicity of routine stimulating to the youthful imagination. For recreation Sir Henry recollects best 'Don Quixote' and an old volume of English ballads, and these inspired a longing for adventure and romance. Outside were a wild and desolate landscape and a rough mining population redeemed in the youngster's eyes by its eerie tales and legends.

'Halsetown gave me a good physical start in life, at any rate,' said he to me, ' whatever else I owe it. I attribute much of my endurance of fatigue, which is a necessary part of an actor's life, to the free and open and healthy years I lived at Halsetown, and to the simple food and regular routine ordained by my aunt. We rambled much over the desolate hills, or down to the rocks at the seashore. There was plenty of natural beauty to look for, and I suppose we looked for it. I know the sea had a potent attraction for me. I was a wiry youth, as I believe, when the time came for me to join a London school.'

This was in the year 1849, when he was eleven years old, and joined Dr. Pinches' school in George Yard, Lombard Street. I do not propose to follow him there, or show how early he evinced that predilection for the stage which, happily for us, surmounted all obstacles. But whatever theory of environment you hold, it cannot be denied that the Duchy of Cornwall has contributed to Sir Henry Irving's ultimate and splendid success.

ARTHUR BRASHER.

COLLINGWOOD

THE *Ville de Paris* lay off Port Mahon
With the great sea-captain dying—strange that he
Who fought the French his whole life long should be
So berthed for the last battle; there, as noon
Waned to the sunset, they were ware he grew
Conscious once more, and bending o'er his bed
The grave fleet surgeon touched his heart and said,
' Hope is not over.'
    The old sea-dog knew
His voice, and smiling in the pause of pain,
Asked, ' Can I live to fight the French again ? '

RENNELL RODD.

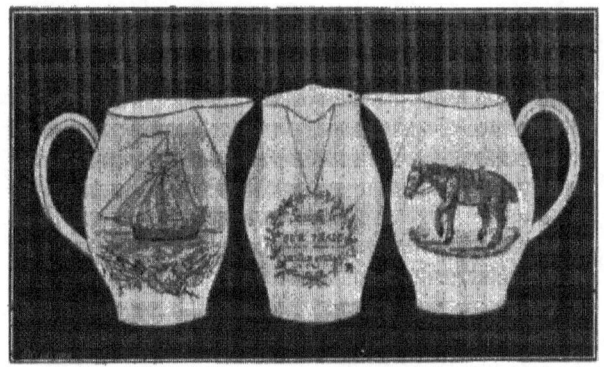

ANNALS OF THE SMUGGLERS

I. THE CAWSAND MEN

QUITE a halo of interesting associations encircles the twin villages of Cawsand and Kingsand. It was in Cawsand Bay that our fleets were wont to assemble during the old wars before going forth to encounter the foe; and it was to Cawsand the vessels returned to refit, provision, and take in water in readiness for fresh duties. For a couple of centuries Cawsand was so closely bound up with the navy, that for the navy it may be said to have lived and moved and had its being; and assuredly such prosperity as the place ever attained to was chiefly due to its connection with the naval service.

But there was another phase of Cawsand life which, though long forgotten, once played a very important part in the economy of its inhabitants—namely, smuggling. At what period of the world's history the men of Cawsand took to illicit trading cannot be now affirmed with any certainty; but to them, when the final history of Cornish smuggling comes to be written, the place of honour will probably be awarded. Nor has the haven long ceased to cherish the recollection of its 'golden age.' There was a time, within the memory of persons still living, when old cronies, gossiping with the stranger, would speak regretfully of the 'good old days' when money was 'that plentiful' in Cawsand that if one woman went to borrow of another the friend in need would measure out guineas by the basinful.

'When I was stationed at Cawsand, long ago,' said a very old Coastguard pensioner to the writer, 'I well remember a poor old fellow named P——, almost bent double with age, who often came down to the beach to hunt about for spade guineas. You see, guineas were so plentiful in old times that I've heard it said chaps used to play pitch-and-toss with them, just as the youngsters do now with ha'pence.'

Whence arose this tradition? Possibly the reckless way in which the smugglers in the halcyon days of the 'trade' were wont to squander their ill-gotten gains—for the profits of a successful trip were often enormous—may have given rise to an exaggerated notion of the wealth of the community. And I am the more inclined to accept this as the true explanation, seeing that precisely the same story has been told to me in other Cornish havens.

Not till we come to the present century do we find any solid basis of fact to build on. All anterior to this is mere tradition and does not concern us here.

When the long war with France came to an end, early in the present century, and the fighting services of the Crown were reduced, an immense number of privateersmen and other lawless characters which a long war invariably brings to the surface—men whose vocation was fighting, and who infinitely preferred a life of excitement and danger to the more prosaic paths of honest industry—were let loose upon the country. And these men, for want of more exciting occupation, naturally drifted into the ranks of the smugglers, with the result that, within a short time of the return of peace, there was a great recrudescence of smuggling all along the coasts of the United Kingdom.

But the termination of the war also enabled Government to devote more attention than had been possible hitherto to the frightful leakage which had been going on for years past in the revenue in consequence of the activity of the smugglers; and as the services of a large number of soldiers and sailors who had been fighting their country's battles were now available there was at once organised, for the first time in the nation's history, a really efficient preventive service.

The new force was established along the south coast of England in 1816–17, and it is from the official records of the force that it is now possible to compile a consecutive history of smuggling. But documents of this sort are terribly dry reading, and, although they afford an accurate measure of the extent of the leakage that went on, and even give some idea of the marvellous activity with which smuggling was conducted, to make a history of this sort interesting something more is needed than official statistics. The personal recollections which constitute the life-blood of such a story must be sought for, and, fortunately, these have been forthcoming in abundance. For it was the writer's good fortune in days gone by to be brought into contact with the class which has always furnished the most numerous recruits to the smugglers' ranks. And as there were many old men—'ancients of our villages'—then living who had taken a very prominent part in the trade, and who, after a short acquaintanceship, proved nothing loth to discourse without reserve on the subject of their youthful delinquencies, from these sources of information some very interesting facts were elicited.

Of the causes which contributed to the pre-eminence of Cawsand in smuggling annals, not the least important was its proximity to Plymouth and other populous places, in which there was a ready market for the sale of French brandy and such other odds and ends as it pleased the smugglers to bring over, and of which the inhabitants showed a decided preference for cheap spirits. With such facilities for disposing of their wares, the men of Cawsand would have been more than human had they neglected to take advantage of them; while the high duties which were imposed at this time on nearly all imports, but especially on spirits and tobacco, with the resultant enormous profits that accrued to the successful smuggler, gave an additional stimulus to the trade all along the coast.

But what chiefly enabled the Cawsand men to take the lead was their possession of a class of boat which exactly suited the requirements of the trade. The large craft, cutters and luggers, of a hundred tons and more—half smugglers and half privateers—which had been employed during the war, and carried guns, not always for fighting the French, were no longer available. An armed smuggler was a pirate, pure and simple, and could never be tolerated in peace time. Moreover, most of these vessels, even if not worn out and consigned to the ship-knacker's yard, were far too large for *bona-fide* smuggling. A much smaller class of vessel was now required, as being less liable to detection and handier in every way for the 'running' of illicit goods on a guarded coast.

It so happened that the Cawsand Bay fishing-boats exactly met these requirements, and, being half-decked, excellent sea boats, and of remarkably good sailing qualities, they came into immediate request.

Now, in an industry such as smuggling, where high profits tempted men to run great risks, every sort of craft, as may be supposed, was brought into requisition, and it is a well-established fact, incredible as it may seem to landsmen, that there were men always to be found who were both willing and eager to risk the crossing in small open boats. Some heroes of these expeditions have recounted to the writer their experiences, and very thrilling were the stories they told. But, of course, only a few tubs could be brought over in such frail craft, for the passage across the intervening hundred miles of stormy sea was hazardous in the extreme. The more ambitious traders who aimed at cargoes of a hundred tubs or more required for the safe conveyance of their wares a larger class of boat than was to be met with at that time at the fishing villages along the Cornish coast. And, as suitable vessels could always be got at Cawsand, 'freighters' flocked there from all parts of the county, and found the owners nothing loth to direct their energies into a line of trading which, if the risks were great, tempted them with profits far exceeding anything likely to arise from a more legitimate industry.

It might be thought that the proximity of a great naval port, with men-of-war constantly going and coming, and a large staff of Customs officers—to say nothing of the presence of an officer and several men in their very midst, and a revenue cutter or two at anchor in the bay—I say it would be natural to suppose these would act as a wet blanket. But, as a matter of fact, these obstructions only gave additional zest to smuggling, and for many years the business went on as merrily as ever, a large proportion of the Cawsand fishermen occupying themselves with little else.

A RUN OF GOODS
From an old engraving

Cawsand having thus become the headquarters of smuggling in the west, there was witnessed here during the next twenty years a remarkable display of enterprise and daring on the part of the men who conducted the trade. The reputation for skill, energy, and knowledge of their 'craft' which the Cawsand men enjoyed far and wide, brought about a constant demand for their boats; and, naturally, while profits were high, there were never wanting men to risk the crossing.

The establishment of the Coastguard soon made it evident to the experienced smugglers that the free-and-easy methods of old were no longer applicable. With watchmen posted at every creek and headland, it was impossible to effect a direct landing now, even at night, while the strength, discipline, and fighting equipment of the new force disinclined all but the most fire-eating of smugglers from risking a conflict. The danger, moreover, of approaching a rock-bound coast in the dark was one the owners of boats seldom cared to face. Hence there came into vogue at this time the practice of sinking cargoes, and afterwards 'working' them—that is, picking up the goods and landing them as opportunity offered, to avoid suspicion.

Now, for the purpose of 'working' the goods, the Cawsand smugglers employed a special kind of boats, six- and eight-oared galleys of light frame-work and great speed, which were built ostensibly for working the seine nets. These galleys played a very important part in the economy of Cawsand smuggling, and there arose so great a demand for them that the writer has been assured by old men, whose acquaintance with this particular branch of smuggling was both extensive and peculiar, with pardonable exaggeration, that X——, of Anderton, a well-known boat-builder of former days, turned out these galleys as fast as ever he could build them.

Having regard to the peculiar nature of their occupation, the galleys, as may be supposed, soon became objects of almost affectionate solicitude to the preventive men: all their movements were watched, while the prolonged absence of a galley was sure to cause a flutter in the Coastguard dovecots. An old general order of the period contains the following significant remark: 'A rocket and blue light will be fired from the Ramehead when the galleys go afloat, as a signal to Polperro.'

It was kind in the Coastguard to concern themselves so much with the galleys, but all this solicitude was not entirely disinterested. There were such things as 'Rewards for seizures,' or, as we should call it, prize money, awaiting the active and zealous preventive man who made captures, and, if tradition lies not, a good many rewards of this description fell to the share of the officer and boat's crew stationed at Cawsand in old days.

The activities of the Cawsand men were, however, by no means confined to their own neighbourhood. They often wandered round into the 'North Channel,' and 'ran' cargoes as far afield as Padstow. But the sphere of action of the galleys was necessarily more circumscribed, being practically confined to the coast comprised between the Mewstone and Polperro, the scene of most of their enterprises lying between Plymouth Sound—where a great many cargoes were successfully run—and Looe Island, a spot with quite an interesting history of its own. But the happy hunting-ground *par excellence* was in Whitsand Bay, along the shore of which the cargoes were usually sunk.

At a later period, owing to the vigilance of the ' enemy,' the smugglers were driven further afield, to the Eddystone, around which enormous quantities of goods were sunk, a fact which has been unaccountably overlooked by historians of this well-known beacon.

Naturally, the display of so much enterprise and activity in the cause of 'free trade' on the one hand, and the keenness of the preventive men in pursuit of prize money on the other, led to some interesting situations, from whence arose many sensational and romantic incidents. In fact, the story of Cawsand smuggling, as related to the writer by old men who helped to make its history, and subsequently verified by official documents, constitutes one of the most curious chapters of our domestic annals during the present century, and affords a striking illustration of the oft-quoted aphorism about truth being stranger than fiction.

Of course, a smuggler's career was a chequered one. For instance, the fate of a galley or boat, when taken *in flagrante delicto*, was a sad one ; though, as the old saying has it, ' You must first catch your hare ; ' and therein often lay the difficulty, for the smugglers, by dint of long practice, had become so crafty that it was no easy matter to catch them red-handed. Of ruses for throwing the Coastguard men off their guard there was no end. 'A favourite dodge,' said an old Coastguard man, 'was to carry the boat down to the water's edge, and then, directly the watchman's back was turned, to carry it away, and launch it at another spot some distance off.' Sometimes a boat would be transported all the way to Whitsand, and launched there. In fact, every conceivable trick was resorted to by the smugglers for veiling their intentions and concealing their movements from the enemy.

If a cargo was to be 'worked,' reports would be spread abroad of intended operations in an entirely different quarter to that where the run was to be effected ; and if the Coastguard watch was too close to admit of a start being made unperceived, two boats would be launched simultaneously, and rowed off in opposite directions. The boat that was 'shadowed' by the Coastguard galley would row away in a wrong direction, and, after leading her chaperon a wild-goose chase for a sufficiently long distance, would double back to where her consort was lying and help to work the goods. Strategy and cunning necessarily played a conspicuous part now in the successful prosecution of smuggling, and fortune did not always side with the 'big battalions.'

As years rolled on, and the increased efficiency of the preventive cordon put further difficulties in the way of trade, the smugglers found it necessary once more to adapt themselves to their new environment. But the fates were against them—the trade was doomed ; and what, perhaps, tended more than anything else at this time to break the neck of smuggling was the strict enforcement of the 'limit laws,' under which boats unprovided with a special licence found outside of the nine-mile limit were liable to seizure, and, if proved to be engaged in illicit practices, condemnation, followed by sawing into three parts. The feelings, and language, of the owner of a smart little vessel as he watched the centre of all his hopes, and the source of so much profit, being slowly sawn through into three equal portions, must be left to the imagination of the reader.

Amongst other curious reminiscences of those frolicsome days which have come into the possession of the writer, is a list of some fifty Cawsand boats known to have been in the habit of making clandestine runs to the French coast for contraband, together with many interesting particulars relating to their adventurous careers, and, in some cases, their capture and destruction, derived from official sources, as well as from old men who had sailed in them. One of the smartest and most successful of these craft was captured by the Cawsand Coastguard and converted into a tender, in which capacity she made several valuable prizes, on the principle of setting a thief to catch a thief!

The writer's 'Smuggling Directory' further contains the names of over eighty men from Cawsand and neighbourhood known to have been engaged in illicit trading, and of whom many suffered martyrdom in the cause. Their adventures would supply material for quite a bulky volume; and when we compare the experiences of these old Cawsand smugglers with the contracted field open to adventurous spirits at the present day in England, but one inference can be drawn, namely, that we have fallen on sadly prosaic times.

As time went on, fortune declared more decidedly against the Cawsand men, and in the year 1839 the following suggestive Memorandum was sent round the Coastguard stations: 'In consequence of the large number of Cawsand and other boats taken, lost, and made to throw over their cargoes, the Coastguard are warned against the smugglers employing French boats.'

As a matter of fact, the smugglers everywhere had begun to change their methods; and, instead of risking their own boats, they chartered French vessels, which the revenue cruisers had no power to interfere with while out of territorial waters. In these the freighters brought across their goods, and sank them, as usual, in convenient spots; and by this means the trade was continued for many years, with varying success, the 'working' and 'running' of the goods being carried out as before by the galleys, the backwaters running up to St. Germans and other places behind Whitsand offering splendid opportunities for getting the goods safe away after landing, for the whole countryside was riddled with caves and secret places, and there were plenty of friends always ready to facilitate the despatch of goods into the interior. Millbrook was a noted depôt at that time for spirits, which were conveyed into Plymouth by old women, in skins concealed under long cloaks.

The following observations of an old man who had known Cawsand in the days referred to will form a fitting conclusion to this sketch: 'It was a very good thing for the place that smuggling was put down, for it was the ruin of a lot of people, especially young fellows who served in the Navy. For, you see, in those days men only shipped for a commission, and when they came home again they wouldn't be over and above flush of money; and, finding smuggling going on briskly, they would take a trip across to France. If the goods were landed safe there would be grog going all night afterwards, aye, and all next day, too, for those who liked it. So it was difficult for a young fellow of spirit to keep out of the business, whether he intended to go smuggling or not. I can tell you this, though, none of the smugglers bettered themselves by it. There was an old saying that " Smuggling money never did good to anyone." One moment there would be money and to spare, but it would all be lost later on; and every smuggler that I remember died poor.'

H. N. SHORE.

II. THE MEN OF MOUNT'S BAY AND 'THE KING OF PRUSSIA'

When we read in our daily paper that the Coastguard yesterday seized a quantity of smuggled tobacco at one of our fishing ports, and that H.M.S. 'Leda' has gone round to render assistance if necessary, we feel a delicacy in speaking or writing on the subject, lest our natural Cornish sympathy should give to our remarks a tone which would belie our claim to rank as peaceful and law-abiding subjects. Fortunately, we can find an escape from this dilemma in the difference between the smuggling of the eighteenth century and the mere revenue cheating of to-day.

What importation of foreign goods free of duty (to give it a name which makes romance impossible) there is to-day is much too small a thing to win our admiration, or even our passing sympathy. Whether the reason be, as Uncle Tom Warren said to the writer, that ' it wouldn't pay, there are too many people about,' or not, the fact is with us that no one nowadays fits out luggers with eighteen carriage guns, or charters French brigs or Irish wherries ' heavily armed and full of men' for the trade, or imports 218 ankers of brandy in one cargo without the knowledge of the officers of H.M. Customs, as the ' Proustock' men did on June 10, 1762.

A mackerel driver dodging the watchful searchlight of the gunboat, to buy a few bad cigars from a Dutch cooper off the Wolf, is a very poor thing compared with the first Friday in March 1767, when ' no less than nine sail of large boats and sloops went from this port [Penzance] to France in a fleet in open defiance at mid-day, even in the sight of the man-of-war.'

It is the difference between wholesale and retail which Sydney Smith has pointed out—the difference between murder and war. To-day, smuggling is on a level with the neglect to take out a dog licence; but one hundred years ago it was straightforward and above board. Scores of well-found vessels and hundreds of honest, daring, reckless men made no secret of their calling. The scale on which they worked required the sterner virtues, and excluded the petty vices. Even the natural and lawful enemy of all smugglers, the Collector of the Customs at Penzance, writes in 1771 that ' Richard Penheath of Mousehole, otherwise "Doga," bears the character of an honest man in all his dealings. He is a notorious smuggler,' and Thomas Mann, of the same place, ' a reputed smuggler, is also an honest man.'

John Carter, the great King of Prussia Cove, himself set the high example

A SEIZURE
From an old aqua-tint

On one occasion, during his absence from home, the excise officers from Penzance came round in their boats and took a cargo which had lately arrived from France to Penzance, where it was secured with other captured goods in the Custom House store. In due course, John Carter returned to the Cove and learned the news. What was he to do? He explained to his comrades that he had agreed to deliver that cargo to his customers by a certain day, and his reputation as an honest man was at stake. He must keep his word. That night a number of armed men broke open the Custom House store at Penzance, and the 'King of Prussia' took his own again. In the morning the officers found that the place had been broken open during the night. They examined the contents, and when they noted what particular things were gone they said to one another that 'John Carter had been there, and they knew it, because he was an honest man, who would not take anything that did not belong to him.'

These eighteenth-century smugglers were brave as well as honest. All their courage was not used in defying the Custom House, nor all their powder and shot expended against humble sitters in the boat or slow-sailing revenue cutters. Harry Carter has told us in his own words how, while smuggling along the coast in 1783, his two new vessels, a cutter of 160 tons carrying nineteen guns and a lugger carrying twenty guns, 'after discharging our cargo,' were lying at anchor in Newlyn Road, 'when we had an express sent us from St. Ives of a large cutter privateer from Dunkirk, called the "Black Prince," had been on that coast, and had taken many prizes, to go out in pursuit of her. It was not a very agreeable business; notwithstanding, for fear to offend the collector, we put round the both vessels to St. Ives Roade, and, after staying there two or three days, the same cuttar hove in sight Christmas day in the morning. We, not having our proper crews on board, collected a few men together and went to sea in pursuit of him. Soon come up with him, so that after a running fight for three or four hours, as we not being half manned and the sea very big, the shots so uncertain, the luggar received a shot that was obliged to bear up, and in the course of less than an hour after I received a shot that card of my jib and another in the hull, so that we could hardly keep her free. So that we bore up after the luggar, not knowing what was the matter of her running away. We came up with her about five in the evening. Desired the Captain to quitt her, but he, in hope to put her into Padstow, continued pumping and bailing until about six, when he hailed me, saying, stand by him, he was going to quitt her. So that they hoisted out their boats, but the sea being so bigg and the men being confused, filled her with water, so that they could not free her no more. I got my boat out in the meantime, sent her alongside the luggar, so that some of the men jumpt overboard, and my boate pickt them up, and immediately the luggar went down. I hove to the cuttar and laid her to, that she drifted right over the place that the luggar went down, so that some of the men got on board by virtue of ropes hove from the cuttar, sume got hold of the jib tack and sume pickt up by the cuttar's boate, so that we saved alive seventeen men and fourteen drowned.'

For at least one hundred years every port and creek and cove from 'Proustock' to the Land's End knew the trade, and, with one glorious exception, every one figures more or less often in the records of the Penzance Custom House, which, by the courtesy of the officials, I have been permitted to inspect. That one exception is Prussia Cove, the most famous of them all.

Between Penzance and Porthleven, dividing Mount's Bay into two halves, is Cuddan Point, and immediately to the eastward of Cuddan are three small coves, now called Pisky's Cove, Bessie's Cove, and Prussia Cove. Pisky's, too exposed and rocky for a harbour, was useful, and is famous, for its caves. Bessie's, called after Bessie Bussow, who kept the 'Kiddleywink' on the cliff which was the great resort of the smugglers, bears on its face to-day the traces of its history. A spot so sheltered and secluded that it is impossible to see what boats are in the little harbour until one literally leans over the edge of the cliff above; a harbour cut out of the solid rock, and a roadway with wheel-tracks partly cut and partly worn crossing the rocks below highwater mark; and, climbing up the face of the cliff on either side of the cove, caves and remains of caves everywhere, some with their mouths built up, which are reputed to be connected with the house above by secret passages—these are the trademarks of Bessie's Cove, and the world has not yet known the degree of innocence which could believe that these were made for the convenience of a few crabbers.

The eastern and the most open is Prussia Cove. Here still stands to-day the house in which John Carter, 'the King of Prussia,' lived and reigned from 1770 to 1807. He was succeeded by his son-in-law, Captain Will Richards, under whom Prussia Cove maintained the reputation which the earlier generations had won, and Captain Will Richards's son, Captain Harry, still lives in the house which his father built, on the site of Bessie Bussow's 'Kiddleywink.' Long may he yet flourish, to light and delight this decadent age with the tales of his grandfather's glory and his father's fame!

This Prussia Cove, first among our smuggling centres, and these heroes, John Carter, Harry his famous brother, Will Richards, 'Tummells' and 'Old Bird,' whose names and deeds of derring-do have been familiar to me from the days before I went to school, have no place in the books and reports of the Penzance Custom House. Time after time the Collector records his utter inability to cope with the coast to the east of the Mount, echoing, with plaintive appeals for soldiers and ships of war, an official version of the sailor's litany—
'From Praa sands and Breage hands,
Good Lord, deliver us!'
Prussia Cove was too far from the places where his few men were stationed, and occupied by men too greatly daring and too reckless for his small force to cope with, and Prussia Cove boasts that the officers never seized but one keg there, and that was a leaky one in a pool at Pisky's, which they smelt as they were passing by.

The history of Prussia Cove is bound up with John Carter. The very name is his. The story goes that when he was a boy, playing at soldiers with other boys, he would always claim to be the King of Prussia, and in later years for his sake the Cove lost the older name of Porthleah, and became 'The King of Prussia's Cove.' Little doubt Porthleah was not idle. Smuggling was no novelty in 1770, when the Carters began to grow famous. As early as April 21, 1739, the Penzance Collector records the capture of eight bags of tobacco, 'just put out of a small boat that was observed to come from a sloop then at anchor some distance from the shore, but the boat was put off before the goods were found, and no person in possession '—quite as if it were a matter of everyday occurrence. But all the earlier history of the Cove is hidden behind the great figures of the King and his brother. This brother, Captain Harry Carter, has left his own record in the little autobiography which was so well received by the reading public when it was published four years ago. And such a man as he would give a lustre to many a worse calling. Harry spent his time at sea; John lived at the Cove, and more often managed the actual landing and disposal of the cargoes which Harry brought. Once, when the boats were expected, a supply of provisions, beef, bread, and so on, was stored in John Carter's shed, waiting for them, and safely under lock and key. The Custom House officers happened to pay a visit to the Cove, and, finding the shed locked, demanded to be allowed to inspect the contents. The King refused, stating that the contents were provisions for his brother's vessel. This was more than any officer could be expected to believe: a locked outhouse at Prussia Cove was much too sure a thing, and they proceeded to break open the door, in spite of the repeated warning that they would be called upon to make good any damage and any loss which might occur through leaving valuable provisions in an unprotected shed, where any passer-by might steal them. They, however, persisted, and were bitterly disappointed to find that they had been told the merest truth. That night John Carter slept peacefully in his bed, but next morning the shed was empty, and he made those unfortunate officers pay for his lost provisions. He had no difficulty in finding them when his brother's vessel did arrive a few days later.

Probably the most famous episode is the firing on the revenue cutter from the little battery on the point between Bessie's and the King's Cove. As I have heard the tale, it came about in this way. A smuggler chased by a revenue cutter, being somewhat pressed, ran through a narrow channel amongst the rocks between the Enys and the shore. The cutter, not daring to venture amongst the shoals, sent her boat in. And the King, with his merry men, opened fire on the boat. They loaded up the little guns so that every time they fired the guns kicked over completely backwards, and had to be replaced. The boat was driven back, and the cutter held off for the night. Next morning the fight was renewed, the cutter opening fire from the sea, while a company of 'riders' fired from the hedge at the top of the hill on the rear of the men in the battery. This turned the tables on the smugglers, who sought shelter in Bessie Bussow's house. The boys, of whom Will Richards was one (he died about 1855, aged eighty-five), were out behind the house; and as the cutter's shot struck in the soft cliff, they ran with a 'tubbal' and dug them out. All this time Uncle Will Leggo was ploughing in the little garden just above the house, and his old sister Nan was leading the horses. Some one went to him and suggested that it was dangerous, and he had better 'leave out.' 'Now, theer,' said Uncle Will, 'I've bin thinkan of Nan and the 'osses this bra while,' which shows a fine contempt either for the serious intentions or for the marksmanship of H.M. seamen and the riders. The firing produced little effect, or was apparently not followed up in any way, for there the story somewhat abruptly ends.

In the days of the King the smuggling was carried on in large cutters and luggers armed with eighteen or twenty guns apiece; but at a later period it was found more convenient to use twenty-seven foot gigs and small open sailing boats. Two of the Covers, rowing home from Roscoff, went into Mullion; here they found two officers. They offered 5*l*. to be allowed to land, but bribery was of no avail, and they had to row off for the Cove. The officers, on horseback, rode round by the cliffs to meet them. When the smugglers got near home they found a Cover in a boat hauling crab-pots. Their pursuers happened just then to be out of sight behind a headland, and the smugglers used the opportunity to change boats with their neighbour, who, with his crab-pots, got into theirs. They rowed to Prussia Cove, where the officers, who arrived shortly after, searched their boat in vain. When the coast was clear, the innocent crabber came ashore, and they helped him to land a catch which is not often taken in crab-pots.

These open-boat expeditions were in the days of Captain Will Richards. There lived with him at Bessie's Cove an old man-of-war's man called Hosking, and Hosking had an apprentice. He was nominally a ship's carpenter, but that apprentice probably learnt much that wasn't ship's-carpenter work and little that was. One evening, while these two were rowing home from France, some one came into the house, and asked Will Richards what time he expected the boat. 'With this south-east wind, they ought to be here about nine to-night,' thought Captain Will. And the newcomer then warned him that the Custom House boat had been off Cuddan all the afternoon, on the look-out for something. At this time the penalty for showing a light or signal of any kind on the coast at night was 100*l*., with the pleasant alternative of twelve months' hard labour, and yet Hosking had to be warned of his danger. Without a word, Cappen Will threw a large armful of 'after-windings' (threshed straw and chaff) on his kitchen fire. The blast which roared up the chimney no doubt nearly burnt his house about his ears, but the blaze was visible many miles at sea, and Hosking saw it in good time. The cargo was safely landed, and temporarily stored in the old shaft just behind Cappen Will's house. Next day the horses from the country were at Trenowl's farm, on the top of the hill, and everything ready to carry the kegs, when four Custom House men arrived at the Cove. That was an unusually idle afternoon at Bessie's Cove. Chatting with the enemy, Cappen Will learnt that they had been sent off in such a hurry that they had neither food nor drink, and it was coming in a cold and stormy night, too. As evening closed, Mrs. Richards made some broth for the poor fellows out there in the cold, and her good man invited them in, but thoughtfully added that it wouldn't do for all four to come in at once, in case one of their officers came along. 'Oh,' said they, 'no officer won't come along to-night.' 'Good,' thought Cappen Will. But all the same he pressed his advice, and two went in. After a good dish of broth and a warm grog, they relieved their companions, who were treated with the same hospitality, and even more.

These two stayed so long, the night turning still wetter and colder, that the two outside grew impatient, and went to the house to fetch their erring comrades; but time was passing more quickly inside than out, and supper hadn't been half finished. This happened a second time, and then Cappen Will brought out a something warm, which was good and welcome to men waiting out there in the rain and the dark. A third time they went to the door, and this time they too found that songs and grog before a good fire were stronger attractions than watching nobody on such a night, and they yielded to the hospitable persuasions of that merry company. Long before those four men left that kitchen the kegs were up from the old shaft, and the horses loaded and gone.

All these tales which we hear along the coast are the smugglers' version of affairs, and we are naturally led to deduct some discount before giving them credit as authentic history; but the official records of the Custom House are not open to the same criticism, and they bear overwhelming testimony to the daring and the success of the smugglers. One report from the Collector at Penzance to his superior in London, out of many, will give some idea of how things appeared to him. Writing on June 29, 1775, he refers to the 'great audacity of the smugglers on this coast,' and goes on: 'Last Saturday two Irish wherries full of men and guns (one about 130 tons, and the other less) came to anchor within the limits of this port, and within half a mile of the shore, and lay there three days, in open defiance discharging their contraband goods. We are totally destitute of any force to attack them by sea, and, as the whole coast is principally inhabited by a lot of smugglers under the denomination of fishermen, it is next to an impossibility for the officers of the revenue to intercept any of these goods after they are landed, unless by chance a trifling matter. The smugglers escort their goods in large parties when on shore. A few nights ago, while the above-mentioned wherries were on the coast, the officers, being on the look-out, saw a boat come off from one of them and come ashore near where the officers had secreted themselves, and the crew began to land the goods. The officers interfered, and attempted to make a seizure of said boat and goods; but a blunderbuss was immediately presented to one of their breasts, and the smugglers, with great imprecations, threatened their lives. The officers, not being in sufficient force, were glad to get off, and the boat reshipped the goods and went off again. We humbly beg leave to remark the smugglers were never on this coast more rife than at present, nor less goods taken in proportion to the quantity supposed to be smuggled.'

The Collector might have used even stronger language than 'audacity,' and probably did, on November 29, 1777, when he saw a large Irish wherry, well manned and armed, come into Penzance harbour and carry out the 'Brilliant,' 'a shallop employed in the service of the revenue,' with the captain on board. The 'Brilliant' had just come in with a captured cargo, and the Penzance people had the pleasure of seeing the smugglers take all the goods out of her and turn her adrift.

The value of the 'trifling matter' of goods seized by the Custom House people in the port of Penzance in 1767 was 2,233*l.*, and in the three years 1776, 1777, 1778, 2,179*l.*

The poor Collector reiterates almost to monotony requests for the assistance of soldiers to suppress the smugglers. These requests appear to have been granted from time to time, but the soldiers were always soon taken away again. At one time, August 1740, he had around the Bay a company of a captain, an ensign, two sergeants, two corporals, fifty-five men, and 'one drum,' in addition to the twenty-three men in the regular employ of the Custom House. But even when the soldiers were here it was not all plain sailing, for 'Captain Lynn, whose company has lately been here, has no orders from the War Office to assist us in cases of shipwrecks or smuggling.' In 1769 he writes, 'the soldiers now quartered in this town are most useful. They are a great terror to the smugglers. The Mayor of Penzance has always paid for fire and candles for the guardroom, but the present Mayor refused to do so. At this I do not wonder, as he is at present bound over in a large sum not to be again guilty of smuggling.'

No wonder the Collector found it so difficult to get a conviction that he could not prosecute after a free fight, in which the smugglers had recaptured their property, because his men could not positively swear what was in the kegs. It might have been water, though we may be very sure it wasn't.

It is pleasant to notice that these records are very free from tales of bloodshed. Whether credit is due to the gentleness of the 'fishermen,' or, as is more probable, to the tact with which the revenue men abstained from impolitic interference, we cannot tell, but in all the seventy years I have been through I only find three cases recorded of violent deaths. In January 1774, a smuggler was shot by a marine. In April 1775, Henry Higgs, boatman at Marazion, was found one morning on the beach dead, with marks of violence. It was only suspicion that laid his death at the smugglers' door. But on March 12, 1769, William Odgers, one of the officers stationed at Porthleven, was killed, while endeavouring to seize some smuggled goods. The Collector says, 'murdered in a most barbarous manner,' and the Coroner's jury agreed with him, and found a verdict of 'wilful murder' against 'Melchisidek Kinsman of Gwennap and others unknown.' Melchisidek and his friends kept well out of sight. On April 7, the Collector is 'afraid that two of the murderers are in Guernsey and the other two in France, at Morlaix.' But on the 25th 'some think they are still skulking underground in the tin works.' Thus they managed to keep safe for nearly a year.

In the next January 'an agent of the murderers offered Alexander Hampton (the principal witness for the Crown) 500*l.* to go out of England for two years, but he refused, saying he would not take the price of blood. Several times since his refusal the smugglers have threatened his life, and have appeared armed, surrounding his house. The murderers are seen publicly in the neighbourhood, and it is thought sleep at night in their usual habitations.'

In January, and again in March, 1770, the Collector made an attempt, with the assistance of a party of soldiers, to catch them, but without success.

Then three of them seem to have decided that it was safer to trust a Cornish jury than their own humble efforts to get off, and they surrendered for trial at the assizes.

The fourth at first held a different opinion, but 'the three who had surrendered in order to protect themselves arrested Melchisidek Kinsman. In this attempt a horrible conflict ensued, and one was greatly wounded;' and all four appeared at Bodmin and were tried before a jury —a Cornish jury, mind—and duly acquitted. Our poor Collector! 'Everyone was amazed and shocked,' he reports, 'at the acquittal of Kinsman.' He knows the jury were bribed; that was clearly shown by the facts that 'three of them disappeared immediately after the case, and one was seen in a public-house drinking with Kinsman's friends.'

No wonder Mr. Edward Giddy wrote on March 4, 1778, recording some particularly flagrant daring, 'I fear a criminal prosecution would be useless at best, for a reason which it shocks me to mention, that a Cornish jury would certainly acquit the smugglers.' And not smugglers only, Mr. Giddy, for there are no smugglers now, but there are still Cornish juries to temper a very little justice with 'an intolerable deal' of mercy.

JOHN B. CORNISH.

In Cawsand Bay lying, with the Blue Peter flying,
    And all hands on deck for the anchor to weigh,
We spied a young lady, as fresh as a daisy,
    And modestly hailing, this damsel did say—

'Ship ahoy! bear a hand there! I wants a young man there,
    So heave us a man-rope, or send him to me:
His name's Henry Grady, and I am a lady
    Arrived to prevent him from going to sea.'

Now the Captain, his Honour, when he looked upon her,
    He ran down the side for to hand her on board.
Cried he with emotion, 'What Son of the Ocean
    Can thus be looked arter by Elinor Ford?'

Then the lady made answer, 'That there is a man, sir,
    I'll make him as free as a Duke or a Lord.'
'Oh no!' says the Cap'en; 'that can't very well happen;
    I've got sailing orders—you, sir, stop on board.'

But up spoke the lady, 'Don't you heed him, Hal Grady;
    He once was your Cap'en, but now you're at large:
You sha'n't stop on board her, for all that chap's order!'—
    And out of her bosom she drew his discharge.

Said the Captain, 'I'm hanged now, you're cool, and I'm banged now!'
    Said Hal, 'Here, old Weatherface, take all my clothes!'
And ashore he then steered her: the lads they all cheered her:
    But the Captain was jealous, and looked down his nose.

Then she got a shore tailor for to rig up her sailor
  In white nankeen trowsers and long blue-tailed coat ;
And he looked like a squi-er, for all to admi-er,
  With a dimity handkercher tied round his throat.

They'd a house that was greater than any first-rater,
  With footmen in livery handing the drink,
And a garden to go in, with flowers all a blowing—
  The daisy and buttercup, lily and pink.

And he got eddication befitting his station,
  — For we all of us know we're not too old to larn ;
And his messmates they found him, his little ones round him,
  All chips of the old block from the stem to the starn.

OLD DITTY

REVENGE IN ARCADY

A PASTORAL

QUIET fields, sunshine, comfortable warmth everywhere; large stacks of corn studded thickly around the farmsteads in the middle distance; recumbent cows close at hand; ewes with their hobbledehoy offspring across the valley. In the valley a large orchard with plots of vegetables in little clearings between the trees.

An unusually plump pony attached to a light cart and tied to the gate of the orchard, looked longingly at the golden fruit over the top bar—she had cleared every blackberry from the long trail of bramble which opportunely spread from the hedge to the gate-post—but Cherry was very fond of fruit, and in that pleasant spot things generally went as they were particularly wanted to. However, Cherry had now been waiting at the wrong side of the gate for so long a time that she had given up all hope of attaining her desire, so she resigned herself to what, after all, was not an uncomfortable situation. She gave a stamp or two, and then settled down to a siesta, lulled by the sound of bees and birds in the air, and voices in the orchard.

Inside the orchard two young women gathered apples, and, when the elder occupants, their master and mistress, were out of earshot, talked in low but emphatic tones of some matter that was evidently of absorbing interest.

'I never would have believed it of 'un,' said the taller and paler of the two, 'not if I hadn't seen it myself. But there, he was so bold as brass, and she walking close alongside, laughing. And worst of all, Billy Matthews was watching of 'um, and after they'd gone up the road, he stood still and laughed to hisself, and then he looked at me and Cowling, and laughed again. I didn't know what to do with myself for spite, Priscilla. I'd almost have given a month's wages to be able to hit 'un as hard as ever I could right in the middle of his silly simpering face.'

'Never mind, Lizzie. Don't care so much about it,' said the rosy Priscilla, although it was abundantly plain that she cared very much herself. 'I should 'a thought Cowling could 'a told 'ee there's as good fish in the sea as ever came out. For my part if Dick is such a fool as to lose his head, and pick up with any bold hussy that holds up a finger to 'un, he's not the fellow I took 'un for, and I am well quit of 'un. For quit I'll certainly be—not that Theresa shall have 'un, neither.'

'I should be glad to see any way of helping it,' sighed the mournful Lizzie, who seemed unable to be happy even in the thought of her own unimpeachable lover, while Priscilla was suffering from the slighting of handsome but foolish Dick.

'I've been thinking of something ever since Billy Matthews come sneaking and sniggering up to tell me when I was feeding the calves Monday morning,' said Priscilla. 'If I ain't so pretty as some I won't mention, on the outside of my head, perhaps I've got just as good inside. I'll tell 'ee after Polwhele and George are gone to bed,' she added hastily, as her master and mistress approached, and began to comment on and criticise her work.

'You pick all you can of these Redstreaks,' said Mr. Dean, 'and for the ones you can't get at we must have George down—unless you'd rather have Billy Matthews to help, Priscilla?'

This was intended for a little joke, but even good-natured Mr. Dean felt it had fallen rather flat when Priscilla indignantly cried:

'You know I would not, sir.'

'I think you had better have down the steps yourself, and pick the gilliflowers and stubbards that grow too high for the maidens,' interposed Mrs. Dean, in a voice that all parties felt to be a reproof. 'Neither George nor Billy Matthews is fit to be trusted with my best fruit. Still, it's full early for picking them—they would only shrivel, so keep to the Redstreaks this afternoon; you've nearly enough for the baskets already, if Cherry is not to shake them out again,' and she passed on to inspect a promising bed of beet which would also want harvesting before long, while Priscilla and her companion picked on in comforting assurance that they would have no lovelorn widower suitor or troublesome boy to plague them during their labours. What Mrs. Dean thought the best thing to do, somehow also seemed right and desirable to Mr. Dean, and Lizzie never thought of questioning the matter, though Priscilla might sometimes question, but even she never put her doubts into words—still less would she have acted on them.

So the peaceful afternoon wore away, each half-hour bringing some fresh beauty to earth and sky. And the four in the orchard took no notice of the glories around them, until the position of the sun reminded Mrs. Dean that it would soon be time for Lizzie to go to her milking, and Priscilla's calves would be bleating for her.

Then the laden baskets were collected, and carried out to the cart, where Cherry was dozing with her nose against the gate.

Mrs. Dean picked a few sprays of thyme and marjoram from the fragrant beds as she passed, thinking of the stuffing for to-morrow's roast fowl rather than of the gorgeous peacock butterflies and 'painted ladies' so thickly fluttering in that favoured corner.

'Now be careful you don't shake those baskets about, William. Redstreaks will stand a good deal, but not everything, and they must be kept steady going up the hill—you had better get in, Lizzie, and hold them in their places, and Priscilla can drive, and you can give me your arm, Mr. Dean—if you are walking with me you won't have to climb down from the cart to open the gate of the Homepark. Drive slowly, Priscilla'—apparently quite an uncalled-for command, for Cherry had never moved quickly under any provocation, and was not likely to now, with a gently rising ground before her.

But though Cherry's pace was slow, Mrs. Dean's was even slower, and the two girls, still absorbed in their talk about the fickle Dick, reached the gate first, and had to wait while Mr. Dean helped his portly partner up the meadow. Unhappily Cherry was now thoroughly aroused from her slumber, and thinking of supper, or, at least, some little handy snack that might be snatched in yard or stable, even before her regular mealtime. As she thought of it her eye lighted on a juicy branch of blackberries, rather high in the hedge to be sure, but with a step or so she could reach the tempting morsel. With Cherry, under the circumstances, to think was to act, so having already realised Priscilla's preoccupation, she just took the step or so, and picked her blackberry, but at the same time tilted up the cart so suddenly, that maidens and apple baskets were all thrown out together, and came rolling down the slope towards their astonished master and mistress.

Cherry was as surprised as anybody, but she had sense enough to stand still after the mischief was done.

'My poor maidens! I hope you are not hurt,' was Mr. Dean's first cry.

Mrs. Dean said nothing about them, but after a hasty glance in their direction, set to work to bewail the damage done to her apples.

'Such fine Redstreaks! and very fair keepers—and now Priscilla will have to take them all in when she goes with the butter, and just make what she can of them as windfalls! Wherever could your thoughts have been woolgathering, Priscilla, not to have known what she would do if you gave her the chance? Come at once, and pick them up again, unless you want the poor calves to suffer as well for your stupid negligence:' and poor Priscilla with a guilty conscience, which for once admitted that the rebuke was deserved, scrambled to her feet, and restored the apples as hastily as possible to their baskets.

Lizzie was slower in thought and action, and sat woefully rubbing herself, until she realised that the stout Mrs. Dean was laboriously stooping and trying to help to repair the damage. Then she began to help too, still uncertain whether to laugh or cry, and between them all the cart was soon refilled, and driven to the house.

'It is no good to take them to the storeroom, Priscilla; just carry them into the cellar and leave them there till you can take them in to market, that is if Mr. Dean thinks you can be trusted to that extent again after letting Cherry tip you out like that. If it had happened to be on the turnpike road instead of a nice soft meadow I dare say you would remember the matter a bit longer than you will now.'

Priscilla carried in the baskets and then hurried off to her special charges, who were complaining loudly by this time, and Mr. Dean took Cherry to the stableyard.

Mrs. Dean was vexed, and having nobody at hand to blame but Lizzie, who was hurrying from parlour to pantry, preparing tea, she continued her oration for her benefit.

'Whatever is ailing that girl?—she has done ever so many stupid things only this week. Some nonsense about sweethearts, or perhaps only finery. You are all alike—never happy until you have managed to catch some fool's attention, and then you give him no peace until he has crowned his folly by giving you the right to throw away every penny he gets as fast as it comes in.'

Lizzie would have had plenty more of the same quality if she had not told her mistress of Priscilla's trouble about Dick and Theresa Bunt.

Mrs. Dean dearly loved a confidence, and she was fond enough of her really good maids to resent a slight to either. So her wrath soon evaporated, and she heartily wished, for quite unselfish reasons, that she could help and comfort the girl in her trouble.

'I never had a very high opinion of Dick, but Priscilla seemed set on him, and I thought she was strong enough to keep him in order. But if he flouts her before marriage he would do worse after, and she may be glad it has gone no further. I should think one of my maids, with my favour, and a nice little bit of money in the savings bank, need not wait long to do better than that;' and Mrs. Dean, feeling that she had had quite an emotional afternoon, put an extra spoonful of tea in the pot—an action not unnoticed or unappreciated by Lizzie. She, with Priscilla, enjoyed the reversion of the teapot, and she felt that a slight extra stimulant would be grateful all round.

So with a consciousness that she had almost justified her friend and altogether gratified her mistress by the little confidence, she tied on her cotton bonnet again. It was with the mild elation which was the nearest approach she ever made to high spirits that she went off to seek her shining milkbucket on the bench outside the back door, where it always stood in the sunshine and air when off duty.

While she milked her cows she wondered what plan Priscilla could have thought of for punishing her insulters—she could never initiate an idea herself —if she were only clever like Priscilla she would, at this moment, be contriving some excellent reason for getting that tiresome old Polwhele, and still more tiresome boy, off to bed an hour before their usual time. What was the good of their staying after they had 'suppered up' the cattle? Just sitting about in the most comfortable places—right in the way of those who had work to do, and saying things nobody wanted to be hindered to listen to, and on the lookout to hear things they were not meant to. Mere encumbrances in the kitchen, where she and Priscilla would get through their dish-washing, and settle to their sewing, and enjoy their talk over their trouble ever so much better if those two were out of the way.

However, the wish to be rid of them fathered no thought of any means for accomplishing so desirable an end; and when the frothing pail was full, she roused herself from her useless reverie and sighed deeply, as was her wont when in perplexity. Poor Lizzie's thoughts seemed always to travel in very small circles, and no effort of her own would make them take any other direction, so she had to wait as patiently as she could for Priscilla's disclosures.

That astute maiden gave her no sign. In spite of the forcible reminder of the afternoon, of the folly of trying to do one thing while absorbed in contemplation of another, she was as absent-minded as ever, while her heightened colour, and an occasional toss of her head, showed the anxious watcher that there was a good deal of mental activity going on.

It seemed a very long evening. Never had a pipe of tobacco so much smoke in it as that nasty little black one which spent just as much time in Polwhele's mouth as in his pocket, and George's monkey tricks were almost unbearable. He brought in more mud on his feet than he should have done in a fortnight, and he placed tin things on edges of tables and benches, so that they might fall with a clatter and make the maids jump, with the delightful added possibility that they might get a rebuke from Mrs. Dean for not making 'that boy behave himself.' At last he took the tidying of the kitchen workbox in hand, at a hint from Priscilla. She knew perfectly that nothing would be found in its place the next time it was wanted, but the tangling of her worsteds and soiling of her buttons seemed preferable to his restless fidgetings. The master and mistress came from the parlour to receive reports or give advice and directions—often quite unnecessary in that well-ordered household. The daily life had gone on in just the same groove for years—boys grew too big, and were sent off on the doubtful errand 'to better themselves,' and Polwhele got stiffer and more selfish, the maids thought, and that was all with which to relieve the monotonous prosperity of their lives—except the difficulty of reconciling sense and sentiment in the choice of a lover for Priscilla. Lately she had been allowing sentiment rather too much liberty, with the result which her sense had told her was sure to follow. The handsome simpleton she had favoured had quickly tired of her good ways and propriety, and taken his attentions to another damsel of his class whose tastes were more in accord with his own.

At last the evening came to an end. 'The boys,' as Polwhele and George were always called collectively, were gone to bed, doors and windows fastened and inspected, and the supper-tray carried into the parlour. Lizzie sat staring at her friend in honest admiration and expectation.

'Well, Priscilla, what is it? I'm sure you've thought of something.'

'I generally do when I put my mind to it for a whole afternoon,' she said, with an air of superiority; she never could understand Lizzie's wavering cogitations—brooding on a matter for hours and getting no further.

'I don't want to hurry you, Priscilla, but I'm aching to know,' responded the meeker maid.

'Well, you'd never guess, so I may as well tell you. Not that I want you nor anybody else to guess too much, for that matter. You know Theresa has been to ever so many places, and never stayed anywhere long. Wherever she went things had a habit of getting lost. Then Mrs. Young's chain was not only lost but found again where it had no right to be, and it was all proved plain, though she would not have the police, being sorry for the girl on account of her upbringing—the father's family was always held light-fingered. Still Theresa was off to a minute's notice. And though she got a place in a new neighbourhood and no questions asked, she couldn't keep it, and now she's been home this pretty while, wearing out her clothes and no money coming in to buy more. And there's enough at home without her, and perhaps they don't make her too welcome. So she just looks around for somebody to take and maintain her. And if Dick would do it, there'd be an end of the money worry—at least till she taught him to help himself, and he'd be sure to get into trouble. And besides she'd have the pleasure of flouting me that have always kept respectable, and looked down on the likes of her! Oh! I do get out of all patience. However, I'll make her the talk of the parish, and if Dick likes to take her after that showing up, he can—I misdoubt if he comes to good anyway, and he'll be well jeered at, too.'

'But you can't go round and tell everybody that,' sighed Lizzie; 'they'd think more about your spite than Theresa's wickedness.'

'That's just it. Nobody is to know that I've got anything to do in the matter. You can't make poetry, can you?'

'No, indeed,' Lizzie cried, startled and shocked at the idea that Priscilla was going to make some demand on her friendship with which she would be unable to comply. 'You know I can't even read or write easy, much more make up anything. It isn't a bit of good—I couldn't do it whatever——' and Lizzie began to laugh hysterically when Priscilla pulled her up testily.

'Don't be so silly. Who wants you to? All I meant was, I can, and I've made several verses, and will make a few more, and write them out in printing hand, and stick them up in two or three places where they will be sure to be read. About seven or eight verses will do, just what folks can remember with reading two or three times, and I'll end up every verse alike—that makes it stick. Oh! I'll do it beautiful.'

'It would be beautiful, but you could never do it. Seven or eight verses! And if you could, how could you get 'um stuck up? Billy Matthews might do it to please you, or Cowling to please me, but I shouldn't like to tell a man about it, and let 'un know how vexed we was.'

'Billy Matthews, indeed! Nor Cowling, neither! I should think not. I'd rather risk missus finding it out, and get out of bed and do it myself in the middle of the night! I've a great mind to tell missus—I've made her laugh before now with things like that about other people. I wonder if she could be brought round to let us go—you and me together, after dark? I'll think it over, and make some more verses to-night—some way I will find;' and then they had to go to bed, for where there is much to do, early to bed and early to rise is the rule.

There could be very little talking in their own room, for the mistress slept in the next, and she expected her maids to be quiet and let other folks sleep, even if they couldn't themselves—indeed toothache was the only reason she allowed for keeping awake when the time came for sleep. 'If you do your duty in the day you'll be glad enough of the chance to sleep in the night,' she would say, so Lizzie had to smother her sighs and curiosity at the same time.

The circumstances did not seem very favourable for anything striking in the way of poetical composition, but Priscilla's Pegasus was a homely animal, and all she wanted it to do now was to carry her over a rough place, and at the same time fling all the mud possible at those who had insulted her. She lay quietly in the dark, and before she went to sleep she had arranged her set of verses, and even decided on what she should say to Mrs. Dean to get her to consent to her plan for posting them over the parish. She repeated them to the admiring Lizzie in the dim light next morning, while they dressed, and Lizzie was so overwhelmed by the cleverness and audacity of her friend that she promised to go with her to pin up the papers, although she felt afraid in the dark, and more afraid still that it would not be dark enough to hide them from prying eyes.

Priscilla had more trouble than she expected in bringing Mrs. Dean to consent to the expedition. Indeed she would not have consented at all, if she had not at last realised that to let her have her way would be the speediest way of ending the whole matter. For days the girl had moped, and done her work miserably, so when she was so anxious to work off her ill feeling in this manner, her mistress at last gave a reluctant consent, only stipulating that if they were found out, nobody was ever to know that she knew anything about it.

As soon as permission had been wrung from Mrs. Dean, Priscilla became a different creature; she got through her work quickly and well, and even made time to help the dazed Lizzie with some of hers, before she ran up to her room, and printed her posters, in the usually short time that could be made between tidying up after dinner and preparing supper for the calves, pigs and poultry—her special charges. Nothing was neglected to-day, and Mrs. Dean rejoiced to think that her clever maid was more deeply wounded in vanity than affection.

If the previous evening had seemed long, this one was still worse, and the restlessness of the girls soon told George that something unusual was agitating them, which made him determine to watch, and find out what it was —experience had taught him the futility of asking questions. Happily for the success of the girls' plan, a day's work in the open air had made him so drowsy that in spite of his determination to be watchful he was sound asleep before ten o'clock. In that primitive place ten was considered so very late that all right-thinking people were sure to be asleep, and therefore that was a propitious time for the girls to start on their errand, Mrs. Dean herself letting them out by the front door, and telling them to put the key under the scraper, so that they could let themselves in by the quietest entrance, and avoid the chance of disturbing Polwhele, whose rheumatism made him a light sleeper.

Of course it was not dark, and the girls instead of wearing their ordinary clothes had thought it better to disguise themselves with dark shawls over their heads—a precaution which would have called attention to them instantly if anyone had seen them, but their path led through fields seldom traversed even in the daytime, and the stiles were sufficiently complicated to be dangerous to any belated customer of the Church Town public-house. They had the world to themselves as far as the church.

Poor Lizzie felt almost faint with the excitement and the speed with which Priscilla had whirled her along, so when the churchyard was reached she was left in a dark corner outside while Priscilla ran through and rapidly fixed her paper on the gate fronting the road.

Then they retraced their steps for a short distance, and skirted a rough piece of ground, the scene of the village wrestlings at feast-time, and then they were obliged to go for a short distance on the highway between the Church Town and another village. They listened, but could hear nothing, so ventured boldly out, and there strolling towards them was Billy Matthews.

There was no time for consultation; they must run or be caught.

It was well Lizzie had had her little rest; she ran now and never stopped until they were a good half mile away, and the startled Billy had almost decided that they were a pair of good-for-nothings who had been making a raid on somebody's hen-roost. 'Yet they were uncommonly like our maidens,' he said to himself, 'the very image of Priscilla and Lizzie, only what could they be out for? I'll be bound Lizzie wanted to see Cowling, and Priscilla hadn't the heart to let her go by herself. Whatever would missus say! But I won't tell—I know better than that. What a good hold I've got now on Priscilla!'

Almost before he had got so far in his meditations the girls had reached the Bryanite chapel, and stuck the second set of verses on its gate. Another minute saw them over a stile and safely hidden in a field where arish mows were still waiting to be carried. This was on the farm of the laggard of the parish, who was justly held in much scorn by his fellow farmers. But the girls were so glad of the shelter that they could have blessed him for his laziness.

'That's getting on well,' whispered Priscilla, leaning against one of the mows to rest herself after such a run. 'All the women are bound to see them either on the church or chapel. Now we will go and put up the other on Mr. James's barndoor—that's where all the men go to see about sales and such like —then we shall have done.'

'But what shall we do about Billy?' moaned Lizzie. 'I'm sure he saw us, and when he hears about the verses he'll know in a minute. I wish we hadn't come.'

Priscilla was not dismayed, 'We'll just run along as fast as we can, and put up this, and then get home to bed. I dare say missus is listening for us, and not over comfortable. And you leave me to manage Billy—most likely he won't say a word to you—he's not going to put me out of temper if he can help it, and I'll show 'un that 'tis for his own good to hold his tongue. I shall have to be civil to 'un for a little while—the old plague—but I ain't a bit afraid of 'un.'

Priscilla's spirits were rising, and with them her confidence in her ability to guide events to her own liking, and the sequel proved that her confidence was not misplaced.

All happened as she expected; her mistress was watching for their return, and did not attach any importance to the meeting with Billy.

The verses were in everybody's mouth before the next night.

Billy's daughter told him the gossip when he came in to dinner, and added that Priscilla must be fine and vexed about Dick or she would not be so cross with Theresa. This threw a new light on last night's proceedings, but Billy would not gratify his daughter by admitting that Priscilla had anything to do with the matter. 'She's clever enough,' he said, 'but she've no call to concern herself about Dick—she cud take her pick of the sensible men of the parish.'

But he made a slight ailment of one of his horses an excuse for going back to the farm in the evening.

A short visit to Nelson prefaced what he meant to be a much longer one to Priscilla in the calves' house. She saw him arrive with much inward disgust, but until the calves had drunk all the milk in her buckets she was obliged to stay and listen.

He poured out the woes of a 'widowman,' as he called himself, with three children, and only a giddy girl to look after them, and refused to see the point of Priscilla's suggestion that he should either make the girl less giddy, or marry some staid woman who could do better. When he said she was exactly staid enough herself, she did not like the compliment, and had some ado to put her reply into language of sufficient mildness. Then Billy produced his trump card and told how he had seen her and Lizzie the night before, and could show her up to her mistress and Dick and everybody.

'And what time was it you saw me running the roads, as you say?' inquired Priscilla, with rising temper in every tone.

'About half-past ten, I should think—leastways they told me so just as I came out, down to Church Town.'

In his eagerness to make a damning point against Priscilla, Billy forgot the frightful admission he was making against himself.

'So you, who on your own showing were at the public house till such an hour as that, expect anybody to take any notice of what you say you saw on your way home! Respectable girls are to have all sorts of tales told up about them by the likes of you! Mrs. Dean would be very pleased to hear what an old fool of a carter had to say about her maids, and master would be glad to find that one of his men was so fond of drink that he wanted more after he had had as much as was good for 'un here already. Yes, Billy, your place would not be worth much for pleasure or profit if I chose to tell a little of what I know,' and she caught up her buckets and whisked off to the house, leaving the crestfallen Billy staring vacantly after her—convinced that he was in the right, yet made to appear in the wrong.

Of another thing he was also convinced—that he would lose all favour, not only with Priscilla, but, more serious still, with his master and mistress also, if he mentioned his knowledge of the maidens' escapade, so he set to work at once to persuade himself that he must have been mistaken overnight, or if he could not quite manage that, he could at least keep his impression to himself.

. . . .

Some years after Mrs. Cowling was visiting her friend Mrs. Wood in a flourishing porkbutcher's shop, in one of the suburbs of Plymouth.

'What times we'd got,' she sighed. 'I'd no notion how pleasant it all was at the time. Even the trouble you'd got with your sweethearts, Priscilla. There was Dick, and Billy, and then the shipwright whose mother was so keen to have you marry her son—all they before you took up with Mr. Wood. Oh, it was funny! and do you remember those verses:

> *Theresa went to Truro once,*
> *But soon came back again;*
> *Could it have been her mistress heard*
> *Theresa stole a chain?*
>
> *So now Theresa stops at home,*
> *And wants a place in vain;*
> *It is not thought she'll have the chance*
> *To steal another chain!*

I believe I could say off everyone of them now, and I never think of them without wanting to laugh. And Billy had to marry Theresa after all, and a pretty staid wife she made 'un—and sarve un' right, too. How kind missus was, in spite of being so strict! There's very few like her now—we often tell of it. As soon as ever my Marina is big enough, straight she goes to service, and to the most particular missus I can hear of. I keep my eye on all the missuses round already, and there's but few to trust a girl to. Cowling's doing well, and we're saving steady, but for training and real good times a girl is best off with an understanding missus.'

Mrs. Wood, looking round on her prosperous business, admitted the value of the training, but could not help thinking that the girl had something to do with the result, as well as the mistress.

FANNY SPETTIGUE.

NEWQUAY

'THERE is a charm in the Cornish coast which belongs to no other coast in the world.' So wrote Dean Alford, of Canterbury, many years ago; and the declaration thus made has since been practically endorsed by numbers of persons who return year after year to revel in the grandeur of its scenery and to recuperate their jaded energies in its health-giving air. When Dean Alford spent his famous 'week' on this coast, the district was *terra incognita* to the multitude. Though Cornwall contained, in the picturesque Bodmin and Wadebridge Railway, the third line opened for passenger traffic in the kingdom, it was not for a quarter of a century after this opening that the county was connected by railway with Plymouth and the world beyond. And even then the north coast was left far beyond the ken of railway systems. Where the Cornwall Railway did touch coast at all, it was on that southern shore which is washed by the waters of the English Channel.

But the 'splendid isolation' of the north coast, which provided Dr. Pusey with an ideal retreat during his inhibition and at other times, and which Dean Alford and other wanderers appreciated so thoroughly, has become a thing of the past. It has been pierced by branches of the Great Western Railway to Newquay and St. Ives, and a further extension of the same system is about to open up Perranporth by means of a link connecting Newquay with Truro; while, farther east, the South-Western Railway runs through King Arthur's country, though it does not actually touch 'wild Dundagil by the Cornish Sea.' Cornwall has been discovered; and dwellers in the great centres of population hie thither in annually increasing numbers to seek for rest and relaxation. They find both in the pure and bracing air which, as Dean Alford remarked, 'nobody has breathed since it left the Yankees.'

Owing largely to its accessibility, Newquay has become the centre of attraction on the north coast. Four trains—one of them stopping only once between Paddington and Plymouth—arrive daily from London, bringing passengers from the Midlands also through the junction at Bristol; while in addition to this excellent service on the Great Western line, the coach from Wadebridge brings the South-Western contingent from Waterloo and elsewhere. Abundant facilities are thus available for getting to Newquay, and every succeeding year sees them taken advantage of to a greater extent than before. Then there is a choice of no fewer than five trains by which passengers can travel daily from Newquay to London by the Great Western line, in addition to the morning coach which meets the South-Western train at Wadebridge *en route* from Bodmin to Waterloo. Not many health resorts situated 300 miles away from London can be better served by the railways than Newquay is; and the companies find their reward in the increased and increasing volume of traffic. The incursion of multitudes of tourists

[*Photo by*] NEWQUAY BEACH [*Waren, Newquay*]

and health-seekers promises to compensate Cornwall, in some measure, for the decay of its mining and other industries. But the Cornish people should study and provide for the requirements of their visitors, and should cater particularly for invalids, if the potentialities—as Dr. Johnson would say—of their new 'industry' are to be fully realised.

Of all the north coast of Cornwall there is, perhaps, no part that possesses greater 'charm' than the section that can be seen from Newquay Beacon, extending from Trevose Head on the east to Pentire on the west. Yet this charm is essentially characterised by impressive grandeur. Thus sang Mr. Sewell Stokes, viewing the scene from a neighbouring eminence:—

> Tregurrion's hamlet from yon cliff stands white,
> And indistinct the fisher-cots are seen
> Cluster'd like sea-fowl on that breezy height;
> Beneath, as with a long wide belt of sheen,
> Saint Mawgan's Porth girds round the water's green.
> . . . .
> Eastward, Bedruthan's wild and caverned shore
> Reverberates the sea's primeval song;
> Saint Eval's echoes swell it evermore;
> To high Endellion soon it sweeps along;
> Or west revolving, yet more deep and strong,
> By Newquay's rock-piled wall its murmurs flow,
> Round bold Pentire, where Cubert's pilgrims throng.

There can doubtless be found elsewhere more towering cliffs than can be seen from Newquay Beacon, though those which fringe Watergate Bay rise to a height of several hundred feet. Yet between Trevose and Pentire the lofty cliffs, bold promontories, splendid beaches, tidal inlets, and a singularly blue sea form a combination of attractive features which can hardly be equalled in any other section of that coastline. The *hinterland* of Newquay—to use the jargon of diplomacy—is likewise of varied beauty, and is invested with an

Photo by] [Waren, Newquay

CLIFFS AT NEWQUAY

interest that is saturated with tradition and appeals alike to the antiquary and the lover of Nature.

Newquay cannot be truthfully described as a pretty town. It is, in fact, a very striking contrast to its romantic surroundings. Such a magnificent site might have been expected to inspire a design in keeping, to some extent, with what Nature had made so beautiful. But there is little or no evidence of such inspiration. What remains (though that is very little now) of the old village is picturesque in comparison with the modern rows of houses which constitute the main thoroughfare. And this street seems to have been formed without any particular plan, and without taking the future into account. The local authorities do not appear to have considered even the possibility of future growth to any appreciable extent, otherwise they would surely have guarded against such a contraction of the thoroughfare as is seen in the very centre of the town where comparatively new houses leave room for only two rows of vehicular traffic. A narrow street with dangerous curves is not in accord with the pretensions of Newquay to be the first of Cornish watering-places. It is, too, a great drawback to the town as a pleasure and health resort that it possesses no 'front.' The greater part of the ground along the edge of the cliff, from one end of the town to the other, has been built upon. A laudable attempt—or rather proposal—was made at the time of the Diamond Jubilee celebration to utilise the piece of frontage not yet occupied and provide for at least a small piece of 'front' while there was a possibility of doing so. Some day Newquay will regret this lost opportunity. With a broad promenade between houses and the cliff the attractions of the town would have been far greater, especially to invalids, than they are now. Perhaps when the importance of this matter is fully realised, care will be taken to safeguard the future in regard to ground outside the town which the builder has not yet invaded. The preservation of a 'front' does not block the sea view of the houses that may be built farther back; it simply increases the attractions of the place, and enables the public to enjoy the prospect while inhaling the ozone.

Within living memory Newquay was little more than a cluster of thatched cottages nestling near what is now the centre of the town. A few of those still remain, constituting links with the past, and leavening, so to speak, the mass of more modern houses. But Newquay, in the main, is new as a town; and it is also relatively new as a popular watering-place. The railway, of course, has made the place what it is to-day. People have been enabled to get there with facility; and its popularity has grown concurrently. Its merits as a 'recuperative station' are recognised and proclaimed by those who have tested their efficacy. So the crowd of visitors becomes larger in each successive season. Increasing numbers must necessarily involve more accommodation, and the house-covered area is perpetually widening. We seem to be centuries away from the time when Newquay was nothing but a small fishing village, situated so far out of the world that the post reached there but once a week. Yet several persons are still living in the place who remember it under those conditions—testimony alike to the growth of Newquay and to its life-giving air.

One of the chief glories of Newquay is its grand headland. Running right out into the Atlantic it forms a bold, natural pier, in comparison with which the costly artificial piers which are to be found at most watering-places of repute are mere toys. Nothing can be more exhilarating than a walk to the extreme end of this jagged promontory. It is like breathing a vitalising essence. At present this headland is the appanage of those only who are physically strong. It has never been made available for the use of feeble invalids. Yet it seems to have been specially designed and provided by Nature for their enjoyment and benefit. When, in the course of time, a smooth and broad path shall have been made out to the Point, Newquay will surely be largely patronised by sufferers from nerve affections and other complaints which yield to the curative influence of pure and bracing air. The imagination, as well as the nerve centres, is stimulated and strengthened by the grandeur of the scene and its surroundings. What a promenade it might be for those folk who are obliged to use bath chairs! From the western end of the town such a promenade could be made along by the sea to the farthest extremity of Towan Head, and at comparatively little cost. When the City Fathers of Newquay realise the importance of making this improvement, the place will soon be 'advertised;' for it would be an ideal resort for people in need of the very best of nerve tonics. On the Beacon, which may be described as the root of the headland, stands the Atlantic Hotel, with its unique view of sea and land, of cliff and beach. Near by is the 'look-out' station of the coastguard, and also in close proximity is

Photo by]   *[Warren, Newquay*

THE HEADLAND

the picturesque huer's house from which a sharp watch was formerly kept, at the proper seasons, for the advent of the pilchards. But, alas! the huer's trumpet has not been much heard of late years. A neighbouring resident used to say that 'Newquay lives on fat fish and flat fish, the fat fish being pilchards and the flat fish lodgers.' By far the greatest profit is now derived from the 'flat fish.'

The view from Newquay headland comprehends scenery of the most varied description. There is the grand expanse of ocean, studded with craft of all kinds. Then, at one sweep of vision, can be seen those great stretches of yellow sand which have made Newquay famous for its beaches. The cliffs in all their ragged and rugged splendour, with their extensive and weird caverns, present an ever-varying aspect which never satiates and never tires the observer. Beyond is an undulating section of the *hinterland*, with St. Eval Tower and Carnanton Woods on the sky-line in one direction, and a number of castle-like buildings, grand and gloomy, in another. But inquiry reveals the fact that these buildings are not, and never were, fortresses of any kind; they are simply dismantled engine-houses of mines that are no longer worked. Such buildings are, unhappily, very numerous in Cornwall now, performing the function of tombstones which perpetuate the memory of defunct enterprises. From the Beacon can be seen the entire town of Newquay, perched on the cliffs and ascending in a more or less fragmentary way to the crest of the hill,

NEWQUAY

which is locally designated Mount Wise. Nestling at the foot of the Beacon, on the town side, is the harbour, whence considerable quantities of china clay and other products of the district are shipped, and through which coal and other commodities are imported to satisfy the needs of the population for some miles around. Consequent on the construction of a new quay two or three generations back, it is popularly supposed that the name of the place became changed from Towan Blystra to Newquay; but a similar belief was current three hundred years ago. In Carew's 'Survey of Cornwall' reference is made to 'newe Kaye, a place in the North coast of this Hundred (Pider), so called, because in former times, the neighbours attempted, to supplie the defect of nature, by Art, in making there a Kay, for the Rode of shipping.' So that even Carew referred to 'former times' for the traditional origin of the name. Whatever that origin may be, it is clear that the place itself is of considerable antiquity.

A very fine and very valuable feature of Newquay is found in its magnificent beaches of yellow and firm sand. West of the headland is the Fistral beach, which at low water shows to great advantage. This beach is bounded on the east and the west, respectively, by Towan Head and East Pentire. Between East Pentire and West Pentire spreads out the estuary of the River Gannel; and here also at low water there is an extensive beach. But the Gannel beach is regarded as pertaining to the villages of Crantock and West Pentire rather than to Newquay. The Fistral beach, however, is distinctly a Newquay possession, the golf links sloping down to its edge. But it is some little distance away from the town, and is consequently not so much frequented as the beach at the foot of the cliffs on which the town is built. This beach extends from the harbour to Porth; and here the people chiefly bathe and disport themselves, generally during the earlier half of the day if the tide is suitable. The cliffs bounding this beach on the south are of very irregular formation, numerous small bays and other indentations giving them anything but a uniform or uninteresting appearance. Further variety is given to the beach by clusters of huge rocks that dot its surface. These rocks have taken fantastic shapes, and afford perennial interest to certain classes of visitors.

BEACH BY PORTH [Waren, Newquay]

The whole of

Porth Inlet, which intersects Sir Richard Tangye's demesne at Glendorgal, is a bed of sand at low water, but at high tide is completely washed by the waves, as all the other beaches are. Beyond Glendorgal and east of Trevelga Head appear the immense proportions of the beach in Watergate Bay. The interest of this beach is increased by the grandeur of the cliffs, the rock-islands which break the stretch of sand, and, above all, the remarkable caverns. This part of the coast is, indeed, peculiarly romantic and attractive. Sir Richard Tangye's commodious house, built in bungalow style and containing his famous Cromwell Collection, is an ideal summer residence, the extensive grounds being preserved in their wild beauty. A subterranean passage near the 'point' of the private portion of these grounds connects Porth Inlet with the great beach between Glendorgal and Newquay. On the other side of the inlet is 'Porth Island,' terminating in Trevelga Head. This promontory is not nearly so extensive as Towan Head, on the near side of Newquay Bay, but it is a delightful and very favourite place of resort, and is about a mile distant from the town of Newquay. In certain conditions of wind and tide some curious and interesting natural phenomena may be seen near the point of this headland. There are two apertures—one much larger than the other—in the rock, known as 'blowing holes.' The air in these apertures is compressed by the inrush of water, with the result that great clouds of spray issue from the 'holes,' which are thus said to 'blow.' A deep chasm, through which the tide flows when nearing high water, cuts off the promontory from the mainland ; hence the designation of 'Porth Island.' The island, as already intimated, is a part of Glendorgal, but it is open to the public. A wooden bridge spans the chasm, and Sir Richard Tangye, with characteristic consideration for others, has had steps and pathways cut in the rocks to facilitate access. He has also provided shelters for the convenience of persons who may be overtaken by rain, or who may engage in picnic festivities. Similar thoughtfulness has prompted him to substitute, at his own expense, nearly a dozen wicket-gates for the horrid and dangerous stiles that formerly encumbered the footpath between Newquay and the parish church of St. Columb Minor.

Close to the chasm separating Porth Island from the mainland are sundry remains of ancient defensive works, which are supposed to have been constructed by the Vikings. On the adjacent cliffs, at almost their highest point, are some ancient tumuli that are believed to have been constructed for the sepulture of chiefs among Norse warriors. In one of these tumuli, indeed, a skeleton and a stone axe were found when Mr. Borlase opened it a quarter of a century ago. Some years previously an ancient 'kist' was discovered on the high ground close to Glendorgal House ; and in this an urn was found, containing—as was supposed—human ashes. This urn is now one of the objects of interest in the museum of the Royal Institution of Cornwall at Truro, while Sir Richard Tangye has reverently placed a strong iron grating over the kist to prevent its desecration. Still nearer to Newquay there are other tumuli which excite the interest of antiquaries, and in these also urns have been found. The fields in which these tumuli are situated are close to the eastern end of the town. They are still called the 'Barrow' fields, and are the property

of the Duke of Cornwall. It is hoped that these fields will be acquired some
day for the purposes of a public recreation and pleasure ground ; and then,
perhaps, greater care will be taken of these relics of a bygone age.

The caverns which constitute such an attractive feature of the cliff scenery
in and about Newquay are of various shapes and sizes. Some are of comparatively small dimensions, and serve as convenient dressing-rooms for bathers.
Others are of really grand proportions. The Tea caverns, which open from the
north side of Newquay Beacon, are of curious formation, and extend to a point
beneath the Atlantic Hotel. Improvement in the approach has of late induced
increasing numbers of visitors to inspect these splendid caverns, which in

Photo by] [*Frith & Co.*
CATHEDRAL CAVERN, PORTH

former days provided convenient storage for large quantities of smuggled goods ;
and for such a purpose they were obviously well adapted in the olden time.
But the caverns which attract the largest number of people are situated beyond
Glendorgal. A land-slip has somewhat lessened the noble proportions of the
Cathedral cavern, but it still excites much interest and commands admiration.
The Banqueting-Hall cavern is so large and accessible that successful concerts
are regularly held in it during the Newquay 'season,' the proceeds of these
entertainments being usually devoted to local charities or other objects deserving of public support. The acoustic properties of this cavern are excellent, but
were never demonstrated more magnificently than when Clara Novello sang

there to an entranced audience. (It may be remarked parenthetically that this famous songstress still lives in the repose of a calm and beautiful old age. Long may it be before we shall have to apply to her the apt epitaph which Douglas Jerrold suggested for Charles Knight, and say 'good night' to the gifted lady who made multitudes of a past generation fancy that they had heard an angel sing.) Among other caverns that are worth inspection, the Fern cavern and the Boulder cavern, the respective designations of which will be readily understood, may be mentioned; but there is such an infinity of interest created by an exploration of Watergate Bay that much must necessarily remain undescribed or even indicated here in any detail.

In connection with the cliff and beach scenery of Newquay, reference may be appropriately made to Bedruthan Steps. Bedruthan, as has been already intimated, is within sight of Newquay Beacon, and is fairly included among the attractions of Newquay itself. A visit to this romantic spot is paid, as a matter of course, by people lodging in the town; and the recompense is great. That 'wild and cavern'd shore' must be seen at low water if all its sublime beauty and grandeur is to be revealed. One striking object on the beach is the 'Queen Bess Rock,' so named because of its resemblance to the Virgin Queen, with her ruff and extended skirt. The drive of seven miles or so to Bedruthan Steps, with the return journey deviating to Mawgan and through the Vale of Lanherne, is more popular with visitors to Newquay than any other outing. It is a trip of delightful contrasts. A corresponding trip westward from Newquay brings

Photo by]   BEDRUTHAN STEPS   *[Waren, Newquay*

the splendid cliffs and beaches of Perranporth within purview; while among the sandhills between the two places may be seen the 'buried church,' or what remains of it, of St. Piran, which was long covered with sand and which Mr. Warden Page speaks of as 'the oldest known religious building in England.' This interesting district, as well as that of Bedruthan, is regarded as being within the Newquay 'beat.'

Close to the western limits of the town of Newquay is the eastern boundary of the parish of Crantock. But to get from Newquay to Crantock 'churchtown' the river Gannel must be crossed. When the tide has receded, the Gannel is but a small stream which pedestrians cross by means of a plank bridge; and it is as much a matter of course for visitors to Newquay to go to Crantock as it is for them to go to Bedruthan Steps. Crantock village is very ancient and picturesque; but it is the grand old church which excites the interest alike of the antiquary and the merely curious sightseer. Unfortunately, the condition of the fabric is almost ruinous; and the vicar is heroically endeavouring to raise sufficient funds to restore it to something like its pristine beauty. In an appeal for help, issued last Christmas, Mr. Parsons explained that 'the foundation dates from the sixth century, when the Celtic Bishop, Carantoc—or Cairnech—whose name the church bears, and who was a companion of St. Patrick, first founded a religious cell here. The church became collegiate before the time of King Edward the Confessor, and continued so, with large endowment, until it was utterly despoiled, and its community scattered by King Henry VIII.' But we are also told that 'the walls and arches, dating from the twelfth century onwards, remain in their severe and massive beauty, and the extreme dignity and devotion of the unique plan—like a cathedral—are very striking.' The date inscribed on the font is A.D. 1474. Various remains of early work are likewise to be seen within the building, and are worthy of careful preservation. In the churchyard are the remains of an ancient stone coffin, discovered a few years ago just beneath the spot where they now lie; but it is not known whose body the coffin contained. The idea that it may have been the 'casket' of St. Carantoc himself, though poetically attractive, does not seem to be tenable; for it almost certainly belongs to a later date than the century in which the Saint lived and died. In the centre of the village is an old well, which is often designated 'holy,' though its claim to the designation is disputed. It is said that the site of the old well of St. Ambrose, near the church, as well as his old sanctuary in the churchyard, was demolished within living memory; but it cannot be now exactly located. There is a suspicion, however, that it is covered by a large pig-stye!

It has been pointed out that the trip from Newquay to Bedruthan Steps usually includes a visit to Mawgan, a pretty village lying in the heart of the Vale of Lanherne. Here the ancient parish church and a Roman Catholic convent and chapel stand side by side. The convent building was formerly the manor house of the Arundells; and in the last century a Lord Arundell of Wardour presented this residence to a body of Carmelite nuns who had come from abroad. The convent chapel contains some fine pictures, one or two being attributed to Rubens. Ancient crosses, beautifully sculptured, are to

Photo by]   *[Warm, Newquay*

ST. MAWGAN.

be seen in the graveyards attached to both the church and the chapel ; and here also the antiquary will find his curiosity excited, if not satisfied.

Comment is sometimes made on the absence of trees in and about Newquay ; but in the Vale of Lanherne, trees of the stateliest proportions, with numberless varieties of vegetable life, exist in the greatest profusion and of exuberant growth. Few lovelier valleys can be found in England. The woods belong to the estate of Carnanton, once the residence of Noye, Charles I.'s Attorney-General. The neighbourhood of Trerice, another old seat of the Arundells, in another direction and at a less distance than Mawgan from Newquay, is also prettily wooded. But daily 'excursion' tickets are issued at specially cheap rates from Newquay station so as to bring the exquisite woodland scenery of the Luxulyan Valley and the Valley of the Fowey into conjunction, as it were, with the bolder and wilder scenery of the north coast. There are some compensating advantages, however, in the lack of trees at Newquay. To this the town is indebted for its freedom from that autumnal dampness which is often a characteristic of wooded districts. A former owner of Glendorgal, whose principal residence was situated among trees in a distant part of the county, always migrated to his house on the comparatively treeless Atlantic coast as soon as 'the fall of the leaf' set in.

The climate of Newquay is, indeed, wonderfully fine. Almost total immunity from severe frost and snow is due, no doubt, to the Gulf Stream which washes that coast, and which takes the warm water up the tidal river Gannel as well as into the bay on the northern side of the peninsula. Thus Newquay is in the fortunate position of having the influence of the Gulf Stream operating both in front and behind the town. But the storms of winter, though producing spectacular effects of the sublimest grandeur on those majestic promontories that are struck by the full force of the Atlantic, must always militate against the place becoming a popular winter resort unless and until the slope from Mount Wise to the Gannel—where these storms are not usually felt, but where a southern aspect is combined with shelter, sunshine, and genial warmth—is dotted with pretty houses in which winter visitors can find accommodation. When this is done, and when the suggested lock is constructed at the narrow part of the river below Trethellan, charming residences will overlook a pretty lake on which boating will be safe and enjoyable, and along the sides of which there may be sunny drives and beautiful promenades. Who knows but that the 'Gannel crake'—a weird, unearthly sound which is sometimes heard there in the dead of night and is supposed to be the cry of some species of night-bird, though it is traditionally represented by the superstitious as being the cry of a troubled spirit that haunts the scene—will be considered an additional and unique attraction?

With all its great natural advantages, Newquay must have an assured future as a popular health resort; for not even a continued display of the ingenuity already shown in spoiling a site which nature has made so grand can arrest the force of advancement. Newquay is bound to grow, and to confer inestimable benefits on untold multitudes in the years to come. That there is an awakening to a sense of its privileges and responsibilities, as well as of its 'potentialities,' was indicated last year by the wise proposal to secure a 'front' before it was too late, and also by another felicitous suggestion that the headland should be made available for the use of invalids and other feeble folk in bath-chairs; while there was shrewdness at least in the idea that Newquay might worthily celebrate the Queen's Diamond Jubilee by getting her son, the Duke of Cornwall, to present the Barrow fields to the town for perpetual use as a public park! So the leaven of practical farsightedness is evidently working and the prospect is encouraging. But, even as it is, Newquay possesses so many attractions, that an eminent member of the medical profession, who was soon to become President of the Royal College of Physicians, thus wrote regarding his own visit to the place: 'I never spent an entire month in one place before; but at the end of a month in Newquay I found that its charms were by no means exhausted.'

J. HENWOOD THOMAS.

CRYING A NECK

Towards the beginning of the present century the Member for North Devon was extremely unpopular, especially with the lower classes, and there had been a disturbance on the occasion of his election, in which he had run some personal risk.

Not long after the election he went to Dunsland, the seat of William Holland Coham, by virtue of his marriage with the heiress of Bickford.

Whilst strolling near the house, he came near a harvest field, whereon he saw a rush of men, and he heard a cry of ' Us have'n ! Us have'n ! A neck ! A neck ! '

Panic-stricken, he ran, nimble as a hare, to the house, and shouted to Mr. Coham, ' For God's sake hide me, anywhere, in the cellar or the attics ! There is a mob after me who want to string me up ! '

What the M.P. for North Devon saw and heard was the ' Crying a Neck,' a custom universal in Devon and Cornwall till reaping machines came in and abolished it. It is now most rarely practised, but I can remember it in full swing some forty or fifty years ago.

Mrs. Bray, in her ' Borders of the Tamar and Tavy,' thus describes it in 1832 : ' One evening, about the end of harvest, I was riding out on my pony, attended by a servant who was born and bred a Devonian. We were passing near a field on the borders of Dartmoor, where the reapers were assembled. In a moment the pony started nearly from one side of the way to the other, so sudden came a shout from the field which gave him this alarm. On my stopping to ask my servant what all that noise was about, he seemed surprised by the question, and said : " It was only the people making their games, as they always did, to the *spirit of the harvest*." Such a reply was quite sufficient to induce me to stop immediately, as I felt certain here was to be observed some curious vestige of a most ancient superstition ; and I soon gained all the information I could wish to obtain upon the subject. The offering to the " spirit of the harvest " is thus made.

' When the reaping is finished, towards evening, the labourers select some of the best ears of corn from the sheaves ; these they tie together, and it is called the *nack*. Sometimes, as it was when I witnessed the custom, the nack is decorated with flowers, twisted in with the seed, which gives it a gay and fantastic appearance. The reapers then proceed to a *high place* (such, in fact, was the field on the side of a steep hill where I saw them), and there they go, to use their own words, to " holla the nack." The man who bears the offering stands in the midst and elevates it, whilst all the other labourers form themselves into a circle about him ; each holds aloft his hook, and in a moment they all shout as loud as they can these words, which I spell as I heard them pronounced, and I presume they are not to be found in any written record. "Arnack, arnack, arnack, wehaven, wehaven, wehaven." This is repeated several times; and the firkin is handed round between each shout, by way, I conclude, of libation. When the weather is fine, different parties of reapers, each stationed on some height, may be heard for miles round, shouting, as it were, in answer to each other.

'The evening I witnessed this ceremony, many women and children, some carrying boughs, and others having flowers in their caps or in their hands or in their bonnets, were seen, some dancing, others singing, whilst the men (whose exclamations so startled my pony) practised the above rites in a ring.'

Mrs. Bray goes on to add a good deal of antiquated archæological nonsense about Druids, Phœnicians, and derivations. She makes 'wehaven' to be 'a corruption of *wee ane,*' 'a little one,' which is rubbish. 'Wehaven' is 'we have 'n,' or 'us have 'n,' 'we have got him.' As I remember the crying of the neck at Lew-Trenchard, there was a slight difference in the procedure to that described by Mrs. Bray. The field was reaped till a portion was left where was the best wheat, and then the circle was formed, the men shouted 'A neck! A neck! We have 'n!' and proceeded to reap it. Then it was hastily bound in a bundle, the ears were plaited together with flowers at the top of the sheaf, and this was heaved up, with the sickles raised, and a great shout of 'A neck! A neck!' &c., again, and the drink, of course.

The wheat of the last sheaf was preserved apart through the winter, and was mixed with the seed corn next year.

My old coachman, William Pengelly, who had been with my grandfather, father, and then with myself, and who died at an advanced age in 1894, was wont annually, till he became childish with age, to make the little corn man or neck, and bring it to be set up in the church for the harvest decorations. I kept a couple of these for some years, till the mice got at them and destroyed them. In Altarnon Church, on the beam ends, the corn man or neck is represented several times.

The custom is not peculiar to Devon and Cornwall. It is found very widely spread. In the North of England the little figure is called the Mell-doll. Grimm, in his 'Deutsche Mythologie,' says: 'Formerly it was the custom at harvest to leave a bunch standing on the field, round which the reapers danced, throwing up their caps and crying, "Waul, waul, waul."' And again: 'Throughout the whole Ukermark, and in many of the parts adjacent, the custom prevails at the end of rye-harvest, and, in some places, at the carrying in of every kind of grain, to make a puppet out of the last sheaf, and either to carry it home rejoicing with the last load, or let it be borne to the village by the girl who is the last ready with her binding. In accordance with the one or the other of these usages, the custom is called, "Bringing the old man," or else of the girl it is said, "She has the old man." Customs closely akin to the above-mentioned prevail in several other places.'

In the North of England the figure of the corn man or neck is called, as already said, the Mell-doll or Meal-doll, from melr, the Norse for corn.

The whole matter has been gone into by Mannhardt, whose study has been popularised in England by Mr. Frazer in 'The Golden Bough,' 1890.

In so brief an article as this, it is not possible to do more than mention a few of the facts on which Mannhardt based his argument, and to give his results in a brief summary.

The harvest usage now gone out in the West of England is almost identical with a great many others observed throughout Europe, and even in India. These point to a common origin, and are the embodiment of one idea.

This idea seems to have been that the spirit of the harvest resided in the corn. This spirit was regarded in some places as male, in others as female. In some it is the corn man or Hnikr, in others it is the corn mother or Guda.

To ensure fertility and there being a good harvest in the next year, to this spirit an offering had to be made, and this offering was a human victim.

When human sacrifices were abolished, then some modification was introduced into the custom : either a straw figure was made and burnt or buried, or a stranger was caught, wrapped in straw and maltreated, or else the last reaper was so treated. Let us see how this idea is still at the bottom of harvest customs not quite obsolete.

In Essex, a stranger passing a harvest field stands—or a few years ago stood—the chance of being run up to by the harvesters, caught in a loop of straw twisted, and held till he paid a handsel as forfeit. To the present day in Devon, at haysel, the haymakers will make a twist of dry grass, and with this band catch a girl—or a girl will catch a boy—and hold her or him till the forfeit of a kiss has been paid, and this is called 'making sweet hay.' But in other parts of Europe the penalty of being caught is more severe : the stranger captured is tied up in straw, buried to his waist, or thrown down and beaten and kicked, or cast into the water.

Our Guy Fawkes is simply the straw man removed from harvest time to November, and the persistence of the custom of burning Guy Fawkes is due to the stubbornness with which people hold to old customs, and, rather than abandon them, give to them new significations. The Celtic Well, the work of a water spirit, became with Christianity the Well of the Saint, and is now the Wishing Well. The straw Guy Fawkes takes the place of the straw man at harvest, and the straw man at harvest is a modification of the human sacrifice to the Spirit of Vegetation.

In spring in like manner there was an oblation to the same spirit. The May Queen is really the virgin elected and decked with flowers who was given a brief reign and honour, and was then sacrificed. Jack in the Green is the man enveloped in leaves, just as the victim at harvest was enveloped in straw, and both were originally destined to be sacrificed. On Shrove Tuesday in some places it is customary to lay hold of a stranger, bear him aloft, and carry him away till he redeems himself with a kiss or money. I remember a Government Inspector of Schools arriving in a Yorkshire town—a very stiff and stately clergyman—on Shrove Tuesday. At once a rush on him was made by mill girls : they seized him, lifted him on their shoulders, and declared that unless he kissed them all round they would throw him into a very nasty canal, black and reeking with dye from the mills. He struggled, all in vain. To kiss! He could not do it, his professional dignity forbade him. He was carried through the town by the girls, and deposited more dead than alive at the school door, but only when he had emptied his pocket among his merciless sustainers. I myself have been thus lifted by Basque girls near Bayonne, when I was a boy of seventeen, but I did not find any difficulty in complying with the demand for a kiss all round. But anciently this was a form of capture, without benefit of redemption by kiss or money, by a stranger, who was held in durance till the time came for the sacrifice.

In a vast number of cases the predestined victim was treated with great honour, was well fed, well clothed, almost adored, till the day of the sacrifice arrived, when he was despoiled of his garments and put to death. Then he was literally hacked to pieces, and portions of his flesh were carried off to be buried in the fields and gardens, to ensure good returns for the ensuing year. In Spain a figure of a woman is made on Shrove Tuesday: this is sawn in half; one half destroyed at Mid-lent and the other half burned on Easter Eve. Here, again, we have the sacrifice. The person is caught on Shrove Tuesday, but the image is a substitute, and that is burned. Among the Russians Judas Iscariot is hanged on Good Friday. In this case, again, it is the victim offered to the Spirit of Vegetation in the spring replaced by an image of wood, and then to this image an entirely new idea has been attached. The custom, greatly modified, remains, but its meaning has been entirely forgotten.

I take from Mannhardt a very few illustrations of the custom at harvest, which can now be understood, knowing as we do what was the original purpose of the ceremony.

At Hadeln, in Hanover, the reapers surround the last sheaf, and thrash it to drive the Corn Mother out of it. They shout as they do so, 'There she is; hit her! Take care she doesn't catch you.' In Danzig the person who cuts the last ears of corn makes them into a doll, which is called the Old Woman, and is brought home on the last waggon. In Bohemia the Baba, or last sheaf, has the figure of an old woman, and the last binder in the field has to dance with this figure. Sometimes the woman who is last to bind is wrapped up in the sheaf so that only her head projects. The Bulgarians also make a similar doll, which they call the Corn Queen, and after it has been carried through the village it is thrown into the river. In Poland the man who gives the last stroke at threshing is wrapt in corn and wheeled through the village. In Bavaria he is tied up in straw, carted through the street, and cast out on a dunghill. The custom in its unmitigated and unaltered form is not quite extinct. The Pawnees practised it till as late as 1838. A girl was kept in preparation for six months, then burned over a slow fire, and shot to death with arrows. The chief sacrificer then tore out her heart and ate it. Whilst her flesh was still warm it was cut to pieces and the bits carried away to be buried in the cornfields. At Lagos, in Guinea, it was the custom to impale a young girl alive soon after the opening equinox, in order to ensure good crops. A similar sacrifice is still annually offered at Benin. The Marimos, a Bechuana tribe, sacrifice a human being for the crops. He is captured, then intoxicated, carried into the fields, and there slaughtered. His blood and ashes, after the body has been burned, are distributed over the tilled land to ensure a good harvest next year. The Gonds of India kidnapped Brahman boys for the same purpose. The British Government had to act with great resolution in putting down the similar sacrifices of the Khonds, some half-century ago.

The mode of performing these sacrifices was as follows. Ten or twelve days before the sacrifice, the victim's hair was cut. Crowds assembled to witness the sacrifice. On the day before, the victim was tied to a post and anointed with oil. Great struggles ensued to scrape off some of this oil or to obtain a drop of spittle from the victim. The crowd danced round the post, saying, 'O God, we offer this sacrifice for good crops, seasons, and health.' On the day of the sacrifice the legs and arms were first broken, and he was either squeezed to death or strangled. Then the crowd rushed on him with knives and hacked the flesh from the bones. Sometimes he was cut up alive. Another very common mode was to fasten the victim to the proboscis of a wooden elephant, which revolved on a stout post, and as it whirled round, the crowd cut the flesh off while life remained. In some villages as many as fourteen of these wooden elephants were found, all of which had been used for this purpose. In one district the victim was put to death slowly by fire. A low stage was erected, sloping on each side like a roof; upon this the victim was placed, his limbs wound about with cords to prevent his escape. Fires were then lighted and hot brands applied, to make him roll up and down the slopes of the stage as much as possible, for the more tears he shed the more abundant would be the supply of rain. The next day the body was cut to pieces. The flesh was at once taken home by delegates of the villages. To secure its rapid arrival, it was sometimes forwarded by relays of men, and conveyed with postal fleetness fifty or sixty miles. In each village all who had remained at home fasted until the flesh arrived. When it came it was divided into two portions, one of which was offered to the earth goddess by burying it in a hole in the ground. The other portion was divided into as many shares as there were heads of houses present. Each head of a house rolled his share in leaves, and buried it in his favourite field. In some places each man carried his portion of flesh to the stream that watered his fields.

Since the British Government has suppressed the human sacrifices, inferior victims have been substituted, such as goats.

Here, then, we have almost before our eyes a change of the victim. A still further change takes place when an image is used as a substitute; and there is again modification when the person captured and destined for sacrifice is allowed to redeem himself with a handsel or a kiss. But the fact that in Europe, aye and in England, we have these modified customs only now dying out is an almost sure proof that at a remote period our ancestors practised the awful rites at Harvest and in Spring of which a description has been given as still in use in Africa, and as only just put an end to in America and in India.

S. BARING-GOULD.

HOW TO DEVELOP CORNWALL AS A HOLIDAY RESORT—(*continued*)

OPINIONS OF EMINENT CORNISHMEN AND OTHERS

Mr. Joseph Pennell I would suggest the building of a few roads round your magnificent coast if you wish cycle tourists, and the improvement of those you have if you wish to be ranked with civilised countries—as the condition of the roads is typical of the county through which they pass.

Mr. T. Hodgkin, D.C.L. One great recommendation of Cornwall as a place of holiday resort lies in its unlikeness to the rest of England. This sounds rather uncomplimentary to 'the rest of England,' yet it may be said with perfect loyalty to our native land. For, as all holiday-makers know, half the charm of a holiday lies in the stimulus given to the wearied brain and nerves by contact with unfamiliar sights and sounds. It is this which makes even a few days spent in Normandy and Belgium so delightful, though, as far as natural beauty of landscape is concerned, these districts cannot compare with our own Kent or Surrey; and it is this, I imagine, which the American traveller in his own land generally looks for in vain. He may travel many thousand miles by railway in the United States, but he looks on the same kind of civilisation, the same sort of cities, the same 'clearings,' the same farmhouses at the end of the journey that he saw at the beginning.

Now this cannot be said of the eight hours' journey by the 'Flying Dutchman' which brings the jaded Londoner to one of the many picturesque nooks of the county of Cornwall. Our county was once called 'West Wales,' and it still has many marks of separateness from the rest of England. One of these, strange to say, is the very goodness of the English spoken by its least educated children. It is true that it is spoken 'with a difference.' There is a delightful turn-up inflection of the voice which gladdens one's heart when one lands at the station at Truro, or Falmouth, or Penzance, and makes one feel one is really back again among kinsfolk and friends. And there are also many charming turns of expression which, in Milton's phrase, would make a Londoner 'stare and gasp' when he heard them for the first time. But the Cornish peasant's English, compared with the English of a man of his own station in Devonshire or Dorset, is the English of an educated man; just as the people of Caithness are conspicuous for their good English among the Lowlanders of Scotland. In both cases the reason is the same. The man of Caithness and the man of Cornwall had to unlearn a language of their own and to learn English, after it had become a literary language, as a foreign tongue, and therefore they speak it with what we call correctness; while the man of Somerset and the man of East Lothian had each an English of his own which he inherited from his forefathers who had crossed the sea from Holstein or Jutland, and which differs from the dialect that happens to have obtained currency as literary English. Long may he keep it, in spite of Board Schools, and railways, and newspapers, and all the distant assimilating influences of modern civilisation.

Let the holiday-maker, then, who wants to combine some of the stimulus of foreign travel with some of the comforts of home travel, visit Cornwall. He will find fiords not quite unworthy of comparison with those of Norway, except that we have no line of snowy peaks on the horizon, no glaciers descending to the sea. He will see the Atlantic wave dashing in the fullness of its strength against the sentinel cliffs of the Land's End, and will understand what Homer meant when he talked of the 'winedark deep.' He will discover a whole nest of churches (many of which have suffered little at the hand of the 'restorer') hidden away in flowery recesses of the hills and dedicated to all sorts of Celtic saints of whose names he never heard. He will talk to the fishermen of Mousehole and Mevagissey, a hardy and courageous race. He will see tin mines, some of which may have been worked in the days of the Phœnicians a thousand years before the birth of Christ; though the miner of Cornwall, alas! has now fallen on evil days. And also he will find a warm-hearted and nimble-witted people, courteous but not servile, with a strongly marked character of their own, whose somewhat clannish disposition is aptly expressed by their favourite motto 'One and All,' but who know how to give a hearty welcome to an appreciative stranger.

R. D. Boase, M.O.H., Penzance I desire to express my complete agreement with all that is written under this head in your excellent first issue. I even include the brief but significant testimonial of Sir Joseph Pease to Cornwall in its 'undeveloped' state. None the less can one at times sympathise with the bitter cry of the outcast authoress of the ' Unsentimental Journey.'

Sir Edwin Durning-Lawrence deftly hits the mark when he tells us that our first requisite is accessibility. For this we require, and ought to receive, special favour from the Great Western Railway Company. For us in the furthest west the Company has not yet solved the problem of entraining passengers at a reasonable morning hour in London and discharging them at the western terminus in time to tidy up for an ordinary hotel dinner. This it could readily effect at once by running on a train to us from Truro on the arrival of the 10.30 from Paddington.

I cannot but again agree with Sir Edwin Durning-Lawrence in regarding our reception of visitors as not always in all respects complete. We should strive to make them not merely with us but, as closely as possible, of us. Various clubs here and there do something in this direction, but I am of opinion that sociable approach on our part is still inadequately developed. Here, too, we should not rest content with sharing our customary 'home comforts' with the new comers, but should even make allowances for their prepossessions—it may be, their infirmities. Above all, I would plead for their possible infirmities of digestion. I have known visitors (invalids in particular) driven from the field of Cornish lodging house industry—vanquished in a brave and painful struggle with 'food comforts' readily assimilated by our robuster selves. We residents know where to obtain the best of food, and can, if we will, supply it. But there is (*inter alia*) beef imported to us which the best cooking in the world would not suffice to conquer. And ours is not always the best cooking. I mention these things because they are more to visitors than piers and bands and winter gardens, of which they are at all times and everywhere supposed to stand in urgent need.

Fortunately, in West Cornwall at least, Nature has (I think it must be allowed) very fairly developed her 'show places.' Our chief concern should be to see that they be not spoiled. Here, again, the greatest accessibility of course is requisite, but does not this also imply a reasonable and respectful subsequent retreat? To share, not to monopolise: to live if he will at a little distance, not to overshadow our loveliest coves completely — that surely we may in fairness ask of the visitor and of the promoters of his hotels.

Something, no doubt, may still be done to 'discover' Cornwall by advertisement. We have one of the finest climates in the world, not merely 'seasonal,' but all the year round. Is not this as yet a thing not generally known? For the last quarter we registered in Penzance 686 hours of sunshine and a death-rate of 13·4. And the visitors' 'season' will begin in August, and last three months! That I may assist in the revealing of Cornwall may I direct attention to an excellent pamphlet 'Cornwall as a Health Resort,' compiled by Mr. Kitto, of Falmouth, published by the G. W. R. Co., and worthy of a much wider distribution than it at present seems to get.

Our West of England newspapers render the county good service by the publication of meteorological results. More might be done in this direction. More stations of the Royal Meteorological Society should be formed in Cornwall, and tabulated returns (daily, monthly, quarterly, and annual) regularly published. These a competent person should collate and issue with explanatory notes and comparisons with other localities.

One is glad to note, of late, increasing signs of consciousness of the reality of a tide that is striving to flow toward us. I hail as a happy event the successful launching upon its waters of the *Cornish Magazine*.

Mr. John Davies Enys The development should concern Cornwall as a health resort also. Several instances of the benefit of residence in the county can be given. Canon Phillpotts was sent down as a last resource and lived to over eighty; the Rev. W. Wingfield, of Gulval, sent down in the same way, has lived as vicar of Gulval fifty-three years or more. A list of places where clean and good accommodation can be obtained, and information showing how people may get to and from various places, would be most useful. The large hotels will, of course, advertise themselves fully. Cost of living is a great item in holiday-making.

Mr. J. L. W. Page I am perfectly satisfied with Cornwall as it is, and think that it has developed as a holiday resort quite enough. For goodness' sake, let us have some place that knows not the tripper—that is innocent even of a 'season's band.' Cornwall is not at present overrun by the former, or rendered melodious (?) by the latter. Long may it remain the happy hunting-ground of those who, like myself, love peace and quietness.

(*We hope to conclude this discussion next month*)

CORNISH DIAMONDS

'You say you consider the defendant was not drunk. Will you tell the magistrate when you consider a man is drunk?'

'Wael, when 'ee takes 'es muther fur 'es father.'

It used to be the practice of boys in the Cornish fishing ports to use a small net on the end of a long stick for the purpose of scooping up pilchards when they could get near big catches; and by this means, which was known as 'kyben,' hundreds of fish were at times stolen. One day Mr. B—— arrived on horseback at St. Ives as those who manned his boats were dealing with a large school of pilchards on the beach. Riding down, he called to a boy to hold his horse.

'What 'el 'ee give me?' inquired the youth.

'Give you? Oh, give you sixpence.'

'Shaent do et. I ken get more 'en that kyben Mr. B——'s pilchers.'

A mayor of Market Jew, who was noted for his snuff-taking propensities, had before him a boy charged with playing 'jeeps' (pitch and toss) in the streets. 'I seed 'ee playen "jeeps," boy,' said the mayor, as the offender drew the sleeve of his coat across his eyes. Believing that the time for her to act had arrived, the mother of the boy rose in court with an insinuating smile and, holding out a capacious snuff-box, inquired, 'Will yer wurshop 'av pench o' suuff?' 'No thanks, Mary,' replied the chief magistrate, 'I've just put chaw uv baccy in me mouth.'

A labourer, on his first visit to a harness-room, was much puzzled by the stirrup-leathers hanging there. 'Wha's the use of these here holes in 'en?' he asked. Then with a bright smile of comprehension, 'Why, of coorse—silly of me not to knaw! First you lowers 'em to ground, and then, when the gentry's put its feet in, hoist away an' make fast!'

When Squire —— attended Bodmin Assizes as High Sheriff, the Judge on the bench was troubled with a slight huskiness in the throat. Squire —— considerately handed up a lozenge. 'You mustn't chow 'en, my lord. Keep 'en in your lordship's mouth and let 'en *conjale*.'

A vicar, thought lightly of as a preacher, had as his severest critic a farmer of rather intemperate habits who was regarded as a judge of pulpit oratory. One boisterous night they met in the nearest market town, and the parson accepted the farmer's offer of a lift back to the village. The recipient of the favour thought he could not make a better return than by giving his friend some advice, and accordingly delivered what he regarded as a particularly moving sermon on intemperance. The farmer was silent until they reached the place where the vicar had to get down. He then said, 'Good night, sir, good night. You'm a very nice man, but you'm a hopelessly poor preacher.'

Complainant (cross-examining defendant's witness): 'What colour was the horse?'

'Black.'

'Well, I'm not allowed to contradict you; but I say it wasen't.'

ONE MAN ONE VOTE
(From a Water-Colour by WALTER LANGLEY, R.I., *in the possession of E. Atkinson, Esq.)*

MR. LEONARD COURTNEY

N an evening in June of the last session, the House of Commons enjoyed one of its private little jokes, the dearer to its heart by reason of monopoly of appreciation. The business before it was consideration of a cluster of Water Bills. Mr. Chaplin, in his capacity as President of the Local Government Board, moved the first of a long series of new clauses. These, he explained, were the fruit of consideration of the epidemic that had devastated Maidstone, following on the use of impure water. Mr. Mellor, speaking with the weight of authority pertaining to an ex-Chairman of Ways and Means, protested against altering the law of the land through the agency of a private Bill. This view was accepted on both sides of the House, and in the end Mr. Chaplin found it desirable to capitulate.

At this stage a sturdy figure, principally, certainly most prominently, arrayed in a yellow waistcoat, the like of which was never seen on sea or land, uprose from a corner seat below the gangway, and in grave, solemn voice observed—

'I cannot help thinking that in this matter the House is moved by a sort of pedantry.'

A smile flashed back from the crowded House upon the sheen of the yellow waistcoat. A titter followed, then a laugh. In a moment, to the marvel of the stranger in the gallery wondering where the joke came in, the chamber was filled with a merry roar.

The member on his feet was Mr. Courtney, and there was something about him, of all men, rebuking 'a sort of pedantry,' that tickled the legislative midriff. The member for Bodmin, of course, does not mean to assume a pedantic air when addressing the House, and doubtless is unaware of the tendency. Nevertheless there it is, ingrained in the constitution, current in the blood. The accident of training and position has much to do with it. For some time in early life Mr. Courtney was a private tutor at his University. In his fortieth year he was appointed to the chair of Political Economy at University College, London, and, of course, had to lecture. Earlier he was engaged as a writer in the leading columns of the 'Times,' a position from which the most modest-mannered man learns to regard his fellow-kind with a certain air of superiority. For two years he was Examiner in Constitutional History at the University of London, and, finally, came to be Chairman of Ways and Means in the House of Commons; an autocratic position, second only to that of the Speaker.

In view of this succession of circumstances it is not to be wondered at if, when addressing the House of Commons in his capacity as a private member, Mr. Courtney should lapse into something of a Moses-on-the-mountain manner. At the outset of his parliamentary career this irritated the House, but by long wont and usage has come to be regarded with amused benevolence.

Born a Cornishman, Mr. Courtney has loyally devoted his parliamentary services to his county. He appeared on an electoral platform for the first time in 1874, when he fought Mr. Horsman at Liskeard. It is interesting to recall the fact that not quite a quarter of a century ago Liskeard returned a member of the House of Commons on a total poll of 663 votes. With almost even-handed impartiality these were divided between the two candidates. But Mr. Horsman, having five more than Mr. Courtney, also had the seat. Two years later Mr. Horsman's occasionally brilliant, on the whole disappointing, career closed in death, and Mr. Courtney was elected on much the same poll by a majority of over a hundred.

This was on December 22, 1876. Mr. Courtney was too good a citizen to leave the House of Commons long lacking the benefit of his counsel. I have no recollection of his maiden speech; but as early as the first week in June, in his first session, not quite four months old, he suddenly achieved fame. It was a Wednesday afternoon, and the House was engaged on the second reading of the Woman's Suffrage Bill. That is one of several subjects on the flank of Imperial politics Mr. Courtney has made especially his own. He was anxious above all things that a division should be taken on the second reading. He succeeded in talking out the Bill.

It was a quarter-past five when he rose with a portentous sheaf of notes in his hand. At that time debate on Wednesdays might be continued till a quarter to six, when, if not otherwise concluded, it would automatically close.

Mr. Courtney had something under half an hour at his disposal, and had he been left undisturbed, might have used the opportunity to advantage. It happens that thus early in his career he had succeeded in alienating the House, a position long ago retrieved by fuller acquaintance with his sterling qualities and his high capacity. There are few things the House of Commons resents more hotly than haste on the part of a new member to assist it with his counsel. At this epoch Mr. Courtney had strong views on the Eastern question and was not diffident in setting them forth. Some weeks precedent to this Wednesday afternoon he had, in spite of protests not least persistent on the Liberal side, insisted on bringing forward a motion raising a delicate phase of the Eastern question. When he now appeared on an off day, plainly predisposed to deliver a lecture on women's rights, members, in any circumstances shamelessly predisposed to make fun of the topic, resolved to 'have a lark.'

Mr. Courtney had not proceeded far when there were cries for the division. This interruption he met with angry rebuke that fanned the flame. For twenty minutes by Westminster clock he stood and faced the storm. Opposite and around him was a crowd of hilarious gentlemen shouting ''Vide! 'vide! 'vide!' When the roar of sound momentarily fell Mr. Courtney, raising his stentorian voice to thunderous heights, attempted to get in the fragment of a sentence. Then, as the winter storm surging through the forlorn trees, having apparently blown itself out, suddenly rises with angrier roar, so Mr. Courtney's voice was drowned in a fresh shout of ''Vide! 'vide! 'vide!'

It was characteristic of his courage that, though still a new member, presumably in awe of the House, he for twenty minutes faced the music, the roar rising to a final yell of exultation when, as the hand of the clock pointed a quarter to six, the Speaker rose with call of 'Order! order!' and Mr. Courtney sat down, having talked out the Bill he had risen to advocate.

Apart from its personal connections, this scene is historic as beating the record in its own line, and as marking a state of things that would not be possible to-day. There was no closure in the session of 1876. A rough substitute was found in this deafening shout for the division—a rude expedient which the Speaker of the day did not feel himself authorised to rebuke. With the closure at hand, the Speaker of a modern Parliament would not permit for the duration of three minutes such a scene as was in Mr. Courtney's recollection prolonged for half an hour.

When, in 1880, Mr. Gladstone came back to power, master of a great majority, Mr. Courtney had so far redeemed this early failure as to be regarded among the Premier's inevitable choice for the new Ministry. This was verified to the extent that he was offered a Lordship of the Treasury. He declined to begin a Ministerial career at the very bottom rung of the ladder, and through the session of 1880 enjoyed a season of independence below the gangway. In December of that year, he was appointed Under Secretary at the Home Office. Less than a year later came promotion to the Colonial Office, and in May 1882, when poor Lord Frederick Cavendish went to the Irish Office on his way to assassination in Phœnix Park, Mr. Courtney became Financial Secretary to the

Treasury. Here he had full scope for his business habits and capacity. The post does not loom large in the public eye. Apart from those of first-class rank it is one of the most important in the Ministry. It has been held by men of the stamp of W. H. Smith, and Sir Henry Fowler. It is regarded, and has occasionally proved, a training school for the Chancellorship of the Exchequer. Mr. Courtney fully equalled the expectations formed of him. He proved a model Financial Secretary, and under his care the machinery of legislative business in the House of Commons worked with unbroken smoothness.

In 1884 he resigned the Financial Secretaryship, which proved to be his last Ministerial office. When, in 1886, the split in the Liberal Party on the question of Home Rule opened and widened, Mr. Courtney threw in his lot with the section of the party who seceded from the leadership of Mr. Gladstone. The 'Unionists' coming into power in 1886, he was rewarded for this preference by being appointed to the chair of Ways and Means.

This was a position that brought into play all his special gifts and faculties. To begin with, he is a man of almost aggressive integrity. There are conceivable circumstances in which he would, on the whole, rather go to the stake than not. If he had lived through the reign of Queen Mary, he would certainly have been done to death under the gentle rule of Queen Elizabeth. Through his chequered political career never once has been heard whisper of accusation that he was, in word or deed, actuated by other than conscientious motive. He is further endowed with a mind at once acute and judicial. So prevailing is this last quality that he revolts from the inequalities of our existing electoral system and bankers after proportional representation.

When he took the chair in Committee of Ways and Means, he found some thorns in the cushion. The ceremony of the induction of a Chairman of Committees is appropriately businesslike. When a Speaker is elected there is a certain stately ceremony. He is proposed and seconded by two of the most important members on his own side. If, as in the case of Mr. Gully, his election be opposed, members of equal standing on the other side espouse the cause of his rival. Debate being thus formally opened, any member may take part in it. On one occasion, when Mr. Peel was re-elected, an Irish member seized the opportunity of protesting against the choice on the ground that earlier experience of his manner had found him somewhat repressive of Irish eloquence. Had this ceremony of introduction pertained to the installation of a Chairman of Committees, the Irish members would undoubtedly have had something to say when it was proposed that Mr. Courtney should take the chair.

What happens on such occasion is that the Leader of the House observes, studiously *sotto voce*, 'I move that Mr. So-and-so take the chair.' The Chairman designate, fortuitously close at hand, and, by good fortune, arrayed in the evening dress indispensable to the work of Chairman of Committees, even at a morning sitting, pops into the chair, submits the question that a private Bill shall pass an immaterial stage, and before the House quite realises it has got a new Chairman, he is out of the chair, and, as the Parliamentary reports put it, 'the House resumes.'

Mr. Courtney came into the House on the Radical platform. Up to the end of the session of 1885 he steadfastly voted with that section of the party which always went further in the direction of supporting the Irish Nationalists than did any other. The Irish members with special chagrin saw him take his place in the ranks of the anti-Home Rulers. To find him, as they put it, benefiting thereby to the extent of a snug berth, to which pertained a salary of 2,500*l*. per year, and an average of five months' holiday, was more than they were disposed to bear with equanimity. Had he been a weak, irresolute man, the Irish members would have made his occupancy of the chair a melancholy experience. He is not a weak man, either physically or mentally, and in matters of opinion irresolution is the last charge that might be brought against him.

I remember only one occasion when, in the habitual struggles with the Irish members, Mr. Courtney gave himself away, and that was a trivial matter. One night Sir Richard Webster was defending himself against an attack made upon him from the Front Opposition Bench. Mr. Biggar, still with us, and some other members of the Irish Party, who had perforce maintained long silence in the Probate Court what time the Attorney-General laboriously indicted them before the Commission of Judges, eagerly seized this opportunity of paying off old scores. They accompanied the Attorney-General's remarks by a running commentary varied by outbursts of ironical cheering. After long endurance the Chairman—the House was in Committee—rose, and in stern voice said, 'I must order the honourable member for South Mayo to retire.'

The member for South Mayo was Mr. J. F. X. O'Brien, who to this day sits aloft in high supremacy over his fellow-members. Some of them have been in prison. The many initialled O'Brien was ordered to be hung, and might have been drawn and quartered. Thirty-one years ago he was tried for high treason and sentenced to death. At the last moment the sentence was commuted to penal servitude for life, amnesty following some years later. Mr. O'Brien is the mildest-mannered man that ever looked the gallows in the face, not to mention contemplation of ultimate dismemberment. That in such a *mêlée* he should have been picked out as a ringleader struck the House, even in a moment of excitement, with a sense of the ludicrous. This was increased when Mr. O'Brien, pale and frightened, whimpered 'I did not open my lips.'

Testimony from those seated near him convinced Mr. Courtney that he had made a mistake. That is more or less permissible with ordinary humanity. It is fatal to the reputation of a Chairman of Ways and Means. To persist in enforcing the consequences of a proved mistake was, of course, not to be thought of. To acknowledge error would be embarrassing. Mr. Courtney must say something, for he had ordered a member to withdraw. He was equal to the occasion. Having publicly accused Mr. O'Brien of having done something it was clear he had not done, he ' accepted the honourable member's disclaimer,' and called on the next speaker.

More blessed than Mesopotamia was the word 'disclaimer.'

This incident is chiefly interesting as showing the constant strain under which a Chairman of Committees sits hour after hour in the fierce light that beats upon the chair. In nightly practice the position of Chairman of Committees is even more arduous than that of the Speaker. Being hedged about with less authority, the atmosphere and tone of the Committee differs in subtle fashion when the same body of men are earlier or later on the same day sitting in the same chamber in the full majesty of the House. Moreover, the style of debate varies, being more conversational in manner, with quicker touch-and-go, calling for closest attention on the part of the president and lightning-like readiness to decide a delicate point of conduct or procedure suddenly submitted.

One of Mr. Courtney's monumental achievements in the chair was the smooth, business-like passage of the English Local Government Bill. It is probable that, with the exception of Mr. Ritchie, the Minister in charge, he was the only man who thoroughly grasped the nightly, hourly changing aspect of this stupendous measure, with its one hundred and sixty-two clauses, its five schedules, its eighty folio pages of amendments. For ninety-nine out of a hundred members in that session of 1888 duty to their country was discharged if they remained within sound of the division bell, in the reading-room, the smoking-room, or on the terrace. The Chairman of Committees must needs sit hour after hour through the long night, not only watching the drift of debate round the particular amendment under discussion, but recalling the slow course the Bill had already fought its way through, and the devious plain that lay before it. He must be courteous but firm, steeped in lore of Parliamentary procedure, watchful and ready: out of the chair an ordinary member, subject, like the rest, to rule and discipline; in the chair absolute autocrat, subject only to formal and final appeal to the regularly constituted House.

These were conditions Mr. Courtney through his six years' tenancy of the chair of Committees admirably filled. He did not please everybody—a success rare of human achievement. His manner lacked the polish of Mr. Arthur Balfour, or the grand urbanity of Mr. Gladstone. He ruled with an iron hand, not wasting precious time in pulling on silken and, on the whole, inefficacious silken gloves. But never once through his chairmanship did breath of suspicion of his strict impartiality or of his honesty of purpose find its way into the sometimes heated chamber.

The highest tribute that could be paid to his success in the chair was the conviction held by some old parliamentary hands in the Parliament of 1892, that had he been retained as Chairman of Committees, the career of the Home Rule Bill through Committee would have been far less turbulent. It was at the time a common thing to hear Mr. Gladstone blamed for lack of judgment in this matter. I have good reason to believe that when the new Parliament met after the election of 1892, Mr. Gladstone was personally disposed to move Mr. Courtney into the chair of Committees. In this, as in some other matters of importance vital to the Liberal Party, his hand was forced from below the gangway on his own side of the House. Irish Nationalists and British Radicals were one in their determination to oust from the chair of Committees the once Radical-Nationalist member for Liskeard.

By a painful coincidence, Mr. Courtney's promotion to higher place was barred by an analogous demonstration made from quite a different quarter. On the retirement of Mr. Arthur Peel from the Speaker's chair, it seemed inevitable that Mr. Courtney should succeed him. Even his personal enemies—and there are such—would admit that by his tenancy of the chair in Committee of Ways and Means he had shown himself qualified for the canopied chair behind him. His political friends were in a majority that rendered opposition futile. It was no secret that opposition to such election would not come from the leaders of the party opposite. Sir William Harcourt, sinking all feelings of resentment at the secession of a former colleague, warmly espoused Mr. Courtney's cause. Opposition came from within the Cabinet. According to common report, a Minister not, as a rule, slow to urge the claims to promotion of members of his own section of the 'Unionist' Party, stood in Mr. Courtney's way to the Speaker's chair.

We know now that he was only anticipating another and a darker influence. Had Mr. Courtney been elected Speaker in the spring of 1895, he must needs, owing to physical infirmity, have, long ere this, retired. There are few sorer calamities that could befall a man of active habits, a scholar, and a lover of books, than the deepening shade of blindness. For more than two years past it has been gathering over Mr. Courtney—a calamity met with a courage and serenity of mind that extort the admiration of all who have eyes to see.

Henry W. Lucy.

Photo by] [*Burrow, Camborne*

THE GREAT DOLCOATH

To the north-west of Carn Brea, and very near it, lies one of the most interesting areas in Cornwall. For a couple of miles or so the surface presents a strange appearance by the side of the small fields and cottages. In all directions there are heaps of stones and sand, ranges of irregular buildings, tall chimneys, and gigantic machinery belonging to the chief mines of the county, one of which, Dolcoath, is the richest and deepest tin-mine in the world.

If an article is to deal exhaustively with the history of Dolcoath it ought to commence with the times when 'the inhabitants of that extremity of Britain called Bolerion' sought in streams and amongst rocks for tin to cast into cubes for the foreigners that came to Iktis, because it was then, assuredly, that Dolcoath's history commenced. But as there is a distracting variety of theories about the doings of the 'hospitable and civilised' early inhabitants of Cornwall and the whereabouts of Iktis, I prefer to let each one believe what pleases his fancy and pass to years of which more is known.

Dr. William Borlase, writing in 1746, mentioned Dolcoath as a 'very considerable mine,' and Dr. William Price thirty-three years later stated she was nearly one hundred fathoms deep. Subsequent progress must have been comparatively rapid, for when Dolcoath was stopped in 1787—because the

THE GREAT DOLCOATH

heavy outputs by the Anglesea mines had reduced the price of copper—she had reached a depth of 132 fathoms and yielded 1,250,000*l*. worth of copper.

In this year the copper standard was 67*l*.—lower than it had been for fourteen years—and in the succeeding twelve months sank to 57*l*. But a continuous rise set in after 1788, and by 1799 the standard was at the giddy height of 121*l*., far beyond what it had been for at least a quarter of a century. Stimulated by the prospect of big profits, a number of gentlemen restarted the mine, under the cost-book system, and worked her on a large scale. For labour alone in 1801 they paid 12,277*l*.; in the succeeding twelve months their produce of copper ore was sold for 21,149*l*.; and in 1803 there was a profit of 2,000*l*. But these figures look insignificant by the side of those of a few years later. The copper standard, which had been slowly improving, jumped from 136*l*. in 1804 to 169*l*. in 1805, and in the latter year Dolcoath made, on ore sold for 114,121*l*., a clear profit of 35,769*l*. It is sometimes stated that at mine meetings in the old days, when times were prosperous, the ruddy faces of adventurers beamed through the steam of many grogs from mid-day until far into the night, and, whether this was so or not, one feels sure that the Dolcoath meetings in 1805 were very interesting little gatherings. That those who attended took no heed of the morrow is proved by the division of the whole of the enormous profit except 6*l*., and I am tempted to suggest they stopped where they did because there were vast fields of fractions to be waded through before the 6*l*. could be distributed. Had the adventurers been possessed of that power of looking into the future which the Scotch call second-sight, they would have found the mine was never to have such days again while worked for copper. The standard diminished in the following year to 138*l*., and in 1807 to 120*l*., but even these prices permitted large profits, and Dolcoath was worked briskly year after year, over 1,600 men, women, and boys being employed.

Hitherto the profits had swelled and contracted with the price of copper, but now another and a very important thing had to be reckoned with. The vast lodes—the pride of the shareholders—became poorer, and by 1832 had so seriously decreased in value that people talked of an early abandonment of the mine. Every effort was made by the manager and the agents to discover further rich deposits of copper, but without success; and after years of anxiety it was, in 1836, agreed to let the water accumulate in the bottom of the mine, where the lodes were poor, and confine operations to ground above the 125 level.

In the year following that of enormous dividends, there had come to work at Dolcoath the twelve-year-old son of one of the agents, and after spending nine years on the mine he was made an underground agent. This studious young man, Captain Charles Thomas, had taken it into his head that if the copper deposits were followed down, rich tin ground would be met with; and, though men of science shook their heads and declared Dolcoath was practically a thing of the past, he persisted in the notion. When, in 1836, the adventurers resolved to abandon the bottom of the mine, he drew up a statement to show that the lower levels could be worked without loss, and armed with this and

[Photo by] DOLCOATH MINERS [Burrow, Camborne

goaded on by a conviction that the future of Dolcoath and Camborne depended entirely on deeper mining, he went to the adventurers when they met to confirm their resolution and persuaded them not to allow the water to rise above the 155 level, thus saving thirty fathoms from inundation. But even then there had been surrendered, much to his disappointment, twenty-five fathoms of the most promising part of the mine. A profitless period followed, and throughout the district it was believed nothing could save the mine, as no valuable copper was being found in the upper levels and the shareholders had set their faces against deep mining.

Evidently, however, the advocate of deep mining was thought well of, for when the manager, William Petherick, died, in 1844, Thomas was appointed to the position; and it was soon made evident that the experiences of the past few years had strengthened, if it were possible, his belief in deep mining. But as on this matter the proprietors were obdurate, if not inexorable, the manager endeavoured to reach his goal by easy stages. It has long been the practice of some miners to enter into contracts with the managers to work pieces of ground for a share of the profits made on the ore they send up. Thinking this would prove an admirable way of getting the 145 level worked, Captain Charles Thomas asked a number of 'tributers' to take pitches there and, when they agreed to do so, the shareholders, who could not lose a penny by the arrangement, consented to his proposals. In a short time these men opened very productive ground, which served the double purpose of infusing hope into all associated with the mine, and attracting tributers to other levels the manager was most anxious to see worked. Taking advantage of this success, Captain Thomas induced the adventurers to spend money on improved appliances for dressing the tin, and to let him pump out the twenty-five fathoms of water that had been in the mine since 1836. But he failed to bring all the shareholders to his side, and some were so strongly opposed to any attempt to convert Dolcoath into a tin-mine that they sold their shares and ended their connection with the company immediately it was decided to pump the water out. This, however, did not cause the manager to relax his efforts in the least.

When all the levels were open to the miners again, the manager found that the great metallic veins—which in the upper levels yielded rich copper ore, and in lower ones a not very valuable mixture of copper and tin—gave more tin as they were explored in depth; but his opinion was that a large sum would have to be spent before the mine could be placed on a firm footing, and he therefore advised the shareholders to lay out several thousands of pounds in going deeper. Many were afraid to try the experiment, and in that respect were in striking contrast to the average Cornish mine adventurer of a later date, whose pluck never falters while he is able to pay the calls made upon him. The largest individual shareholder at that time was Lady Basset, who had thirty-two of the 186 shares, and she came to the help of her co-adventurers by guaranteeing the repayment of all capital expended out of the dues which would come to her as owner of the land. Thereupon 3,084*l.* was spent as advised by Captain Thomas, who in 1853 had the supreme satisfaction of

TRAMMING TIN STUFF, 375 LEVEL

seeing the first dividend paid on tin. Profits were regularly made after that, and for many years the adventurers duly received large dividends every quarter.

To show at a glance what 'the pioneer of deep mining' did for Dolcoath it need only be stated that the value of the mine, calculated on the market prices of shares, rose from 4,000*l*. in 1846 to 90,000*l*. in 1868, and that during the intervening period 147,854*l*. was paid in dividends to the shareholders.

The news of what had been done in a Cornish mine spread throughout the mining world, and Captain Charles Thomas' advice was widely sought, with the result that he inspected nearly three hundred mines in Cornwall and Devon, besides others in Wales, Scotland, Ireland, Norway, and Prussia.

While Captain Charles Thomas was an underground agent his health began to fail, and though for a long time there were no symptoms of serious disease, he was, in 1867, obliged to give up his work at the mine, and in the succeeding year he died, respected by thousands of mining men and beloved by the Methodists of Camborne, with whom he had laboured practically all his life.

Within twelve months of the payment of the first dividend on tin Captain Charles Thomas brought his son, then fifteen, to learn mining at Dolcoath, and five or six years after he became an underground agent. In that capacity he was acting when his father retired, and the adventurers paid a compliment to his ability in making him manager. Captain Josiah Thomas proved himself a firm believer in deep mining by sinking shafts and driving levels with all possible speed, and he discovered tin ground the richness of which surprised men.

It seems that this revelation of immense wealth in a mine so recently regarded as exhausted caused adventurers throughout the county to feel what had yet been done in other mines was comparatively little, and that deeper down there lay limitless riches; for Dolcoath was again and again the burthen of their speeches, and they paid willingly, even gladly, to enable managers to carry out what a few years before would have been deemed the schemes of madmen.

Up to 1876 the miners' chief tools were a few bars of steel and a sledgehammer, with which men worked for hours in making a single hole to receive

THE GREAT DOLCOATH

the explosive. But in that year Captain Josiah Thomas introduced machines, driven by compressed air sent in pipes from the surface, for boring the rocks, and thus increased the output of the mine considerably. What this meant can be appreciated when it is remembered that two men with a boring machine make twenty holes while two men without a machine are making three. In another direction an advance was made at Dolcoath some years later. When the tin stuff is received from underground it is crushed into fine powder in order that the tin may be separated from the useless material with which it is associated in the lodes; and in 1892 Captain Josiah Thomas erected a set of Californian stamps which, it is claimed, crush at half the cost of the Cornish stamps in general use throughout the county. Numerous other improvements were made in the machinery and appliances by Captain Josiah Thomas, who, like his father, came to be regarded as the leader of Cornish mining. Besides directing the affairs of Dolcoath he preached from Methodist pulpits regularly, and filled prominent positions on the Mining Association and Institute of Cornwall and other bodies, whilst inspections of mines took him to various parts of the United Kingdom, the European Continent, and once to Dakota, in the United States.

Between the owner of the mine and those who had invested money to work her the relations were most amicable until about 1883, when a dispute arose to which, even at this distance of time, the older shareholders cannot refer without ' chewing the cud of bitter fancy.' To the advisers of the late Mr. G. L. Basset, the father of the present lord, it seemed that to open the mine ' in a miner-

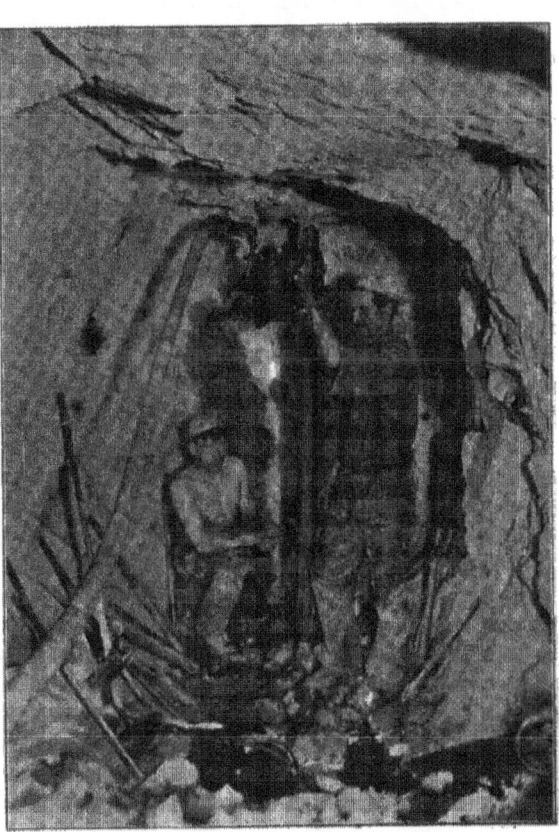

Photo by]   *[Burrow, Camborne*
USING A BORING MACHINE, 336 LEVEL

like manner' a new shaft would be necessary in the south part of the property, and the adventurers were informed that unless they agreed to make such a shaft 40,000*l*. would have to be paid to the lord when the new lease was taken up. The attitude of the owner of Tehidy was regarded with consternation, and the majority of those financially concerned did not hesitate to express their indignation frequently and forcibly. They admitted the dividends had been large—more than 30,000*l*. a year—but in the same breath emphasised the fact that Mr. Basset was taking 20,000*l*. a year in dues from mines and tin streams in the county, of which between 8,000*l*. and 9,000*l*. was paid by Dolcoath. As those working the mine were averse to spending scores of thousands of pounds to make a new shaft, and the lord showed no disposition to relent, the future of the concern was discussed with considerable uneasiness, and the price of shares rapidly fell 14*l*., representing 65,800*l*. on the total number held. At length the lord agreed to accept 25,000*l*., and that was paid with a long wail.

After this 'fine' had been met there was a resumption of dividends, which continued unbroken down to 1894, when thousands of tons of ground fell away with a mighty roar, and, breaking down the massive timber-work, buried the richest tin ground and eight miners. The disaster was the most terrible in the history of the mine, both from the number of lives lost and the difficulties it placed in the way of future profits. A popular description of the catastrophe was 'the bottom of Dolcoath has gone together,' and that best conveys an idea

[*Photo by*] [*Burrow, Camborne*

WHERE THE 'RUN' WAS, 412 LEVEL

of the hopeless jumble of timber, rocks, and rubbish that faced those who went to ascertain whether any of the missing men had escaped instantaneous death. While the seriousness of the situation thus created was distressing the officials, another 'run' of ground choked one of the principal shafts, and as no tin stuff could

A RICH LODE, 412 LEVEL

be drawn through it, the output of the mine fell off greatly.

It was now seen by the manager that practically a new mine would have to be opened under these runs, and the shareholders decided, in May 1895, to convert the company into a limited liability one and raise capital sufficient to accomplish this and make a new shaft, away from the old levels, in the south part, so as to avoid the possibility of communication between the 'new mine' and the surface being cut off by runs in the old workings. When the change in the company was effected Captain Josiah Thomas was appointed managing director, and the management of the property was entrusted to his son, Captain Arthur Thomas, who for some years was manager of a mine in South Africa.

This is a convenient point at which to review the working of the mine in the twenty-six or twenty-seven years while Captain Josiah Thomas was manager. In his father's reign the dividends amounted to 147,854*l*., making a total paid in dividends since 1799 of 305,395*l*. But so astounding was the progress from 1867 to 1894 that profits amounting to 644,000*l*. were made, while the mine doubled in extent and importance.

As this article is to include an account of a personal exploration of part of Dolcoath, I will endeavour, for the sake of those unacquainted with Cornish mining, to outline a few salient features of the operations.

Tin lodes are mineralised substances that have been deposited in fissures in the crust of the earth, where they stand for miles in length and no one knows how deep. Speaking generally, in the two western counties they run from east to west, and whilst some 'underlie,' or lean towards, north, others favour the south. The face of the 'country' resting on the side of a lode is termed the 'hanging wall,' because when the lode has been removed it overhangs; and the side of the country upon which the lode appears to be resting is known as the foot-wall.

The opening of a mine commences with the sinking of a shaft and the driving of tunnels, or 'levels,' twelve to twenty fathoms below one another. Levels are at first made seven feet high and six feet wide, and into them tramways are put to facilitate the removal of the tin stuff to the shaft. By degrees the spaces are increased in height, while the width is regulated by the size of the lode. In Dolcoath they are often more than thirty feet across, and enormous quantities of timber have to be employed to prevent the ground running together. The chief supports are balks of American pitch pine, thirty to forty feet long and eighteen inches to two feet square, which stretch from the foot-wall to the hanging wall and are supported by smaller timbers where necessary, the whole making a framework technically called a 'stull.' When miners have to take away a section of ground between two levels they cut a narrow shaft, termed a '.winze,' through the lode from one to the other, and this is gradually widened along the length of the level. Such a place, where men work week after week and month after month hacking away the lode, is a 'stope,' and down its rugged length the tin stuff falls to shoots opening on to tram-roads.

Of the many legends connected with St. Piran, the miners' saint, there is one I always think of when I see the slow and costly process by which tin is separated from the useless materials surrounding it in the lodes. When St. Piran lived in the wind-swept district bearing his name he collected a number of uncommon stones from the beach and the hill-side, and one day when 'preparing a humble meal' there flowed from a large black stone forming part of the fireplace a stream of liquid which was found to be pure tin.

Miners know of no such simple means of preparing tin for the market. The tin ore found in Cornwall contains, on an average, only three per cent. of tin, and the other ninety-seven parts, being practically useless, have to be got rid of. When sent up by the miners the tin stuff is of various sizes, and a number of 'bal girls' look it over—rejecting what is not worth dealing with and breaking the large rocks to lessen the work of the stamps. Water runs over the tin stuff as it is being pounded to powder by the great stamp-heads, and gushes through a fine screen, or 'grate,' on the other side loaded with tin and waste. The surcharged water spreads itself over planes of wood, known as 'frames,' and, as the tin is specifically heavier than the waste, the grains of mineral lodge on these prepared surfaces while the waste flows away. But the tin is not yet ready for the market. The stuff caught has to be freed from deleterious substances by burning, and then there are further washings in tin-dressing sheds, where women are employed largely. From the mine the tin is sent as dark grains—'black tin'—to furnaces in different parts of West Cornwall, where, by smelting, blocks of pure tin are obtained.

Several times it had been suggested to me that I should go to the bottom of Dolcoath to see the rich ground spoken of at shareholders' meetings, and when I declared a readiness to do so, the manager, Captain Arthur Thomas, kindly offered to accompany me.

It was a novel experience to find myself in miners' flannels and fustians —with a 'bowler' of hard rough felt for head-gear and half a dozen candles

THE GREAT DOLCOATH

suspended to a button of my jacket—kneading a lump of clay that was to be my candle-holder.

You can go down Dolcoath Mine by ladders fixed on one side of the shaft or, as we did, in a gig, which is an iron box thirteen feet long hanging in the shaft to a wire rope worked by a powerful engine. A shelf divides the gig into two equal compartments, and, with an adjustable iron bar across the open front of each, eight men usually ride in it.

The descent commenced slowly, but when we had got beyond the last glimmer of daylight the speed grew faster and faster until we must have travelled at the rate of two hundred fathoms a minute. Riding in the gig was not like sliding down a modern cliff railway. The angle of the shaft is not uniform, and consequently the gig bumped and jumped between the wooden guides and we lurched correspondingly, whilst the candle's light showed us the slimy, rugged nature of the shaft through which thousands upon thousands of tons of tin stuff had been drawn and hundreds of men had ridden to and from their work at all hours of the day and night.

Gradually the speed slackened, and presently we halted at a point where there opened away before us a long dark cavern whose roughly-hewn sides re-echoed the steady fall of sledge-hammers, the rattle of trams coming towards the shaft, and the voices of miners. We pulled a lever communicating with the men at surface, and down slid the gig with its half a dozen miners to deeper levels.

Measurements given in speeches at a meeting convey no adequate idea of the immensity and solemnity of those great spaces men have hewn out of the earth half a mile below surface. And the excellent photographs Mr. J. C. Burrow has produced, although imparting a knowledge more clear than words can, deprive the mine of some of its eerie

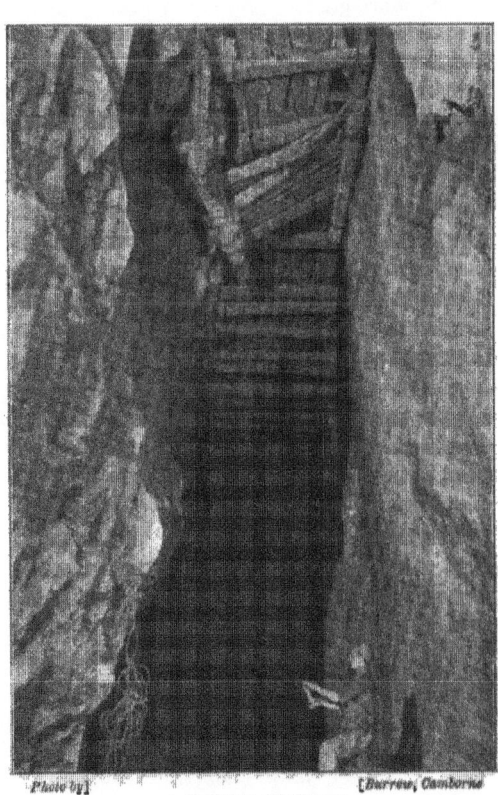

A HANGING TRAMROAD

grandeur. For light is essential to photography, and darkness is a part of mining.

Each with a candle, we trudged along—now passing through openings that stretched away into empty blackness, and now bending our backs to pass through tunnels leading to other and larger spaces.

Going along one level I discerned miners working far up the rocky surface of a large stope by the light of candles stuck to their hats or to projecting rocks, and then, further on, we came to another stope where, sixty feet or more down, I caught sight of a group of men in a circle of dim light, the sounds of whose voices were borne to us as hollow whispers between the regular beats of the hammers, and served to emphasise the distance between us. There was a constant traffic along the level dividing these tin-producing areas, and more than once we had to step aside while the trams, with candles stuck to their sides, came from out the gloom and disappeared in the darkness beyond.

Near the shafts the air is fresh, and pleasant to breathe; but when you get away from those main channels and reach the narrow tunnels being driven to open more ground, you find the atmosphere hot and oppressive, and I felt the perspiration trickle down my face even at the sight of the half-naked miners working there.

Close to one of the shafts we rested after visiting hot 'ends,' but presently loud reports boomed like thunder through the levels, the walls seemed to tremble, and the air pulsated about my face, whilst pieces of rock fell close by. So, thinking we were too near blasting operations, we adjusted our candles and resumed the journey.

I mentioned that ladders occupy a part of each shaft. They run almost perpendicularly to the bottom of the mine and are shut off at each level by a trap-door. Raising one of these iron doors my companion went down, asking me to follow. The sound of his footsteps soon died away in the distance, for the progress I made was not rapid. Left in that long narrow way I began to wonder how far I should fall supposing my wet hands failed to grasp firmly the bars shown by the light of the candle in my hat; and when the skip thundered through the shaft I had visions of myself falling and knocking the mine manager off his legs—to fall, perhaps, a score of fathoms below.

But we reached the 412 without such a swift transition, and went to the place where, in 1894, the eight men were buried by thousands of tons of rock. The stull under which the men rushed for protection when they heard the terrific noise of ground falling was regarded as an excellent piece of workmanship, and it happened that Mr. Burrow photographed it not long before the disaster. But all the great balks were broken as matches in the hand of a strong man, and those who cut a passage through the mass were day after day and night after night alternately blasting rocks and sawing timber—fearing all the while that they might dislodge more ground, and thus place additional obstacles between them and where they could hear a voice at rare intervals. As I looked into the little cavity amongst rocks and timber from which the only man who escaped alive was taken, an involuntary shudder came over me at the thought of being doubled up in that hole, with darkness and death for companions, for a whole week. 'Where is he now?' I asked, remembering how frail he was when brought to surface. 'Oh,' came the answer, ' he went to America some time after, and is now working in South Africa.'

Although we were half a mile below daylight there was yet the 455 level, where the miners were working in hot ends with boring machines, and sending to surface the richest stuff found in the mine. For under the 'run' there is being opened ground that promises to lead to the payment of further big dividends.

Whether the men who work there at a settled price per day find a potent spell in the rich ground, I know not ; but tributers do, and I well remember an old tributer telling me, as I sat by his peat fire in a lonely Dartmoor cottage, that when he worked in a silver-lead mine near Tavistock, the bright ore and the prospect of a good pay-day were so fascinating that he could scarcely tear himself away from the mine to go home to sleep.

Half a score of miners working 'afternoon core' got out of the gig as we reached the shaft, and, with kegs of water for drinking slung across their shoulders, went along the level towards their work, singing blithely. In three minutes we were at the top of the shaft in the brilliant sunshine of a July day.

Do not imagine that only what is worth seeing at Dolcoath is underground. There are massive high-class pumping, winding, and air-compressing engines at surface, besides the tin-dressing machinery, in which changes are about to be made which will, it is contended, revolutionise the whole process and effect great saving in the cost of treating each ton of stuff. With the advent of mechanical stone-breaking and the new tin-dressing appliances, the number of girls who 'spall' the tin and work on the tin-dressing floors must be reduced greatly,

Photo by]   *[Burrow, Camborne*
FILLING A TRAM, 412 LEVEL

and the mine will lose some of its features that are novel and attractive.

This wonderful mine is at present yielding tin ore at the rate of 75,000 tons a year, and, notwithstanding the introduction of labour-saving machinery, provides employment for 1,300 men, women, and boys, whose wages reach nearly 45,000*l.* a year. From 1799 to the end of 1897 there was taken from her

Photo by]   SPALLERS   [*Burrow, Camborne*

mineral sold for 6,118,366*l.*, of which 3,766,487*l.* was for tin, 2,328,435*l.* for copper, and the remainder for arsenic, silver, and cobalt. The proportion of silver was slight, but at one time the ore sent up contained an appreciable quantity of that metal, and out of part of it a centrepiece was made and presented to the lord of the mine.

In a roll-call of those who have worked at Dolcoath would be heard more than a few noteworthy names besides those I have referred to. A cursory glance shows me Richard Trevithick, sen., father of the famous engineer, was manager there in 1765, whilst some years later his illustrious son occupied the position of chief engineer. And then there was Rodolph Eric Raspe, a 'learned and scientific German,' who left his fatherland somewhat hurriedly after pawning valuables belonging to the nation, and was officially described as 'a man with red hair who usually appears in a scarlet dress embroidered with gold, but sometimes in black, blue, or grey clothes.' He came into Cornwall in or about 1781, and while employed as 'storemaster' at Dolcoath wrote and published his 'Travels of Baron Munchausen.'

ALBERT BLUETT.

THE PISKIES

WE were not good enough for Heaven,
    Not bad enough for Hell:
And therefore unto us 'twas given
    Unseen on earth to dwell:

To listen by the moonlit thatch,
    By window-blinds to lurk,
To watch men on their knees, and watch
    Men go about their work.

We watch in hope to be forgiven;
    But still we cannot tell
Whose deeds are good enough for Heaven,
    Whose bad enough for Hell.

Q.

POLLY POSTES

THE great road from London to Falmouth, after leaving Launceston, ascends continuously, except only for a dip into the valley of the Inney, till it reaches the ridge of the Bodmin moors.

From Five Lanes in Altarnon parish it leaves culture and trees behind, and climbs the desolate moors for some thirteen or fourteen miles, from eight to nine hundred feet above the sea.

Although crossing moors it commands no beautiful scenery. In its construction what was sought was a tolerably even surface, and the dips to basins containing bogs and the rises to craggy tors were alike avoided. The traveller in quest of the real splendours of these moors must desert the road and go some four or five miles north or south, towards Brown Willy or Killmar.

Although at one time this excellent road was much traversed by coaches every day, and it was a main artery of communication, at present scarcely any two or four wheeled conveyances pass over it; it is a convenience to the cyclist and to the pedestrian only. No coach, no van, no waggon conveys passengers and goods along it; and the lonely dwellers in scattered farms or cottages are as much cut off from the circulation of life and ideas as if they were banished to Scilly or to Lundy.

About five miles on one side of this highway, but whether to the north or to the south I will not say; near, however, to the steep flank of the granite mass where it heaves itself out of the altered slate and volcanic beds that engirdle it; lived Roger Kerneu, a stonecutter, along with his aged mother. Their cottage, called 'Nankivel,' or 'Nancivale,' was built against a steep bank, and was constructed of rude blocks of granite, quite unshaped, but neatly set together, and the joints filled in with turf. It was thatched with reeds from the bog, and was of one storey alone. It possessed but a single chimney, and comprised but one room, which served every purpose. The window was exceedingly small, and such panes of glass as remained in the casement were so dirty as to admit hardly any light. But the door was usually kept open, partly to afford light, mainly to assist the smoke from the open hearth in getting out of the cottage.

Roger Kerneu roved over the moorside for a mile or two and took stone wherever he listed. Not an errant block was spared, and when a node of granite showed through the moss, he attacked it and sliced out of it gate-posts or window-sills. The entire district was marked by his chisels, and not a piece of native rock remained that did not bear tokens of having been split by his 'jumper.' As to the precious relics of prehistoric populations within reach, he effaced them all.

Roger Kerneu possessed a rough moor cob, and this brute he fastened by chains to a strong 'truckamuck' he had, on which he bound the pieces of stone he had shaped or at least cut, and he made the cob drag the load down the steep and rugged track from the moor to the lowlands, and deposited the stones beside the way, where that way began to be practicable for wheeled conveyances, and thence farmers or builders fetched them at their convenience.

No one who has not seen a moor stonecutter at work has any conception of the facility with which he manipulates prodigious masses of granite. Any block, so long as he can succeed with a lever in moving it sufficiently to slip a marble under one corner, is at his mercy. Masses of rock that to the eye of the inexperienced would seem impossible of being turned about and moved from place to place, yielded to the unaided labours of this one man, helped indeed occasionally by Sparrow, his horse.

I have said that Roger's house door was usually open, but after a certain period this ceased to be true. Thenceforth it was not only shut but locked. This was what produced this change: Roger's mother died.

Now it was some time after only, and uncertainly, that the rumour got about that the old woman was dead; but Roger had made no movement towards burying her.

At length the report gained consistency and force, so that the police and the registrar deemed it expedient to mount to the moor to inquire into the matter.

They found the house open, but no Roger there; he was away 'nogging out' gate-posts. They made free to enter, and, to their horror, discovered the body of the old woman lying in a sort of bed dug out of the bank in the rear, littered with heather and bracken, and the rats had gnawed and horribly defaced the corpse.

The man was at once sought out, and an explanation demanded.

Now Roger was a fellow of few words, morose, shy, uncivilised. All the explanation he could give was that 'it warn't convaynient to bury her. He had an order for a lot of stone quoins for a new bridge as was bein' built; and he thought there wor' no hurry—her wouldn't run away, and the longer her wor keeped, sure the more her'd shrump up.'

If this had happened anywhere else there would have been a grand disturbance over it; but no one in the parish desired to have a fuss. An obliging surgeon signed an affidavit that the woman had died of old age, and the registrar gave the required order for her interment, and the old woman, or what remained of her, was consigned, earth to earth, ashes to ashes, in the parish churchyard.

This interference of the authorities with his liberty and this invasion of his house so offended Roger that henceforth he kept his door locked; and once, when he saw two pedestrians approach his house, though it was merely to inquire their way, he rushed out upon them with his gun and threatened to shoot them if they came nearer.

In the West of England the natives dearly love a nickname, and after this Roger was often called 'Shrump.'

Now in a very short while the stonecutter found that there was inconvenience in solitude. He had to light his own fires, cook his own food, go his own errands. This inconvenience induced him at length to resolve on altering his condition.

Within three miles was a farm, half-way down the side of the moors, called Cargantic, and in it lived a farmer of the name of Trewen, who had a daughter Mary. Trewen was a man of limited education; his daughter was by no means comely, a rough 'blowstering' girl, but handy and muscular.

One day Roger Shrump appeared before the farm, and called out Trewen. He led him into the yard.

'Look'y 'ere,' said the stonecutter, 'do'y see your cart-linney restin' on them postes?'

'Yes, I reckon; what o' that?'

'Well now, I say, them postes be poor miserable bits o' wood.'

'To be sure.'

'And what be more, they'm rotten.'

'I reckon they be going home.'

'They'll fa' and bring the whole concarn down.'

'I'll get fresh postes.'

'And have the same trouble again. Why not have two purty stone postes.'

'They'd cost a cruel sight of money.'

'No they won't.'

'But they will.'

'Not if us can make a deal.'

'As how?'

'Now look'y 'ere. I've got two beauties, proper beauties, just about the right height, and not too wide and big. Now I don't mind, I'm a bit dull up yonder to Nankivel, and I want some 'un to rin errands, and boil my pertaties. If you'll give me Polly—you shall have them two postes.'

'What do you mean? Make her your wife?'

'Ees, I reckon.'

'Have you spoke wi' she.'

'Noa—but look'y 'ere; I'll bring they two postes down on my truckamuck, wi' Sparrow, and I can drag Polly back on it. 'Twill save a lot o' trouble.'

'You must see her.'

'Well, send her out to me.'

So the farmer went within, and called his daughter and gave her a flying hint that there was a suitor outside soliciting the honour of her hand. So Polly at once put on a clean apron, combed her hair, and went forth.

Roger was measuring the supports to the cart-shed, beneath which, out of the rain, reposed not only the cart, but also the little gig in which Trewen was wont to drive to and from market on Saturdays.

'Well, Roger Shrump, what do'y want, now, wi' me?'

'First and foremost, can'y peel and bile a pertato?'

'I reckon I can. But bain't this goin' first and foremost like the bullock as slided back'ards down a well?'

'You must take what I say in the order I gives,' said Roger; 'then as to the bit o' rent I has to pay the Squire, I hev to go to the court twice a year and pay up, and it don't 'gree wi' my constitution to go among genlevolks. Could'y now take the bit o' rent for me them days.'

'If you made it worth my while.'

'O, I reckon I cu'd do that by givin' myself in.'

'How do'y mean?'

'Well, now, look'y 'ere. If you'll go to the shop for me when I want to buy a bit o' baccy, or some odds and ends; and if you'll keep the fire from goin' out, and you'll bile my bacon and pertaties, and look after the geese, and take my rent to the court—I don't mind, I ain't so cruel partic'lar, but I'll take you to live along wi' me.'

'Well, I don't mind,' said Polly.

'Then you get along wi' what you want on to the truckamuck when I drag down the postes.'

'That won't do,' said Polly, 'we must be married by the passon.'

''Twill come expensive.'

'Not so amazin!'

'If you partic'lar wish it, I'll do so, though I don't see the sense of it. But I don't care, I've got a crooked bit o' coorse granite, as I've begun to make into a pig trough. If he'll do the job for that, he shall have the pig trough, and Sparrow shall drag 'n down.'

Thus the matter was settled. All were satisfied, Trewen got his 'postes,' the parson his crooked pig trough, and Shrump his 'missus.'

'But mind you this,' said Roger to his wife, 'I won't have no strangers meddlin' here. If any comes, you knack their little 'eads off, or shoot 'em through the middle.'

The life of Roger Shrump ran smoothly enough; perhaps he had not anticipated greater things of Polly than that she should boil potatoes and bacon, run errands and carry his rent, and these were things she could perform. Nor had she idealised Roger into a hero of romance. She knew beforehand what he was, so that in her married life there was no disillusioning. The story of the postes had spread, and Polly was called Polly Postes accordingly.

They were certainly happy together in a quiet undemonstrative manner.

When the trifling occupations of the household were over, she would go with her knitting to where he was at work, seat herself on a block of stone, and there continue her knitting and occasionally exchange words with him. She was even summoned occasionally to assist with the lifting of a block by inserting stones beneath it whilst Roger heaved with his lever or 'bar of ire' as he termed it.

So a twelvemonth passed, and then Polly fell ill. She had caught a severe chill.

Her father came up to Nankivel, and finding her in a high fever and with short breathing, said, 'It's inflammation. I know it. I had a cow tooked thus, and there's nothing for inflammation like an embrocation. I've tried it on the cow and also on my 'oss when her strained her fetlock.'

So Trewen descended to Cargantic and returned with a bottle.

'There, Roger,' said he, 'there you be, terrible good for inflammation. Embrocation for external application only—writ large—there you see. Hope Polly'll be better to-morrow. If you've time you come and let me know, or I'll send up one o' the boys.'

Some time in the evening Trewen found Roger in his house.

'What ha' brought you here? How's Polly?'

'Well—you've gone and made a purty mess,' said Shrump.

'Why, what have I done?'

'You've gi'ed me the wrong bottle.'

'No, I have not. That's the embrocation.'

'I don't know what you may call it, but you have killed Polly! Her's dead as a biled rabbit!'

'Polly dead?'

'Ees, I reckon. After her took that there bottle, her was ravin' mad like, and then after a bit went tottle, and died right on end!'

'You don't mean to say you made her drink the embrocation?'

'Ees, I did. You gave 'n me.'

'But it was for external application only.'

'What do I know of 'starnal application? I'm no schollard.'

'But it was written on the bottle—that is to say it was printed.'

'I can't read.'

'And Polly be dead?'

''Ees, I reckon.'

'Whatever is to be done? She'll be crowned.'

'I don't know. I'll have no strangers come ferriting in my house, I knows that!'

'But go there they will.'

'I shall shoot 'em if they do!'

'You're a terrible obstinate man!'

''Ees, I reckon.'

'And haven't no more edication than a flea!'

'No, I reckon.'

Then ensued silence.

'Now look'y 'ere,' said the stonecutter after awhile. 'I don't want no onpleasantness, nor do you. So let me heave Polly on to my truckamuck. I can fasten her there tight enough wi' my chains, and I'll put Sparrow in, and run her down to Cargantic.'

'You may do that if you please,' said Trewen. 'But the crowner will be here to a certainty.'

He also mused and bit at his thumb.

Another pause ensued.

After much consideration, Trewen said: 'Right you be, Shrump. Us don't want no onpleasantness, and onpleasantness there will be when that confounded crowner comes here, and larns all about that there bottle! He'll have you up and try you for murder!'

'I reckon it'll be purty bad for you, farmer. He'll say it was you as brought that there dratted bottle as did it!'

'But I said it was embrocation.'

'He won't be content wi' that. You never told I what embrocation was for!'

'But I said for external application only.'

'You used larned words as warn't English. How was I to understand that?'

'Well,' said Trewen. 'Don't us have no onpleasantness about it. I'll tell y' what us'll say and swear to! I'll admit right enough as I brought up the bottle, and I'll say as how I left it at Nankivel. But you was out, noggin' of stones.'

'Aye—right enough,' threw in Roger.

'Well, and while you was out, what did Polly do, but her drinked it up, every drop, thinking as how it was cough mixture!'

'That'll do bravely.'

'And when you comed in, you was struck all of a heap, and took on terrible!'

'Right—that'll do fust-rate.'

'And then us got Polly up on the truckamuck to run her down to the doctor, but her died on the way.'

'That's prime,' said Roger.

'Well now, Shrump,' said Trewen, 'you just run the little tale over wi' me once right through, then we'll have it one like the tother, all alike, and they won't get nothin' else out of us, 'cos there was no one else up to Nankivel but Sparrow, and he don't count. You see, Shrump, I don't want to have no onpleasantness in the family, and if you was hung it might make onpleasantness, you know. Beside, there'd be the lawyers; and what iver we do, we must keep them out of the fingering of it!'

So the whole concern was arranged. Polly was taken down to Cargantic, and there a coroner's inquest was held, and all that came out was what was agreed upon between Trewen and Kerneu. They stuck to their tale; there was no bringing them from it. Polly had been a little off her head with fever, and had inadvertently swallowed the embrocation. No one was guilty. The coroner did think fit to rebuke Kerneu for leaving his wife alone in the house when ill; but, as he said, there was absolutely no one he could have called in, and he really did not suppose that his wife was in danger. The coroner also animadverted on the chaining of a sick woman on to a truckamuck. But here, again, a reply was ready—before a doctor could be communicated with and brought to that remote spot, her condition would have been worse. It was done to save time—perhaps as much as four important hours—and as to the truckamuck, no other conveyance—nothing on wheels—could possibly travel over the rough track. The truckamuck was the sole vehicle practicable. The verdict was 'Accidental death.' After the funeral, as farmer Trewen and stonecutter Kerneu were standing together outside Cargantic, before the latter pursued his way uphill to the moor, Roger said:

'Look'y 'ere, farmer, I reckon now I'll have them two postes back.'

'What postes?'

'Them I gave you in exchange for Polly. Them as supports the beam o' your cartshed.'

'I'll be hanged if you do!' retorted Trewen. 'A deal is a deal. You had my Polly and I had your postes!'

'That's all very well, but you tooked your Polly back after you'd killed her!'

'I killed her!' echoed Trewen; 'I like that. It was you as made her drink the embrocation.'

'But I'd never have gived it her if you hadn't a brought it.'

'You made her drink it, and you must take the consekences. I keep them postes.'

'Will you? we shall see. I've had a order for two just about their length.'

'Then you must nogg out two more.'

'But I can't come on a bench of granite fitty.'

'That's your concarn. Them postes be mine, and mine they remain. You had my Polly.'

'But you took her back to Cargantic.'

''Twas your truckamuck and Sparrow as did that.'

'Because you agreed to have her returned.'

'I don't care, I keep them postes.'

'We shall see.'

'I don't want no onpleasantness,' said Trewen.

'No more do I, but onpleasantness there must be unless I get my postes back again.'

So they parted.

Nothing happened further for a fortnight. Then, one day Roger Kerneu drew some blocks of granite down to the place where he usually deposited the stones, but instead of returning the same night to Nankivel, he remained below and put his horse into a field. He himself disappeared. He lay in a barn till about midnight, and then, armed with a 'bar of ire,' he took his way to Cargantic, and entering the shippen set to work at the foundations of the posts that supported the cart-shed. Having freed one from the ground, he lowered it by means of a chain fastened about it and passed over a beam, till it lay its length on the ground. Everyone in the farmhouse was asleep, and he was undisturbed. Next he attacked the second post.

There was a difficulty in the matter: the main beam of the linney rested on these props, but then it was also supported by the walls at the extremities. On this Roger calculated when he began to loosen the second post. Unhappily for him the beam was not continuous, but was composed of two loosely united by a splice.

He worked hard till he had disengaged the post, but no sooner had he removed the head of this from the beam, than down came the latter upon him, struck him to the ground, and fell across him so as to make him incapable of rising. Indeed, so severely had it injured him, that even had it been lifted off he could not have stood.

Very early Trewen came out, and to his dismay saw that his cartshed was wrecked and that the wrecker was his son-in-law, who lay prostrate under the beam.

'What darned mischief ha' you been up to there?' he asked.

'I'm been trying to get away the postes,' replied the injured man. 'You know very well they belong to I, since you took back Polly.'

'I don't know nothing of the sort,' retorted Trewen.

'Well now, look'y 'ere,' said Roger, 'I've been lying 'ere for a gude many hours, I reckon, and will you believe me—I seem'd as I saw Polly—her came to me from out o' the graveyard, and her sent a message to you.'

'Did she? then why didn't she come straight to me.'

'Because you was sleeping as sound as a pig, her said, so as her couldn't do nothing with you, her camed to me.'

'Well, and what did her say?'

'Her said, said she, "Tell my vayther, as how it be my wish he should let them postes go, that there may be no onpleasantness between you."'

'I bain't going to let 'em go,' said Trewen.

'You listen to me,' pursued Roger from under the beam, 'her argued the whole matter beautiful, just like scriptur'. Her said, when Roger—that is me —tooked I up to Nankivel, then everyone sed as I was Polly Postes, 'cos as how he had gived up two fine granite posts in exchange for I.'

'Well, what of that?'

'You're comin' to it, if you'll be patient and listen,' said Roger. 'Then her said, "When I was crowned, none o' the jury, no, nor the crowner, sed a word about me as Polly Postes, but spoke o' me as Polly Kerneu; and tell vayther to look in the parish register and see if I be buried under the name of Kerneu or Postes. And if he finds Postes there, then I'm content they two pieces of granite as Roger nogged out shall remain at Cargantic; but if he finds that the name Postes is gived up, that's an evidence and a token as how the two postes is to be a-gived up and returned to Roger Kerneu." There now, what ha' you to answer to that?'

'What I've got to answer to that,' replied Trewen, 'is that this be all rotten nonsense. I don't call that an argiment, I don't. And now I think I'll call up the men and have you out from under that beam. But I ain't going to surrender the postes.'

Accordingly the injured man was relieved from the mass of wood that had fallen across him, and he was removed into the house and put to bed, as it was discovered that he was so injured as to be unable to maintain himself on his feet.

'You ain't goin' to give me no embrocation?' asked he, 'as you did to Polly.'

'I give embrocation! It wor you, like an ignorant stoopid idjot as you wos. No, I've sent for the doctor.'

The surgeon arrived a couple of hours later, and at once pronounced the case as hopeless. Roger had received internal injuries that must prove fatal within a very few hours.

Soon after, the rector arrived. He had heard of the accident.

When doctor and parson were gone, then Roger called out for Trewen to come to him.

The farmer mounted the stairs to the bedroom, and entered it with an expression of dogged determination on his face.

'Now look'y 'ere,' said the dying man. 'I've been turning over them postes in my 'ead, and I sees it all clear as daylight.'

He put up the thumbs of both his hands from above the bedclothes.

'There's a little bit o' red paper as was on top of the cork o' yond bottle. Will you oblige me wi' tearin' off a mite and lickin' it and stickin' it on this 'ere thumb?'

The farmer complied.

'And there's a bit yond of bright green band as was round an antilope packet' (he meant envelope). 'Will you now tear off a bit o' that and lick it and stick it on the end of 'tother thumb?'

The farmer did as was desired.

The two thumbs protruded from the bedclothes, each furnished with a little paper cap, one of red, the other of green.

'Now then,' said the dying man. 'This 'ere thumb o' mine wi' the green paper on it be Nankivel, and this 'ere bit o' paper on it be the postes. That there other thumb o' mine be Cargantic, and thickey red paper atop o' he be Polly. Will you now just oblige me wi' liftin' the bits o' paper, and changing of them?'

The farmer complied with this request.

'Now, then,' said Roger, triumphantly, 'you see, Polly—the red paper — hev come to Nankivel, and so the green paper, as is the granite postes, be gone to Cargantic! That's right, I reckon. Please to change 'em again.'

'Now, I don't want no onpleasantness—' began the farmer.

'Change 'em, it's an argiment,' said Shrump.

'Well—' said Trewen sulkily, and shifted the bits of paper to their former position.

'Now, you see,' exclaimed Roger, 'when Polly be come back to Cargantic, in course and naturally back goes the postes to Nankivel. If that ain't an argiment as you can understand, you're a born fool!'

'It's not an argiment,' said the farmer. 'It was you as brought Polly here, with your own truckamuck, and your own 'oss, Sparrow. Now to be right you must fetch the postes back, same way!'

'I don't see it,' said Roger, with a little doubt in his voice.

'But I do! It is plain as my nose on my face!'

'Well, look'y 'ere,' said the dying man. 'Let's split the difference.!'

'I won't split no difference! You go on, and think of 'eaven : the parson told you to.'

'How can I think of 'eaven till them postes be settled?'

'Oh, they'll be settled fast enough.'

'Look'y 'ere, we'll split the difference,' persisted Roger. 'I reckon my time is short, and I'll soon be in the graveyard. You stick one of them postes above Polly's head and the other above mine, and say no more.'

'I'll think about it,' was all that could be wrung from Trewen.

Before nightfall Roger Kerneu was dead; before the week was out he was buried.

The posts were refixed to sustain the roof of the cartshed.

'I don't want no onpleasantness,' said Trewen. 'And to have to pay half a sovereign for two new ones would be cruel onpleasant, so here they bide. Roger—he didn't understand an argiment. Bless you, he were no schollard.'

S. BARING-GOULD.

TO CORNISH MAIDS

Now listen, all fair Cornish maids,
    Down in the West Countree,
It is a lover who upbraids,
    So turn and pity me.

I loved the fairest Cornish maid
    In all the West Countree;
And at her feet my heart I laid,
    But she never did pity me.

Her eyes were like the soft grey dawn
    Where the sun shall surely be;
But neither life nor light was drawn
    From those dear eyes for me.

Her hands were sea-foam, and her voice
    Like the sighing summer sea;
The one ne'er bade my heart rejoice,
    And the other ne'er welcomed me.

There came a stranger, lean and old,
    To spoil the West Countree;
He dazed her eyes with pearl and gold,
    And she turned away from me.

The servants stand about her door,
    She fareth daintily;
But sorrow bideth ever more
    With her, and eke with me.

But still my love's the fairest maid
    In all the West Countree;
And I pray by love her soul be stayed,
    Though she never did pity me.

RICCARDO STEPHENS.

WRESTLING

THE CORNISH AND DEVONSHIRE STYLES

WRESTLING is a very ancient game. Jacob wrestled with an angel, recorded in Scripture of great antiquity. The Greeks wrestled at the Isthmian and Olympic games, and later the Amphitheatre of Rome was a wrestling ring. It was a game in those days for the amusement of the public, though it was a matter of life and death. The wrestlers played without clothing, and they anointed their bodies with grease to make the hold or grip a slippery piece of work.

At the present day in India wrestling matches can be seen between the natives, who play as the ancients did, without clothing, and their play is a serious affair.

The player's hold was round the body, and the fall was severe. The player who gave the fall fell as heavily as he could on the fallen man, and if the fallen man was maimed, or, better still, killed, great was the joy of the public.

The word *wrestle* is English, not of the Greek or Roman classics, and is always pronounced by the players of Cornwall and Devonshire *wrastle*. It is wrestling in Chaucer, and in old verse; there is also in Dr. Murray's 'Oxford English Dictionary,' under the word ' HEEL, 20, 1600,' a quotation from Shakespeare's 'As You Like It '—' It is young Orlando who tript up the *wrastler's* heeles, and your heart, both in an instant.' It would appear, therefore, that *wrastling* is good old English, and so let our West Countrymen wrastle. The word is a fine word, and lends itself to metaphor, as when a holy man wrestles

ABRAHAM CANN
Height, 5 ft. 8¼ in.; weight, 12 st. 7 lb.; age, 30
(*From an old print.*)

in prayer, though the allegory may be somewhat obscure to Worldly-wiseman. I knew an under-gardener, given to quoting Scripture, who said he had been 'wrestling with the Devil all the morning, and had a draw'd un a vine turn.' What sort of temptation the Devil may have represented in his case did not appear. Wrestle, therefore, is a fine word, and to wrestle an undoubtedly fine and ancient game.

There are only two styles of wrestling in England worth talking about. The West Country—Cornwall and Devonshire style; and the North Country — Cumberland and Westmoreland style. There is, or was, a Lancashire style, which calls for no particular notice. The contrast between the North Country style and the West Country style is great, and explains by comparison the characteristics of the West Country style. In the West Country players play for a hitch. In the North Country the hold is taken more after the manner of the ancients; each player rests his chin on the right shoulder of the other, and grasping him round the body, each having his left arm over the right shoulder, and the right arm under the left shoulder of the other, clasps hands at the back. This is a firm hold, without playing for a hitch, and the wrestle for a fall is a matter of skill, strength, and weight. A fall is a fall, there is no question of a 'fair back,' and sometimes a wrestler, in giving a fall, fell also on his man as heavily as he could, inflicting much injury.

In Shakespeare's 'As You Like It,' Charles, the Duke's wrestler, breaks the ribs of three sons of an old man.

Orlando says, 'But let your fair eyes, and gentle wishes, go with me to my trial: wherein if I be foiled, there is but one shamed that was never gracious ; if killed, but one dead that is willing to be so.'

On the Duke saying in the case of Orlando, 'You shall try but one fall,' Charles answers, 'No, I warrant your grace; you shall not entreat him to a second, that have so mightily persuaded him from a first.'

WRESTLING

But Charles is thrown, cannot speak, and is borne out.

This wrestling in Shakespeare's day—and Shakespeare was sure to know all about it—was evidently in the North Country style, and rough play enough.

Rosalind says, 'Young man, have you challenged Charles the wrestler?'

'No, fair princess,' says Orlando, 'he is the general challenger: I come but in, as others do, to try with him the strength of my youth.'

In the West Country style there would have been a ring prepared, and anyone might have thrown in his cap as a challenge to any other who was ready to take his part in the play.

There have been, and there are still, instances in the West Country when a wrestler of repute will challenge another, and will play it out, the best of three falls, as it is in the North Country; but a proper wrestling match in the West Country is a different affair altogether.

Polkinghorne and Abraham Cann played a famous challenge match at Morris Town, Devonport, in 1826. Polkinghorne, an enormous man of great power and fame, was the Cornish champion, and played the Cornish play. Abraham Cann was above the middle height as a man, endowed with surprising strength of limb, especially in the legs, and played the Devonshire play.

There has always been a dispute about this match, and the best authorities seem to pronounce it to have been a drawn game. Enthusiasts on one side or the other claim the falls, the best of three, for their own county champion. Abraham Cann is said to have kicked mightily on the occasion; some say he was allowed but one shoe, and it is not unlikely that the three falls, or the two out of three, were not given by either.

Gundry, the champion of Cornwall, played a match with a North Country player. The North Country man, justly confident perhaps in his own powers, said that Gundry might take any *hitch* he pleased. As he was to play the North Country style against the West Country style, he had to wear the West Country jacket for Gundry's accommodation. Gundry took his own particular hitch, and reduced the North Country man to something like clay in the hands of the potter.

Gundry is here dressed in his ordinary clothes, with his champion's belts and his wrestling jacket.

GUNDRY, CHAMPION OF CORNWALL

SHAKING HANDS

West Country wrestling in the style proper and peculiar to Cornwall and Devonshire is played in a large ring, sometimes on the turf, or on a spot of ground under cover or otherwise prepared for a fall with sawdust. It used to be (it is sad to write such bygone words) at well-known times, at well-known places, such as Whitsuntide at some great fair, where all the wrestling world in Cornwall or Devonshire, or both, would assemble.

In describing the West Country play it will be seen that it is quite distinct and different from any other style of play. Also that the Cornish and Devonshire styles are the same, though a variation has taken place, not improbably the consequence of some champion players in each county playing the play that suited them best, followed afterwards by all players of their county.

The ring is open to all comers, and any man may throw in his cap, to try a turn with any other who does the same.

The wrestling dress is peculiar to the West Country, and marks the style of play. It consists of breeches or trousers. In the days of breeches the leg was a handsome limb to be admired, not concealed by that ugliest of all contrivances by way of costume—the trouser. Then there was the all-important wrestling jacket, the only part of the dress by which a hold, or West Country *hitch*, could be got by the rules of the play. This jacket, with the hitch, is a West Country peculiarity, which distinguishes it from all other play. The jacket is short and loose, made of exceedingly tough linen stuff, untearable; it has short loose sleeves reaching nearly to the wrist, it extends to a little below the waist, and is tied firmly but loosely by tough strings round the neck. Wrestlers are clothed in nothing else, except worsted stockings or socks, in Cornwall, with the addition of shoes in Devonshire.

Three good and true men are appointed as *sticklers*, who are the only persons allowed in the ring besides the players, and it is their office to watch the players and decide whether the play be fair, and, in the case of a fall, whether it be a *fair back* or not. For a fair back both shoulders and one hip must touch the ground at the same time, or both hips and one shoulder. Such a fall is called a three-point fall, and is the usual fall. But sometimes a four-point fall has been agreed upon, which requires both shoulders and both hips to touch the ground when the back fall—it is always the back of course—is given. The sticklers are old well-known players, and their decision, in the palmy days of wrestling, was not questioned. The word *stickler* is a good word, to be found in Sir Philip Sidney's 'Arcadia,' for an umpire or arbitrator.

The men having stepped into the ring, they shake hands, then separate, and the play begins by playing for a hitch. Each player wants to get his own favourite hitch, and to prevent the other from getting his. This leads to a good deal of dodging play, the players crouching and avoiding one another, very interesting to the lookers-on who know the game, and amusing to ignorant idlers. Gundry has been known to play half an hour for his hitch, which, when got, was a sore discomfort to the other man. The hitch having been got, whether the right one or not, the play for the fall begins. A player who gives a fall stays in the ring for the next player, and when he has given two falls he is a standard. There are never too many players, and the first day is usually taken up in making standards. In the case of a great well-known player, that he may be free for the better play to follow, it is by the consent of the sticklers allowed that a *faggot* may give him his back. The word *faggot*, known so well in the wrestling rings of the West, is to be found in Dr. Murray's 'Oxford English Dictionary': '7. A person temporarily hired to supply a deficiency at the muster—a dummy. 1700.' But a faggot, giving his back without the consent of the sticklers, just to serve a friend or for a bribe, would be hissed out of the ring.

A HITCH

Standards having been made, the double play begins. And here I will quote an old song, 'The Press Gang,' which aptly illustrates West Country wrestling:

> When I went up to Plymouth Town,
>   Along with a great man a ostling,
> I went over to Cremyl green
>   For to have a turn to wrastling.
> A gold-lace hat, he was the prize,
>   Never the worse for wear.
> Dick Symons and me drawed two valls apiece,
> And the blind-man come in vor a share.
>
> Just as the double play begins,
>   The glock he had knocked down zix,
> A passel of chaps come up to the ring,
>   And they'd a got zwords and sticks;
> They aboosed Dick Symons and darned his eyes,
>   And called un all zorts o' names.
> 'Darn 'ee,' says I, 'Dick Symons,' says I,
>   'They've a parfetly spiled the games.'
>
> Then up comed a feller with a great cocked hat,
>   He zeemed for to be the King.
> 'Darn 'ee,' says I, 'eff you've any consait,
>   Will 'ee plaze to stap into the ring?'
>
> . . . . . .
>
> But they hauled us down to the water zide,
>   And draw'd us into a boat.
> 'Darn 'ee,' says I, 'Dick Symons,' says I,
>   'They've a got the both ov's a-vloat.'

The prize of a gold-laced hat is explained by the following extract from the 'Monthly Packet.' 'In the diary of Penelope Sydenham, daughter of John Sydenham of Dulverton, describing a visit to London with Mrs. Yarde of Trobridge, Crediton, in the summer of 1762, the following statement occurs: "Bucks with hats looped up with gold lace, a sign to protect them from press-gang capture, were presented to her."'

In the days of the song it seems there was a well-known blind wrestler. What have not blind men done!

Supposing there were twenty standards left in, the double play would begin by the sticklers matching them with each other, and ten would be left for the treble play.

The players then would be reduced to five, and then to three, naturally a very select company, when very fine play might be expected.

Large rings might be formed, and very good play seen, but when a champion, or a very great man, was expected to appear, the excitement was intense, and the public of all ranks eagerly watched the play.

The play of Cornwall and Devonshire is the same, with a difference. The wrestlers step into the ring in the same way, they wear the same clothing and jacket, and they play for a hitch in the same fashion. Sticklers are appointed, who keep the ring, and the public are present in crowds. In Cornwall, however, the man steps into the ring in his stockings or socks. In Devonshire he

WRESTLING

wears his shoes, made for the express purpose. He is bound by rule not to have any iron or other metal whatever in his shoe, but he has the soles so hardened by baking that they are very formidable weapons.

The difference in the

AFTER TEN MINUTES

play has been called the in-and-out play, the off-and-on play, the toe-and-heel play. Or the Cornish play—the hugging and heaving; the Devonshire play—the kicking and tripping. It might be thus defined: in Cornwall the shoulders and arms are chiefly relied on, in Devonshire the legs.

In Cornwall the Cornish game is always played, in Devonshire the Devonshire game is played; but on the borders of the counties, in Plymouth especially, where a great deal of play used to be seen, Cornwall and Devonshire met one another, and sometimes each would play his own game.

It is not difficult to understand the difference in the play, bearing in mind broadly the Cornish hug and the Devonshire kick. If an unlucky victim had to choose as a fate between one and the other, he might not be able to make up his mind in a hurry. But as the resort to kicking, instead of the true play, fell away sometimes into a kicking match, the Devonshire play got into disrepute, and the kicking was very properly held in scorn, especially in Cornwall.

The style of the two counties being the same, as explained, it cannot be said that in Cornwall the leg-play was not known, or in Devonshire the shoulder-play was not known, but it came to pass that in the one the shoulder-play was chiefly followed, and in the other the leg-play. The shoulder-play and the leg-play are here used shortly to refer to a great many different ways of throwing a man a back fall.

In Cornwall a player having got his hitch would proceed to very close quarters, the *in*-play or *on*-play, and taking his man round the body, not lower than the waist, throw him over his shoulder, giving him the *flying mare* (which is poetical enough, considering that Pegasus was a flying horse), and, turning him over on his back while falling, get the back fall. The flying mare might be an affair of some danger. There was a little man at Truro some years ago who could throw the biggest of men by the flying mare. He did not take more than a few minutes about it, and if he failed at first he failed altogether. Big men stood off from him. He was so short that before they could get a hitch of him he was under them, and the flying mare was their due.

In West Country wrestling it would appear that small men can enter the ring with big men, and that would be especially the case in the Devonshire play. At Penzance in the year 1839 I saw a great wrestling at fair time (I also saw 'The Stranger' played at the immortal Lawrence's *barracade*).[1] It was given out that the St. Just men would play the world—the Cornish world of course, though they were ready for all the world, no doubt. A very fine young St. Just man stepped into the ring with great confidence, and was followed, to my great surprise, but not to the surprise of the company in general, by a very small man. The small man gave himself up to the big young man without playing for a hitch, and was taken into the arms of the big one to be dealt with. Suddenly I saw the big one on his back, a fair back fall. It was done by the inside lock, leg-play.

In shoulder-play a little man could have but small chance with a big one, except in the case of the Truro man described, but in the leg-play he might trip up the giant.

Besides the *flying mare*, there is the *cross-buttock* fall in shoulder-play, the *back heave*, and others. In the leg-play, there are the *fore-lock*, the *back-lock*, *heaving toe*, the *back-heel*, and others. Cornish players know them all, and Devonshire players know them all. Some are not readily played without the shoe, hence the lapse into kicking.

On the borders of the Tamar, at Plymouth, for example, famous wrestlings have taken place, and the best players of both counties have met there. In making the standards usually Cornwall would play Cornwall, and Devonshire Devonshire. And in the double play the sticklers would match them in like fashion, but in the end Cornwall must meet Devonshire, nothing loth on either side. The Cornish player would play for his hitch to draw his man *in*, the Devonshire man would play for his hitch to keep his man *off*. As long as the Devonshire player could keep his man off, he could play with his toe. The Cornish player did not seem to fear the kick, the stop to which is the knee. The kick, supposing the toe-play to be played without the savage kicking which was discountenanced for good-fellowship sake, is directed against the inside of the knee just under the joint. The stop is bending the knee to meet the kick, stopping the toe by receiving the shin against the knee, a most effective and punishing stop. In kicking the player must of necessity have but one leg on the ground, and having an off-hitch might be thrown by a quick player with a trip or a lock. The Devonshire play is a lively play: the kick and the leg-play in general must be very quick, and it is undoubtedly fine play when properly played. If the Cornish player were not thrown in the Devonshire out-play, he would get his man too close to him for a kick, and try his own Cornish play on

[1] Cornish for the strolling players' booth. French, *baraque*.

him. The Devonshire player would still play his leg-play, and a couple of hours might pass before one or the other got his back fall. The play would be well understood and be intensely interesting to a large company, the rivalry between the two counties always being at fever heat.

I well remember Johnny Jordan, an enormous Devonshire player, who used to walk about Plymouth in his old age. I also remember James Cann, a brother of Abraham Cann, and himself a well-known wrestler, who in his later years was an under-gamekeeper, respected for his fearlessness when poachers were to the fore.

I am much indebted to Mr. Michael Henry Williams, of Pencalenick, who is a great admirer of wrestling, and wrestled himself as a boy, for much information that he has given me, also for the photograph of the Indian wrestling which heads this article, and the portrait of Gundry.

Has football taken the place of wrestling, even in Cornwall where kicking is despised? In football there are symptoms of a degeneration into kicking matches. Is the fine manly game of wrestling to be one of the victims of this nineteenth century, civilised off the face of the earth? I have even heard that the police constable has taken upon himself to put a stop to young men *playing to wrastling* in their own fields. Have we come to this? Is Bumbledom to reign over us? And is the law really 'a hass'? I appeal to Cornwall to re-establish wrestling as a famous and manly West Country play.

W. F. COLLIER.

A FALL

GRAMMER GRACE'S CHEELD

I

The ' Seamew ' was ready for sea, and Cap'n John Joly was ' as vexed as fire.'

Two things had happened trying to the temper of an old salt used to authority : the little schooner had been caught by the heel when the tides were ' taking off,' and there was ' a row in the caboose among the wimmen to home ' about Grammer Grace's Cheeld going to sea. What made things worse was that the ship was eating up her freight, when there was a fine wind blowing with which to ' shape her course keenly to th' land, and then up Channel, my hearties, all canvas drawing ! '

As the tides would ' take off ' he didn't blame them—he had too much respect for his Almanac—but he was ' as mad as a curley ' with the land lubbers for not getting the cargo on board in time. The more he cried out ' hurry-all ! ' the slower they were ; so the ' Seamew ' was caught by the heel and then settled restfully in the thick slimy ooze waiting for the tides ' to make ' again.

Cap'n John Joly never let barnacles grow on his sea boots, not he. All St. Porth knew when Cap'n Jack was about. The sailmaker, having him at his elbow, patched the spare jib with a needle so hot that it blistered his ' palm ' —so he said—in order to be in time, and now there were days to spare. Some said the Cap'n had a seagull's feather in his brain, so restless was he upon land. The gossips at the Ship only added fuel to fire when they said : ' Take things a bit quiet like, Cap'n,' and ' Doant'ee chafe th' rope before tha' reeves th' block.' There was no comfort in the words. Cap'n John Joly was vexed, sure 'nuff, and he let everyone about him know it.

But the second trouble gave him an inward fret ; for it touched his authority, which he thought should be as absolute among the women folk as on board ship. This was a serious matter, and made him take long breaths and blow them out quickly, as though there was a fire raging within, too hot to be borne.

' A purty kettle ov fish,' said he to his wife, ' when th' wimmen folk put their hands upon th' helm on board ship, and mark out th' course upon th' chart ! John Joly have a-sailed his own course for twenty year, and now you come prateing and praiching about "th' tender cheeld." Make a maid ov'n to wance.'

' Coo, coo, John Joly. I wish you was to sea ; there's no rest nor peace in th' housen when your great boots es stomping about th' planchen,' said

Mrs. Joly, who had been worked up by Grammer Grace, Cap'n Joly's own mother.

'Wimmen's tongues es too slipper in what don't consarn em.'

'A purty spache, sure nuff, about your own mother, John Joly—the tender dear and blind, seventy-five this very year and her breath failin'. Coo, coo, you doant mean it, John.'

'The boy's kit es ready and he'll go this voyage in the " Seamew," the same as his father afore him' [this firmly, with a stamp which made the timbers ring]. Then he added : 'The boy's heart es in it, I tell 'ee.'

Mrs. Joly put her hand to her side and sighed. She did not like to be on bad terms with her husband at any time ; and now that he was ready for sea and vexed about other things, there were good reasons for not 'blawing' fresh wind from the bellows of strife.

After all, why shouldn't the boy go to sea? There never was a Joly of St. Porth but went to sea. Some were drowned, of course, but some died in their beds and made good endings, though, as a rule, they did not take kindly to feather beds and 'doctor's trâde.' When a Joly coiled up his ropes and stayed ashore the dry rot got into him, and his temper suffered, so that his own people were the happier when he took his last voyage, feet first, and became but a memory in the land of the living.

Cap'n John Joly was a chip from off the old block—every inch a sailor like his fathers before him, and his own sons who now sailed with him in the 'Seamew,' which belonged to the family. The trouble had arisen over a curly-headed boy, his own grandson, whose father had been drowned off Lundy. Grammer Grace in her old age and dotage had set the family by the ears, saying, 'Ceant I have one cheeld to stay to home and comfort me?' And Grammer was a woman of authority in the small household, because of her age and her blindness and of a certain intuition which seemed like a gift of second sight. She was not a Joly, and had a dread of the sea which had swallowed up her man in his prime, two of her sons and a grandson, the father of the youngster whose kit was ready for the voyage.

At the last moment she spoke as one inspired and foretold disaster, which sadly upset the nerves of all the women. She counted over again and again the horrid death-roll : 'My man, my two sons, my grandson, all drowned at sea. Now you do want to take my cheeld and drown'n too. Woe's me! What am I to touch ov my own flesh and blood to comfort me, now that my sight has gone, ef you do take this tender lamb also?'

''Tes enough to make one wisht to hearken to Grammer talking like this,' said Mrs. Joly to her husband. 'Why ceant th' cheeld stop ashore and l'arn a trade? We might put 'n to the blacksmith's or shipwright's or sail-maker's, and it would plaise th' poor soul to hear his mouth spache at meal-times, and put her old fingers through his curls that purty, you ceant think. Leave 'un bide, John, do'ee,' said the good woman pleadingly, her eyes filling.

But Cap'n John wouldn't have it so. His word had been law on board of the 'Seamew' for twenty years, and he had hardened with authority. He had passed his word that the boy should go to sea, and that was sufficient.

The boy was a proper Joly, never happy but amongst spars and rigging and when sporting with the billows. There was a place for him in the caboose, which he was able to fill. When he was on board, the crew would be as follows :
John Joly, master.
John Joly, mate (master's eldest son).
William Joly, A.B. (master's third son).
Henry Joly, promoted to A.B. (master's fourth son).
James Joly, boy (master's grandson, whose father was drowned at sea).

It had been one of Cap'n John's ambitions to man the 'Seamew' with the issue from his own loins. He had had four sons, and his wish might have been gratified long ago only the second was washed overboard, but not without leaving a successor to fill in the blank in the roll-call at the proper time. He had had to wait, and the desire grew stronger within him with delay. It would be a proud moment for him when he could lay his hand upon the wheel of the 'Seamew' owned by the Jolys from truck to keel, and manned by the Jolys from cabin to caboose.

Now, and at the last moment, Grammer Grace—his own mother, who should have been heart and soul with him—interfered, and demanded, with the authority of age and the pathos of blindness, that the boy should bide with her.

If Cap'n John had not been a firm man he must have yielded, for his own wife also took up the parable and gave him no rest at meal-times. But he kept on his sea boots, which with him was a sign of authority, and escaped from the house whenever he could. Still he was grieved that the women folk did not share his ambition, and vexed to be compelled to resist them. Then, when he thought he would be free and the 'Seamew' flying with outstretched wings, he was caught as in a trap. The vessel had taken the ground.

Cap'n John Joly was 'as vexed as fire,' and no one wondered.

II

GRAMMER GRACE'S cheeld, the cause of all this to-do, was on the side of authority as represented by the Cap'n's great sea boots. The sea boots were his fetish and, after the 'Seamew,' first of all earthly things in his young affections. He had played with the Cap'n's old worn-out sea boots before he could walk, hidden his treasures in them, measured himself against them as he grew, and longed for the day to come when he could wear boots like them and be called 'Cap'n.' The music of the word to the child!

He was ten years old now, and Cap'n John Joly had promised to take him to sea and rate him as cook the very next voyage. 'Ess, fath, you shall, and be a man and eat plum duff and salt beef till Grammer Grace weant knaw 'ee.'

These were blessed moments, and the youngster jealously watched the knitting of his socks and jerseys, and the preparation of his kit. He was going to sea like all the rest of them, and he put on consequence and grew manly, as a child will.

When all were told, there were four generations under Cap'n John Joly's roof, and such was the nature of the man that he would have welcomed a dozen. First of all, there was his own mother, Grammer Grace; himself and his wife; his son Henry, who had not finished courting yet; and James, his grandson, who was adopted when his father was drowned, so that the widow might be more helpful for herself. The great-grandmother took to the child and clung to him, and was so greedy of his presence and love that he was given up to her and became 'Grammer Grace's cheeld.' And as her sight failed, mysteriously it seemed, so bright were her aged eyes, her love for the boy increased and she was filled with dread at separation.

This feeling, which she could no longer control, was the source of all the present trouble. It seemed to her such a little thing to ask, 'Let me keep th' cheeld that I may hear the voices of all the others whom I have loved and lost.'

And when they denied her, for his destiny was fixed, she said, 'You're hard to me, and me blind. Four sons I bore to my man, and the sea has my man and two of them, and a third has drifted I know not whither. And three living maids I bore, and two are this day widows—their men swallowed up by the sea—and the third is not. Then my grandson James was drowned off Lundy and left this tender lamb to me—and what for?'

'Doant 'ee take on so, Grammer,' said her daughter-in-law. ''Tes hard on me also, for the cheeld es my James's, precious dear, and he drowned.' Then she threw her apron over her head and wept.

'Spake to Cap'n when he do come home,' said Mrs. Joly, greatly distressed, yet knowing not what to say.

'I knaw it'll be of no sarvice. He's got salt water in his blood, and there's no cheeld born of woman too good for th' "Seamew." I hate the very sound of the name.'

'Coo, coo, Grammer, doant 'ee fash th'self so. Th' craft es th' living of th' Jolys.'

'I knaw—and their destroyer, and, let me tell 'ee, she'll be their coffin.'

The old woman lapsed into silence until her son came in, full of hurry and bustle and preparation for the voyage. She laid her hand upon his arm and her lips quivered.

'Ess, mother, I knaw,' said he, 'but 'twill break th' boy's heart to draw back now. I couldn't do it.'

''Tes but a little thing, John; only to say "yes" to a blind old mother!'

'What's to become ov 'm, mother, ef he doant go to sea? He's mazed for ships and do knaw every spar and rope and patch in all the spare sails. He'll do credit to the Jolys, never fear, mother.' Then he drew her withered and sightless face down to him and kissed it.

'I knaw th' cheeld, who better? John Joly, and I'm not afeared that he'll turn coward. No, no, the cowardice es in me, but it es the cowardice of love.'

'He'll grow brave and big on board ship—I fath he will.'

But Grammer Grace was not to be put off. 'Have 'ee ever thought,' she asked solemnly, 'what will happen ef th' "Seamew" was to founder?'

Cap'n John Joly laughed—he could not help it. The " Seamew " founder! He knew every plank, every bolt, every rivet in her. She was as dry as a herring-bone. He had only just tried the pumps and they 'sucked.' The 'Seamew' founder, and John Joly on board! 'No, no, Grammer,' said he. 'You'm a bit wisht to-day. I'll mind th' boy, never fear, and he'll be a comfort to 'ee yet!' He rose to go, but she held him.

'John, John, I see inwardly and I knaw. Think! Ef th' "Seamew" should go down weth all hands! Think! I am left blind and withered. Thy wife widowed and without a son. John's wife a widow and his children fatherless. William's wife a widow and his little maid fatherless. Henry cut off weth th' warm kisses of his maid upon his lips; and James, thy own dead son's innocent cheeld, dead in his infancy. Canst tha' not leave one Joly to home to comfort the wimmen?'

It was his own mother entreating him, and she told the truth, every word as true as the Gospels. But then it was absurd to listen to women. If the ship came to grief the Jolys might as well come to grief also, for she was their life. The boy would go to sea—he had promised him, and his kit was on board; so blow wet, blow dry, he'd have to go.

He hardened up again whilst the trembling fingers were on his arm, and went about letting everyone know that John Joly was Cap'n on board his own ship, and that he'd rather sail to the Devil in a gale of wind than live in a house with women with tears in their eyes. He told himself that if he showed any sign of weakness now he must strike his colours, and all authority would pass from the hands of John Joly, master mariner, captain, and best part owner of the good schooner 'Seamew.'

He also told himself he would die first!

III

The 'Seamew' was family property and was built according to the very convenient plan of co-partnership on the 'Cost book' system which prevailed in the county of Cornwall and worked well. She was divided into sixty-fourths, and before her keel was laid upon the stocks every share was taken up, and paid for from time to time either in 'money or marbles,' as the old men used to say. The system suited the democratic and independent spirit of the people, who still carry on an extensive fishing industry without regular wages, preferring to 'consarty' and receive their shares according to old-established and invariable rule—capital and labour each receiving its proportion of the results!

When the century was young, some of the smartest craft in European waters were called into existence, like the 'Seamew,' by a trading co-partnership, but with unlimited liability. For example, the shipwright would take so many sixty-fourths, the sailmaker so many, the blacksmith and roper so many, then the merchants and general public would be applied to until the whole sixty-four shares were subscribed. The hum of labour would then rise, and the little craft shape towards completion under kindly but critical eyes.

In small ports every family with any pretensions would have a direct interest in a new vessel. Every share was registered, and might be transferred from hand to hand at small cost and with the stroke of a pen. The simplicity of the whole system has never been excelled. Take another example: A family wished to build a ship for the benefit of one of its members. They would subscribe so many sixty-fourths—the whole, perhaps, and if not the rest would be taken up by the shipwright and sailmaker. The control of the vessel was usually in the hands of the largest shareholders, who appointed a 'ship's husband.' The 'Seamew' was built like this, built for Robert Joly her first master, the family owning fifty sixty-fourths, and in time they acquired the remainder. When John Joly succeeded his father, the ship was 'family property,' and you could not speak of one without thinking of the other. The very life of the family was bound up in the ship.

When the 'Seamew' met with disaster there was gloom, a pinching of stomachs at meal-times, a saving of candle-ends, and a paring down of expenses in all directions. When the 'Seamew' had good freights and quick passages money was easy and her name passed current for a benediction. Children lisped her name in their prayers at bedtime. They were taught to say: 'God bless father, God bless mother, and send the "Seamew" fine weather.' She became the pivot on which everything turned—the motive power, the inspiration. What wonder that Cap'n John Joly saw in her only what was admirable, and had ambitions, and looked with a certain disdain upon the women folk who would keep the boys at home and not risk a little--if there were risk—to keep the craft for the family and the family for the craft.

When he said 'No' to all gentle entreaty, he told himself that he had reason on his side, and no man in St. Porth would have gainsaid him.

IV

THE Boy was the hero of the hour. He put on his new jersey, rolling it up from the bottom so that his hands were free of his pockets, and stayed on board of the ship when the crew went ashore, to keep watch with Rover, who was glad of his company. The two passed hours looking over the taffrail, the Boy warning all other boys to get out of the ship's jollyboat swinging at the stern, and Rover barking in savage chorus. The dog was as jealous as any Joly over everything appertaining to the 'Seamew.'

The crew went to their homes to sleep, and when there was only one night more before the ship would lift from the ooze the last to leave her were Cap'n John Joly and the Boy. How the lad envied Rover as he ran along by the Cap'n's side, but looking back every minute so long as he could see the dog's great paws and head above the bulwarks and his great, flashing, watchful eyes!

He must say 'good-bye' to Grammer now, and he wished she could see him in his new jersey frock, but then she could feel it. He felt himself a man, and talked like one. She should hear him say 'Heave ho, my hearties!' and 'B'lay that!' like Cap'n Joly.

It was September now, and dark in the little room but for the sea-coal fire, only he knew well enough where to find Grammer. He saw the outline of her white frilled cap, and the white wool turnover folded across her bosom and pinned behind as she always wore it in the afternoons. She was sitting in her high-backed chair, and her bright eyes, which saw not, were turned towards him.

'My cheeld!' said she, throwing her arms around him and bringing him close to her bosom. A spare, frail, upright little figure of a woman, but 'straight as a dart' always, was Grammer Grace, only now her voice trembled a little.

'Grammer,' commenced the boy, putting his hand against her cheek.

'Ess, my cheeld, I knaw it all. You'll come again to-morrow to say good-bye. Only now let me love 'ee.' So yielding to gentle pressure he knelt by her side, and her thin fingers passed over his face, lingeringly on his lips and eyes, and then softly through the crisp curls of the little round head.

'My cheeld, my cheeld! 'tes like cutting away my own flesh to lose 'ee.'

Then she rose from the chair and went to a drawer, and took therefrom a belt, in the lining of which was sewn a charm.[1] No man had ever been drowned at sea whilst wearing this. She had brought it from the westward when she married and settled at the Porth, but the Jolys laughed at and her own husband would not wear it—except once to please her—saying: 'To be drownded is a swate enough death for a sailor man, ay fath it es.' Nor would her own children wear it, having had instilled into them a wholesome disdain of charms and incantations and dealings with 'wise' women, except in the matter of herbs for wounds and sickness. The Joly blood was manly, and had no dread of the sea in it; the men trusted the sea and loved it, and it was life to them.

Now the aged fingers clasped it around the boy's waist as a consecrated zone, which would preserve him in the hour of peril. 'Sleepin' or wakin', wear it always—promise me, my cheeld.'

'Ess, Grammer,' said the boy, delighted with a parting gift when he had expected tears, and had prepared himself to run away if he had been clutched at.

In the night Grammer Grace came to his bed and felt for the belt, and found it where she had fastened it, which gratified her; then with her scissors

---

[1] Traffic in charms against drowning at sea is very small now, and faith in them has probably quite disappeared from amongst our sailors and fishermen. I once saw a 'charm' brought from St. Ives, but it originally came from near Penzance. It was composed of two strips of parchment and a child's caul. One strip was an ordinary *Mezuzah*, and had probably been nailed to the doorpost of an orthodox Jew's dwelling. It was out of its case. The other strip had written on it

Ps. cvii. 29

IN TE
DOMINE
SPERAVI.

The two strips were tightly folded in a caul, and the whole sewn up in a piece of old canvas. The charm was in very truth 'good' reading.

she snipped off one of the boy's locks and twisted it around her fingers, saying: 'It will comfort me ef my dreams come true.'

She listened to the boy breathing, and when he gave a great sigh in his sleep she went back to her chamber, for her own heart was very full.

The 'Seamew' rose from the ooze with the morning tide. Every plank in her was living, and every fibre in Cap'n John Joly moved in sympathy. All hands were on board, the white wings were unfurled, and away she flew down Channel with a leading wind.

Now that her berth was vacant, a feeling of loneliness fell upon the Porth. It was such a little place, and when men went out of it not to return again at night they were always missed.

The 'Seamew' made a good passage to Cardiff, and secured a return freight with 'black diamonds,' which was good news, as winter was coming on, and coasting was but 'poor tally' in the winter months. Besides, the women then had the men all to themselves, for they had to play second fiddle when the ship was coasting. In his letter Cap'n John said to his wife:

'Be sure and tell Grammer that her child is doing handsome, sure enough. He is growed bravely, and will make a proper man.'

Then there came another letter—a sailing letter, short, crisp, business-like, 'all, for sure, like Cap'n Joly in a hurry to batten down his hatches and sail.'

Then there was silence.

The 'Seamew' and all who manned her were on their last voyage. When nearly to the Land's End she was driven back with not a creek or cove or harbour under her lee but meant destruction, and no ray of hope but to face the abysmal rollers of the great Atlantic. She took her only chance, and was swallowed up. So much became known for certain, and the tale was all told.

When the news came to St. Porth the heart of the community stood still, and then bounded with compassionate grief.

The first thought was for Grammer Grace, the frail, blind old woman, who, with a sort of divination, had opposed Cap'n John Joly's taking the boy to sea. Who should tell her?

When they trooped into her room she was sitting in her high-backed chair in her deep-frilled white cap and white turnover crossed over her bosom. Her hands were in her lap, and around her fingers was twined the soft brown curl from her darling's head.

Grammer Grace had had an inward vision, and was gone to meet her cheeld.

J. HENRY HARRIS.

FALMOUTH:
ITS PAST, PRESENT, AND FUTURE

ONE could hardly wish fairer encouragement to the beginnings of a descriptive paper than that which is mine this morning of early May, as I try to bring my mind to bear on a note or two *àpropos* of Falmouth. The sun shines brilliantly on the waters of Falmouth's outer bay, now flecked with foam by the gusty north-west wind beating down over the land. To the left of where I stand is the sombre outline of the ancient castle of Pendennis, a relic of Tudor times, surmounting the wooded slopes that rise steeply from the sea-swept rocks below. Midmost in the land-circuit of the bay are the glistening white sandy beaches of Gyllngvase and Swanpool, terminating in the picturesque cliffs of Pennance. And, out yonder on the skyline of the extreme westward view, are the hills which gradually curve downward towards that narrow spit of treacherous rocks, given a wide berth by all inward-bound vessels making the welcome light of St. Anthony, known to mariners as the Manacles. Behind me are the topmost terraces of Falmouth itself, looking down on the beautiful harbour and Carrack roadstead. I know no more lovely landward or seaward scene than this, in the whole of England. I find myself the one sole student of this exquisite bit of landscape, in which the first delicate emerald green touches of early Spring, shown on the trees, shrubs, and meadows around me, comprise not the least attractive parts of the picture. Thought I to myself as I stood contemplating it, if Londoners did but know what this extremity of England can offer them in variety of land and sea views, in comparison with their dearly loved counties of Kent and Norfolk, how they would flock to it! On some accounts it is just as well, perhaps, that they do not realise its many and varied attractions, else might we who happen to be 'in the know' be driven from it by the holiday incursions of the week-end and other trippers. They are the very last persons we wish to meet down here. As times go, we are as yet a fairly primitive people. We know nothing of beach minstrels, black or white, and the 'real gentleman' in frock coat who does the piano business for a wager (which he in the long run, not to seem cynical, will probably win) has not thought it worth while to travel thus far, to troll forth his music-hall ditties to the few bathers and attendant loungers of Gyllngvase. I esteem it fortunate for those who, like myself, relish the quietude of life, that the Falmouthians are only just beginning to wake up to the possibilities of their interesting town and district. They have been

FALMOUTH

Photo by]   *[Harrison, Falmouth*
FALMOUTH FROM TREFUSIS

indulging in a very long sleep, since the old Packets were abolished in 1850. Now that the last of the Falmouth families, which throve well, and lived long and reputably on the profits of their many ventures that way, are departed (rest their souls!), the younger generation are taking to rub their eyes and stretch their limbs, and lament the poverty of their town—as if, by the way, prosperity or riches ever came to any without effort!

Meanwhile, it may be said to be an ill wind that blows nobody good. Visitors have the advantage of finding Falmouth outwardly very little altered from what it was in the days when George the Fourth was king, and the old ' Marlborough ' Packet was making her customary trips to Lisbon: the same narrow, old-fashioned streets, the same curious little houses and shops, the same dear old tumble-down market-place, once very neat and busy, but now weedy and forsaken, and generally an old-time, drowsy, unoccupied air, very agreeable when we can claim our rest, but not altogether desirable or advantageous when we are still youthful, and feel that we ought to be up and doing.

Robert Louis Stevenson came to the conclusion that the Cornish are more clannish than the Scotch. I am disposed to think that a reason for this clannishness may be found in the fact that, until comparatively recent years, Cornwall was, in more senses than one, the *Ultima Thule* of England. People who, crossing the Tamar by Saltash, journeyed westward still, into the sparsely populated Cornish towns and villages, were hailed as visitors ' out of England.' This notion prevailed to some extent even in my day. I well recollect a naval chaplain of a humorous turn preaching a charity sermon in Falmouth Church from the text, 'And the barbarians showed us no little kindness, for they kindled a fire and received us all, because of the present rain and because of the cold.' Whether he really intended to indulge in an inoffensive pleasantry I know not, but certainly it was considered an apt enough text to preach from, and none were offended. News travelled slowly in those days. Falmouth was cut off from all communication with the world of London, save for a considerable distance by coach. There was no telegraph, and no train farther west than Plymouth; of newspapers, cheap or otherwise, there were but few, and those always a day or more old; and as for visitors to the good old town, they came to us only in the season of summer, and then not more in number than an occasional adventurous half-dozen or so.

What wonder, then, that we were facetiously styled barbarians, and the parts in and about which we dwelt Western Barbary? I fancy we rather plumed ourselves on the distinction. At all events, we held our heads loftily with the best. We prided ourselves on being Falmouthians, men of the Duchy; and when we went to London (as we sometimes did), if our coat was a trifle out of date and our wife's bonnet a little less stylish than some seen in Bond Street and the Park, we cared not a brass farthing, so long as we held a tester in pouch, and could pay our way, and carry ourselves bravely and independently, after the manner of Cornish folk all the world over. When we came

Photo by]   *[Harrison, Falmouth*

FALMOUTH

Photo by] FALMOUTH HARBOUR [*Harrison, Falmouth*

back, needless to say we set the more curious townspeople agape in the Church Street promenade, and the aristocratic parts of Woodlane and Greenbank. We had now the satisfaction of setting the fashions for some time to come, alike in coats, hats, gowns, and bonnets. Ours was the style. To be imitated, tickled our vanity and brought some local fame to our eastward enterprise.

. . . .

I think it were best, perhaps, to let my pen run as my thoughts lead me. And, just right here (as our American friends say) might I ask leave to remind my sometime fellow-townsmen, many of whom were friends of my younger days, and for all of whom—if I may be allowed the privilege of saying so—I entertain those kindly feelings which inevitably arise in glancing backward at the scenes, surroundings, and unbroken friendships of one's boyhood and early home: may I remind them that Falmouth's future prosperity as a watering-place is in their keeping? They can make it what they please. Let some spirit of enterprise be shown such as we find in some popular sea-resorts, on the Lincolnshire, Lancashire, and Norfolk coasts, possessing not a tithe of the natural attractions of Falmouth, and there is no reason in the world why Falmouth should not gain a like position in public favour to that held by Torquay, Scarborough, or Bournemouth. Visitors will go to places in increasing number whenever they find local interest awakened in their behalf and contributing to their amusement. Much has been done in various ways of late years to improve the town and to attract strangers; but I venture to submit that more remains to be done. I hold stoutly to the opinion that Falmouthians have only to set vigorously to work to scheme, plan, and discuss, in order to promote their town to the rank of one of the most prosperous of Winter Resorts. It has everything in its favour—an exceptionally mild and sunny climate; many pleasant residential parts; and a neighbourhood abounding in picturesqueness and natural beauties. But visitors cannot be attracted from afar by natural beauties alone. They soon tire of drives, walks, and excursions. In brief, in winter they will have amusement of some kind or other to while away the duller hours—afternoon concerts, entertainments, social recreation in some sort. I am well aware that it is easier to say this than to devise some practical means of doing it. For all that, any seaside town which can lay claim to being a summer and winter resort as well may be

Photo by]　　　　　BEACH AT FALMOUTH　　　　　[Harrison, Falmouth

accounted very fortunate as towns go. Most sea-coast places have no ' season ' but that of summer. No programme of amusement, however varied, would take Londoners to such cold and bleak places, for example, as Filey or Whitby or Lowestoft in winter. With Falmouth, it is altogether different. It might be made a kind of English Riviera, if the Falmouth people could only be brought to bend their minds to such a project. The idea is not altogether impossible of realisation. Where there are wills there are ways, even with very little means. One man, stout of heart, strong of purpose, and gifted with the right spirit of intention to do, may accomplish a great deal. He might, at all events, help to lead his fellow-townsmen on the road to a future prosperity. Until one tries, he never knows what he may accomplish. The most difficult business enterprises are often carried to a successful issue by one man's thought, will, and energy alone.

It is just as well for the people of Falmouth to recognise the fact that its trade as a seaport is gone. Probably it will never be recovered, for it has nothing at back to help it: no coal-mines (we'll say nothing of tin), no great factories, no substantial exports, whether of produce or of trade. In the event of a great war—which Heaven forfend!—it might profit; but only in a limited sense and for a short while, by reason of its docks for repairing. No—Falmouth's one hope now is in creating for itself prestige as a watering-place for well-to-do visitors attracted from all parts of the country. That way lies a revival of its former prosperity, and that way only. It richly deserves such prestige, for no pleasanter place lies anywhere on the coast-line of England. The Great Western Railway Company is fully alive to the fact. Its present express train service to the west is really excellent. Corridor-cars and sleeping-cars mitigate the fatigue of the long journey. None can complain of its tedium by day; for the line west of Exeter and Plymouth abounds in varied interest to the traveller. At night one sleeps, and there's an end on't.

I cannot think that any good end will be served by my attempting a written description of Falmouth and its neighbourhood. Descriptive papers never can satisfactorily reproduce the place itself—its old-time narrow streets, its terrace houses, its pleasant walks, its delightful landward and seaward views, its charming nooks and out-of-the-way spots, its hills, vales, and leafy lanes, its rocky coast-line, inviting creeks, beaches, and extensive bay, and last, not least, the scenery of its beautiful Fal river, and of the land-locked waters reaching up to Penryn. I never tire of looking across from the window where I am now writing, to the harbour's mouth, and St. Anthony point, taking in with one sweep of the eye the picturesquely placed castle of St. Mawes, the lighthouse and Pendennis, and the docks, the harbour itself dotted all over with large and small craft—yachts, boats, and the rest. At nightfall, the ships' riding lights dance over the roadstead like will-o'-the-wisps, and at early dawn on a summer's morning, when the sun rises over the hills of St. Just, the scene is one of surpassing beauty on sea and land. When inquiring Londoners talk to me of summer holidays, I have but one reply to make to all. Go to Falmouth, and make daily excursions in the neighbourhood to Land's End, Helston, Redruth, and so on, and if you be not thankful for these recommendations write me down no good adviser of the uninformed. I venture to repeat the recommendation here. Let the reader once go, and he will probably go again. He will not soon forget his Pendennis drive, his walk across the fields to Budock Church, his sail across the bay to Helford river, his daily dip at Gyllngvase, his stroll along the cliff to Swanpool, his homeward walk by way of Bull's Avenue and the pleasure grounds of Kimberley Vale, his trips up and down the Fal, his afternoon picnicking at Place by St. Mawes, or under the trees at Trefusis. In short, he cannot fail to be delighted with his Cornish holiday, or I am without holiday experiences of this land we live in.

Lovers of research will find the town's beginnings chronicled in the annals of the Civil War. The picturesque old castles that crown the wooded

NEAR SWANPOOL
Photo by] [*Harrison, Falmouth*

heights on the one side of the harbour, and the rocky entrance to St. Mawes creek on the other, are interesting relics of the fight between King and Parliament. Pendennis showed a good front in those days, and gained reputation for its defenders. That Falmouth's heart was with the King may be concluded from the fact that its parish church (lately restored) is dedicated to King Charles the Martyr.

The Falmouth of our boyhood yet gave evidences of the prosperity which belonged to the town when it was the station of the Post Office Packets—ten-gun brigs, officered by naval men, flying the blue ensign, and carrying the mails to various Mediterranean ports, and to the North American and West Indian stations. By some they were facetiously named 'bathing-machines,' by others 'coffins.' In truth, they were not pleasant ships to sail in, in stormy weather. I have frequently talked with old commanders of 'Packets,' and been told of the discomforts aboard of the Northern Ocean winter passage to Halifax. They carried passengers at rates that would stagger a traveller by 'Lucania' to New York in these days. If I am not mistaken, fifty or sixty pounds was the cabin fee to Halifax. The Falmouth Packets often fought their way across the Atlantic in war time. The curious visitor to the town may yet find a well-preserved relic of those good old days in Marlborough Cottage, by Swanpool, built by Commander Bull, by whose descendants it is, I believe, still occupied. A chiselled relief of the old 'Marlborough' Packet may be seen in the top angle of the façade.

FALMOUTH

In the forties Falmouth was perhaps in its most flourishing condition. House rent was cheap, provisions were cheap, school education was cheap, and there was much pleasant society of one kind and another. The town could boast a good many well-to-do residents of the naval and military professions, both officers and men; and trade was brisk, and tradesmen contented. It was not merely a naval station of some importance: the roadstead was frequently crowded with ships of all nations, wind- or weather-bound or calling for orders. An old pilot told me but yesterday that he had known 300 sail in the roadstead. And the town, for a place so remote from London, was exceptionally well endowed with a cultured and prosperous middle-class community, which kept things moving. There was a good deal of party-giving on a small scale, and picnicking and junketing of one kind and another, to which the naval and military element contributed not a little colour. There was a guardship stationed in the roadstead, and a detachment of artillery or militia regiment generally quartered at Pendennis, to say nothing of occasional visits of transports homeward or outward bound. The Royal Mail, with its scarlet-frocked coachman and guard, arrived and departed daily from the 'Royal,' the bar-parlour of which old-fashioned and comfortable hostelry was the daily rendezvous of the gossips of the town. The stout, ruddy-faced guard of the coach, one Brice by name, Falmouthian bred and born, brought us our daily budget of news from afar; and perhaps no man of his day was better known, and more respected. I need not say that we were a self-respecting community. Police officers were rare. In fact, our police force consisted of one constable (if I remember aright) and a deputy. We could boast of a lock-up; but no prisoners other than an occasional drunken sailor found a lodging there. When we went abroad at night on country roads we carried a kind of Dogberry's lantern, for we had no gas-lamps to light us by the way. 'Preventive men' patrolled the coast-line—ancient weather-beaten tars, such as used to be seen on the Adelphi stage of melodrama, armed with big broad-sword, huge pistols, and stout cudgel, clad in shaggy

COLLEGE WOODS, PENRYN VALLEY

pea-jackets, 'sou' westers,' and jack-boots, with a buckled belt about the waist, broad enough to sling a cart-horse. Many a time did I see those naval veterans mustered at nightfall at the watch-house, under the eye of their old commander, Lieutenant Pooley; and seldom without asking myself whereabouts between 8 P.M. and 6 A.M. they slept? We never heard of any smugglers running a cargo ashore. Had there been any bold seaman from the French coast making his way for Pennance Point, I doubt if he would have encountered much opposition in landing. The old 'Preventive' men were not altogether unlike the ancient London watchman, at least in outward seeming. We have another and a very different Coast-guard now.

The opening for traffic of the Cornwall railway to Truro, which closely followed upon the completion of Brunel's famous tubular bridge across the Tamar at Saltash, set Falmouth cogitating great schemes. Spacious docks were to be built—we have them now, but not so extensive as was intended—and the mail steamers from the West Indies, British India, and the Cape, were to find in Falmouth their most accessible and nearest English port of call for the delivery of mails and passengers. Alackaday! the docks in due time came after much expenditure of thought, labour and money; but neither steamships, passengers, nor mails.

OLD DOCK AT LITTLE FALMOUTH

However, there the docks are; and there also is Falmouth's grand hotel, and the beginnings may be noted of a new residential part at Trefusis, and the town is handsomely extending out by Gyllngvase, and promising to extend in other directions. Meanwhile, we have the neat old-fashioned houses still standing at Woodlane and Greenbank, and the highly picturesque and still more old-fashioned architectural relic of the Killigrews of Stuart days at the Bar, and many examples of middle-class Georgian dwellings elsewhere. We note the hotel on the Greenbank, beloved of yachtsmen; Ludgate Hill (is it still known by that name?), steep and narrow as ever, and the busy Market Strand, and the Fish Strand, and the Custom House Quay, and ever so many quaint-looking alleys leading to the water-side, locally known, if I recollect aright, as 'opes' and 'slips'—all sufficiently picturesque and redolent of old-time memories, if nowadays out-of-date and inconvenient. The little township of Flushing should not be omitted in this brief category of Falmouth's points of interest, as I first remember it, peopled by not a few well-to-do families, in which were included those of two distinguished admirals and of other naval officers of subordinate rank. Mylor, not far distant, over the hills of Flushing, is a charming little village, abutting on the beautiful waters of the river Fal. Than that winding waterway to Malpas and Truro, there is none more beautiful. Tregothnan, on the Fal (Lord Falmouth's seat in Cornwall), is a spot to be remembered. I know of no place more picturesque or more lavishly endowed with the varied beauties of woodland scenery. St. Just in Roseland, and St. Mawes, and the fishing village of Gerrans, facing the outer bay, offer many inducements to the tourist from town fortunate enough to find vacant accommodation in that little which is available for visitors at farm-houses and primitive inns in and about such villages. A summer holiday spent in such places as I have named is likely to be a real holiday of rest, recreation, and invigorating open-air life, remote from the 'cheap tripper' and the noisy business of the sands. Yachting, boating, fishing, are within easy reach everywhere; and daily seaward excursions by pleasure steamers serve to beguile the hours of those that way inclined. Of all pleasant excursions, let me not forget to make mention of that to Helford Passage. Were I asked to name the spot which will always live in my memory as the most beautiful I can call to mind, it would be Helford Passage. The road thither from Falmouth is by way of Penjerrick, one of the show-places of the county.

CHARLES EYRE PASCOE.

MORWENNA OF THE SHADES

THERE is a little fishing town on the north Cornish coast which juts out on a slender tongue of land into the blue sea. If you know the coast at all, you will have seen it blinking yellow eyes seawards at nightfall, or rising blue-roofed and sand-bound from the morning mists.

In the doorway of an iron studio, clinging as it were to the bosom of the cliff, Hugh Polcarron, painter, stood one evening gazing wistfully across the blueness of the bay, while the revolving lighthouse off the point flashed its first warning over the waters. His eye lingered with artistic appreciation on a fleet of herring boats standing out to sea with ruddy sails unfurled. No fairer view could be desired by mortal eyes, but the painter turned away with an impatient sigh.

'It's no use,' he muttered. 'Inspiration's dead. I'll go for a stroll.'

He stepped into the studio behind him, where a young and pretty woman stood looking round on the litter of paints and pipes with friendly disparagement, and dainty skirts well in hand.

'How detestably your paints smell, Hugh. I wonder you can go on working in this stuffy den day after day. No wonder you feel ill and low-spirited.'

'I don't, particularly,' said Hugh, looking round tenderly on the 'den.'

An old patched sail stretched its tawny length upon one of the walls, and a fishing net or two represented the principal industry of St. Morwen. The place was full of odds and ends suggestive of the painter's craft, and Hugh's eye lingered tenderly on an old stone jar, to which bits of sponge still clung. It was a relic of a jaunt to Smyrna, and in bygone years someone had been wont to fill it with marigolds or crimson tulips—a person of sympathies, herself an artist at heart, whose very memory was sacred, even from the woman Hugh Polcarron had in later life married.

Mrs. Polcarron gave a dissatisfied look round.

'I really must get a charwoman to come in and clean the place up,' she remarked. 'I couldn't possibly ask the servants to do it.'

'It's very well as it is, Dolly. For Heaven's sake don't send any charwomen here. You ought to be used to my ways by this time, little woman. Two years to-morrow, isn't it?'

'Twenty years wouldn't reconcile me to this muddle,' said his wife, laughing. 'Why, what have you been doing all day? The picture looks exactly the same as it did yesterday morning. If you mean to send it up in time, you'll have to work harder to-morrow.'

The artist flushed.

'It's inspiration that has failed me, Dolly. Give me that and I'll work hard enough.'

'Inspiration?' repeated Mrs. Polcarron, lightly. 'I thought genius was a capacity for hard work. If you didn't dream quite so much, I expect you'd get on faster. Are you going out?'

'Yes,' he said a trifle bitterly, 'I've got the blues.'

Sympathy he had ceased to look for. Once . . . but that was an old story.

He turned his half-finished canvas to the wall and went out.

Just outside, however, he encountered a brother artist whose happy-go-lucky expression contrasted strongly with his own weary one.

'Hello, Polcarron,' cried the other cheerily. 'Whither bound? I've been the other side that headland, sketching. The tints in that pile of rocks are grand. Where are you off to?'

'Anywhere,' said Hugh. 'The fact is, my ideas seem to be giving out, and I fancied a tramp in the half light might give them a fillip.'

'Been sticking too close to work, I suppose. You ought to sketch more in the open. By the way, I've heard no end of a romance this afternoon. Come back with me and hear it.'

Hugh hesitated.

'Perhaps I will. The sight of your face is worth a good deal to a melancholy man.'

'But you've no business to be a melancholy man, Polcarron. You're the first man down here, and safe to get your Associateship in a year or two. Then there's your wife —'

'Let's have your romance,' cut in Hugh.

'Ah, I'd forgotten. Well, I found the neatest little cottage down in that hollow that you ever saw. An old couple of the name of Trevorrow live there. I fancied the old man in my boat scene and found him quite amenable to 'bacca and blarney, and he sat to me. While I was sketching, he told me his history, or rather his daughter's history. The girl was very pretty, it appears, and even in those days there were plenty of men about wanting to paint her, but for some reason she never would sit. Suddenly, however, some lucky devil appeared on the scene and took this Morwenna's fancy.'

'Morwenna?' repeated Hugh.

'Yes. Pretty name, isn't it? So Cornish. Well, this fellow, who ever he was, got round her somehow, and she agreed to sit for some big picture he was painting.'

'An old story, isn't it?' murmured Hugh.

'Yes, but it ended rather queerly. They fell in love, of course, and——'

'The woman went to the wall, eh?'

'No, that's the odd part of it. She didn't. He married her, but she died on the wedding night.'

'Murdered?'

'Apparently not. It seems her heart was weak, and the excitement of "being made a lady of" killed her. By Jove! old chap, that picture you're working at now would just illustrate that story.'

'Would it?'

'Of course it would! Haven't you got the girl asleep on a couch and the husband just bending over her to take her in his arms when Death glides in between them? That's queer, too.'

'Possibly,' said Hugh, with white lips. 'The rub is, that I can't get Death in as I should like. Inspiration has stopped short of the supreme Healer. I can't accept the cut and dried ideas of death. Sometimes I seem to catch a breath—the shade of an idea—from somewhere, but directly I take up my brush it eludes me altogether. And to think that the man of whom you told me—the man I have painted if you will—was once in the presence of Death and had not the power to grasp his personality—was brute enough to sleep in the supreme presence. My God! what a wasted opportunity!'

Fletcher eyed his friend narrowly.

'Look here, old man,' he said earnestly. 'I tell you what it is. This weird coast is getting on your nerves. Take my advice and have a week in town with Mrs. Polcarron. It will be the saving of you.'

'Can't be done; at all events till the picture is finished. I'd give five years of my life for an hour of inspiration. Oh, for the days when men saw visions and dreamed dreams! But there, old man, I needn't infect you with my dismals. Good night!'

The two men parted, and each was swiftly swallowed from sight in the grey mist.

Hugh Polcarron tramped forward, brooding painfully over the central blank on his canvas. How could he fill it with a conception that should be a thing apart?

His mind recurred hungrily to a night long ago when Death had stood at his very elbow as a thief in the night—to rob him in very truth. So treacherous is human nature that to-night the man's chief regret for that episode in his past was for the opportunity he had missed, of meeting face to face with the supreme healer of mankind. Why, he asked himself, had his eyes been holden? In lesser degree his heart was sore with the old wound, which rude hands had touched and torn. Once, indeed, it seemed to him that the plaintive wailing of the gulls, or the washing of the sea, shaped in his ear the word 'Morwenna.'

Suddenly he stumbled, deceived by the treacherous twilight into mistaking the edge of the cliff for the white path line. He slipped bodily over the brink. Fortunately for him his fall was arrested by a protruding ledge more stable than the rest of the towans which spread overgrown with sand rushes to the margin of the sea. To this perilous perch he clung, sending call after call into the growing darkness. His shouts raised echoes all around him, but elicited no reply.

After a moment or so he desisted, reflecting that he was in no immediate danger. A little manœuvring enabled him to attain a sitting posture which was comparatively comfortable. After all, the worst which could befall him would be a night in the open, and who could tell but that the inspiration he sought might not come to him under the mottled arch of heaven, with the unfettered breeze leaving its salt upon his face? All around him sea and sky were grey, excepting where, at the base of distant cliffs, long white breakers curled. One by one the boats of the herring fleet in the bay showed their lights, until the sky itself looked like a faint reflection of the spangled sea.

Suddenly, as it seemed, though in reality the feeling grew upon him gradually, he felt a strange sense of companionship.

He was no longer alone. He felt it, even before he could see a dusky figure making its toilsome way over the towans, where, at the best of times, walking was exceedingly difficult and in the darkness one would have thought impossible for human feet.

So thought Hugh. Nevertheless, the figure that approached him was certainly that of a man of small stature with a face that seemed pale in contrast with his black conventional garments.

This individual came up the crumbling sand-bank with wonderful agility and seated himself beside the painter on the ledge.

'Well,' said Hugh. 'If you can get up, I suppose I can get down that way.'

'You can't,' said the stranger curtly. His face was averted.

'You came up,' said Hugh.

'I? Oh, certainly—*I* did.'

'A madman,' thought the painter.

'No, sir, not mad,' replied the other immediately.

Hugh Polcarron shivered slightly, and he regarded his companion closely. Despite the darkness, his face seemed illumined, possibly by reflection from the water.

'You don't know me?' asked the stranger.

It was the calmest, gentlest countenance Hugh had ever pictured, but beyond this utterly indefinable. He shivered again nevertheless.

'I can't say I do. I should guess you to be a physician, sir, and your face seems somehow familiar, but I can't for the life of me remember when and where I saw you.'

'I am *the* physician,' said the little man serenely. 'My name is Death.'

Hugh stared.

'*Death?*'

'Yes. I suit my dress to every age. You sought inspiration concerning my personality. Are you satisfied?'

Amazement sealed Hugh's lips. It was not horror at all: simply amazement.

'You are not, I see. You doubt my identity. Nevertheless I am he, whom not long ago you called your best friend. You spoke truly; but so blind is man, as a rule, that he looks on me as his worst foe and shuns me as long as he possibly can. Only the understanding minds of children have no fear of my approach. It is a weakness that is the heritage of maturity.'

'And what of women?' ventured Hugh, speaking at random. The madman promised to be interesting.

'Ah, there you have me,' said the little doctor. 'I don't pretend to understand *them*. They come to me sometimes of their own free will, but oftener they fight me with their latest breath.'

'They cling to life then?'

'Yes, but generally for the sake of those who must be left behind. Sometimes it is children, sometimes a husband, sometimes a lover. I could tell you of a woman who lived upon this coast——'

He paused and looked long and steadily at the painter. The latter made no sign.

'She was a bride, poor child, and I would have spared her if I could, but I was powerless to do so. It was her hour.'

'Tell me of her,' said Hugh suddenly. 'Was she loth to go?'

'Loth indeed,' replied the little doctor looking out to sea. 'But I carried her away in her sleep. I always avoid a scene if I can, and I knew her to be wedded to earth and a man.'

'Tell me of him,' broke in Hugh eagerly. 'Supposing that he had waked, could he too have seen—you face to face?'

Death smiled.

'Only once do mortal eyes behold me,' he said. 'At the last. You must know that before I actually reveal myself to any creature, my shadow is upon him for three days, and at the moment when soul and body part company it is in my power to grant one wish to the departing spirit.'

'One wish?' said Hugh eagerly. 'Death would be a cheap price to pay for some.'

'That is true. But some wishes are not easy to grant, especially those which necessitate a certain lapse of time ere their fulfilment can be attained. For instance, only now can Morwenna's last desire be granted her.'

'Morwenna?' repeated Hugh.

'Morwenna—now of the shades. Her desire was to return to the troubled world.'

'Absurd,' said Hugh.

'Yes, but a man was the magnet. Nothing would content her but that she might visit him in human shape, and that of course is difficult to manage.'

'Why?' asked Hugh.

'She had no body, you see, and there was only one way out of the difficulty. It meant that she must usurp for a time the form of whatever being her husband loved best on earth, while its real owner was sunk in a deep sleep.'

'Rather a gruesome idea, isn't it?'

'Does it strike you so? But think of the poor soul's rapture at finding herself in the arms of the man she worshipped. Love, you know, is eternal.'

'I suppose so,' said Polcarron dreamily. 'But why not in the spirit?'

'A question of temperament,' rejoined the doctor. 'I fear her desires were not spiritual. A fisher maiden is apt to have limited ideas of love—limited but enduring.'

'Only the noblest of love could have survived till now,' said Hugh, not ungratefully. 'You are going, doctor?'

The little man had risen. A mere grey wisp he looked in the gloom. He gained the summit of the cliff with apparent ease, and stretched out a hand to Hugh.

'You don't want to stay there all night surely?' he said. 'Come.'

His fingers closed icily on the painter's wrist. His grip was like frozen iron, but it enabled Hugh to regain solid earth.

As the doctor's fingers relaxed, their chill remained. He disappeared in the mist as suddenly and incomprehensibly as he had appeared.

Depression and excitement struggled for mastery in Hugh Polcarron's breast. Had he been dreaming, or was the odd encounter a reality? But for the clutch of those icy fingers, still imprinted on his sensibilities, he would have deemed the whole a fantastic nightmare.

Perhaps after all he had been dreaming, and in his sleep had performed the feat of scrambling up the cliff; at all events here he was safe and sound, with an overweening desire upon him to find himself once more in the shelter of his own home.

He turned back burning with an insatiable desire to finger brush and palette and work as he had never worked before. Already the grey dawn was in the sky. . He must have slept long. He moved as though his feet were winged.

In his studio an unaccustomed light was burning, and, stranger still, his wife was sitting over the little stove in an attitude she rarely affected. Something in her pose sent the blood racing back to Hugh Polcarron's heart. His thoughts flew back a score of years, and lo!—against the tawny setting of the sail upon the wall stood an old stone jar. It was filled with late marigolds.

Acting on a sudden impulse he went forward, and with a boyish gesture covered his wife's eyes softly with his hand.

She clutched them feverishly.

'Hugh, Hugh, Hugh!' she cried, and flung herself into his arms.

'Why, darling,' he murmured, amazed at so unusual an outburst. 'How hot your hands are! You must be feverish.'

'I was cold a moment ago,' she said. 'Oh Hugh, say you're glad to see me—but I know you are! I see it in your eyes.'

'Of course I'm glad to see you, little girl,' he said gently. 'Aren't you my own dear wife?'

'Yes, yes, I am indeed. But I was afraid that you might have forgotten me. But you haven't, dearest—say you haven't.'

'My memory's bad, I own,' said Hugh, looking fondly into her eyes. 'But not quite so bad as that. Are you quite well, darling?'

'Of course. Why shouldn't I be? Oh, my love, my love, my love!'

Her embrace was choking him.

'My dear wife,' he said tenderly, 'something has upset you. I can't bear to see the pain in those blue eyes of yours.'

'*Blue?* They're brown,' she cried pettishly.

'Well, you know best, I suppose,' said the painter, forcing a laugh, while his heart throbbed strangely. 'My impression is that they are blue, little woman.'

The girl burst from his arms and like some wild thing rushed to a broken mirror fixed on the wall.

From its surface gazed out at her a white terrified face, the low brow just touched with burnished locks, the eyes blue as speedwell.

Long and fearfully she looked at those blue orbs through which her imprisoned spirit shone impotently to reveal itself.

'It's not my face,' she shrieked. 'My hair was like seaweed, brown and glossy. You always said so, Hugh.'

For reply he caught her round the waist. The man in him was roused by the unwonted tenderness and passion of his wife's demeanour. In a sudden gust of passion he pressed his lips on hers, his glance bespeaking unutterable tenderness. He had not dreamed that so much emotion existed under his Dora's placid amiability.

'What possesses you, dearest? What is it, Dolly?'

'Hugh, Hugh,' she screamed. 'Don't you know me? It is I—your own wife.'

'My dear, I know,' he said soothingly. 'You are my own wife, my dear little Dora.'

'Not Dora, Hugh! There is no Dora! Oh, my God, make him know me. It is I, Morwenna!'

Her arms flew round his neck. He could feel her imprisoned heart beating madly against his own, but the recognition of a soul struggling to pierce the disguise of another's flesh, stamped with another's likeness, passed human comprehension. How could he know that his very lavishness of love was torture worse than hell to her on whom he showered it, seeing that it was spent on another. Dora's his kisses, hers his tenderness, for her his passion. Morwenna stood outcast in the fervour of his embrace.

Her clasp tightened round his neck and her eyes darkened with a despair worse than death.

A voice from the grave out-shrieked the voice he had loved best and latest, and in her last bitter cry, as the spirit broke its bonds, he knew her.

. . . .

They found him later with brush and palette still clenched in his stiffened hands. Above him towered his finished picture with a weird majestic presence where last night's blank had been.

For in descending into the valley Hugh Polcarron had found his Inspiration.

ARNOLD LYNTON.

ST. BURYAN FROM NORTH-WEST   [J. C. Burrow, F.G.S.

THE COLLEGIATE CHURCH OF ST. BURYAN

ST. BURYAN is one of the most interesting churches in West Cornwall, both architecturally and historically. The church, as we see it to-day, is for the most part of the fifteenth century, but portions of it are probably later even than that, and should perhaps be dated in the second half of the sixteenth. But there is an exception to this late date in a portion of the north wall of the chancel, where a rude semicircular arch, set in rubble masonry and enclosing a smaller arch (see next page), is at least three centuries earlier in date. Within, the larger arch alone is visible, and not only is it interesting in form, but also from the fact that the voussoirs of the arch are not of stone but of concrete made of the shell-sand of the neighbourhood. This interesting arch was only discovered in the progress of the restoration. The church consists of a nave 58 ft. in length, a chancel 43 ft. long, and two aisles, which, like the nave and chancel, are each 14½ ft. wide, and extend the whole length of the church to within a few feet of the east wall of the chancel. The unusual length of the chancel is, of course, due to the collegiate character of the establishment, and the consequently considerable number of clerics who had to be accommodated; though, if we credit Leland, the provision was unnecessary, at any rate in later times: 'There longeth,' says he, 'to S. Buryens a deane and a few prebendarys that almost be nether ther.' As we approach the church from the south, the first object that catches our attention is a cross in the open space outside the gate, and round which bodies have been found buried, suggesting that it was formerly within the consecrated enclosure. And in the churchyard itself is another, of which only the head remains, which was fixed, after the removal of the shaft, on the top of the four steps which constitute the base. It is of much beauty and interest, having the figure of our Lord on one side, and on the other five bosses, typical of the five wounds of Christ. Just behind this is the porch, of a type very common in West Cornwall, buttressed and battlemented and with crocketed pinnacles to the buttresses, of which that at St. Just (in Penwith) appears to be a copy, and perhaps the work of the same man. The windows on the south side are each of three lights with depressed rounded heads, and surmounted with square hood-moulds. Between the second and third windows east from the porch is an octagonal projection containing the stairs that formerly led to the rood-loft. The oak rood-screen, judging from the fragments that still remain, must have been an object of singular beauty, rich with crisp carving and exquisite colouring. In 1814 the church was repaired, and the screen (as well as some carved pew ends) was destroyed—the screen being sacrificed (it is said) because the vicar had a weak voice, with which he thought it interfered. The name of this weak-voiced and inartistic gentleman deserves immortality. He was one Henry Jenkins, D.D., a nominee of George Prince of Wales, who had succeeded in establishing the rights of the Duchy over St. Buryan as against the Crown. The view we give of the interior shows a portion of the screen, which still, fragment though it is, serves somewhat to take from the squareness and monotony which even a lovely church like St. Buryan exhibits in common with so many of our Cornish churches. A good rood-screen will convert an ugly church into a beautiful one, as has lately been well shown in the case of Blisland, where a new screen, designed by Mr. Eden, has been placed in the same position as one that during 'the reign of darkness' had been removed. Under the most easterly of the windows of the south aisle is the priest's door, now built up. The windows on the north correspond with those on the south. The church

Photo by]   [*J. C. Burrow, F.G.S.*
ST. BURYAN, NORTH WALL OF CHANCEL

ST. BURYAN, SOUTH PORCH

is built of granite ashlar, except the older part of the north wall of the chancel already referred to, and the adjoining part of the east wall of the north aisle, both of which are of rubble and of the same age. The regular square-cut stones of the walls detract considerably from the beauty of the church externally, making it look flat and heavy. The north wall of the aisle is of more recent date than the rest of the church, and is believed to have been rebuilt in 1775. The building stands on high land, and the tower is of fine proportions, being of four stages with a basement; it is 80 ft. in height to the top of the battlemented parapet, with a bell-turret at the north-east angle that rises above the tower to the height of the pinnacles. The beauty of this tower is enhanced by the buttresses, which rise by five stages to just below the battlements, and round which the bold string-courses of the tower are carried. Over the west door of the tower is a fine Perpendicular window of five lights. The tower appears to be of somewhat earlier date than the church; and, during some excavations, made for the purpose of fixing a warming apparatus, foundations extending northward for 20 ft. and presenting the form of steps were discovered. Foundations were also partially traced in other directions, and are, in all probability, part of the foundations of the college, in which the dean and the prebendaries resided. As you enter the church observe the stone seats on each side of the south porch, and the interesting, though very mutilated, stoup in the east wall. Standing beneath the fine tower-arch, and looking eastwards along the nave (locally known as 'Athelstan's church,' and believed by the inhabitants to be part of his original foundation),[1] you will see that the roof is of the regular 'waggon' shape so common in the district; that the church is lofty (its height having been somewhat increased by the lowering of the floor at some time, probably in 1875, when the church was restored under the direction of Mr. Butterfield, of London), and that each aisle is separated from the nave by six fine four-centred arches supported on granite pillars, formed of four three-quarter rounds with hollow mouldings between, the capitals and bases being strongly moulded. The east end of the north aisle has been parted off by a modern oak screen to serve as a vestry. The chancel—or, as it was called of old, the choir—is raised above the nave by two steps and separated by four beautiful panels of the old rood-screen, and a portion of the rood-beam and cornice is still suspended in its place, its carved and traceried supports having been removed. At the east end is a wooden altar-table with a handsome modern reredos of marble partially blocking the east window, the tracery of which is neither old nor elegant. Under the third window of the south aisle is a segmental recess, which perhaps at a former time held an effigy. In the

[*Photo by*] [*J. C. Burrow, F.G.*]
ST. BURYAN, INTERIOR

[1] During the restoration a lead coffin, but without contents or inscription, was found here, and this, too, local fancy has seized on as the former holder of the royal bones!

THE CHURCH OF ST. BURYAN

foreground is the font, which is of 'Ludgvan granite,' and probably dates from the thirteenth or early fourteenth century. On three sides the bowl has angels carrying shields carved on it, and on the other side is a shield with a plain Latin cross on three steps. Between two of the angels is the small Maltese cross shown in the illustration. The base and kneeling steps are modern. But perhaps the most interesting objects in the church are the four early Miserere stalls and the Boleit tomb. Of the Misereres, one was no doubt intended for the dean, viz. the first on the south side, and the others for the prebendaries of Respernell, Trithing,[1] and the 'Prebenda Parva.' The seats are now fixed (a foolish proceeding, which was quite unnecessary, and greatly detracts from their interest); formerly they could be raised as required, the small underledge serving the useful purpose of enabling a priest to half sit and rest

ST. BURYAN, MISERERE STALLS

during the long choir services. They have, moreover, been removed from their ancient position as returned stalls, and shifted round to face north and south—another unnecessary proceeding, reflecting no credit on the judgment of the architect. The Boleit tomb now lies on the floor of the tower. It is a coffin-shaped stone, with a much-worn floriated cross in relief on the upper surface. Round the margin is the following legend in Norman-French, and in characters of the thirteenth century: CLARICE : LA : FEMME : CHEFFREI : DE : BOLLEIT : LIT : ICI : DEV : DE : LALME : EIT : MERCE : KE : PVR : LEALME : PRIVNT : DI : IOR : DE : PARDVN : AVERVND. (Clarice the wife of Geoffrey de Bolleit lies here, God on her soul have mercy: who pray for her soul shall have ten days of pardon.) What a glimpse into the old world! Here in Norman-French, written some 700 years ago, we are promised ten days' pardon if we will but pray for mercy on the soul of Clarice. We can all honestly pray for her if she any longer needs it, whether induced thereto by the promised pardon, or merely by a feeling that more things are wrought by prayer than this world dreams of. Hals in his 'Parochial History' tells us that this stone was discovered by the sexton, about 1665, while digging a grave.

THURSTAN C. PETER.

[1] Also called Trethin and Tirthney.

(*This article will be concluded next month.*)

HOW TO DEVELOP CORNWALL AS A HOLIDAY RESORT—*(concluded)*

OPINIONS OF EMINENT CORNISHMEN AND OTHERS

Mr. S. Trevail

In the year 1877, when travelling in Italy with a North of England friend I was impressed with how much we lacked of what was required to 'slock' people westwards, when, in addition to all the competition for tourists of the Highlands, North Wales, and the East and the South coasts of our own snug little island, we had also to contend with the rivalry and the attractions of the best resorts on the Continent. Then we had but two really first-rate tourist hotels in Cornwall, the Queen's at Penzance, and the Falmouth Hotel, but since several have sprung up, for which I may perhaps assume some responsibility, either as the promoter, or in being the cause of others promoting. The late Mr. Alderman Cail, C.E., of Newcastle-on-Tyne, was primarily the cause of this movement, by showing me in North Italy how much we, as a county, lost by not making better provision for visitors; and when we returned, by way of Switzerland, I was more than ever impressed by the importance of his suggestions. Since that, in season and out of season, I have been advocating this object; and it is a matter of great satisfaction to me to find so many of the more eminent of my fellow-countrymen now taking up the latest Cornish 'interest.'

Now, Mr. Editor, you may be saying this refers too much to the past—what about the future? My retort is that by a careful study of the past we are the better able to judge of what is best to do for the future. I should say then for the present that our existing hotel accommodation, and what is now in course of construction, will be equal to probable demands, at least at the better known points, and our next business will be to fill them. We should follow the example of the Swiss, the Scotch, and the Germans, in the sense of doing everything we can to make the stay of the visitor amongst us pleasant and agreeable to himself, and under such financial conditions that after once visiting our glorious coast line he may be induced to come again and to recommend his friends.

Some will say 'continentalise' our pleasure resorts with casinos, theatres, winter-gardens, and all the other costly paraphernalia that goes to make one watering-place so much like the other, as are two railway stations, where you hardly discern the difference unless the name be stuck up prominently somewhere. Nothing is more tiring, in my opinion, to the educated tourist than this sameness; and in our county, where is the money to come from to produce this expensive monotony? What is infinitely better, in my opinion, is, so far as possible, to cultivate every bit of originality that our county may possess, either in the places or the persons, or the local characteristics and customs. This may be done at comparatively little cost to ourselves, and with much pleasure to others. Let the visitor fully appreciate that directly he crosses the Tamar he is in 'Cornwall,' the people of which, by their manners in the twentieth century, have similar charms to those which they are said to have possessed in the seventeenth and eighteenth. Let us take care that only the very best Cornish cream is served, dainty chickens (not old hens), and the choicest of beef, mutton, fish, and vegetables. Let us take care that the very best of these is served to our visitors at home, and not the best sent off to other watering-places competing against us, and only the indifferent kept for home consumption. Let the science of cooking be taught and better understood than it is to-day locally. There is no necessity for bringing in the precise Continental system of serving a meal, but let our caterers take care that the Cornish dishes are properly cooked and served. They will be more enjoyed if not the exact counterpart of what has been had on the last European trip; but they must be tasty, and all the appointments of the table must be scrupulously clean and tidy.

There are many ways in which our visitors may be entertained without incurring the expenses of Continental methods. All along our coasts more might be made than is of the very natural and engrossing sport of fishing. Let there be a good supply of well-appointed fishing-boats, manned or owned by those who can take care of their charges. Let golf be fostered. Let every facility be given for visiting all objects of local interest, and never tire of placing, in convenient and attractive shape, in hotels, lodging-houses, &c., local histories, hand-books, guide-books, maps, &c., that will interest the stranger and induce him to prolong his visit.

There are many other points that one could take up, were your space unlimited, but I will in conclusion content myself with one—our railways. It is, of course, known that it was a dream with me to see both of our great systems down through the county, the western and the southern, as in addition to the advantages of having 'two strings to our bow,' and so much more territory 'up the country' opened up to us, as a gathering ground of tourists, as the South Western would bring, I always looked forward to a clean run right away through our north coast, and on to the north coast of Devon, without break or those vexatious delays caused by trains of opposite systems working in antagonism instead of agreement with each other. But that, by the apathy of the South Western, has been frustrated, and now our hopes must, of course, centre on the Great Western, which, to its credit, has since the big railway fight of 1893 shown a complete change of policy, and now, for its more liberal services, the doubling of the main line, the improvement of the stations, the rebuilding of the viaducts, and the readiness with which its managers listen to suggestions for local development, is to be highly commended. It is to be hoped that this policy will be maintained. Light railways, too, should play an important part in our county's future —coupling up such points as the Lizard and Helston, Penzance and St. Just, Newquay and Padstow, Delabole and Tintagel, and St. Austell and Mevagissey.

Mr. Arthur H. Norway You have asked me to tell you how in my judgment Cornwall might best be developed as a holiday resort. You assume, I notice, that the object propounded is one with which I am in sympathy; but on questioning myself as to whether this is so I do not find a ready answer. Cornwall is to me like a dear mistress. Must I share her with others? I sought her in the solitudes where she has dwelt in all ages till our own. Must I help to send every man a-wooing her who can pay the price of a tourist ticket from Paddington?

You will probably interrupt me here to say this is as inconsequent as the reply of the animals in the poultry yard who were called on to disclose with what sauce they would prefer to be dressed; and, indeed, I perceive that a stream of influences is popularising Cornwall which is far stronger than I could hope to control, even if I would. Not one man nor twenty could preserve for Cornwall the lonely charm of her cliff paths, or prevent the ribbed sands of her beaches from being cut up into tennis-courts; and therefore I will not waste your space with regrets which are of no practical importance, but will tell you very briefly what appear to me to be the points to which we should endeavour to direct our efforts so as to retain for our land as much as may be of the charm which seems in these days to be her only valuable asset.

It is tolerably clear that a great danger is arising of enclosures of the coast-line. For the first time in the history of Cornwall the rough ground bordering the cliffs has acquired a market value, and that value is increasing daily. In ten years time every man who owns a field commanding a fine view will be bartering it to a mammoth hotel, or to a speculative builder of villa residences. Let no one think that speculators of this class will hesitate to close the cliff paths. Let us have no illusions on this subject. Human nature contains no element on which we can rely to ensure the rejection of the largest profit. We must not dream that landowners will refuse to sell to the highest bidder.

But is there no central body which will protect these paths, and reserve for all who come to Cornwall free access to the cliffs? It is a task which presses, and demands both powers and watchfulness beyond the reach of individuals. If prompt and energetic action is not taken, if appeals are not made without delay to that unity of interest which we Cornish boast that we possess more than any other section of the English people, the privilege of wandering where one will upon the summits of the cliffs will be lost for ever. The first point to work for is to keep open a right of way, as wide as possible, all round the cliffs.

The next is to consider our hotels, laying aside for the time as much as we can of our complacency, and trying to regard them as the stranger does—for, after all, it is he who is expected to use them and pay for them, and, however stupid his tastes may be, we had better give the man his way if we desire to make money out of him. If we turn an attentive ear to his complaints, we shall find that he is perpetually recurring to his ideal inns, which are in France and Germany, and asking us why we cannot imitate their freshness, their excellent though simple cooking, and their moderate tariff. Upon my life, I do not know why we cannot. I am quite aware there are many admirable inns in Cornwall; but I imagine the complaint against them to be that they are not modern. I have but to search my memory for recollections of the cordial welcome, the unfeigned desire to please, which the village host in the Black Forest shows towards his guest; the comfortable sweet-smelling chamber, half sitting-room, half bedroom; the delicious dish of cutlets at supper; the trout, the honey, and the mountain strawberries at breakfast; the bill not exceeding five or six shillings for all this luxury. I have but to remember this, and I understand at once why the stranger spends so much time in girding at our Cornish inns; and though he is very troublesome about it, I find myself a little in sympathy with him.

Again, in Cornwall few inns are planted where the tourist needs them most. I know long ranges of cliff, too long by far for a comfortable day's walk, on which no house of entertainment will be passed. I do not wish to see mammoth hotels built upon these cliffs. But there are inns of a type well known to travellers in Norway and in other countries, which are cheap to erect and picturesque to look at, built of wood, something on the pattern of a Swiss chalet. Such inns ought to return a very fair interest on the capital laid out in building them. They would not spoil the views. They would be welcome resting-places in summer, and in winter they could be left untenanted.

It is, I suppose, recognised by everybody that the means of locomotion in Cornwall are more easily to be improved than made worse. If there be anyone of a contrary opinion, he may convince himself of the truth by attempting to go by train from Helston to Newquay. He will have leisure enough upon the journey to count the miles, to reckon his rate of speed, and to resolve that next time he will use his cycle. I know not how far the railway company sees its interest in co-operating in the development of Cornwall; but I am clear that it cannot be said to have begun until it has made these cross journeys possible without the loss of time and temper which they entail at present.

When I visit watering-places in other parts of England, I find far more facilities for excursions to points of interest than I have noticed yet in any town in Cornwall. Let anyone who disputes this reckon the number of chara-bancs which go out of Lowestoft on any day of summer. Let him count the comfortable small pony-carriages standing for hire in long lines at the corners of the streets, and note how popular they are. And finally, to touch the point where we should excel in Cornwall, but do not, let him observe how plentiful is the supply of comfortable small boats.

Miss J. H. Findlater I am not a native of Cornwall; and so perhaps 'should not speak,' as the saying goes. But there is a very true proverb which tells us that lookers-on see most of the game, so let this be my plea for speaking of Cornish matters from the far distance of Scotland.

Eight happy months I spent in Cornwall, and when I had left it far behind me, the sight of a yellow-covered publication entitled THE CORNISH MAGAZINE sent a thrill to my heart. And I bought it: read it: laughed over it: sighed over it: finally almost wept over it.

For the writers are all professed lovers of their native county, or of the land of their adoption; yet I find some of them deliberately advising Cornishmen to the destruction of their 'Delectable Duchy.'

This is my argument: The charm all charms excelling of dear Cornwall is that remoteness—that exquisite peace and sort of primeval calm which now distinguishes it from other counties. The land seems to sleep an enchanted sleep—why, in a restless age, should one such haven of peace not remain untouched? '*Because,*' we are told, '*we wish that Cornwall should be developed.*' This seems an unanswerable argument; and in one way it is unanswerable, for no one, except perhaps Mr. Ruskin, wishes the world to stand still. But what I would urge on Cornishmen who love their county is that they see that no miserable mess of pottage is given to them in exchange for their birthright.

I speak, alas! from bitter experience of what 'discovering' and 'developing' can do for the spoiling of a country—for it is almost impossible to estimate all that my poor Scotland has lost by being 'discovered.' And this not merely, as I shall show, from the æsthetic standpoint, but from the purely mercenary one. Her fair face has been in too many cases her undoing instead of her fortune, and where once the whole land smiled, now you see nothing but rows of villas backed by railway embankments. 'All this means money,' the practical people argue; but not at all, in the long run. What too often happens is this—that *for a short term of years*, before any place is too much built up, a rush of rich people comes to it and money pours into the place; then more and cheaper houses are built, and yet cheaper again and nastier, until the place becomes an abomination; and then it is deserted completely and the houses stand empty, and the proprietors lose their money, which goes on elsewhere.

For, after all, what one wishes in the country is the country; and if the country becomes a sort of mongrel town no one who can afford to live elsewhere will live in it. As this has happened in Scotland, so it will happen in Cornwall if some of the advice which is given in the first number of THE CORNISH MAGAZINE is taken by the Cornishmen. 'Something is to be done to enliven' the little towns. It is suggested that the music of the Atlantic breakers is not sufficiently attractive for Londoners, so they are to be provided with a 'fashionable promenade,' where they may walk to the strains of 'a fine military band.' Further, 'that animation which is wanting in Cornwall' is to be supplied by means of 'open-air cafés, concerts and entertainments of every kind.' Cockney Paradises, in a word, are to gem the shores of happy Cornwall. Is this not disastrous advice to give? For heaven's sake, let those who long for fashionable promenades, military bands, cafés, and nigger minstrels, retire to Brighton, Ramsgate, and Margate, leaving the habitable parts of the earth to those who have simpler tastes, and can still enjoy a walk on the shore and listen to the old music of the world!

Unless Cornishmen look to it, their country will be spoilt before they know it. Already there are signs of it—pitiable signs. Not many months ago I visited Tintagel, which is justly one of the prides of the Duchy. The 'swinging seas' are breaking against the great cliffs as they broke there centuries ago, when Arthur and Launcelot and Knights of the Round Table peopled the place. The castle is mostly crumbled away now, but some fraction of its old strength still stands to face the Atlantic gales, and to show us how walls were built in the grand old days. In the valley the grass is green and the gorse is yellow, and overhead the skies are blue and delightful; but facing Arthur's Castle—grinning down, as it were, in derision at the ruins of its old state—there is being erected a modern hotel—'built in imitation of Arthur's Castle,' as one is told! Bad taste cannot possibly go any farther.

There is not yet a rubbish shoot over the edge of the cliff, but I do not think I am wrong in stating that the drainage is brought down into that cove where, long ago (the story runs), the naked baby Arthur came ashore on the great wave!

Well, is it not a suicidal policy to destroy all the splendid remains of a country in this way? Would it not have been possible to select (for instance) some less glaringly offensive site for an hotel at Tintagel, if hotel there must be? This, as well as the cheap lodging-house horror, is a matter for the proprietors to look to. Could expansion not be carried out within reasonable limits, and could some rules not be adhered to in the case of rising towns to insist that very ugly houses are not built to deform the place? Let me take a very popular health resort in North Cornwall as an 'object lesson.'

Bude is a place with many natural advantages—sands, cliffs, downs, a river —yet by a promiscuous and unrestrained building it has been turned into a perfect eyesore. Great rows of cheaply run-up lodging-houses stand in tiers on the cliff side, and every abomination of the jerry builder is to be seen here to the greatest advantage.

Is all this quite inevitable? and, as I argue above, would it not pay better, *in the long run*, to build houses that were architecturally good?—the people who are willing to pay for good houses being presumably the class of tenant that is most earnestly desired of the natives as 'bringing most money into the country.'

But alas! the principle of 'quick returns' is deeply rooted in us all, and doubtless Bude will 'have its day and cease to be' (fashionable), and another Bude, worse than the first, will rise on the now untouched wildness of the splendid Western shores; or perhaps, now that the railway has reached so near to it, even dear Marhamchurch will be 'discovered' and 'developed' and 'destroyed,' and some proprietors will be the richer, and the many will be poorer far!

The Editor. Let me confess that in summing up this discussion I have (so to say) to cut myself in two and weigh one part of me against the other. If my own private feelings must be uttered, I hate a crowd. I can honestly say, with Sir Joseph Pease, that I have never found any difficulty in liking Cornwall as she is. In my heart I agree with Mr. Norway that her remoteness is a great part of her charm. To me her solitudes are dear because they speak to me. With Mr. Page, I abhor the tripper and the brass band. I am not a cyclist. If I were, the suggestion that the cyclist is civilisation's highest product would doubtless appeal to me with greater force and find me more eager to abase every hill and exalt every valley to make the cyclist's path easy. And a natural love of my native land no doubt blinds me in some measure to the failings which many strangers are bound to discover in her.

But these are private feelings. On the other hand I see Cornwall impoverished by the evil days on which mining and (to a lesser degree) agriculture have fallen. I see her population diminishing and her able-bodied sons forced to emigrate by the thousand. The ruined engine-house, the roofless cottage, the cold hearthstone are not cheerful sights to one who would fain see a race so passionately attached to home as ours is still drawing its vigour from its own soil. In the presence of destitution and actual famine (for in the mining district it came even to this, a little while ago) one is bound, if he care for his countrymen, to consider any cure thoughtfully suggested.

The suggestion is that Cornwall should turn her natural beauty to account, and, by making it more widely known, at once benefit thousands and honestly enrich herself.

Well, on this point I may say at once that, jealous as I am for the beauty of our Duchy, and delighted when strangers admire her, I am if possible more jealous for the character of her sons, and more eager that strangers shall respect *them*. And I do see (and hope to be forgiven for seeing it) that a people which lays itself out to exploit the stranger and the tourist runs an appreciable risk of deterioration in manliness and independence. It may seem a brutal thing to say, but as I had rather be poor myself than subservient, so I would liefer see my countrymen poor than subservient. It is not our boast—we have it on the fairly unanimous evidence of all who have visited us—that hitherto Cornishmen have been able to combine independence with good manners. For Heaven's sake, I say, let us keep that reputation, though at great cost! But let us at the same time face the certainty that, when we begin to take pay for entertaining strangers, it will be a hard reputation to keep. Were it within human capacity to decide between a revival of our ancient industries, fishery and mining, and the development of this new business, our decision would be prompt enough. But it is not.

Well then, since we must cater for the stranger, let us do it well and honestly. Let us respect him and our native land as well. We have on our side unique and magnificent natural scenery, and a pleasant and extraordinarily temperate climate. The Riviera has exquisite scenery: but somehow its scenery lacks the depth, the 'values' of ours. It wears at the best a painted appearance: and the difference between the Mediterranean and the Atlantic is just the difference between flat cider and champagne. It has more sunshine—far more sunshine—than we enjoy: let that be confessed. But the alternations of heat and cold are swift and treacherous. One moment you are basking in warmth: the next the sun has disappeared behind the hills and leaves you miserably shivering.

On the other hand the Riviera provides splendid hotels, good music, magnificent cliff drives. Its inhabitants understand the art and the value of gaiety. Life there is full of small comforts, small pleasures: it is brisk, and full of variety, colour, 'go.' In this business the French show themselves far more sportsmanlike than we. They are willing to risk their money for a prospective harvest. Their municipalities recognise the simple truth that if a town seeks to be attractive—to charm the eye and ear and offend the nose as little as possible (though in this matter of smell the Latin races are a trifle behind the rest of the world)—it must not grumble incessantly at the rates. The rates go up, to be sure: but the money comes pouring back with interest, and the inhabitants have a town which satisfies them as well as the visitor, and on which, as they take their Sunday walks, they can let their eyes dwell with true citizen pride. It is idle, I submit, and in the end it must debilitate our character, if we merely accept what nature has done for us, and sit down with folded hands, while the visitor provides his own amusement and pays a pretty stiff bill for the privilege. It is for *us* to take thought, and bestir ourselves, and provide the amenities of life.

Only we should do so with decent respect for our country and its past. I do not, for example, look forward to seeing Dozmare turned into a sheet of ornamental water, or a casino in full swing of business amid the ruins of King Arthur's Castle. In choosing the sites of our hotels, we should not only consider the view from their windows but the effect of their chimneys upon the surrounding landscape. Nor should landowners at once expect the visitor to put money into their pockets by enhancing the value of ground rents, and affront him by standing too pragmatically on the strict letter of their rights. In short there must be a fair give-and-take, or, as Sir Edward Durning-Lawrence put it, 'a courteous readiness on the part of the inhabitants to surrender a portion of their own home comforts for the benefit of the new comers.'

To come to a minor point, yet not an unimportant one. There are notable exceptions: but as a rule the *cookery* throughout our Duchy cries aloud for improvement. And, oddly enough, I believe it could be vastly improved by the judicious introduction of a few of our own native and traditional dishes, or by experiments having them for a base. On the Riviera I have turned with eagerness from the tasteless and eternal *poulet à cresson* to the *bouillabaisse* which the inhabitants eat on Sundays and high days. Also I would plead for a wider recognition of the great and solemn truth that the label does not make the claret: nay, that the coal-black and rose-pink products of Germany's commercial cunning seldom bear even a visual resemblance to what they profess to be—the sound wines of Bordeaux. With trustworthy wine-merchants at our door there is no good excuse for ignoring the difference. Many Cornish hotels provide excellent wine: and I believe the number to be increasing. But the visitor has a tendency to remember the exceptions.

Lastly, I have dreamed from time to time of a broad and noble coast road: but always I awoke, and lo, it was a dream!

TWO AUSTRALIAN KNIGHTS

Two South Australians, who have during the present year received the honour of knighthood, are not only connected with Cornwall, but, curiously enough, are both associated with the parish of Mylor. Sir James Penn Boucaut was born there, and Sir John Langdon Bonython represents the Bonythons of Bonython, who held Carclew from before 1420 until 1749, when the estate was purchased by Colonel Tremayne's ances-

SIR J. P. BOUCAUT

tor. Sir J. P. Boucaut, who is a judge of the Supreme Court, has been premier and acting-governor. Sir J. L. Bonython is the proprietor of the Adelaide 'Advertiser,' and has done much for the advancement of education. Among the positions which he has occupied for many years is that of President of the South Australian School of Mines and Industries, which is the biggest educational institution in the colony. Both are enthusiastic Cornishmen.

SIR J. L. BONYTHON

CORNISH DIAMONDS

'I sheant go theer nor nawheer else,' said old Jane Caddy, 'I shall go'n up Redruth.'

———◆———

When the railway was opened the whole town was out joining in the procession, and as the volunteers marched up the hill the children were crowding round the band. 'Now get out of the way, you boys,' said the drummer, 'I'm three seats behind as tes.'

———◆———

'What's the greatest amount of cider you ever drank?'
'Haaf a osget.'
'But I mean at one sitting.'
'Tha's what I'm tellin'' 'ee. Father helped, and uncle did a bit, too.'
'Look here—do you mean to tell me that you three drank half a hogshead of cider at one sitting?'
'Iss, tha's of it. Set to work eleven one forenoon, an' drank stiddy: finished 'en clane off some time next evenin'.'
'But why on earth . . . ?'
'Well, you see, 'twas this way. We'd a-finished harvest and there wad'n much doin' 'pon the varm. And so happen 'twas goin' to be a terrible fine season for caider: I never seed the trees lookin' more keenly. Father said 'twould be a zin to waste it. So now you knaw.'
'But I don't understand . . . ?'
'Why, you see, we'd got a use for the caask.'

———◆———

An old couple, aged ninety, had buried their only son, who was close upon seventy years old. On returning from the funeral, they sat in silence for half an hour. Then the old woman remarked, 'I allus told 'ee so. Dedden I knaw 'ow 'twoud be when the baby was born? I told 'ee 'eed never live to be reared.'

A mine captain was one day 'out uv coore' discussing with the other agents the latest phase of military science, and the consequent expediency of large expenditure on extensive fortifications. 'I tell 'ee what et es,' says the captain; 'garrisons aren't no good toall. What es the good fer a man to go a-hidin' uv 'esself behind gaat walls? Why doan't he cum aout when theere's a enemy and crack to 'en? Look to the saige of Paris. Ef they oanly cum aout to fight they wudden haave ben staarved. Wusn't 'ee ruther be kelled then staarved to death?'

———◆———

A covey of partridges rose out of shot, flew over the hedge, and was lost to view.
'Where do you think they have gone?' said the shooter to his keeper. 'There's a man digging potatoes in the next field, ask him if he's seen them.'
'Aw, that's old Sam Petherick; ee asna seed em, ee's 'ard uv earin'.'

———◆———

Uncle Billy had met a stranger on the road, 'a nice little fella, too,' he reported.
'But what sort of man?'
'A round, compact little man 'e was; going to R'druth for a cargo of copper oor; a cap'en of a man-of-woor, so he towld me.'

———◆———

After a very grand lecture on chemistry delivered by a University man to a Cornish audience, the chairman rose and addressed the meeting:
'Friends, what wonders we do live amid! The passage is narra, and the doorway is smal; now go out slaw, so's, and don't stank one pon nother.'

A CORNISH MOORLAND [Harrison, Falmouth

FOOTPRINTS OF THE WESLEYS IN CORNWALL

HOWEVER thoroughly their names have swallowed up those of the lesser men who heralded them, neither of the Wesleys was the pioneer of Methodism in the West, nor can we with certainty identify the first of the missionaries who ventured into these regions with the solemn warnings and glad promises of the newly discovered evangel. But the oldest class-ticket which has been preserved in Cornwall bears the initials 'J. R.,' with the date 1740. Now amongst the earliest and most energetic of Wesley's assistants was one Jonathan Reeves, and it is probable enough that we are indebted to him for the first breaking up of the hard, yet potentially fertile soil, which has since produced such an abundant harvest. The report of Jonathan Reeves, or of whomsoever it was that began the good work, as to his labours in the far west, evidently

interested the great leader of the enterprise, whose restless loving eyes were ever on the watch for means of service, and in 1743 he determined to bring his personal influence to bear on the population of Cornwall. His brother Charles preceded him by a few weeks, but on Michaelmas day in that year John Wesley, with John Nelson as his companion, crossed the Tamar on the first of those numerous visits whose importance in our history can scarcely be exaggerated.

Without a little reflection one might, perhaps, experience some surprise at the fact that Wesley, who was one of the most economic and systematic of men, thought it necessary to devote so much time and attention as he did to our remote and, as we now regard it, sparsely peopled county. But the truth is that we do not easily realise the change which has passed over the condition of the country between that day and this, especially as to the extent and distribution of the population. To-day the inhabitants of England and Wales number something over 30,000,000, of whom about one-sixth live in what is called Greater London. In Wesley's day the census had not been instituted, so that we cannot give precise figures; but the material supplied by the registers of births and the records of the house tax enables us to make our calculations with a considerable degree of confidence, and we cannot be far wrong in estimating the population in 1743 at about 6,000,000. Even now, as we have seen, the predominance of London over other towns is remarkable. It is nearly ten times as large as the next largest city. Then Bristol was the second city in the empire; but London, with a population of 600,000, was fifteen times as large as Bristol with its 40,000 souls. Moreover, whereas there are now very many towns nearly approaching the size of our second city, then there were very few indeed which came near the size of Bristol. Next to it stood Norwich, Exeter, and York, but besides these there was not a single town exceeding 20,000 inhabitants. Now there are many towns whose population exceeds or nearly approaches that of Cornwall. Then Cornwall, which has in the present century so largely contributed to the colonisation of Greater Britain, was probably not much less populous

Photo by]   ST. JUST MARKET PLACE   *[Trembath, St. Just*

than it is at present. While, then, we do not now regard Launceston, Bodmin, St. Ives, or St. Just as very influential centres of national life, at that time Launceston was as big as Sheffield, Bodmin larger than Birmingham, St. Ives considerably more populous than Liverpool, and St. Just nearly as extensive as Manchester. When Wesley first visited Looe he referred to it in his 'Journal' as 'a town about half as large as Islington'! So that after all we need not be greatly surprised to find that in the first Conference, which was held in 1744, the answer to the question 'What is the best way of spreading the Gospel?' was this, 'To go a little and little farther from London, Bristol, St. Ives, Newcastle, or any other society.' From which we may conclude that St. Ives was then not only the chief Methodist centre of Cornwall, but was one of the four principal societies in the United Kingdom. It is, I think, referred to in Wesley's 'Journal' more frequently than any other town west of Bristol.

It was there that Charles Wesley established his headquarters at his first visit; and from thence amidst many wild scenes of opposition he spent about a fortnight in visiting the surrounding villages. At this time no churches were open to him; in fact, the clergy were his chief opponents, and too often the instigators of riotous opposition. His pulpits, therefore, were found occasionally in the rooms hired or built for the use of the Society (they never called them chapels in those days), but more commonly in the market places or on the open downs. It was during this visit that, when Charles was preaching at Pool, a churchwarden, heading a mob, drove preacher and congregation 'out of the parish' (that is, I suppose, to the bottom of Tuckingmill Hill, the boundary between Camborne and Illogan), and then returned to celebrate the victory in the old alehouse at Pool. The following entry in the parish book of Illogan testifies to the methods by which the conquerors' valour was inspired— 'Expences at Ann Gartrell's on driving out the Methodist, nine shillings.' Apparently it was the ratepayers' money which was devoted to the holy purpose, and 9s. in those days would have covered the cost of a goodly amount of ale and smuggled brandy.

A few days later Charles Wesley visited Camborne again, and we met with this interesting entry in his 'Journal': 'An elderly man pressed us to turn into his house near Camborne. It was a large old country seat, and looked like the picture of English hospitality.' Unfortunately neither the name of the house nor that of the host is given, but there is evidence which warrants the conclusion that the 'country seat' was Rosewarne. As the 'Journal' shows, Wesley had brought his congregation from Pool to Camborne, presumably to avoid the effects of the churchwardens' vigour and Ann Gartrell's beer. He speaks of the glorious sight of the 'wide-spread multitude walking up the hill,' evidently the hill on which Tuckingmill now stands. Then he immediately speaks of his preaching and of the invitation to 'turn in' to 'the country seat.' Rosewarne was near at hand. There is nothing else like a country seat within miles. Moreover, from later entries in John Wesley's 'Journal' we learn that Mr. Harris, the then proprietor of Rosewarne, was one of his earliest supporters in Camborne, and more than once or twice he speaks of preaching at his house, and of having partaken of his hospitality. It must be noted, however, that

Photo by] [*Capt. L. Ching, R.N., Launceston*
TRESMERE CHURCH

the house which the Wesleys knew and admired has long since disappeared, the present mansion having been erected and once or twice enlarged within the memory of people still living.

After having spoken of the opposition of the clergy generally, it is pleasant to be able to record some exceptions to the rule. On Charles Wesley's second visit in 1744 he preached in St. Gennys church by the invitation of Mr. Thompson, the rector, and on the next day and several times afterwards in the Laneast church, whose minister, Mr. Bennett, accompanied him to Gwennap. These churches, and also those at Tresmere and St. Mary Week, were frequently opened to John Wesley, but there is no record of his having had similar invitations elsewhere, and it is noteworthy that all these churches lie within a small area in the north of the county. In his later days many of the clergy were more or less favourable to Wesley's work, and extended to him a generous hospitality. For example, he makes special reference to his visit in 1787 to Kenwyn rectory (now known as Lis Escop, and until recently the residence of the Cornish Bishop), which he describes as 'a house fit for a nobleman, and the most beautifully situated of any I have seen in the county.'

But whether the clergy were favourable or otherwise, the Wesleys, especially in the course of their earlier visits, frequently attended the churches, too often hearing themselves and all their works declaimed against. And when the insides of the consecrated buildings were refused them, they often found convenient preaching places just outside the holy ground. The 'north side of the church at Morvah' is more than once spoken of as a favourite spot. At Zennor, at Towednack, at Ludgvan, at Breage, at Buryan and elsewhere, congregations were from time to time assembled close to the churches, which could not have accommodated a tithe of the numbers within.

One can scarcely turn

Photo by] [*Capt. L. Ching, R.N.*
WEEK ST. MARY CHURCH

FOOTPRINTS OF THE WESLEYS IN CORNWALL

from the subject of Charles Wesley's visits to Cornwall without mention of the Land's End, the aspect of which is locally alleged to have given rise to one of the best known verses in his hymns :

> 'Lo! on a narrow neck of land
> 'Twixt two unbounded seas I stand,
> Secure, insensible :
> A point of time, a moment's space
> Removes me to that heavenly place,
> Or shuts me up in hell.'

LANEAST CHURCH [*Capt. L. Ching, R.N.*

But unfortunately for the tradition which presumably the guides on the spot will, after the fashion of guides, repeat to the end of time, there is not a particle of evidence connecting the hymn with the locality. Moreover, the sentiment or illustration is so natural, and has been expressed by so many previous writers, that it does not seem to demand any special inspiration ; and curiously enough there is a promontory in Georgia which also claims, probably with just as much or just as little reason, to have suggested the thought. Yet again ; if it is necessary to associate the idea with some definite 'narrow neck of land,' I am inclined to think that Cape Cornwall, a risky ascent of which Charles Wesley particularly mentions, has from its configuration better claims than the Land's End, where the indicated ridge is so very narrow and rocky that one would scarcely describe it as a 'neck of land.'

This method of commenting on scenery, natural or architectural, is, however, quite characteristic of the Wesleys and their times. No charm of view, no admiration for art could for a moment hide the invisible from their eyes, or distract their thoughts from the eternal. Whatever Charles said or thought at the Land's End, John has given us his comment on the scene. 'We went as far as we could go safely towards the point of the rocks. It was an awful sight! But how will these melt away when God ariseth to judgment!' He walked up St. Michael's Mount, and reflects thus, 'The house at the top is surprisingly large and pleasant. Sir John St.

LIS ESCOP, TRURO

Aubyn had taken much pains, and been at a considerable expense, in repairing and beautifying the apartments; and when the seat was finished the owner died!' Mount Edgecumbe received a visit, of which he writes, 'The situation is fine indeed. The lofty hill, nearly surrounded by the sea, and sufficiently adorned with trees . . . is uncommonly pleasant. . . . And are all these things to be burned up?' He speaks of the ascending of Carnbrea, and refers to the rock basins as Druidic remains possibly coeval with the pyramids of Egypt, adding, 'What are they the better for this? Of what consequence is it to the living or the dead whether they have withstood the wastes of time for 3,000 or 300 years?'

It is interesting to observe the slow degrees by which Wesley's personality and pertinacity overcame the violent prejudices of the Cornish, and at last filled them with such enthusiasm that his visits almost resembled triumphant progresses. At first he experienced almost unbroken hardship and conflict, not only from active opposition, but also from callous neglect. Nowadays whatever faults our people may be charged with, they certainly are 'given to hospitality.' There is reason to think, however, that this as well as other Christian graces was revived, if not implanted, by Wesley's evangelism. In recording the first visit, John Nelson says, 'We usually preached on commons, going from one common to another. Seldom did any one ask us to eat or drink. One day we had been preaching on St. Hilary Downs: as we returned Mr. Wesley stopped his horse to pick the blackberries, saying, "Brother Nelson, we ought to be thankful that there are plenty of blackberries, for this is the best county I ever saw for getting a stomach, but the worst I ever saw for getting food."' Happily, I think tourists would now agree that the county has retained its former characteristic, but has turned over a new leaf as to the latter. Nelson had between intervals of preaching to seek work as a mason, in order to keep body and soul together, and often slept on the floor with no softer pillow than 'Burkitt's Notes on the New Testament.' Once at three in the morning, a whole hour earlier than his usual time of rising, he was awoke by Wesley's crying, 'Brother Nelson, be of good cheer, I have one whole side yet.' I fancy that the experiences of the visiting preachers of the last half century have run in the direction of indigestion rather than of starvation.

The incident above given illustrates one aspect of the evangelist's difficulties; but of course the opposition was not always of this passive character. In 1744, during Wesley's second visit, the whole county was greatly excited at the news of the victory of Admiral Mathews over the Spanish fleet. The crowd at St. Ives could think of no more congenial way of giving expression to their joy and thanksgiving than by demolishing all the windows and furniture of the Methodist preaching room. It was certainly a somewhat characteristic way of celebrating a joyful occasion. Wesley, whose temper and patience were imperturbable, though of course grieved at the destruction, appreciated the humour of the idea, and even found cause for thankfulness, remarking that if Admiral Lestock had fought as well, the mob would probably have killed all the Methodists.

The most dangerous of all the riotous assemblies aroused by the new

FOOTPRINTS OF THE WESLEYS IN CORNWALL

preaching occurred at Falmouth in 1745. The evangelist had a narrow escape indeed, and speaks of his deliverance as even more wonderful than that which he had experienced at Walsall. The house in which he was assailed has been removed, but I am told that in the village of Buck's Head, near Truro, the door is still preserved, indented with the stones which were hurled against it.

Another form of persecution to which some of the early preachers were subjected had a little more semblance of legality in it. The barbarous custom of impressing men for military and naval service was then in full practice. It is true that by a then recent statute the cruelties of the press gangs had been to some extent mitigated, but their operations were still quite brutal enough to present a tempting means of oppression to petty bigots in authority. The Wesleys themselves were, of course, as clergymen exempt from this danger; though on one occasion an attempt was made to bring the law to bear on the elder brother by the circulation of the report that the real John Wesley was dead, and that the little man then travelling about the country in cassock and bands was an impostor personating him. His assistant ministers, however, being in the eye of the law laymen, could claim no indulgence, and on more than one occasion in various parts of the country they suffered intolerable injustice. Maxfield, one of the best of them, was so arrested at Wesley's side, at Crowan (which Wesley described as the headquarters of the men who delight in war), hauled off to Marazion, and adjudicated for a time to naval service by Dr. Borlase, a celebrated man and notorious persecutor. The allegation against him was that he was a vagrant without visible means of support, and as such fair game for the gang. It is pleasant, however, to be able to record

Photo by]   GWENNAP PIT   *[Argall, Truro*

that Wesley was able within a short time to secure his deliverance, and that he was one of the first to receive Methodist ordination.

I have as yet only incidentally mentioned the one place in Cornwall which is, perhaps, more conspicuously than any other associated with Wesley's preaching—Gwennap.

He frequently preached there in his earlier visits, but it appears that he did not utilise the celebrated 'pit' until nearly twenty years after his first tour, and that then its occupation was in a way fortuitous. At an early date there was a 'room' in the near vicinity: but these 'rooms,' though useful and commodious enough for the local preachers, were far too small to accommodate the multitudes who gathered to hear the great missioner. So he usually took his stand on some elevation, a horse-block or low wall, or anything that would raise him sufficiently to be seen and heard by the congregation. Such had been his practice at Gwennap until one occasion in 1762. It was a windy day; the crowd was greater than ever, and it was a question whether he could possibly make himself heard in an unsheltered place. Then some one happily thought of the neighbouring pit, and thither they went; the multitude thronging it as they might an amphitheatre, the preacher taking his stand about a third from the top. To every one's delight the experiment was most successful. The preacher was heard perfectly. It was natural enough that thenceforth the pit became a favourite preaching place; and surely if consecrated ground is anywhere to be found it is there. It is doubtful whether there is any one spot

GWENNAP PIT ON WHIT MONDAY

on earth in which such vast numbers have simultaneously listened to the preaching of the Word, or which has witnessed more wonderful results attending such preaching.

It will not, of course, be supposed that the Gwennap pit of Wesley's day was levelled and trimmed after the fashion with which all Methodist tourists are so familiar now. He speaks of it as a natural formation, but it has since been clearly shown that the depression was caused by the subsidence of the surface owing to some ancient mining excavations. At first, no doubt, it was a roughly circular cavity providing only standing room for the congregation. But as soon as it was discovered to be admirably adapted for an auditorium, some enthusiastic supporters of the cause set to work to improve the accommodation by cutting rows of seats in the banks, and otherwise smoothing and levelling the surface. By this means its holding capacity and convenience were greatly increased, and on subsequent visits Wesley spoke enthusiastically of the services held there as presenting the most lovely and imposing spectacle he had ever witnessed. In 1781, when he was seventy-eight years of age, he wrote, 'In the evening I preached at Gwennap, I think this my *ne plus ultra*. I shall scarce see a larger congregation till we meet in the air.' But in his last allusion to the pit, which was six years later, he says, 'I suppose we had a thousand more than ever were there before; but it was all one; my voice was strengthened accordingly, so that every one could hear distinctly.' He estimated his congregation at over 30,000 people, but I suspect that this was an unconscious exaggeration. Even his own figures suggest as much. He gives the dimensions as 200 feet across one way and near 300 another. If, for convenience of calculation, we assume a mean diameter of 240 feet, which is precisely the estimate which he himself made on another occasion, we shall find that the superficial area of the enclosure must have been a little over 5,000 square yards; so that to accommodate even 30,000 people, six men, and Cornishmen at that, must have been stowed in every square yard over the whole surface! Even half this number seems an outside figure.

It is stated in an article which appeared in the 'Cornish Banner' in 1847, that in 1803 the pit was narrowed and remodelled to the dimensions and form now so familiar. At present it is perfectly circular, with a diameter of but little over forty yards, and a surface area of about 1,200, which is scarcely one-fourth of its size in Wesley's day, if his measurements were correct.

It is an interesting, but it is in some respects a disappointing, task for an admirer of Wesley to travel over the county attempting to identify the precise localities consecrated by his name. In one sense, as I have intimated, we may be said to see him everywhere. There is scarcely a high road which in the course of one or other of his thirty-one visits he did not traverse again and again. There is scarcely a market-place in which he did not preach, and when even market-places were too strait for his congregations many a common or downs served his purpose. But of actual buildings honoured by his use or residence few indeed can be found. Only one existing Cornish chapel was built in his lifetime—that at St. Ives. It was built in 1785, near the close of his ministry, and though it has since been twice or thrice enlarged, it still

TREWIRGIE HOUSE, REDRUTH

comprises a portion at least of the original building in which he probably ministered in the course of his later visits. Within the last few years the old chapel at Sticker near Grampound, which was actually opened by Wesley and thus possessed a unique interest, has unfortunately been removed. Of course there are scores of cases in which the present chapels occupy the sites of the rooms which Wesley used. He says of the preaching-house at Hayle, 'I suppose such another is not in England, nor in Europe, nor in the world. It is round, and all the walls are brass, that is, brazen slags. It seems nothing can destroy this till heaven and earth pass away.' But the vaticination has failed. The name 'Copperhouse' probably enshrines the memory of this singular edifice, but the building itself was within thirty years of Wesley's death replaced by a more conventional and capacious room, the 'brazen slags' being used in the erection of many an adjacent house.

What is true of Wesley's chapels is equally so of the houses in which he was entertained. But few so remain as to be capable of identification. As already mentioned, the old Kenwyn rectory is one. Trewirgie, near Redruth, is another, in or near which he often preached. I hoped to have found in St. Ives 'John Nance's house,' which is frequently mentioned in the 'Journals' as a rendezvous, and was the centre of some violent scenes of opposition. It stood at the top of the Street-an-Garrow, but has disappeared in the effecting of recent improvements.

Both the Wesleys were men of little stature, and naturally found it necessary to seek some elevation when addressing the multitudes that followed them. Sometimes it was the window of the house of a friend, sometimes the low wall of a churchyard, sometimes a mere hedge, sometimes a protruding rock. One of these last has given the name of 'Wesley Rock' to a village which possesses one of the prettiest of modern chapels. It is situated between Madron and Penzance. The rock utilised by Wesley as his pulpit was so closely associated with his memory, that on the erection of a chapel there in 1842 it was removed bodily and built into the floor so as to serve as the foundation of the pulpit. This chapel has recently been replaced by a new building of a very different type; but the 'rock' has again been removed, and still contributes its inspiring memories to all who minister there. Another similar stone pulpit has been removed from the neighbourhood of Sithney to the grounds of Mr. Bickford-Smith at Trevarno. St. Just also boasts the possession of one of Wesley's preaching rocks. He alludes to it as 'the stone by brother Chenhalls's house,' the 'brother Chenhalls' being the grandfather of Mr. Alfred Chenhalls, the present worthy representative of the name. Until a few years ago it continued to occupy its original site, but it has recently been placed, for better preservation, in the new cemetery.

Of Wesley relics, such as small presents, letters, &c., doubtless the county could furnish an interesting collection to a patient inquirer, but this investigation scarcely falls within the scope of the present article. And, after all, to one who is something more than a mere curiosity seeker, the most significant of the vestiges of Wesley in Cornwall are found in the homes and hearts of the people. You can scarcely enter a farmhouse or labourer's cottage amongst the hills of Zennor or the moors of Wendron, or an engine-house amongst the mines of Camborne, without finding amongst the few books displayed a copy of Wesley's hymns. You can scarcely find a village from the Tamar to the Land's End which is not blessed with a little house of prayer and worship, plain and unpretentious indeed, but the cherished centre of a true devotion. These are the real monuments which commemorate the unequalled labours of the great evangelist. The ancient churches perpetuate the names of many saints, the little chapels all preserve the name of one whose heroic life changed the whole life of England, but no part of England so thoroughly and so effectually as the land of Tre, Pol and Pen. The last word about Cornwall in Wesley's 'Journal' is one of good hope which, I think, we shall all agree, has been abundantly realised—'I preached at nine in our new house at Camelford ... and at six in the evening in the new house at Launceston, still too small for the congregation which seemed exceeding lively. So there is a fair prospect for Cornwall from Launceston to the Land's End' (August 1789).

CHARLES WESLEY

H. ARTHUR SMITH.

WISHT WOOD

THOSE slanderous rogues, the Devon folk, are wont to declare that there is not enough wood in Cornwall to make a coffin with. There is as much truth in this as in most of the tales folk tell of their neighbours. Certainly the Duchy is no longer what it was in the old days—the old ancient times of all, as they say—when the oaks rubbed shoulders together from Bude to Sennen, and the Mount was still *Carclowse en Cowse*, 'the Hoar Rock in the Wood,' and the last wolf was not yet trapped in the forest of Ludgvan. But Cornwall is still in a position to provide funereal timber for every one of her tall sons—ay, and for all the fat, wheezy Devon chaps that ever died of a surfeit of sour cider and sourer cream. Her hills are bare; naked and unflinching they stand up against Bucca, the blustering storm-god; but down in the deep valley-bottoms and narrow seaside glens, where Bucca never ventures, grow elms as tall, and oaks as stout, as ever Devon man set eyes on. And I know of a place where there is a wood—not an upstart plantation, nor a straggling copse, but a real wild wood of ancient growth, dense enough to shut the world out, big enough, with the help of a little manœuvring and make-believe, for one to lose oneself in, without its like in all Cornwall. They say there is a wood near Bodmin, but this is not the one. Where it is I shall not tell, for fear the Devon men should come and make a may-game of it, and the foreign visitors drive out in their carriages to stare at it as they stare at the Mên-an-tol and the Dawns-myin, and other Cornish wonders. That would be a pity; for the marvels and secrets of Wisht Wood (so it shall be called, its real name being unspoken) are retired and delicate, only to be comprehended by solitary lovers.

This may be told, that it lies in a hollow on a hill-side, where the land dips from the moors to the pastures; and you may approach it from either direction, according to your mood—down from the heather to surprise it, or up from the grass to woo it gently. If you come from below you see it afar off, and lose it and find it again as the path wanders among the hills; and when you reach it, there is only a little brook to cross and you are within. But if you come from above, you are suddenly aware of the moist, sweet-smelling breath of innumerable green leaves, close at hand, and not one to be seen. You step without warning from heather on to stone; two steps you take, and stop, for the place where next you meant to set your foot is not earth, nor rock, but the top of a tall tree. A wall of granite drops sheer beneath you into twilight. Pines and ash-trees crowd against it; young elders and thorns grow out of its crevices; and beyond, down the slope, stretches the wood—a ruddy mist of ash buds in spring, in summer a leaning roof of green leafage, a dense, unbroken surface, on which the eye rests as on firm ground, denying the airy space below, so that it comes like the shock of a blunt contradiction when a sudden wood-pigeon claps out of the fancied solidity.

Within, the wood's name is justified; it is a wisht place, sure enough, as the saying goes. It wears an appearance of extreme age—age that has surpassed the limits of venerable dignity and fallen into a fantastic dotage. Grey rocks lie half prone in grotesque attitudes among the trees; the trees, too, are grey with moss and shaggy lichen, and scarcely one of them has its natural growth. There are pollard ashes leaning cunningly this way and that, their monstrous heads bristling with stiff twigs. There are elder trees whose trunks run along the ground and suddenly erect themselves, like threatening snakes. There are thorn-bushes on which you would think an agonising spell had been cast, their twigs are involved in such mad twists and contortions. In one remote corner you come across two young trees locked together in a desperate death-grapple. Another has been pinned down by a boulder, and is growing over it, slowly smothering it in thick foliage. Two others, straight-stemmed pines, are crossed like foils at the parry. The heart of the wood is a deep black pool, hardly to be approached, so crowded about is it with peering, stooping trees and bushes. You guess them to be gloating over an unsavoury secret which they would not have you share. Elsewhere there is a handsome, flourishing oak, with one unaccountable dead limb, from which, as you approach, a stealthy hawk always stoops and flies noiselessly away. On still spring afternoons the least stir of wind rouses a faint sound of pattering footsteps, and a faint, sweet perfume; but when you turn your head there is no fair ghost gliding past, only a laurel thicket tapping dry leaf on leaf, and uneasily shaking its tasselled blossoms.

One cannot doubt that other influences are at work in the place beside the ordinary control of sun and wind and rain, who are honest journeymen, loving the straight and comely in their serious work, and reserving all fantastic imaginings for their sky-playground and the clouds that may be carved and dyed to all wild shapes and frolic colours, and no harm done. Trees are not the dull insensible rustics some would have us think them. They breathe a moral as well as a physical atmosphere, and the forest is as impressionable, as sensitive to good or evil influence, as any other crowd. In a park the trees are fine gentlemen, in an orchard they wear the loutish smock-frock and gaiters, on waste lands they are ragged gipsies every one. Natural conditions are not enough to account for the moods and perversities of the denizens of Wisht Wood. The spot is a sheltered one, the soil wholesome and fertile; no visible reason prevents the trees from leading a decent, orderly life. What, ask the few who know the place and frequent it, has driven them thus frantic?

One hints at a dreadful midnight crime; but there is no record of this in local tradition, which is notoriously absorbent and retentive of such things. Another advances a more plausible theory. In the rock wall at the top of the wood there is a cave, blocked at the entrance by a great stone. This, he declares, is none other than the stone, told of in the history of King Arthur, under which Merlin lies imprisoned by the craft of Nimue, the Lady of the Lake. We read :

'And so, upon a time, it happened that Merlin showed to her a rock where was a great wonder, and wrought by enchantment, which went under a stone. So, by her subtle craft and working, she made Merlin to go under the stone to let her wit of the marvels there ; but she wrought so there for him, that he never came out, for all the craft he could do ; and so she departed and left Merlin.'

And later we read of Sir Bagdemagus riding out in quest of adventures, and coming to the same rock where Merlin was,

'and there he heard him make great moan, wherefore Sir Bagdemagus would have helpen him, and went to the great stone, and it was so heavy that a hundred men might not lift it up. When Merlin wist that he was there, he bid him leave his labour, for all was in vain, and might never be helpen but by her that put him there.'

Our friend supports his theory with much earnestness and some display of learning. He scouts the claim of the Welsh folk to the bones of the great enchanter. The story nowhere tells of his death, and the Mynydd Merlin, the hill by Towey, under which it is alleged that he lies buried, is a delusive cenotaph. The Welsh were always vain and superstitious, ready to believe any wild tale that might serve to enhance their glory ; and they had their bards, skilful in fashioning false stories and in imposing them on the world ; so that they have stolen the credit from Cornwall and made a Welsh king of Arthur, and a stuttering Taffy of Merlin, whose only authentic words extant are in good Cornish. It was at Camelot that Merlin met Nimue and fell into a dotage on her, and Camelot is the Cornish Camelford, as all the world knows. From Camelot they went together to Benwick, and afterwards—the history is precise—afterwards they returned to Cornwall, where she grew weary of his importunities, and lured him to his doom under the stone. The learned arguments adduced in proof of the identity of that stone with the stone in Wisht Wood may be omitted here. But granted that this is the place, Merlin must still be here, and alive ; for the Lady would never have released one whom she hated and feared as a devil's son, and neither she nor anybody else had skill to encompass his death. He has ceased long since from useless groanings, but the evil heart of him still beats strong, and he continues to weave his spells, not with the hope of freeing himself, but out of pure malignity, finding solace in the thought that he may yet have power to do harm in the world. The subtle venom of his magic rises in an unseen vapour through the crevices of the rock, poisoning the air, driving the trees to play mad antics, and twisting their innocent growth into the deformed likeness of his ugly passions.

So far our friend ; but though his explanation is attractive and plausible, to my mind it lacks a sound historical basis. The objection must again be raised, that the tale finds no support in local tradition, though it is just the kind of tale of which local tradition would be sure to preserve a vivid memory. To proceed scientifically on our investigation, since documents are wanting, it is precisely to local tradition that we must apply, and to the simple sufficient

WISHT WOOD

solution it offers I pin my faith. In four words, Wisht Wood is piskyridden.

Now by adopting this explanation we get rid of the shadowy Merlin, in whom I for one have never entirely believed; and we are enabled to put a pleasanter construction on the behaviour of the trees. Instead of writhing in atrocious torment under an infliction of black magic, they are simply attempting, in their stolid, clumsy way, to adapt themselves to the freakish moods of the Little People; and all this melodramatic show of anguish and deadly combat is merely a joke and a may-game, a rheumaticky, stiff-jointed old grandf'er playing at Indians and pirates with young Curlylocks. The sport may not be altogether to the old one's liking, but the capricious elf is master, and must be obeyed.

One thing is certain—no place in Cornwall is so pisky-haunted as the neighbourhood of Wisht Wood. In a cottage hard by, an old woman dwelt within living memory, who never looked to dirty but one clean apron betwixt Monday morning and Saturday night, for the piskies did all her churrs for her. Every night she opened the window a little way, set a dish of milk on the table, and went to bed. Every morning the milk was gone, the cloam washed and put by, the slab polished, the floor swept and sprinkled with white sand, and not a cobweb left under the planchin. And there is a man working in the farm below, who is in the habit of going up-along to Churchtown every Saturday evening, to take a social glass, or maybe two, at the inn. And three times out of four, he assures me, he is pisky-led on his way home across the moor; as soon as his feet touch the heather they fall under an enchantment, and lead him this way and that, in stumbling circles and zigzags, till his dizzy senses fail him, and he knows no more till he wakes next morning, with his toes in a puddle and his head in a furcey-bush. As for the wood itself, few of the neighbours will venture within it by day, and none by night. Chattering voices are heard there, for all the world like the confidential twitterings of a flock of pednypaleys, and the scurry of tiny feet, like the sound of mice playing hide-and-seek in the grass; and on Mondays, if you peep into the wood as you pass, you may chance to see scores of little red caps hanging up to dry on the thorn-bushes. From these and other indications, I am inclined to believe that Wisht Wood is the headquarters, the chief camp or metropolis, as you will, of piskydom. And so I come to my story.

But first a note on the origin and history of the piskies. As to their origin, that is obscure and doubtful. Some think their tiny bodies hold the souls of the good heathen who died before the saints came to Cornwall from Ireland, and are fated to remain on earth because there is no appropriate place for them elsewhere. No such thing, others say: there were no piskies at all in Cornwall before the invasion of the saints; but when St. Keverne and St. Just and St. Sennen and the rest sailed across the sea on their goodly millstones (for such was their saintliness that they could not do the simplest thing except in a miraculous way), the piskies came with them, perched on their shoulders, or hanging on to their beards; for in those days sanctity wore a merry face, and holy men were well disposed towards the sprightly little folk, and loved to have them about them, to cheer their vigils with sport and frolic. Others again declare the piskies to be no others than the ancient pagan gods of Cornwall; and this to me is the most probable explanation of all, and sets their history, and especially the story I am about to tell, in the clearest light. Being gods, they subsist on worship and belief; without these they perish. Tiny as they are now, in the old days they were tall and stout, far exceeding mankind in bulk and stature. You have heard of the Cornish giants; well, these were they. But on the day when the first millstone with its saintly cargo kissed the pebbles under Cape Cornwall, they began to shrink and shrivel. As the years passed and the old beliefs faded, they dwindled and dwindled, until at the time of my story, the time when the great Preacher came across the Tamar, they were no bigger than the dolls you buy at Corpo-Crist Fair.

Those were the days before the folk of West Cornwall were so foolish as to make roads, which only serve to let in the foreign gentry and other undesirable persons. But the Preacher, though small of stature and particular in his attire, had the stoutest heart that ever beat under a black gown. By bridle-paths, trodden knee-deep into mire under the hooves of pack-mules, by trackless moors, over rocks and through rivers, he pushed his indomitable way from mining village to upland farm, from upland farm to fishing cove, halting, wherever he found an audience, to plead, exhort, and denounce, and everywhere leaving behind him a trail of flame and sweet odours. So in time he came to the neighbourhood of Wisht Wood, and entered the farmhouse that still stands hard by, first to deliver his message, and afterwards to take rest and nourishment. And as he sat in the kitchen, expounding points of doctrine to the farmer and his hinds, a tapping was heard at the door, low down, just above the drexel, like the tapping of a grey-bird's beak breaking a snail-shell on a stone. So the farmer's wife went to open the door, and screamed and scuttled back; for there on the drexel stood a tiny little man, no bigger than a whitneck when it sits up on its hind paws. Like a whitneck he was dressed in a brown coat and white waistcoat; his breeches were brown also, his stockings were green, and his shoe-buckles were two silver dewdrops. On his head he wore a red cap, which he doffed politely as soon as the door opened, discovering a natty little wig made of grey lichen. And in his right hand he flourished a straight twig, to the end of which a shred of white linen was tied, by way of flag of truce.

'Aw, my life!' screamed the farmer's wife. 'Aw, my dear life, ef 'tedn' wan o' they piskies!'

Now the Preacher was not without acquaintance with the creatures of the unseen world. All his life the evil spirits and the good hovered about him— these with comfort and assistance, those with pricks and buffetings. So he showed no astonishment or dismay at the sight of the little man. He stood up, and in a stern voice, the voice that had made wax of the hearts of thousands, he bade the sprite depart and trouble him not. But the little fellow did not budge. Pressing the red cap to his bosom, he bowed profoundly, and, in a voice like the chippering of mice in the wainscot, squeaked out a string of outlandish words.

WISHT WOOD

'What is all this?' asked the Preacher, looking round.

A very old man—he was the farmer's grandfather—lifted his voice from the chimney corner.

'I d' knaw,' he quavered. ' "Tes a brae long time sence I heerd the like; but I d' knaw. 'Tes the auld ancient spache o' Cornwall. Folk did use to taelk so when I was a lad, but now 'tes most forgot. Manen o' what the li'll chap do say is that the piskies o' Wisht Wood are wanting to 'ave a word wi' your reverence, ef you'll be so kind as to step across for a minute.'

'Don't 'ee goo, your reverence!' cried the farmer's wife. 'They'm artful an' vicious as foxes. They'll do 'ee some harm, sure 'nough, the rogues!'

The Preacher's eyes flashed.

'I will go,' he said. 'This is part of my work; and from my work none shall turn me back.'

So saying, he stepped to the door and took the path across the meadow, the pisky trotting before him, the folk of the farm following after. They crossed the bridge over the little babbling river, and passed one by one through a gap in the hedge into the shadow of the wood.

'Twas a strange sight within. At first, to their sun-dazzled eyes the green twilight seemed studded with innumerable clusters of scarlet berries, on the trees, on the bushes, on the rocks, on the grass, everywhere. When they began to see more clearly, they perceived that what they had taken for berries were little red caps, such as the pisky ambassador wore; and under each cap shone a pair of little eyes, no bigger than a bush-sparrow's, and as bright and unwinking; and the little eyes were set in little wrinkled faces, as like one to another as the faces of a parcel of Chinamen. And all the little faces were turned towards the Preacher, and all the little eyes were taking stock of him, up and down, while the air began to fill with a buzzing murmur, like the hum of midsummer flies.

The Preacher advanced a step and waited; his companions huddled in a whispering, gravely-nodding group behind him. The hum grew louder, and all the bright little eyes turned together towards a square white stone that lay among the grass, ringed about with a circle of toadstools. Suddenly a tall, stout pisky, wearing a carcanet of dewdrops round his cap, leapt briskly upon the stone, and immediately the hum died away into silence. Then the tall pisky hemmed, removed his cap, and began to speak, with quaint, earnest gestures of finger on palm and arms swung abroad—the queer little manikin! But as he too spoke in the ancient tongue, the Preacher turned about and beckoned the old grandf'er forward to interpret. And this is what the tall pisky said to the Preacher:

'To the black-robed foreigner, in the name of the community of the Pobel Vean, the Little People here assembled, greeting. We have a story to tell, a complaint to make, and a petition to prefer. In the beginning we ruled; our stature was great, our power also. Then the white monks from Eire descended on our shores like a flock of seagulls, and hunted us out, and sprinkled us with holy water. As the drops fell on us we shrank, and became as dwarfs, all but a few, who avoided the shower and fled to the Hoar Rock that stands in the sea, and made war thence on monks and people, and perished at last by the sword. But we survived, by virtue of the holy water and of the relics of ancient worship that remained to us. For the white monks were kindly and compassionate; they remembered that we were gods, with the pride of gods and the need of gods. Our power they took from us, but left us a nook in the hearts of men, that we might not altogether perish. It was a compact between us and them, and so long as their creed endured we had no fear. Then we heard rumours of changes, of a new creed, and a new God that hated holy water; and we trembled and hid ourselves. When we ventured forth again, our friends the monks and friars had disappeared, and black-gowned persons were in their place. And looking one upon another, we perceived no change; our stature was not diminished by the breadth of a hair. So we took heart, and went by night and peered into the breasts of the people as they lay asleep; and our niche, the niche the monks had left us, was still there, swept and garnished as of old. There was peace in our niche, but elsewhere in every heart there was a division and a conflict between the old faith and the new. Then we laughed; for, looking again, we perceived that we had waxed a little bigger—our limbs were plumper and our chests broader. This we set down to the dissensions between the Gods who had supplanted us; the people, not knowing which to adhere to, were turning half in jest to us, their forgotten divinities. Some of us said, "We have but to wait; soon the parsons will go where the monks have gone, and we shall be masters again." But others said, "No; our time has gone by for ever; if the parsons go, others will step into their place before us. Let us rest content in our little niche; parson or priest, none will disturb us there." And we took notice that the parsons talked loud for a while, and then they fell asleep talking; and for many years we lived in peace and merriment undisturbed.

'But one day not long ago we woke, and looked upon one another and exclaimed; for it seemed to each that his companions had suddenly grown old in the night, so wizened were our faces, so shrunken our limbs. Also it appeared as if the grass about us had sprouted miraculously; it was breast-high when we lay down, and now it waved above our heads. And as we stared and shouted in wonderment, a jack rabbit hopped in amongst us, and we jumped up and fled in terror; for he seemed as big as a bull calf. Then we knew that what had happened before at the first coming of the monks had happened again. In a single night we had been shorn of half our stature. We doubted and feared, and sent messengers forth. They returned, and told us of a strange Preacher from the East, with yet another new creed, hot and strong; they spoke of shoutings and raptures, of old customs overturned, of old beliefs brushed away by the power of a single voice. Then we called a council of the chiefs, and debated on the danger that threatened. Some were for flight across the sea to Eire, the green island, where our brethren dwell securely. Others were for a call to arms, and open war. Others for waylaying the Preacher on the moors, craftily decoying him among the deserted mine-shafts, and leaving him there in the darkness to break his neck at the first step forward. But others—they were our wisest—counselled prudence. "Let us wait," they said, "until the Preacher comes this way. Then let us demand audience of him, and put our case before him plainly, without craft or concealment; if there is pity in him, if there is room in his creed for loving-kindness and tenderness towards the weak and oppressed, surely he will deal gently with us, and renew the compact the monks made with us of old."

'So said our wisest, and their counsel seemed good to us. We waited, and now the Preacher is before us, our fate in his hands. Consider, O Preacher; we are a small folk, and a harmless; there is no malice in us, and our pride is subdued. The people love us, for the sake of old times, and because we solace them with our merry antics. But now that they begin to think new thoughts, to travel this way and that, and to read in the magic Book you bring them, they are in danger of forgetting us; and forgotten we perish. Now, is there no room for us in your message? Will you not slip in a word here and a word there, commending the Pobel Vean, who were gods once? Gods once, and now we run from a jack-rabbit! Soon the bull-horns will rise up against us, and the muryons send out hunting parties to chase us from wood and moor, and the quilkens run at us open-mouthed when we go down to the stream to drink. There will be no place left where we can lay our heads in safety; we shall be wanderers and outcasts in our own country; no fate is harder. Have pity then, O Preacher; your power is great—a word from you, and our safety is assured. 'Tis little that we ask; no increase or exaltation - only a secure tenure of our present stature, that we may not shrink to dust, and be blown away by the wind into the sea.'

Such was the speech made by the tall pisky to the Preacher in Wisht Wood, the old grandf'er interpreting. The other piskies hummed applause, for their spokesman had performed his office well; and they turned confident faces on the Preacher, for surely here was piteous eloquence to move the hardest heart. But the Preacher's face was stern and forbidding, as he stood meditating his answer. And when it came, it was no answer. The petition he thrust aside, making no reference to it; and instead, waving a hand that seemed to carry a sword, he delivered once again the message that he had come to publish through the land. As St. Patrick preached of old to the birds in Eire, so now the Preacher preached to the piskies of Wisht Wood, in words of fire, with a voice of thunder, terrible to hear.

The piskies listened with puzzled faces, that grew longer and longer as the Preacher went on, pleading, promising, and threatening. When he had finished, the tall pisky bowed politely, and spreading two vague little hands, said:

'We are foolish little fellows; these matters are too deep for us; nor do they seem to concern us. They are for good folk and wicked folk, and we are neither; whether we laugh or cry, whether we do this or that, it is out of pure wantonness, and for no reason at all. How then should all this concern us? One thing only concerns us—our diminishing stature, and the danger we foresee from the bull-horns and muryons. From the fear of this arose our question, which remains unanswered. Was it obscurely put? I will repeat it. Tell us, O Preacher, is there no room for us in your new creed?—no tiny corner-space for laughter, and the telling of gay randigals, and the kicking of heels on the turf?'

Now hitherto the Preacher had been puzzled by the piskies, and doubtful in what light to view them and in what way to treat them. But when the tall pisky spoke thus of randigals and riotous doings, he cast all doubt aside, recognising their corrupt and devilish nature. There never was a better or more saintly man than the Preacher, but there was something terrible in his inflexible goodness. Two things oppressed him—the wickedness of the world, and the awful brevity of human life; between these he found no time or place for laughter. Angrily he turned his back on the tiny tempter, and addressed his followers, vehemently denouncing the piskies to them as evil spirits, imps of the pit, passionately exhorting them to cherish the demons in their hearts no longer, to cast them forth, trample them under foot, and bray them in the mortar of righteousness with the pestle of faith. His words burned the people like hot coals, so that they fell under conviction and groaned aloud. Then he was seized with the spirit of prophecy, and foretold the imminent doom of all piskies, spriggans, knockers, and brownies, that they should be first scorned, and then in a little while forgotten, and so perish utterly from the land.

Then the piskies called anxiously to the old grandf'er, to know what the Preacher was saying; and when he told them they wailed shrilly, and those in the trees dropped to the ground with one accord, as the berries drop from the mountain ash in autumn; and all the company of little men fled shrieking and lamenting into the recesses of the wood, and were seen no more.

So runs the story of the piskies of Wisht Wood, and the doom pronounced on them by the Preacher who came out of England. This was many years ago, and the doom is long in fulfilling itself; for the piskies are still abroad in the land, though they are shy of showing themselves, because of the fright the Preacher gave them. For my part, it is not on account of the Preacher's denunciation that I fear for the piskies; it is not in earnest open combat that old beliefs are overcome. But of late a more terrible enemy has come out against them. The scoffer is abroad; and all the heavy artillery of homily and text cannot work half the havoc of a single volley of light laughter. Nowadays the lads and maids come home from school, 'cutting up,' as they say, talking proud book-talk, and making fun of giants and piskies, tokens and spells; the old speech and the old wisdom of their fathers are not good enough for them. And what is the result? The stature of the piskies diminishes daily; already the bull-horns grow restive, and toss the little men from their backs when they essay to mount them; and the muryons, I am told, are plotting raids and robberies in their caves underground. The time is not far distant when the last of the piskies will be laid in his box; and if you are present at the burying, perhaps you will see a light cloud of imperceptible dust fly up and disperse as the grave-digger gives the final pat with his shovel on the mound. And when the dust has vanished, you will have seen the last of the piskies.

CHARLES LEE.

The Prefs-Gang

COME listen vather, and mother too,
   And Sister Nance, I pray,
And I'll tell 'ee a passel o' strange things,
   Since I've comed home from say.
I'll tell 'ee a passel o' strange things,
   All about the wind and tide,
How the compass steered as thee never heerd,
   And lots o' strange things beside.
        Chorus—Too ral, lal, too ral, &c.

When I went up to Plymouth town,
   There to a inn a hostling,
I went over to Maker Green
   To ha' a scat to wrastling.
A pair o' leatheren breeches was the prize,
   A little the wuss for wear;
Jan Jordan and I drawed two valls a-piece,
   And Dick Simmons comed in for a share.

And jist as the double play had began,
   And Maker clock had nacked six,
Up came a passel o' ugly chaps,
   Wi' lots o' swords and sticks;
They abused Dick Simmons, and darned his eyes,
   And called 'un all sorts o' names.
'Blam 'ee,' ses I, 'Dick Simmons,' says I,
   'They've purfectly spoiled the games.'

Then in comed a chap with a great cocked hat,
   That seemed to be the king;
'Blam 'ee,' ses I, 'if you've a consait,
   Will 'ee stap wi' me into the ring?'

So he turned inside, and I drawed the sword
  Directly out o' his hand,
When a veller behind me nacked me down,
  And another he told me to stand.

Then amang mun all they took me up,
  And lugged me down to a boat,
When ses the meister to the men,
  'Let's set the rascal afloat.'
But though I begged 'em in good stead—
  And I looked like anything—
That they shouldn't top me in the say,
  But send me to serve the king :

There came alang Alias Prowse—
  He was bound for a vurren croos,
And he ran away for a small chield,
  And a devil o' veller he was ;—
Then he took me up both neck and heels,
  And topp'd me into the say ;
But as I always trusted in Providence,
  I wasn't to die thicky way.

Then they took me out to a gert big ship,
  Which lied far out in the Sound ;
The waves did top so cruel high,
  I thought we'd all been drowned,
But I catched hold a rope and climbered up,
  And so I got inside.
Massy upon me, I was so sick,
  I thort I must ha died.

Jist as a nation row began,
  Our ship she jist got out ;
The waves did top so cruel high,
  And the wind turned right about.
One cried, 'Luff ! ' another cried, 'Tack ! '
  And another, 'Helm's a-lee ! '
But luff and tack, or tack and luff,
  Was all the same thing to me.

Now as we on the ocean sailed,
  We spied a French ship comin' ;
Our meister beat all hands to quarter,
  And a veller went round a-drummin'.

Now I began to call o'er my past life,
  My sinful actions all;
My Lor! ses I, if I should die,
  What would become o' my saul?

Then this here French ship up she come,
  And a whole broadside let she;
The sulphur did vly so cruel high,
  I could neither hear nor see.
One got his head a nackèd off
  By means o' a cannon ball;
My Lor! ses I, if it's honour to die,
  I don't like sich honour at all.

Then come along the meister of our ship—
  I seem I see the sword o' en—
'Pray then, Jan,' ses he, 'come along wi' me,
  And I'll warn we'll soon get aboard o' en.'
So I vollered about to my meister's heels,
  While t' other men were out vending;
And there I spied a gert French toad,
  And I thought I could make an end o' en.

Then this French veller up a come,
  And showed me his gert long spit;
But I'd a sword made o' a oaken twig,
  And I didn't mind en a bit;
Not though he shet vore, and tho' he shet back,
  And so the toad kept prancing,
Till my oaken twig valled down on his wig,
  Which sot his daylights a dancing.

Then they ordered me up a-top o' the mast,
  Which I thought was cruel hard,
And there sot a lot of piscy toads
  A-grinning all on the top yards—
Till at last the mast come tumbling down,
  And so did the yards likewise;
And I thought if Maker tower had valled,
  He couldn't have made more noise.

Some valled in the sea, and some on the deck,
  And I had a cruel thump,
When a veller cried, 'There's five feet water in hold!'
  So they called all hands to the pump.

THE PRESS-GANG

So we pumped away till we could hardly stand,
   And we daresn't not to speak,
Till a veller he called out again,
   Sayin', 'I've stopped the leak.'

Then come aboard all the rest of the crew,
   And drove away all the French vellers;
My meister went vore to a gert big post,
   And hauled down all the French colours.
I went vore to a veller who collared my meister,
   And I beat him black and blue,
From the crown of his head to the sole of his foot,
   Till the rascal called out 'murblue.'

So now come all you husbandmen
   And ostlers, that would vight,
I hope, whenever you're called upon,
   You'll maintain old England's right;
For since sich a silly vool as I
   Can do sich deeds of war,
Why if ever the French they do come here,
   We'll give them all 'what vor.'

                              OLD BALLAD.

PORT ELIOT

LONDON towards the close of July somehow fails to give one the environment requisite for a word picture of a beautiful country home; the scanty shade afforded by the City trees scarcely recalls the generous leafy canopies of the Cornish ones; nor is the splash of the park waters so refreshing in sound or invigorating in atmosphere as the river Lynher, which flows past the historical home of the Eliots. Nevertheless, the time of year and the locale being such as they are, Lady St Germans is good enough to devote some portion of her last morning in town to telling me something of Port Eliot, its history and its renovations.

'We are going off to-morrow to Port Eliot,' she says, 'so you are just in time to find me.'

A word or two of apology for troubling her Ladyship at such a busy time, and then we plunge straight into the subject of her home.

'I expect you are very fond of Cornwall, Lady St. Germans?'

'Yes, I am, although, you know, I am not Cornish myself. My father, Lord Taunton's place was in the Quantock Hills. Since my marriage I have, however, spent a great deal of time at Port Eliot, and grown to love the place very much.'

'I am told it is a very interesting old place. What is the reason of its being called Port Eliot?'

PORT ELIOT

THE EARL OF ST. GERMANS

'Eliot is, you know, the family name of the Earls of St. Germans; and Port, I suppose, shows that the old Priory, on the site of which the house now stands, was situated on the river quite near the old church tower of St. Germans, or St. Germaines as it used to be called.'

'Is there any part of the Priory remaining, Lady St. Germans?' for I have visions of the old monks' comfortable refectory doing duty as the cheerful modern dining-room, or of the chapel making a delightful library; but these are dispelled by her Ladyship's answer to my question.

'I am sorry to say that no trace whatever remains of the original Saxon building above ground. The Priory was said to have existed before 936; at least, about 1060 it was converted from a secular into a regular monastic order, which it continued until 1539, when Henry VIII. suppressed many of the religious houses. Of the Norman building which succeeded the Saxon one there are

PORT ELIOT

LORD ELIOT

but few remnants, and these are not easily identified owing to the numerous alterations and additions which have been made quite recently. Three thirteenth century lancet windows have been discovered in what is now the central wall of the house, but must originally, we think, have been the south wall. At the same time as this discovery was made, it was found to be necessary for the safety of the inmates to take down the old and much decayed timber roof, which was believed to be that of the refectory of the Priory.'

'Was the house always known as Port Eliot?'

'The house, yes; but the Priory was called Postle Priory or Port, because the tidal water used in those days—before the Reformation

—to come up to within a few yards of the house. You know the Priory was first granted to John Champernowne, the son and heir-apparent of Sir Philip of Devon in Henry VIII.'s days. He was a noted courtier, this young man, and very friendly with the King; or, to quote Carew, "he won good grace with him." The same quaint authority goes on to say, "Now when the golden showre of the dissolved abbey-lands, rayned welnere into every gaper's mouth, some two or three gentlemen, the King's servants, and Master Champernowne's acquaintances, waited at a doore where the King was to passe forth with purpose to beg such a matter at his hands: our gentleman becoming inquisitive to know their suit, they made strange to impart it.

THE HON. JOHN ELIOT

This while, out comes the King. They kneelle downe, so doth Master Champernowne ; they preferre their petition ; the King grants it : they render humble thanks, and so doth Master Champernowne ; afterwards, he requireth his share ; they deny it, he appeales to the King ; the King avoweth his equall meaning in the largesse. Whereon the overtaken companions were fayne to allot him this Priory for his partage." After this John Champernowne exchanged the Priory with John Eliot for Coteland (now Courtland) near Kingsbridge. By the way I should add that with the ownership of the Priory site the Eliots took over the rights of farming the Manor of Cuddenbeak, also in the parish of St. Germans.'

At this point Lady St. Germans leaves me to find some photographs of the house and of the old Church of St. Germans which is close by Port Eliot. When she returns she brings with her, besides the views, a box which was the property of the great Sir John Eliot who was born at Port Eliot in 1592. 'His great uncle was the John Eliot who had the place from Champernowne, and his father was Richard Eliot. In those days my husband's ancestors were simply squires ; they just farmed their own land and acted as ordinary country gentlemen. The famous Sir John was, however, not content with this sort of life, and he became, as you know, one of the leaders of the anti-Royalists. He

SIR JOHN ELIOT, KT. (1628)

was the great friend of Hampden and suffered several imprisonments ; being finally sentenced to death in the Tower, he succeeded in thwarting this sentence by dying from illness. He must have been dreadfully ill too,' her Ladyship adds musingly, ' for we have a picture of him, painted on wood at Port Eliot, which shows how much he must have suffered. There are several souvenirs of him besides this. I believe many of his printed speeches and debates were preserved there. He changed the name of the house to Port Eliot, and he used frequently to stay there to obtain rest from his parliamentary duties and to brace himself against fresh attacks.'

'Was it this Sir John, then, who made the house what it now is ? ' I ask.

'No, both it and the gardens, and indeed the place generally, are mainly the work of Edward, first Lord Eliot, and a very clever man. He was intimate with many eminent literary and artistic men in his day—the friend of Dr.

SIR JOHN ELIOT
Painted a few days before his death in the Tower, 1632.

Johnson, Sir Joshua Reynolds and of Gibbon. He rebuilt a great part of the house, laid out the gardens, which were reclaimed from the river, made the lawn in front of the house, and, finally, planted the neighbouring hills from designs by Repton, the landscape gardener.'

'It looks to be a very large house, Lady St. Germans,' I say, as she shows me a view of Port Eliot.

'Yes, it is a roomy, comfortable old place, but I do not think it shows any architectural pretensions.'

'And the pictures?'

'All those are good, especially the Sir Joshua Reynolds; they are quite a feature of the gallery. Then there are the portraits of bygone Eliots, including, of course, the one of the great Sir John and one of his friend John Hampden.'

'Now I want to know something about your old church at St. Germans, and of the restoration that has been effected there.'

'The present church dates from 1261, and it stands upon the same ground as the old Cathedral of Cornwall. It is dedicated to St. Germanus, Bishop of Auxerre, in France; and in its construction there are to be noted specimens of Norman, decorated and perpendicular work. The west front, the north, and the lower portion of the south towers are all pure Norman architecture, and the beautiful porch displays the best features of the later Norman period. In 1888 it was found necessary to repair both these towers, in the former of which three bells belonging to the Priory were hung, and unfortunately these repairs led to the removal of the pretty ivy mantle which was so picturesque a feature of the dear old church. Possibly in its original Norman form the edifice consisted of a nave with north and south aisles, having lean-to roofs; but, of course, any conjectures may fall short of the reality, for no records as to the Norman chancel exist.[1] Whilst the preparations for the restoration of 1893 were being made, the remains of two clerestory windows with ornamental work were discovered.'

'What are the restorations which you speak of, Lady St. Germans?'

---

[1] Carew says of this: 'A great part of the chauncell, anno 1592, fel suddenly down upon a Friday, very shortly after publike service was ended, which heavenly favour of so little respite saved many persons' lives, with whom immediately before it had been stuffed, and the devout charges of the well disposed parishioners quickly repayred this ruine.'

ST. GERMANS CHURCH [Coath, Liskeard

'I think principally raising and levelling the portion of the roof between the towers, and the raising of the roofs of the nave and the south aisles. We have all worked hard at collecting the money for this purpose during the past ten years. All the people round about have helped, and we have had no less than three bazaars on behalf of the funds, all of which were most successful. By the way, I must not forget to tell you that we have a beautiful Burne-Jones window, and its completion was William Morris's last work.'

By this time I feel I have more than occupied the leisure which Lady St. Germans has so kindly bestowed upon me, but I feel tempted to learn even a little more of her home life; so I ask her about her children.

'I have two boys,' she says. 'The eldest, Edward Henry John Cornwallis, called after Lord St. Germans' mother, is twelve; and the second, John Granville, who is named in memory of the famous Sir John, is eight years old. They are both very fond of Port Eliot, and enjoy a great deal of riding whilst there.'

'And you, Lady St. Germans, are you a good horsewoman?'

'No, I go in most for driving. You see, I have always a lot of people to visit when I am in Cornwall, and long distances to go. Then there are our poorer neighbours to see after, and a number of things to do. I always look upon my season in London as my holiday, and I do nothing then but just amuse myself.'

'Are you musical at all?'

'Only in so far as that I am very

ST. GERMANS CHURCH [Coath, Liskeard

fond of it, but I do not play or sing myself. I enjoy hearing good music very much.'

'Do you take much interest in your garden at Port Eliot? for I am sure it must be a pleasure to you, Lady St. Germans.'

'I do, I think. I spend a great deal of time in it, and we have of course our specialities. I believe we may pride ourselves justly upon the Port Eliot peaches, for instance.'

LAURA ALEX. SMITH.

THE DAIRY, PORT ELIOT

THE BURGLARY CLUB

'YES,' said the Judge, 'I ought by this time to know something of Cornish juries. They acquit oftener than other juries, to be sure; and the general notion is that they incline more towards mercy. Privately, I believe that mercy has very little to do with it'

'Stupidity,' said the High Sheriff sententiously, and sipped his wine. His own obtuseness on the bench was notorious, and had kept adding for thirty years to the Duchy's stock of harmless merriment.

'Nothing of the sort,' snapped his lordship. 'You can convict a man, I presume, as stupidly as you can acquit him. No: with other juries a crime is a crime, and a misdemeanour is a misdemeanour. You tell them so and they accept it. But with Cornishmen you have first to explain that the alleged offence is illegal; next, you must satisfy them that it ought to be illegal; and then, if you choose, you can proceed to prove that the prisoner committed it. They will finally discharge him on the ground that he never had the advantage of such a clear exposition of the law as they have just enjoyed.'

'Well, but isn't that stupidity?' persisted the High Sheriff.

The Judge turned impatiently and addressed a grey-headed man on his left. 'Did I ever tell you, Mr. ——, how I once enjoyed the hospitality of a Cornish village, through the simple accident of being mistaken for a burglar?'

The grey-headed man—an eminent Q.C. and leader of the Western Circuit—dropped an olive into his glass of sherry. He had been dosing. Two or three guests and members of the junior bar drew their chairs closer.

'It was in 1845,' the Judge began, 'just after I had taken my degree, and I had been walking through Cornwall with a knapsack—no small adventure, I can tell you, in those days. The inhabitants declined to believe that anyone could walk and carry a pack for the fun of the thing, and I left a trail of suspicion behind me. The folks were invariably hospitable, though convinced that I was pursuing no good. You remember, Mr. ——, that when Telemachus visited Gerenia he was generously entertained, and afterwards politely asked if he happened to be a pirate. My case was pretty similar, only my Cornish hosts did not ask, but took it for granted.

'In the first week of August—to be precise, on the 4th—I reached Polreen Cove, and found lodging at the small inn. The spot and the people so pleased me that I engaged my rooms for a week. At the week's end I had decided to stay for a month. I stayed for almost two months.

'Well, as luck would have it, I had not been in Polreen three nights before there happened the first burglary within the memory of its oldest inhabitant—if burglary it was. I incline to think that Mrs. Giddy, the general dealer, had left her shop-door unbolted, and that the culprit, after removing the bell—the door had two flaps, and the bell, hung on a half-coil of metal, was fitted to a socket inside the lower flap—had quietly walked in and made his choice. This choice was a peculiar one—six bars of yellow soap, a cullender, some tallow candles, a pair of alpaca boots, a pair of braces, several boxes of matches, an uncertain amount of cheese, a dozen pocket-handkerchiefs, a coloured almanack, three of Mrs. Giddy's brass weights, and the bell. He was detected two months later at Bristol, in the act of using one of the handkerchiefs, which illustrated the descent of Moses from Mount Sinai; and four other handkerchiefs were found in his possession, together with Mrs. Giddy's brass weights. He had disposed of the rest of the booty, and proved to be a stowaway who had been turned out of a Cardiff schooner on Penzance quay, penniless and starving. Nothing further was proved against him, and it still puzzles me how he made his way through the length of Cornwall, Devon, and Somerset, on the not very nutritious spoils of Mrs. Giddy's shop.

'For the moment he got clear away. Not a soul in Polreen had set eyes on him, and as he entered the village by night so he departed.

'I know now that the excitement in the Cove was intense; that for weeks afterwards the women carried their silver teaspoons and chinaware to bed with them; and I should explain that the housewives of Polreen are inordinately proud of their teaspoons and chinaware—heirlooms which mark the only degrees of social importance recognised among the inhabitants of that happy Cove. A family there counts its teaspoons as our old nobility counted its quarterings; a girl is judged to have made a good, bad, or indifferent match by the number of teaspoons she 'marries into'; and the extreme act of disinheritance is symbolised, not by the testamentary shilling, nor by erasing a name from the Family Bible, but by alienating the family plate-basket. In short, teaspoons are to the Covers what the salt-cellar was to the ancient Latin races.

'But at the time, though I could not help observing symptoms of suppressed excitement, the Cove behaved with an outward calm which struck me as highly creditable. To be sure, the men seemed to spend an extravagant amount of their time in the tap-room of the inn, which happened to be immediately beneath my sitting-room. Hour after hour the sound of their muffled conversation ascended to me through the planching, as I sat and studied Justinian's "Institutes." Low, monotonous, untiring, it lasted from breakfast time until nine o'clock at night, when it ceased abruptly, the company dispersed, and each man went home to reassure and protect his wife. I suppose some liquor was required to start this conversation and keep it going, just as seamen use a bucketful of water to start a ship's pump; but I must admit that during my whole stay at Polreen I never saw an inhabitant who could be described as the worse for drink.

'I did not know that this assemblage in the tap-room was unusual and clean contrary to the men's habits, and therefore may be excused for not guessing its significance. Nor was I familiar enough with Polreen to note an even more frequent change in the atmosphere and routine of its daily life. When the weather is fine, down there, the men put out to sea and the women go about their work with smiles. When it blows, the women go about their work, but resignedly and in a temper which the men avoid by ranging up shoulder to shoulder along the wall by the lifeboat house, and gazing with approval at the weather; with approval, because it relieves them of the fatigue of argument. But should the day break doubtfully, and the men incline to give themselves the benefit of the doubt, then, indeed, you will learn who are masters of the Cove. For in extreme cases the women will even invade the 'randivoo,' and shrill is the noise of battle until the weather declares unmistakably for one side or the other. Does it refuse to declare itself? Then I can promise you that half an hour will see the men routed and straggling down the beach to their boats, arching their backs and ducking their heads, may be, under the parting volley.

'But, as I say, I did not know Polreen and its ways. It awoke no wonder in me to see the bulk of its male population ranged like statues, day after day, and from dawn till eve, against the wall by the lifeboat house, talking little (or ceasing at any rate to talk when I approached), smoking much, conning a serene sky, and the dimples spread on the sea by a gentle nor'-westerly breeze. At intervals one or two would leisurely fall out of the line and saunter towards the inn, leaving their places to others as leisurely sauntering from the inn. It did, indeed, occur to me to wonder how they earned their living, for during the first fortnight, beyond the occasional hauling of a crab-pot, I saw no evidence at all of labour. It was on the tip of my tongue, once or twice, to question them; but, though polite, they clearly had no wish to be communicative.

'I found great difficulty in hiring a boat and the services of its owner. I wished to be rowed along the coast; to try for pollack; to inspect some of Polreen's famous caves. The men were polite again; but one boat leaked badly, another had been pulled up for the carpenter to insert a new strake, a third was too heavy, the owner of a fourth could not leave his business—it wouldn't pay him! At length I patched up a bargain with an old fisherman named Udy—or rather Old Tom Udy, to distinguish him from his son, who was Young Tom. He owned the most ramshackle old boat in the Cove: if the others were out of repair, his was manifestly beyond it. I took my life in my hands and struck the bargain.

'"When do 'ee want her?"

'"Now, at once," said I; "or as soon as you have had your dinner."

'He went back to the company by the lifeboat house. He reminded me of some ancient king consulting a company of stone gods. They looked at him and he looked at them. I suppose a word or two was said; half a dozen of them spat reflectively; nobody moved. Old Tom Udy came down the beach again; we embarked and pushed off, and the row of expressionless faces watched us from the shore.

'In silence we visited the famous caverns. As we emerged from the last of these I essayed some casual talk. To tell the truth, I was beginning to feel the want of it, and, of course, I began on the first topic of local interest—the burglary.

'"The odd thing to me," said I, "is that you seem to have no particular suspicions."

'"I'd rather you didn' talk of it," said Old Tom Udy. "I got my living to get, and 'tis a day's journey to Bodmin. Tho' you musn' think." he added, "that we bear any gridge."

'"It seems to me that you men in the Cove treat the whole affair very lightly."

'"Iss, tha's of it," he assented. "Mind you, 'tisn' *right*. Seemin' to me 'tis a terrible thought. Here you be, for the sake of argument, a Christian man, and in beauty next door to the angels, and the only use you make of it is to steal groceries. You don't think I'm putting it too strong?"

'"Not a bit."

'"Well, I'm glad o' that, because, since you ask me, as a professing Christian, I cudn' say any less. But you musn' think we bear any gridge."

'"I'm sure I wonder you don't. And the police still have no clue?"

'"The police? You mean Sammy Crego, the constable? Why, I've knawed en from a boy—pretty thing if any person in Polreen listened to he! No: us han't falled so low yet as to mind anything the constable says."

'"Then the whole affair is as much a mystery as ever?"

'"Now look 'ee here; I don't want to tell nothin' more about it. A still tongue makes a wise head; an' there's a pollack on the end of your line."

'The wind stuck in the north-west, and day after day the regal summer weather continued. I grew tired of hauling in pollack, and determined to have a try for the more exciting conger. The fun of this, as you know, does not begin till nightfall, and it was seven o'clock in the evening, or thereabouts, when we pushed off from the beach. By eight we had reached the best grounds and begun operations. An hour passed, or a little more, and then Old Tom Udy asked when I thought of returning.

'"Why, bless the man," said I, "we've not had a bite yet!"

'He glanced at me furtively while he lit a pipe. "I reckoned, may be, you might have business ashore, so to speak."

'"What earthly business should I have in Polreen at this hour?"

'"Aw, well . . . you know best . . . no affair o' mine. 'Tis a dark night, too."

'"All the better for conger, eh?"

'"So 'tis." He seemed about to say more, but at that moment I felt a long pull on the line, and for an hour or two the conger kept us busy.

'It must have been a week later, at least (for the moon was drawing to the full) that I pulled up the blind of my sitting-room a little before midnight, and, ravished by the beauty of the scene (for I tell you Polreen can be beautiful by moonlight), determined to stroll down to the beach and smoke my last pipe there before going to bed. The door of the inn was locked, no doubt; but, the house standing on the steep slope of the main street, I could step easily on to the edge of the water barrel beneath my window and lower myself to the ground.

'I did so. Just as I touched solid earth I heard footsteps. They paused suddenly, and glancing up the moonlit road, I descried the gigantic figure of Wesley Truscott, the coxswain of the lifeboat. He must have seen me, for the light on the whitewashed front of the inn was almost as brilliant as day. But whatever his business, he had no wish to meet me, for he dodged aside into the shadow of a porch, and after a few seconds I heard him tip-toeing up the hill again.

'I began to have my doubts about Polreen's primitive virtues. Certainly the village, as it lay bathed in moonlight, its whitewashed terraces and glimmering roofs embowered in dark clusters of fuchsia and tamarisk, seemed to harbour nothing but peace and sleeping innocence. An ebbing tide lapped the pebbles on the beach, each pebble distinct and glistening as the water left it. Far in the quiet offing the lights of a fishing fleet twinkled like a line of jewels through the haze.

'Half-way down the beach I turned for a backward look at the village.

'Now the wall by the lifeboat house looks on the Cove. Its front is turned from the village and the village street, and can only be seen from the beach. You may imagine my surprise, then, as I turned and found myself face to face with a dozen tall men, standing there upright and silent.

'"Good heavens!" I cried, "what is the matter? What brings you all here at this time of night?"

'If I was surprised, they were obviously embarrassed. They drew together a little, as if to avoid observation. But the moon shone full on the wall, affording them not a scrap of shadow.

'For a moment no one answered. Then I heard mutterings, and as I stepped up one of the elder men, Archelaus Warne by name, was pushed forward.

'"We wasn' expectin' of you down here," he stammered, after clearing his throat.

'"No reason why you should," said I.

'"We done our best to keep out o' your way—never thinkin' you'd be after the boats"—he nodded towards the boats drawn up on the beach at our feet.

'"I'm afraid I don't understand you in the least."

'"Well, you see, 'tis a kind o' Club."

'"Indeed?" said I, not in the least enlightened.

'"Iss"; he turned to his companions. "I s'pose I'd better tell en?" They nodded gravely, and he resumed. "You see, 'tis this way; ever since that burglary there's no resting for the women. My pore back is blue all over with the cloam my missus takes to bed. And ha'f a dozen times a night 'tis 'Arch'laus, I'm sartin I hear some person movin'—Arch'laus, fit an' take a light and have a look downstairs, that's a dear!' An' these fellows 'll tell 'ee 'tis every bit so bad with they. 'Tis right enough in the daytime, so long as the women got us 'ithin hail, but by night there's no peace nor rest."

'One or two husbands corroborated.

'"Well, now—I think 'twas the third night after this affair happened—I crep' downstairs for the fifth time or so just to ease the old woman's mind, and opens the door, when what do I see but Billy Polkinghorne here, sittin' on his own doorstep like a lost dog. 'Aw,' says I, 'so thee'rt feelin' of it, too!' 'Feelin' of it!' says he, 'durned if this isn' the awnly place I can get a wink o' sleep!' 'Come'st way long to Wall-end and tetch pipe,' says I. Tha's how it began. An' now, ever since Billy thought 'pon the plan of settin' someone, turn an' turn, to watch your window, there's nothin' to hurry us. Why, only just as you came along, Billy was saying, 'Burglary!' he says, 'why, I han't been so happy in mind since the *Indian Queen* came ashore!'"

'"Watch my window? Why the ——" And then, as light broke on me, "Look here," I said, "you don't mean to tell me you've been suspecting *me* of the burglary all this time!"

'"You musn' think," said Archelaus Warne, "that we bear any gridge."

'Well,' the Judge concluded, 'as I told you, the thief was apprehended a week or two later, and my innocence established. But, oddly enough, some thirty years after I had to try a case at the Assizes here in which Archelaus Warne (very old and infirm) appeared as a witness. I recognised him at once, and when I sent for him afterwards and inquired after my friends at Polreen, his first words were, "There now—I wasn' so far wrong after all. I knawed you must be mixed up with these things, wan way or 'nother."'

A. T. QUILLER-COUCH.

THE OWNERS' 'COUNT STEP [1]

A MINER'S DITTY

Ef you want for to knaw, ef you want for to tell,
    What fortin will follow a chap,
You needun thraw niddles nor pins in a well,
    But look for the Awners' 'Count Stap;
Ef ees tredling along, like a cow in the grass,
    Weth es hob-boots clidged fast to the ground,
You can tell, onless miracles cometh to pass
    In the mud ee will allus be found.

There's Timothy Jinkin, up Pednandrea Lane,
    Ee bought a lil hoss for to ride,
But ee wudden move quicker in shine than in rain,
    An' ee just fooched along till ee died;
For the hoss used to pull the ould whem all the day,
    An' 'twas nawthen but round after round,
So ee maade up es mind not to gallop nor play,
    An' ee stuck to et, Timothy found.

Ee stuck to et, soas, like a cobbler to wex,
    An' I've seed a bra' few like that hoss;
An' ef you remark, they will stan' by the tex'
    That 'a rollin' stone gathers no moss':
Which is all very true, but they seem to forget
    That other tex' wrote by a chap:—
'No maiden nor man es wuth feedin' weth bran
    Ef they walk weth the Awners' 'Count Stap.'

Now, up to the bal, ef you trammey or spal,
    Or fillee or pack down the tin,
Doantee go for to say 'Aw, I'm paid by the day,
    So touchpipe till the croust time begin.'
Ef you caant move along weth a bit of a song
    To shaw you're a wideawake chap,
You'll be left in the lurch; lose your maid at the church;
    Cause you've stuck to the Awners' 'Count Stap.

HERBERT THOMAS.

---

[1] The general labourers employed above ground in a Cornish mine are called 'owners' account men.' They are paid by the day, and have not the same incentive to work as a miner, whose wages fluctuate according to his energy and the nature of the ground.

THE JUGGLER

A TRAGI-COMEDY

(Illustrated from photographs by
J. H. Coath, Liskeard)

Act I

Says Jack to Jill,
' Behold me try my skill . . .
A simple stick, a plate,
And now—you wait ! '

Act II

' Observe, I raise with care
The plate in air,
And keep it balanced, so—
Eh ? Steady . . . woa ! '

THE JUGGLER

Act III

'And now the trick begins--
Observe, it spins;
The quickness of the hand,
You understand . . .'

Act IV

Says Jill to Jack,
'Now, where you learned
 the knack—
My goodness! See it hop!
If it should drop!
Please, Johnny, don't be
 rash!
It's mother's favourite——'

Act V

Crash!

'I began doing these things,' Mr. Coath explains, 'in 1888. I experimented on my own tiny children. Yes, it needs patience, and an eye for the exact moment. Above all, there must be no anxiety about spoiling a few plates.'

A CORNISH GHOST STORY

The following narrative is not only remarkable in itself: it has a remarkable history. In April, 1720, Daniel Defoe published his 'History of the Life and Adventures of Mr. Duncan Campbell, a gentleman who, though deaf and dumb, writes down any stranger's name at first sight: now living in Exeter Court, over against the Savoy in the Strand.' In August a second edition was called for, of which some copies included a pamphlet which had been printed in June, 'Mr. Campbell's Pacquet, for the Entertainment of Gentlemen and Ladies': and this pamphlet or 'pacquet' contained our ghost story.

It has been commonly supposed that Defoe wrote the story himself. But as Defoe asserted, and as Mr. Robbins will prove, it was actually written by the Rev. John Ruddle, of Launceston. The scene of the story can be identified by anyone who chooses to visit the parish of South Petherwin. For its age it is one of the best-authenticated statements of its kind, as it undoubtedly is one of the most striking. We will first print the tale as it stands, and then let Mr. Robbins unfold its history and the evidence bearing on it.—Editor, 'Cornish Magazine.'

A REMARKABLE PASSAGE OF AN APPARITION,

RELATED BY THE REV. DR. RUDDLE, OF LAUNCESTON, IN CORNWALL,

IN THE YEAR 1665

In the beginning of this year, a disease happened in this town of Launceston, and some of my scholars died of it. Among others who fell under the malignity then triumphing, was John Elliot, the eldest son of Edward Elliot of Treherse,[1] Esq., a stripling of about sixteen years of age, but of more than common parts and ingenuity. At his own particular request, I preached at the funeral, which happened on the 20th day of June, 1665. In my discourse (*ut mos reique locique postulabat*), I spoke some words in commendation of the young gentleman; such as might endear his memory to those that knew him, and, withal, tended to preserve his example to the fry which went to school with him, and were to continue there after him. An ancient gentleman, who was then in the church,[2] was much affected with the discourse, and was often heard to repeat, the same evening, an expression I then used out of Virgil :—

'Et puer ipse fuit cantari dignus.'

---

[1] *Trebursey*, C. S. Gilbert's *Historical Survey of the County of Cornwall*.
[2] Gilbert adds (*Mr. Bligh, of Botathan*).

The reason why this grave gentleman was so concerned at the character, was a reflection he made upon a son of his own, who, being about the same age, and, but a few months before, not unworthy of the like character I gave of the young Mr. Elliot, was now, by a strange accident, quite lost as to his parent's hopes and all expectation of any further comfort by him.

The funeral rites being over, I was no sooner come out of the church, but I found myself most courteously accosted by this old gentleman; and with an unusual importunity, almost forced against my humour to see his house that night; nor could I have rescued myself from his kindness, had not Mr. Elliot interposed and pleaded title to me for the whole of the day, which, as he said, he would resign to no man. Hereupon I got loose for that time, but was constrained to leave a promise behind me to wait upon him at his own house the Monday following. This then seemed to satisfy, but before Monday came I had a new message to request me that, if it were possible, I would be there on the Sunday. The second attempt I resisted, by answering that it was against my convenience, and the duty which mine own people expected from me. Yet was not the gentleman at rest, for he sent me another letter on the Sunday, by no means to fail on the Monday, and so to order my business as to spend with him two or three days at least. I was indeed startled at so much eagerness, and so many dunnings for a visit, without any business; and began to suspect that there must needs be some design in the bottom of all this excess of courtesy. For I had no familiarity, scarce common acquaintance with the gentleman or his family; nor could I imagine whence should arise such a flush of friendship on the sudden.

On the Monday I went, and paid my promised devoir, and met with entertainment as free and plentiful as the invitation was importunate. There also I found a neighbouring minister who pretended to call in accidentally, but by the sequel I suppose it otherwise. After dinner this brother of the coat undertook to show me the gardens, where, as we were walking, he gave me the first discovery of what was mainly intended in all this treat and compliment.

First he began to tell the infortunity of the family in general, and then gave an instance in the youngest son. He related what a hopeful, sprightly lad he lately was, and how melancholic and sottish he was now grown. Then did he with much passion lament, that his ill-humour should so incredibly subdue his reason; for, says he, the poor boy believes himself to be haunted with ghosts, and is confident that he meets with an evil spirit in a certain field about half a mile from this place, as often as he goes that way to school.

In the midst of our twaddle, the old gentleman and his lady (as observing their cue exactly) came up to us. Upon their approach, and pointing me to the arbour, the parson renews the relation to me; and they (the parents of the youth) confirmed what he said, and added many minute circumstances, in a long narrative of the whole. In fine, they all three desired my thoughts and advice in the affair.

I was not able to collect thoughts enough on the sudden to frame a judgment upon what they had said, only I answered, that the thing which the youth reported to them was strange, yet not incredible, and that I knew not

TREBURSYE HOUSE

then what to think or say of it; but if the lad would be free to me in talk, and trust me with his counsels, I had hopes to give them a better account of my opinion the next day.

I had no sooner spoken so much, but I perceived myself in the springe their courtship had laid for me; for the old lady was not able to hide her impatience, but her son must be called immediately. This I was forced to comply with and consent to, so that drawing off from the company to an orchard near by, she went herself and brought him to me, and left him with me

It was the main drift of all these three to persuade me that either the boy was lazy, and glad of any excuse to keep from the school, or that he was in love with some wench and ashamed to confess it; or that he had a fetch upon his father to get money and new clothes, that he might range to London after a brother he had there; and therefore they begged of me to discover the root of the matter, and accordingly to dissuade, advise, or reprove him, but chiefly, by all means, to undeceive him as to the fancy of ghosts and spirits.

I soon entered into a close conference with the youth, and at first was very cautious not to displease him, but by smooth words to ingratiate myself and get within him, for I doubted he would be too distrustful or too reserved. But we had scarcely passed the first situation, and begun to speak to the business, before I found that there needed no policy to screw myself into his breast; for he most openly, and with all obliging candour did aver, that he loved his book, and desired nothing more than to be bred a scholar; that he had not the least respect for any of womankind, as his mother gave out; and that the only request he would make to his parents was, that they would but believe his constant assertions concerning the woman he was disturbed with, in the field called the Higher-Broom Quartils.[1] He told me with all naked freedom, and a flood of tears, that his friends were unkind and unjust to him, neither to believe nor pity him; and that if any man (making a bow to me) would but go with him to the place, he might be convinced that the thing was real, &c.

By this time he found me apt to compassionate his condition, and to be attentive to his relation of it, and therefore he went on in this way:—

'This woman which appears to me,' saith he, 'lived a neighbour here to my father, and died about eight years since; her name, Dorothy Dingley, of such a stature, such age, and such complexion. She never speaks to me, but passeth by hastily, and always leaves the footpath to me, and she commonly meets me twice or three times in the breadth of the field.

'It was about two months before I took any notice of it, and though the shape of the face was in my memory, yet I did not recall the name of the person, but without more thoughtfulness, I did suppose it was some woman who lived there about, and had frequent occasion that way. Nor did I imagine anything to the contrary before she began to meet me constantly, morning and evening, and always in the same field, and sometimes twice or thrice in the breadth of it.

Photo by] [*Hayman & Son*
UNDER HORSE ROAD

'The first time I took notice of her was about a year since, and when I first began to suspect and believe it to be a ghost, I had courage enough not to be afraid, but kept it to myself a good while, and only wondered very much about it. I did often speak to it, but never had a word in answer. Then I changed my way, and went to school the Under Horse Road, and then she always met me in the narrow lane, between the Quarry Park and the Nursery, which was worse.

'At length I began to be terrified at it, and prayed continually that God would either free me from it or let me know the meaning of it. Night and day, sleeping and waking, the shape was ever

[1] *Higher Broomfield*—Gilbert.

running in my mind, and I often did repeat these places of Scripture (with that he takes a small Bible out of his pocket), Job vii. 14: "Thou scarest me with dreams, and terrifiest me through visions." And Deuteronomy xxviii. 67: "In the morning, thou shalt say, Would God it were even; and at even thou shalt say, Would God it were morning; for the fear of thine heart, wherewith thou shalt fear, and for the sight of thine eyes, which thou shalt see." '

I was very much pleased with the lad's ingenuity in the application of these pertinent Scriptures to his condition, and desired him to proceed.

'When,' says he, 'by degrees, I grew very pensive, inasmuch that it was taken notice of by all our family; whereupon, being urged to it, I told my brother William [1] of it, and he privately acquainted my father and mother, and they kept it to themselves for some time.

'The success of this discovery was only this; they did sometimes laugh at me, sometimes chide me, but still commanded me to keep to my school, and put such fopperies out of my head. I did accordingly go to school often, but always met the woman in the way.'

This, and much more to the same purpose, yea, as much as held a dialogue of near two hours, was our conference in the orchard, which ended with my proffer to him, that, without making any privy to our intents, I would next morning walk with him to the place, about six o'clock. He was even transported with joy at the mention of it, and replied—'But will you, sure, sir? Will you, sure, sir? Thank God! Now I hope I shall be relieved.' From this conclusion we retired into the house.

The gentleman, his wife, and Mr. Sam [2] were impatient to know the event, insomuch that they came out of the parlour into the hall to meet us; and seeing the lad look cheerfully, the first compliment from the old man was, 'Come, Mr. Ruddle,[3] you have talked with him [4]; I hope now he will have more wit. An idle boy! an idle boy!' At these words, the lad ran up the stairs to his own chamber, without replying, and I soon stopped the curiosity of the three expectants by telling them I had promised silence, and was resolved to be as good as my word; but when things were riper they might know all. At present, I desired them to rest in my faithful promise, that I would do my utmost in their service, and for the good of their son. With this they were silenced; I cannot say satisfied.

The next morning before five o'clock, the lad was in my chamber, and very brisk. I arose and went with him. The field he led me to I guessed to be twenty acres, in an open country, and about three furlongs from any house. We went into the field, and had not gone above a third part, before the spectrum, in the shape of a woman, with all the circumstances he had described her to me in the orchard the day before (as much as the suddenness of its appearance and evanition would permit me to discover), met us and passed by. I was a little surprised at it, and though I had taken up a firm resolution to speak to it, yet I had not the power, nor indeed durst I look back; yet I took care not to show any fear to my pupil and guide, and therefore only telling

---

[1] Gilbert omits brother's name.
[2] Mr. *Williams*—Gilbert.
[3] Spelt *Ruddell* by Gilbert.
[4] Gilbert—*Talked with Sam*.

him that I was satisfied in the truth of his complaint, we walked to the end of the field and returned, nor did the ghost meet us that time above once. I perceived in the young man a kind of boldness, mixed with astonishment; the first caused by my presence, and the proof he had given of his own relation, and the other by the sight of his persecutor.

In short, we went home: I somewhat puzzled, he much animated. At our return, the gentlewoman, whose inquisitiveness had missed us, watched to speak with me. I gave her a convenience, and told her that my opinion was that her son's complaint was not to be slighted, nor altogether discredited; yet, that my judgment in his case was not settled. I gave her caution, moreover, that the thing might not take wind, less the whole country should ring with what we had yet no assurance of.

In this juncture of time I had business which would admit no delay; wherefore I went for Launceston that evening, but promised to see them again next week. Yet I was prevented by an occasion which pleaded a sufficient excuse; for my wife was that week brought home from a neighbour's house very ill. However, my mind was upon the adventure. I studied the case, and about three weeks after went again, resolving, by the help of God, to see the utmost.

The next morning being the 27th day of July, 1665, I went to the haunted field by myself, and walked the breadth of the field without any encounter. I returned and took the other walk, and then the spectrum appeared to me, much about the same place where I saw it before, when the young gentleman was with me. In my thoughts, it moved swifter than the time before, and about ten feet distance from me on my right hand, insomuch that I had not time to speak, as I had determined with myself beforehand.

The evening of this day, the parents, the son, and myself, being in the chamber where I lay, I propounded to them our going all together to the place next morning, and after some asseveration that there was no danger in it, we all resolved upon it. The morning being come, lest we should alarm the family of servants, they went under the pretence of seeing a field of wheat, and I took my horse and fetched a compass another way, and so met at the stile we had appointed.

Thence we all four walked leisurely into the Quartils, and had passed above half the field before the ghost made appearance. It then came over the stile just before us, and moved with that swiftness that by the time we had gone six or seven steps it passed by. I immediately turned head and ran after it, with the young man by my side; we saw it pass over the stile by which we entered, but no farther. I stepped upon the hedge at one place, he at another, but could discern nothing; whereas, I dare aver, that the swiftest horse in England could not have conveyed himself out of sight in that short space of time. Two things I observed in this day's appearance. 1. That a spaniel dog, who followed the company unregarded, did bark and run away, as the spectrum passed by; whence it is easy to conclude that it was not our fear or fancy which made the apparition. 2. That the motion of the spectrum was not gradation, or by steps, and moving of the feet, but a kind of gliding, as

A CORNISH GHOST STORY

children upon the ice, or a boat down a swift river, which punctually answers the descriptions the ancients gave of their *Lemures*.

But to proceed. This ocular evidence clearly convinced, but, withal, strangely frightened the old gentleman and his wife, who knew this Dorothy Dingley in her lifetime, were at her burial, and now plainly saw her features in this present apparition. I encouraged them as well as I could, but after this they went no more. However, I was resolved to proceed, and use such lawful means as God hath discovered, and learned men have successfully practised in these irregular cases.

The next morning being Thursday, I went out very early by myself, and walked for about an hour's space in meditation and prayer in the field next adjoining to the Quartils.[1] Soon after five I stepped over the stile into the disturbed field, and had not gone above thirty or forty paces before the ghost appeared at the farther stile. I spoke to it with a loud voice, in some such sentences as the way of these dealings directed me; whereupon it approached, but slowly, and when I came near, it moved not. I spake again, and it answered, in a voice neither very audible nor intelligible. I was not in the least terrified, and therefore persisted until it spake again, and gave me satisfaction. But the work could not be finished at this time; wherefore the same evening, an hour after sunset, it met me again near the same place, and after a few words on each side, it quietly vanished, and neither doth appear since, nor ever will more to any man's disturbance. The discourse in the morning lasted about a quarter of an hour.

These things are true, and I know them to be so, with as much certainty as eyes and ears can give me; and until I can be persuaded that my senses do deceive me about their proper object, and by that persuasion deprive myself of the strongest inducement to believe the Christian religion, I must and will assert that these things in this paper are true.

THE narrative which has been accustomed to be attributed to Defoe, but which he himself rightly declared to have been 'related by the Rev. Dr. Ruddle, of Launceston in Cornwall, in the year 1665,' merits especial mention in these pages because of its absolutely Cornish origin and development. It has been declared by literary critics to be the best ghost story in the language, and characterised by professed believers in the supernatural as not only one of the most remarkable tales of 'the unseen world' that have been recorded, but as 'bearing the very impress of truth.' This last point is the one which will the most fully be brought out by examination; for, whatever its merits as literature, there can be as little doubting the sincerity as the simplicity with which the relation is given. It deals with a real place and with real people, and its narrator was a man of mark in the Cornwall of his day.

---

[1] Gilbert who (*supra*) called it *Higher Broomfield*, here says *Quartiles*: thus confirming the assertion in our text that the real name was *Higher Broom Quartils*.

These points the more need emphasis because of the distortions which have been the fate of the tale as originally in plainest fashion set down. Nothing could be more straightforward than the narrative as written by John Ruddle and published by Daniel Defoe. A young Launceston clergyman, who kept a school in the town, preaches a funeral sermon over a scholar which so impresses a parent present that he is requested to exorcise a ghost, which troubles that parent's son, and with this request he successfully complies. Every name and date in the original can be tested and proved to be correct, and it might have been thought impossible for any erroneous accretion to have been made. But the mere fact that it was a ghost story, and therefore one in which no 'man of common-sense' would confess to believe, appears to have rendered more than one re-teller suspicious to the verge of stupidity. Mrs. Bray, when writing her 'Trelawny of Trelawne,' which deals with the tale, held the opinion, originating with the Rev. F. V. Jago-Arundell, that the name of the sprite could not have been 'Dorothy Dingley,' because she had 'never heard of the name in Launceston or the neighbourhood;' and yet a James Dingley was instituted to the vicarage of the very parish of South Petherwin, wherein the ghost appeared, in the same reign as the sprite was seen, and assisted Ruddle in his ministrations at Launceston, the name existing in that town and district unto this present. In the same heedless fashion, Cyrus Redding, in 'An Illustrated Itinerary of the County of Cornwall,' wrote in 1842 that, while the story was 'told with so much simplicity of truth that it is difficult to believe that the tale is not, as novel writers say, "founded on fact,"' 'no clergyman of the name of Ruddle had been an incumbent in Launceston for 200 years past, at least in St. Mary's Church,' though Ruddle occupied the living of St. Mary Magdalene from 1663 to his death in 1699. But there has been worse than carelessness in the matter, for Samuel Drew, in his 'History of Cornwall,' having mistakenly placed the scene of exorcism 'in a field about half a mile from Botaden or Botathen' in the parish of Little Petherick, between St. Columb and Padstow, instead of at Botathan in South Petherwin, Hawker of Morwenstow employed his genius in literary fabrication by inventing a 'Diurnall' of Ruddle, which not merely included this palpable error, but clumsily altered

Photo by]   *[Hayman & Son*
BOTATHAN HOUSE

the date of the apparition so as to make it hopelessly disagree with the facts which stand upon record.

'Facts' as concerning a ghost story would not seem to be customary; but, for the fit comprehending of such a tale, some of the atmosphere of its period must be imbibed, and then both the facts and the inferences will be found to agree. There was nothing unbelievable in itself in a ghost story in the days of Ruddle, for materials in fragmentary fashion exist for a Cornish tale of that time of a kind in which Defoe would have delighted, and which his genius would have made to live. Hidden in the depths of the State Papers of the Commonwealth, and of a date only about ten years earlier than the Botathan apparition, is a baldly grim confession of John Baldock, a seaman on board the battleship 'Tiger,' which is a study in remorse. The repentant sailor told how three years previously he had served in the privateer 'John'—'under Captain Jno. Shipman, of East Cowes, Isle of Wight'—and, putting into Guernsey with some prizes, he went on shore with one William Gibson. After drinking very hard they met an English soldier, whom Gibson stabbed, and the deponent consented to the act ' by washing his hands in the blood.' The dead man was robbed and thrown into a ditch, and the two sailors parted, Gibson to settle down at Fowey and Baldock to join the 'Tiger,' thereon to be so haunted or troubled with the ghost or appearance of the murdered soldier that he could get no rest until he had publicly confessed. Captain Gabriel Saunders, of the 'Tiger,' then engaged in watching the coast between Beachy Head and Newhaven, and searching French fisherboats and all vessels of which he had suspicion, at once laid his man by the heels, and forwarded the confession to the Admiralty, with the common-sense remark that it was a matter to be tried in the place where the murder was committed. A fortnight later he sent to London a reminder of the circumstance, but there the affair disappears into the night : whether the ghost-haunted Baldock was tried in Guernsey or the murderous Gibson continued to flourish at Fowey remains unrecorded.

But it was not only a time when the existence of ghosts was an article of faith, but when every other form of what nowadays is roughly labelled 'superstition' was regarded as credible. Ruddle finally laid the sprite of Dorothy Dingley on July 29, 1665, and he wrote his narrative on the following September 4. Now, between those two dates there had occurred in Cornwall an incident, having its own connection with Launceston, calculated to awe every believer in the direct interposition of Providence in human affairs. For on August 16 was gored to death by a bull Thomas Robinson, a Member of Parliament for Helston, who had distinguished himself by zeal in the sending to Launceston Gaol of recalcitrant Nonconformists. One of these, a former incumbent of St. Hilary and subsequent preacher at St. Ives, looking his persecutor full in the face, exclaimed upon committal, 'Sir, if you die the common death of all men, God never spake by me.' And a few weeks later, while on his way for a warrant to despatch to Launceston another clergyman ejected under the Act of Uniformity, the judgment fell upon Robinson—a bull, previously regarded as tame, pushing gently aside with his horns a maid standing near her master, whom he tore to pieces. And that no touch of the supernatural should be lacking, a witch apprehended near Looe subsequently claimed that it was she who caused the animal so to act, because Robinson 'prosecuted the Nonconformists, she being one herself, either a Presbyterian or Baptize.'

In days when haunted mariners and witch-stricken magistrates furnished material for State Papers—the vast repository of many a romance yet to be told—it was little wonder that a rural clergyman should not merely credit the existence of an apparition but have faith in his power to exorcise it. John Ruddle, though, as he himself says, ' young and a stranger in these parts '— 'natu Severianus,' as he is described on his Launceston monument—was not in the least likely to be diffident as to his own abilities. Fresh from Caius College, Cambridge, where he had graduated Master of Arts, he had been instituted to the vicarage of Altarnun on May 24, 1662, upon the presentation of the Dean and Chapter of Exeter; and the incumbency of St. Mary Magdalene, Launceston, becoming vacant by an ejection under the Act of Uniformity, he, as the parish register attests, ' began his ministry at Lanceston at ye Feast of Our saviours Nativity 1663.' The ejection of his predecessor, William Oliver, had opened the way for Ruddle also to become master of the Launceston Free School, an institution subsidised by the Treasury and under the control of the local Corporation. And in 1665 a veritable *annus mirabilis* for Ruddle, he figured in the latter capacity in 'The Bishop of Exeter's certificate of the Hospitals and Almshouses, Pluralists, Lecturers, Schoolmasters, Physicians, and Non-Conformists in his Diocese,' now to be seen among the manuscripts at Lambeth Palace. ' There is a free schoole within ye Borough of Lanceston,' it is therein recorded, ' and ye Exhibition of about 16 li. yearly is paid out of ye Kings Audit, and Mr. John Rudle A.M. keepes ye said schoole being Licensed thereunto ; ' and it is added that Ruddle was ' well affected to ye Governmt and a frequenter of publique Prayers '—the latter circumstance being one that should scarcely have surprised the Bishop, seeing that the schoolmaster referred to was the incumbent of two livings.

Both as clergyman and schoolmaster, Ruddle figures in his own narrative; and it is possible, therefore, to test his accuracy in points of detail. He sets out with two specific assertions—that there was in his school a lad named John Eliot, son of Edward Eliot of Treberse (or, as it is more usually called, Trebursye), and that he ' preached at [his] funeral, which happened on the 20th day of June, 1665.' Now, the name of Edward Eliot, of Trebursye, was one not lightly to be used at Launceston, and in connection with a story, he being one of the most prominent of all the neighbouring gentry. He was the third son of Sir John Eliot, the illustrious patriot, into whose family the possession of Trebursye had come through his marriage with the daughter of Richard Gedie, one of the victims of Charles I.'s oppression. While in his fatal confinement in the Tower, Sir John Eliot had written to his father-in-law, with whom the ten-year-old lad was staying at Trebursye, ' I hope God will bless him with his growth to overcome the defluxion in his eyes, against which I see no practice does prevail ; ' and when grandfather and father alike had passed away, and Edward Eliot had seen the troubled times of the Great Rebellion, the local love for his forbears caused him to be returned for Launceston to the Convention Parliament—'by the proper officer,' as it was reported to the House of Commons. But a son of Sir John Eliot was not likely to be in favour at Westminster just then, and the Restoration party ousted him from his seat upon some undiscovered pretext, and gave it to one of Monk's active intriguers, while almost simultaneously the Lords were petitioned by some Cornish widow with a grievance to exempt him and his eldest brother from the General Act of Indemnity until her claim against them had been satisfied. From that time Edward Eliot, save for occasional appointment as a Commissioner of the Subsidy, settled down to a quiet life at Trebursye; and the parish register of South Petherwin, in which that estate is situated, attests, as Ruddle relates, that 'John the son of Edward Elliot Esq and of Anne his wife was buried the 20th day of June 1665.'

It was as Ruddle left South Petherwin church that he encountered the 'ancient gentleman,' who was the father of the ghost-ridden boy, and who, if Edward Eliot had not insisted upon the clergyman spending the remainder of the day at Trebursye, would have carried him off at once to see his son. It will be noted that in the narrative no name is given of either the family or the estate, while even the ghost was indicated only by initials in an early copy of the story locally preserved. The first publication of the former names was by C. S. Gilbert in 1817, when, in his 'Historical Survey of the County of Cornwall,' he mentioned—upon the authority, as he stated, of one of Ruddle's own manuscripts—Bligh as the name of the boy, and Botathan as that of his residence; and there can be little doubt as to the accuracy of this assertion. Thomas Bligh, the then possessor of Botathan, was a very likely person to be at young Eliot's funeral, for he was not only a neighbour, but was at that moment joint holder with Edward Eliot of 'the Deere-parke' in the contiguous parish of St. Thomas-by-Launceston, in which parish, as extant records show, was situate a 'Quarry Park,' in a narrow lane near which the story avers the sprite to have appeared. Moreover, there is still a Higher Broom Field on the estate of Botathan; and it was in 'the Higher Broom Quartils' that Dorothy Dingley's apparition was first seen. Tested, indeed, at every available point, the truth of the tale appears, even in such a personal touch as Ruddle's reference to his wife's illness, for there is incontestable evidence in the Launceston parish register that that lady was at the time indisposed, and she died just two years later.

The belief that Ruddle was the author does not depend, however, even upon the strength of the case from internal evidence or the plain statement of Defoe. There still exists at Launceston a manuscript copy of the story, which corresponds exactly—save for occasional initials in place of names—with that published by Defoe, with the addition of the signature 'John Ruddle' after the date at the end, and the sentence, 'This is a copy of w^t I found written by my father and signed John Ruddle. Taken by me, William Ruddle,' who had become vicar of South Petherwin in 1695, on the presentation of the University of Oxford, and who subsequently was incumbent also of St. Thomas-by-Laun-

Photo by]   SOUTH PETHERWIN VICARAGE   *[Hayman & Son*

ceston, the two parishes with which both the Eliot and the Bligh families were intimately connected. This copy bears the following attestation : ' The readers may observe y^t I borrowed ye remarkable passage of ye grandson of John Ruddle who had it from his Uncle William Ruddle. I think I'm exact in its transcription. I well knew the s^d John Ruddle to have had (and I daresay deserved) the character of a Learned and eminent Divine, and I also knew his son ye sayd William Ruddle, a Divine whose character was so bright y^t I have no room to add to its Lustre, and I hereby certify y^t I copyed this from ye very hand-writing of the sayd William Ruddle. *Quinto die Februarii Anno Dni :* 1730. James Wakeham.' And this formal style must have been congenial to the writer, for —though, as an Election Committee of the House of Commons once had occasion to be told, Wakeham had been ' outlawed for debt, 13th Anne, 1715, and the outlawry was not reversed '—he mentioned to the same body, in 1724, that ' he served his clerkship to Mr. King, the town clerk.'

The completeness of the body of proof of the Ruddle authorship leaves nothing, therefore, to be desired ; but it may be added that his taste for writing was not exhausted by this effort. It appears from an account book in his own hand, which passed into possession of a present-day successor in the living of Alturnun, that in 1683 he published a sermon, and was ' by agreement to have 160 books at 3^d ye book ; ' and among those he distributed were ' 8 to the Mayor and Aldermen of Lanceston, 1 to Mr Dingley, one to Capt Blighe '—a combination of names specially worthy of note. Moreover, not only did he write himself, but he was the cause of writing in others. Having married as his second wife the widowed daughter-in-law of the Treasurer for Sequestrations in Cornwall in the days of the paramouncy of Parliament, he became possessed of documents which he put at another author's service. And the Rev. John Walker, in his preface to 'The Sufferings of the Clergy,' thus acknowledged the obligation: 'Such [of the Manuscript Papers] as I have made use of were . . . the *Original Account of the Treasurer to the Sequestrators in Cornwall*, for the Years 1646, 1647, 1648, and Part of the Year 1649, communicated to me by the Reverend Mr. *Ruddle* of that County.'

But how did Defoe become possessed of the Botathan manuscript? This much can be said for certain: he visited Launceston while Ruddle's son, who was obviously proud of his father's feat of exorcism, was a clergyman there, and, though the stay was brief and somewhat agitated, it gave sufficient time to study not only the political aspect of the town but the architectural distinction of the church. In the autumn of 1704, Defoe, as a secret agent of the Minister Harley, undertook a tour in the eastern counties for the purpose of inquiring into the opinions and feelings of the voters in the principal boroughs, to spread 'principles of temper, moderation, and peace,' and to persuade all and sundry that the Government was actuated by these ideas. During the following summer, and a few weeks after a general election, he performed a similar office in the West, and naturally paid special attention to Cornwall. On the very day after he had been in Launceston—August 8, 1705 —and while crossing the border into Devonshire, a Crediton justice, not suspecting his true position as a ministerial spy, issued a warrant against him as 'a person of ill fame and behaviour now lurking within some or one of your parishes, tythings, or precincts,' for the offence of 'spreading and publishing divers seditious and scandalous libels and false news to the great disturbance of the peace of this kingdom.' Defoe was too expert a practitioner in the arts of the spy to be greatly troubled by this; and he reported to his employer that 'Providence, and some dexterity of conduct (pardon my vanity), have hitherto rendered all the measures of the [opposing] party impotent and unsuccessful, and yet I have not omitted one part of my work, nor balked one town I proposed to call at, Barnstaple excepted.'

From a political point of view, this visit to Cornwall was a failure, for, when Defoe presented to Harley 'An Abstract of my Journey with casual Observations on Public Affairs,' all he could report concerning Saltash, Liskeard, Bodmin, and Launceston, the four Cornish boroughs at which he stayed, was, 'There is nothing to be done in these towns, they are wholly guided by the gentlemen, and the townsmen know little, but act just as they are bid. My Lord Granville governs several of them, my Lord Treasurer more. I thought it was throwing away time to stay among them.' But the most expert journalist of his period, the greatest genius in journalism the press has seen, never wasted time anywhere; and, when he came to write 'A Tour Thro' the Whole Island of Great Britain,' he gave a description of Launceston—'a pretty neat town, situate on a rising ground, great part very old, ragged, and decayed'—which showed how he used both eyes and ears while on his travels. ' There is a fine Image or Figure of MARY MAGDALEN upon the Tower of the Church at LAUNCESTON, to which the Papists fail not to pay Reverence, as they pass by. There is no Tin, Copper, or Lead found hereabouts, as I could hear; nor any Manufacture in the Place. There are a pretty many Attorneys here, who manage Business for the rest of their Fraternity at the Assizes. As to Trade, it has not much to boast of; and yet there are People enough in it to excuse those who call it a populous Place.'

Defoe, always a snapper-up of unconsidered trifles, thus visited the town in which manuscript copies of the Ruddle story were current; and there is no difficulty in assuming that one of these came into his possession, to be used when, in the first flush of ' Robinson Crusoe's ' success, his publisher was eager to secure further work from his pen, and when he compiled from various sources ' Mr. Campbell's Pacquet.' The original author thus became lost sight of in the compiler, but the honour of writing the ' Remarkable Passage of an Apparition ' cannot be taken from him now. Only two years after that effort, he poured forth his heart in ' The Husband's Valediction,' still to be seen in his own old church of St. Mary Magdalene, as a memorial to his first wife:—

> Blest soul since thou art fled into the slumbers of the dead,
> Why should mine eyes
> Let fall unfruitfull tears, the offspring of despair and fears,
> To interrupt thine obsequies.
> No, no, I won't lament to see thy day of trouble spent;
> But since thou art gone,
> Farewell! sleep, take thy rest, upon a better Husband's breast,
> Until the resurrection.

The display of Latinity in the ghost narrative had no echo in his first wife's monument, though it had on his own; but it is recalled by some hexameters in the private note-book earlier described. In a more simple style, and conveying a hint that may be useful to many even now, is to be quoted his cure for the gout, forwarded from Launceston in 1678 to a relative at Exeter, and his only other extant composition: ' I am sorry to hear of your Fathers gowt, and would recommend to him for inward medicine his neglected friend Rheubarbe, and for outward application ye incomparable engine called a Flesh Brushe the gentle use whereof doth infallibly open ye pores and free ye part afflicted from ye venemous matter of ye gowt and that without weakening ye joynt which all playstires, oint^{mts} and poultices are guilty of. Let him take it upon mine and my wifes 8 months experience, but espetialy hers, who for ten together never had so much freedome as since she hath rejected all receits and made use of this little artifice. It is a very soft hand brush made purposely for ye gowt and scurvey, and by ye gentle use of it before ye fire evening and morning in chafeing ye hands knees ankles &c. causes an easy sweat or at least a warmth whereby ye transpiracon is much forwarded and by consequence ye joint relieved.' Whether in the exorcism of a ghost or the elimination of gout, John Ruddle, vicar of Altarnun, incumbent of Launceston, and prebendary of Exeter, was ready with advice and aid; and, as long as our language remains, his tale, buoyed up by the mighty aid of Defoe, will never be lost.

ALFRED F. ROBBINS.

TO A GIRL IN THE WEST

ONCE, when my home was by the sea
(In the old days that were so blest),
Whene'er the wind was in the West
Then would my father say to me,
'If you could travel without rest
At swallow's pace, unceasingly,
You'd come not for a week or more
Where this cool wind last touched the shore.'

But now the sea is far away,
And when I know, by heart's unrest,
The wind is blowing from the West—
O then all bitterly I say,
'O happy wind! thou hast caressed
To-day, or may be yesterday
A maiden still more far from me
Than the last star the eye can see.'

H. D. LOWRY.

THE LATE VISCOUNT FALMOUTH

THE MAGPIE JACKET

THE power of that attractive institution the English Turf is never more clearly indicated than by the faculty it possesses of conferring widespread public distinction upon individuals who would otherwise be but little known, if at all, to the world at large. Whether for good or for evil, the Turf occupies in the public mind a place second only in importance to politics; and, as in politics, individualities stand out with great prominence. Many who could be mentioned, the possessors of honoured names, have gained public reputations more notorious than desirable; but happily those reputations have made no lasting impression. In the Turf, as in every mundane institution, it is the good that remains; and when we speak seriously of the past it is upon those pillars on which the fabric once rested that we dwell. Of the many prominent persons that have helped to build up this great institution the names of three stand out beyond all others—viz., Lord George Bentinck, Admiral Rous, and Lord Falmouth. Lord George Bentinck was the autocrat of his time, as Admiral Rous was of his; and the Turf was none the worse for being ruled by a man of such unswerving integrity as the Admiral, who will be remembered so long as there is racing in England. But though Lord Falmouth did not figure as a ruler of men, but as a breeder and owner of racing thoroughbreds, his name will be handed down to racing posterity with the same certainty and reverence. Surrounded as the sport of racing is with pitfalls of duplicity and chicanery, it is something to contemplate that it is not the man who succeeds best by these doubtful methods whom we honour, but he who pursues an undeviating course of uncompromising rectitude. There always have been plenty of owners to whom this description applies, and probably their number was never greater than at the present time. So, in this one respect, the late Lord Falmouth was not absolutely exceptional; and it would be sad indeed if it were so; yet he stands out with great prominence by reason of his wonderful Turf career.

'To race like Lord Falmouth has almost passed into a proverb,' wrote Lord Suffolk, an intimate of Lord Falmouth, and himself since passed over to the majority; and many a wealthy man has done his best to do so, and is now trying; but it is not in the power of money, even when combined with a firm resolve to do everything in the best style, to command the fulfilment of this laudable desire. Many an owner would like nothing better than to do as Lord Falmouth did; but all are far from being Lord Falmouths. And that is wherein the secret lies. Lord Falmouth came of a country stock, from whom he inherited that English deep-set love for all that pertains to a country life. On the breeding of every kind of farm stock he was an expert; and there is no need to dwell upon the interest he took in the subject, for many there are still with us to testify to the heartiness and urbanity with which he received farmers and others at Mereworth Castle, his Kentish home, and Tregothnan, his Cornish seat, to which he succeeded in 1852. The matter is here touched upon because it is sought to show why it was that Lord Falmouth succeeded in the way he did. With him there was no gambling in 'four-figure' yearlings, on the off-chance of purchasing a good one; the thoroughbreds that gave him such prominence as a winner on the Turf were the result of unusual knowledge of the subject, not unaided by other contingencies hereafter to be mentioned. Nowadays we have a section of owners who are people of suddenly acquired wealth, who race because it is the thing to do. With the best will in the world how can such expect to 'race like Lord Falmouth,' knowing nothing, and never likely to know anything, about horses or any other blood animal? Breeding was Lord Falmouth's hobby and study, and thoroughbreds held his special favour.

Photo by] [*De'Ath, Maidstone*

MEREWORTH CASTLE

At Mereworth, which came to him with his wife in 1845, he established his stud, and it is easy to understand that the addition of 35,000*l*. to his annual rent roll in 1852 would enable him to launch out in this direction.

Though it is improbable that he waited until 1857 before running something in the shape of a racehorse, it is in that year that we first meet with an authentic record of his doing so. He had a few ordinary animals in training with Goodwin at Newmarket, and one named Sichæus is credited with first carrying his colours, the magpie jacket, though running in Goodwin's name. In the following year his name first appears as a subscriber to the 'Racing Calendar,' a fact significant of increasing interest in racing matters. In those days John Scott of Whitewall, Malton, Yorkshire, had a great name as a trainer, and deservedly so, and thither Lord Falmouth in 1860 sent his horses. As 'Mr. T. Valentine' he raced with moderate success until 1862, when he made his first hit with Hurricane, a filly by Wild Dayrell out of Midia, who won the One Thousand Guineas. In consequence Hurricane was made favourite for the Oaks, but was beaten by Feu de Joie; and it is suggestive of the sporting spirit of the time that a match for 500*l*. a-side, at one mile and a half, was made between the two, and decided at the Newmarket Houghton Meeting, Hurricane winning.

This year, though the fact could not be then suspected, was really the determining one of Lord Falmouth's Turf career, for it saw the first appearance of Queen Bertha, by Kingston out of Flax (a daughter of Surplice), whom he had purchased from Mr. Blenkiron, and she won her race in a canter. The next year she carried off the Oaks, much to the surprise of everyone, her owner and trainer included, so hopeless had been her trials; but her jockey, Aldcroft, came to the rescue, he snatching a slow run race by a head. These notable successes were of the flash-in-the-pan nature, for they were not followed up for some years, Queen Bertha being beaten by Lord Clifden in the St. Leger. The breeding went on at Mereworth just the same, however, the greatest attention being paid to the acquisition of brood mares, of whom in 1863 there was already a goodly collection. John Scott grew old, and Lord Falmouth trained with W. Boyce for a few years, but did moderately only. Then in a moment, as it were, all was changed, simply by Lord Falmouth in 1869 giving his horses into the charge of Matthew Dawson, a Scottish trainer, settled, like his brothers, at Newmarket. The very next year he won the Derby with Kingcraft, and his winnings for the season just exceeded 11,000*l*. In Tom French, Dawson had the best of jockeys; and no one knew better than that astute trainer the high value of a really good jockey. It was therefore extraordinarily fortunate that, when French succumbed to consumption a few years later, another even greater one should be found growing to hand. This was Fred. Archer, who had come into Dawson's stable as a lad of ten. Archer quickly showed wonderful aptitude for race-riding, and with nearly all Lord Falmouth's subsequent triumphs he was connected. Indeed, it is difficult to decide to whom the most credit is due, the owner who bred (for he ran nothing that he did not breed at Mereworth, which is a remarkable fact to chronicle), the trainer who trained, or the jockey who rode. It was the wonderful

MATT. DAWSON

combination that achieved such results; and it is impossible to conceive a more perfect instance of unification. This was the secret of the magnitude of the success attained. In order to understand both Matt. Dawson and Fred. Archer it is necessary to have known them, and, possessed of that advantage, it is not difficult to comprehend how they fitted in with a Lord Falmouth and with each other. Not that Mr. Dawson claimed pre-eminence for Archer over every other jockey, for he was firm in the opinion that he had his superior in George Fordham.

As has been suggested, the acquisition of Queen Bertha was the corner stone of Lord Falmouth's great successes, for she produced a number of wonderfully successful colts and fillies, especially fillies, the fillies including such remunerative winners as Wheel of Fortune, the best thoroughbred Lord Falmouth ever possessed, and Spinaway. Besides this, her produce got numerous other winners in their turn; Gertrude, one of her fillies, for instance, producing Childeric in one year and Charibert in the next. These results took time to mature. In 1873 Cecilia won the One Thousand Guineas, and in 1874, when the winnings jumped from 7,676*l*. to 15,775*l*., Atlantic, the produce of Hurricane, his first notable winner twelve years before, won the Two Thousand Guineas with Archer on his back, but he was robbed of the Derby through sickness. He was sold at a handsome price to go to France. Spinaway came out in this year as a two-year-old, winning one race out of three; but in 1875 she had a great run of successes, winning ten times in thirteen starts. Her successes included the One Thousand Guineas and the Oaks, eight races being won consecutively. She contributed nearly 10,000*l.* to the total of 21,152*l.* for the year, the contributions of Farnese being also significant, for he won eight races out of eleven, including the Prince of Wales's Stakes, Goodwood, the Champagne Stakes, the Buckenham Stakes, and Clearwell Stakes, all valuable prizes. Skylark, the produce of Wheatear, running as a two-year-old, won all four races for which she started. One of them, the Post Stakes at the Newmarket Second October Meeting, was worth 2,655*l.*

1876 was a moderate year compared with 1875, a little over 10,000*l.* being won. Lady Golightly, a filly that was destined to do Lord Falmouth eminent service, had been foaled by Lady Coventry two years before to King Tom, and now made her appearance on a racecourse. After running second to Warren Hastings in the July Stakes, she won five races in succession. Two of these were won at Doncaster—viz., the Champagne Stakes, a valuable race, and the Wentworth Produce Stakes; this race being immediately followed by that for the Doncaster Cup, which Lord Falmouth also won with Great Tom, another of the produce of King Tom. That she succumbed to a horse of the calibre of Chamant in the Middle Park Plate was no disgrace to Lady Golightly. In this year also Skylark won six races.

1877 was Lord Falmouth's second best year, the amount won in stakes being 34,388*l.* Of this, nearly 30,000*l.* was won by five horses. Silvio, whose dam was Silverhair, purchased as early as 1859 and sent to the stud in 1863, won the Derby, value 6,050*l.*, the Ascot Derby, value 1,050*l.*, and the St. Leger, value, 5,025*l.* Chamant had fallen lame, or Silvio might easily have been second best in the Derby; but the piece of good fortune, accounting it as such, merely counterbalanced the ill luck with Atlantic, three years before. Redwing, a two-year-old filly, won five races out of six, these including the Hurstborne Stakes, value 1,350*l.*, and the Astley Stakes, value 2,155*l.* Lady Golightly ran fifteen times, winning on ten occasions. Jannette, the produce of Chevisaunce, obtained from General Pearson, came out as a two-year-old in splendid fashion, winning each of the seven races for which she started, including one of the value of

FRED. ARCHER
[From ' Vanity Fair ' Cartoon]

2,140*l.*; and another two-year-old, Childeric, out of Gertrude, won four races out of six, including the Chesterfield Stakes of 1,500*l.*, and three other races aggregating over 2,000*l.* Skylark, as a four-year-old, won five races out of seven, and Hydromel, a two-year-old, added grist to the mill by winning all three races started for. By way of trophy Skylark annexed the Ascot Gold Vase.

Though 1877 was indeed a great year, it was to be surpassed by 1878 in the matter of stakes won.

Photo by De'Ath] [*From a painting at Merewortk*

SILVIO

For some time nothing looked less probable than this result, for, with the exception of a few moderate stakes picked up by Silvio, it was not till June 7 that Jannette broke the ice by winning the Oaks, value 5,000*l.*, Childeric having been fourth in the Two Thousand Guineas and third in the Derby. At Ascot Lord Falmouth was represented by Lady Golightly, Childeric, Jannette, Silvio, Muley Edris, and Redwing, but nearly all their efforts missed fire, the bright exception being the success of Redwing in the Coronation Stakes, value 2,550*l.*, her solitary success in nine attempts. At the Newmarket July Meeting, Charibert, another of Gertrude's produce, appeared on the scene in the July Stakes, but the success was scored by Leap Year (out of Wheatear) in the Chesterfield Stakes, value 1,490*l.*

At Goodwood the peerless Wheel of Fortune, the produce of Adventurer out of Queen Bertha, made her first appearance, and a significant one it was, she winning the Richmond Stakes, value 1,980*l.* Pacific won the Gratwicke Stakes and Charibert the Prince of Wales's Stakes, value 1,000*l.* Wheel of Fortune, who won all six races for which she started, won the Prince of Wales's Stakes at York, value 1,530*l.*, a horse called Falmouth running second. In the St. Leger 'Falmouth' was again first and second, but more legitimately, Jannette being first and Childeric second. Jannette also won the Park Hill Stakes, Charibert the Champagne Stakes, and Childeric the Doncaster Stakes. At the Newmarket First October Meeting, Wheel of Fortune won the Buckenham Stakes of 1,050*l.* and the 31st Triennial, Leap Year the Boscawen Stakes, and Lady Golightly the 29th Triennial. At the Newmarket Second October

Photo by De'Ath]   *[From a painting at Mereworth*
KINGCRAFT

Meeting, Jannette won the Champion Stakes and the Newmarket Oaks on the same day, the two races aggregating 3,385*l*., Leap Year winning the Prendergast Stakes of 1,075*l*., and Childeric the Royal Stakes. At the Houghton Meeting five races were won, the principal being the Dewhurst Plate, value 2,040*l*., by Wheel of Fortune, Hydromel rounding up the season by winning the last race of all, the Winding Up Free Handicap. The bulk of the total of 37,981*l*. was contributed by Jannette (6,686*l*.), Wheel of Fortune (6,665*l*. 10*s*.), Leap Year (3,165*l*.), and Redwing (2,550*l*.).

In 1879 Wheel of Fortune supplemented her two-year-old career by winning the One Thousand Guineas, the Oaks (Lord Falmouth thus winning this race two years in succession), and the Prince of Wales's Stakes at Ascot, the three races aggregating 11,750*l*. Charibert won the Two Thousand Guineas, value 6,250*l*.; but Jannette won only two races out of seven; whilst Silvio out of four races, and Leap Year out of five, did not score once, which was a falling off indeed. At the York Summer Meeting Wheel of Fortune won the Yorkshire Oaks, and two days later won her last race in the Great Yorkshire Stakes. She broke down, and what her loss meant can scarcely be estimated. That she was the best racer ever owned by Lord Falmouth was the emphatic opinion of Matt. Dawson, who should have known.

About this time Lord Falmouth purchased from Lord Ailesbury Cantinière, who had thrown nothing of any note, but for her new owner she at once produced Bal Gal and Dutch Oven in consecutive years. Each in her turn won the Richmond Stakes at Goodwood, the years being 1880 and 1881, Lord Falmouth thus winning this race four years out of five, and each time with a filly. The interloper was Bend Or in 1879. Bal Gal also won the July Stakes at Newmarket, and the Champagne Stakes at Doncaster, as a two-year-old, finishing up the year by winning the Dewhurst Plate. In winning this race she was followed in 1881 by Dutch Oven, who, in the following year, created a great surprise by winning the St. Leger, beating Geheimniss and Shotover, Shotover having beaten her placeless in the Derby.

In this year appeared Galliard, and he won the Chesterfield Stakes, Newmarket, following this up in 1883 by winning the Two Thousand Guineas, beating, amongst others, St. Blaise and Highland Chief. It was, therefore, a great surprise, not to say disappointment, to see him finish third to this pair in the Derby; the disappointment being aggravated by the form afterwards shown by Galliard at Ascot, where he won the Prince of Wales's Stakes, and afterwards, on one day, the St. James's Palace Stakes and the 30th Triennial.

1883 was to be Lord Falmouth's last year on the Turf, for ill-health, which affected his nerves and prevented his giving that whole-souled attention which had been one of the secrets of his success, caused him to arrive at the sudden determination to sell off the whole of his splendid stud in the following spring. At this time his stable showed signs of continuing on the old lines. The Clearwell Stakes (1883) he won with Harvester (who, as the property of Sir J. Willoughby, was destined to run a dead-heat in the next year's Derby with St. Gatien), and the Middle Park Plate and the Great Challenge Stakes at the same meeting with Busybody.

The estimation in which the stud was held by other owners was evinced plainly enough at the sale, which realised 111,880 guineas. Of the choice brood mares to whom Lord Falmouth owed so many of his successes, Spinaway fetched 5,500 guineas, Wheel of Fortune 5,000 guineas, Jannette 4,200 guineas, and Cantinière 4,100 guineas.

Summarising Lord Falmouth's successes in the 'classic' races, he won the Derby twice, with King-

Photo by De'Ath] SPINAWAY *[From a painting at Mereworth*

craft in 1870 and Silvio in 1877; the Oaks four times, with Queen Bertha in 1863, Spinaway in 1875, Jannette in 1878, and Wheel of Fortune in 1879; the St. Leger three times, with Silvio in 1877, Jannette in 1878, and Dutch Oven in 1882; the Two Thousand Guineas three times, with Atlantic in 1874, Charibert in 1879, and Galliard in 1883; and the One Thousand Guineas four times, with Hurricane in 1862, Cecilia in 1873, Spinaway in 1875, and Wheel of Fortune in 1879.

Photo by De'Ath]   [From a painting at Mereworth
WHEEL OF FORTUNE

The system pursued by Lord Falmouth was to fly at the highest game only, and he never ran a horse on any but the best courses, save Epsom, the fact of the Derby and Oaks being run there giving him no choice. His operations were confined to Newmarket, Ascot, Goodwood, York, Doncaster, Epsom, and Lewes, and one never found him scheming to win a handicap by means of some carefully kept animal, after a due course of hoodwinking of handicappers. This sort of thing is of little use to anyone who does not bet, and Lord Falmouth never wagered. His outlays on bloodstock and the incidentals of racing he sought to cover by stakes won, and he was firmly of opinion that, in this way, the public should indirectly share with owners the heavy expenses of racing. That he was greatly influenced by the astute advice of Matt. Dawson is not to be doubted, and this incomparable trainer's assistance was appreciated to the full. As an instance, when the great sale took place Lord Falmouth presented Dawson with the sum of 6,500*l.*, by way of commission. The services of Fred. Archer were equally appreciated, as they deserved to be, and Archer refused all offers for first claim from others, however tempting, though his retaining fee from Lord Falmouth was an insignificant one.

The great lesson taught by Lord Falmouth's Turf career is the high value of brood mares; and a perusal of the foregoing will show that to fillies he owed nearly everything. And another lesson to be learned is that the breeding of thoroughbreds is not a matter to be lightly undertaken by anyone not conversant with it. The reign of the 'Magpie Jacket' was the dominance of a combination of everything that was of the best, from the largest to the smallest detail. Lord Falmouth's heart was in the pursuit, and he paid the minutest attention to it, and those around him were inspired by the same ardour. The result is before the world.

E. T. SACHS.

P.S.—Since the foregoing was written, Matt. Dawson has passed away, in the fulness of years and with the glory of his career as a trainer undimmed. By a melancholy coincidence, I was the last person outside his family to see him, for he immediately took to his bed and never rose again. Though the hand of death was firmly upon him and he was in pain, he exhibited all the old courtesy for which he was famous, and conversed on Turf matters with the perspicuity and facility of expression which he possessed far beyond any other member of his class. He was the last of the wonderful triple combination that produced the results briefly recorded above, and by his departure Newmarket loses more than it may care to acknowledge. Matthew Dawson may be said to have made Newmarket as a training centre, and that he lived to see it reach its zenith as such is not an isolated opinion. He was a man of liberal, comprehensive ideas, without a symptom of bigotry, and in his dealings with all, whether high or low, set an example the following of which would be of inestimable benefit to a calling where temptations are unusually strong.

THE COLLEGIATE CHURCH OF ST. BURYAN

(*Concluded*)

OF the saint who gives the church her name we really know nothing, except that she was a king's daughter, and in the fifth century dwelt here, and here built an oratory.[1] At the same time it is not improbable that she is the same person as 'Bruinsech the Slender,' commemorated in the Martyrology of Donegal under May 29, the day that in an English Martyrology of 1608 is set down as St. Buryan's feast, though this is now held on the nearest Sunday to May 12. Colgan ('Acta Sanctorum Hiberniæ,' vol. i.) conjectures that she can also be identified with Bruinecha, one of the holy women who lived with the mother of St. Piran. Dymna, the chief of Hua Fiack, admired her beauty and carried her off to his castle by force. Piran then went to the castle to demand back his sister (for his mother had adopted her), but the savage chief refused, unless, as he said sneeringly, he should be awaked from sleep next morning by a swan—a thing he deemed impossible, it being then the depth of winter. Holy Piran and his comrades stood around the castle all night, and shortly snow began to fall and covered the whole ground except where these holy men were posted. As morning broke, it was seen that a miracle had been wrought, for there on every roof and turret of the castle was perched a swan whose plaintive cries aroused the inmates. Beside himself with fear, the chief craved pardon of the saint and let the lovely Bruinecha free. Lust, however, was too strong for him; his heart was hardened, like Pharaoh's of old, and in a few days he was seeking her again; but at the news of his approach the lady died. Shocked by this, the chief turned over a new leaf and showed such genuine signs of repentance that Piran, feeling he might be trusted, by prayer restored the lady to life. The story suggests Juliet and Friar Laurence; but, as we are dealing with the doings of saints, related for our edification by other saints, it is safest to believe the story as it has come down to us. The Cornish tradition that Buryan was one of Piran's companions to this shore is consistent with the identity of Buryan and Bruinecha. Tradition tells us nothing of her life in this county, except that it was one of holy benevolence. How many noble men and noble women pass from us every year in the same way, forgotten except for a dim tradition of holiness and kindness, while persons of less worth but greater 'splash' have pretentious monuments erected to their memory!

About a mile or so south-east of the church is a little spot called 'The

[1] A hospital bearing the names of St. Buriana and St. Alexis was founded at Exeter in 1164 (Reynolds, *Anc. Dio. of Exeter*, p. 166).

THE CHURCH OF ST. BURYAN

Sanctuary,' on the farm of Bosliven, and here by the side of a gently running brook are still visible the remains of what may possibly have been a small oratory. It is far from improbable that this is the place where once lay the mortal remains of St. Buryan, at whose shrine it was that Athelstan, in A.D. 939, vowed that, if successful in his contemplated conquest of the Scilly Islands, he would, on his return, found here a college of priests as an act of gratitude to God.

On August 26, 1238, the church of St. Buryan was dedicated by the Bishop of Exeter, the Act of Dedication being still extant, as is also a Vidimus of the original dedication by King Athelstan.¹ The clergy of the church were secular canons of the Order of St. Augustine, bound to pray daily for their founder. We trust they were mindful of this obligation. We know from the Valor Ecclesiasticus that in the time of Henry VIII. the college distributed yearly 4s. to the poor on the Obit of Athelstan. The chief feature of interest in the Founda-

tion was that it was for a considerable time a Royal Peculiar. The King (or the Duke of Cornwall) could appoint whom he would as Dean, without any interference on the part of the Bishop; and the Dean, when appointed, had absolute ecclesiastical jurisdiction over the parish of St. Buryan, with its dependent parochial chapelries of St. Sennen and St. Levan, both of which were served by clergy from the college. An appeal from the Dean was direct to the Crown (or the Duchy), and not, as in the case of ordinary peculiars, to the Archbishop. The patronage of the benefice, now a rectory and shorn of its two dependent chapelries, is still in the Duchy of Cornwall.

The first incumbent of this benefice of whom we have record is Walter de Gray (February 12, 1213), who at the same time held St. Probus. Whether he was Dean or not we do not learn; but we assume that, whether so called or not, that was really the position he held. We believe he subsequently became Bishop of Winchester. William, Provost of St. Omer, succeeded (1214). In December 1220, William de Sancto Albino (St. Aubyn) was instituted, on the collation of the Legate, Pandulph, in the name of the King (Rot. Claus. 5 Henry III. m. 18). In 1301 King Edward I. granted the 'Deanery of our Free Chapel of St. Buryan' (*decanatum Libere Capelle nostre Sancte Beriane*) to Ralph de Mantone, Clerk, and commanded the Chapter to induct him into corporal possession of the same, and to render him due obedience as their Dean.

As might be expected, the Bishops of Exeter did not calmly suffer this

---

¹ Grandisson's *Regr.* vol. ii. fol. 25, b, 26. There is nothing in Athelstan's grant (if, that is, we may assume it to be correctly set forth) that anywise justifies the claim of the Deanery to freedom from episcopal control, and the words of Domesday certainly do not support such a position.

Deanery to remain exempt from their ordinary jurisdiction, and constant quarrels were the result. On the death of Edmond, Earl of Cornwall, without heirs, and the consequent escheat of his earldom to the Crown, Edward I., claiming St. Buryan as a Royal Free Chapel, gave the Deanery to Sir William de Hameltone, his Chancellor and Dean of York. In 1292, Bishop Thomas de Bytton objected to the Dean as non-resident, and litigation ensued which was still pending when the Bishop died in 1307, litigation being apparently as slow then as it is now. On July 6, 1310, a Royal Writ was issued, dated at Westminster (received at Paignton July 28), calling on Roger Gruglan, Roger le Somenur (i.e. Apparitor) of Kerrier; Thomas, Vicar of St. Erth; Ralph, Rector of St. Gwinear, and several other clerics to appear before him, and explain how it was that, though St. Buryan was a Royal Free Chapel and had been so in the times of all his ancestors, Kings of England, and exempt from the ordinary jurisdiction, yet they had *vi et armis* broken into the said chapel, and had presumed to exercise the ordinary jurisdiction therein, and had more-

over insulted the Dean, his men and servants whom they had found there, and had beaten them, so badly indeed that the lives of some of the servants were despaired of; and subsequently, because the said Dean and his men and servants had refused them admission at the time of the visitation, had pronounced sentence of excommunication against them, and had been guilty of other enormities, to the prejudice of the said King and of the Royal Dignity, and in manifest derogation of the liberty of the said chapel, and to the serious hurt of the said Dean, and against the peace &c. The return to this writ is that their goods were sequestrated; Ralph of St. Gwinear's to the value of 20s., and of the others in smaller sums. But no execution had been effected against Gruglan, because he had no benefice in this diocese, or against Thomas, Vicar of St. Erth, or Nicholas, Rector of St. Constantine, because no such persons could be found in the diocese. It is clear from the writ that St. Erth is named twice in error, as two persons are named as vicars of that parish—namely, Thomas, who could not be found, and Henry, whose goods were sequestrated to the value of 10s.—while 'Nicholas' is a clerical error for Henry, who at that time held Constantine. The Bishop was probably only too well pleased to take advantage of these clerical slips, as he always did with obvious relish.

On June 24, 1318, Edward II. issued his prohibition to the Bishop of Exeter, forbidding his exercising any jurisdiction in the chapel of St. Buryan or over the ministers thereof, or attempting anything to the King's prejudice in connection therewith, pending the decision of the plea in the King's Court between him and the Bishop—the King asserting the chapel to be his free chapel, exempt from all ordinary jurisdiction, and the Bishop, on the other hand, claiming such jurisdiction and alleging that he and his predecessors always had exercised the same. The King at the same time issued his order to the Sheriff of Cornwall to maintain and defend the immunity and liberty of the aforesaid chapel, pending the said plea, or until further orders, and not to permit anyone to usurp upon the King by lay force.

In 1325 we find a foreigner, one John de Mante, as Dean, and a dispute on the subject going on between Queen Isabella and Bishop Stapeldon. Bishop Grandisson seems to have kept a careful eye on St. Buryan, with a view to finding grounds for intervening. An opportunity soon occurred which led to the Bishop excommunicating Mante for neglect of duty and disregard of the episcopal monitions. Many of the parishioners of St. Buryan seem to have taken the Dean's side in the dispute, for in 1328 the Bishop issued a mandate for the citation of John le Archer, Roger de Penros, and others, including a lady, Margaret de Desdenewel, to appear before himself or his commissary. But they do not seem to have been as much frightened as they ought to have been at the episcopal thunderings, and, on August 17 of the same year, we find an order declaring them and others suspended and excommunicate. One of them, Vivian de Penros, was suspended from entering the church (*ab ingressu Ecclesie*); others were to be declared excommunicated in church, in chapel, and in all other public places; while the sentence on Richard Vivian, his son Hugo, and other ringleaders, was that they were to be declared 'excommunicate, with tolling of bells of churches and chapels, with candles lighted and extinguished in public, and with all due solemnity.'[1]

---

[1] The cursing by 'bell, book, and candle' has been said to be a Protestant fabrication, and there are many who believe it can be found only in works of fiction, such as *Tristram Shandy* and *The Ingoldsby Legends*. The above, however, is one only of the several instances where it is referred to in the Episcopal Registers. In his illustrations to Shakespeare, Halliwell quotes the following from Nares, who in his turn quotes from the *Canterbury Book*: 'The prelate stood in his pulpit in his albe, the cross was lifted up, and the candles lighted, when he proceeded thus:—" Thorow authoritie of Lord God Almighty, and our Lady S. Mary, and all the saints of heaven, of angels and archangels, patriarches and prophets, evangelists, apostles, martyrs, confessors, and virgins; also by the power of all-holy church, that our Lord Jesu Christ gave to S. Peter, we denounce all those accursed that we have thus reckned to you: and all those that maintaine hem in her (id est, 'them in their') sins, or given hem hereto either helpe or councell, so that they be departed from God, and all-holy church, and

On September 3, 1328, several of the parishioners were inhibited from communicating. The parishioners in this strait obtained the services of one John Kaer, 'declaring himself to be the parish priest of St. Buryan.' On November 4, 1328, Bishop Grandisson, being then at St. Michael's Mount, did, in the presence of his chaplains and other clergy, vested in stoles and with burning candles in their hands (*stolis indutis et candelis accensis in manibus eorum*), fulminate sentence of excommunication against the rebellious people of St. Buryan, and against the said John Kaer for that he did 'celebrate the Divine Service, nay, rather, profane it, in the presence of certain excommunicate and schismatical parishioners of St. Buryan in a place now accounted prophane and under an interdict,' both the church and the churchyard having been polluted by bloodshed. Especially severe was his Right Reverence against Richard Vyvyan, who is described as 'the author, promoter, and inciter of the many evil and flagitious deeds perpetrated in the said parish;' but all who ventured to communicate with the offenders were included in the curse, which he solemnly pronounced, using the accustomed formula : 'As these lights are extinguished before our bodily eyes, so, in the presence of God and of Blessed Mary, the Blessed Angels and all Saints, may their soul be extinguished and delivered to the devil and his angels for endless punishment in everlasting fire, unless they repent and come to a better mind. Fiat ! Fiat !' However, forgiveness for the good people could be obtained by acknowledging the Bishop as their spiritual father, and taking the oath of submission to the mandates of the Church.

In the following year we find the King, Edward III., interfering to protect the Dean. The Dean and a large number of other people, including Richard Vyvyan, having been indicted for seizure of the goods and chattels of Richard de Beaupre at the town of St. Berian, Trethin, Tendraenen and Tredeney, and for other trespasses, before Thomas le Ercedekne and his fellows, justices of the peace for Cornwall ; and the King, understanding that the indictments were made at the procuration of the said Sir Richard de Beaupre, pretending to be the prebendary of Trethin in the King's free chapel of St. Berian, and that the goods and chattels in question had been sequestrated by the Dean as fruits of the prebend, Sir Richard's right to which he disputed, and willing that the matter should be settled before himself, by letter dated March 8, 1329, ordered the sheriff to release those whom he had imprisoned by reason of the premises, upon their finding mainpernors to have them before the King in fifteen days from Easter, to stand to right concerning the said indictment. We do not know the immediate sequel of these proceedings, but they probably did little to turn the Bishop from the course he had laid down for himself.

Some time in the year 1333 the Bishop ordered De Mante, 'who represents

that they have noe part of the passion of our Lord Jesu Christ, ne of noe sacraments that been in holy church, ne noe part of the prayers among christen folke, but that they be accursed of God and of holy church, from the sool of their foot unto the crown of their head, sleeping and waking, sitting and standing, in all her words, and in all her workes, and but if they have grace of God for to amend hem here in this life for to dwell in the pain of hell, for ever withouten end, *fiat, fiat*. Doe to the book, quench the candle, ring the bell. Amen, Amen !"'

himself to be Dean of the parish church of St. Buryan' (*qui pro decano Ecclesie Parochialis Sancte Beriane . . . se gerit*), to be denounced as excommunicate for refusing to pay the 'tenths' imposed by the Pope. The ceremony was to be accompanied by the usual bell-ringing and candle-extinguishing. But 1336 found the parishioners in a happier frame of mind. In this year, on July 12, the Bishop visited St. Buryan again, and this time as ordinary and diocesan; and the good folk (including John Kaer the parish priest) came in and acknowledged their wrong and were again received into the bosom of the Church. An interesting feature of the ceremony was that some of the penitents did not know any language but Cornish, and Henry Marsley, rector of St. Just, had to act as interpreter. The ceremony closed with the singing of *Veni, Creator Spiritus*, and a sermon from the Bishop, who took his text from the First Epistle of St. Peter : ' For ye were as sheep going astray ; but are now returned unto the Shepherd and Bishop of your souls.' The interpreter repeated the sermon in the Cornish tongue when the Bishop had finished, and then followed a great many confirmations, and several natives of St. Buryan were also admitted to the first tonsure.

But among the penitents was not found John de Mante; far from it, for, as the Bishop sadly puts it, he was neither ashamed nor afraid to remain excommunicate, and to withdraw himself, in his disobedience, from the unity of the Church (*decedere ab unitate Ecclesie per inobedienciam non erubescit nec expavet*). So Henry Marsely, whom we have just encountered as an interpreter, was, on July 14, 1336, appointed by the Bishop as guardian (*yconomus*) of the Church, with full canonical powers.

But even this troublesome and contumacious Dean could not hold out for ever against the firm and persistent Bishop Grandisson; and on August 16 following, he came to Bishop's Clyst, and in the presence of the Bishop took a solemn oath of submission and obedience, promising amendment for the future. He would faithfully obey the Bishop's advice, counsel, and decrees; but he was permitted to add : ' saving the royal rights in the said Deanery and his own person.' So he got plenary absolution and (what he possibly valued more) was restored to the enjoyment of the profits of his benefice.

The visitation of his diocese is and has always been one of the chief duties of a Bishop—a duty implied of course in the very name.

On the occasion of these Visitations, Bishops frequently travelled in great state with a large retinue, and taking with them what was called their ' Chapel,' so much so that many Councils found it necessary to admonish them not to be too burdensome to their poorer clergy.

The Bishop was met with much ceremony on his entry into the parish, and was escorted to the church, where service was held and he gave the people his blessing, and explained the object of the Visitation, and prayed for its success. The most gratifying part of the service to the parishioners was probably the grant by the Bishop of forty days' indulgence—a word which, by the way, is not to be understood in its modern sense ; it meant pardon—the remission of penance imposed for *past* sins. Service over, the Bishop was vested in his amice and a purple (or black) stole and cope, and proceeded to the churchyard, where he said the *De profundis* (i.e. Psalm 130) and prayers for the faithful departed.

In the dispute as to the patronage of the Deanery, victory was, in the end, with the Crown and Duchy, and continued so from the time of Edward III. till A.D. 1850, when by Statute (13 and 14 Victoria, c. 76) the Deanery was divided into three Rectories, of St. Buryan, St. Levan, and St. Sennen ; the office of Dean being abolished as from the death of the then Dean (the Hon.

THE CHURCH OF ST. BURYAN

and Rev. Fitz-Roy Henry Richard Stanhope, who died in 1864) ;[1] all peculiar and exempt jurisdiction was taken away, and all wills, seals, &c., ordered to be transferred to the Registry of the Archdeaconry at Bodmin.

The college shared in the general suppression of the Reformation, and its officers were pensioned off; the Dean, Thomas Bauge, receiving in 1553 25*l*. 17*s*. 4*d*. ; William Woodward, 5*l*. ; Philip John, 4*l*. 10*s*. ; Lewis Jenkins, 2*l*. ; Robert Whitster, 2*l*.

In 1555 there was paid to Philip John, a stipendiary in the church of St. Burian, called the King's Priest, 4*l*. 10*s*., and to David Barrghe, formerly Dean, 25*l*. 17*s*. 4*d*. The others were perhaps dead ; at any rate, their names are not on the Roll of Fees paid out of the Exchequer (Add. MS. 8102, British Museum). David Barrghe is probably a mistake for Thomas Bauge.

It was evidently contemplated to make some change in connection with this parish somewhere between 1538 and 1566, as among the State Papers in the Public Record Office is a petition of the 'whole paryshe of St. Buryan' to the Lord Treasurer and the Barons of the Exchequer, asserting theirs to be a parish church and to have been so time out of mind, the parson having 'the cure and charge of fifteen hundred comunycatinge people being within his said cure as the estate thereof may most manyfestly appear unto your honoure by deposicons remayning of record which hath byn so tryed heretofore as by the record and judgement in the Courte of Exchequer appeareth. So yt ys righte honorable Lorde that certen covetuouse personns for theire owne gredines have procured an informacon agaynste our incumbent John Guyer touching the estate of our Church supposing the same to be a Deanrye.' The 'power orators' pray that an early day may be fixed for determining the matter. Probably they did not care whether the establishment was called collegiate or not ; they were only anxious that the cure of souls should be recognised as part of the duty of the Dean and Prebendaries. There is among the papers a plan of this and the adjacent parishes of apparently the same date.

From photo by]   [*J. C. Burrow, F.G.S.*
ST. BURYAN FONT

[1] Stanhope does not appear to have ever come into residence. It is said that no English Bishop could be induced to ordain him, and that his Royal friend sent him to Ireland for the purpose with this note of introduction: 'Ordain Stanhope, Yours York,' to which, in due course, came the reply : ' Stanhope's ordained, Yours Cork.'

During the Commonwealth two Deans of St. Buryan seem to have suffered ejection—namely, Robert Creyghton and John Weekes.

The sacred vessels of the church now are two flagons of pewter presented in 1684 by Dr. Phillips, a chalice of silver of the same date, weighing fifteen ounces, the gift of Dr. Nicholas Phillips, and a silver paten weighing 12 oz. 5 dwt., the gift of Francis Hocken in 1740.

The bells are three:—

1. Legend: MR. RICHARD O DAVIES O SAMPSON O HVTCHENS O WARDENS O 1681 o in flat Roman capitals 1¼ inch high. The coin impressions between the words are from a half-crown of Charles II., 1676. Diameter at mouth, 37¾ inches.

2. VOCEM EGO DO VOBIS VOS DATE VERBA DEO R (skeleton of a bell) P. 1638, in broad Roman capitals. Diameter at mouth, 40⅜ inches. The trade mark is that of Roger Purdue of Bristol.

3. Legend: VIRGINIS O EGREGIÆ O VOCOR O CAMPANA O MARIÆ o Richard: Dennis: Iohn: Kevan: C: W: with the date 1738 below. Lettering rather irregular. Coin impressions as on No. 1. Diameter at the mouth, 46 inches. This bell was cast in the village, and a flaw in it is said to have been caused by a man jumping off a hedge and shaking the mould before the metal was cool. In Dunkin's 'Church Bells of Cornwall' (London, 1878) is a copy of the churchwardens' accounts of 1738 with reference to this bell, from which we learn that the chief expense was 'Paid the Bell founder in money 15*l*. 7*s*., the ropes, blocks, &c., being most lent by friends at Newlyn, Penzance and Hayle.' The total cost of casting the 'Great Bell' (as the churchwardens call it) and fixing it up amounted altogether only to 33*l*. 19*s*. 11*d*.

One interesting relic is an altar-cloth worked by two maiden ladies, the Misses Davies, towards the end of the seventeenth century, and still in occasional use. In the Transactions of the Penzance Natural History Society (vol. ii. p. 293) is an account of the discovery of two urns in ground then (1886) recently added to the churchyard, and on the supposed site of the ancient chapel of St. Clare. We can trace no reference to this chapel in any ancient document.

There were also formerly the ruins of at least two other chapels in this parish, one by the seaside on the manor of Treviddron, dedicated to St. Loy or St. Dillower, and the other on the estate called Vellanserga.

THURSTAN C. PETER.

OLD MAN'S CORNER

Every old Farm or Manor-house in the Duchy had its Old Man's Corner by the inner side of the chimney, where the gaffer of the household smoked his pipe and talked of the past.

Such a corner we propose to allow in our Magazine. The following notes are authentic. Some are taken from the MS. of an old man who died in the year 1870, at the age of eighty-two. We shall be glad to receive similar notes and jottings from those who sit quietly and watch a younger generation.

' *And sometimes I remember days of old,*
  When fellowship seemed not so far to seek,
  And all the world and I seemed much
    less cold,
  And at the rainbow's foot lay surely
    gold,
And hope felt strong, and life itself not
    weak.'

Remarkable receptions were given in many parts of Cornwall to some of the habits and conveniences of modern times. The introduction of the first umbrella into Polperro caused quite a sensation. It was presented, about the year 1800, to Mr. Charles Guy, who kept the Ship Inn; and when he walked the streets with the umbrella over his head all eyes were on him, as if some strange animal was there, while almost everyone exclaimed against 'the pride of some people.' Those who loudly railed at Mr. Guy would, no doubt, have gladly accepted the umbrella, however. But probably they would have regarded it as too precious a thing to use, and locked it away in their chests.

During the war of the French Revolution gold became exceedingly scarce in Cornwall, so much so that not a single gold coin might be seen, even by a man of position, for twelve months together. Paper money then came into common use, and that led to the establishment of banks, which grew so numerous that scarcely a town was without one, while some had two. A few of the banks lived prosperously, others ended amidst disaster and ruination. All the banks issued notes, and we give reproductions of two. The note for one pound bears the impress of a fivepenny stamp, and the note for five pounds has two stamps —one being for a shilling and the other for threepence. At the outset no licence was required to be held by those who issued notes, but subsequently a licence, with a 50*l*. stamp annually, became necessary. The licence, or perhaps the cost of the stamp, led some bankers to

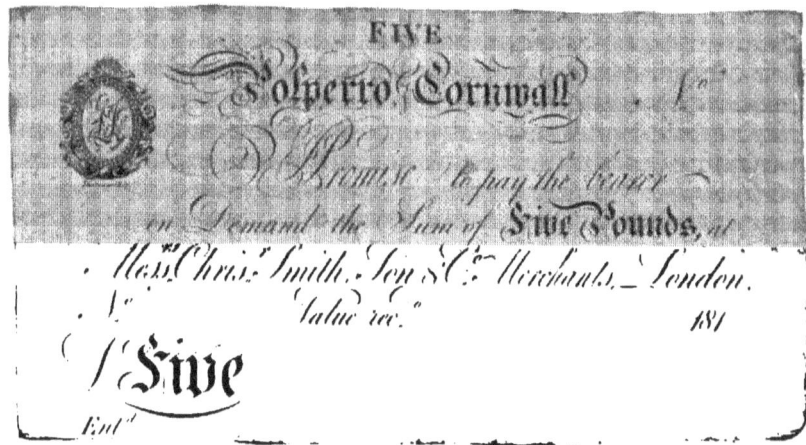

withdraw their notes from circulation, Mr. Richards, who had a bank at Port Looe, being amongst them. During this reign of paper the guineas sold at a high premium. They were constantly being collected by Jews, who gave as much as 27s. each for them, and it was said that the Government employed the Jews to obtain the guineas in order that they might be sent to the armies.

When oxen had been supplanted by horses in other parts of England they were still highly esteemed in Cornwall, and continued in general use on the farms. At the beginning of the century oxen could be seen in all directions drawing butts, wains, and waggons on the roads or walking in front of ploughs and harrows in the fields. It was the custom to bring them to the yoke and bow when three years old, and as a rule they proved docile and active. A plough team consisted of four, and sometimes there was a horse as leader. The oxen were shod or, as it was termed in the county, 'cued.'

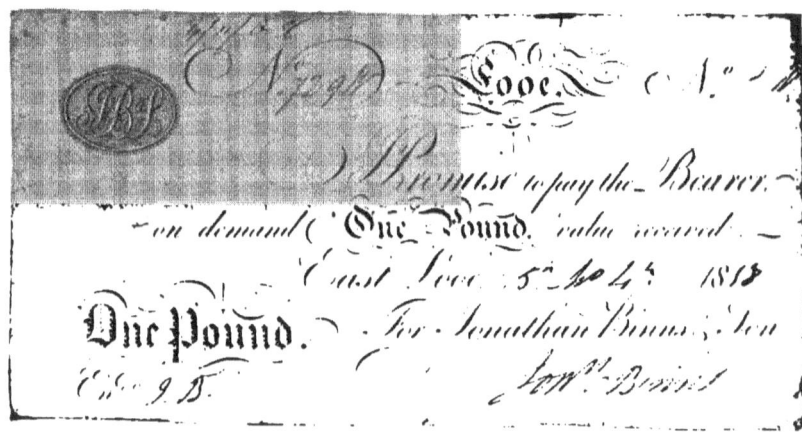

'My recollections of the West Country ceremony of crying the neck differ a little from Mr. Baring-Gould's. It was not the cutting of the last sheaf, but the saving or the housing of it, as in the case of the harvest home, that was the cause of rejoicing. The neck was a bundle of the largest ears of bearded wheat to be found, just a dozen or twenty, enough to make a good handful plaited together. Bearded wheat is generally of inferior quality, known to the trade as cones or rivets, which grinds rather rash, or *raish*, as the millers call it. But associations with a beard are venerable, and bearded wheat has a venerable appearance. The last sheaf having been *saved*, the expression used in the West, the harvesters assembled in a ring, and some called in a loud voice, "Us have un, us have un, us have un"; which was answered by others, who called, "What have ee? what have ee? what have ee?" to which all replied by crying out, "A neck, a neck, a neck"; and then followed a "wurrah," as they call hurrah, and drink. This was done three times, with three drinks following. The neck was afterwards hung up in the farm kitchen, and was looked upon as rather a sacred thing. When I was a small boy there was a bonfire on the occasion of crying the neck, to light which no straw happened to have been provided. I said, "Light it with the neck." There was an immediate uproar of indignation. I heard "Who says light un with the neck?" and I slunk away mightily ashamed. This must have been nearly seventy years ago. It has left a deep impression.

'W. F. COLLIER.'

CORNISH DIAMONDS

'Please God,' said Aunt Mary Bunny, 'if I live till this evenin', and all's well, I'll send for the doctor.'

A West-country squire on his death-bed was visited by the Parson. 'You are going to a better world,' said the Parson.
'I don't want no better world. With my whit-vaced mare and a thousand a year I don't want no better world. Her'd go over gates one arter t'other—tip—tip—tip.'

As our readers know, John Carter the famous smuggler of Porthleah went throughout Cornwall by the name of the 'King of Prussia.' A Mousehole man on hearing news of the real King of Prussia's defeat at Jena, remarked, 'Misfortunes never come single. I'm sorry for that man. Not more'n six weeks ago he lost three hundred keg o' brandy, by informa- tion, so I'm towld.'

A commercial traveller, having lost his way on a Cornish moor at night, rode up to a cottage and tapped with his whip at a bedroom window.
'Can you tell me the way to Redruth?'
'Who's theer, stankin' down my lil liks an' lil taties?'
'I've lost my way to Redruth.'
'Where be comin' from?'
'From Liverpool.'
'What be goin' to R'druth for?'
'To sell needles and pins.'
'Niddles an' pins! Niddles an' pins! Come all the way from Liverpool to sell niddles an' pins! Go's 'long with 'ee, stankin' down my lil liks an' lil taties!'

Uncle Billy was discussing pronuncia- tion with a ship's captain from Dundee. 'See here,' the Scotsman said, 'in the West of England, now, div ye say "nay- ther" or "neether"?' Uncle Billy: 'Nather; us dawn't use the expression.'

Report of a public speech:
'" What shall I say?" sez a—" What shall I say? I don't knaw *what* to say"; and the old fule, he *didn'* know what to say, an' he sot down.'

Chairman of Parish Council: 'What? You keep us here till nine o'clock at night and then cast the town drains in our teeth? You keep us here ploughin' the san's, and then, at nine o'clock at night, you drag in that everlastin' red herrin' and expect us to swaller it? You rake up a motion that was carried *non com* at the last mittin', and away you go into the public drains, causing unneces- sary friction. 'Twon't do, I tell 'ee. 'Tis too barefaced to hold water.'

First Miner: 'Who's that fella you was talkin' to just now?'
Second Miner: 'Cap'en Trevanion.'
First Miner: 'What, the new cap'en over to Wheal Rose?'
Second Miner: 'No, that's another man.'
First Miner: 'What's this one cap'en of, then?'
Second Miner: 'He's a hoorse-sojer.'
First Miner: 'There, now, I thoft he was only a army cap'en. He didn' look like nothing more'n that.'

THE BATTLE OF ALGIERS

From a painting in Greenwich Hospital. By permission of the Lords Commissioners of the Admiralty

Photo by]   NARCISSUS TIME   *[Gibson & Sons, Penzance*

THE DAFFODIL IN CORNWALL

IT occurs to me, as I sit down to write, that to the daffodil, and the daffodil alone, I owe my introduction to Cornwall, and more than one delightful friendship with the genial Cornish folk. 'Is it too late to go round the garden?' asked my hostess, the desire for tea and saffron buns being assuaged, on that March evening after my journey of over two hundred miles to judge at the first Cornwall Spring Flower Show. It is never too late to go round a garden. The new beauty of plants by lantern-light may have struck other stalkers of the midnight slug than myself. That first vision of a Cornish spring garden is unforgettable; the fair reaches of Falmouth Harbour and the pale gleam of the lighthouse in the distance, the mild air loaded with the scent of violets—those same wonderful violets which came in first by several lengths, or rather breadths, at the show next day—*Marie Louise* and *Neapolitan* the size of half-crowns—and, everywhere luminous in the half light, the daffodils, massive in bloom, tall in stem, and broad in leaf, having the air of opulent contentment peculiar to plants that have found all their heart's desire in both soil and air. Here, then, was the promised land of daffodils ; here was the Mecca to reward a nearly twenty years' pilgrimage through long tracts of less perfect flowers. To predict of the treasury of spring blossom unlocked at Truro next day, that this must forthwith rank as the premier English Spring Show, was no breach of the sound rule, not to prophesy until you know. It is outside the limits of this article to descant upon the glory of the great Rhododendron trusses, ruby, pink, and white, or dappled with a score of lovely tints, except to note that they seldom or never reach London shows in perfection, and are literally a revelation to the March visitor from the bleaker shires, and a sight well worth a journey across the breadth of England, whether massed on the show tables, or, still better, shining against their superb foliage in the Cornish valleys. Nor must I dwell upon the *Anemone fulgens*, larger and of more dazzling scarlet than any before seen by me, except to here tender my regrets, *à propos* of this flower, for a misconception of the Cornish character. When the competitors for the Anemone prize, and, indeed, in other departments of that first show, insisted on putting into their bunches more than the twelve blooms prescribed by the schedule, it is recorded in the book of the Hon. Secretaries that the judge betrayed impatience. From his after experience of invariably receiving thirteen to the dozen in all Cornish courtesies and hospitalities he is now well aware that the occurrence was owing, not to perversity or arithmetical incompetence, but purely to the fine lavishness of the Western temperament.

But to return to the daffodils. The Truro Shows of 1897 and 1898 have convinced me that the daffodils of Cornwall are, or certainly ought to be, unsurpassed. The qualification of the 'ought' will be explained presently. This judgment may be arrived at by the several criteria of excellence. Earliness is a point of great value, to the market-grower especially, and it is needless to demonstrate this quality of Cornish spring produce. Size is usually ranked next, and being fully familiar with the growth of all parts of England, of Ireland, the Channel Islands, and Holland, I can confidently give the palm for size, compatible with quality, to the flowers of Cornwall. The wonderful trumpet *maximus* of Captain Pinwell, Mr. Charles Dawson's giant *Sir Watkin*, and Mr. Andrew Lawry's *Grand Monarque* may serve as examples. In actual measurement of flower some Dutch blooms may possibly exceed these, but the latter are coarse in texture and literally dropsical, being grown in land half sand and half manure, their roots almost in the water. Colour counts next, though in my judgment it should reckon before mere size, and here the Cornish flowers hold the field. Mr. T. A. Dorrien-Smith has written of the Scilly Narcissi, 'I have never seen such colour as we get in *C. J. Backhouse, Barri conspicuus*, and other of the crimson-rimmed varieties. . . . The great feature in all the flowers is the purity and intensity of colour ; whether this is caused by the salt in the air, or by a porous soil . . . I cannot say.' This holds good also of the mainland of Cornwall. I cannot answer the question whether this enhancement of the colouring is due to the air or the soil, but it is certain that some kinds put on a vividness which makes them almost unrecognisable by, say, the London grower. An instance is *Cynosure*, a tall-growing *incomparabilis*, with flowers of flimsy substance, worthless in my Hampshire garden, but having the characters of earliness and freedom of bloom, and in Cornwall developing so bright an orange in the rim of its cup as to be a very valuable market sort. The magnificent collection of cut Narcissi from Scilly, contributed to the Truro Show this year by Mr. Dorrien-Smith, included specimens of the shapely *Princess Mary*, with a depth

NARCISSUS GRANDEE

quite unknown to me of orange red in their broad saucer-eyes. The red and yellow of the bunch-flowered *Soleil d'or* from Scilly and the mainland are extremely pure and rich.

Of the first impression made by the Cornish daffodils as seen growing a word has already been written, but for magnificence of these plants grown to perfection on a large scale I have seen nothing to equal Mr. Andrew Lawry's flower-farm in Mount's Bay. The view of acre upon acre of the silver *Poeticus ornatus* and the great waxen clusters of *Grand Monarque* stretching, under the brilliant spring sky of Cornwall, far away towards the blue bay and the ancient mount of St. Michael upstanding in the sunlight, would need the idyllic gift of a Theocritus to describe worthily. There can be no finer Narcissi in flower, leaf, or bulb than those grown in this warm, alluvial soil. On the higher grounds, too, of the county, especially on the slopes of the southern valleys, and where there is much detritus of moist sandstone and granitic rock in the staple, they flourish exceedingly; indeed, no spot has come under my notice where they do not appear at home and happy. One garden has proved a perfect sanatorium for consumptive bulbs of certain beautiful, but, in my less kindly soil and harsher climate, delicate varieties. The daffodil, to use the name in its modern application to all plants of the genus Narcissus, can but do well in a land to which it is in a manner indigenous. The cream-white *Tazzetta*, nearly if not absolutely identical with the *Scilly White* of the winter market, is an immemorial dweller on the rocky slopes of St. Michael's Mount. Not to assign it to the inevitable Phœnician, that *deus ex machinâ* to cut all Cornish antiquarian knots, who is unlikely to have traded in 'Dutch bulbs,' its age is respectable enough if we suppose it to have been introduced by the monks half a dozen or more centuries ago. They probably had not our æsthetic enjoyment of its great tufts of pale bloom against the lichened stone, but employed it for medicinal or 'still-room' concoctions. One ingredient of the celebrated liqueur of the *Grande Chartreuse* is said to be the expressed juice of a yellow daffodil. But possibly it is a true native, a western outlier of the widely distributed race of *Narcissus polyanthus*, which extends from Portugal to China, and from Switzerland to North Africa. The point, however, is that the 'Mount lilies' are glad in their Cornish environment, untended, except by Lord St. Levan's anxiety, which it is hoped all will respect, that they shall be held sacred and inviolable by the tourist.

By the side of the long approach to one of the most beautiful homes in South Cornwall, in the clear spaces between rhododendrons, hydrangeas, and what not of choicest flowering shrubs, may be seen in February great colonies of the prettiest and best, to my mind, of all quite early-flowering trumpet daffodils, broad-petalled and of the softest pale yellow. This is a local kind, collected from meadows of the same estate, where it has been 'always' (no : neither the writer nor the Editor will give the address or forward begging letters for a bulb or two). It was the existence in the isles of similarly wild or long-established sorts which suggested to Mr. Augustus Smith the enterprise, since so splendidly successful, of the Scilly narcissus industry. It is owing to no lack of appreciation of this work that it is scarcely mentioned here, but only because it has been written of again and again, from both the picturesque and the statistical points of view, and my subject is rather its extension to the mainland, which, it must be confessed, has but taken a leaf out of Scilly's book :—

'Most can raise the flower now,
For all have got the seed,'

Photo by] [Gibson & Sons, Penzance
PART OF A FLOWER FARM

from the foresight and the labours of the Scilly dynasty, to whom all gratitude is due from the Cornish flower-farmers.

There is little doubt that the surface soil of Cornwall must, in the long run, yield vastly greater wealth than its mines, for the former, if treated with fair consideration and elementary knowledge of scientific farming, is inexhaustible. The increase in population of our great towns is expressed in bewildering figures; and though these millions may still be mostly fools, yet they buy flowers and have an insatiable appetite for the first flowers of spring. Climate is not to be made artificially, nor can flowers, like fruit, be brought thousands of miles over sea to under-sell home produce. Moreover, the growing demand is not for cut flowers only, but also for plants, or, in the case of daffodils, for bulbs. This is an age of gardening : dwellers in the country make more of their gardens than in any past time, and never before was his daily or week-end escape to his garden so prized by the man whose business or profession holds him in town. Put briefly, all respectable people nowadays have gardens, and all respectable gardens must have their complement of daffodils. The competition for new and fine varieties is sharp, and long prices are cheerfully paid. However lugubrious the talk of badness of times and reduction of establishments, rarities do not remain unsold. ' Give us the luxuries of life and we will dispense with the necessaries.' Ten or twelve years ago half a guinea each was about the top value, until, with the advent of the white trumpet *Madame de Graaff*, it rose to 5*l.* 5*s*. Messrs. Barr's large yellow trumpet *Monarch* now fetches 15*l.* 15*s*., and it is known that desirable seedlings, not yet in the general market, are sold at something like 35*l.* per bulb. The shapely, clear-skinned bulb, weighty for size, small at base, can be harvested nowhere more surely than in Cornwall, and nowhere can valuable stocks be increased to better advantage. The excellence of the flowers shown at Truro has already induced at least one London firm to make overtures for a Cornish nursery. The bulk of the more ordinary commercial sorts has hitherto been supplied by Holland, but it is yearly more evident that the Dutch soil, a sand loaded for many generations past with cow manure, is not permanently suited to the cultivation of the daffodil. The Dutch bulbs are large, but rough, and, unless difficult precautions are observed of fallowing and alternate cropping, unwholesome of complexion and beset with the deadly ' basal rot.'

Great and increasing multitudes of bulbs are now grown on the alluvium round the Wash, mostly in the neighbourhood of Spalding and Wisbech—good bulbs, but in my judgment inferior to the best Cornish samples. The Cornish soils will probably prove more enduring, *i.e.* possessed of a larger reserve of daffodil-food in their phosphatic and potassic constituents, and climate is all in favour of the western county. The daffodil is rightly called a hardy plant ; few of its varieties are killed by cold, but it is a mistake to credit it with *enjoyment* of frost and cutting winds. The winter temperature of the high mountain pastures, whence the ancestors of most of our garden daffodils came, is very low, but it must be remembered that they are protected throughout the inclement months by a thick coverlet of snow. The habitat of those found on lower ground, as *N. maximus* from near Biarritz, is outside the zone of severe frost. A mild, moist winter, with a sunny March and April, are the most favourable English conditions. And the earlier the plant matures, the earlier the bulb can be lifted and placed on the market, a very important consideration. It has suited the convenience of the retail dealers to catalogue and distribute daffodil bulbs in autumn, together with their hyacinths and tulips, and

NARCISSUS TRIANDRUS

unknowing customers still plant largely in October and November. But the daffodil by nature starts quickly into growth, and much of the preparation for its spring effort is made before winter. In proof, let any reader lift a few bulbs at the end of July and note the length of fresh white roots. For the finest bloom and fullest increase planting should be completed by the end of August; my own more valuable seedlings are planted, when possible, in July. The time is not distant when this will be generally understood, and the district which can lift early in June and sell in July will forestall the market. The quite brief period of quiescence is indicated by the *partial* withering of the leaf, not by its total disappearance, and this may happen in Cornwall as early as the end of May. For the first bloom under glass, bulbs should be potted or boxed proportionately early, and for the earliest supply of good bulbs there is and will be an unlimited demand. Mr. Dorrien-Smith alone forces *a million Poeticus ornatus* annually! In short, then, looking to the opportunities of the daffodil trade alone, every foot of suitable soil in Cornwall must steadily rise in value.

It may, however, be asked, what warrant is there that all this affection for daffodils is not the unstable fashion of an hour? Why should not the daffodil be dethroned and another favourite reign? An amateur who has in his garden never less than some 30,000 of his own seedlings, a link in a chain of experimental work reaching over more than a decade and a half of years, must often have pondered this question. But after long thought and conference with the most piercing horticultural intellects, I have retired into the solacing conviction that while roses are gathered and strawberries eaten the daffodil's empire will not be seriously threatened. The spring flower seems not to exist in nature, and cannot be evolved from the most fertile inner consciousness, which shall supersede the daffodil. Sumptuary laws are not for our times; though prices should mount to 1,000*l.* a bulb the traffic will not be put down by Act of Parliament, as was the tulip craze of the first half of the seventeenth century in the Netherlands. Mr. George Monro, the salesman and prophet of Covent Garden, is of opinion that with regard to cut bloom we are but at the beginning of the demand for the best produce, that is, for the finest kinds perfectly grown and consigned to market in perfection. The costly elaboration in letter and picture of the daffodil specialist's catalogue, and the undeprecating boldness of its prices in guineas of two figures, argue that the daffodil cult is not on the wane, and the guarantee of its permanence lies in the intrinsic excellence of the flower. What other has the abundant market qualifications of great earliness in the open air; fresh and delicate colour; ability to store water in its cells and keep fresh two days without a drink, like a camel crossing the desert; and, by no means least, a flower at right angles to a long stem, so that it makes up into long bunches facing one way for display, and travelling uncrushed in shallow boxes? The outdoor hyacinth is profitless for cut bloom; it comes much later, will not bunch, and is too rank of scent in rooms. The attempts made of late to 'boom' the tulip have fallen flat. The florist's tulip proper runs into the plethora of early summer flowers; its bloom is fugitive, and, to quote from a Cornish amateur, 'in a quite common combination of sun and rain is ruined by a kind of small-pox.'

A character which has endeared the daffodil to our gardens is that of all spring flowers it is the most lily-like. Botanically it is separated from the true lilies by certain features, as that of the seed vessel being formed outside instead of within the corolla. But the popular names 'Lent Lily' and 'Mount Lily' show that it has by a true discernment been recognised as a lily, a flower of queenly rank, removed from the crowd by a certain aristocratic grace of presence. The first flower of note to appease our winter-long hunger, the very tips of its strong leaves are rejoiced in as they break the soil:—

'When daffodils begin to peer,
. . . . .
Why, then comes in the sweet o' the year.'

'E molto bello: è il primo fiore della primavera,' was the appreciative comment of an Italian labourer as he watched me digging up a wild yellow daffodil by the roadside outside Lucca. This fearlessness of our rough English spring— March is 'the roaring moon of daffodils'—has made it pre-eminently an English flower, and the hands of Englishmen have fashioned it to its present beauty. Over two and a half centuries ago Parkinson had anticipated Mr. Peter Barr in employing Pyrenean 'root-collectors,' and describes some hundred kinds of daffodil. The magic art of cross-fertilisation was then undreamed of, and the possibilities latent in Parkinson's store awaited the coming of Herbert, first

Dean of Manchester. Herbert, who in one side of his versatile genius was something of a pre-Darwinian Darwin, published, in 1843, the results of many years' experiments at his Yorkshire rectory of Spofforth, and demonstrated that the short-crowned narcissi of the reputed 'species' *N. incomparabilis* are really hybrids between the trumpet daffodils and the pheasant-eye, or *N. poeticus*. The first to avail themselves of this discovery, of such paramount importance for the enrichment of the spring garden, were Messrs. Leeds, of Longford Bridge, near Manchester, and Backhouse, of Walsingham. By effecting this cross in variety, and intercrossing the resultant seedlings with other flowers and one another, they obtained the host of lovely forms now in common cultivation. These, again, are being sedulously used by the hybridist for the further evolution of size, form, and colour. The subsequent workers in the same field have all been Englishmen. A few fine trumpet daffodils have been raised in Holland, notably the very beautiful white *Madame de Graaff* by Messrs. de Graaff, of Leyden, but these seem to have been chance seedlings, and it is a curious fact that the Dutch, reputed quick to discern any avenue of profit, have never deliberately taken in hand the hybridisation of the Narcissus. The best *Polyanthus Narcissi* or *Tazzettas* are, it is true, of Dutch origin, but these do not rank in general esteem or money value with other daffodils, and have scarcely been improved for a century. Leeds sold his entire collection for a hundred guineas, and the sum was thought so large that it was found by a small company of purchasers. Twenty times the amount would now be thought a small price. At the death of John Horsefield, the Lancashire weaver, who raised the fine white and gold trumpet daffodil bearing his name, the few bulbs were sold by auction for eighteenpence apiece—*sic vos non vobis*.

A propos of the essentially English associations of the daffodil, I have been told by Mons. H. L. de Vilmorin, of the great French firm of seedsmen and florists, that the venture of growing it on a large scale for the Paris market failed entirely. The more fanciful and fickle Parisian tires of a continuance of one flower, liking here a bit of white lilac, there a spray of mimosa or a bunch of Riviera anemones, but only now and then a daffodil. In France, too, there has never prevailed, as in England, what may be termed *intensive* gardening, the loving and ex-

ONE OF THE AUTHOR'S SEEDLINGS

haustive study of some one particular flower in all its phases and potentialities. The sight is inconceivable in France, which may be witnessed any April at a Royal Horticultural Society's gathering, of four men standing rapt and abstracted, their heads in close contact over a match-box containing a single 'pip' or floweret of a new auricula seedling. The minutiæ of distinction between daffodils like 'tweedledum and tweedledee' to the casual eye, their more subtle *nuances* of shape, tint, and growth, are for the specialist, the daffodil florist proper, and it is vain to reproach him for distinguishing between things indistinguishable. Wherever the mind's full interest is long bent upon a numerous class of objects, the critical faculty develops, and the eye, without either

Photo by]   [*Gibson & Sons, Penzance*
'THE SWEET O' THE YEAR'

straining or make-believe, acquires powers both telescopic and microscopic.

But there is no lack of more obvious charms in the daffodil. In its resources of form and colour there is a limitation, a certain restraint and sobriety, which belong to the highest beauty no less in nature than in art. It loses nothing when compared with the orchid's fuller colour-palette and bizarre eccentricity of form. In its general chalice or bell-like contour it presents but two elements, the inner crown, cup, or eye, and the outer whorl or *perianth* of six petals, or, more accurately, sepals. The crown may be a long tube or funnel, as in the trumpet daffodils, or a shallow eye defined by a rim not a quarter of an inch deep, as in the *poeticus*. But cross the trumpet and the *poeticus*, and again intercross parents and progeny, and the central portion of the flower exhibits every gradation in depth of cup, bowl, saucer, and plate, to draw a familiar comparison from the wholly inadequate resources of the modern crockery cupboard. An apter but over recondite illustration might be found in the more varied and graceful curves of the equivalent Greek and Roman vessels. The colour elements are only yellow, white, and red. The yellow—a cheerful and satisfying colour in flowers—is of large range, from the richest gold of the stately *Maximus* or *Santa Maria*, a still deeper toned flower discovered in Spain by Mr. Peter Barr, to the cream of *Pallidus præcox*, which consorts so exquisitely with the purple of violets or *Iris reticulata*. In one catalogue I find the yellows described as orange, lemon, primrose, canary, gold, sulphur, with light, full, rich, clear, soft, and a dozen other modifying adjectives. The daffodil's whitest white, almost the negation of colour, is found in the *poeticus*, especially the late *P. recurvus*. Elsewhere the whites are those of the ecclesiastical embroiderer, the faintest possible creams, greens, and, in the cups of some of the *Leedsi* class, citrons and pinks. When left to dress itself the daffodil employs red with quite niggardly discretion, as though to merely accentuate and set off its yellow and white. The purple brown thread which rings the eye of *N. poeticus* sometimes appears in its seedlings and hybrids as a ribbon-edge or a suffusion of red. By intercrossing such flowers an accumulation of the colour may result, and some of my own most recent seedlings have cups of almost true scarlet. This intensified red is held to be one of the goals of the hybridist and is greatly coveted, but I must own to private misgivings whether violence has not been done to the daffodil's better taste, and the lighter touches of colour are not more pleasing. Should a seedling ever attain to full red in both cup and petals, it would command an enormous price, but artistically considered would be somewhat of an outrage. The most disdainful of all daffodils in its rejection of red is the dainty little *N. triandrus*, with pale, clustered, cyclamen-like blossoms, as common in parts of Portugal as the primrose in Cornwall, but practically unknown in England until fifteen years ago. From this, crossed with the larger garden kinds, I have a series of perfectly lovely hybrids with pendent fuchsia-like flowers of the most refined cream and ivory whites. But cross it as you will with the most brilliant of the red-cupped sorts, the seedlings perpetuate its own simpler apparel, and never show a trace of red.

A race more delightful to myself than perhaps any other are the *Leedsi* varieties, intermediate between *N. poeticus* and the white trumpets. It is remarkable that in this cross the former parent effaces the weakliness of the latter, and supplies a diversity of vigorous and very lovely white flowers. In the cups of some of these a quite exquisite range of colouring occurs, which can be only imperfectly conveyed by such words as salmon, citron, apricot. Recent seedlings perhaps foreshow the coming of true pink in the daffodil. To appreciate these delicate tints the flowers should be studied in the late afternoon when the sun is off them and they seem to create a still, magical atmosphere about themselves.

A discourse upon the whole art and mystery of seedling raising would far transgress the bounds of this paper, but it should be urged that the time is at hand when this department will be necessary to every gardener abreast of the times in the culture of flowers, fruit, or vegetables, to the least amateur and to the largest farmer. Seed-selection and cross-fertilisation are as certain to supersede, or at least supplement, the mere propagation of existing plants as the electric light is to extinguish gas. Absolutely nothing has been done in this province in comparison with what awaits the educated and industrious worker. A certain fortune, for instance, is in store for the young man who will devote his life to the scientific improvement of our fruits. In Narcissi there are still many desiderata: large early yellow trumpets of sturdier constitution; finer and stronger white trumpets; short-crowned flowers, of the size and vigour of *Sir Watkin*, of uniform clear white, and others with cups of full red. The *Polyanthus Narcissus* is still capable of advancement in size and colour; I cannot join in the current depreciation of this beautiful plant; its earliness and perfection of growth in Cornwall should draw more attention to its possibilities. The *poeticus* may be enlarged and the eye deepened in colour.

My remark at the outset, that the Cornish daffodils *ought* to be unsurpassed, was not of the ungrateful nature of general faint praise, but referred to one point only. The *répertoire* of the market growers has struck me as rather meagre. The truth is questionable of the common objections that it does not pay to buy new varieties, and that the public do not distinguish between one kind and another. The wise grower will not invest largely in an untried bulb, however striking the flower may be at a show, but he will not neglect to have a small experimental bed of the newest introductions. It is strange that the bright yellow and red and the immense vigour of *Barri conspicuus* have not caused it to be more largely grown. That very fine golden trumpet *M. J. Berkeley*, of the *maximus* order, but less shy in bloom, should well repay an enterprising buyer. The new *bicolor*, *Victoria*, is dear at present, but increases fast, and for size and substance will supersede *Horsfieldi* and *Empress*. More attention should be paid to the best *Leedsi* kinds, such as *Minnie Hume* and *Duchess of Westminster*. The spot or mildew which has lately invaded

NARCISSUS MRS. J. B. M. CAMM

the former may be a transient effect of season. The Covent Garden salesmen tell me that good white Narcissi, such as these, are wanted. It may be an excellent investment to give 5*l.* or 10*l.* for a bulb of a small new stock. An instance is known to me of 5*l.* being paid for one *Madame de Graaff*, and at the end of three years three of its increase being sold for 12*l.* and three still retained. A midland florist expresses to me his regret that he purchased only one bulb of *Weardale Perfection* on its first appearance at 12*l.* 12*s.* apiece.

On the subject of cultivation I am reluctant to say much. The dilemma besets me that upon the general requirements of a plant it is superfluous, and upon its local requirements presumptuous to speak. Let me not fall into the pit of the technical education lecturer on horticulture, who, in my country side of chalk downs, with the nearest water 100 feet from the surface, devoted the whole of his introductory lecture to methods of drainage. Mr. Andrew Lawry was amiable enough to follow my suggestion and plant his *ornatus* deeper, but found he had made a mistake. That the following practices are beneficial, I do not doubt: Early planting and early lifting; rotation of cropping, *i.e.* not growing daffodils, or at least not similar kinds, upon the same plot for long together; an occasional entire change of stock with a distant grower, if feasible; manuring from the surface with soluble phosphate, such as dissolved bone. The much advertised basic slag is valueless on most, perhaps on all, Cornish soils.

Lastly, I would ask both professionals and amateurs to support the Annual Spring Flower Show by subscription, exhibition, and personal presence. Apart from the extreme beauty of the display, the show serves, and will serve increasingly, to bring all that is newest and most meritorious under the eye of the Cornish flower-lover, and to advertise the wares of the Cornish producer. If it be possible that any Cornishman cares nothing for daffodils for their own sake, let him still of duty support an institution sure to bring grist to the mill of a worthy Cornish industry.

GEORGE ENGLEHEART.

THE LUCK OF TREYOLLA

I SUPPOSE they've told you up-the-country tales of how there used to be wreckers in these parts, and an old horse, hobbled, used to walk o' nights with a lantern round his neck. I don't believe that no such thing ever happened. I'm an old man now, and I never saw such a thing, nor heard of it, though I've seen wrecks enough to fill the bay, if they or the ghosts of them could come to the surface again.

I don't believe that ever a wreck on this coast happened except by the hand of God, for there's neither man nor woman but knows the bitterness of death on the sea, when a man goes down with the cry of his children in his ears, knowing they will lack bread. But 'tis true enough that if there is a wreck the people do think it only right they should help themselves to whatever may come ashore. 'Tis little enough we get out of the sea with all our labour and loss, and this is, as you might say, an unexpected harvest. I've helped myself often, and I should again if I had strength to go down to the sands, or climb the cliffs, and the luck to find anything.

But there's one curious thing about wrecks. We hardly ever have one here at Tresidder: if a ship gets into trouble in the bay you may be almost sure that she'll end up under Treyolla, at the other side. That is the meaning of the old saying, 'Like the luck of Treyolla, you find it waiting at the door.' There are reasons in plenty why Tresidder folk should think little of Treyolla, and 'tis little indeed they do think of it. So when Treyolla do get another wreck you can understand 'tis hard to put up with.

There was one time, however, when Treyolla didn't have the usual luck, and that was in '78, when the 'Gretchen' was wrecked. She was a big cargo boat, and what she didn' have aboard was what nobody needed. There were things fit for women folk, and things that men were glad of; things that children loved; things for use and things for ornament. She fought all day in the bay, but towards dusk the crew lost hope. Tresidder people watched all day—for nobody could help—and they were bitter enough when she drifted on the rocks close to Treyolla just before dark and started to break up. Even the dog and the cat were brought ashore, so there was no call for any but worldly thoughts, and no noise of drowned men calling their names in the night to make men remember death.

There was little sleep in Treyolla that night. Long before dawn the village was awake, and mothers gave their children a holiday from school.

Those that went down early found that others were before them, for the sea had been at its wildest when the 'Gretchen' took the rocks, and everyone knew that she would be gone to matchwood by the time the dawn came.

'Twas a busy day for Treyolla. Everybody worked from dawn to dusk, and there was never a hole of the rocks that was not explored, nor any that did not prove a gold mine in some sort of way. Moreover, as fast as what there was had been picked up and put away, the sea was casting up more, so that they could hardly keep pace with it. Tresidder folk went about their work with thoughts that were hurtful to their feelings, but they did not go near the place. However, an old pedlar came over to the 'One and All' at night, and told what there was to tell.

'What did she carry?' he asked, when the landlord had given him his pint in a cloamen jug. 'Better fit you should ask me what she didn' carry, for then I might be able to tell 'ee. Her hold must have been like my pack—filled up with all that man, woman, or child could desire, and with many things, like the blue pills I carry, that their poor systems might be crying out for all the time and they never know it in the foolishness of their hearts. There's combs and collars and curtains—Nanny Pengegon's front parlour 'll be a palace so I'm told; there's tea in tins, and cases of spirits, thermometers, hair-brushes, walking sticks, and biscuits. I can't think of all, but if you could name a few things to me I'll warrant I shall have to answer "Yes" as a man born truthful. There's candles by the hundredweight, and rugs, and picture frames, and a great big roll of silk that'll be fit for the Queen when it has been dried again. I tell 'ee there's no end to it: towels, and zinc pails, and a carpet, and a leather bag or two, and varnished trunks. What she didn't carry 'twould puzzle the wit of man to say, and 'tis all of it stored away in Treyolla.'

The old man was for going on, but Joe Symons, the vicar's churchwarden, stopped him. 'Thee's told us enough, Sam,' he said. 'Drink up thy beer and le's think 'pon it. 'Tis the luck of Treyolla again, and all the luck of Tresidder is to hear old wandering men like you tell of the good things happening on the other side of the bay. 'Tis kind of 'ee to come, and I'm sure we thank 'ee kindly. But we don't want no more detail: simme you've told us just as much as 'tis good for us to hear.'

The matter was not one that we cared to talk about, and though rumours came of the splendour of Treyolla's luck, little was said in the village for the next few days. Then George Laity came over one evening and dropped in at the 'One and All.' He was a son to the leading man in Treyolla, but he was courting a daughter to old Joe Symons, and the village having taken time to consider the idea of a stranger coming to its midst for a wife, had made up its mind that he could be put up with. All the same, George was none too sure of his welcome at the 'One and All'—there were one or two that had a wonderful gift of speech—and if he came in he was only too glad to have news to tell that would make him sure of his reception.

He came in and gave his order, and took a chair in the corner. Before he had time to speak Jim Jose was on him. 'I suppose,' he said, speaking sarcastic, and in fine up-the-country way, 'I suppose the marriage is coming off nex' week?'

George looked at him, puzzled-like. 'Nex' week?' he said. 'I didn' know it, and I don't think Martha does.'

'Aw,' said Jim, 'I'm surprised you should be content to wait. There can't be any need for it. I was given to understand that every man in Treyolla over eighteen years of age was going to retire upon his means, and that more than half of them had bought their houses and put up a little board in the garden with "Gretchen Cottage" painted upon it.'

The company laughed, but George was not so much taken aback as you might have expected. ''Tis very plain you haven't heard the news,' he said.

'Not another "Gretchen"?' said Jim.

'No,' said George, ''tis all a part of the same story. If there's any man here that can take a holiday he wouldn' do badly if he was to take a stroll over to Treyolla to-morrow afternoon. I'll warrant he'll find plenty to amuse him.'

'If 'tis anything new,' said Jim, 'out with it. But I can't fancy Tresidder people coming to Treyolla over the "Gretchen." That is hardly the way they think about the matter.'

'Well,' said George, 'I suppose they'll do as they like, but there'll be things to see to-morrow. There's a German gentleman come down to Trenear inquiring after what was saved from the "Gretchen," and he's coming to see what he can find. He has found out about some trifling articles that were sold in Trenear, and he swears he will get back all that was picked up.'

Now, it was not a common thing to sympathise with Treyolla, but this was no ordinary case. 'A German going to search Treyolla?' cried everyone.

'Well,' said George, 'I can't say 'tis altogether unreasonable. The "Gretchen" was a German ship, underwritten in Hamburg, and they say that the little man that's come over to Trenear will be several thousand pounds out of pocket. I can't say that Treyolla is likely to give him the kindest of welcomes, but if you put yourself in his place, you'll understand that he would naturally want to get back all that is possible.'

'So the luck of Treyolla is no luck at all?' said Jim Jose, with an air of satisfaction.

George Laity looked from one to another with a smiling face. 'I couldn' exactly say that,' he said. 'I've heard tell of people before now that went forth to seek what they couldn' find when they got there. He has the warrants——'

There was a shout of laughter. 'But the stuff is all put away?' said Jim.

George was still smiling. ''Twas a sinful trade, the smuggling, but 'tis wonderful what cunning hiding-places they used to hit upon in those days. The coastguard have forgotten, if they ever knew, but I dare say some of you do know as well as we do in Treyolla what splendid cavies there are in the valley at the back of the village. There's no need to say more, but I don't fancy the German 'll find much in any house that he may visit, and I suppose that some will be angry to be inspected and troubled with the law when they can prove themselves innocent as daylight.'

There was a shout of laughter, and then the matter began to be discussed, and a score of ancient stories were brought up. There's no denying that there used to be a brave deal of smuggling done in these parts, and the cavies had been so well chosen or made that there was never anything captured by the revenue-men unless they chanced to come along before it had been put in hiding. I had a touch of the bronchitis myself, and could not afford to be out late at night, but most of the folk stopped, and George Laity was still talking of the way the underwriter was to be balked, when landlord Penhale called time, and began to put the lights out as a hint that they must go.

The next day was just like fair-time. For once in a long while Tresidder and Treyolla were in sympathy, and everyone who was not bound to stop at home went across the fields to see his neighbours. I noticed that Jim Jose and a few others that might have been expected to take an interest were not there, but when the German turned up matters became amusing and I forgot to miss them.

He was a little bald-headed man, with a stubbly beard and spectacles, and a very nervous manner. There have been times when Treyolla folk have showed themselves a bit violent when there was anything going on that they couldn' bring themselves to approve of, and I suppose the fame of such deeds had reached him. However, for all the violence there was he might have executed the warrants himself, without the help of the policemen he had brought with him. There might be a few small boys that mocked his spectacles and his broken English, but there are always small boys who are rude when a crowd is come together.

Most people were unusually polite, if you recollect how little Treyolla is famous for manners. The German had got a list of the names of people who were supposed to have done best off the wreck (he had been very accurately informed too), and by the time he was finished with one house there were always a couple of score ready to show him the whereabouts of the next on his list. I wouldn' say that all this politeness didn't try his temper just as much as violence would have done, but he didn't go away without a talking to. He went through house after house, looking everywhere, from the top of the dresser to the straw in the stable where Willie Dunstan kept his little dunkey. He could find nothing, and his temper was sore tried, for even the police were laughing at him.

At last he came to Williams's cottage, that was a miner and had been away from home at his work when the rumour of the search warrants came. Mrs. Williams was ready for him. She was a big dark woman, with a temper of her own, and a wonderful name for the cleanness of her house. She had eight children, all under twelve. One was in her arms and the rest were gathered round her in a body, like as if the German was a foreign foe and come to slaughter and slay. 'Wipe your feet on the mat,' she said: 'I'll have no dirt in my house. Wipe your feet, and you can come in and search where you like. I'm a poor woman, and there's things in the house I wouldn' own for a moment if I had money. But I'm honest, and you can go where you like.'

THE LUCK OF TREYOLLA

Of course the German did not understand the half of what she said, but there was something of a crowd around, and Mrs. Williams was a woman to be feared. He took his hat in his hand and began a little speech, bowing and scraping like a Frenchman. But Mrs. Williams wouldn' hear of that. 'There's no need to talk,' she said. ' You've paid your money, and you've got the law behind you, and you can go where you will. Search the house, I tell 'ee, and be so kind as to be quick. I can't abide a pa'cel o' strangers in my house.'

So they went into the house and made their search, with Mrs. Williams following after, the baby in her arms and the other seven around her, three of them crying. Of course they found nothing, and in a few minutes they would have been glad to go in peace ; but Mrs. Williams had something to say, and so the crowd leaned over the whitewashed wall of the garden and made ready to listen. Mrs. Williams looked them up and down, and spoke.

'Is this the law?' she said hardly looking at the German. 'Is this what they call the law in a Christian land? You've come, and you've pried into every corner of my little home, and you do know things that I've kept from Treyolla people for ten years past. I aren't ashamed to be poor, but there's things that are as well kept quiet. Why don't 'ee tell them what you've seen? Neighbours, there's a great piece gone out of the bedroom jug, and there has been for years, for I could never afford a new one. The counterpane is patched, and there's a plank in the floor that's rotten. I couldn' afford to have it made right, for I've reared eight children and my man has never earned a pound a week. And after these people have gone everywhere in their dirty boots, I can't even say that the place is clean. Is that the way to treat a woman?'

She put her apron to her eyes and sobbed, and a murmur came from the crowd. The underwriter spoke to himself in a foreign language, and it was plain enough that he was swearing terribly. Mrs. Williams understood the meaning of it in a moment, and began to talk to him again. ' If one of my boys was grown up,' she said, ' you would be sorry for those words. I can't tell what the meaning of it may be, but I know what you was saying. My man is away at his work, and there's no one to take up for me ; but if he was at home you would be ducked in the harbour, for all you've got the law at your back.'

The German moved off then, glad to get away. The crowd was harmless enough still, but Mrs. Williams had set a sort of example, and there was a little horse-play, though nothing to hurt. He tried another cottage, and when he had found nothing and had another talking to, he decided to go back the way he had come. All the village went with him to the inn and waited in the street while his horse was being harnessed. When he drove out with the two policemen they gave him a hearty cheer, and he was last seen leaning over the back of the trap and using the most dreadful language. It was fortunate no one could exactly make out what he was saying, for there were young people about.

As soon as he had gone every one was hungry, and a good part of the Tresidder folk went homewards. I was thinking to do so myself when I knocked up against Jim Jose. 'I didn' know that you was here,' I said. 'I thought that you had missed it, though it didn' seem likely that you would.'

'Not me,' said Jim, who seemed to be mighty pleased with himself. 'I had work to do that kept me later than some; but I wouldn' have missed this afternoon, not for money paid in my hand.'

Upon that he went on his way, and then I happened up against a man that I knew well. 'What a day!' he said. 'Do 'ee feel like a cup of tea and a pilcher'?'

By this time I was fine and hungry, so I thanked him kindly, and accepted the offer. We enjoyed our tea, and he told me in private that he had done fairly well over the 'Gretchen.' We were just lighting our pipes when we heard a noise in the street and went out, to find Mrs. Williams crying like rain, and in a terrible flurry.

'Aw!' she said, 'there's thieves in the land! 'Tis they Tresidder people, if I do know what's what. I put a few little things in a cavie up the valley last night, not caring to have all my belongings pawed over by a German, and now they're all gone.'

She was not half-way through with her story when a man came running down the street in a worse state of mind than she was. 'All my little savings is gone!' he said. 'I put away a few trifles up the valley last night, and now they're all gone. Some one has stolen them: I could see the tracks of wheels in the road.'

In another ten minutes there were as many as six of them, all raving together; but there was no one to listen, for it turned out that everyone in Treyolla had got a little hoard up the valley, and all the village was off to see if the cavies had been ransacked. I heard afterwards, from more sources than one, that only one or two of them found anything left, but I concluded not to wait any longer just then, and started homewards.

I must say that Jim Jose behaved very well. Of course, he and the other men who had gone round with carts while Treyolla was amusing itself kept most of the plunder for themselves, but I found a very nice little present in my back-garden a night or two later, and I believe there were few in Tresidder that didn' get some sort of a remembrance. Since then there's been a second saying about Treyolla, and if ever you meet a man from those parts, and he won't fight, and you mean that he shall, you've only got to ask him what he knows about the wreck in Treyolla valley. He will fight then, right enough, and you might even find your work cut out for you if you meant to beat him.

H. D. LOWRY.

MR. GEORGE TANGYE

ROMANCE IN HARD METAL

AN INTERVIEW WITH MR. GEORGE TANGYE

THE success of the Tangye Brothers, the great engineers, is one in which Cornish folk must needs feel a particular interest, for the Tangyes are an old Cornish family, and yet—as we all know—it is essentially a success which does not merely pertain to a county or a nation, for it is an episode in the great engineering forward movement of the past hundred years, an epoch initiated and very largely encompassed by the genius of James Watt. It is indeed one item in an imperishable record, this record of two generations, and one which goes to make up what is, in many respects, the most important chapter in the history of the world's progress.

Mr. George Tangye's residence, Heathfield Hall, near Birmingham, for the past twenty-five years has been rented by him from the Watt family. It was formerly the dwelling place of James Watt, and the Watt room—the classic garret at the top of the house—is, in every detail of its contents, just as Watt left it, and for many reasons may be described without much fear of contradiction, as the most interesting relic to be found in this country. I allude to this matter first because the historic interest of this room and its associations, added to the fact that the genius of Watt and the success of the Tangyes is in some respects indivisible—the inventions of the one being developed by the other to suit the necessities of modern requirements—increases the otherwise wide scope of the subject matter of this article.

The success of the Cornwall Works, Birmingham, which has grown from a bit of a workshop, the size of which can be gauged by the fact that four shillings a week was adequate rental for it, to the present day, when the works cover twenty-five acres and find employment for 2,500 hands, is not due to the work of one man, but to the brains and energy of four of the five sons of the late Mr. Joseph Tangye, of Redruth. The two younger brothers, Sir Richard and Mr. George Tangye—the subject of this interview—went into business for themselves in the little Birmingham workshop in 1852 and 1853 respectively, and were joined very soon afterwards in 1855 and 1856 by their two elder brothers, James and Joseph, who have since retired. Happily no invidious distinction can be made as to which of the four brothers has had most to do with this great engineering success. Each has had his own special work, and each has been indispensable to the other. There is only this to be said, and I am quoting my very kindly and courteous informant, Mr. George Tangye: 'My eldest brother, James, was one of the cleverest engineers of his day, and the earlier success of the Cornwall Works certainly emanated from his skill. Joseph was equally skilful, but not so inventive.'

In briefly sketching the history of the 'beginnings' of this great inventive and industrial enterprise, I would refer the reader who may desire more information on the point, to a book written by Sir Richard Tangye, aptly named

HEATHFIELD HALL

'One and All,' published by Messrs. Partridge and Co., from which I shall venture, in the earlier part of this article, to make one or two brief quotations.

Perhaps the first one of the family who displayed the trend for mechanics was the grandfather, born at St. Columb in 1776, whom Sir Richard describes as being a tall, strong man, active and intelligent. In the interval of tilling his own bit of ground the grandfather obtained a situation as night-driver of a mine pumping engine. His account of his day's work deserves repetition. He used to say, 'I drove the engine for ten hours, worked on the farm seven hours, and wasted the rest.' But this notion of an 'eight-hours' day did not seem to disagree with him, for he lived to be nearly ninety-five, and never required the services of a doctor.

Cornwall has occasionally been guilty—shall we say—of being at least a few days behind the times, but often the county has redressed the balance by taking the lead. One of the first railways opened in England was in Cornwall, 'as indeed was only fitting,' writes Sir Richard, 'seeing that Murdock invented the locomotive there, and Trevithick and Vivian greatly improved it.' One of the earliest railway lines ran through the late Mr. Tangye's farm, and so the sight of what was locally described as this 'wicked invention' is amongst the earliest of the recollections of the brothers.

The elder brother, James, much against his will, was placed with a country wheelwright; while Joseph, the second brother, equally unwilling, was bound for a term to a shoeing smith; but having completely mastered these trades while yet in their teens, they determined to follow their natural inclinations by obtaining employment as engineers. Their love for mechanical engineering, Sir Richard ascribes to the maternal grandfather, to whom reference has already been made, and in his book 'One and All' he continues:

'While my brothers were engaged in their uncongenial occupations with the wheelwright and shoeing-smith they spent their evenings in a workshop at home, where they made working models of engines and other machines, while the younger ones turned the wheel. My father was unable to see that any practical advantage was likely to accrue from this occupation, and often used to lament the waste of candles; but my mother, with a keener perception, recognised the natural bent of her sons' minds, and encouraged its development. Unhappily neither of them lived to witness the ultimate results of her foresight. But it was not long before the brothers demonstrated that the candles were not wasted, for a little beam-engine which they made was sold for a sum that much more than paid for all the candles they had used.

'My brother James, while still a youth, obtained a situation at an engine factory at Devonport, the manager of which was Mr. Smiles, a brother of the author of those interesting works, "Self-Help" &c. Mr. Smiles had gone to London to get married, and during his absence a twenty-five horse-power engine had to be completed. A difficulty having arisen as to the parallel motion, the master asked the men in the shop if any one among them could strike out the proportions of the links and the radius rods. To this there was no reply until James, who had mastered the principle in making the little engine of which

HEATHFIELD HALL

I have spoken, called out that he could do it. Coming from a lad who was looked upon, from his age, as being little more than an apprentice, this was received with a murmur of derision. However, he was requested to give the dimensions, and the work was completed accordingly.

'When the engine was finished, and the trial was about to take place, there was no little speculation as to how the parallel motion would work. At the first starting there was some amount of unsteadiness, and the croakers looked for a triumph, till James, suspecting foul play, sprang up and examined the blocks, when he found that one of them had been unscrewed, either purposely or by accident. The mischief was quickly remedied; the engine "went off"; and once again it was demonstrated that the candles were not wasted.'

After leaving Cornwall, the first experience the brothers had of the work which was afterwards to make the name of Tangye known wherever there is a demand for steam power, was gained at a little engineering works in Birmingham, owned by Mr. Thomas Worsdell, whose father made the first railway coaches for the London and North-Western Railway.

Sir Richard Tangye was the first to enter Mr. Worsdell's service as a clerk. He was joined shortly afterwards by Mr. George Tangye, and quickly followed by the two elder brothers, James and Joseph, who, after throwing up their situations in Cornwall to join Mr. Worsdell, gave such evidence of mechanical and engineering skill that James was made the foreman of the works, while Joseph gained a leading position there in consequence of his being able to do a class of work (hydraulic) that his new employer had not done before.

Mr. Joseph Tangye, besides being an able designer of new tools, was an exceptionally clever mechanic. His lathe was a first-class tool. It was therefore hoped that enough work would be obtained to keep them employed, and accordingly the brothers determined to launch out for themselves. A portion of a manufacturer's packing-room into which a revolving shaft projected, by which Mr. Joseph could drive the lathe, was rented for a sum of 4s. a week, though in the course of my inquiries at Birmingham I was told that the manufacturer referred to has smilingly disputed this. The actual rental was not quite so much. The rent was 3s. 6d. a week, and there was another 6d. paid for gas.

ROMANCE IN HARD METAL 343

The first big opportunity which the new 'firm' obtained came through the difficulties of Mr. Brunel in launching his leviathan, the ill-fated 'Great Eastern.'

Mr. James Tangye had invented a new hydraulic lifting jack, which happened to be just the thing Brunel required. This was in 1856. Brunel's first attempt was an utter failure, but, as Mr. George Tangye told me, apart from the superiority of the Tangye lifting jack, the secret of their success simply lay in the application of a number of small jacks to each cradle rather than a smaller number of large jacks, because the bursting of one of the latter would mean a serious failure, whereas with the small jack it would not make much difference. Acting on the brothers' advice, Mr. Brunel succeeded in floating the big ship on January 31, 1858, and this launching of the 'Great Eastern,' and the consequent demand for this species of hydraulic jack, constituted the first foundation of the big Tangye business.

The next opportunity, which had even greater results, came about in 1859, when Mr. T. A. Weston, the inventor of the Differential Chain Lifting Block, brought this partially developed invention to them.

The idea was new, but there were mechanical difficulties in the way which had to be overcome. After Mr. George Tangye had made many experiments and attempts, a method was discovered by which the links of the chain could be made with the necessary exactness, and very soon thousands of these lifting blocks were being supplied. In passing perhaps I may be permitted to remark that nothing I saw in Birmingham impressed me more than this Weston block, on account of the simplicity of the means and the magnitude of the effect. The Weston chain lifting block is certainly an exceedingly interesting instance of what can be done by mechanical means. Perfectly simple! Mr. Tangye would tell you. Perhaps it is; but imagine a man being able to lift a weight of several tons with blocks constructed mainly on this principle! Yet this is the result of an application of the great mechanical principle that the effect of a mechanical contrivance depends on the excess of the velocity of the power

TEA ON THE LAWN
Mr. George Tangye, Mr. Lawrence, Mr. Clement Tangye, Miss Daisy Tangye, and Mr. Edgar Tangye

over that of the weight. It is not indeed surprising that the Weston block effected a revolution in the previous methods of liiting and moving heavy weights. It would be impossible to compute the terrible strain and toil this invention must have saved, or the number of accidents which its use has avoided.

So much for the beginnings of Messrs. Tangye's great engineering success, and, at this point, I am happy in being able to continue the narrative, by quoting the remarks which Mr. George Tangye made to me the first evening I spent with him :

THE DRIVE

'It was not until this time—the time I am speaking of would be about 1862—that we turned our attention to steam engines. Only a few small engines were made by any one firm in the course of a year, leaving out of account those turned out by the agricultural engineers, who devoted their attention almost exclusively to portable engines and boilers. My brother James was set apart to design a suitable model, and no man was more capable, for he knew the secret of people's wants, and also the means of manufacture, and was, too, an excellent draughtsman. In less than a year everything had been discussed, the model fixed upon, and a striking novelty brought before the public.

'Well, of course the arrangement was laughed at by the critics. It is an open secret,' Mr. Tangye added, 'that English manufacturers are conservative, and, in short, nothing but failure was prophesied.

'However, a discriminating public thought otherwise, and the Americans, who are always exceedingly ready to adopt things which are new and good, immediately made use of this new invention, and to this day, in most of the Science Schools throughout the States, the Tangye steam engine and governor is the adopted model.

'Besides the steam cylinder, James also metamorphosed the regulating governor, and instead of the slow and cumbrous revolving balls fixed on a separate foundation, he designed and made perfect the "quick speed" governor, and this was readily attached to the engine itself. It was a really pretty piece of accurate mechanism for controlling the speed of the engine under all conditions.

'And so it happened that after the complete engine had been actually launched, distrust and prejudice concerning it soon passed away, and the result was that a very large works became necessary—and soon was an accomplished fact—at Soho, adjoining the site of the works erected by Boulton and Watt. Thousands of these engines have been supplied by us since then.

'The governors were and are made in thousands, the greater number being supplied to engineers who, while making steam engines, find it cheaper to buy articles such as governors from those who manufacture in large numbers.'

Such was Mr. Tangye's quiet business-like way of explaining—I had almost written explaining away—one of the main causes of the success of this mighty business. During the time I was with him he made no sign—nor would anyone knowing him, his modesty, and strength of character, expect him to make any sign—that there was anything in all this that any intelligent group of men might not have done—if they only 'had the mind' to do it; nor does one ever get a hint from him of the business aptitude, the moral and physical fibre, and the exceptional mechanical skill—more a birthright than an acquirement—to which the rapid growth of this mighty business testifies.

'Well, now,' Mr. Tangye exclaimed after we had been talking for some little time after dinner, in his study, 'I will show you the Watt room, if you like.' Looking back, I don't think that from my own point of view a better moment could have been selected for seeing it, although the fact that the hour was late when we entered the Watt room was due to the accident of my having chosen to go down to Birmingham by a late train. It was not far from the hour of twelve, everyone had by that time retired to rest, and each of us bearing a candlestick—for one cannot expect to find electric light in that garret, nor any modern contrivance whatsoever—and much in the manner of two conspirators, we went upstairs, until we came to the door of James Watt's ancient sanctum.

Even before Mr. Tangye opened the door there was something to be seen which struck me as being characteristic. Merely a piece of wood, in the shape of a small square shelf, fixed between the door and the stair-rail. It had been placed there in order that the inventor might not be interrupted by entrance of a servant with a meal for him. The food was left on this shelf, outside the door, so that he could fetch it if he remembered it, though not infrequently it was forgotten.

The photograph of the Watt room, taken by one of my host's sons, Mr. Harry Tangye, will give a better idea of its appearance than any laboured description.

In the flickering candlelight the three busts shown in the illustration naturally claimed first attention. They seemed endowed with life, and one felt it necessary to pay one's regards to the presentment, at least, of the old owner, before proceeding to examine his room. The middle bust is considered to give the best picture extant of James Watt, and was executed by Chantrey in 1818, only a year before the death of the inventor. The one on the left, also of Watt, is by Turnerelli, in 1807; and making allowances for the fact that it was done eleven years before Chantrey's, is certainly less life-like, less imposing, and, judging from other portraits, less faithful. The third bust, on the right, of Sir John Rennie (a handsome man, who earned the sobriquet of 'the ladykiller!') is also by Chantrey.

Even so clever a photographer as Mr. Harry Tangye cannot do other than submit to physical laws, and so—probably because the light from the little window does not reach it—the stove which Watt used is not shown in the photo. It is immediately to the left of the door as you enter.

[*Photo by*]   [*Mr. Harry Tangye*]

WATT ROOM

This hundred-year-old stove, like everything else in the room, has not been disturbed since the death of its owner; the cinders of the last fire burnt in it remain in the grate, and on the top of it, in a little crucible, are the ashes of Watt's last assay.

These ashes may be said to have come from Cornwall, for, as Mr. Tangye pointed out, 'Watt would take his royalties from Cornwall in "kind," but before doing so he would have a sample of the stuff sent on to him, as it was never his habit to take anything on trust, or without examining into the matter very shrewdly himself; and so, when the sample of the mineral came to hand he would assay it, to see how much pure metal it contained, before writing to the sender as to how many tons he would accept of the ore in lieu of cash.'

In these days, when a man is reckoned an inventor who happens on something approximating to the shadow of an idea—placing a piece of rubber in a pencil-holder, for example—and lives for the rest of his life on the royalties which he gets out of it, not the least impression left on one's mind after an examination of this room is the way in which the great man turned out invention after invention of the greatest importance by way of mere recreation in his old age.

Here is a big nest of drawers. Mr. Tangye pulls open one drawer after another. They seem filled with unconsidered trifles, odd bits of metal, nuts and screws, scraps of wood, mathematical instruments, and the like.

JAMES WATT

'Here's a little thing,' Mr. Tangye exclaims. 'Watt invented the metal pen, and here is the first nib ever constructed, made out of a threepenny bit. If we had some ink here you could write with it.' It is exactly and beautifully made. A little thing, certainly, but the moment Watt made it he had, in effect, delivered a deadly blow to the quill trade, and created a far larger industry, to say nothing of having revolutionised the handwriting of the next generation.

'The first copying press—Watt's invention.' There it is, with the dust of years on it, much the same as the copying presses used in every office at the present moment, but before Watt constructed it every letter had to be copied by hand. Previously, like everyone else, Watt had been compelled to laboriously copy his own letters before entrusting them to the post, but, as he did so, his busy brain was at work, and he soon invented a means of escape from this weariness. As the result of a few hours' labour on his own part, here is the simple contrivance which has since saved an amount of time and labour quite beyond all calculation.

'He invented the copying ink, too, without which, of course, the book and press would be useless.' Mr. Tangye opens another drawer, and I look at a packet of it. It was made up in the form of a powder, selling at ninepence, with printed instructions for liquefying it, a process which involved some little trouble and the use of hot water. It is amusing to remember that when Watt's copying press was first put on the market it was attacked as an improper invention, on the somewhat mysterious assumption that the use of it would encourage forgery.

Near the window is Watt's lathe, with its lamp and tools left untouched as he himself placed them, and with the stool on which he sat. His old leather apron (at the right hand side of the room) hangs up where he left it.

Then Mr. Tangye explains the method of working and the purpose of the two machines which stand out prominently in the centre and left side of the room. The one in the centre is the first copying or medallion machine which Watt invented, the working of which is most easily explained by saying that the principle is practically the same as the popular pentograph used for copying drawings, worked by means of a pointer at one end of the bar and a pencil at the other, the copy being larger or smaller than the original, according to the relative lengths of the parts of the bar from the fulcrum. On this principle—his own invention—Watt devised this medallion machine, but instead of a pencil there is a cutting tool which bites its way into wood, marble, or iron. The machine is worked by a foot treadle, and a similar machine is extensively used at the present day for making a large number of articles from a standard pattern. Any number of objects from one original can be carved, at the same instant, by increasing the length of the bar and multiplying the number of cutting tools.

The machine seen on the left is of the same type, but so constructed that it is not limited to raised surfaces (medallions), but can be used for copying statuary—working 'all round' the original. The finest examples of work which Watt made with it were copies of his own bust, by Chantrey, and these copies Watt used to give to his friends as the 'works of a young artist in his eighty-first year.'

Amongst the many interesting things to be seen in this old room are evidences of the processes by means of which the inventor arrived at the invention of photography upon metal about the same time as Daguerre, with whose name the invention is more immediately connected. Whether first in point of time or not, Watt seems to have invented the system of engraving on metal by means of acids without any outside hints or assistance.

'He never wasted anything,' Mr. Tangye declares, pulling open more drawers, 'not even the end of a nail. He knew all these odds and ends would come in useful as he went along. Here is some drawn steel pinion wire, for example; well, you see, he could cut little wheels off it by the dozen.'

We came upon a packet of snuff; then, avoiding the somewhat severe gaze of the Chantrey bust, I essayed a pinch—in which there seemed something disrespectful to Mr. Watt—but not a sneeze disturbed the sanctity of the room: its aroma had long since departed; in fact, as Mr. Tangye remarked, it was 'dead.'

Even a bit of china which came out of one of those many wonderful

ROMANCE IN HARD METAL 349

JOSIAH WEDGWOOD

receptacles implied a great deal, for the rim of it was beautifully gilded, and this calls to mind the friendship which existed between James Watt and Josiah Wedgwood, for whom Watt perfected the process of gilding on china.

It was in this room that the meetings used to take place of the Lunar Society, so called because it was held on the full moon of the month, so that those who resided at a distance could ride home in safety. It is due to the work of the great men of that period (William Murdock, the inventor of gas-lighting, in particular) that the moon is less useful in this way than formerly.

What would one not give to have been present at one of those friendly scientific meetings held between Josiah Wedgwood, Matthew Boulton, Dr. Erasmus Darwin, Dr. Priestley, and James Watt! Dr. Darwin was regarded as the patriarch of the society, but was somewhat incommoded in his attendance by the necessities of his medical practice. The words which Dr. Darwin uses in a letter to Boulton (April 1778) may be quoted, to the extent of one sentence, as fairly liberally describing the purposes of this influential coterie.

'Lord, what inventions, what wit, what rhetoric, metaphysical, mechanical, and pyrotechnical, will be on the wing, bandied from one to another of your troop of philosophers, while poor I, I by myself I, imprison'd in a post-chaise, am joggled and jostled, and bump'd and bruised along the King's high-road, to make war upon a stomach-ache or a fever!'

There was Dr. Priestley, a man of extraordinary gifts, and one of the most brilliant chemists of his time—nine gases, so familiar to us now, oxygen, nitrogen, and others, were discovered by him. Times and manners have so changed during the last century that it is difficult to believe Dr. Priestley's invaluable chemical experiments were so much objected to, that his house at Fairhill was invaded and entirely wrecked by the mob, so that he was fortunate in escaping from Birmingham with his life.

Before concluding this brief reference to the great genius, James Watt,

whom men of science acknowledge to be the greatest inventor the world has yet seen, one feels tempted to inquire in what manner his personality impressed his contemporaries.

When close upon his eighty-second year (at a time when he used this place of retreat so considerably) Dr. Smiles tells us that Watt formed one of a distinguished party assembled in Edinburgh, at which Sir Walter Scott, Francis Jeffrey, and others were present. He delighted the northern literati with his kindly cheerfulness, not less than he astonished them by the extent and profundity of his information. 'This potent commander of the elements,' wrote Sir Walter Scott, ' this abridger of time and space, this magician, whose cloudy machinery has produced a change in the world, the effects of which, extraordinary as they are, are perhaps only now beginning to be felt—was not only the most profound man of science, the most successful combiner of powers and combiner of numbers, as adapted to practical purposes—was not only one of the most generally well-informed, but one of the best and kindest human beings. . . . Methinks I yet see and hear what I shall never see or hear again. The alert, kind, benevolent old man had his attention alive to everyone's question, his information at everyone's command. His talent and fancy overflowed on every subject.' 'It seemed,' said Jeffrey, 'as if every subject that was casually started had been that in which he was occupied in studying.' Yet the man was, in accordance with the necessities of his work, retiring and devoted to study, and when in company his information was at everyone's service, but forced upon no one. When no one addressed him he would abstract himself in his meditations, and yet never earned the charge of being 'absent-minded,' nor did his natural alertness desert him to the last day of his life.

In one corner of the room is a model of the famous governor, or steam regulator; in another is a model of the parallel motion, and then one gives a final look at the sculpture machine, the wooden framing of which is worm-eaten and dropping into dust, like the hands which made it. As another visitor has said,

'The interest of the room is unique, its relics are priceless as personal memorials, and to enter it and look around is indeed to stand in the presence of genius at work, although the busy brain and skilful hand have been at rest for nearly eighty years.' Again to quote Dr. Smiles: 'But although the great workman has gone to rest with all his griefs and cares, and his handiwork is fast crumbling to decay, the spirit of his work, the thought which he put into his inventions, still survives, and will probably continue to influence the destinies of his race for all time to come.'

Next morning I accompany Mr. Tangye to the works. Some few hundred yards from the entrance lodge of the carriage drive, we get on to one of the Handsworth cable trams. The company having been duly made richer to the extent of two pence, I discover that the cable and plant were put down by the firm one of whose directors sits beside me, and I glean the further and not less cheerful intelligence that the tram company earns forty per cent. on the cable section of its system!

This prompts another question, and Mr. Tangye tells me that the first tramways in Birmingham were laid down by George Francis Train, who came over from Omahu, in Central America, about thirty-five years ago. 'People wouldn't go into the trams at that time,' Mr. Tangye observes, 'and the lines had to be pulled up again, but no doubt the more intelligent had perceived the advantages before this was done.'

We pass the site of the old 'Waggon and Horses.' It was there, Mr. Tangye tells me, that one of Watt's carpenters 'opened his mouth too wide,' as the phrase has it, concerning one of his master's inventions, the crank, with the result that a Frenchman who was present rushed off to London and patented it. 'Because of that,' Mr. Tangye added, 'Watt would not use the crank motion until the patent for it had run out, but, instead of it, invented the sun and planet motion, which he always made use of.'

In accompanying Mr.

DR. ERASMUS DARWIN.

Tangye over the works I was not only struck with the good relations between the men and himself—of which even in a few hours' visit one can get at least some impression—but also by the entire absence of anything like servility amongst the men. It is my own notion—I know not how far people better able to speak of these things will agree with me—that where one finds a body of men cap-touching, cringing, showing increased energy at the sight of their employer, and evincing similar symptoms, it will be generally found there is a strong probability that they are demoralised and discontented, and will be the first to revolt upon the slightest pretext. There is no suggestion of this in the men whom I saw at the Cornwall Works. It is true that a large number of them are skilled workmen, earning exceptionally good wages; but whenever Mr. Tangye had occasion to speak to anyone on the premises there seemed to me a thorough mutual understanding, and, in a word, every one of them—some of them looking burly enough to suggest that they could even dispense with any steam power in their engines—respected Mr. Tangye not less for himself than for his authority, and, above all, respected themselves none the less because of their deference to him. Anyone who has ever come into contact with a body of workmen will thoroughly appreciate what I mean. It is an *esprit de corps* which one recognises intuitively, and without which the life, the inspiriting buzz and throb of the workshop would be but a very sordid 'romance' indeed.

One special feature which Mr. Tangye explained to me should be recorded. For some time past a medal has been awarded to those who have been in the workshops during a period of twenty-five years and over, and the most tangible testimonial of the fact that the men do not find the place disagreeable is that over two hundred of them are the owners of these medals.

The foundry is a scene which one would like to describe, but that most of us are probably acquainted with something like it. The furnaces, the subdued roar arising from them that tells of the intense heat, only revealed when the molten metal is allowed to run from them, the radiant white light throwing into strong relief the men who are standing nearest it, with their bared arms, grimy faces, and almost weird alertness, as against the deep shadows, produce an 'effect'—to use the cant word—which, apart from Rembrandt, few painters have ventured to attempt upon canvas. Then the fascination to the outsider of the rivulets of molten metal running into the prepared mould. Everyone here seems to deal with this molten metal as if quite prepared to use it as one might use water. Two men pass us carrying a vessel filled with it, and when a little is spilled it seems almost to explode as it touches the ground, distributing itself freely in small sparks and cinders.

In the smithy, which is a long shop forming a double row of men at work, the smiths are thrusting huge iron bars into the fires, and withdrawing them white-hot, working them into a variety of shapes. In an adjoining shop there are several hydraulic presses. Here I saw one of the presses at work, giving the bar a squeeze of about two hundred tons pressure; the hot metal appears to leap into flame, the scale on the surface—which is now a mere common fiery

THE SMITHY

red—is knocked off, showing that the body of the metal is still white-hot underneath; it is given another giant squeeze, and is now of the required shape for the machinery of which it is to form part.

Almost uncanny are the machines—some of them of American design—which go through half a dozen different evolutions mechanically; and although the machine is under full pressure and requires little attention, it is so graduated and arranged that it gives the necessary time for the renewing of the various operations. Such is, for example, the American milling machine, cutting every tooth in a revolving pinion with perfect accuracy.

In the chainmakers' making shop I watched a skilled smith drawing a long pencil-like piece of metal from the furnace, and with his hammer dexterously shaping links from the heated end of it. The chain trade, I learnt, is in a pretty bad way, but the Tangyes do not make chains for general use, but simply the chains needed for lifting blocks, such as the Weston (which I have already alluded to), where the links have to be specially strong and very accurately made. The necessary exactitude will be appreciated by a consideration of the fact that the links must be accurate to the thousandth part of an inch.

Mr. R. H. Kirton, one of the staff, was kind enough to show me William Murdock's Birmingham house, notable in that it was the first house lighted by gas, Murdock's invention, and a method of lighting which, if he had patented it, would probably have been known as Murdock to this day. His name must still be remembered in Cornwall, for this extremely brilliant inventor was Boulton and Watt's ablest assistant, and in the beginning of his career his special work lay in Cornwall, where he married and settled down in Redruth. As far as this Birmingham house is concerned Murdock brought the gas for it from the works, where he made it. People could not be persuaded that the pipes were not red-hot, imagining that fire and not coal-gas was conveyed through them. Murdock also lit up his house and offices at Redruth with gas. He also constructed a lantern with which he lighted himself home at night across the moors when returning from his work to his house at Redruth.

In conversation with Mr. Kirton I gathered what I should not have learnt from Mr. Tangye himself : namely, his exceeding activity in the good work of

PETROLEUM ENGINE TESTING SHOP

the town. He is J.P. for both the city and county, and his opinions carry exceptional weight. He is a member of Sir Josiah Mason's Orphanage—and no visitor is more welcome or better appreciated at the famous Birmingham General Hospital—and he is the Superintendent of the Soho division of the Severn Street First Day Schools (founded by Joseph Sturge), in which work he is assisted by his two elder sons, Harry and William. But although Mr. Tangye is ranged on the right side politically (I shall not here reveal which I consider to be the 'right side'), I learned that when he was asked to stand for the constituency he declined.

There are many more points which I could have wished to set down, and points which I should like to have elaborated concerning all that is comprised and implied in the progress and growth of the Cornwall Works, Birmingham. There is more that I should like to have written about the four Brothers Tangye, and, as I have had the pleasure of knowing him (at least, in some slight degree), of Mr. George Tangye more especially.

MR. TANGYE'S FARM-HOUSE, AT WYRE FOREST, SHROPSHIRE

But perhaps at least enough has been expressed, or indicated, to justify the title at the head of this article.

So far as the employment of that badly battered word 'romance' is concerned, it is impossible to view from any other standpoint the work and personality of such men, whether it be James Watt and his contemporaries, or the greatest inventors and engineers of the present day. The extraordinary difficulties, struggles, and the triumph of the genius of the first owner of Heathfield Hall, and of his partner and friend, Matthew Boulton, have already been the subject of more than one fascinating volume. But of the work and personalities about which I was more immediately concerned in my visit to Birmingham, there could hardly be anything conceived more interesting, encouraging, or instructive. In speaking of the big events which have been the result of certain causes there is no need to exaggerate anything. The Tangyes had the happiness of excellent parents and received a good education, which was none the less advantageous for being eminently practical. Mr. Joseph Tangye, of Redruth, owned his shop, a little farm, and some other property. He must have trained his children exceedingly well, and, best of all, there was no smirch of any kind on the good name which he left them. Yet, as Mr. George Tangye expressed it, when the little workshop was taken in Birmingham by the four brothers, 'we had little more than what we stood up in,' and the progress made from that to the present attainments of the Tangye business testifies, in an uneffaceable record, to the sterling qualities of the four men who have been the life and soul of it.

Alongside the story of the way in which men of all time have seized, controlled, and made use of the great forces of Nature, every other form of romance seems to me dim in comparison. It is obvious to us all that these achievements have not only needed big brains, but also uncommon force of character; and in describing the story of the Tangye works as a 'Romance in Hard Metal,' the title must be taken to indicate the strength and sterling integrity of the men who have forced their way forward with such rapid strides, as well as to the wonderful achievements in hard metal of which the bloodless weapons of their great and benevolent warfare on behalf of civilisation are composed.

ARTHUR LAWRENCE.

O Falmouth is a fine town with ships in the bay,
And I wish from my heart it's there I was to-day;
I wish from my heart I was far away from here,
Sitting in my parlour and talking to my dear.
    For it's home, dearie, home—it's home I want to be;
    Our topsails are hoisted, and we'll away to sea.
    O the oak and the ash and the bonnie birken tree,
    They're all growing green in the old countree.

In Baltimore a-walking a lady I did meet
With her babe on her arm as she came down the street;
And I thought how I sailed, and the cradle standing ready
For the pretty little babe that has never seen its daddie.
    And it's home, dearie, home &c.

O, if it be a lass, she shall wear a golden ring,
And if it be a lad, he shall fight for his king;
With his dirk and his hat and his little jacket blue
He shall walk the quarter-deck as his daddie used to do.
    And it's home, dearie, home &c.

HOME, DEARIE, HOME

O there's a wind a-blowing, a-blowing from the west,
And that of all the winds is the one I like the best,
For it blows at our backs, and it shakes our pennon free,
And it soon will blow us home to the old countree.
    For it's home, dearie, home—it's home I want to be;
    Our topsails are hoisted, and we'll away to sea.
    O the oak and the ash and the bonnie birken tree,
    They're all growing green in the old countree.

W. E. HENLEY
(by kind permission).

THE FIDDLE ROCK

SET in the cliffs that look over towards Lundy are here and there bands of a hard stone better defying the Atlantic, and running out to sea in jagged ridges, where the crumbling shillett of the shore has been worn away. A few of these are uncovered even at high water and in stormy weather, and stand up like black and broken teeth among the breakers. That long known as the Fiddle Rock, from its rough resemblance, as seen from the heights above, to a violin, lies some five miles south of the river mouth, with its neck turned landward and thrust into the huge slope of pebbles that form the beach.

For about an hour at low water you may scramble out along this neck to the body of the fiddle. Its resemblance there to any of man's making is of the smallest. The strata composing it are all on edge, and its surface is rather like that of a gigantic currycomb. Among the gaunt slabs is a nook or crack, you may hardly call it a cave, sheltered from all winds but the south-east off shore, some twelve feet long by five broad, at the entrance of which stands an old iron stove, such as those used for roasting chestnuts.

For upwards of ten years a man stood in that crack for the space of a tide each day, and played the violin to the shags and sea-gulls so that now the rock has a better title to its name.

I first knew Thomas Dalton at Cambridge. We called him Terrible Tom. He was an enthusiast and something of an outcast. Not being a public-school man, he lacked the ballast which convention demands even at the University. He had spent most of his life till then learning to play the fiddle, and reading the classics with an antiquarian uncle somewhere in Wales; and he came to Cambridge because he had persuaded himself that he had a call towards the ministry, and wanted a degree therefor. Yet, like most of us, he was idle, and little inclined for set courses, and all his time suffered from an inability to get up in the morning. I have found him breakfasting at three or four. Then he would sit up all night reading indiscriminately, or playing, with muffled windows, and go for a walk as soon as he could leave his rooms in the morning, tramping about till eight, when he would come in and go to bed.

By consequence he was the enemy of all routine, and was constantly interviewing deans and tutors. He played no games, although, except for a dreadful stoop, he was one of the finest men I have seen; with a deep, soft voice and a chest capacity, as I remember on an anthropometrical occasion when he tried the spirometer, about a third larger than anybody else's there;

which he accounted for by his singing so much in the open air. He had the long thighs of a foot-baller, and arms two yards across, with feet that would have helped him to wondrous jumping, and hands that could stretch elevenths, which was one of the distracting feats he delighted in, running up and down your piano with both of them in a triumph of discord. Despite his height, which was not quite six feet, he gave you the impression of a giant; and despite his gauntness, he had the gracefulness of a peculiar aptness and precision in all his movements that made them almost womanly. Those long fingers were as clever as a girl's in arranging the flowers with which his room was always filled, and on his violin seemed verily possessed. His face was thin and bony, his eyes set close together and deep, his nose straight or slightly aquiline and sharply pointed, his mouth little bowed and very wide; altogether the face of an aristocrat with a touch of the Jesuit in its expression, which was one of intense self-control and power of patience and purpose. His hair was blackish then and quite flat, and he always shaved clean—and very blue.

We called him Terrible Tom because of his social uncouthness, and a certain habit of his of inflicting his dogmatic views on out-of-the-way subjects at inordinate length and inappropriate times; and partly because, in spite of his manner of life, he was possessed of a natural and reckless austerity and strange indifference to custom that we could not catalogue. We did not think him mad—only a bit cracky. He never drank anything but water or milk, never smoked, was almost a vegetarian, not on principle but from choice. He had long been an orphan, and had about 600*l*. a year under some settlement, quite a third of which he spent, I believe, in charities; a heap on flowers, old books, and music; next to nothing on clothes; and what was left over from college bills on what he called freaks, which took the form of elaborate practical jokes with a present at the end. As once when he wagered he would ride down the King's Parade in his cap and gown and a donkey cart, selling apples in company with an old woman known as Mrs. Gummidge, who kept a greengrocer's shop in a back street, and made a very poor thing of the business, until this performance brought her notoriety and custom, and the donkey cart to deal with it. Again, when a young lady, a don's daughter, and not of his acquaintance, had sung 'Cherry Ripe' charmingly at one of the Wednesday 'Pops,' she was bombarded in her house in Trumpington Street by little boys bearing baskets of cherries at intervals of a quarter of an hour the whole of one summer's day.

He had a passion for 'Poker.' And though this might seem inconsistent with his aims, he never admitted that it was so, nor argued at all about it. He did not play for money's sake nor love of gambling, but purely because he took pleasure in the exercise of the faculties requisite. He played it extraordinarily well, with a sphinx-like impenetrability; and was the only one of us who, so far as I remember, was never detected bluffing. He won pretty often, and kept account of his winnings, adjusting these every term. If he had lost, he played on through the next light-heartedly; if he had won, as was usually the case, he took pains to find out odd ways in which he could make return to those who had lost to him, or set aside the money for the next freak. And the amount of method he would put into some matters was as startling as his carelessness in others. He was always shabby, except as to his cap and gown, which seemed to excite in him a respect we kept for any other garments by preference.

He was a year senior to me, and so remained on the superior footing that gives, apart from other reasons; and I think it was owing to the fact that I played accompaniments to his liking that we became as intimate as we did; perhaps also to the fact that I was receptive and impressionable, and willing to listen and say 'yes' with interest, if not intelligence, while he talked. I was, however, always conscious of a condescension on his part and an inequality on my own. And so, though I became aware of the strength and weakness of his character, which was a fine mixture of determination and pride and passion, I never felt that I had the smallest influence upon it, nor indeed was entitled thereto. His purpose in life was the passionate self-sacrifice of an ideal priesthood, and his pride would not admit of any human quality that could not be bent to absolute subservience for this end. Proportionably he looked for reward not of any ordinary sort, but that reward which is the knowledge of wise influence and the natural effect of sweet power. He was immensely ambitious for the effect of a good, of the possession and development of which in himself he had never a doubt. And this did not seem in him so much arrogance as an unwarrantable optimism and belief in human nature and its capacities. The reward he looked for was love, and the thought of it consumed him. He would declare that no man ever did anything for nothing, that effort for nothing was fictitious and impossible; that 'Right' and 'Duty' were only words that hid our real object, which was that we might be loved by God or man; and that this was the only thing worth doing anything for, or indeed possible to do any real thing for. As to his own love for God he was always very reticent, and seemed to treat the declarations of others, with reference to theirs, as of too subjective and self-evolved a nature to be regarded as considerable realities. He denied that it had any necessary bearing upon the question of one's life-work. And as to his love for man, he said once quietly, and as if to put an end to any further inquiry, 'I think, I say, I think it will be enough.' Only by what he did could one judge that it was at all events of a more practical kind than with many who protest more.

He attended no lectures that he could avoid, never entered into discussions, and joined no club but the Union. At twenty-one he was more independent than most men at thirty. How he managed to keep the necessary countenance of the authorities to his life's purpose I do not know; for I read for law, and did not come across him in his work. But his theology was so liberal that he must have had considerable difficulty in conciliating them. I fancy the Jesuit in him came to his aid then. He recognised that the path to his end lay through the Church of England, and this being so, he did not scruple to acquiesce outwardly in any tenets that might be required of him. He considered all creeds as necessarily of the nature of temporary makeshifts, and that the laws of evolution applied to them as to all else. And so, although he felt himself at liberty to advance as his individuality dictated, partly for policy's sake and partly out of pure complaisance towards what he regarded as essentially immaterial, he submitted to such acknowledgments as were conditions, and such methods as precedence and custom necessitated. This he did with no disdain or mockery of others or himself. His reverence for human nature was too big. If human nature regarded many things as perfected or unmistakable, he was ready to agree, in order that, like St. Paul, being all things to all men, he might by any means save some. The efficacy of works was paramount; the dogmata of the church like clothes, which wear out, to be renewed on a different pattern with the progress of time.

His views likewise underwent such constant modification that even while he had immense confidence in his personality, he fettered it not at all with a craving for consistency. He recognised that he too must develop, and by consequence change continually. Yet this led to an intimate doubt of the passing theory he could assert, and at the same time divided him between honour and mistrust of those who were content to accept any system as permanent and unimprovable. He was in fact a free-thinker, with a keener sense than is usual for the worth of things that are, because they are; for the worth of charity, because it is, like honest policy, not only the best to choose, but vitally so, the instinct of the future; for the worth of faith, because at least we see through its glass darkly. He temporised therefore, not from motives either good or evil in themselves, but because he felt, and very deeply, that to temporise is the only essentially true and consistent course for any man born into the world, where time and circumstances are the necessary conditions of his existence; where a soul, if eternal, is by implication but on its way.

And as he made no public parade of unorthodoxy, and his behaviour, though eccentric, was unimpeachable except on the insufficient ground of its unusualness, he passed through his time at Cambridge without any open rupture with authority, took a decent degree in classics, and about a year afterwards was ordained.

His first curacy was in Bristol, but he afterwards passed on to East London. He wrote to me once or twice, but I did not see him for some years after he left Cambridge, and knew nothing of his success or mental development, his letters telling me little beyond the commonplace of his surroundings and fellow-workers. In truth we had been friends of occasion rather than choice, for there was that in his morality which jarred upon an ordinary man, and made me gasp too often for whole-hearted confidence. I remember that once when I was bold enough to ask him seriously whether, considering his attitude towards the creeds, he could affirm that he had a 'call,' or assent to the declarations required by the Church, he replied by asking me in turn if any one had ever been able to prove that he had a call otherwise than by his personal assertion; and on my inability to answer, he added that neither could he, and that such personal assertion was of the usual value of human evidence. We were on a week's walking tour at the time, four of us, one Easter, along the coast of Devon. The two others were on ahead, having chosen the road; but Dalton had persuaded me to do a big scramble by the cliffs, and we were standing looking out over the Fiddle Rock when he said this. I remember I made no reply, and we both of us stared at the rock for some time. And then he suddenly turned upon me: 'If ever I was convinced that I was mistaken,' said he, 'I'd go and live on just such a place as that. How can anybody know?'

It was more than six years afterwards, and nearly five after he had obtained his second curacy, that I saw him again. By that time he had passed, as I thought, quite out of my life, like so many others of one's college friends. An old school fellow of mine, who had been with us at Cambridge, happened to call on me in Lincoln's Inn one day, and mentioned Dalton. He had come across him in connection with some mission work. Dalton was in a bad way, he said: he could make nothing of him. He seemed breaking up. He had worked himself to death, and was in a state of mind bordering on lunacy. And yet he refused to consult a doctor, or indeed any one, and was consumed with some great spiritual trouble, that nothing could abate.

So I took his address and went down to Bethnal Green at once, and there I found him in a little dingy room lying on a sofa. There were no flowers here, and on the four walls nothing but a broken crucifix.

Seeing me, he sat up, but he gave me no greeting, nor offered me his hand. Yet his indifference touched rather than chilled me. I do not know why I should be half ashamed to own it (besides, my mother was French) I sat down beside him, and before he could speak I put my arm about him and kissed him. He flushed and bowed as he sat, and then he hoisted himself up by his hands and stood by the table, swaying slightly. He steadied himself a moment, but immediately recognising that I might take his doing so for physical weakness, he stood straight up, and pointing to the crucifix said, his face quite white again, but absolutely calm: 'I did that. Hadn't you better go?'

But as I made no motion, being quite uncertain how to act, and only desirous of gaining time, he walked up and down the room for a while as if debating with himself. His clothes hung loose about him, he stooped worse than ever, and I could see that he was terribly wasted. He was not thirty then: he looked double. His forehead was ruled with lines and a sickly shining white; his cheek bones were like knobs, his lips barely visible for the habitual tension that had drawn two long furrows down each side of his face. His eyes I could not see until he presently flashed them upon me; and then I did not understand. They were almost devoid of expression, and his face, though so worn, was imperturbable: as sometimes we see in those who have travelled much in the tropics, a multitude of puckers and wrinkles, which give a permanent look of pain that is not being felt.

'A pitiful thing to do,' said he, stopping opposite the crucifix; 'I keep it there to remind me. We do such pitiful things at times.' And he resumed his walk. Again I waited.

'I may as well tell you,' said he, 'as you are here—there's no reason against your knowing—I've resigned.' Still I had nothing to say, and after a space he went on deliberately:

'This is not enough for me. That's what's the matter, and so I do not choose to continue. The vicar does not understand, and I dare say you will not understand. He thinks me everything that is good, and will give you an excellent account of me, I don't doubt, if you care to ask him. He knows nothing of me. I have not chosen that he should. He will say I am his right hand, and all that sort of thing. And perhaps I am. As they reckon success hereabout I am successful. Well, I've worked for it, fourteen hours a day have I worked getting on for five years. I've not spared myself; I see that you can see that; I've given it a fair trial. So far as the folk here can worship any one they worship me. And I don't care that for their worship. I might as well have tickled their rickety babies all the time.' A long pause, then again:

'I find words difficult. I know I cannot make myself clear. Roughly the thing is like this: here am I close on thirty, and I've the half-animal homage of, say, a thousand mixed indescribables. It is not good enough. I'm not going to pay the price. That sounds commercial may be, and not very deep. Yet it goes deep enough too. I am conscious of a power within me that may not be used, that is just so much waste. I don't find fault with them. They're average human beings, some better, some worse. And don't think I consider myself thrown away because I work in Bethnal Green instead of Belgravia. I am thrown away because I was born. There, I told you I had not words. That sounds portentous nonsense, doesn't it? I am not alone. We are all mocked with the possession of a power—to waste. Every man has it, but few realise that they have it, and fewer that they may never use it. I don't arrogate to myself any quality I do not share with our fellow men, but simply I revolt against our inability to use what we have for proportionate ends. We are a contradiction in terms. We have been given infinity, limited with the finite! We are immortal—that we may cook our dinners! We are a living testimony to a superhuman joke, a set of dolls made in the God-like image, with the God-like attributes, but denied the means to employ them like gods; as we might be said to deny our dolls aught but their outward resemblance to ourselves. Or, to take another idea, I am like a man trained as a clockmaker and set in a land where there is no time. Like sheep, we submit because there is no escape. Only the heathen could imagine the man who dared raise a hopeless defiance. But in spite of his hopelessness he is the finest creation of man's brain, and the most profound.'

'And yet,' he went on presently, and in the same calm tone, 'men do retort unconsciously. Every soldier that dies in battle retorts in a way. For some silly squabble (the origin of which lies where?—in this human nature!) he flings back his life in God's face. He has done what was expected of him. There is at bottom no greater retribution for the fowler than that the game fall into his snare. Have you never laid a trap yourself? But I am shocking you horribly, I'm afraid. You must remember that my God is not your God, not the God of your New Testament and of love and all tenderness, but that Almighty who is beyond our ideas of benevolence, as our ideas of benevolence are beyond the social instincts of ants or bees, though, indeed, they have been put in the same catalogue, and "utility" written above them. Utility for what? For life in general. We call pain Process now, but it hurts all the same. We recognise its utility towards a goal of which we can just conceive, and so hesitate to call even evil evil, for the definition of evil must be opposition to God, and we cannot face a duality. The old dilemma persists. But just by so much as our benevolence or morality is below God's, by so much is He removed from fatherhood. The more we think, the less anthropomorphic becomes that terrific Personality, the more removed are we from any sense but that we learn by looking at the stars. And yet are we conscious of this divinity within us, and the size of the mockery too. I, like every man, must fail; I will fail in my own way. I have given life a trial. I have succeeded as they think; but *I* know that I have failed, and must fail. And so I will waste my life.'

'And what good will that do?' I mumbled.

'How absurd of you!' said he.

'Then who will be mocked?' I cried in desperation. 'You don't imagine that this Omnipotence you speak of will be—be—damaged.'

'Of course not,' said he; 'I forget how many millions there are in the world just now, and I am sure I can hardly conceive of the millions that have been or will be. They are all assisting Process, unconsciously more or less. They are the means for evolving a future type. Is there not then something unique, if one but considers one's vanity, in standing consciously aloof from every dictate of instinct or experience, so far as they may by any possible means be so abandoned? One unit shall hinder Process to the extent of his individual capacity! Surely Nature must be anxious! She whose regard for life in general is so great, that to preserve it she has evolved all these incessantly complicated methods, physical and moral and intellectual, is yet absolutely reckless of the unit, or even the type, as you know well enough. I refuse to go to school. She will come and whip me, no doubt. Well—' and he laughed, 'let her whip.'

'You acknowledge the infinite littleness of the result then?'

'Yes,' said he. 'But that a created being should be so little is a reflection of rather a subtle character on creation, is it not? I had thoughts of suicide when I was at Cambridge. You never knew, of course. But suicide is petty. Suicide is but refusal to live. I will do more, I will live, if I am permitted, in order that I may insult this thing men bless as life. And even if that be like the ridiculous profanities of a naughty child, remember who made the child. Is it only the child who is ridiculous?'

'I cannot understand,' said I, 'how any man——' But he broke in:

'I did not suppose you would. There is no need. This thing is between me and the dark. "Work while it is day; the night cometh when no man can work." What a strange reason to give for work! For five years have I wasted my life more or less in God's way. I say more or less, for perfect success, of course, is withheld even thus. I have lived half my life, I shall waste the rest of it in my own way. There's but one thing in the world to stop me, and that is like Pharaoh, King of Egypt; so don't ask.'

Throughout all this declaration he was as collected as if he had been discussing a change of domicile, perfectly free from embarrassment or compunction. If he had displayed a trace of emotion I could have appealed to him. I recognised something of the impotence he spoke of in my own heart, as I struggled to think of any argument to touch him. But his impassivity froze me. However, I made an effort.

'Dalton,' I cried, 'I'm going to pretend this is all morbid rot. You've been overdoing yourself and knocking up all round, and imagining the universe a manure heap to get on top of and crow. Now you just come back with me into the West, away from all this, and come and have a jolly good dinner, and see " Our Boys " (which was running then).'

Rather to my surprise he said at once : ' Right you are.' And the rest of the evening he was as gay as in the best of the old days at Cambridge. I remember we talked of Hammond and his engagement to a certain Miss Chanter, who afterwards married Lord T——.

The air seemed clearing, so that suddenly I ventured between the acts to suggest that he should take advantage of his present resignation to do a fortnight's walk abroad with me; and I named Holland, because I remembered he loved old cities once. But he laughed.

'You're not a bit satisfied,' said he. 'Here have I come out and spent a whole evening with you, and now you want me to spend a fortnight.'

'Yes, I do,' said I.

'I thought you didn't understand a bit,' he replied. 'Good night,' and he got up, and went straight out of the theatre. I was so nonplussed and annoyed at my own helplessness that I let him go; and when I went down to Bethnal Green in the morning he was gone, and had left no address. There seemed nothing to be done. I was deeply sorry for him, but I confess I was not sorry to be free of a task for which I felt myself so unequal, however I wished to serve him. I might more easily have attempted to play his fiddle.

And so for the second time I lost sight of him.

I am aware that I have given above but the shadow of what he said, for although I made notes next day of all I could remember, with the idea that I might submit them to some one spiritually able to help him, the thoughts were unfamiliar, and dealt with matters so far beyond the commonplace of my life, that I missed much of his meaning, and am not at all sure that I have adequately represented his difficulty, even if I have understood it. And when I came to read them over, they seemed so insufficient that—I did nothing. Somehow I was ashamed. And besides, I should not have known whether to take them to the Cowley Fathers or the doctors at Hanwell.

Many years afterwards I was on a cricketing tour one summer with some old school-fellows. We were most of us well getting on in life, and only played what might be called second or third-rate teams. We had spent a week playing near Barnstaple, and on the Sunday afternoon, remembering my walk along the coast, I went for a long tramp westward over some of the old ground, recalling old times and Cambridge by the way. It was a fine, hot August day, and when I came above the Fiddle Rock I was seized with a boyish longing to scramble out and have a bathe among the pools. The invitation of the low-tide and the beautiful air was irresistible. So down I went by a path a little way back, which seemed well-worn, and out over the pebbles on to the rocks and strewn seaweed.

And there, as I paused to look for the easiest way, came through the hot air to the lazy swash of the swell the tone of a violin, and with it stole into the beauty of earth, and sky, and sea a human horror that I recognised at once, and gasped. The sound was of the air of the flute solo in the *entr'acte* of Gluck's 'Orfeo,' that lamentation of an exquisite despair. Dalton's words on the cliff above came back wailing. Dalton was here playing his life away! I stood stock still and waited and listened, and as I listened the tide crept up about my feet.

Presently the sound ceased, and there clambered out from among the rocks the man himself. Seeing me he came rapidly towards me, waving his violin case; but on his face was no greeting, as there had been none that other time. The face was weather-worn now, but not as lined as when I saw him last. I cannot describe its expression, which was too vacant for cynicism, a sort of placid weariness as of a hero asleep. But the eyebrows rose as he called out banteringly: '"Hast thou found me, O mine enemy?" Did you hear the old tune we used to play? The day is abominably still. I always play that last—when the tide turns.'

My face must have betrayed something of the shame I felt for the thing I knew had come to pass, for he frowned slightly, and then looked upwards towards the cliff as if to go. So I stifled all but sympathy.

'My dear Dalton,' I cried, 'what the ——'

'I owe you a dinner,' said he, 'as you're here, come and have it. It won't match yours at the Monico. Still, you've let yourself in for it. Come along.'

When we had climbed to the top he stayed a while, and looked me over with some amusement. 'Professional whiskers,' said he; 'otherwise the same old W.G., I'm thinking. I thought of growing a beard too, but it hinders one's playing.' He looked down at the rock below, and the smile faded. 'Yes,' said he, 'you have let yourself in. Like the American, you "want to know." It'll save us both some bother perhaps if I tell you. But there's nothing much to tell, you can't guess for yourself. I've been here since you saw me last, that's all. How many years ago is that?'

'Is it nine?' said I.

'That's about it. I live close by here, at a farm. At low water I can get over into a sort of cave on the rock there, and there I play for about eight or nine hours every day—to nobody. That is my life.'

'About eight or nine hours a day of it,' said I, more for the sake of steadying my nerves than anything.

'Yes,' he said. 'Then there are meals and sleep—and the rest! Oh, I read the paper to see what's going on, and do acrostics and puzzles and things to keep my wits going,' and he almost laughed again. 'The people round here, what there are, think me a bit mad, of course, but most of them imagine

I am taking inordinate pains to become a professor on the violin. So I am, but not for their reasons. No one here has ever heard me play. The sea usually makes too much noise for the sound to come across when the tide's up, and no one interferes, so that all is as convenient as possible.'

He spoke lightly, as if by the commonplace mention of such things he would hinder me from kindling, and I felt more than half inclined to bid him good-bye then and there, and hear no more. He must have divined my thoughts instantly.

'As you please,' said he. So I walked on with him.

'But why play the violin?' I asked. 'That seems rather a refined way of—of spending the time.'

'Exactly,' said he, 'as refined as I could manage. Think—no one hears. To play as well as I do now—and no one hears! Isn't that exquisitely futile enough?'

'You fiend!' I exclaimed, but I clutched his coat as I cried. 'Dear old chap,' I cried again, 'haven't you a spark of manhood left?'

He put up his hand and released his coat.

'For some time after I left London,' he went on imperturbably, 'I sat thinking how best to carry out my purpose. I had various ideas, all more or less impracticable. I did not think of the fiddle at first, I had not touched it for years. Instinct naturally suggested publicity. To have by some means held up human nature to ridicule elaborately and systematically would have pleased me beyond measure. But I required that there should be consciousness of the ridicule. An audience, however, would have either been conscious and avoided me, or it would have heard me in ignorance; and so I should have missed my aim either way. I do not think I could possibly have made disciples—I am too different,' he added: 'and besides, to have tried would have involved me in endless worries and pesters, and I did not care about such trouble. I know human nature pretty well. It would have had no appropriate sympathy with my wishes. I know myself, too, pretty well, and I knew I could win with myself. And so I was content, perhaps more than content, to deal with myself alone. Isolation magnifies. My single isolated victory is more than a dozen modifications. And yet to have mocked them, even without their consciousness, would have been much. To have played before them as a splendid triviality would have been exaltation. Still the notion was too subtle, and I abandoned it. I had thoughts of doing worse.'

'How possibly worse?'

'You know the power of music over sensuous London,' said he. 'To prostitute a magnificent gift to sensuality would have been worse. Imagine all my thoughts, knowing as you do my fixed intention of insulting Nature (with a capital N), as I could have done by the choice of the music I might play. Perhaps you wonder why I refrained; simply for this reason: we are possessed of passions. Essentially their utility is for the multiplication and perpetuation of life. Foster them in however degraded a form, you still foster them. My aim would have been rather for their freezing and death. In any other direction I should have but pandered to Nature after all, and in that one direction I recognised at once my absolute impotence. No: with myself alone could any reasonable satisfaction be obtained. But my method, of course, has serious drawbacks. It is extremely dull. I have to fight that, and it takes some fighting. Mere physical apathy is my danger, and that is why I compromise so far as to read the paper, lest my brain should take to jibbing. To rise daily and go forth to be useless is only possible with a brain thoroughly alert. But I always loved music for its own sake, and that helps me much. I can play for hours without a thought of aught but playing well, and the beauty wrapping me about. I play pretty well now,' he said proudly. 'I have the sense to see that my victory is limited and partial, and must be; that I am bound and encompassed with a heritage I can never be free from. But such as it is, my defiance goes up continually; and as long as I can stand upon the rock there—it will.'

The path still wound by the cliff, and he looked seaward.

'It is grand,' said he, 'to be there when one of our south-westers is flinging the Atlantic up, and I can hardly hear my notes for the tremendous smashing of the sea; to feel that in presence of all that power I am still as strong. And I never play wildly then, as you might think. But when the storm is gone, and the after-swell comes thundering in, then I play my wildest, for I have outlived it, and feel the right to boast. And it is almost as grand in some still winter mornings, when the light is very faint, to be awake and playing there unsubdued amidst that dead tranquillity. Or again, in the summer evenings, such as we have had lately, to sit and play towards the setting sun, and feel above all part with it! The gulls and the curlews and the oyster-catchers have lost their wonder at me, and the shags will sit near me while I play. But often just at the best that wretched little string snaps, for the sea air plays havoc with them; and then I laugh, for the vanity of it never fails to catch me then, I hardly know why.'

'But sometimes,' he continued slowly, with his eyes far away, 'I have a deep doubt that I am, after all, in an odd way, submitting myself like others to the great object of all process, even by this futility of my own, since all is futile finally. And in my antagonism I grow conscious of a deep communion with all about me. That rock there on which I sit, I seem to see it forming slowly in layers of deposit, flat and gradual. I see it overlaid in the ages and crushed by layers above and metamorphosed by heat and masses of which one can hardly conceive. I see it buried and raised again, and crushed sideways and bent and contorted, and left and contorted again, while ceaseless other changes have played about its bed. And again I see it worn away by streams from above and the sea from below, and the still slower might of the air, till all but the hardest is left to stand out into this Atlantic of our times. Then come I, and sit my days upon it with this mortal immortal mockery. And I see myself gone, and itself worn away in time, and strewn afresh upon the sea floor, to be made up perhaps again and again. And so all is change and an endless making to unmake, an endless, endless futility. And I am a part, but by scorn I am conscious.'

He was unhasping an old rickety gate, and suddenly looked me full in the face. His eyes were inscrutably tender as he uttered the words, as if with a pity that seemed to me divine. But seeing my utter want of comprehension he added with a smile, 'Here is the farm.'

The farm was a slated, whitewashed barrack, set in mud. I have hardly ever seen a place muddier—and it was August. He led me upstairs to a long room bare as a prison, and then went down to make arrangements with the farmer's wife for my entertainment.

The window looked out on a grass slope lined at the top with a row of Scotch firs, crippled with the salt wind. It had neither blind nor curtain. The walls were plastered blue, and patches had fallen away. The boards were bare except for a strip or two of carpet, and a worn sheepskin before the tiny hearth. A bed, a chest of drawers, a washing-stand of stained wood, a small table, and a few Windsor chairs completed the furniture. There were no bookcases nor cupboards, only a large pile of papers in a corner. Over the mantel was a card with the misapplied words upon it, 'Do what thou dost as if the stake were Heaven, and that thy last deed ere the Judgment Day.' There were two photographs upon the table, one of an old man with a kind intellectual face and hoary beard, the other of a most spiritual and tender-looking woman. Stamped on her frame in gold letters was 'La Belle Dame sans Mercy'; upon seeing which I began to think things of Dalton which had never occurred to me before. It was all very cheerless even on that bright evening, and my spirits fell to zero. What were the winters like here? I was overwhelmed with pity as I sat and waited for him.

He returned with some gaiety. 'Pork chops and cold figgy pudding,' he cried; 'there's glory for you.! And you may try the cider. My meals are usually rather unconventional. You see, to catch the tide, I have to go out at such odd hours sometimes. I often sit playing hours before sunrise by the light of my stove there. In the winter I have to carry a regular load of wood and coal down with me in a sack on my back; and then it gives out before the tide's up, and my fingers have to give in.'

The feast was brought upstairs on a tray by an untidy woman, who looked at me with a furtive curiosity, but said nothing. He ate well, and I had a holiday appetite in spite of my surroundings, and so did not betray myself.

When we had finished, and I was smoking, he took up the portrait of the spiritual-looking woman, and put it into my hands.

'She stood between me and this once,' he said. 'But that is long ago. Is it not a beautiful face? Her character was like it, but she was human. She failed. I will tell you about her. When I was in Bristol I met her, and fell in love with her. She shared my views about my vocation; she was a saint. She, too, felt that priesthood and celibacy were inseparable. It was her will, as it was mine, that every sacrifice should be made for Heaven's sake. And so we separated. But I loved her, I told her so; and she loved me, she told me so. I knew it when I foreswore her. She had been to me the sister of Sir Percivale, and I believe at one time I was her Galahad until then. But then she gave way, and I knew what I know now. It was a terrible time.

There is no conflict beside it, this daily fight is nothing, the fight in London was nothing beside it. But we won—that we might fail later! We parted. I went to London, she gave her life behind in Bristol, and so the years ran on. Well, when I gave up my work at last, you see what happened—I was free—to marry her—but upon what conditions? She only in fact stood between me and this. I did not go to her—I wrote to her. That was folly, the world would say; it was heroism. I wrote to her fully all my thoughts, as fully at least as one can write; and I wrote because I wanted her to judge the whole matter calmly, and without that personal appeal my presence would necessarily have brought. She wrote to me the letter I have upon me till I die. It is a most extraordinary letter. I shall never understand it. It is a splendid lie. It contains an official version henceforth to be accepted. She told me she had never loved me, not that her love was dead, but that it never existed. You see the position was hopeless on all accounts. If I continued priest I forswore her by the very act; if I ceased to be so, I became for ever unworthy of her. I forsook my calling, and she could not stoop. She is magnificent for not stooping. And yet the magnificence is that of failure. Had she been better than mortal she could have stooped; but she knew she was mortal, and that mortal strength was insufficient. It was not she but her human nature that was, by God's grace, inadequate. And so, probably that the matter might be finally closed by an impenetrable misunderstanding, she wrote me this official version.'

'But perhaps,' I interjected, 'it was, after all, the true one. Perhaps she had been carried away before, and it was you that misunderstood her when you thought she loved you.'

He opened a drawer and took from it a book, the fourth volume of Mrs. Browning's poems, and opened it at the thirty-eighth of the Portuguese sonnets. I read it, and a date, and two sets of initials pencilled below, Dalton's and another's, not in Dalton's handwriting. He regarded me scornfully.

'That's contemptible of me,' said he. 'But why should not I be contemptible? I was not contemptible then, nor when I wrote to her. I paid her the grandest compliment possible to man. I likened her love to her God's, a thing which could never fail, however contemptible I might become; a thing which could live on for ever for me however fallen. An ordinary woman could not rise to that. But she was not an ordinary woman. Her power of forgiveness I thought limitless as His. A strange compliment, but a big one. She could not take it—and I am here. I installed her as divinity. She did not cavil at my conception of divinity, but by a lie she made polite disclaimer—poor human soul—and I am here.

'And yet I could have won. By the flesh I could have won. I might have gone to her, and put my arm about her; and that had been stronger than pen or tongue, and a kiss had conquered where prayer failed. She knew not that in God's sight my appeal made, standing aloof, was more pitiful than bent knees and cries for mercy. Her human nature stood by her, and she was humanly wise. Yet this same human nature would have bowed at the breath of a lover, and human eyes mixed her tears with his. I, who could not win by the spirit, might yet have won through the flesh; for on earth the flesh reigns paramount, and beside it the spirit must content itself with its immortality! Impotence! Impotence! Once Sir Percivale's Sister, again The Blessed Damozel, and again La Belle Dame sans Mercy for ever. And now,' he cried with a laugh, into which stole that same divine pity that still haunts me at times, till something of his own madness catches and chokes me, 'you can understand better why "the sedge is withered from the lake, and no birds sing."'

Yes, I understood. As I looked at the patience, and pity, and indomitable defiance on his beautiful face, I understood that for any help I could give him I was as impotent as he considered me.

He took the photograph from my hand, and with a bow put it back on the table. The matter was ended.

'I managed to get my money sunk in the Panama business,' said he presently. 'That seemed as useless as any other. There are labourers employed certainly who live feverishly; but nature is putting things on the old footing fast. I kept 100*l.* a year for my life. I have no relations. My uncle died four years ago. I never saw him after I came here. He was beautiful. I shall not see you again,' he added, ' when you leave me to-night. You will not give me the trouble of avoiding you, it is such a nuisance to be moving. Chance directed you here. You will not take advantage of it. When and if any change occurs, you shall know.'

What could I do but promise? But when we parted in the mud at the gate I caught his hand.

'Dalton, Dalton,' I implored, 'dear old Tom, is there nothing I——' But his hand was upon my mouth. Then he pointed upwards to the new moon. 'She is as good as dead,' said he. 'They say she was once alive, as we think of life. I am as good as dead. And you might as well think of warming her up again with a gas kitchener.'

With what a healthy selfishness did I not enjoy the cricket and good humour and homely happy commonplace of next day! It was like stepping from a sepulchre into the sunshine.

That was August. The following June I had a letter from him. Here it is :—

'DEAR G.,—When I leave here you will come and take the book I showed you and the photograph. I am giving instructions that you may be informed when I am gone. You will come and take possession of my effects and destroy them all, except the photograph and the box of violin strings you will find labelled. You will advertise for a lady to claim them, you will know her by the photograph. For many reasons I did not tell you her name. You will present her with both. The strings are those I have broken in my playing here. They are the sort of things a woman would care to keep.

'Yours,
'THOMAS DALTON.'

And about a couple of months later—something tells me that the time was specially arranged with reference to my holidays—I received a scrawl from his landlady. Dalton was gone, would I be pleased to come?

No one knew anything more. His violin had been picked up smashed upon the beach one morning, and suicide was a natural inference, or perhaps misadventure. But I have my doubts of his suicide, and an accident with the tide to him, who knew it so well, seems unlikely. Moreover, the weather had not been particularly boisterous. Neither his body nor any trace of him has appeared; yet there is a strong current southward, and it may be he was washed away.

The silent slovenly woman helped me to carry out his requests. We burnt his things in the yard. Of all places upon earth that muddy farm is the most horrible to me. She hoped that I would be able to recommend her other lodgers in the place of the one she had lost. She had no fault to find with him.

It is no use accusing myself now. It almost seems to me that if I had been able to help him he would not have confided in me as he did. He is gone, and nothing remains but to do as he requested.

Who is the lady who will come to me and claim her photograph, and 2766 pieces of broken fiddle string?

GRAILY HEWITT.

THE HEROIC ACTIONS OF LORD EXMOUTH

ENGLAND sent forth many noble lads to fight her battles in the last quarter of the eighteenth century; but among them all there was no one more plainly marked out from his youth for greatness than Edward Pellew, whose family traditions were of that wild and lonely coast which stretches from Penzance towards the Lizard. Many tales, and some not over creditable, have been told of the dwellers on those solitary cliffs, where the law had little power, and most men did what seemed good in their own judgment. But whatever qualities which go to make the perfect man may have been lacking on the Lizard shore, courage and seamanship were there in fullest measure; and it could not be that Pellew should have failed to inherit both. Moreover, his father, commander of a Dover packet, led a wild, adventurous life. For the captains who made the Channel passage in the last century, when war was the rule, and an horizon clear of privateers a rarely met with blessing, were of more martial and heroic stuff than the very worthy seamen who command the steamers of to-day; and so the lad, born at Dover in 1757, found his ears ringing with grand traditions of the sea, when many children know only nursery rhymes, and by the time he lost his father at the age of eight his mind was set already in the direction which he followed with strength and single purpose all his life, till in the end he left a name which will stand as a proud possession of Cornwall and of England.

Much of his boyhood was spent, as Bottrell tells us, in a cottage at Penzance, where he dwelt with his grandmother, Madam Woodhouse, and distinguished himself by an even unusual reluctance to go to school, slipping off on every proper and improper occasion to the quay, where the sailors loved the reckless lad, and encouraged him in his wild ways. Once only in his career did his stout heart fail him, and set his heels in motion in face of an enemy; and that was on one unhappy day when, having wandered with a friend up Castle Horneck avenue, he was inspired to discharge a few shots through the latticed window of a cottage inhabited by two excellent old maiden ladies. The pellets were aimed at pewter plates, and struck those only, but the insult knocked at the heart of one of the old ladies, who seized the firehook, as the nearest weapon, kilted up her gown, and gave chase. Pellew's courage dissolved at the first sight of this gaunt apparition, running as he thought no lady of her age could run. He fled like a hare; she cast away her firehook and followed; he threw away his musket and gained some ground; she caught him up again, and in Madron Churchtown was almost on his back, when there came a kindly hill. The old lady's wind was gone, she could spurt no more, so while the culprit fled away in shameful rout without his arms, she retreated honourably, the one person (if she could have known it) who ever terrified Pellew.

'I think you will kill many,' said his grandfather when the lad insisted on going to sea; and indeed, it was obvious enough that if he did not do so, the fault would be neither in his strength nor courage. He won credit from the first days of his service; and at the battle fought on Lake Champlain in America, he distinguished himself so greatly by his gallant conduct on the 'Carleton' schooner that he was ever afterwards a marked man. For this valour he won his lieutenancy; not long afterwards he gained another step for distinguished service on the 'Apollo' frigate, and in 1782, when he had served twelve years only, he attained post rank as the reward of an act of signal courage and good conduct. All these early services contain tales well worth the telling, but they must be read elsewhere, or there will be no space to speak of the greater deeds on which Pellew's true fame must rest. When the peace came he attempted farming, but made no more of it than sailors commonly do of landsmen's work; then thought of entering the Russian navy, but abandoned the idea at the solicitation of his brother Israel, a gallant sailor like himself; and finally rose up with new life and hope when war descended from the clouds in February 1793; and hastening to London, obtained command of a fine frigate, the 'Nymphe.'

The whole country was waiting with eagerness and some anxiety for the news of the first engagements. It was known that there were already several powerful French frigates cruising in the Channel; and the armaments at the disposal of the Navy Board were so imperfect that there was difficulty in equipping ships to meet them. Pellew found he could not at once get good seamen. He had

ADMIRAL EDWARD PELLEW, FIRST VISCOUNT EXMOUTH, G.C.B.

no mind to wait while others struck the blow for which the country watched. He meant to strike that blow himself; and knowing well, what few knew then, namely that Cornish miners, used to hardship and danger of every kind, possessed a bulldog courage which he could turn to excellent purpose on board ship, he gave them a chance of joining him. He had but to hold up his hand, when eighty splendid fellows answered; he got as many more stout seamen as he could, and came round to Falmouth, where he picked up as a volunteer his younger brother Israel, a commander on half-pay, and took counsel with his elder brother, who was collector of customs at Falmouth, as to the quarter in which the enemy might most probably be met with.

There may have been some who had apprehensions about the policy of facing trained French seamen with a crew consisting largely of miners who had never been afloat before. But on the 'Nymphe' herself there were no doubts, for the miners were proving noble fellows, and there was none among the whole ship's company who did not watch for the enemy as eagerly as if he were looking for his sweetheart among the dusky hedgerows on a summer night. Two at least of the impatient Cornishmen saw the coming enemy in their dreams, and knew her readily when they saw her heave in sight in the summer daybreak off the Start, a noble frigate finely equipped and handled perfectly, for her commander had learnt his business under Suffren in the East, and the lessons taught by that great commander had made him a worthy adversary for any Englishman.

'There are too many of us here,' said Pellew a little wistfully, as his brother Israel ran on deck at the first hail to see the stranger. He meant that there would be hot work, and he wished in his heart that Israel were with his wife and children. But Israel had no time for sentiment. He was interested only in the verification of his dream, in which he had shot away the wheel of the approaching frigate. He knew her at once, and meant to serve her as his dream had prophesied; and so without much heeding his brother's observation, he proceeded to take charge of a gun (which he was well qualified to do, being an excellent artilleryman), and waited grimly till the moment came for action. It was not long in coming. At six o'clock the two ships were within hail. Pellew saluted the French captain, who waved in answer a red cap of liberty, and in the next moment gave it to a sailor, who ran up aloft and nailed it to the masthead. The two ships were all but abreast by this time; and as the 'Nymphe' forged up on the starboard quarter of the 'Cléopatre,' Pellew, who stood bareheaded on his quarter deck, raised his hat to his head. That was the appointed signal; and in the same instant the frigate rocked and quivered as her full broadside crashed at that short distance into her antagonist. Captain Mullon was not backward in replying, and for some forty minutes there ensued a fierce and deadly cannonade.

While the two ships lay pounding each other at close quarters, Israel Pellew was grimly serving the gun which he had taken for himself, and whenever the wind blew aside the dense smoke that wrapped the ships, he seized his chance and fired. He had killed more than one French steersman already; and at length, a few minutes before seven, his dream came true, and the wheel itself of the 'Cléopatre' flew into splinters. In that moment the day was lost and won. The 'Cléopatre' swung round with her bow to the Cornish broadside, the guns roared out, the French mizzen mast crashed down upon the deck, and the doomed frigate was a scene of wild confusion. There was scarcely need for Pellew to call for boarders. Every man saw the opportunity, and Pellew himself, quick as he was in every moment needing prompt decision, was hardly on the bulwarks before his men were crowding after him. There was a short but bloody fight. The French fought fiercely, but they were outmatched, and the gallant Mullon died tearing up in his last agony what he deemed to be his code of private signals. It was, in fact, his commission, which his failing sight could not distinguish; but he has the honour of having given his faculties to the very last to the service of his country.

Such was the first action of the great war on which we look back with envy of the men who saw such glory; and any one who knows the Falmouth of to-day may try to form a picture of the scene when the 'Nymphe' came in beneath Pendennis, followed by her prize, and Pellew stepped on shore upon the Market Strand. No man living has looked on such a scene; yet it may well be that we shall see it ere we die. Heaven grant that our fortunes may be in the hands of others like Pellew! Within a few hours, the excitement which roused Falmouth first was echoing through every part of England; and men welcomed this brave fight as an earnest of what was to come. As for Pellew, he was knighted, while his brother Israel obtained post rank.

Now this, the first summer of the war, was not far spent when it became evident that serious measures were demanded to check the ravages of French frigates, which were cruising in the Channel in unprecedented numbers, and which threatened to cripple British commerce as effectually as the French Government desired. It was this danger which put the seal on Pellew's greatness. We may believe if we will that there were a dozen other officers of the English Navy as capable as he of encountering and hunting down these pests. We cannot deny that there must have been some others, when we remember what Cochrane, then a mere lad, achieved a few years later. But it is certain that Pellew possessed in a very rare degree that peculiar combination of quick courage with fine seamanship which was needed for the task; and when he proposed to Sir John Borlase Warren the formation of that which was known as the Western Squadron, a group of frigates operating from Falmouth, which port appeared to Pellew to possess unequalled advantages for those who sought to watch the Channel, he was able to enforce his somewhat novel proposition with arguments which made it irresistible.

So a squadron was formed to hunt the Channel, and from the first moment it proved its use. To such profit indeed did these ocean hounds go out from Falmouth, that in another year the pack was divided into two, and while Warren retained the one, Pellew was appointed huntsman of the other. I would that I had space to follow closely the story of his hunting. Under Pellew's flag the frigates became familiar with every mile of coast from Calais to Finisterre. They knew the navigation and the currents; they scouted with such will up and down the coast that the French frigates, so far from preying

THE HEROIC ACTIONS OF LORD EXMOUTH

on English commerce in the Channel, were, for the most part, locked up with their battle ships in Brest. One instance must serve of the cool audacity with which Pellew performed this service. It was at the end of 1796. The blockade of Brest was looser than it became under the iron hand of Lord St. Vincent. Admiral Richery, who had slipped out of Toulon with six sail of the line in the previous year, and who had since been occupied pleasantly enough in plundering British commerce in Newfoundland, as well as on the Atlantic, had with unbroken good fortune slipped into Brest, and reinforced the French fleet lying idly in that harbour.

All these movements were fully known to Pellew, who was scouting in the 'Indefatigable' off the harbour; and on December 16, the wind being favourable for the sailing of the French, he judged it well to run into the harbour and see what they were about. As he suspected, he found the fleet in motion. Four-and-forty ships were getting under way, and some great movement was clearly begun. All that winter day Pellew hung on and off the port, waiting till he could be certain what course the fleet intended to set, so that he might take to the rendezvous fixed by Admiral Colpoys, eight miles east of Ushant, some certain information as to the objective. But the French ships hung about unaccountably, and the early dusk came on long ere they were clear of the harbour. As it began to get dark, guns were fired from the flagship and blue lights burnt as signals to the fleet; and Pellew, seeing that it was clearly of some consequence to the French that the true meaning of these signals should be appreciated, conceived the brilliant idea of perplexing them.

CLOSE OF THE ACTION BETWEEN THE 'NYMPHE' AND 'LA CLÉOPATRE'

Accordingly he ran up within half gunshot of the admiral; and as often as the French fired signal guns he fired others; he sent up rocket against rocket, and copied their blue lights till he left the signalmen in absolute bewilderment, and the vessels following knew not what to make of the wild medley of lights and cannon shots that illumined the night sky. The consequence of this pretty prank was that few, if any, of the French ships comprehended that their admiral had abandoned his original design of issuing from Brest by the southern entrance, the passage Du Raz, which in those days was scarcely practicable, save in broad daylight and with an easy sea. The greater part of the ships stood on through the rocky channel, while the admiral ran straight out to sea; and one of them ran ashore on the 'Grand Stevenet,' where she was lost with near seven hundred lives. Her guns firing for help amid the darkness increased the confusion; and Pellew having done with his single ship as much mischief as a squadron could have hoped for, set sail for the rendezvous, where Colpoys should have been in waiting with his fleet.

Colpoys was not there. How great a blow might have been struck had he but held St. Vincent's sailorly maxim, 'Well up with Ushant on an easterly wind.' If Pellew had found him, the whole French fleet might have been annihilated on the next day as it lay at anchor in Camaret Bay. As it was, this great armada was let loose in the Channel; and had those who commanded it possessed the qualities of great leaders, or met with even tolerable luck, a deadly peril might have risen up for England. But it is one of the reassuring facts of warfare that mistakes are never wholly on one side; and fortune served England at this crisis so well, that within two weeks this fleet of enemies, shattered and broken by the fury of the elements, was in full retreat for France again, having won no glory and dealt no blow at England.

Such was the end of Hoche's great invasion; and yet not quite the end, for it was Pellew, with his accustomed luck, who saw the very last of the great scattered fleet which he had watched issuing in its pride from Brest. It was on the afternoon of January 13, 1797, that the 'Indefatigable,' cruising in company with the 'Amazon,' came in sight of 'Les Droits de l'Homme,' a 74-gunship, lumbering homewards over the stormy sea. A heavy gale was blowing, which increased during the night to a fierce storm; and the grey winter dusk was almost dark already when the 'Indefatigable,' outsailing her consort, laid herself alongside the vast bulk of the battleship and opened fire. Pellew cared little for the difference in force between his 44-gun frigate and the 74 which he attacked; yet it was a bold adventure, for a full hour is said to have elapsed before the 'Amazon' could render him assistance; and the French captain, having a large body of troops on board, possessed the advantage of a vast overweight in musketry as well as cannon. But doubtless, in the failing light, and over a sea which began to roll mountains high, accurate aim was scarcely possible. I have heard it said that Pellew's men fought up to their waists in water; and James tells us that the frigates rolled so terribly that some of the guns on the 'Indefatigable' drew their ringbolts from her side, while others broke their breechings no less than four times.

When this had lasted for an hour, the 'Indefatigable' shot ahead, and the

'Amazon' came up on the quarter of the battleship, where she hung maintaining the fight till she too forged ahead. Then, after some manœuvring, in which Pellew saved himself by smart seamanship from being run aboard, the two frigates fastened like wolves one on either flank of the tall quarry, and there they hung for five hours cannonading fiercely in the night, while all three vessels ran before the storm without care or notice of their course, though knowing well that a lee shore studded with perilous reefs could not be far distant. It was then past midnight, and the storm was at its height. The ships were rolling terribly. All the 'Indefatigable's' masts were wounded, the 'Amazon' had lost many of her spars, and the crews were almost spent with fatigue. But they had no thought of letting the great battleship escape; and having secured their wounded masts and loose rigging as they might, they ran down and resumed the fight. So the three ships drove on fighting desperately in the stormy night, till at half past four in the morning the moon broke suddenly through the clouds, and Lieutenant Bell, who was on the forecastle of the 'Indefatigable,' reported to Pellew that there was land ahead. What land it was no one knew; but guessing that it might be Ushant, Pellew made sail to the southwards, which would have given him a free course had the guess been right. But they had not run long to the southward when the breakers were seen upon the other bow. They wore to the northward, and watched for dawn with the desperate hope of men who see but little chance of life. When the slow day broke they saw their foe, 'Les Droits de l'Homme,' lying broadside uppermost in the surf, while not far away the 'Amazon' lay in the same helpless state. Pellew passed within a mile of them, but was powerless to render any help; for he knew now where he was, he had recognised the contour of Audierne Bay, and he knew well that his only chance of life was to weather the dreaded reef called the Penmarks. It was not the first time he had been in danger of wreck in that locality; but with shattered spars and rigging badly cut, it seemed impossible to set a steady course in such a storm. But no chances were neglected under Pellew's command. The carpenters were doing what was possible. Pellew himself and his master, Mr. Gaze, who sailed with him throughout the war, had few equals in the art of handling ships, and knew well how to save their rickety spars from any unnecessary strain. It was touch and go, but the spars held, the 'Indefatigable' kept her course, the Penmarks drifted by a short half-mile to leeward, and the valiant Cornishmen gained the open sea, giving proof of seamanship at least as fine as the courage and audacity manifested in the fight.

One of the most terrible of stories is told of the suffering of the crew of the great French battleship, of whom some five hundred perished in the surf. The officers and crew of the 'Amazon,' on the other hand, saved themselves by a raft, losing only six of their number.

Such was the life of Sir Edward Pellew as commander of the Western Squadron, and this may serve as an example of the skill and spirit which he infused into his hunting up to the time when his growing fame called him to larger enterprises and more extended commands. He had obtained a baronetcy in 1796 for an act of signal daring performed at Plymouth, where an Indiaman

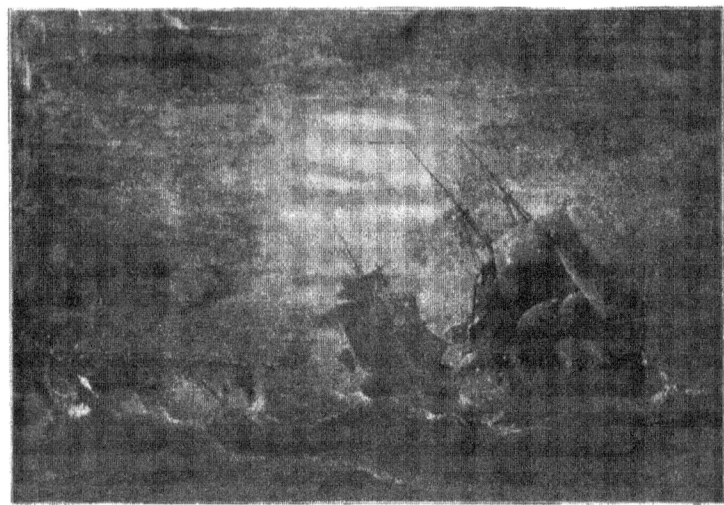

[Photo by Durrant & Son, Torquay] [From a painting by H. Pocock, 1811, in the possession of Lord Exmouth]

'LES DROITS DE L'HOMME,' OF 74 GUNS AND 1,300 MEN, CAPTURED BY THE FRIGATES 'INDEFATIGABLE' AND 'AMAZON,' JANUARY 17TH, 1797

laden with passengers had driven on shore beneath the citadel, and was in danger of going to pieces. The chief officers were on shore; the crew had got at the spirits; the decks were covered by a frightened and unruly mob, who seemed only too likely to perish by their want of discipline, when Pellew went out and climbed on board by a hawser, took command, devised fresh means of rescue, and finally brought off the whole frightened mob in safety. Acts such as this impressed upon the minds alike of people and of Government that Pellew was lucky as well as brave; and before the century closed there were certainly only one or two officers at most whose reputation stood as high as his.

Of his actions during the rest of the war I shall say but little; for it is from his greatest deeds that the quality of the man must be estimated, and the bombardment of Algiers claims what little space I can command. Few remember in these days what England, and Cornwall in particular, suffered once from Sallee pirates; and fewer still can realise that the whole foul system of Christian slavery continued still unchecked into the present century, and that while England possessed a fleet which was capable of blowing the fortifications of Algiers, Tunis, and Tripoli into ruins at any moment, she yet permitted English men and women to languish there in slavery. It is a miserable story. It is true that from time to time a British envoy was directed to express to the petty tyrants who ruled these nests of pirates that his Majesty of England would be really pleased if they would take to better ways and cease to plunder and enslave his loving subjects. But when a blank negative was returned to this friendly suggestion, no measures were taken to enforce it, and England suffered ignominy at the hands of the Dey of Algiers which would have been washed out in seas of blood had it been offered by a Christian potentate, however mighty. Such a mild suggestion of reform Pellew, as Commander in the Mediterranean, was directed to carry to Algiers, Tunis, and Tripoli, in 1816, together with certain other proposals of less consequence to-day. At Algiers, whither he went first, the suggestion met with the customary blank refusal. The other proposals were accepted; and Pellew went on to Tunis, where a curious accident occurred. The interpreter, who was directed to make to the Bey of Tunis the same suggestion which the Dey of Algiers had scoffed at, blundered into firmness, and presented an actual demand for the abolition of Christian slavery. The ministers expressed surprise; but Pellew, who never feared responsibility, and whose blood must have boiled at the timid part he was called upon to play, leapt at the chance, detected signs of irresolution, and pressed his unauthorised demand. To his astonishment he gained the point; and at Tripoli, whither he went next, he was equally successful. A weaker man would have referred to England for instructions at this stage, but Pellew preferred to do the work himself, and leave to ministers the shame of disowning him if they dared. And so he went back to Algiers, and fortified by his triumph at the other ports renewed his demand more boldly.

To the Dey of Algiers it appeared incredible that he had at length encountered a man not tainted with that strange infirmity of purpose which affects most Christian negotiation with Mohammedans, and which had encouraged him and his predecessors so long in the belief that the fangs of England were not for the Moors, who might insult her with impunity. He therefore answered with more or less contempt that the demand was impossible; and when Pellew hinted that if that were so, it might be necessary to continue the argument with cannon, the Dey pointed confidently to the batteries which bristled with heavy guns all round the harbour and up the steep hill on which the town is built, and answered that he did not fear the English ships. To this Pellew replied that with five battleships he would lay the town in ruins; and after a sharp altercation, he took out his watch and gave the Divan two hours to decide. Such language had not been heard before in Algiers, and the anger of the people rose at once to fever point. When the two hours had expired, Pellew, who had received no answer, took the British consul, Mr. McDonnell, and walked down through the town towards his boat. They were followed by an angry mob; and at the town gate they were stopped by the guard, who flatly declined to let them pass without express orders from the Dey. While a messenger was despatched to the Divan, the crowd seethed furiously round the British officers, crying out aloud that they should be slain upon the spot. At one moment their actions were so threatening, that the whole party believed they were about to be attacked. The captain of the port had actually cocked his pistol; and Israel Pellew, who accompanied his brother, strove to draw his sword, crying out, 'At least let us die with arms in our hands.' But the press of Moors against them was so great that he had not space to unsheathe his weapon. At length one of the principal officers of state appeared, thrusting back the crowd, and begging for two days in which to consider a question of such moment. But Pellew, furious at the indignity offered to his person, replied sharply that he would not give two hours; and went on board his ship, with the avowed intention of firing on the town. The consul was detained on some plea of a debt due from Portugal, which country he also represented, and was flung into prison as a malefactor.

It is a commonplace in naval strategy that the power of ships in reducing batteries is very limited, and Pellew was well aware of the strength of those which protected Algiers. At the same time he had his own views about the possibility of reducing forts which some experts held to be impregnable; and, indeed, he was far too good an officer to have committed himself to the chance of an attack without very clear ideas in regard to how it should be carried out. In fact, some months earlier, he had sent Captain Warde to Algiers, with instructions to map out the harbour secretly and take full soundings, a service which Warde performed most ably, spending all his nights upon the water in a little boat. Pellew was therefore in possession of full information as to where he ought to place his ships, and looked forward confidently to the attack. However, the wind was adverse all that day; and before the ships could gain their proper stations, a new ambassador from the Dey came off, protesting that he could not grant so important a demand without authority from Constantinople, whither he wished to send an ambassador. In the end Pellew, who had his reasons for doubting how far he would be supported in England, agreed to a suspension of hostilities for three months, and sent the Algerine ambassador to the Golden Horn on the British frigate 'Tagus,' while he himself returned to England with the remainder of his fleet.

He may very well have doubted with what face ministers would receive him; for there was no courage nor any pride in Whitehall which could be appealed to against the Moors. Indeed, there were actually people to be found in England who maintained that the monstrous barbarities of the Algiers pirates were a help to British commerce, which would suffer if they were suppressed; and this is an argument of a kind which seems irresistible to politicians. But while Pellew had been exceeding his instructions out of zeal for England's honour, the stars in their courses had been fighting for the same cause. The Algerines had slaughtered without provocation a whole colony of coral fishers under British protection, and Lord Brougham in one of his most fiery speeches had won the House of Commons over to counsels of bravery and honour. Thus the ground was prepared when Pellew reached London. He had no need to defend his action. He had only to disclose his plans, and persuade ministers that he could smoke out the wasps' nest which had stung so fiercely. In two months he was under way again, pledged to the accomplishment of a task which many of the wisest heads in England believed would end in defeat and loss of credit.

Pellew knew otherwise. Nelson had declared he would not attack Algiers with less than five-and-twenty ships; but Pellew knew both the soundings and the channels better, and would not have more ships than he could place effectively in the stations at command. He took five battleships, five frigates and several smaller vessels; while under his command was also a Dutch squadron of five frigates and one sloop. He sent on in advance a swift corvette, with orders to bring off the British consul and his family ; but when this corvette rejoined the fleet off Cape De Gatte, the officers reported that the consul lay in the dungeons used for malefactors and in risk of death. His wife and daughter had been brought away gallantly enough disguised as midshipmen, and had reached the boats in safety ; but the party who followed them carrying McDonnell's infant child had been betrayed by the crying of the infant as they passed beneath the gateway, and had all been arrested. The child was sent off to its mother, but the party of brave men who had tried to save it were with McDonnell in the dungeons whence few men came out alive.

Doubtless the peril of their comrades added to the wrath which was widespread upon the fleet as they sighted the white hilltown which had stood during so many generations for a type of all barbarity ; and the lust of fighting was quickened by some trace of the Crusaders' passion ; for those who looked out from their ships upon that August morning, and saw the sea lapping blue and sweet around the mole of Algiers, or followed the line of the mountains towering over the steep town, saw in that lovely spectacle nothing but a hell of sorrows for every nation which sailed by upon those seas, and they meant to strip the terror from it ere another dawn. They trusted their commander perfectly ; otherwise, as they lay off the port waiting an answer to the demand which had been sent on shore for unconditional assent to the terms already proffered, there might have been some among them who looked upon the batteries and the narrow space for manœuvring with doubt how the ships would get out again.

There is no natural harbour at Algiers. A broad pier lined with storehouses juts out some three hundred yards ; and from its extremity a mole is carried in a sort of semicircle in the direction of the town, while on the opposite side another small pier leaves an entrance no more than a hundred yards in width. Both these piers, as well as the mole, were bristling with cannon, mostly, says Osler, disposed in a double tier, with ports below and embrasures above, while the eastern batteries, next the lighthouse—which was itself a fort of considerable strength—had an inner fortification with a third tier of heavy guns. On the sea wall there were nine batteries ; along the shore there were three, as well as a very heavy fort ; in short, the town had been fortified with very considerable skill. Its approaches were defended by scarcely less than five hundred guns, placed in situations so commanding as might well justify the widely held belief that Algiers was impregnable.

Three hours had been given for a reply ; and when the boat returned without an answer, the 'Queen Charlotte,' steered by Lord Exmouth's veteran master, Mr. Gaze, moved forward silently to her position ; she anchored by the stern, just half a cable's length from the mole, in such a position that her broadside flanked all the batteries from the mole head to the lighthouse. The crew gave three cheers. The sound of the defiance had scarcely died away when a gun thundered out its answer from the eastern battery, followed by another and a third. At the first flash Pellew cried out, 'Stand by ;' at the second, 'Fire.' The bombardment of Algiers had begun.

Only one other ship had reached her station. To see the others coming up steadily and without confusion under the tremendous fire which rolled already over the whole harbour from every battery that could bring its guns to bear, was a very noble sight. There was intense eagerness to secure places in the front row. Some succeeded, others failed; but it may be observed that Captain Wise, of the 'Granicus,' a small frigate which could not naturally aspire to a prominent place in work so deadly as was then in progress, had the self-control to wait behind till all other ships had taken up their stations; and then, setting his topgallant sails and courses, steered audaciously for Lord Exmouth's flag, which he saw towering over the thick smoke, and anchored in the open space between the 'Queen Charlotte' and the 'Superb,' so equalling his small craft with battleships of the largest size; thus the last were among the first.

The fire from the 'Queen Charlotte' was so well directed that, if Osler's account be accurate, the batteries on the mole were silenced in a few minutes, and the gunners were at liberty to concentrate themselves on those in the neighbourhood of the lighthouse. Now, the Dey did not rely on his batteries alone, but had confidence in the traditional prowess of his Moors in boarding onslaughts, whereby they carried nearly all the vessels which they attacked upon the sea. He had accordingly equipped a fleet of thirty-seven gunboats packed with men, all picked and desperate fighters; and seeing that his batteries were tumbling faster than he liked into a row of rubbish heaps, he

[Photo by *Durrant & Son, Torquay*] [From a painting in the possession of *Lord Exmouth*]

CAPTURE OF 'LA VIRGINIE,' FRENCH FRIGATE, OF 44 GUNS, BY H.M.S. 'INDEFATIGABLE,' COMMANDED BY SIR EDWARD PELLEW, BY MOONLIGHT, APRIL 21ST, 1797

concluded that the moment had arrived for sweeping the infidels off their decks. The gunboats were accordingly ordered to advance, and the whole flotilla swooped down with what suddenness they might on the 'Queen Charlotte' and the 'Leander,' which formed the centre of the fight. But quick as was their onslaught, the defence was quicker. Pellew's gunners had the range. A storm of heavy shot swept over the waters of the harbour; and when the smoke drifted up, thirty-three out of the fleet of gunboats had gone down, their crews were struggling in the water, and the risk of boarders was at an end.

About four o'clock, having got the batteries in his immediate neighbourhood pretty well in hand, Lord Exmouth was at liberty to turn his attention to the shipping in the port, which he accordingly proceeded to set on fire. As one by one the long pirate galleys were ignited, and the flames spread upwards to their masts and rigging, the scene became very grand and awful. It was growing dusk. Though silenced here and there, the batteries were very active still, and the air was thick with the din of cannon and the loud reports of burning timbers. The hottest fire was that directed on the 'Impregnable,' which had drawn upon herself the fire of batteries so heavy and well served that she had lost 150 men killed and wounded; and Admiral Milne now sent word to Lord Exmouth that he would be glad if a frigate could be sent to draw off some of the attention he was receiving from the Moors. Unfortunately the wind was almost still; the landward breeze on which Pellew had counted for extricating himself from the harbour had not risen yet; and no frigate could reach the station where the 'Impregnable' lay. It mattered little at the stage now reached. The day was lost, and the Algerines knew it. One by one as the sky darkened the batteries ceased to spit out flame, but the harbour was ablaze like one huge bonfire; and to increase the grandeur of the scene a terrible storm of thunder and lightning burst over the ruined town, bringing with it the wished-for breeze, so that as the ships moved out upon the open sea they looked back upon a sight which Pellew said truly was like Pandemonium.

In this great engagement the English loss amounted to no less than 128 killed and 690 wounded; while the Dutch, who fought with a skill and courage which it is almost impertinent to praise, lost upon their smaller squadron thirteen killed and fifty-two wounded. It was a heavy toll of blood, and yet a small price for the service done; for the great tyranny was shattered, and the breaking dawn was the signal for release to many a wretched captive who had taught himself to expect nothing from each recurring day except increase of misery. There was a Neapolitan lady of distinction there, carried off and enslaved with her eight children, of whom six were living still. A British officer had lately seen and spoken to her in the thirteenth year of her foul slavery. Hers was not a solitary case. One can scarcely realise the alternations of hope and fear which these miserable people suffered during the bombardment, or the stunned bewilderment with which they learnt on the following morning that deliverance had come indeed.

For the Dey had yielded utterly. And that morning there were set at liberty Christian slaves in the numbers set forth below:

Neapolitans and Sicilians	1,110
Sardinians and Genoese	62
Piedmontese	6
Romans	174
Tuscans	6
Spaniards	226
Portuguese	1
Greeks	7
Dutch	28
English	18

Rarely has it fallen to any warrior to deliver so many who were oppressed, or play the knight errant on such a scale as this. As for the merits of the fight itself, they were extolled most highly by those who knew best the risk and difficulty which had been surmounted. There was one man qualified above all others to estimate them; and this is what Lord Cochrane said: 'No one was better acquainted than himself with the power possessed by batteries over a fleet; and he would say that the conduct of Lord Exmouth and the fleet deserved all the praise which that House could bestow, for he never knew or had heard of anything more gallant than the manner in which Lord Exmouth laid his ships alongside the Algerine batteries.'

When one hero speaks to praise another with the full knowledge which his own deeds give him, lesser men may be content to listen silently. I add nothing therefore to this brief outline save a hope that Lord Exmouth, that strong fighter, may not be forgotten by Cornwall, whom he himself never forgot; but that in the present time, when examples of strength and fortitude are sorely needed, his great actions may serve to stimulate others among his own people, so that when the storm bursts and the day of trial comes, Cornish sailors may stand once more where Pellew and Boscawen stood.

ARTHUR H. NORWAY.

BY PLEASANT STREAMS

Flumina amem silvasque inglorius

I. BY ONE WHO ANGLES

IT is very difficult to convince those fishermen or laymen whose estimate of trout is cramped by what they see as they stand on the bridge at Salisbury, or by what they catch in the Test, that there is any particular *kudos* in taking the little three or four ounce trout of the moors in Cornwall. There is a chance for some little condescending congratulation from a cosmopolitan who, in his pursuit of fresh fields, takes things as they are wherever he is; but from the angler who is compelled to fix his limit to eleven or twelve inches in length, or a pound in weight, there comes only a lofty sympathy for him whose lines are cast in such unfortunate places.

Now, all this kind concern is sympathy wasted. The fisher for little trout has large pretensions. He backs his basket by weight, and his sport by number, against that of his rival, and would certainly not make a change of residence to the neighbourhood of big fish a permanent one. Would he give up the rough, breezy, rocky moorlands, or the woody, winding, flower-bedecked valleys, for the rushy, flat marshes, the rich pasturages, and the lawn-like meadows? Would he leave the noisy, eager, sparkling stream for the dignified, placid, weedy river? No, certainly not; not even if his only end in fishing were fish.

His primary intent is trout, of course, and he likes to get a big one now and then for the sake of the fight, and because he knows that, for the welfare of the others, the big chap is better out than in; for he is a terribly malignant cannibal, and very indifferent at table. But the big one is a scarce fish, and, besides that, he is a recluse, and gets off as soon as possible into the deep pool which he abides in and monopolises. The clear, pebble-bottomed, shallow runs, which his little congeners will dart and bustle through, will hardly, excepting in a freshet, cover him deeper than his lateral line. In fact, generally speaking, he is not at home, and he is not wanted to be by either fish or fishers.

There is a typical little trout stream which rises some eight or nine hundred feet up on the moors under the Cheesewring. It can, without much difficulty, after a mile's career as a stream, be jumped across, yet there are pools here some five and six feet deep, and in them are hundreds of pretty little trout, five or six inches long, and perfectly mature. Huge moss-covered, granite boulders are littered round, in the stream and out of it. The soil is peaty, and the trout are consequently dark-backed, but the edging of the dorsal fin, and the gold and yellow spots are exquisitely brilliant.

Pick out a breezy day, hide yourself as cunningly as possible behind a rock or where else may be convenient, and offer them a single yellow dun or other such moor fly. You may at first suffer some qualms of conscience about basketing even the best of the little fellows, but when you are reconciled to the fact that they are all small, that they fight splendidly, and last, but by no means least, that they make a breakfast fit for the most fastidious, your conscience will cease from troubling.

A little further down, the stream reaches the margin of the upland moor, and plunges, step after step, around and over boulders, rushing through gullies, hurrying and tumbling along for nearly half a mile. In every pool of this locally and very reasonably called 'cascade' there are trout, and every pool may be fished! Down at the bottom in the meadow it weds with another stream coming from somewhere else, and together they go on merrily, stopping every now and then to take matters easily in a long deep pool, until some poisonous pollution is met and all fish life finishes. Hemmed into the upper waters of the Lynher the fish grow and multiply.

THE CASCADE

Let us look at the course of the stream which joined with it at the bottom of the cascade. That, too, is of moorland origin, and when it leaves its upland course is utilised to make the beautiful and indispensable watercourse through the park at Trebartha. First, it runs through a succession of ponds, bounded thickly by rare rhododendrons, and holding innumerable trout. Here, with plenty of room and food, they grow to be very much bigger than the average of those living entirely in the stream. From one pond to the other there are capital spawning grounds, and progress and egress are easy. Each pond is several feet below the other, and capital sport is got in the whole of them—the supply being easily kept up from

TREBARTHA

the prolific breeding of the indigenous fish only, and not by the addition of outsiders. At the bottom of the ponds the stream runs through the park, and here, as the course is somewhat level, hundreds of tons of granite boulders have been artificially introduced, making the pools, and runs, and eddies the most perfect fishing that can be desired.

There are hundreds of trout here; none of them big, but all pretty, and game as can be. No fish of any other class or species have ever been introduced. Talk to the owner about putting in some Loch Levens, or Rainbows, or any other of the pool-loving, quick-growing trout, and he will doubtless, by implication only, of course, advise you to mind your own business.

Without going many miles from this stream you shall find another, the offspring of a desolate moorland pool above Temple—a stream which, as it runs along through undulating gorse, and ferns, and peaty marshes, bending round hillocks, and falling over rocks, shows itself from a distance as a long silvery line, at places thin and almost lost

THE CASCADE.

to the eye, at others a wide reflecting, glittering streak. It is lonely fishing, of course, and perhaps the angler may look along for a mile, even on the best of sporting days, and not see a soul to relieve the moor monotony. But there are fish here by the hundred.

One day I tried this water. There was a stiff breeze up stream, and the tiny little wavelets made every dark and deep pool fishable. As I swished the line over the left shoulder, and let the couple of small flies go in almost anyhow, the trout seemed at times to struggle for precedence in the matter of taking. There was none of the dignified scrutiny, and the contemptuous refusal, or slow, bulging take of the educated and pampered trout about these fellows: they simply took. After an hour and a half they absolutely, and as if by common agreement, declined to take, neither coming up to look, nor even condescending, or conascending, to investigate. These little fish are not so unsophisticated that they will take whatever is offered whenever it is offered. They, as well as their big relations, have their humours.

Photo by] [J. H. Coath, Liskeard.
GOLETHA FALLS

I shall never forget one little incident of the rise. I had cast into a long, deep, dark pool, and my fly seemed to stop where it fell, and become fast. Then it moved up stream and I felt the weight of a big fish. It did not disturb the surface, nor did it put on any pace, and I was at a loss to know what the fish was like. By-and-by it came to the top, and I saw it was a trout. Dipping gently but resolutely down, and showing its wide tail above the water, it again took matters easy up and down the pool. It was evidently too lazy to jump a bit and show fight, or to change its venue of operations to another pool, and it may have underestimated the power of the wretched little attachment it could not rid itself of. At any rate, its movements were confined to going evenly, and without spurting up and down. When it was done up it came towards me along the surface, open mouthed, and I hauled it clumsily enough on to the bank, where it gave a gasp or two and died. It weighed two pounds three ounces and was the ugliest, biggest headed fish I ever saw. If trout can experience and express feelings of relief there must have been a pæan of rejoicings among the rest when that beast was taken out.

Then, what more desirable homes can trout want than the upper moorland parts of the Camel and the Fowey? Here are the maximum of seclusion with the minimum of molestation, and, for the angler, perfect quiet. Here the little inhabitants will mount indefatigably to the very sources and revel in their confined quarters. From Palmer's Bridge, under which the Fowey as a trickling streamlet crosses the Bodmin road, down through a heavy, rocky bed, by moorland banks, leaving the Dozmare Pool with its legends on the right, and the Hurlers with their history on the left, on to Redgate and Goletha Falls, where the pools get deeper, the trout get bigger, and an occasional salmon finds its way up to associate with the trout, all is as varied and delightful as the most ardent landscape-loving wanderer and fisher can even hope for.

Photo by]   [*J. H. Couth, Liskeard*
BELOW GOLETHA FALLS

The feature of moorland trout is the evenness of the stock. If there is plenty of natural food there is always plenty of trout, and as the moors are parts of a landscape which are rarely ever meddled with by the builder or the cultivator, there are as many trout now as there were hundreds of years ago.

NUSS MAYO.

OLD MAN'S CORNER

CORNISH CAVE-DWELLERS

People in the habit of frequenting the shore of Whitsand Bay between Looe and Downderry are familiar with the sight of a couple of women moving about amongst the rocks exposed at low tide. They are shell-fish gatherers who live in a small cave a little to the west of Seaton. The illustration shows almost the extent of this cleft in the shaly cliff, and anyone who examines the place must wonder how two human beings can exist there. Along one side is a strip of sand, and from that the floor slopes upward at an angle of about sixty degrees. Whether by years of practice the women have attained such perfection in the art of balancing their bodies that they go to sleep on the slanting rock without fear of falling, or whether they rest on the sand (wet, when I saw it, from a late storm), I was not informed; but it is evident that they know no comfort at any time. When I came suddenly upon the cave one morning in October the smouldering ashes of a drift-wood fire, a kettle, a teapot, and two cups were dotted about just inside; further up the floor their 'cupboards'—a couple of iron boilers —were standing; and in a niche near the fire was a pipe—short, dark, and odorous. The women who have made this their dwelling-place are Irish widows, 'born in Ireland and married in Ireland,' as one of them said. They are between fifty and sixty years of age, and for the last thirty years have managed to gain a sustenance by gathering limpets week after week and taking them to Plymouth. When the sea is rough they obtain few or no fish, but under favourable circumstances the two sometimes get fourteen shillings a week between them. In fine weather, when from Rame Head to Looe Island the sea lies calm and glistening under a summer sky, this smoke-blackened cave is an uninviting hovel; and in the winter, especially when there is a gale from the south-east, the women must be almost blown out of the hollow or frozen to death. On some such occasions they are forced to leave the cave, and then they go to a disused pigsty near by. In talking with them while they dexterously chipped limpets from the weed-mantled rocks, I mildly remarked that workhouses were now made very comfortable. Immediately the younger woman stood erect and, with something akin to pride and determination, exclaimed in a voice more than tinctured by the Irish patois,

Photo by]   *[Coath, Liskeard*

'Never, sir, will us go to the workhouse while us can get as much as one crust in twenty-four hours.' Hitherto I had seen her only in a stooping attitude, and I was surprised now to see how tall a woman she was, and what strength of character was indicated by her features. As she stood there amongst the sea-weed, with feet and legs bare and her hair confined by a handkerchief, beating the palm of one hand with the knuckles of the other to emphasise her words, it dawned upon me that I had named the thing against which those two women have fought grimly for more than a quarter of a century.   A. B.

TO THE QUEEN'S MOST EXCELLENT MAJESTY

The humble and dutiful Petition of the Working Miners, their Wives and others employed in the Mines of Cornwall.

Most Gracious Sovereign.

WE, your Majesty's faithful and dutifully attached Subjects, whose daily bread and every earthly comfort depend upon the working of the Mines in the County of Cornwall, venture to approach our Queen in the full confidence that Her gracious protection will be vouchsafed to us at this moment of peril to our most vital interests, on our humbly and dutifully representing to your Majesty that the wages of the Cornish Miner are so low at present, that every measure which would seriously depress the produce of the Mines, will deprive most of us of our means of subsistence.

That, in many instances, he labours during eight hours out of the twenty-four at the depth of 1,800 feet below the surface ; and, as he is obliged to undergo the exhausting fatigue of climbing ladders to and from that great depth during two hours more, in addition to the task of his every-day walks from his dwelling to the Mine, and home again,—we humbly submit that none of your Majesty's subjects earn their livelihood by more severe bodily exertion.

That nearly a Million Sterling has been the annual remuneration exchanged for this daily labour, and is the working Miners' only capital ; but we look forward with alarm at the prospect of the Home Market for Tin and Copper being inundated by the introduction of such Metals from abroad, in consequence of the proposed reduction of those protecting duties which have hitherto induced our richer fellow subjects to embark large Capitals in the Gigantic Mining Undertakings of Cornwall, with the hope of deriving a benefit from the Speculation.

That the intended future comparatively free importation of foreign ores into your Majesty's United Kingdom of Great Britain and Ireland will expose us to a competition with Countries, whose ores not only contain a far greater portion of Metal than what is contained in the Cornish ores, but are obtained so much nearer to the Earth's surface, that the very expensive and complicated Machinery, so essentially necessary for the working of the Cornish Mines, is not there required.

That it is impossible to calculate the extent of the supply ; but so rapid has been the increase of Copper, that from 373 tons of metal in 1834 it increased during the last year to more than 10,000 tons, whereas from the consequent gloom thereby thrown over British Mining, its produce, during the same period, became reduced from 13,341 tons to 10,799 tons, and during the single month of March last, the ores from Cuba and Chili alone sold for 85,196$l.$, whilst those raised in Cornwall produced but 61,959$l.$, and that during the first fortnight of the present month, the ores from the Foreign Mines sold for 59,145$l.$ 4. 0, whilst those from Cornwall made only 28,062$l.$ 17. 0.

That, under these circumstances, we humbly submit to your Majesty, that the introduction of the produce of Foreign ores into the Home Market, considering the richness of the Mines abroad, and the easy manner of obtaining them, must have the effect of soon stopping the deep Mines of Cornwall, unless much better protection than that proposed by the present Tariff be immediately granted to the British Miner.

That, as the present shallow Mines, by proper working, will soon become deep, their destruction must, from the same causes, consequently follow,—and, as there will be no inducement to risk the opening of new Mines in Cornwall whilst the Foreign Miner is afforded such encouragement by the Government of this Country ; Mining, in Cornwall, cannot probably long survive the loss of that protection which the present Tariff is intended to destroy.

That your Majesty's Ministers calculate on the increased employment which an extra quantity of Foreign Copper ores would give to the English smelters, without considering that every ton of such Copper Ores must, from their superior richness, displace nearly 3 tons of British ores ; and, consequently, a less number of Smelters would be required,—such extra quantity of Foreign ores would, indeed, not only require less Smelters to bring them into metal ; but for every Smelter so employed, about 25 of your Majesty's loyal, faithful, and dutiful Subjects, the Miners of Cornwall, must lose their employment, although capable of raising within the Cornish Mining District, under fair protection, both Tin and Copper ores sufficient to supply the whole world with metal.

That we believe that your Majesty's Ministers, when they first determined on depriving us of that protection under which such immense sums of money have been expended in opening the Cornish Mines, were not duly advised as to the amount of protection necessary to be substituted in lieu thereof; and, that they not only allowed their first Tariff to be essentially altered at the request of those who have already reaped enormous profits by the employment of *Slaves* (to our great injury) in the Foreign Mines; but when the defects of such and subsequent alterations were pointed out to them by our Employers, we are informed that your Majesty's Ministers' proposals to extend the amount of the present intended protection, so far as they themselves admitted that they could do with safety, were actually frustrated by the unconstitutional and unjust interference of the *Slave* Employers in the Cobre Mine! That, therefore, your Majesty's dutiful, loyal, and humble Subjects are driven to the sad conclusion, that your Majesty's advisers are about to pass a law, without duly considering or knowing the evils which it will produce,—or that they have been improperly influenced, directly or indirectly, by the very workers of the Foreign mines, to frame that part of the Tariff for their benefit, and not ours,—in coming to which last conclusion, we are borne out by an attempted apology for the conduct of your Majesty's Ministers in their own daily organ, the Standard Paper, which on Monday last, after speaking of the ruin of the Cornish Miners, and the loss that it would be to the Crown, stated " that the money power of some Rich Mine Owners was the author of the evil, and that Ministers being unable to resist the money power must yield to it."

That, as we are fully prepared to establish beyond dispute the facts stated in this petition, we humbly but fervently pray, that your most gracious Majesty will not allow the projected Tariff to receive the Royal assent, because it is full of danger to the prosperity of your Majesty's most loyal County of Cornwall, and calculated to ruin about one hundred thousand of her population, whose daily livelihood is directly provided by our earnings in the Mines; and to impoverish just as many more, who, as Merchants, Ship-owners, Carriers, Founders, and Tradesmen in every branch of commerce, are indirectly benefited by supplying our wants, and the various Machinery and Stores necessary to carry on works of such national importance, which, if now destroyed by improper legislation, would (should a war break out) be found wanting when too late to be restored.

That such interference on the part of your most gracious Majesty to prevent the Tariff becoming Law will save from its, otherwise, most disastrous effects the Inhabitants generally of your faithful and peaceable County of Cornwall, and more particularly ourselves and families, who have no other view of gaining a livelihood but by the Mines, whilst the introduction of Foreign Tin and Copper ores, at the low rate of duty proposed by your Majesty's Ministers, will not confer any adequate advantage upon so numerous a class of your Majesty's subjects, even supposing it were justifiable to ruin one class for the benefit of another.

Devotedly attached as we are to your Majesty and to our Country, and ever ready to sacrifice our lives in the defence of either, we venture to assure your Majesty of our determination to act in obedience to the law, and to all who are duly commissioned to administer it, without listening to the false advice of those who may endeavour to promote disaffection, notwithstanding the distress to which we may be exposed, well knowing our duty towards our most Gracious Sovereign, for whom we shall ever pray.

June 24th, 1842.

In June last Mr. Box, of Clubworthy Farm, North Petherwyn, discovered a jug (see sketch) under the eaves of a thatched roof of an outhouse on his farm. It had a piece of rag for a stopper, and contained 199 shillings of the reigns of Edward VI., Philip and Mary, Elizabeth, James I., Charles I., and Charles II. The greatest number by far were of the time of Charles II. The jug and the coins were at first claimed by the Treasure Trove Office, but have since been returned to the finder. It is a brown glazed earthenware jug, and was made at Cologne about 1660. There is an inscription in German, somewhat

Two-thirds of the actual size. *Side View*

blundered, as follows : 'Des heren Wort Bleit im ew(igkeit),' which is twice repeated in circling the jug. Mr. H. C. Gruelier, of the British Museum, gives as the translation of the inscription, 'The word of God remains for ever.'

The legends on specimen coins are :—

Two-thirds of the actual size. *Front View*

EDWARD VI.
Reverse obliterated.

Edward VI.—Edward. VI. D. G. Agl : Fra : Z. Hib : Rex :

PHILIP AND MARY

Philip and Mary.—Philip et Maria D.
G. R. Ang: Fr: Neap: Pr: Hisp: 1554.
Philip. et Maria D. G. Rex et Regina
Ang: 1555.

ELIZABETH

Elizabeth.—Elizab: D. G. Ang: Fr:
et Hib: Reg: I. Posui Deū adivtorem
meū: I.
Elizabeth D. G. Ang: Fra: et Hib:
Regina.

JAMES I.

James I.—Jacobus D. G. Ang: Sco:
Fra: et Hib: Rex: XII. Exurgat Deus
Dissipentur inimici.

Jacobus D. G. Mag: Brit: Fra: et
Hib: Rex: XII. Quæ Deus coniunxit
nemo separet.

CHARLES I.

Charles I.—Carolus D. G. Mag: Br:
Fr: et Hi: Rex: XII. Christo auspice
Regno.

CHARLES II.

Charles II.—Carolus II. D. G. Mag:
Bri: Fra: et Hib: Rex: XII. Christo
auspice Regno.

I believe it was formerly a custom for
persons living in the country districts of
this neighbourhood not to keep money in
the house. Last week an old lady told
me she remembered that her grandmother
used always to keep the money under the
thatch of the barn roof.

OTHO B. PETER.

Northernhaye, Launceston.

CORNISH DIAMONDS

'Ee was a kind-hearted man, he was,' said Uncle Billy. 'Ef you was going to kill a flea he'd say, "Lave un lone, poor thing, e's got to arn es livan."'

———

'I thot 'twere she, and she thot 'twere I,' said Gracey Temby, 'but when we come close 'twadn't narry wan oo us.'

———

Two miners met on Illogan Downs at ten o'clock in the morning.

'Where going this time o' day cummraade?'

'Goin' 'ome; ben to bal, fust coor; got hit spar in me eye; goin' 'ome to bed to slape en out.'

———

'I d' hear tell the Emperor of Germany's gone dead.'

'Ah! Gone dead es a?'

'I ss.'

A pause.

'Ah! And who's carrying on the business?'

———

'I'm afraid, Jenny, you irritate your husband with your long tongue.'

'Aw, no, my dear Miss Vivian. I'd never say nawthen to en. T'other day I was 'ome waiting for'n to come 'ome to supper. Eight o'clock come, an' no Jan; nine o'clock come, an' no Jan; ten o'clock come, an' no Jan. I put up me bonnet an' shoul an' went to every kiddly-wink in town, thout Dyke Winsor's. When I come there, there wor Jan. Says I, "You uggly murderen vellan, theest killed thee fust wife an' now theest want to kill me too;" an' he up an' knacked me down.'

———

'Where gwain, you?'

'Down along.'

'What for?'

'A happerd a salt.'

'How ar'ee gwain to buy so much en?'

'Granny likes it fresh and fresh.'

———

'I'd as soon dig a grave for you, Cap'en Toby, as any man I know,' said a sexton to a mine manager in a burst of admiration.

———

Labourer (mopping his brow): 'Aw, missus, do 'ee give me a drink; I'm dying uv thirst.'

Farmer's wife hands him a jug of cider from a barrel not popular with the household.

Labourer (returning the jug after the first mouthful): 'Thank 'ee, missus, I baint quite so thirsty es I thought.'

———

In the days when tallow candles were used to light churches and chapels, the wife of a vicar in a certain fishing village gave a pair of snuffers to the old man who had charge of the candles, and, after examining them with silent wonderment, he promised to use them on the following Sunday. Going down the aisle in proud possession of the snuffers, he shortened the wick with his thumb and forefinger, and, opening the box of the snuffers, dropped in the piece of charred wick with the remark: 'Bless me, what a 'andy place to put 'en!'

A Grace for a Child.
by Robert Herrick

Here a little Child I stand
heaving up my either hand;
Cold as paddocks though they be,
Here I lift them up to Thee,
For a benison to fall
on our meat and on us all. Amen.

Photo by] [Gibson, Penzance

AROUND THE MANACLES

IN St. Keverne parish and the district round, when the fishermen and farmers talk by the winter fire, they talk of shipwrecks. Old men and women, and those who are not old, reckon by the score vessels that have been lost in their time between Nare Point and the Black Head; and sometimes, when the flames dance on the logs and light up the faces of a family group, an old man, or maybe an old woman, almost forgotten in the corner, recalls things told by a former generation, and so the story is traced back far beyond the memory of those now living. But long as is the list made on such occasions, it is far from complete. If you search old documents that deal with such things, your attention will every now and again be arrested by references to ships 'wrecked on rocks about three and a half leagues north-east of the Lizard,' whilst the oldest registers of the parish of St. Keverne record not infrequently the burial of 'a mariner and stranger.'

It should not be supposed that every vessel lost on or near the Manacles has left her name to tell her fate. When, in 1620, Sir John Killigrew was pleading for a lighthouse on the Lizard he wrote: 'Nether is y^t possibell to get parfitt notice of the whence and what the Ships ar that yearly do suffer on and near the Lizard, for y^t is sildom that any man escapes and the ships split in small pieces.' Things are not so bad as that now. For we have a lighthouse on the Lizard; coastguards watch along the cliffs; and lifeboat crews are ready to imperil their lives in going to wrecked vessels. But the least romantic of those dwelling near the Manacles will tell you that even now there occasionally goes down some craft that leaves nothing behind her but the bubbles that rise to the surface and disappear. Certain it is, at any rate, that cottagers and farmers have been aroused by the knockings of a few survivors who battled their way to shore from ships that in the darkness disappeared entirely amongst the rocks; and only a short time ago there was found just west of the Manacles a wheel bearing the name of a vessel no one remembered as having been wrecked on the coast.

'The Manacles' is the inclusive title of a number of rocks that stand between a quarter of a mile and a mile from the shore, and extend for a mile along it, beginning a little to the south-west of the small cove and fishing village of Porthoustock. All except one, Carn dû, are covered at high-water springs, but several are exposed at other stages of the tide, and always treacherous points and ledges lurk below the surface. Between some of the rocks there is water deep enough for the passage of large vessels, though only men who know the rocks thoroughly can with safety venture amongst them. It is said that in the early part of the last century, when mails were carried in the face of great dangers, a Falmouth packet, run close by a French frigate, was taken through the Manacles, and thus the French vessel was lured to destruction.

'Manacles' is a corruption of two Cornish words *maen eglos*, meaning 'church stones,' and it is a matter of controversy whether they were so called because mariners remembered their position by the spire of St. Keverne Church, on the high ground immediately behind them, or because they are visible from the church tower. Each stone has its separate name, and to show

ST. KEVERNE FROM THE CHURCH TOWER

that landmarks are connected with the designations of some stones it may be mentioned that Maentrenoweth is in line with Trenoweth, half a mile from St. Keverne Church.

When Napoleon had scared half the world, and England waited with anxiety for news from Spain, there befell on the Manacles disasters that shocked the whole country, and caused men to forget for a brief space the state of things abroad and the inquiries that were being made by Parliament into the conduct of a person of high degree who had been writing to the wife of a London stonemason as 'My dear, dear Polly.' About two hundred officers and men of his Majesty King George's army were drowned and two ships and their contents were lost in a few hours. More than half the men were of the 7th (Queen's Own) Regiment of Hussars, who had been fighting in Spain under Sir John Moore. The others were outward bound for foreign service.

To appreciate adequately the condition of those who had been doing duty from Sahagun to Corunna it is necessary to recall the circumstances under which the British army marched and fought. And that is done effectually by reading the statement, published in the 'Royal Cornwall Gazette' in January 1809, of a soldier who had returned: 'He marched from Lisbon, with General Hope's brigade, to Madrid, thence to Salamanca, and ultimately to Corunna. In all this march, 1,300 miles, they had never seen a Spanish regiment; the fatigues and privations which the British army sustained were extreme; and, although amongst the Spanish gentry the officers sometimes met with civility, the peasantry (indifferent to all parties and alarmed at the appearance of soldiers) would shut their doors against them. In the meantime the strictest discipline was observed, and every attempt at plunder was severely punished. The country in general exhibited nothing but poverty and wretchedness; the roads were bad, often flooded with rain, and sometimes covered with snow; the British soldiers were frequently a whole day without sustenance, and slept at night on the bare ground, happy if they could approach a horse and sleep under his neck for warmth and shelter. In this combination of evils many men died; horses were knocked up, were shot, and left with all their accoutrements upon the road.' It is elsewhere recorded 'that fine regiment, the 7th, had scarcely one hundred horses left fit for service.'

On January 14, 1809, two days before the death of Sir John Moore, three officers, seventy-two non-commissioned officers and privates, and thirty-six horses of the 7th Dragoons left Corunna in the transport 'Dispatch,' George Fenwick, master, for England. Two other officers, Cornishmen, of the same regiment, Lieutenant-Colonel Vivian and Captain Treweeke, also went on board the 'Dispatch' with the idea of going home in her, but their friend, Captain Linzee, invited them to return in the 'Barfleur,' and they did so.

The weather in England at this time was exceedingly rough and cold. Its nature will be gathered from the fact that on January 19 a miller's boy in Kent picked up ninety-five larks, twenty-six rooks, three partridges, and two pheasants that had been frozen to death in one field. Similar reports came from all parts of the country. Snow fell on the 21st and continued throughout

COTTAGES AT PORTHOUSTOCK

the night, accompanied by wind that blew with hurricane force. At half-past three on Sunday morning the 'Dispatch,' an old ship in bad repair, was driven on the rocks near Lowland Point, and speedily became a total wreck. While men and women were rushing through the gale with news of this disaster, and men and horses were being dashed about by the roaring sea, there came tidings that at the other end of the Manacles another ship filled with soldiers was foundering. In those days there was no Lifeboat Institution with its record of gallant services all along the coast. But there were men of the sort that the grandest lifeboat crews are made of, and six Porthoustock fishermen, taking the best boat they could find, went out from their cove across the wind-torn sea towards the rocks barely discernible in the early morning light. Little it was that they could do, though, and worn out with their strivings against the wind and sea, they returned with only one boy and the news that the vessel disappeared almost immediately after she struck, at five o'clock, and all except the boy were lost. There was uncertainty amongst them and the group that had watched for their returning as to what the name of the vessel was. From papers washed ashore she seemed to be the 'Triumph,' but when the boy, John Meaghen, was able to talk he told them that she was his Majesty's brig of war 'Primrose,' eighteen guns, James Mein, commander, outward bound. On board the 'Primrose' when she struck there were 120 officers and men and six passengers. Of these the boy alone remained, and from the 'Dispatch' only seven private dragoons came ashore alive. So the total loss of life around the Manacles in the early hours of that Sunday morning was about 200. The officers of the 7th Light Dragoons drowned were Major George Henry Compton Cavendish, son of Lord George Cavendish, of Eastbourne, afterwards created Earl of Burlington; Captain S. G. Dunkenfield; and Lieutenant the Hon. Edward Waldegrave, third son of the fourth Earl of Waldegrave. On that and succeeding days there were scenes along the shore that made men's minds reel. At one time fifty bodies of officers and men lay strewn along a beach, and Captain Treweeke, who came to Plymouth in the 'Barfleur,' and reached Truro an hour or two before news of the disasters was brought to that place, recognised amongst them Major Cavendish, his brother officer. In his hasty journey to Coverack, Captain Treweeke was accompanied by Mr. John Vivian (a brother of the Lieut.-Colonel Vivian who returned in the ' Barfleur '), and as soon as possible six of the surviving dragoons were conveyed to Truro, where they were entertained at the house of Lieut.-Colonel Vivian's father. The other dragoon was too badly bruised to travel, and between him and the boy from the ' Primrose ' there is woven in ' The Roll Call of the Reef ' a strange and pathetic friendship which one likes to believe had an existence in reality.

Until 1808 no provision was made by the laws for the suitable interment of unclaimed dead bodies cast ashore by the sea, but in that year an Act was passed stating that they must be buried in the parish churchyard. In some places it was the practice until then to inter them on the cliff or in any convenient piece of ground, though the registers of the parish of St. Keverne prove that long before that time such bodies were buried in the churchyard.

About one hundred and ten bodies of those who belonged to the ' Dispatch ' and the ' Primrose ' were found in the immediate neighbourhood, and 104 of them were buried by the Rev. William Whitehead, minister, in St Keverne Churchyard between January 24 and April 2. The bodies of officers of the Dragoons were taken to the vaults of their families, and that of Captain Mein, of the ' Primrose,' was interred at Falmouth with military honours. In St.

Photo by] [*Burrow, Camborne*
ST. KEVERNE CHURCH

Keverne Church, against the western end of the south wall, a tablet was placed by the officers, non-commissioned officers, and men of the 7th Dragoons to the memory of their comrades who were drowned. Near the top of it there is a ship on a stormy sea, and below the inscription a rifle, pistol, sword, and flags are carved in the marble.

Photo by] ONE OF THE 'MOHEGAN'S' STEEL BOATS *[Gibson, Penzance*

I stated that six Porthoustock fishermen went out to search as soon as they heard that a vessel had gone down not far from their cove. They were George Tonkin, Stephen Old, Edward Tonkin, William Matthews, Bartholomew Tripp, and Joseph Matthews, and when what they had done became known the Government sent ten guineas for each man and expressed admiration of the way they risked their lives for the only survivor from the 'Primrose.' It is remarkable that amongst the men who did noble work in the lifeboat when the 'Mohegan' sank there were five named Tripp.

In these days it is a quite common occurrence to meet with landsmen full of knowledge as to how a vessel came to get upon the Manacles. And as they run their forefingers across a chart and talk about 'opening out the Eddystone and Lizard lights' one becomes convinced that it is a simple and a safe thing for any one to attempt to bring a large steamer from the Strait of Dover to the Atlantic. Men of this kind were not scarce in 1809. And because it is much easier to invent theories than to ascertain the truth the race will flourish and increase to the end of time. One chronicler states 'it was conjectured that the captain of the "Dispatch" kept near the shore for the purpose of stranding his vessel in order to obtain the exorbitant value contracted for with the Government, and that in attempting this fraud he fell on the rocks.' The historian who sought to explain the cause of the loss of the 'Dispatch' did not say why the 'Primrose' was near the shore. Nor does he tell us how the 'Nancy,' of Plymouth, and the 'Catherine,' of Bideford, came to be wrecked at Scilly; through what dishonesty 'a trade vessel of considerable tonnage' was dashed to pieces on rocks near Mullion; what was the cause of the 'Rose,' Captain Knight, sailing from Plymouth to Falmouth with twenty-six passengers, being lost with all on board near Looe Island; and what compelled the 'Orion,' transport, Captain Martin, from Corunna with camp equipage, to go ashore at Crow Sound, Scilly. All these things happened

AROUND THE MANACLES

within a few days of the 'Dispatch' and 'Primrose' being lost, and they testify conclusively that terrific weather prevailed along the southern coast of Cornwall.

New countries with wide prospects were attracting large numbers of people from England and other places about forty years ago, and the records of ships wrecked at that time outline lamentable stories. During the six years from 1852 to 1859 no fewer than 2,892 emigrants lost their lives from eleven ships, one of which was run on the Manacles. This was the 'John,' of Plymouth, 468 tons, which used to run between Plymouth and Quebec, taking over emigrants and bringing back timber. When she came home early in 1855, her owners had her overhauled, with the outcome that 2,000l. was spent in repairs. The 'John' was to start for Canada on the afternoon of Thursday, May 3, and through all the forenoon men were finishing the repairs, so that emigrants and cargo had to be hurried aboard. There were two hundred and sixty-eight passengers (including 112 children, of whom sixteen were infants) and a crew of eighteen under the master, Edward Rawle. The weather was fine, and when the 'John' sailed out of Plymouth Sound there was every prospect of a passage as comfortable as was possible in a small ship crowded with men, women, and children. Gaily the square-looking ship went westward with her sails bellying before the N.N.W. breeze, and the passengers watched the sun set, and the moon, one day past her full, rise behind the fleeting clouds. The captain had charge of the vessel all the way down the Channel, but in spite of that she went out of her course, and at ten o'clock struck on one of the outer Manacles, and then drifted shoreward until held fast by other rocks. With proper management almost every one on the ship might have been saved. But the master was not equal to the emergency, and nearly every one of the crew was selfish. Into one boat five of the crew and one passenger scrambled and she drifted to Coverack, where the plight of the emigrant ship was cried. In the meantime the 'John's' lifeboat, neither in its proper place nor prepared for immediate service, was launched with only two, instead of twenty, people in her; and then the captain forbade the launching of any other boats. He appears to have believed he had a safe position and that only patience was needed, for he assured the terror-stricken passengers

COVERACK

there was no danger, and advised them not to try to reach the shore until daylight.

A boat could not be taken against the wind from Coverack to where the 'John' lay, and therefore a messenger was despatched to Porthoustock, three and a half miles off. By half-past twelve, however, when the state of things was made known to the men there, the wind had so risen that it was not possible for them to reach the 'John.'

On board the ship there were panic and despair. She was slowly sinking, and, when the waves covered her deck, men and women gathered their little ones and clambered into the rigging or slipped with them and disappeared in the swirling sea. A father and a mother put their small children into a sheet and tried to hoist them into the rigging, but the fastenings slipped and the children were drowned. Every hour claimed many victims, but still some contrived to cling to the rigging and encourage one another to hold fast and hope. After repeated unsuccessful attempts the Porthoustock men reached the wreck, and by the light that foretold sunrise saw about seventy people in the rigging. No anxiety for the passengers was manifested by either the captain or crew, most of whom were anxious to save themselves and their clothes. The Porthoustock men made three trips between the land and the ship and rescued all they found in the rigging. The captain took care that he

Photo by Harrison, Falmouth]   THE 'JOHN'   [From a painting by Philp in the possession of Dr. Owen, Falmouth

was not the last to leave the 'John,' and he and the mate were the only ones who saved anything besides what they were wearing. In all 91 reached land alive, the remaining 196 being drowned. At the inquest passengers stated that the captain and some of the crew smelt of liquor, and a verdict of manslaughter was returned against Captain Rawle, but at the assizes he was acquitted. Amongst the fishermen whom the jury commended for going from Porthoustock to the wreck was one named James Hill, now coxswain of Porthoustock lifeboat, who, with his crew, worked heroically in saving some of the passengers and crew of the 'Mohegan.'

There is no mural tablet in the church or distinctive headstone in the churchyard concerning the 'John,' but if you bend your back and search diligently amongst the stones bearing names of men and vessels that have a sound strange to English ears, you will discover a piece of slate that has upon its face a ship in a storm and 'Sacred to the memory of 120 persons here interred, who were drowned in the wreck of the "John," May 3, 1855. Erected by one of the survivors.' That is the plain but forceful memorial of those who, from various parts of Devonshire and Cornwall, were on their way to begin the battle of life anew on the other side of the Atlantic.

Even in a locality where wrecks and the loss of life are amongst the yearly happenings it is happily rare that three vessels are split into fragments on the same day. But this was the case at Porthoustock and close to it during the blizzard of March 1891. About noon, people in the cove were startled by seeing a smack in a dangerous position close to the shore. When those on board of her realised that a chance to save their lives could only be seized by beaching her, the second coxswain of the lifeboat, James Henry Cliff, putting a rope round his body and giving the ends of it to men on the beach, rushed into the surf and first brought in a boy, next the mate, and then the captain. The three hands left the 'Dove' just in time to save their lives, for shortly after she was dashed abroad. Hardly had the survivors and spectators realised what had happened when a couple of smacks were seen in a helpless plight in the storm of wind and snow, and before anything could be done for them across the turbulent water they and all on board went down. Stones that could not be moved by the unaided strength of any two men were driven up the beach with boats, spars, and fish ; the great doors of the lifeboat house were broken down ; and the tide rose higher than it had ever before been known to rise. Nothing could be launched from the cove, and those who resided there realised that hard would be the lot of any vessels driven on the rocks. Telegraphic communication between Porthoustock, St. Keverne, and Helston was broken that afternoon by posts being blown down, and consequently the outer world knew nothing of the destruction of life and property that had taken place.

Next morning a farmer, going down on the side of the cove towards Helford River to see how his sheep had fared in the snowstorm, was astonished to see a four-masted ship stranded near Penare Point. He ran for help, and men came and gazed at the stranger covered with snow and long icicles. In the rigging they could see some of the crew, and one or two of the local men

Photo by]   THE 'BAY OF PANAMA'   [*Harrison, Falmouth*

volunteered to swim through the icy water to the ship with a line. Later on the rocket apparatus was used, and nineteen of the crew were saved. Eighteen, including the captain and his wife, perished either from drowning or exposure, several being frozen to death in the rigging. The ship was the 'Bay of Panama,' 2,282 tons register, of Liverpool, on her way from Calcutta to Dundee with about seventeen thousand bales of jute. In the heavy weather of Monday night she sustained damage and lost her captain and boats by seas washing them overboard. Attempts were made to signal to the shore, but wind prevented the rockets rising, and about this time some of the crew, worn by their buffetings by the sea and distracted by the cold and their own helplessness, became delirious and jumped overboard. At half-past two on Tuesday morning the 'Bay of Panama' was driven on the rocks, and before she was discovered some of her crew had been frozen to death in the rigging and on the deck.

Now it was more desirable than ever that news of the disasters should be taken to Falmouth and elsewhere, and Joseph Hendy James, a member of the present Porthoustock lifeboat crew, volunteered to go to Helston with telegrams. By overcoming difficulties scores of men would have declared insurmountable, he reached Helston, and found the railway line blocked, all the telegraph wires broken, and the inhabitants and their visitors snowed up in private houses and hotels. He then tried, against the advice of friends, to ride his pony from Helston to Falmouth, but a mile on the road had to dig the animal out of a drift and resort to walking. For mile after mile he struggled through the feet-deep drifts, and when half the distance had been done began to fear he had undertaken an impossible task. But he was not to be beaten; when almost senseless from cold and exhaustion he was admitted to a house on the roadside, and after resting he continued the journey. To him, however, walking by-and-by became impossible, and so he resorted to crawling on his hands and knees. Two miles and a half were covered in this way and then he reached Falmouth, and delivered the messages from Porthoustock and St. Keverne, and from commercial travellers and others who were snowed up in Helston. For this daring deed he was publicly presented with a purse of gold.

The survivors from the 'Bay of Panama' were conveyed to a farmhouse and then by 'bus to Gweek, from which place they had to walk to Falmouth, as no vehicle could go over the road. Three of them were without boots; the clothing of all of them was thin, and when they reached Falmouth, after the ten-mile walk, their condition was pitiful.

As soon as the gale had ended the owners of the 'Bay of Panama' sent salvors to deal with her cargo, and so successful were they in their work, carried on by night as well as day when the tide suited, that nearly all the jute was taken out of her before she went to pieces in rough weather towards the close of the year. Timbers near Penare Point are shown to visitors as part of the 'Bay of Panama,' but when they have disappeared there will still remain something to remind men of the stranded vessel and the sufferings of her crew, for in the tiny turret of the chapel of ease that Mr. Pendarves Vivian, of Bosahan, had built by the water's edge at Helford, there is the bell that belonged to her, bearing in letters, plain for all to read from the roadway, 'Bay of Panama, London.'

THE 'BAY OF PANAMA,' PORTHOUSTOCK IN DISTANCE.

Not on account of nearness of time does the 'Mohegan' disaster stand prominently amongst the Manacles' victims, but because of the dreadful loss of life associated with it. The 'Mohegan,' a new steamer of about 7,000 gross tonnage, belonging to the Atlantic Transport Company, left Gravesend at noon on October 13 last with fifty-three passengers, a crew of ninety-six, six cattle-men, and a stowaway. She was in charge of the commodore of the fleet to which she belonged, Captain Griffiths, who at half-past two the next afternoon signalled 'All well' to Prawle Point. Four and a half hours later, when the light was good and the wind not high, the 'Mohegan,' going thirteen miles an hour, dashed into Vase Rock, one of the outer Manacles, and within twenty minutes all except the upper portions of the masts and funnel were under water. Half an hour after the 'Mohegan' had sent up signals of distress the Porthoustock lifeboat was launched, but a strong tide, and the fact that every light on the 'Mohegan' went out when the electric light machinery stopped, made the work of rescue comparatively slow. By their bravery and determination the lifeboat crew succeeded, in two journeys, in rescuing forty-four of the passengers and crew from the sea, water-logged boats, and the rigging. One hundred and six persons, including the captain, perished. For conspicuous services on this occasion the Royal National Lifeboat Institution presented the coxswain, James Hill, now sixty-four years of age, with a silver medal, and each one of the crew with a sum of money.

I have mentioned only a few of the vessels known to have been wrecked

Photo by] THE 'MOHEGAN' *[Harrison, Falmouth*

THE 'ANDOLA'
Wrecked in an easterly gale on January 30, 1895. Crew of twenty-eight saved by the Porthoustock Lifeboat.

on the Manacles. But the experiences and the ultimate fate of the others differ only in details. There is nearly always a quick foundering, a struggle of men in the cross-currented sea, and the absence of several who belonged to the vessel when the survivors come to land and look around.

A Porthoustock fisherman not yet past the prime of life gave me from memory the names of thirty steamers, schooners, barques, brigs, brigantines, smacks, and ketches he remembered as having been totally lost close to his home. The names of some of these I found on the board, in Porthoustock lifeboat house, that mentions the services of the 'Mary Ann Story' and the 'Charlotte' since a lifeboat was placed there in 1868; others have their names on headstones on the north side of the ancient church of St. Keverne; but of several there is no record in the locality except in the memories of the people.

Any one who has not been to sea can prove in the course of half an hour's conversation that no vessel going up or down the Channel need be within miles of the Manacles. But many get there; and some are fortunate enough to pass through the maze of rocks without suffering damage. A farmer going along the cliff in thick weather caught sight of a ship's masts just below him when the fog lifted for a moment. He ran to a cove close by and said there was a vessel on the Manacles; but the lifeboat crew was not needed, for the captain of the vessel dropped anchor on finding he was in a dangerous place, and when the fog disappeared took his vessel out beyond the reef. On another occasion a large steamer came so close to the shore that the noise of her engines could be heard distinctly on the cliffs, but she was warned by landsmen and went away.

Captains who get amongst the Manacles do not want any one to know it, and more than one has had a sail dropped over the name of his vessel when threading a course between the rocks of which they had been warned by the firing of guns on shore.

As soon as vessels grate upon the Manacles the crews hastily leave in the boats, but it is not always that the ships sink. A boat was rowed out to a small vessel fixed on the Manacles, and the only man remaining on her was taken off. When close to land the boatmen looked to see whether the vessel had disappeared, and to their surprise and amusement saw her being taken to Falmouth by a pilot boat.

We have the uncontradicted statements of seamen of all classes that the bell-buoy, fixed to one of the outer Manacles, is utterly inadequate to warn vessels of their nearness to danger. And when the sounds of that bell came in the landward breeze to where I stood looking across the reef they seemed, not a message of warning to those who cross the deep, but as the death-knell of the hundreds of men, women, and children who have breathed their last in the sea around the Manacles. That is the only purpose the bell has been serving for the past thirty years or more, and now an additional burden is laid upon it. In wintry days, when the grey-backed sea roars amongst the rocks; through the peaceful hours of starry nights; and in the summer, when the sapphire sea reveals the masts of lost vessels deep down, it will toll on and express something of the desolation of homes in England and America and of the sorrow of a thousand broken hearts.

ALBERT BLUETT.

Photo by]   *[Harrison, Penzance*

A PAIR OF HANDS

AN OLD MAID'S GHOST-STORY

'YES,' said Miss Le Petyt, gazing into the deep fireplace and letting her hands and her knitting lie for the moment idle in her lap. 'Oh, yes, I have seen a ghost. In fact I have lived in a house with one for quite a long time.'

'How you *could*——!' began one of my host's daughters; and '*You*, Aunt Emily?' cried the other at the same moment.

Miss Le Petyt, gentle soul, withdrew her eyes from the fireplace and protested with a gay little smile. 'Well, my dears, I am not quite the coward you take me for. And, as it happens, mine was the most harmless ghost in the world. In fact '— and here she looked at the fire again—' I was quite sorry to lose her.'

'It was a woman, then? Now *I* think,' said Miss Blanche, 'that female ghosts are the horridest of all. They wear little shoes with high red heels, and go about *tap, tap*, wringing their hands.'

'This one wrung her hands, certainly. But I don't know about the high red heels, for I never saw her feet. Perhaps she was like the Queen of Spain, and hadn't any. And as for the hands, it all depends *how* you wring them. There's an elderly shopwalker at Knightsbridge, you know——'

'Don't be prosy, dear. What you know is that we're just dying to hear the story.'

Miss Le Petyt turned to me with a small deprecating laugh. 'It's such a little one.'

'The story, or the ghost?'

'Both.'

And this was Miss Le Petyt's story:—

'It happened when I lived down in Cornwall, at Tresillack on the south coast. Tresillack was the name of the house, which stood quite alone at the head of a coombe, within sound of the sea but without sight of it; for though the coombe led down to a wide open beach, it wound and twisted half a dozen times on its way, and its overlapping sides closed the view from the house, which was advertised as "secluded." I was very poor in those days; your father and all of us were poor then, as I trust, my dears, you will never be; but I was young enough to be romantic and wise enough to like independence, and this word "secluded" took my fancy.

'The misfortune was that it had taken the fancy, or just suited the requirements, of several previous tenants. You know, I dare say, the kind of person who rents a secluded house in the country? Well, yes, there are several kinds;

but they seem to agree in being odious. No one knows where they come from, though they soon remove all doubt about where they're "going to," as the children say. "Shady" is the word, is it not? Well, the previous tenants of Tresillack (from first to last a bewildering series) had been shady with a vengeance.

‘I knew nothing of this when I first made application to the landlord, a solid yeoman inhabiting a farm at the foot of the coombe, on a cliff overlooking the beach. To him I presented myself fearlessly as a spinster of decent family and small but assured income, intending a rural life of combined seemliness and economy. He met my advances politely enough, but with an air of suspicion which offended me. I began by disliking him for it: afterwards I set it down as an unpleasant feature in the local character. I was doubly mistaken. Farmer Hosking was slow-witted, but as honest a man as ever stood up against hard times; and a more open and hospitable race than the people on that coast I never wish to meet. It was the caution of a child who had burnt his fingers not once, but many times. Had I known what I afterwards learned of Farmer Hosking's tribulations as landlord of a "secluded country residence," I should have approached him with the bashfulness proper to my suit and faltered as I undertook to prove the bright exception in a long line of painful experiences. He had bought the Tresillack estate twenty years before —on mortgage, I fancy—because the land adjoined his own and would pay him for tillage. But the house was a nuisance, an incubus; and had been so from the beginning.

‘"Well, miss," he said, "you're welcome to look over it; a pretty enough place, inside and out. There's no trouble about keys, because I've put in a housekeeper, a widow-woman, and she'll show you round. With your leave I'll step up the coombe so far with you, and put you in your way." As I thanked him he paused and rubbed his chin. "There's one thing I must tell you, though. Whoever takes the house must take Mrs. Carkeek along with it."

‘"Mrs. Carkeek?" I echoed dolefully. "Is that the housekeeper?"

‘"Yes: she was wife to my late hind. I'm sorry, miss," he added, my face telling him no doubt what sort of woman I expected Mrs. Carkeek to be; "but I had to make it a rule after—after some things that happened. And I dare say you won't find her so bad. Mary Carkeek's a sensible comfortable woman, and knows the place. She was in service there to Squire Kendall when he sold up and went: her first place it was."

‘"I may as well see the house, anyhow," said I dejectedly. So we started to walk up the coombe. The path, which ran beside a little chattering stream, was narrow for the most part, and Farmer Hosking, with an apology, strode on ahead to beat aside the brambles. But whenever its width allowed us to walk side by side I caught him from time to time stealing a shy inquisitive glance under his rough eyebrows. Courteously though he bore himself, it was clear that he could not sum me up to his satisfaction or bring me square with his notion of a tenant for his "secluded country residence."

‘I don't know what foolish fancy prompted it, but about halfway up the coombe I stopped short and asked:

'"There are no ghosts, I suppose?"

'It struck me, a moment after I had uttered it, as a supremely silly question; but he took it quite seriously. "No; I never heard tell of any *ghosts*." He laid a queer sort of stress on the word. "There's always been trouble with servants, and maids' tongues will be runnin'. But Mary Carkeek lives up there alone, and she seems comfortable enough."

'We walked on. By-and-by he pointed with his stick. "It don't look like a place for ghosts, now, do it?"

'Certainly it did not. Above an untrimmed orchard rose a terrace of turf scattered with thorn-bushes, and above this a terrace of stone, upon which stood the prettiest cottage I had ever seen. It was long and low and thatched; a deep verandah ran from end to end. Clematis, banksia roses and honeysuckle climbed the posts of this verandah, and big blooms of the Maréchal Niel were clustered along its roof, beneath the lattices of the bedroom windows. The house was small enough to be called a cottage, and rare enough in features and in situation to confer distinction on any tenant. It suggested what in those days we should have called " elegant " living. And I could have clapped my hands for joy.

'My spirits mounted still higher when Mrs. Carkeek opened the door to us. I had looked for a Mrs. Gummidge, and I found a healthy middle-aged woman with a thoughtful but contented face, and a smile which, without a trace of obsequiousness, quite bore out the farmer's description of her. She was a comfortable woman; and while we walked through the rooms together (for Mr. Hosking waited outside) I " took to " Mrs. Carkeek. Her speech was direct and practical; the rooms, in spite of their faded furniture, were bright and exquisitely clean; and somehow the very atmosphere of the house gave me a sense of well-being, of feeling at home and cared for; yes, *of being loved*. Don't laugh, my dears; for when I've done you may not think this fancy altogether foolish.

'I stepped out into the verandah, and Farmer Hosking pocketed the pruning-knife which he had been using on a bush of jasmine.

'"This is better than anything I had dreamed of."

'"Well, miss, that's not a wise way of beginning a bargain, if you'll excuse me."

'He took no advantage, however, of my admission; and we struck the bargain as we returned down the coombe to his farm, where the hired chaise waited to convey me back to the nearest town. I had meant to engage a maid of my own, but now it occurred to me that I might do very well with Mrs. Carkeek. This, too, was settled in the course of the next day or two, and within the week I had moved into my new home.

'I can hardly describe to you the happiness of my first month at Tresillack; because (as I now believe) if I take the reasons which I had for being happy, one by one, there remains over something which I cannot account for. I was moderately young, entirely healthy; I felt myself independent and adventurous; the season was high summer, the weather glorious, the garden in all the pomp of June, yet sufficiently unkempt to keep me busy, give me a sharp appetite for meals, and send me to bed in that drowsy stupor which comes of the odours of earth. I spent the most of each day out of doors, winding up each day's work as a rule with a walk down the cool valley, along the beach and back.

'I soon found that all housework could be safely left to Mrs. Carkeek. She did not talk much; indeed her only fault (a rare one in housekeepers) was that she talked too little, and even when I addressed her seemed at times unable to give me her attention. It was as though her mind strayed off to some small job she had forgotten, and her eyes wore a listening look, as though she waited for the neglected task to speak and remind her. But as a matter of fact she forgot nothing. Indeed, my dears, I was never so well attended to in my life.

'Well, that is what I'm coming to. That, so to say, is just *it*. The woman not only had the rooms swept and dusted, and my meals prepared to the moment. In a hundred odd little ways this orderliness, these preparations, seemed to read my desires. Did I wish the roses renewed in a bowl upon the dining-table, sure enough at the next meal they would be replaced by fresh ones. Mrs. Carkeek (I told myself) must have surprised and interpreted a glance of mine. And yet I could not remember having glanced at the bowl in her presence. And how on earth had she guessed the very roses, the very shapes and colours I had lightly wished for? This is only an instance, you understand. Every day, and from morning to night, I happened on others, each slight enough, but all together bearing witness to a ministering intelligence as subtle as it was untiring.

'I am a light sleeper, as you know, with an uncomfortable knack of waking with the sun and roaming early. No matter how early I rose at Tresillack, Mrs. Carkeek seemed to have prevented me. Finally I had to conclude that she arose and dusted and tidied as soon as she judged me safely a-bed. For once, finding the drawing-room (where I had been sitting late) "redded" up at four in the morning, and no trace of a plate of raspberries which I had carried thither after dinner and left overnight, I determined to test her, and walked through to the kitchen, calling her by name. I found the kitchen as clean as a pin, and the fire laid, but no trace of Mrs. Carkeek. I walked upstairs and knocked at her door. At the second knock a sleepy voice cried out and presently the good woman stood before me in her nightgown, looking (I thought) considerably scared.

'"No," I said, "it's not a burglar. But I've found out what I wanted, that you do your morning's work over night. But you mustn't wait for me when I choose to sit up. And now go back to your bed like a good soul, whilst I take a run down to the beach."

'She stood blinking in the dawn. Her face was still white.

'"Oh, miss," she gasped, "I made sure you must have seen something!"

'"And so I have," I answered, "but it was neither burglars nor ghosts."

'"Thank God for that," I heard her say as she turned her back to me in her grey bedroom—which faced the north. And I took this for a carelessly pious expression and ran downstairs, thinking no more of it.

'A few days later I began to understand.

'The plan of Tresillack house was simplicity itself. To the left as you entered was the dining-room; to the right the drawing-room, with a boudoir beyond. The foot of the stairs faced the front door, and beside it, passing a glazed inner door, you found two others right and left, the left opening on the kitchen, the right on a passage which ran by a store-cupboard under the bend of the stairs to a neat pantry with the usual shelves and linen-press, and under the window (which faced north) a porcelain basin and brass tap. On the first morning of my tenancy I had visited this pantry and turned the tap; but no water ran. I supposed this to be accidental. Mrs. Carkeek had to wash up glass ware and crockery, and no doubt Mrs. Carkeek would complain of any failure in the water supply.

'But the day after my surprise visit (as I called it) I had picked a basketful of roses, and carried them into the pantry as a handy place to arrange them in. I chose a china bowl and went to fill it at the tap. Again the water would not run.

'I called Mrs. Carkeek. "What is wrong with this tap?" I asked. "The rest of the house is well enough supplied."

' "I don't know, miss. I never use it."

' "But there must be a reason; and you must find it a great nuisance washing up the plate and glasses in the kitchen. Come around to the back with me, and we'll have a look at the cisterns."

' "The cisterns 'll be all right, miss. I assure you I don't find it a trouble."

'But I was not to be put off. The back of the house stood but ten feet from a wall which was really but a stone face built against the cliff cut away by the architect. Above the cliff rose the kitchen garden, and from its lower path we looked over the wall's parapet upon the cisterns. There were two—a very large one, supplying the kitchen and the bathroom above the kitchen; and a small one, obviously fed by the other, and as obviously leading, by a pipe which I could trace, to the pantry. Now the big cistern stood almost full, and yet the small one, though on a lower level, was empty.

' "It's as plain as daylight," said I. "The pipe between the two is choked." And I clambered on to the parapet.

' "I wouldn't, miss. The pantry tap is only cold water, and no use to me. From the kitchen boiler I gets it hot, you see."

' "But I want the pantry water for my flowers." I bent over and groped. "I thought as much!" said I, as I wrenched out a thick plug of cork and immediately the water began to flow. I turned triumphantly on Mrs. Carkeek, who had grown suddenly red in the face. Her eyes were fixed on the cork in my hand. To keep it more firmly wedged in its place somebody had wrapped it round with a rag of calico print; and, discoloured though the rag was, I seemed to recall the pattern (a lilac sprig). Then, as our eyes met, it occurred to me that only two mornings before Mrs. Carkeek had worn a print gown of that same sprigged pattern.

'I had the presence of mind to hide this very small discovery, sliding over it some quite trivial remark; and presently Mrs. Carkeek regained her composure. But I own I felt disappointed in her. It seemed such a paltry thing to be disingenuous over. She had deliberately acted a fib before me; and why? Merely because she preferred the kitchen to the pantry tap. It was childish. "But servants are all the same," I told myself. "I must take Mrs. Carkeek as she is; and, after all, she is a treasure."

'On the second night after this, and between eleven and twelve o'clock, I was lying in bed and reading myself sleepy over a novel of Lord Lytton's, when a small sound disturbed me. I listened. The sound was clearly that of water trickling; and I set it down to rain. A shower (I told myself) had filled the water-pipes which drained the roof. Somehow I could not fix the sound. There was a water pipe against the wall just outside my window. I rose and drew up the blind.

'To my astonishment no rain was falling; no rain had fallen. I felt the slate window-sill: some dew had gathered there—no more. There was no wind, no cloud: only a still moon high over the eastern slope of the coombe, the distant plash of waves, and the fragrance of many roses. I went back to bed and listened again. Yes, the trickling sound continued, quite distinct in the silence of the house, not to be confused for a moment with the dull murmur of the beach. After a while it began to grate on my nerves. I caught up my candle, flung my dressing-gown about me, and stole softly downstairs.

'Then it was simple. I traced the sound to the pantry. "Mrs. Carkeek has left the tap running," said I: and, sure enough, I found it so—a thin trickle steadily running to waste in the porcelain basin. I turned off the tap, went contentedly back to my bed, and slept.

'——for some hours. I opened my eyes in darkness, and at once knew what had awakened me. The tap was running again. Now it had shut easily in my hand, but not so easily that I could believe it had slipped open again of its own accord. "This is Mrs. Carkeek's doing," said I; and am afraid I added "Bother Mrs. Carkeek!"

'Well, there was no help for it: so I struck a light, looked at my watch, saw that the hour was just three o'clock, and descended the stairs again. At the pantry door I paused. I was not afraid—not one little bit. In fact the notion that anything might be wrong had never crossed my mind. But I remember thinking, with my hand on the door, that if Mrs. Carkeek were in the pantry I might happen to give her a severe fright.

'I pushed the door open briskly. Mrs. Carkeek was not there. But something was there, by the porcelain basin—something which might have sent me scurrying upstairs two steps at a time, but which as a matter of fact held me to the spot. My heart seemed to stand still—so still! And in the stillness I remember setting down the brass candlestick on a tall nest of drawers beside me.

'Over the porcelain basin and beneath the water trickling from the tap I saw two hands.

'That was all—two small hands, a child's hands. I cannot tell you how they ended.

'No: they were not cut off. I saw them quite distinctly: just a pair of small hands and the wrists, and after that—nothing. They were moving briskly—washing themselves clean. I saw the water trickle and splash over them—not *through* them—but just as it would on real hands. They were the hands of a little girl, too. Oh, yes, I was sure of that at once. Boys and girls wash their hands differently. I can't just tell you what the difference is, but it's unmistakable.

'I saw all this before my candle slipped and fell with a crash. I had set it down without looking—for my eyes were fixed on the basin—and had balanced it on the edge of the nest of drawers. After the crash, in the darkness there, with the water running, I suffered some bad moments. Oddly enough, the thought uppermost with me was that I *must* shut off that tap before escaping. I *had* to. And after a while I picked up all my courage, so to say, between my teeth, and with a little sob thrust out my hand and did it. Then I fled.

'The dawn was close upon me: and as soon as the sky reddened I took my bath, dressed and went downstairs. And there at the pantry door I found Mrs. Carkeek, also dressed, with my candlestick in her hand.

'"Ah!" said I, "you picked it up."

'Our eyes met. Clearly Mrs. Carkeek wished me to begin, and I determined at once to have it out with her.

'"And you knew all about it. That's what accounts for your plugging up the cistern."

'"You saw . . .?" she began.

'"Yes, yes. And you must tell me all about it—never mind how bad. Is——is it—murder?"

'"Law bless you, miss, whatever put such horrors in your head?"

'"She was washing her hands."

'"Ah, so she does, poor dear! But—murder! And dear little Miss Margaret, that wouldn't go to hurt a fly!"

'"Miss Margaret?"

'"Eh, she died at seven year. Squire Kendall's only daughter; and that's over twenty year ago. I was her nurse, miss, and I know—diphtheria it was; she took it down in the village."

'"But how do you know it is Margaret?"

'"Those hands—why, how could I mistake, that used to be her nurse?"

'"But why does she wash them?"

'"Well, miss, being always a dainty child—and the house-work, you see——"

'I took a long breath. "Do you mean to tell me that all this tidying and dusting——" I broke off. "Is it *she* who has been taking this care of me?"

'Mrs. Carkeek met my look steadily.

'"Who else, miss?"

'"Poor little soul!"

'"Well now"—Mrs. Carkeek rubbed my candlestick with the edge of her apron—"I'm so glad you take it like this. For there isn't really nothing to be afraid of—is there?" She eyed me wistfully. "It's my belief she loves you, miss. But only to think what a time she must have had with the others!"

'"The others?" I echoed.

'"The other tenants, miss: the ones afore you."

'"Were they bad?"

'"They was awful. Didn't Farmer Hosking tell you? They carried on fearful—one after another, and each one worse than the last."

'"What was the matter with them? Drink?"

'"Drink, miss, with some of 'em. There was the Major—he used to go mad with it, and run about the coombe in his nightshirt. Oh, scandalous! And his wife drank too—that is, if she ever *was* his wife. Just think of that tender child washing up after their nasty doings!"

'I shivered.

'"But that wasn't the worst, miss—not by a long way. There was a pair here—from the colonies, or so they gave out—with two children, a boy and gel, the eldest scarce six. Poor mites!"

'"Why, what happened?"

'"They beat those children, miss—your blood would boil!—*and* starved, *and* tortured 'em, it's my belief. You could hear their screams, I've been told, away back in the high-road, and that's the best part of half a mile. Sometimes they was locked up without food for days together. But it's my belief that little Miss Margaret managed to feed them somehow. Oh, I can see her, creeping to the door and comforting!"

'"But perhaps she never showed herself when these awful people were here, but took to flight until they left."

'"You didn't never know her, miss. The brave she was! She'd have stood up to lions. She've been here all the while: and only to think what her innocent eyes and ears must have took in! There was another couple——" Mrs. Carkeek sunk her voice.

'"Oh, hush!" said I, "if I'm to have any peace of mind in this house!"

'"But you won't go, miss? She loves you, I know she do. And think what you might be leaving her to—what sort of tenant might come next. For she can't go. She've been here ever since her father sold the place. He died soon after. You mustn't go!"

'Now I had resolved to go, but all of a sudden I felt how mean this resolution was.

'"After all," said I, "there's nothing to be afraid of."

'"That's it, miss; nothing at all. I don't even believe it's so very uncommon. Why, I've heard my mother tell of farmhouses where the rooms were swept every night as regular as clockwork, and the floors sanded, and the pots and pans scoured, and all while the maids slept. They put it down to the piskies; but we know better, miss, and now we've got the secret between us we can lie easy in our beds, and if we hear anything say 'God bless the child!' and go to sleep."

'"Mrs. Carkeek," said I, "there's only one condition I have to make."

'"What's that?"

'"Why, that you let me kiss you."

'"Oh, you dear!" said Mrs. Carkeek as we embraced: and this was as close to familiarity as she allowed herself to go in the whole course of my acquaintance with her.

'I spent five years at Tresillack, and all that while Mrs. Carkeek lived with me and shared the secret. Few women, I dare to say, were ever so completely wrapped around with love as we were during those five years. It ran through my waking life like a song: it smoothed my pillow, touched and made my table comely, in summer lifted the heads of the flowers as I passed, and in winter watched the fire with me and kept it bright.

'"Why did I ever leave Tresillack?" Because one day, at the end of five years, Farmer Hosking brought me word that he had sold the house—or was about to sell it; I forget which. There was no avoiding it, at any rate; the purchaser being a Colonel Kendall, a brother of the old Squire."

'"A married man?" I asked.

'"Yes, miss; with a family of eight. As pretty children as ever you see, and the mother a good lady. It's the old home to Colonel Kendall."

'"I see. And that is why you feel bound to sell."

'"It's a good price, too, that he offers. You mustn't think but I'm sorry enough——"

'"To turn me out? I thank you, Mr. Hosking; but you are doing the right thing."

'Since Mrs. Carkeek was to stay, the arrangement lacked nothing of absolute perfection—except, perhaps, that it found no room for me.

'"*She* —Margaret—will be happy," I said; "with her cousins, you know."

'"Oh yes, miss, she will be happy, sure enough," Mrs. Carkeek agreed.

'So when the time came I packed up my boxes, and tried to be cheerful. But on the last morning, when they stood corded in the hall, I sent Mrs. Carkeek upstairs upon some poor excuse, and stepped alone into the pantry.

'"Margaret!" I whispered.

'There was no answer at all. I had scarcely dared to hope for one. Yet I tried again, and, shutting my eyes this time, stretched out both hands and whispered:

'"Margaret!"

'And I will swear to my dying day that two little hands stole and rested—for a moment only—in mine.'

Q.

THE LATE MR. EDWARD SPENDER

THE 'WESTERN MORNING NEWS'

THE scene was a railway carriage. A stranger and the representative of a newspaper were talking.

'What are the principles of your paper?' asked the stranger.

'Oh, we have none,' came the unexpected answer. The pressman forgot, or never knew, that a paper may be independent and yet have principles, probably the more principles the greater the independence.

In 1860, as a two days after date New Year's Gift to the people of the West Country, came the first issue of the 'Western Morning News,' and it heralded its birth by asserting its determination to be independent in politics and religion, and yet to have principles. It was a bold venture to appeal to no particular party or religious sect, but to endeavour to hold the balance evenly, praising whatever was honourable and of good repute in all men and parties, and ready always to lend its influence to aid every movement for the common weal.

'Although we have drawn up no confession of faith,' it was remarked in the first issue, 'we shall not be found wanting in the expression of opinions. Bound to no party, we shall have no hesitation in criticising any. We have set before ourselves a high standard. Being but human, we shall no doubt often fall short of it. Nevertheless, we believe that English men and women are always ready to forgive occasional failings, when they see the hearty desire manifested to serve the cause of truth with vigour and honesty.'

Every morning since then the 'Western Morning News' has come up for judgment, and though, as every journalist confesses in humility, only journalists are ignorant of the way in which a newspaper should be run, the 'Western Morning News' lives and has flourished amazingly.

In these days when Devon and Cornwall are circled and intersected at every point by the railway, the telegraph, and the telephone—all of them necessary helpmates of the journalist—the appearance of the freshly printed daily paper at the breakfast table in remote towns and villages is no more marvellous than the newly laid egg that shares the honours of the meal. We have ceased to wonder at the strides which life in the West has made in the past forty years. Yet you may still meet men who remember the first train that ran from Exeter to Plymouth in 1849, and many more to whom the spanning of the Tamar by Brunel and the opening of the Cornish railway in 1859 is as an event of yesterday.

When Cornwall—hitherto practically an island—was linked to Devonshire, the time was ripening for a daily paper, but the foundation of the 'Western Morning News' was a bold venture. The two counties were large, their populations sparse and scattered, paper still bore a tax of three farthings a pound, there was no swift impetuous machinery to print off the day's news in a bewildering whirl, no branch railways to take the newly printed broadsheet to out-of-the-way towns, and the telegraph was in its swaddling clothes. There were not a few journalists connected with weekly papers in the two counties who recognised the opportunity, but they saw in their mind's eye all the difficulties and drew back. They were content that others should be the pioneers, and thus it came about that Mr. Edward Spender and Mr. William Saunders, neither of them journalists by training, stepped forward to meet a need that the majority of people in the two counties had hardly felt.

They had to educate their public. They were both exceptional men, born journalists, men who led in whatever environment they happened to be. Their courage was rewarded by immediate success. Fortunes have been sunk in establishing many, if not most, papers—and there is nothing like a newspaper for devouring money,

CHIEF OFFICE, GEORGE STREET, PLYMOUTH

not even Cornish mines or Hooley companies—but the 'Western Morning News' paid from the very first.

After months of anxious thought and unceasing labour, a date, January 3, 1860, was fixed for its appearance. A glance at the life of Macaulay will show that he died the day after the newspaper was issued, and the newly fledged enterprise vindicated its right to live by announcing the news in the West at the same time that Londoners were reading their 'Times.' It was a distinct triumph, the precursor of many. The people of the West were not slow to appreciate the advantage of having all the previous day's news of their well-beloved two counties, and of all the far-off corners of the world, served up to them with their breakfasts, and they set even greater store by the market reports and other commercial and financial intelligence which enabled them to carry on their business with almost the same ease as though they traded in the precincts of Capel Court, the antechambers of the Corn Exchange in Mark Lane, or were near neighbours of Lloyd's.

SHAPE OF A SATURDAY'S PAGE

As one turns over the thin tawny brown pages of the first little four-page papers—the page measured only 34½ inches by 16½ inches—one can imagine the genius for organisation that enabled the founders to produce them, and one is reminded that all the pens of those who then dared Fortune to deny them success have been dipped in ink for the last time and laid aside. Mr. Edward Hawkings, the present secretary to the 'Western Morning News' Company, is the only personal link between the staffs of the eight-page paper of to-day and of the modest little sheet of nearly forty years ago.

The 'Western Morning News' was born to fortune and more fame than most papers in the provinces. Mr. Spender, one of its founders, will always have a place in the annals of journalism, not only as a very prince among London Letter writers, but as the pioneer in this branch of journalism. In 1864 he left the office at Plymouth in the charge of Mr. William Hunt, who in his turn gave way to Mr. Albert Groser (who had joined the staff of the paper four years after it was started), and went to London. His ambition was to let the people of the West know from day to day what was happening where the whirl of the Empire's loom is heard weaving the nation's story. He was the first journalist to introduce the London Letter as a leading feature of provincial papers, and it soon became one of the chief attractions of the 'Western Morning News.' Though many years have passed and Mr. Spender has had hundreds, if not thousands, of imitators, he has had few equals for purity of diction, grasp of affairs, and fairmindedness in handling controversy.

The first change in the affairs of the 'Western Morning News' occurred late in the sixties when Mr. Saunders withdrew from the proprietorship. The paper was then bought by a company in which Mr. Spender and a few personal friends were the shareholders. For the next ten years or so Mr. Spender directed the policy of the paper with increasing success, and then came a wrench that might have shaken many papers less wisely organised. While on a visit to Plymouth at Whitsuntide 1878, Mr. Spender, accompanied by his two sons, aged 13 and 11 respectively, and by his brother-in-law, Mr. E. M. Russel Rendle — who had been associated with the paper almost from the first

Photo by Heath, Plymouth.

Albert Groser.

and is to-day the Chairman, thus preserving the family connection—went for a walk to the Whitsands. Mr. Spender and his two sons decided to bathe, and a few minutes later Mr. Rendle joined them. As the latter entered the water, he stumbled and fell forward. When he raised himself he saw Mr. Spender facing the shore in about four feet of water. A wave was advancing upon him from behind. As it approached, Mr. Spender seemed to rise with it, but after it had passed over him neither he nor his two sons could be seen. It would be useless to endeavour to describe the efforts of the only survivor of this quartet to save his companions, or his fruitless search in company with the coastguards. A granite column on the hill above the Whitsands commemorates the tragedy and acts as a warning against bathing at this dangerous part of the coast.

Twenty years have run their course, but to this day the memory of Mr. Spender is revered by those of the staff—and there remains a considerable number—who worked under him, and you may turn to any treatise on the modern newspaper and find his name included among the band of men to whom we owe the excellence of provincial papers to-day. He and Mr.

Saunders were among the first to appreciate the need of co-operation among newspapers. To one or other of these pioneers was due the foundation of the Central Press Agency, the Central News, and the National Press Agency, three associations that have done not a little to enable provincial newspaper proprietors to keep pace with the exigent demands of a public always asking for more news served to them piping hot from the seat of action.

Mr. Spender's death caused a serious breach in the organisation of the 'Western Morning News,' for his position was unique. He was not merely one of its founders and the principal proprietor, but he preferred to represent it in London, where he could enjoy a fuller literary, social, and political life than in the provinces. While in London he always remained in the closest touch with Mr. Groser at Plymouth. When the tragedy of the Whitsands robbed the paper of its dictator, Mr. Groser's fourteen or fifteen years of unremitting service as Plymouth editor led to his being entrusted by the Directors with the control of the paper in a fuller sense than before.

Mr. Groser was a born organiser, and seemed never happier than when planning some fresh enterprise. He would have been a good general manager to a railway company. He was never more pleased than when surrounded by an assortment of time-tables endeavouring to master all the difficulties of intercommunication in the hope of hastening the delivery of news at Plymouth, or accelerating the subsequent despatch of the papers. During the many years that Mr. Groser and Mr. Hawkings were associated in the conduct of the paper there was never a year but some fresh triumph was won.

IN THE LINOTYPE ROOM.

It would be an injustice to the paper and those who have been connected with it—and many of their names are widely known beyond the Western counties—were no mention made of its triumphs, from any feeling of modesty. Any man can put together news that is brought to his hands, but it took little short of genius for organisation in the early days of the 'Western Morning News' to get that news from the hidden-away nooks and corners of the two counties, and from the far-off fields of enterprise where men were building up the Empire which we have so richly inherited. There were no branch railways, but there were coaches and postmen and other means, and these were all pressed into the service of the paper. Many a writer has described the early morning coaches dashing through sleeping villages and past lonely wayside houses, the conductor, with a dexterous jerk of his arm, sending the neatly folded paper hurtling through the air to some doorstep with unerring aim. To this day there is the same method of distribution in some parts of the West Country. Travellers by the Dartmouth and Kingsbridge coach still watch with interest the papers that are aimed so cleverly over hedges and quiet old-fashioned gardens to the doors of isolated houses.

But since these early days railway enterprise has not stood still. When the new London and South-Western Railway Company's line from Exeter to Plymouth was opened in 1890 it was seen that this offered an opportunity of sending the 'Western Morning News' more quickly to North Devon and Exeter and beyond, and it was decided to charter a special newspaper train. It was a bold step, but its boldness was its charm. The 'Western Daily Mercury' showed a

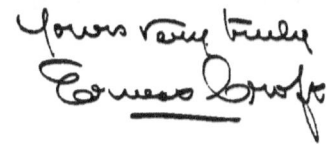

disposition to join in the enterprise, and thus it happens that every morning what is known as the 'newspaper train' steams out of Devonport station at 3.48 A.M. with many parcels of papers on which the ink has not had time to dry. A casual observer might regard this proceeding as parallel with carrying coals to Newcastle, since North Devon is in such close proximity to Bristol and Exeter and on the way to the metropolis. But the expense has been well justified, and every year the present manager, Mr. Ernest Croft, is able to point to improvements in the modes of distribution—I say *modes*, because they are still bewilderingly various.

The 'Western Morning News' has always had an eye to the weather, and those who do not regard weather prophecy as only one degree less trustworthy and demoralising (at least to all pleasure-seekers) than witchcraft may be interested in knowing that this paper was the first in England to print daily weather reports and prophecies. The staff of the paper early every morning 'make' the weather for the day with the aid of a little pencil which records on a rotating roller all the variations of the barometer. Those who are in the habit of frequenting George Street, Plymouth, shortly after midnight may see the 'weather prophet' scanning the horizon, studying the wind, and deciding on all the information at hand the weather best suited to the day. Thus are the hopes of picnickers often lightly wrecked.

It is interesting to glance back over old files, torn and discoloured with age—and sometimes it is sad work. Ten days after the 'Western Morning News' had birth it devoted a leader to the project of encircling Plymouth with fortifications, and strongly denounced the scheme as undesirable and unnecessary. 'If Plymouth,' it was urged, 'is to maintain her position as the Capital of the West, if we are to avail ourselves of the advantages offered by the opening of the railways and docks which are now giving us new life and energy, we must keep our town unfettered by these military works that have usually been fatal to every place that has been surrounded by them.' Well, there was some truth in this protest, as was seen when the Admiralty 'sat' on the lately deceased Cattewater development scheme, but the works were carried out and Plymouth and Devonport have increased in naval and military importance. The 'Western Morning News,' having shown its abhorrence of the 'strait-waistcoat' placed upon Devonport and Plymouth, made the best of the matter, and is known wherever red and blue coats go as the leading provincial paper for Service news. In far-off colonial and Indian garrisons, in warships ploughing the seas north, east, south, and west, are correspondents who send home despatches of all Service events, and times without number this paper at Plymouth has received information long before it has reached the Government offices; and before now, in times of great activity, detectives have done their best to find the means by which the stream of Service news has reached the offices—but that is quite a musty proceeding by this time.

In all the great wars of the last thirty or forty years, from the Ashantee Expedition in the early seventies to the last triumphal march to the ruins of Khartoum, the 'Western Morning News' has had one or more special representatives besides the news furnished by Reuter's and the Central News Agency.

It may not be inappropriate to recall incidents in connection with the first Ashantee War which are still remembered by the Commander-in-Chief — Sir Garnet Wolseley, as he then was. Every general likes to get home his despatches smartly—Lord Wolseley was no exception. But Mr. Groser had laid his plans better than those of the Government, and day after day the 'Western Morning News' published intelligence of the fighting, hours, and sometimes days, before its contemporaries in London, and before the official despatches came to hand at Downing Street. In the House of Commons members asked the Government if they could confirm the news of the Plymouth paper, but Ministers, with as good grace as they could muster, had to plead ignorance of the movement of events. When the Government makes up its mind to be first, it can of course achieve its purpose; but it was not until a vessel was chartered to wait, with steam up, at Cape Coast Castle, to travel at her fastest the three thousand miles to Gibraltar, that the 'Morning News' had to confess itself beaten. As soon as Coomassie was captured the steamer left, and from Gibraltar the news was flashed by cable to Downing Street, and Downing Street was proud that it had beaten its competitor

THE 'WESTERN MORNING NEWS'   433

Since this early exploit the 'Western Morning News' has not been without its triumphs; for example, when it sent a commissioner to meet Stanley as, after years of silence, he emerged from ' Darkest Africa ; ' or when it sent a representative round the British and Irish coasts to

A VICTORY MACHINE

inquire into coast communication, and with the co-operation of the 'Times' obtained the appointment of a royal commission, a commission which, unlike some others, led to most admirable results ; or again when it came to the assistance of the distressed shareholders of the West of England Bank, and raised a larger sum than had ever been subscribed through the channel of a provincial paper; or later still when it received the special thanks of the Lord Mayor of London for so materially increasing the Mansion House Fund for the starving millions of India.

Throughout its career of nearly forty years each year has shown an advance in the circulation of the paper, and with the advance has come the need for more accommodation for the 150 workers — apart from about 1,000 correspondents and others, who are more or less intimately connected with the paper.

PART OF THE CASE ROOM

VOL. I.

Photo by] [*Heath, Plymouth*

Whereas in its early days the 'Western Morning News' was laboriously printed by flat two-decker presses fed by hand, to-day its rotary presses eat up miles of paper in huge rolls as though they were eager for more. The 'Western Morning News' was the first to introduce wet printing into the West, and to-day in its chief office it has three of the most modern printing machines, capable of converting rolls of snow-white paper into printed, folded, gummed newspapers at a bewildering rate, each one counted mechanically as it comes out of the machine. A few steps from the chief office is a reserve establishment with another printing machine and all the accessories ready, so that in case of a fire in the main building the 'Western Morning News' could still be produced.

The case-room, where the news is set up in type and the paper put together ready to be stereotyped on to semi-circular metal matrices that fit on to the rollers of the printing machines, has recently been enlarged, and now accommodates fourteen linotype setting machines—those marvellously ingenious 'compositors' that are fast supplanting hand labour in newspaper offices throughout the world.

What more shall be said? More could be written of the two offshoots, the 'Western Weekly News' and the 'Naval and Military Record,' the latter a weekly 2*d*. paper that has more than trebled its circulation during the past six years; of the special telegraph wire (the only one in the three Western counties) that connects the London and Plymouth offices for the quick transmission of news; of the commercial and reporting staffs busily at work at day, and the editorial and case-room staffs similarly active throughout the night, when every properly regulated man and woman is taking his or her rest.

A great deal might be said of the personalities who all these years have been behind these closely printed sheets of news and advertisements that tell each day how all the worlds are wagging. Many of the old familiar faces are gone. Mr. Spender, Mr. Saunders, and Mr. Groser have passed away. After a period of over thirty years, during which his name, without interruption, appeared in the imprint in the last column of the last page of each paper, Mr. Edward Hawkings retired in 1891 from the management, to be succeeded by Mr. Ernest Croft, who brought to his work all the energy and acumen gained in London and more northerly towns. On the last day of March 1895 Mr. Groser, after a long illness, passed away at Cairo, and his mantle has fallen on Mr. R. J. Michie, M.A., who has shown that in his hands the traditions of the paper are in safe keeping. There have been many other less important changes, but though the faces that are masked by this paper are continually changing, the 'Western Morning News' still continues its career—still conquering difficulties, and every issue reminiscent, to those who now control it, of its reputation.

There are reputations and reputations, and that of the 'Western Morning News' is still cherished by those who wear the mantles of its founders and pioneers.

ARCHIBALD S. HURD.

MR. ALBERT GROSER
A playful sketch by Mr. Walter Crane

AD FINEM

A PARABLE

In the night, and in a lonely place, one man killed another who had injured him. Having done this, he said to himself, 'Now I can sleep, for his tongue and hand are quieted for evermore,' and, going home, he slept.

But before night had passed he awoke, cold, and saw that, while his wife slept by his side, at the other side of the bed stood the Dead Man, whose hand was laid upon him. Then he laughed, saying, 'You are dead, why should I fear you?' and fell asleep again, though the cold crept about his heart and numbed his brain—and when he awoke the sun shone brightly, a blackbird sang lustily outside the window, and he said, 'Here is an end of dreams!'

That day, while eating, he felt a cold wind upon his cheek, and turning to look he found that the Dead Man touched him. At this he said nothing, others being there, but presently got up and left the room. In another place, he and the Dead Man going side by side, he said again, 'You are dead, why should I fear you?' But this time the Dead Man answered, saying, 'Because I am dead,' and vanished.

After that the Dead Man came often, choosing, mostly, the times when the other would be for amusement or sleep, sometimes coming while he laughed, when the laugh died in his dry throat, for the thing began to wear him away, as many light feet will wear away a stone. Often he looked at his flesh where the Dead Man touched him, wondering to see no mark there, until, even by looking, he saw one.

Then, at last, he told his wife all, hurriedly, under his breath, bending to her ear, but with a wandering eye for the Dead Man, who never came.

'For this thing,' he said, 'I cannot sit quiet in my house by day, or sleep in my bed at night; but I have a way that will fool him. There is a trick that I learnt in the East, by which I can, myself, be like a dead man, breathless and with a still heart. In that state you shall have me buried deep, the earth well trodden down. Let it be on a hill-top, so that at nights I may sleep alone with the wind and the stars. A twelvemonth hence you shall come and dig me up again. By that time the thing will have forgotten me, and I, sleeping, maybe shall have forgotten it.'

At this the Dead Man, standing unseen at his elbow, laughed, but said nothing.

Afterwards the other seemed to die too, the breath leaving his body, the blood ebbing from his cheek, until his enemy came and stood one day looking down upon him, while he looked back from half-closed eyes, upon which they had already put death pennies, to keep down the lids.

'You have escaped me!' said the other in his ear, but went away, laughing quietly.

Then his friends found a lonely resting-place, and carried him up where sunrise and sunset could be seen, and where one felt every wind that blew, and was watched by all the stars.

'I shall sleep here,' said the man to himself, 'for I shall have peace.'

He had none.

The blades of grass as they sprouted over him called to one another, saying that they covered the man who was hiding from the dead. The threads and beginnings of springs babbled of it as they began their journey, and he knew that their voices would grow louder, even unto the sea. The passing wind told it to the stars, who knew it already, and the earth whispered it in her sleep at night.

As for the man, he could neither sleep nor move, and at last he prayed for the year's end, which came neither sooner nor later for his praying, but in its own appointed time.

With it came the sound of a releasing spade, and the man sobbed in his grave, saying, 'Now I shall see my wife, and look upon the world once more.'

But it was the Dead Man who dug down to him.

RICCARDO STEPHENS.

THE SEVEN VIRGINS
AN OLD CAROL

ALL under the leaves, and the leaves of Life
  I met with Virgins Seven,
And one of them was Mary mild,
  Our Lord's mother of heaven.

'O what are you seeking, you seven fair maids,
  All under the leaves of Life?
Come tell, come tell, what seek you,
  All under the leaves of Life?'

'We're seeking for no leaves, Thomas,
  But for a friend of thine;
We're seeking for sweet Jesus Christ
  To be our Guide and thine.'

'Go down, go down to yonder town
  And sit in the gallery,
And there you'll see sweet Jesus Christ
  Nailed to a big yew tree.'

So down they went to yonder town,
  As fast as foot could fall,
And many a grievous bitter tear
  From the Virgins' eyes did fall.

'O peace, mother! O peace, mother!
  Your weeping doth me grieve;
I must suffer this,' He said,
  'For Adam and for Eve.

'O mother, take you John Evangelist,
　All for to be your son,
And he will comfort you sometimes,
　Mother, as I have done.'

'O come, thou John Evangelist,
　Thou'rt welcome unto me;
But more welcome my own dear Son
　Whom I nursed on my knee.'

Then He laid His head on His right shoulder,
　Seeing Death it struck Him nigh—
'The Holy Ghost be with your soul,
　I die, mother dear, I die.'

O the rose, the gentle rose,
　And the fennel that grows so green!
God give us grace in every place
　To pray for our King and Queen.

Furthermore for our enemies all
　Our prayers they should be strong.
Amen, good Lord; your Charity
　Is the ending of my Song.

The Flora of A Cornish Cliff

by Edward Step, F.L.S.

AMONG the minor attractions of the Cornish coast I should like to direct attention to the claims our southern cliffs have upon the flower-lover. In few places will he find so great a variety of plants assembled together in a small area. From the very beginning of the year to its end he may here find something to gladden his eyes and occupy his mind. I am often asked by London friends who have sought me in my village home, if I do not find the place intolerably dull during the winter months; and I reply that to a nature-lover there is no dull month in South Cornwall, surrounded as he is by wooded valleys, deep-cut lanes with green rocky banks, and above all by a magnificent range of well-clothed sea-cliffs, below which are sandy beaches or an endless variety of rock-pools teeming with many forms of life, animal and vegetable. In winter the hedge-banks are still bright with fresh green ferns, illuminated by the abundant flowers of red campion and herb Robert, and at Christmas the fields are often white with myriads of daisies.

In the early days of the New Year the visitor from north, east, or mid-England is astonished to see 'the rathe primrose' flowering at the foot of the sea-cliffs, within a few yards of high-water mark. In most cases he will find a convenient sheep-track giving him access to the face of these cliffs midway between the shore and the elevated pasture lands; and here he can sit among the rustling stems of the great reed, and vary his studies of the waves and the shore-birds by making acquaintance of the seedling forms of many a plant well known in its adult condition. In February the lesser celandine is, of course, in flower all around, and is not very greatly in advance of up-country dates; but when the visitor leaves his reed ambush to get a better view of the pied oyster-catchers that are thinning out the limpets on the rocks below, he is delighted by the sight of a spreading clump of pure-white sea campion in flower. Everywhere at the foot of taller plants is the small white-flowered

'THE RATHE PRIMROSE'

scurvy grass, not yet grown long enough to go scrambling over its neighbours, as it will do a little later. Crossing a natural groyne, he sees the furze getting well covered with golden blossoms; but in March he will find parts of the cliffs that are specially well clothed with this spiny mantle aflame as though it were cloth of gold, and strongly, deliciously odorous. At the roots of the furze the wood-violet and dog-violet are well to the fore, and by this time red campion is getting to the height of its lavish display, which lasts for several months.

The end of March or beginning of April sees every ledge of the cliff that is as large as one's hand occupied by at least one plant of thrift or sea-pink—a rounded clump of curling, shiny, grass-shaped leaves, over which sway the rounded heads of rosy blossoms. In some places great stretches of cliff are covered by this beautiful plant—one of the finest examples our native flowers afford of naturally massed colour which is yet light and free. Along the tops of the cliff, and on many a rough stony terrace more than halfway up, the white stars of the blackthorn gleam against the dark background presented by the grim, leafless branches. Where the cliff has a gentler slope a sheet of wild hyacinth extends from top to bottom, and into the fern-brake above. Its rarer and much smaller congener, the vernal squill, may be found among the short grass at the top of most rocky headlands hereabout. The woolly yellow masses of flowers hanging from the cliff-face above are those of the kidney vetch, and here is its variety—Dillen's kidney vetch, with cream-coloured red-tipped flowers.

With the coming of May we are in the full summer-tide of our floral

SEA CAMPION

display, and the cliffs are crowded with all sorts and conditions of flowers, among which as new appearances may be noted the large white umbels of the wild carrot, spreading sheets of white ox-eyes, Smith's pepperwort, and the tall gracefully swaying spikes of foxglove, which the people here strangely call poppy! Where bare rocks crop out of the cliff wall they are surmounted by the little white English stonecrop. The cliffs have now begun to overflow upon the rocks beneath, and from the base and fissures of each, just above high-water, up springs the sea milkwort, with its flesh-tinted, rose-dotted, cup-shaped flowers. In June the scentless mayweed takes the place of the ox-eye, with its similar though smaller blossoms; and from the thick, circular, buckler-like leaves of the wall pennywort the long narrow spikes of strangely tinted flowers shoot up. Now the rosy blooms of the prim little centaury make their appearance; and so the well-staged flower-show continues. Every week some species finishes up its flowering and appears to fall back out of sight—at least

TEASEL

it is masked by some more assertive plant that has yet to show its flowers, and must have a conspicuous place for them.

July sees the advent of several tall and stately subjects that tower up above those already in possession. From the centre of a rosette of large, heavy, flannel-like leaves the mullein erects its spike of clear yellow flowers to a height of three or four feet; and the taller teasel rears its toothed stems and spiny flower-heads two or three feet higher still, its lower pairs of leaves forming basins which fill with water and drown many an aspiring insect, whose body will make a weak bouillon, which the plant will absorb by special glands and devote to its own nourishment. Hemp-agrimony has been progressing slowly, but now has become a tall clump of considerable circumference, and begins to produce its pale purple flower-heads, beloved of bees and butterflies, and esteemed by the Cornish as an invaluable medicinal 'tea,' with power to cure the majority of human ailments, and a few bovine ills as well. The

PURPLE LOOSESTRIFE

ragwort, four feet high, grows in battalions, its flat clusters of rich yellow flower-heads making really fine patches of golden colour, chiefly at the top of the cliffs, where we may find the 'everlasting' flower-heads of the carline-thistle, with their long shining yellow bracts and spiny leaves. There, too, among wild carrot and field convolvulus grows a large form of hard-heads or knapweed, the solid heavy character of its head effectually masked by the graceful lightness of the outer florets.

Our reference to the small field convolvulus, with the furze-like odour of its abundant flowers, reminds us that all the three native species of the genus convolvulus grow here. A little way down the cliff the hedge convolvulus or bindweed with its large pure white flowers twines tightly round the reeds, and down on the sands below runs the sea convolvulus with fleshy leaves and pink flowers, but with scarcely a twist in its stem. Their nearest ally, the com-

mon dodder, twines its parasitical leafless crimson threads in a hopeless tangle over bushes of furze and patches of sweet wild thyme. This plant must have had honest ancestors who laboured for their living, getting it from the earth and air as most plants do, but for ages it has been a degraded parasite, living on the industry of others. Its honest ancestry is suggested by the fact that it begins life with roots, but as soon as it can attach itself to

THRIFT, OR SEA PINK

another plant it quits the earth and fixes its suckers into its victim, from whom it draws its entire nourishment. It has none of the chlorophyll necessary to honest vegetable labour, and no leaves, but it produces bunches of tiny flowers at the expense of its victim, and those flowers enable us to fix its true position as a degraded convolvulus.

Here where the soil is thin and the rocks crop out without any of the taller plants to clothe them is the true samphire in abundance and in flower, and it may be gathered without any of the risks suggested by Shakespeare's well-known reference to samphire-gathering as a 'dreadful trade.' Round about are the fluffy flower-heads of hare's-foot trefoil, presenting little resemblance to its next-of-kin, the clovers of the fields above. There are sheets of the trailing spineless form of wrest-harrow covered with its rosy flowers, and near them, as a matter of course, the clear yellow bird's-foot trefoil.

More or less in evidence all along from summit to base is the great reed —locally known as goss—our largest native grass, now eight feet high, crowned with the large feathery brushes of dark purple flowers. Always treated in the text-books as though it were only to be found on the margins of lakes and rivers, it must greet the inland visitor as one of the most striking features of the cliff flora, forming as it does little jungles in which the otter and many another wild creature finds cover. Sheltered by the taller-growing reeds may be found numerous clumps of tall, straight-growing purple loosestrife with its interesting 'trimorphic' flowers made famous by Darwin years ago. Its case is too complex to be set out fully here, but we may just briefly say that, though to the cursory beholder its flowers are all alike, closer inspection reveals the fact that one plant produces them with that part of the pistil called the style long, a second plant will have the style short, and a third of medium length. There are corresponding differences in the length of the stamens which produce the fertilising pollen, and in the size and colour of the pollen-grains —the whole having relation to the cross-fertilisation of the plants by insect-visitors, and the prevention of in-breeding. Thus No. 1 can only be properly fertilised by pollen brought from No. 2 or No. 3; No. 2 requires pollen from 1 or 3; and

SAMPHIRE

No. 3 must have it from 1 or 2. Bees and humble-bees are the chief carrying agents of the pollen, what time they are searching for honey.

To the reed-stems also cling the tendrils of the narrow-leaved everlasting

NARROW-LEAVED EVERLASTING PEA

pea, a rosy flowered smaller edition of the broad-leaved everlasting pea of our gardens. Near the foot of the cliff, in a spot where the soil is a bit richer and damper, grows the yellow bartsia, covered with downy glands, which excrete a sticky moisture wherein many small flies come to grief. Its relative, the red bartsia, may be found in abundance in all the drier parts above, and its flowers, though small, are well worthy of close scrutiny on account of the manner in which they have become specialised to take full advantage of the visits of bees and thus secure cross-fertilisation. The deep pink flowers are borne on the flower-spike in pairs, and the petals are joined together to form a tube with a two-lipped mouth. The lower lip serves as an alighting platform, and at its base there are several purple streaks pointing the way to the honey which is secreted at the bottom of the tube. But the honey is not so accessible as it appears, for though it is but a short distance from the base of the arching upper lip to the honey, yet insects standing on the lower lip are prohibited from putting their long tongues in at that point, the way being almost blocked by the stamens, which are here thickly studded with sharp teeth. Higher up, just under the pollen-bearing anthers, the stamens are quite smooth and wider apart. The anthers come together and are connected by long interlocking hairs at the back of each, whilst they open in front to discharge their pollen. Herein is seen the cunning of the plant, for when a bee pushes his tongue in here it touches some of the hairs, and by this interference all the anthers are shaken, and pollen falls upon the bee's proboscis and is thus conveyed to a younger bartsia flower, where the sensitive stigma occupies the position assumed later by the anthers. These bartsias and some of their near relations are partial parasites. They are more virtuous than the dodders, for they have green leaves—a certificate among plants that the owner works for its living; but there are degrees of probity among plants as among men. Bartsia taps the roots of other plants, and its relatives eyebright, rattle, lousewort and cowwheat do likewise, showing there is an evil tendency in the family, inherited from a common progenitor; in truth, one of the group, toothwort, has become an utterly abandoned criminal, without leaves or a particle of green colouring matter. This is a subject that should engage the attention of Professor Lombroso, for it seems probable that plants which rob others of the raw material out of which leaves, stems, and flowers are made will go on in their evil course until, like toothwort, they steal the ready-made protoplasm which meets every requirement of the thief and absolves him from the necessity for working. How like this is to the case of the rival broom-sellers immortalised by Dr. Wolcot?

Right down among the hot dry sand, and partially buried in it, is the leather-leaved sea-holly, glaucous, blue veined and blue flowered, a plant whose quiet beauty strikes everyone, but whose relationship to carrot and hogweed would not be suspected by the non-botanical. All along the sands at the cliff foot are special sand-loving plants like sea purslane, sandwort, and salt-horn, their leaves and stems uniformly swollen, and their skins thickened to enable them to retain their

WALL PENNYWORT

moisture when the sun makes the sand as hot as an oven. The last named, salt-horn, is also called marsh samphire, and on some parts of the English coasts where the genuine samphire does not grow, it is palmed off upon visitors as the real thing. Where the sand has been blown into turf-covered dunes the air will be redolent of the aromatic sweet camomile; and any of the valleys that open out upon the shore will afford us introductions to quite another series of plants.

There are ferns, too, along the cliffs—bracken, of course, and hart's-tongue in abundance; prickly shield-fern, and here and there the lady-fern and black spleenwort. Wherever a mass of hard rock juts out from the cliff and is pierced by a cave—or 'hole' to use the local designation—we may look for the bold, smooth, varnished fronds of sea spleenwort, hanging always in elegant clusters from the arch of the entrance, with its roots deeply imbedded between the flakes of rock. There are lichens in plenty on the rocks, and mosses to be discovered nearer the face of the cliff beneath the larger growths of flowering plants.

It may be objected by some botanical reader that many of the plants mentioned above are not essentially maritime. To my mind the latter fact should be a recommendation to the flower-lover to give the South Cornwall cliffs a trial, for he will there find a great variety of plants in a very small compass, some of them growing under conditions that will surprise him if he has come from an inland home.

SEA SPLEENWORT

E. STEP.

THE WELL-CHAPEL OF ST. CLETHER

ABOUT the middle of the fifth century there was a rising of the Native Welsh against the Irish Picts, who had for some time harassed the sea-coast, and had occupied what we now call Cardigan, Anglesea, and Pembrokeshire. The sons of Cunedda drove the Irish out of Anglesea and Merioneth, and the whole, or nearly the whole, of the northern kingdom of Gwynedd.

At the same time Clydwyn, son of Brychan, King of Brecknock, attacked the same invaders in Carmarthen and expelled them.

Clydwyn was himself in part Irish: his father was the son of Aulac Mac-Cormac, an Irish chief who had married the heiress of Brecknock, and had occupied that basin of the mountains with his Pictish followers, and claimed it in virtue of his wife's rights.

Clydwyn ruled over Carmarthen, and perhaps also over a part of Brecknockshire.

Clydwyn had a sister Cymorth, married to an Irish priest, Brynach or Branock, and another, Marchell, married to a petty king, Gynyr of the Red Castle—probably St. David's Head in Pembrokeshire.

Brynach by his wife had children, who probably settled in Cornwall. Gynyr by his wife had a daughter Non, the mother of St. David by Sandde, the grandson of Ceredig ap Cunedda, conqueror of Cardigan.

The expulsion of the Irish from South Wales, and the racial hatred it provoked, may account for the fact that Branock (we will call him by the name familiar in Devon) left Wales and came to Cornwall and Devon. He went further, on to the Continent; but he seems to have established a settlement at Braunton in North Devon.

It is probable that one of his sons is the Beryn of the Cornish Calendars, and the patron of St. Merryn near Padstow, and his daughter was the foundress of St. Minver.

On the death of Clydwyn, his son Clether or Clechr succeeded. He had sons.

Then Branock desired to return to Wales; he accordingly crossed over, but being an Irishman was very badly received; and there seems to have been a domestic brawl; his wife set men on to murder or maltreat him. Driven from pillar to post, poor old Branock arrived one evening in a dell, where he lit a fire and spent the night.

Next morning the sons of Clether saw the rising smoke, and rushed to the spot full of wrath, for to light a fire on ground without permission was esteemed tantamount to claiming a right to settle. An explanation ensued, and the young men brought their Irish great-uncle to Clether, their father.

What ensued we are not told, but we can conjecture. Branock must have spoken to his nephew of the God-forsaken condition of North Cornwall, of the paganism and the savagery that reigned there, for an overwhelming impulse came over the King of Carmarthen to surrender his principality to his sons, and to depart for Cornwall, there to labour for the evangelisation of his Welsh brethren in the peninsula.

In his own little kingdom he founded a church, now called St. Cleer's, and then departed, taking ship at the mouth of the Towy. We know pretty well what the ship was like; it was of wickerwork covered with three coats of hide, held about thirty men, and had a single mast with a tanned hide sail. This was the sort of vessel in which St. Brendan sailed over the Atlantic in search of an unknown land beyond the ocean, and in which St. Breoc came from Ireland to Padstow.

He probably reached Cornwall in Bude Harbour, and thence made his way inland over the bleak ridge where, somewhat later, his cousin David would found a church, and he settled in the warm sheltered valley of the Inny, near the large settlement of his first cousin, St. Nonna, though we cannot say whether she had made her foundation there before or after the arrival of Clether.

It may be as well to remind the reader that in the British Church it was not usual to dedicate ecclesiastical foundations to *dead* saints, but churches bore the names of their founders. In the Inny valley the igneous rocks stretch forward, leaving shelters under them, just the sort of places that palæolithic men would have occupied, and almost certainly on Clether's arrival he would take advantage of one of these natural shelters. Our early British saints were vastly particular about water—they would have none but the clearest and coldest—and a never-failing spring gushing forth between two great horns of rock that project into the valley attracted Clether's attention and decided him to settle there.

Here he built his little rude church, such as that of St. Gothian near Hayle, or that now almost destroyed of Peranzabulo. And here he baptised those who at his preaching believed in Christ. How long he remained at this spot we do not know. He probably welcomed his cousin Non, who came to Altarnon, and rejoiced that another first cousin, St. Wenn, was married to the Cornish King Solomon, who lived at or near Callington. He may have welcomed David on his arrival. Other kinsfolk arrived, St. Enoder, also a first cousin, and St. Carantoc, who was for a while a companion of St. Patrick in his labours. His uncle Gwynys was at St. Genes on the coast, and his aunt Morwenna at Morwenstow.

Probably he moved on to St. Cleer, near Liskeard, and there died ; we do not know the precise date, but we learn that it was at an advanced age, about A.D. 550. He is represented as having received episcopal consecration, but from whom we do not know.

One word must be said as to a confusion that has been fallen into in identifying him with Clether of Clodock in Herefordshire. This latter was esteemed a martyr because killed by the Saxons ; he belonged to another family altogether, and was son of Gwynnar, and from him the poet Taliesin was descended.

When we do not know, but probably when Cornwall fell under Saxon domination, the site of the church was moved further down the valley to where it now stands. Anyhow the church was built or rebuilt in Norman times. It was again rebuilt in 1239 and reconsecrated on October 23 in that year. It underwent a not very happy 'restoration' in 1865, of which the utmost that can be said is that it was 'well-intentioned.'

As in the adjoining parish of Laneast, so at St. Clether, the tradition remained that for baptisms water should be brought from the holy well of the first founder and apostle of the district ; but gradually access to the spring became more and more impossible, and all the surrounding ground was converted into a bog. Thorn-trees rooted themselves in the crumbling walls, and as they grew, with their strong roots dislodged the stones, and the interior of the chapel became a dense wilderness of brambles set with sharp and rending claws.

Such was the condition when the Misses Couch, in their book on the Holy Wells of Cornwall, lamented the condition of the chapel and well as a scandal to the parish. Last year (1897) T. H. Spry, Esq., of Wetherden, the owner, was approached, and readily consented to have the bog drained and the ruins examined. Accordingly, in November, drains were cut, and by March 1898 the ground had become sufficiently solid and dry for operations to be commenced.

Thorns and brambles were cut away, and then it was seen that what remained was the ruin of a chapel with a holy well in the hill side near the north-east end.

When the pick and spade were brought to work, it was ascertained that the chapel was not the original structure of the apostle and founder, but had been reconstructed in the fifteenth century; yet in all likelihood had been built up in part out of the very stones first employed by Clether. The wall on the south side was still standing, nine feet from the ground, and the western door-jambs were in place; and, singular to relate, the old stone altar, rude, and something like a cromlech, remained *in situ*, never having been overthrown. It was marked with five crosses incised.

Mr. T. H. Spry, when he learned what had been discovered, very generously offered to bear a part of the expense of the reconstruction of the chapel. This was advisable, first because the roots of thorn and ivy had penetrated through the masonry to the very foundations, and would inevitably throw down what remained, which had been thrust out of the perpendicular; and secondly, because it was found that almost the whole of the original stonework was there, and the entire structure might be put together again like a child's puzzle.

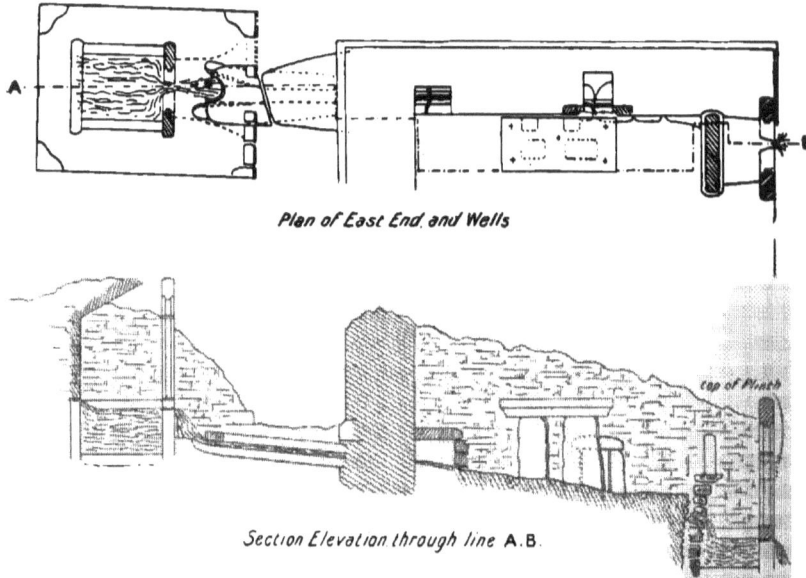

EAST END OF CHAPEL AND WELLS, PREVIOUS TO RESTORATION, PLANNED BY REV. A. H. MALAN.
SCALE ⅜ INCH TO FOOT

The reconstruction was at once undertaken, in the most conservative spirit. Every stone was replaced whence it had fallen, and the only new cut stones introduced were a part of the west window, which was in Polyphant stone, and which had been shattered in falling, as also a few feet of the east gable, the stones for which had been carried away, probably at the reconstruction of the parish church.

The Rev. A. H. Malan, Vicar of Altarnon, was in almost daily attendance, to see that nothing was done in the rebuilding for which there was not warrant.

The chapel points east and west. The external measurements are 25 ft.

THE WELL-CHAPEL OF ST. CLETHER

9 in. by 17 ft. 9 in. There is a west door of granite, over it a Polyphant stone window of two lights. To the south is one small square-headed single-light window. To the north a large granite door, by which access was had to the upper well. At the east end is a large square-headed three-light window, cusped. On each side of the window a bracket to support an image of a saint. The altar measures 4 ft. 9 in. by 2 ft. 4 in. and rests on four granite supports In the place where in a church is found the piscina is an opening above a second holy well, outside the chapel at the south-east end. Before the altar in the wall are two brackets, presumably to support a beam, from which a light might be suspended.

At the north-east of the chapel, not quite parallel with it, is a rather fine holy well, about 3 ft. 6 in. from the north wall. The water from this well was conveyed in a cut granite channel under the east wall, it showed through a small opening on the north side of the altar, it was carried along and flowed through an opening at the south side, and then was conducted under the floor in a cut channel to the second holy well, formed in the thickness of the wall outside the chapel. The idea in the minds of the builders was certainly to carry out the description of the living waters in Ezekiel's vision. ' He brought me unto the door of the house: and, behold waters issued out from under the threshold of the house eastwardly, for the forefront of the house stood toward the east, and the waters came down from under from the right side of the house, at the south side of the altar.' (Ezekiel, xlvii. 1.) This is an exact description of the flow of the St. Clether's waters. Perhaps the meaning of the openings and of the second well would not have been discovered had it not been that at the cleaning out of the upper well the water at once began to run in its ancient channel, to bubble out from under the altar, and discharge into the lower well.

But what was the special object of the two little openings into the channel, one on each side of the altar?—be it observed, one of the legs of the altar is put out of its proper place to allow of the lower opening being visible and being used. Moreover, the floor on the south side of the altar is sunk a step to admit of access to this opening or locker in which the water comes up.

I can, of course, here only offer a suggestion. The upper well, the original holy well, I take it, was

THE HOLY WELL

retained as that for baptismal water. It was where the baptistery of the first fathers of the village had been.

With regard to the higher opening inside the chapel at the east end, which is plain, that I believe was intended for keeping the channel clear; but the lower one with its moulded jambs and lintel had another purpose.

CHAPEL AND HOLY WELL

We learn from the life of St. Patrick that he found in Ireland a sacred well, in which the pagan inhabitants soaked the bones of a dead Druid, and then used the water for healing purposes. He turned out the bones and consecrated the well as a baptistery. Now the old pagan belief that water could be made good for the curing of diseases, by soaking in it the bones of a saint, was not so easily conquered. It lingered on, but a Christian saint was substituted for one who was pagan; and the dipping of holy bones in water, which water was afterwards drunk to cure epilepsy or other disorders, has remained in practice in Brittany and elsewhere to this day. Indeed, within the memory of man, the reputed skull of St. Teilo has been so employed at Penally, in South Wales, by Mr. Melchior, the hereditary guardian of the relic. Patients drink water from the saint's holy well out of his skull, or rather a portion of it that remains.

I suspect, but cannot prove it, that a relic of the saint was inserted in the little aumbry under the altar where the waters flow, and that those who desired to find benefit for their maladies by the sanctified water drew it from the second well in the chapel wall. Such a practice would be entirely in accord with Celtic belief and custom, and it will explain what otherwise would be inexplicable in the very curious and unique structure of St. Clether's chapel.

St. Clether's chapel has now been roofed in, and doors will be fitted and the windows glazed. Those who have done the work have spent a good deal of money on it, and would be glad if Cornish people interested in the recovery of so singular and striking a monument of the past, and one so associated with the founders of Christianity in the peninsula, would help towards the completion. It is the largest well-chapel in Cornwall, and in its structure has none like it.

A melancholy interest attaches to the famous St. Piran's Church at Peranzabulo; it was excavated in 1835. It was left exposed, its uncemented walls unroofed. Boys and visitors pulled down the rude stones of the structure unsecured save by their own weight, and now of that venerable relic only a portion of a wall remains. St. Gothian's, also, after having been cleared out has been left, and the walls are menacing complete ruin. Some years ago the beautiful well of St. Cleer, near Liskeard, was a mass of fallen stone, its design hardly recognisable, but it was taken in hand by Captain Rogers, of Penrose, who owns property in the parish, and was reconstructed; it is now an interesting and beautiful monument.

The little well-chapel of St. Clether lies in the midst of exquisite scenery, and now itself adds greatly to the picturesqueness of the spot where the Gospel was first preached in the Inny Valley.

The owner of the land most generously has offered when it has been completed to hand it over to the Church, that it may be secured against further ruin, and may be licensed for occasional service.

S. BARING-GOULD.

REMEMBER

I'm full to the brim wi' the joys o' my life;
'Cause a home an' a bairn an' a peart li'l wife
Be more, by a deal, than my share o' gude things.
Theer idden nought sweeter as airth ever brings.

Come trouble, come sorrows, come change an' come chance;
Come the ups an' the downs of this plaguey auld dance,
I'll never forget to the end o' my days,
My journey wance took me by butivul ways.

Ban't fair to your reason, when all's said an' done,
To cry out you'm cold at the set o' the sun.
So when the dark sorrows do find 'e at last,
Just mind as you've had plenty gude in the past.

EDEN PHILLPOTTS

FRUSTRATED

FLORA EDITHA MALLAS looked singularly plain and unprepossessing as she sat up in bed in her greyish-white night-gown, and 'sauced' her mother. Flora Editha had lived eleven experienced years, and they had not mellowed her—indeed, they had graven an unlovely line between her eyebrows. She had lank, straw-coloured hair, too, hanging about her sallow little face, and a button-nose, and none of the graces of childhood.

Kit Mallas, on the contrary, was a handsome, deep-breasted woman, with ripples in her mass of fair hair, with lively eyes, too, in spite of her widowhood, and a strangely undisturbed manner of bearing her small daughter's invectives. She was moving to and fro before the small square of looking-glass in the sloping-roofed bedroom of her cottage, and the boards creaked beneath her tread as she crossed them to take from the deep untidy drawer, or unhang from the overweighted peg, some garment as she needed it. It was quite early in the morning, and Kit Mallas was no early riser as a rule, but it was Cranza market-day, and Cranza lay some miles off, and Rickard's van had ways of its own which ways were never shaped to the comfort of the unpunctual.

Flora Editha, with bitterness in her heart and abuse on her tongue, sat between the sleeping forms of her small brothers, Albert and Horatio, and watched her mother as she laced her full figure into the stiff casing of coarse linen and whalebone, and rolled and pinned her rippling hair into showy twists and ringlets.

'*You* don't care if me an' Awlbut an' Rashio gets drownded, or catches afire, or anythin', so long as you can gad off to Cranza market ev'ry week an' see the sights.'

'Law, now, there ain't no need for 'ee to go doin' nuther of it,' replied Kit soothingly, with a tolerant smile on her good-tempered face; but half her attention was given to the laying on of her neck-ribbon.

'Nor *you* don't care if we starves.'

'There's bread—an' tea-water,' said Kit slowly and somewhat absently, as she leaned towards the little square of looking-glass and rubbed an artificial rose upon her cheek-bones, by way of borrowing its bloom.

'Bread an' tea-water,' repeated Flora Editha in scorn. 'We'm sick of bread an' tea-water.'

'An' I'll bring 'ee back some raz'bry rock from Cranza market.'

'I won't eat it!' declared the small fury. 'An' some day when you comes 'long home from your gaddin's an' finds me an' Awlbut an' Rashio has run away, you'll be scared p'raps, but we won't never come back, never!'

'Law, you queer, ancient little soul,' remarked Kit complacently, as she straightened the stems of the more than full-blown roses in her hat before arranging it on her head.

'Leave us a penny for a rasher for dinner,' commanded Flora Editha.

'No, I can't leave 'ee no pennies,' said Kit apologetically. 'But,' she added for consolation, 'I'll give 'ee a penny an' rasher too when I come 'long home.'

'Pah,' sneered Flora Editha in incredulous scorn, noting the inconsistency. 'How's that likely?'

Kit Mallas stopped smiling for a moment or two. 'Come, I've a-had enough of your sauce, miss. There's Awlbut wakin'. You'd best get out an' dress. Rashio 'll be belvin' an' bawlin' next, an' 'tis time for me to be off.'

Rickard, the carrier, did not approve of Kit Mallas any more than did any other respectable Drant man or woman. To his mind, she and her dank little cottage down by the mill-pool made a blot upon Drant's escutcheon. But in the matter of selection of passengers, Rickard was uncertain of his legal rights, and, being a cautious and unhurrying man, he made no aggressive signs of his taste. So Kit Mallas's unrighteous but complacent face looked out from the little high square window of his van, and her full-blown roses nodded in her hat, as the old horses set their backs to Bercom Hill on their way to Cranza market.

Back in the cottage Flora Editha 'minded' her brothers, but her heart was rebellious and her thoughts were unfilial as her mind's eye saw her mother smiling through the whirl of Cranza gaiety, and her body's eye fell upon the hunk of stale bread on the shelf beside the jug of tea-water. Flora Editha disapproved of her mother as entirely as did Rickard; she knew nothing about blots on escutcheons, but the injustice of life raged in her, and as she soaked her crust she thought many bitter thoughts, but above and beyond them all shot the determination to bear no more of it—to strike for freedom—to——

At that point Rashio's fat fist fell into his mug, causing a diversion, and Flora Editha's big plans needing quiet for their maturing, she held them aside as she mopped the table, and still turned from them as she put away the breakfast things. When that was done she led forth Awlbut and Rashio, guiding them by threats and cajoleries up the village street, past the 'Seven Stars' courtyard, where a brewer's waggon with an alluring pair of dappled greys had just halted, and on to the unfailing paradise of the blacksmith's forge, where she arranged them and herself upon the topmost of the mounting-steps beside the open doorway. And here, while the children found their first wide-mouthed satisfaction in the hurry of the sparks and the glowing iron turning grey upon the anvil, she rested her sharp chin on her bony little hand, and reconsidered desperate measures.

She—and Awlbut and Rashio, of course—would walk away to London, or

Cranza, or somewhere big and dirty, where ladies would want their houses washed out. Flora Editha could do that she knew, and they'd have to pay her for it, too. And she'd do it so well that——

'Aw! Aw! Look 'ee there, 'ee's afeard!' Awlbut, victorious on the ground, shouted his derision at Rashio, trembling on the third step.

'Bide quiet, Awlbut,' snapped Flora Editha; and again she settled her chin in her hand and saw visions.

She'd do it so well that the rich lady would cry out, 'Who've a-bin an' scrubbed my house so white as snow?' And then it would be told her that the new charwoman, Flora Editha, had brought the white wonder to pass; and then—— But at that point the visions became a little dazzling, confused by their very radiance, and Rashio, sitting back suddenly upon her shoulder, roused her to the exigencies of the present. Flora Editha gasped as she shut out the kaleidoscopic future and steadied Horatio upon his dilapidated boot-soles; and when she had harangued Awlbut on the subject of his sins, the thoughts to which she next gave her attention were more practical, more mundane.

She would work all day long, and they would have hot tea with sugar in it, and an egg apiece on Sundays; and why should they wait any longer in Drant? Mother never did anything for them, she never cared. They would start right off, or as soon as ever they could get a penny or two for the journey; Awlbut's appetite was so insistent. Perhaps they could start to-morrow! Oh, if only they could start to-morrow before mother got up!

A boy with a freckled face and fustian clothing which creaked sauntered in at the forge doorway, and he carried a horse-shoe in his hand. Awlbut and Rashio closed up about the doorway, and Flora Editha from the summit of the steps looked at the new-comer absently over their heads. The blacksmith, pausing to straighten his back, passed his knuckles across his beaded brow, and said, 'Hullaw, Billy!' Then there followed a short parley between him and the freckled boy, and the horse-shoe changed hands, and the blacksmith dived one grimy hand into his pocket, and, drawing it out again, picked one coin from many and handed it to the boy.

'How much did 'ee giv' 'ee?' asked Awlbut in open envy.

'Aw, a purty sight of money,' grinned back the boy, opening and shutting his hand close under Awlbut's nose.

'F'ousan' hun'red poun'?' queried Rashio, gazing up into the freckled face, and clasping his fat hands tight upon his waistband.

''Bout that much,' grinned the boy; then he slid his hands and his wealth into his pockets and went off whistling.

'He got money for it!' exclaimed Awlbut, turning to Flora Editha.

'I seed 'en,' said Flora Editha, breathing hard.

'F'ousan' hun'red poun',' declared Rashio, rounding his eyes.

But Flora Editha's shrewd brain was working quickly; it had travelled beyond the boy with the freckled face, and was gauging possibilities.

After a return walk to the cottage, during which Flora Editha's eyes were never raised from the ground, and a dinner which was but breakfast duplicated, the Mallas family sat again on the steps by the forge, and Flora Editha's face was fox-like in its shrewdness.

Early in the afternoon the brewer's waggon rumbled out from the 'Seven Stars' courtyard, and the blacksmith sauntered to his doorway to watch it pass.

'H'm, slack shoe,' he murmured to nobody in particular as the dappled greys went by. Then he turned in again to his work, and whistled as he stirred his fire.

Flora Editha had slidden to the ground, and her sallow face was a dull red.

'Awlbut,' she said sharply, 'you bide here an' mind Rashio, an' don't you move away for whatever. I'm a-goin' 'long the road a bit, an' I'll be back quick. You bide here, mind, or you'll wish as you had when I come 'long back.'

Before Awlbut had shaped his curiosity to questions, Flora Editha was speeding along the road in the waggon's wake, her eyes scanning the ground carefully as she went.

At the foot of Bercom Hill the horses slackened pace, and Flora Editha walked at the tail-board of the waggon and listened for the click of the slack shoe, her eyes still bent groundwards. But through her intentness there still danced the glory and the gladness of the life which might begin to-morrow—the independence, the luxury, the revenge.

There had been heavy rains through the night, which had washed the hawthorn hedges sweet and clean, and softened the calyxes of the spring buds in the mossy banks; but Flora Editha had no concern with them, for those same rains had washed the dust from the roads, and the crunch of the wheels upon the gritty ground went near to deadening the click of the shoe for which her ears were straining; she needed all her alertness.

The remaining nails in the grey horse's hoof must have been well driven home, for level followed hill and hill followed level, and still the shoe clicked. Now and again a thought of Albert and Horatio made Flora Editha uncomfortable. Would they 'bide quiet' so long? But she could not turn back; another bit of hill must loosen the nails; it would be waste to turn now she had come so far, and resign the wealth which was so necessary. They *must* start to-morrow; half a day's familiarity with the scheme had made it imperative; it would be dreadful to go back and live as if she had thought no thoughts and planned no plans; she could never stay on with Kit Mallas now.

The afternoon was closing in when the first doubt of success crossed Flora Editha's mind; her back was aching by that time and her toes were sore; the up-hills had been steep and the down-hills had forced her feet into her boot-toes. The waggoner looked back once or twice and offered a lift, but to have accepted would have meant missing the great prize, so she declined.

'I b'aint goin' back without 'en now,' she said to hearten herself, as she limped on. 'Aw, I do wish he'd be quick an' drop his ole shoe.'

Then the shoe seemed to click with a looser note, and her spirits rose again.

'I b'aint goin' to bide home 'long with mother, I b'aint, not whatever,' and she clenched her hands tight.

At length the hedges gave place to low stone walls, with a house here and there. Then came more houses, closer, then in rows; and here and there a light already shone from a window, and the daylight grew deceptive. Flora Editha bent her eyes closer to the ground lest the treasure should escape her, for the click of it was already lost in the rattle of wheels on the cobbled street and the tread of many feet.

' 'Tis a town!' thought Flora Editha, half affrighted; but she still trotted on behind the waggon, for 'sure enough,' she thought, ' 'twill drop off goin' over these here stones.'

The noise, the stir of life, the confusion, so wild in comparison with Drant, seemed to roar and heave about her; the whole of her prematurely old little being was wrought with anxiety; she longed for the shoe with that odd, faithful longing which belongs to childhood, as she hobbled over the stones with her eyes straining to the ground.

Then came a swerve, the horses slackened pace, the wheels rattled along an uneven gutter, the waggoner shouted 'Whoa, now! Whoa!' then drew up before a brightly lighted door; and then, in one little moment, Flora Editha's hopes were killed.

The halt being unexpected she fell with a jerk against the tail-board, striking her forehead; but the pain of the blow was nothing compared with the surging disappointment in her heart. Steadying herself, she limped round the waggon, and followed the waggoner as he went in at the doorway.

'What 'm 'ee stoppin' for?' she panted desperately. 'Why don't 'ee go on?'

The man looked down with a laugh. 'We'm come to a place called "Stop,"' he answered, 'an' I for one b'aint sorry.'

'B'aint 'ee goin' no fu'ther?' she pleaded.

'No fu'ther than stable an' bed,' he declared cheerfully as he walked away down the stone passage to the lamp-lit bar.

Flora Editha stood where he left her, and the stripe on her forehead began to swell, and her ankles seemed to be doubling down under her; then her lower lip proved stronger than her will, cords seemed to be pulling it down and puckering up her chin; then she leaned her head against the doorpost and began to cry. And then it was easier to go on than to stop.

'Why—'tis Kit Mallas's maid!'

A heavy hand turned her to the light, and looking up she saw a blurred Rickard stooping to scan her face.

'Come 'long with me,' he commanded, and he half carried her down the passage to the dazzling bar. Here the confusion of voices and faces dazed her, but as she sat down where Rickard placed her she saw a flushed, half-startled face turn towards her; then a hat with gay roses in it came and bent over her, and then she shut her eyes, and only heard the guffaws which followed, and Kit's loud protesting voice, which seemed to hold its own.

'Clunk down a drop o' this, Flora 'Ditha,' said Kit, holding out her own thick tumbler. But Flora Editha struck at it passionately.

'I won't,' she sobbed, 'I hates 'ee. Let me bide.'

'Dear soul, her's wore'd out an' down-danted with tiredness,' cooed Kit.

'Clunk it down, missie,' cried a big, red-faced man, ' 'twill soon set 'ee to rights.'

'I b'aint goin' to,' cried Flora Editha. 'I hates her! Her's—her's——'
She wanted so desperately to call aloud to them all of Kit's wickedness and her own wrongs, but the words tumbled together and would not sound right.

'Van's waitin',' snapped Rickard. And Kit began to straighten her hat and collect her parcels. And the red-faced man picked Flora Editha from the settle and carried her out, Kit following ; and Flora Editha hated them both. She shook and wriggled herself from the man's arms, and she jostled Kit roughly as she scrambled up into Rickard's van. Then she shrank back into a corner and glowered, and would not give so much as a word to the red-faced man when he said 'Good-night.'

'Here's your raz'bry rock,' said Kit conciliatingly as they jogged away over the cobbles. But Flora Editha snatched the pink sweetstuff from her mother's hand and dashed it on the floor.

The whole course of things was so bitter. She had started out in such hope and triumph ; she was being brought back as a naughty child. Life seemed too black to hold a future. Flora Editha hid her face and sulked.

. . . .

'Like mother, like child, I misdoubt me. All for gaddin' an' gay town life,' muttered Rickard next morning, as he picked the pink raspberry rock from the straw in his van.

And Awlbut and Rashio, whining to their mother, painted Flora Editha's desertion in dark colours.

No one understood Flora Editha ; and she did look remarkably plain when she sulked.

LILIAN QUILLER-COUCH.

BRESSEL THE FISHERMAN

Although you hide in the ebb and flow
Of the pale tide when the moon has set ;
The people of coming days will know
About the casting out of my net,
And how you have leaped times out of mind
Over the little silver cords,
And think that you were hard and unkind
And blame you with many bitter words.

W. B. YEATS.

A HOLIDAY CAMP AT PORT GAVERNE

THE Hawkstone Hall Institute (Christ Church, Westminster Bridge Road, London) has for eight years held a fourteen days' holiday camp for its members, visiting the duchy in 1893 and 1894 near the Lizard, and again this year at Port Gaverne.

In a sentence, the object of the Institute Camp is to provide a healthy holiday amidst the environment of nature's most romantic surroundings, to give a maximum of real pleasure at a minimum of cost to those who otherwise would not have the opportunity of visiting such places. The railway companies made favourable concessions to the party so that the total cost of the holiday, including return rail, board, lodging, and all necessary expenses, was 25s. one week and 33s. two weeks for the younger lads, whilst the older members paid 33s. and 43s. for a week or fortnight respectively.

By the dim light of a hurricane lamp and some guttering candles, on the night of July 22 last, a small band of young fellows might have been discerned (to use the language of the late Mr. G. P. R. James) gazing with mixed feelings upon an immense pile of luggage and boxes in a huge fish cellar on the north coast.

At daybreak, however, this advance party was busily engaged transforming the cellar from its native ugliness into a cosy dining hall or refectory.

In a few hours the walls were covered with 'tapestries,' flags and pictures; tables and benches arranged in place; whilst groceries, provisions, and utensils were stored away in an improvised kitchen, hereafter set apart as sacred to the cook and storekeeper.

Numerous Chinese and other lanterns, suspended from the beams, gave a general air of warmth; and homeliness reigned where, not long before, chilly bareness had held sway. A similar transformation had taken place in the large loft above, to be used as a dormitory, where the canvas stretcher beds were being fixed ready for the sixty enthusiastic campers coming by the night-excursion train.

The reader may well ask: 'Why this labour and energy in putting up at so strange an abode? Why invade the quietness of a tiny hamlet, and so double or treble its population for a fortnight?' In reply it may be explained that 'camping *out*' is a somewhat misleading term to apply to a party who lived *in* a fish cellar. It was thought that tents would hardly provide sufficient shelter for a holiday camp in the event of unpropitious weather. Inquiries were therefore made for a building such as a barn or lifeboat house, fairly weather proof, and close to the sea.

A HOLIDAY CAMP AT PORT GAVERNE

CAMP BUILDINGS, PORT GAVERNE

The building fortunately secured for the camp's headquarters was spacious and convenient. It was airy (very much so when the wind blew strongly from the northwest), but otherwise all the comfort and accommodation were amply provided. Being situated at the charming little cove of Port Gaverne, just above the beach, facing the wide blue Atlantic, and at the foot of a lovely valley intersected by pretty glades, it has proved to be an ideal spot for young fellows to spend a pleasant, invigorating and inexpensive holiday.

It was soon discovered that the bracing air sharpened the appetites of the new arrivals. According to the camp rules the time for breakfast was 8 A.M., dinner 1 P.M., tea 5 P.M., and supper 9 P.M. Four fellows were appointed in turn to help in preparing the meal, to ring the bell when all was ready, and to serve at table.

Free criticism was often indulged in if the amateur waiters seemed remiss in their duties. A breakfast menu would invariably consist of oatmeal porridge as a foundation, eggs or fish, and preserve, with coffee and cocoa.

On excursion days the orderlies packed the lunch in the baskets ready for carrying. On such occasions the company returned

HAMMOCK ROOM

to dine at 'quality' hours. During meals it was usual to call the roll, make announcements of excursions, and often after-dinner speeches, famed for wit and eloquence, provided a continual feast for merry hearts, and so materially aided digestion. The special duty of the night orderly was to light the lamps

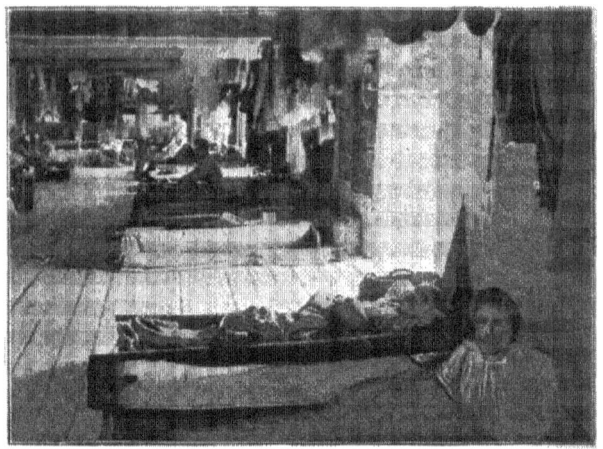

DORMITORY—FIVE A.M.

in the different rooms, call the roll at 9.30 P.M., see that lights were extinguished at 10.15, and endeavour lastly to impress upon the members the rule of '*no* talking after lights out.' The canvas hammock beds were unique in construction, and very comfortable. Members supplied their own blankets and rugs.

The morning bathe was a recognised institution. How delightful to turn out of bed and plunge into the sparkling water, when

> With a swimmer's stroke,
> We fling the billows back from our drench'd hair,
> And laughing from our lip the audacious brine
> Which kiss'd it like a wine cup, rising o'er
> The waves as they rose, and prouder still
> The loftier they uplifted us.

Some of the swimmers especially interested the visitors and seamen by their antics at bathing parade, and in demonstrating life-saving and playing water-polo.

The campers made fast friends with the worthy fishermen, and were invited, for a small consideration, to accompany them on fishing expeditions, visits which often yielded welcome additions to the larder.

But some of the amateur fishermen had strange ideas of their pastime. The tackle once consisted of a piece of string, brown paper and 9*d*. in coppers. This bait not being taken, another 1*d*. was added and the fish was landed! Although taken in a somewhat peculiar way, the fish when cooked and served was much appreciated.

The sea excursions somehow were always provocative of extravagant hilarity and almost boisterous mirth.

Perhaps the wonderful breadth of sea and coast, with glorious sky-scenery above, unconsciously affected the temperaments of the men. The trips to

Tintagel, Boscastle, Trebarwith and Polseath will always be looked back upon with keen enjoyment, even by those who were at the time overcome by *mal-de-mer*.
Many delightful walks were enjoyed and excursions taken by brake and cycle to St. Columb, Newquay in the west, and St. Nighton's Kieve,

BATHING PARADE

CLIFF CLIMBING

Tintagel, Boscastle, and other places less frequented but quite as interesting. The cliff paths around Porthquin and Pentire were often traversed by young pedestrians, on exploring bent; whilst some, leaving their more staid companions sunning themselves on the grassy slopes, would find their way across to Rock Ferry, Padstow and Trevone; returning with sunburnt faces and eager to relate the adventures of the day. Ready were they also to do more than justice to the substantial joint and Cornish delicacies in the shape of junket and cream. The Delabole slate quarry was the destination of more than one instructive and interesting visit. The holiday time thus flew apace with the attractions of cricket, football, cycling and exploring. Of the genuine kindness and hearty Cornish welcome shown by the many friends at Port Gaverne, Port Isaac and St. Endellion, there was a daily practical experience ; and the campers were glad, one and all, to show their appreciation of such kindness by giving a concert for local charities and helping in a cycle gymkhana and sports.

There were frequent visitors 'within the region of the camp,' to whom the orderly officer for the day acted as host.

The ladies of the neighbourhood too, accompanied by their fellow-citizens, graced the ' at homes' and musical evenings.

Truly in Cornwall there was spent a fortnight of unsullied happiness, such as no fashionable watering-place could have provided. In a small way, too, the camp has helped to develop the duchy as a holiday resort. For the 'sixties' (as the people called the party) are not backward to dilate upon the wonders of Cornwall to their friends when they return home.

It is the custom also to place all orders with local tradespeople and farmers instead of bringing everything from town.

The object of writing this article will have been attained if it shows, even in a slight degree, how much pleasure can be obtained at a small cost if a band of young men are willing to exercise the best of the Christian graces, and to forfeit for the time being a few of the luxuries of life.

CHARLES N. WEBSTER.

RECOLLECTIONS OF A PARISH WORKER

I HAVE gathered together a few reminiscences of old friends and good friends in Cornwall. Some of these memories reach back almost a quarter of a century, to the time when the miners used to pray for visitors in their villages as ' English ' and ' Outlandish folk come among them,' and asked ' the Lord ' that these might not remain ' foreigners to Him.' Some are of the present day, of which the ' ould sober side ' people tell us ' Times edn' like they used to belong to be when we was youngsters, then a boay's eddicashun was reading, riteing, rithmetic and rassling, and the chamshun played purty play, feer and proper, and dedn' fagot enny, but tes oal football now, and there's more brawken lembs and scat heads een waun year than there used to be een twenty.'

I was visiting a woman once who did not respond much to the religion I was putting before her. She did not say 'Hallelujah,' neither did she ' praise the Lord.' She sat uninterested. I read on, and at last I came to the words : ' Man shall not live by bread alone, but by every word that proceedeth out of the mouth of God.' Her face brightened. She leaned forward. ' Iss,' she said, ' I do belaive that ! Tes true, shure nuff ! That's what *I* do say—I caant abear *bread alone,* give me a *savour* to my tay if tes only a bit of ould fish.' (' Ould fish ' to the Cornish is what stockfish is to the Germans, and speldings to the Scotch. You may see the ling or cod from which it is made drying in the sun on the rocks at St. Ives, and, what is more, you may smell it.) To a Cornishwoman a ' savour ' with her tea is, like a bit of home-made saffron cake in the cupboard (that she may take a ' crib ' as she goes about her work), almost a necessity of life. It is said that the Cornish like to have the frying pan *on the table* beside them, and to ' drink a cup of tay ' at every meal. I had a servant once, a dear old *friend* of the family, who spoilt my boys unblushingly, even when they were what she called ' anointed ' and deserved the ' lacing ' she promised them but never gave. My eldest son's first tall hat ' frightened ' her. It was the badge of his responsible manhood growing before her eyes, and when he first donned it she hid herself to shed a tear. She was ' tored up ' when they played football, between her tender anxiety about ' scat heads ' and her desire for their honour and glory. If I ventured to rebuke the youngest, she would thus turn on me : ' Laive the cheeld alone, Missis, do'ee coe. Cum 'ere, my 'ansome, the deer on un, clucky down theer my worm, pitch I tell 'ee and I'll give 'ee a curranty biscuit *(Anglicé,* a bun) for a crib.' Her meals, if meals they could be called, spread over the whole day, especially if she was busy. She was continually taking a ' crib ' and a ' leak of tay-water. What a feature these 'curranty biscuits' are to Cornish life may be understood when we see how tea and saffron cake are woven even into their religious life. 'Tesn't the praichin' an tesn't the prayin',' said a man rebuked for frequenting a distant chapel instead of attending his parish church. 'Tesn't the praichin' an tesn't the prayin', but 'tes the caake there es that good and saffrony I culdn't stay away.'

Speaking of the respective merits of church and chapel brings to my remembrance the story of Mary Thomas Martin's conversion told me by herself. I was told if I waited and asked a gentle question and drew her on, she would tell it to me. And she did. 'How do you like the vicar?' I asked. 'Oh he's a lovely man,' she answered, 'and a 'ansome praicher—and such a voice! But did 'ee hear how he lost un to-day. Iss, I thought he would have failed all to-wance, an' that wad have bin a gashly job. But I prayed for un an' the Lord guv it back to un again, twice as loud, an' dedn't 'ee holler. But 'ee dedn't convart me. I convarted meself. Iss a ded. I was a poor wisht bad woman. Never went to a place of worship. Not for thirty years a hadn't a bin. One day theer came word that my brother Willum was hurted to the mine. So I up an' went to un an' theer he was, all scat abroad an' laid out in scritches. He was in a purty stank, sure 'nuff. But all my trouble was his poor sowl. I felt I must get he convarted before he passed. I went where he was to, an' I shut home the door, an' I hollered an' I rassled an' I prayed to him, an' he nivver spoke. I got no mouth spaich out of him at awl, but I screeched and screeched an' prayed until I convarted myself! An' then I be to go to church. Iss, we awl have to come to it, first an' last, though I used to say for christenings an' marryin's an' berrin's we must go to church, but for praichin' an' ennytheng for the nex' wurld give me the chapel; still, I waanted to go to church an' laive everybody knaw I wur proper chaanged. So I pitched to put up my Senday go-to-mittun bonnet, an' I went. An' when I got theer aw! my blessed life t'was Harvest Thanksgivin', an' when I saw the flowers an' the fruit an' the vegetables an' the cotton wool I was haived up on end!' And heaved up on the right end she was. She lived for many years after, a God-fearing Christian life. She became a regular communicant and a pillar of the Church, and I found her one day, many years after, consoling her aged mother, and promoting her cheerfulness by reading her the Burial Service. She is dead now and had a 'proper berrin'' herself, such as is dear to the heart of a Cornishwoman. 'Iss, I always go to berrin's,' said a woman to me, 'tes like this, see, go to other folks' berrin's that they may come to yours.' And when I laughed—'like a pixy,' as she would have said—at that: 'Aw, my son,' she said, 'you do taake my meanin'; but theer, I do dearly love a berrin'.' Yes, a funeral is as dear to the Cornish heart as a preaching. Two boys were quarrelling once, and one, after exhausting every injurious word in his vocabulary and calling his companion 'out of his name what he was neither called nor christened,' ended with this climax of judgment: 'You shent come to my berrin', you shent.'

During the Octave of the consecration of Truro Cathedral, special sermons were preached daily, and country folks from the different deaneries came up to hear them. On one of these days the special preacher was long, and dwelt on the wanderings of the Children of Israel for upwards of an hour. An old Wesleyan who came to the service, and, as he put it, 'harkened like a fox,' thus described his pleasure at the sermon : 'Fifty-five minutes as I do live, and not one to be regretted, and when the mixed multitude fell a lustin' in the wilderness, I almost gave tongue in the church and said "Hallelujah," but I caught Squire Z.'s eye upon me, and I thought I might be putten out, so I dedn't seng out.' The humours of one cripple woman that I know, and her quaint, earnest religion, would fill a book. There she sits at a meeting held in her room, drinking in every word that is said and joining audibly in prayer and praise. She is a bit of a Pharisee certainly, but an earnest Christian woman in spite of her censoriousness. 'Wake up, Emma,' she cried, during the discourse to a sleeping sister who had succumbed to the heat of the room and the drowsy influences around her, 'Wake up, Emma, you'm missing your privileges.' When the same Emma, while enjoying a tea on Jubilee Day, expressed a wish to have, if she were permitted to choose, cream every day, Susan Jane, the mentor of that little band, rebuked her thus : ' 'Tesn't for the likes of you to have cream often,' she said, 'and you dedn't ought to desire it,' and then in an aside to me she excused this erring one : 'She aint exsackly, Missis, you'll understand. She's half-baaked, poor sowl—put in weth the bread and taken out weth the caake.' No one attended that meeting under sixty years of age, and to that had to be also added a certain amount of serious-mindedness. 'I could not have worldly conversation round me,' says Susan Jane, 'I'm not too well, and I mightened be here very long, 'tesn't fitty for me to hear.' 'How are you to-day?' I ask. 'Well, not as I belong to be, Missis,' she replies, 'I are wake and trimbly, I be shaking like a aspen, but I shall come better as the meetin' goes on.' 'I am sorry you are so poorly,' I say. ' 'Tesn't poorly. 'Tes *ill* I am,' she answers indignantly. 'It hes in my head. I'm mizzy mazed with it. My head is leading of me astray and making me speak out of it, sayin' what I dedn't ought to say. I'm all ovver bad, creeny and wisht-like. I've got no sprawl in me at all.' I shall not soon forget one day when I arrived at the meeting to find only Susan Jane and one other woman, Jane Ann, there, and both in tears. It was soon explained. A lady had come and 'slocked' the rest of my flock away to go to the Museum or some such wicked diversion. 'I towld her,' said the weeping Jane, 'that the rest of the Apern Traade culd do as they'd a mind to, but that you come here and did your best discoosin' to we and I meant to encourage you.' 'But theer,' said Susan, 'what can 'ee expect from flitterin' ould pieces like they, with no stay in them ? Nater haave done more for their bodies than for their heads.' 'Confirmed, was she,' said Susan Jane one day to the astonished curate, with withering contempt, when he asked her about a neighbour who had claimed church membership while leading a doubtful life. 'Aw iss, confirmed, back along a braave while ago, but she've forgot all that. She've ill-used herself prettily with drink sence then, an' falled away like a *limpet !* ' Very forcible, too, was her denunciation of the Board of Guardians for giving outdoor relief to a drinking pauper instead of taking her into the House. 'Aw iss, 'tes a wisht poor job, shure nuff. Eliza Smith hev ben before the Board, and they've given her eighteenpence a week and laive to damn her sowl with drink, and she's begined to do it towance.'

Loss of the soul means something to a Cornish man or woman. 'Is that your handkerchief?' I asked my old servant once about an unmarked handkerchief which had come from the wash. 'Now, Missis,' she replied, looking at me 'some sollum,' as she would have expressed it, 'you have asked me something. Now I'll not sweer to un lest I should run my sowl into sin, but if Meary (her fellow servant) will come down and sweer to un I'll sweer to un.' 'Come down towance,' cried a pious old woman to her husband, who still clung to his drop of drink and unconverted ways, and who, perched in a tree, was sawing off a branch. 'I be awl of a sweat to see 'ee up there. You do know you'm not saved, and ef you do fall down you'm be damned. You'll lost you soul, I tell 'ee. You'm a carnal-minded man. Come down towance and leave a saved man go up.' 'Is your husband not a good man?' I asked. 'Aw iss,' was the answer, 'a very good man—that is to say, very well for a "carnal-minded man,"' meaning he was not yet converted. The village in which she lives reminds me of Mary Menadue, a figure once well known there but now passed away. In her house, too, I have held many a prayer meeting. Her plants flourished in the window, every chair shone with rubbing, her table was as white as brick could make it. I went once to hold my usual meeting, and entering the first house in the village found one of my congregation sewing and evidently not going to the meeting. 'Aw dear,' she cried as I entered, 'you be come then, and I aint claned myself for the day. Well, 'tis Meary's fault. She've a said as you had sent a postcard to say you waan't coming.' This I denied. 'Well,' continued my friend, 'Meary can't read, but she took it in to Mrs. Blacks, and her sister's second son's wife read it to her and said you wasn't too well and couldn't come. At least, so Meary told me: but go up to her, and tell what I do say, and if she says she dedn't say it, tell her to come down here and deny it in front of me, and I'll tell her she's a liar!' Meary did not withdraw her statement, and this plain speaking was not necessary, and after a little persuasion Mrs. W. 'cleaned herself,' aired her bonnet, and a handkerchief in case she 'might drop a tear,' and came with the others to the meeting. 'There,' she said at the close, 'We've had a 'ansome meeting, shure nuff.' 'He's a gracious young man,' said Meary another day of a young medical student who filled my place. 'He discoosed like a theng, he ded, and he made a *solid* prayer.' I found afterwards the solid prayer came out of the Commination Service. Speaking of prayer reminds me of a bedridden woman who refused the ministrations of the curate. 'Well,' said Susan Jane, 'she does not need he, for she is a highly connected woman. She is first cousin to the town crier, and he's a proper Christian man and can put up a 'andsome prayer. She don't need no curates prayin to she.' It was Susan Jane who, speaking of one of their number that had married, said: 'She's married since she left thes town to a traveller in oils!' I found this was a man who carried round a can selling paraffin!

I have dwelt on what was to me the humorous side of the pungent sayings of these women. But there was sometimes tragedy in their lives also. Certainly poor Mrs. Terry, one of the 'flittering things' that was slocked away on that fine St. Michael and All Angels Day, ended her *century* of life tragically enough. With bated breath Susan Jane told the others how she had been 'put away,' and was 'propurly gone en.' This awful fate, which means sent to the workhouse, came upon her because, said severe Susan Jane, she had 'nothing to do' (she was eighty-seven years old and had parish relief) 'and she got wandering about looking in the shop windows and going to church every day instead of minding her house. They told her she must go to her daughter's to live, but she culdn't abear the thoughts of going to her daughter's, for she never favoured her man, and culdn't put up with a passel of children round her; so she was "put away."' Her daughter came to see her and tried to persuade her to 'come along of she,' but she never spoke and she 'neither asked her daughter to sit nor stand,' but just sat 'glaazin' in front of her like a stecked pig.' And then she took down 'the cloam from the chimbly and *stanked* it under her feet, so as no one shouldn't hev it after she war gone. Iss, 'twere a naashun hurd job to get her to go, but she's there.' A story full of pathos. I can see her, poor little woman, breaking her *lares et penates*, and stamping on them that they might not fall into the hands of the enemy—the parish. Yes, they are leaving us now, that little band of simple folk. The old Bible-reading, prayer-loving generation, so kindly, so easily contented, so believing and so easily moved, speaking out their feelings even while you spoke or prayed—yes, even 'en the church.' 'God be with them till we meet again,' as they love to sing, and may the new generation rising up amongst us, with what Susan Jane would call 'privileges,' with School Boards to correct their errors of grammar and belief, with churches and far grander chapels to bring the Unseen before them, be as God-fearing, as upright, as faithful—they can never be so original—as these dear old men and women I have tried to tell something about—and shall hope to tell more again.

M.

BY PLEASANT STREAMS

Flumina amem silvasque inglorius

II. BY ONE WHO SAUNTERS

I AM sadly in want of an excuse to spend whole days by the banks of rivers, and especially by this river, this friendly little Cornish trout stream. Angling seems the most obvious excuse, but I cannot become an angler, having a rooted aversion to killing things, and objecting on principle to sportswomen. It is most repulsive to me to think of a girl, an English girl, taking a pleasure in killing live creatures. Indeed I don't quite believe in the *pleasure*, and think very often it is assumed, either out of bravado or that they may be able to hold their own with men, even among the coverts and on the mountain side. I do not want to find fault with the modern girl because I am an old-fashioned woman. I like to see girls riding and driving, playing tennis and golf, and I think the out-of-door life girls lead now is most wholesome, and keeps off the morbid ideas and ill tempers so many unmarried women used to fall a victim to in the old days, when to be feminine meant very often to be nervous, silly, and hysterical—but I do draw the line at the young lady who to enjoy herself wants to 'go out and kill something.' These being my sentiments I must not take even to the 'gentle art' of angling, and find myself still in want of an excuse to spend some of my days loitering by the Camel.

To some people a river, to others the sea, has an irresistible fascination. I can never walk over a bridge without lingering to watch the stream flowing beneath, and the noise of the water as I come near is like the voice of a dear friend. There is an interest, a personal history, belonging to every river, whether it is one of the giants carrying mighty ships, or only a little brawling stream like this one. I do not think 'The Mill on the Floss' would be half such a delightful book were it not for the great river whose history is interwoven with that of the hero and heroine. Then there is so much variety in a river, sometimes flooded and angry, the water sometimes dark, coloured with débris from the moors above, sometimes exquisitely clear and bright, a source of so much pleasure and beauty, yet capable at times of becoming dangerous in its headlong career. Even this tiny river has caused havoc and destruction ere now. Old men tell how once, long ago when the century was young, a waterspout broke somewhere among the tors, and the river, becoming flooded, dashed along destroying all before it, carrying away bridges, houses, cattle. At one farmhouse the water rushing in nearly drowned a girl in the kitchen before she had time to escape, but she clung to the bacon rack fixed just below the ceiling, and was able thus to hold herself out of the reach of the flood until some one came in a boat and rescued her. A waterspout is a mysterious visitation and happily very unusual; but the tale is undoubtedly true, and has been told me by several of the 'oldest inhabitants.'

My river has an element of romance mingled with it early in its career, for the first bridge that spans it after its existence begins among the grey tors commemorates by its name of 'Slaughter Bridge' the 'dim weird battle of the West,' where King Arthur met his death blow, and whence he retreated with his faithful Sir Bedivere to the mystic lake among the hills, and was borne away by the three queens to the island-valley of Avilion.

THE UPPER CAMEL. I.

The mystic lake may still be seen, but the island-valley 'where falls not hail, or rain, or any snow, nor ever wind blows loudly,' is beyond our mortal ken, even in Cornwall! Perhaps (who knows?) Guinevere (if the Arthurian legend is not all a pretty fable) may have sauntered along this river bank, with her court, and delighted, even as we do to-day, in the wealth of lovely ferns and wild flowers. From the snowdrops in January to the purple loosestrife in late summer, there is a constant progress of beauty. In March the woods are golden with Lent lilies, and very soon the great king fern will be sending up its huge fronds, which grow six feet high along the river bank like the bamboos of tropical countries. I love to sit close by the edge of the water and watch the speckled trout, all with their heads up stream, wagging their tails just energetically enough to keep them from drifting with the current. One movement from the human watcher, and they are gone like a flash. There are salmon, too, in the river, but the poachers get most of them—slip nooses over their tails or spear them. I never can imagine how the salmon find enough water to come up to the higher reaches, unless they—as the Cornish people are said to do on account of the damp climate—develop webbed feet and walk up. There is always the delightful chance of seeing a kingfisher, though this happens too seldom. The little dipper is generally to be seen on a stone curtseying up and down. He builds

THE UPPER CAMEL. II.

in the arches of the bridges and is a very fascinating little bird. The neighbourhood is a happy hunting-ground for the naturalist or botanist, and I think in one or other of these pursuits my wanted excuse for loitering by the river may be found. Rare ferns and flowers are there in plenty, but I will not too definitely indicate which they are, or where to be discovered, lest an army of tourists should arrive with baskets and trowels and remove them all. I know of one squire who would not confide even to his own sister where a certain rare fern grew, and such reticence is wise in these days when rare plants are daily growing rarer; when we hear that primroses are almost extinct in some counties near London, since a rage for primrose decorations has set in—though why they should tear up the plants when only the flowers are required I fail to see.

Among the objects of interest to be seen in a day's stroll by our river is the great granite quarry which supplied the stone for the present Eddystone Lighthouse and a monument to the late Prince Imperial at Farnborough. The quarry is cut in the face of a beautiful gorge in the hills through which a rapid stream runs, a tributary of the Camel, and even better than the larger stream for trout fishing. The quarry is well worth a visit. It is practically inexhaustible, and has some of the finest granite in the world, and the only limit to the size of the stones quarried

THE UPPER CAMEL. III.

is the difficulty of dealing with the enormous weight. The machinery is very wonderful and has the newest improvements, but the quarry, though interesting from an industrial point of view, has spoiled the picturesqueness of the valley.

Should one feel sociably inclined there will be many opportunities in a river stroll to enter into conversation with some angler, or farmer, or labourer from the many pretty little farmhouses; or there are several inns, much frequented by anglers in the season, where an idler may hear the gossip of the neighbourhood, and a Cornish anecdote or two, with the real local flavour, if he is lucky enough to meet with one of the local raconteurs, some of whom have quite a store of amusing tales and descriptions of the eccentricities of the olden days. A tale is told of three Cornish gentlemen who were delegated to arrange as to the best route for a new bit of road about to be made to avoid one of the many precipices in which our roads abound. They were to meet on the spot and decide where the new piece was to diverge, and where rejoin the old; but two of them were noted for their West-country stories, and in an unlucky moment one bethought him of a new tale which he felt sure would make his rival green with envy. The latter, of course, felt bound to 'go one better,' and and so the afternoon passed, the unfortunate third man seated by the wayside, waiting in despair till the flow of anecdotes came to an end, which was not till the shades of night were falling, when the matter of the road was settled in a hasty manner; the consequence is that we still have to climb a precipice only a small degree less steep than the old one. Cornishmen may take life seriously, but they have an unconscious cynical humour of their own. Witness a farrier's bill sent to a friend of mine, which ran—'To curing your old cow till she died, fifteen shillings!'

The accompanying photographs give some idea of the character of our little river, but cannot take in the extreme beauty of the valley it runs in, the hanging woods in spring bright with wild flowers, and in winter a lovely purple brown, silvered here and there from the grey lichen hanging in festoons from the branches; the patches of wild land brilliant in spring with acres of golden gorse, granite boulders piled in fantastic groups over many of the hillsides, which in summer are nearly hidden amid the bracken. Here and there one catches a glimpse of a far-away tor, also piled with granite rocks. In its own style I fancy the scenery of this bit of Cornwall is unsurpassed, and I am looking forward, with or without an excuse, to many pleasant hours to be spent next year on the banks of the Camel.

OCTAVIA ONSLOW.

Photo by] CHURCH OF ST. LEVAN *[Burrow, Camborne*

NOTES ON ST. LEVAN

As will already have been learnt from the essay on St. Buryan, this church was formerly a parochial chapelry only, dependent on the Collegiate Church at that place, and the parish was only converted into a rectory, in the patronage of the Duke of Cornwall, in 1864. The church was restored in 1874 by Mr. John D. Sedding, who (as every architect should do) left on record some notes of the state of the church previous to restoration.

The church is built into—we had almost said has grown out of—the side of a hill, in a lonely and secluded valley, and until recently there has been no rectory house.

The church consists of a disengaged western tower of two stages, the lower stage being 16 feet 4 inches square and the upper slightly less; nave, chancel, south aisle and north transept. The transept is connected with the nave by two arches, carried on octagonal granite pillars with capitals of three different designs. These capitals appear to be of earlier date than those of the south arcade, though of later than the transept itself, which is of the thirteenth century. It looks as if an aisle had at one time been contemplated on the north, and subsequently abandoned. The whole arrangement should be compared with that on the south side of Zennor, Germoe, and St. Mawgan-in-Kerrier. The arrangement of the walls at the angle of transept and chancel inclines us to think that there was at one time a hagioscope here. Previous to the usual cutting-down by churchwardens, the roof was of high pitch, and was left untouched in that respect when the new roof of the nave and that of the south aisle were constructed in the fifteenth century.[1] The decorations of the walls of the transept (revealed when the plaster was scraped off during the restoration) were also apparently of thirteenth-century date, or perhaps early fourteenth, as is also a portion of the chancel wall. The font of porcelain stone, with circular bowl (18½ inches inside diameter), bearing a 3-inch band of shallow tooth ornament round the top, and a bold cable-moulding round the bottom, with four sunk cusped circles enclosing geometrical designs in low relief on its sides, is probably of the same age, though the cusping of these circles may indicate a somewhat later date. The perfectly preserved and very beautiful square stoup, with panelling of three pointed arches on its front, we unhesitatingly regard as of the thirteenth century. With these exceptions (and perhaps we may include the tower) the whole church is of Late Perpendicular of the fifteenth century; but the tracery of the windows is quite modern, the architect having had to substitute stone mullions and tracery for the window frames of wood which had been placed throughout the church by the church-wardens of the eighteenth century. The restoration of these windows (as indeed of the whole church) has been carried out with great taste. We cannot, however, but regret that the lancet light in the west wall of the transept has been so restored as to lose the interesting feature that marked it when each side of its arch was formed of a single stone—a local peculiarity of rare occurrence in such early work. Perhaps, however, the old window was ruined beyond repair, but the restoration should have followed the original lines. Certainly the whole church, when restored in 1874, was in such a condition that it was proposed to build a new one in its stead in another part of the parish. This fortunately was prevented.

The tower is probably older than the main part of the church. It is of admirable proportions, and, especially when seen from the west, is a most effective structure, its windows, with tracery of Catacleuse stone, being of very good design. The western doorway, with its arch of a single cavetto moulding with chamfered edges, skilfully stopped at the base, is specially worthy of notice. It contains three bells :—

THE STOUP

Tenor C, 5 Cwt. (approximately), inscribed '1641' in broad flat figures. Diameter at the mouth 33¼ inches.

II D, 4c. 1q. 7l. 1881 (cast by Messrs. Mears

[1] Of course, the ends of the roof timbers rotted away through damp and neglect, and the rude remedy adopted was to cut them shorter and refix them. The original pitch of the roof of the nave is evidenced by the tower, where the dripstone that was carried over the old roof is now more than a foot above it, and also by the relative positions of the roof of transept and nave before the former was restored. There is a good illustration of the transept before its roof was lowered in Blight's *Churches of West Cornwall*. Blight's illustrations of the capitals of the piers of the transept arches are incorrect.

Photo by]   **NORTH TRANSEPT**   *[Burrow, Camborne*

& Stainbank). This bell replaces one of 1754, bearing the trade mark of Abraham Rudhall (whose business Messrs. Mears & Stainbank now carry on) and the names of the then churchwardens.[1]

Treble E, 4 Cwt. (approximately). Inscribed 'Thomas. Iohn: C W 1696.' Letters much corroded. Bell cracked. Diameter at the mouth, $28\frac{1}{2}$ inches.

The tower is separated from the nave by a round-headed arch springing from pentagonal imposts, and its floor is two steps above that of the nave. The staircase is newel, in the thickness of the wall, at the north-west angle.

Entering the church by the south porch, notice the stone seats on each side and the stoup already referred to; also the fact that the floor of the church is by two steps lower than that of the porch.

Within the church the most interesting objects (besides those already mentioned, to say nothing of the general effect, which, by some mystic touch

---

[1] The churchwardens of the eighteenth century and early nineteenth century, who did more to destroy the beauty and history of our churches than the much abused Puritans of one hundred years earlier, seem everywhere to have been proud of their work. At St. Buryan they recorded their names and the date of their mischief on the tower steps; at Wendron their initials are conspicuous on a pinnacle of the tower; and here at St. Levan their names may be seen also on a stone of the lich-gate: their favourite place of record was the sun-dial. Here, however, the sun-dial escapes, and bears merely the legend 'Sicut umbra transeunt dies.' Had these worthies known what would be the feeling of the present generation towards them, they would, for very shame, have erased their names even from the parish registers.

of art, conveys no sense of smallness) are the rood-stairs in the south wall of
the aisle; the arcade of six low four-centred arches supported on monolith
octagonal granite pillars, only 6 feet 8 inches apart; the carved bench-ends
(some of which are shown in the illustration), and the chancel-screen, which is
partly new and partly made up from the beautiful remains of the fifteenth-
century rood-screen. On one bench-end may be seen a monk with breviary
and 'discipline,' on another a woman with her hair neatly gathered in a net,
such as was worn about the middle of the fourteenth century, and on the top
of her head a cap in evident imitation of the style of a man's helm as shown
on the adjoining panel; while the ends of two other benches have spirited
representations of two jesters: these were formerly placed near the door, but
are now doubtless merely restored to their original use. It has been suggested
that the jesters so often represented in church are symbolic of the scoffer at the
sacred mysteries; but probably they are merely the squire's jesters. The local
craftsmen of those days knew nothing and cared less for the conscious scruples
that define one thing as suitable in dramatic art, another as suited for the
church. The two were identical, except that they put their *best* work into the
church. In many churches the element of comedy is boldly introduced, for
the time had not then come when laughter was regarded as a sin, and those
who would be thought religious must assume an unnatural gravity and lay
their humanity aside. One other bench-end is interesting, having on it the
initials 'AV.' Of this Blight gives an illustration, but omits a *heart*, cut in
the lower loop of the V, which, as St. Levan was a chapelry of the Augustinian
Canons of St. Buryan, and a heart was the emblem of St. Augustine, is of
interest, even if its presence here is a mere coincidence, as it probably is. The
bench-ends seem to be of the first half of the fifteenth century. We regret
that the benches are, for the most part, quite unworthy of the ends; anything
more ugly than the dark green paint which has been applied to them it is
impossible to imagine. The Communion-table is of wood, with a vulgar-
looking attempt at superaltar and reredos. In the south wall of the chancel is
a modern piscina with credence shelf above it; and in the north wall is an
ogee-headed niche (removed from the south side and placed where it is for
preservation), which until recently bore slight traces of colouring, thirteen
inches across and containing two shallow basin-like depressions without drains.
In spite, however, of no drains being now traceable, we have no doubt this is a
piscina of the fourteenth century, when two basins were not uncommon. The
hexagonal wooden pulpit bears the date 1752, and is in better taste than was
then usual.

The church plate consists of a paten and chalice, both of silver, presented
to the church in 1887, and an undated chalice of impure metal, $6\frac{1}{2}$ inches in
height and with a flat cover, which was formerly used as a paten. It is of
good shape, with a neat scroll pattern encircling the bowl. It bears the
initials T.G.C + O + S.T

In the Parish Registers the first entry of Baptism is April 7, 1700; of
Marriage, September 9, 1701; and of Burial, July 1, 1700.

In the churchyard are two remarkable crosses: (1) a beautifully

SOUTH AISLE

proportioned wheel cross by the south porch, nearly 7 feet high, having on the front a rude figure of Christ wearing a tunic with sleeves and very full at the bottom; there is an incised pattern on the lower part of the shaft; on both sides, also, are incised patterns, and on the back a very exquisite cross in relief, the head being like (2) that at the north-east entrance by the side of the lich-gate (see illustration). These crosses are apparently both of comparatively late date. On the north side of the gate is a stone with a figure in a tunic, the head and parts of the arms having been broken off. The ancient lich-stone is coffin-shaped, and on each side of the entrance are stone benches. One of the stones on the south side bears the initials of the churchwardens and the date 1794. At the south-west entrance is another roofless lich-gate with stone seats and oblong lich-stone. To the south-east of the church is a curious granite boulder, split part way through, as to which the natives hold that when the two pieces go entirely apart the end of the world is at hand, in accordance with St. Levan's prophecy:—

> When with panniers astride,
> A pack-horse one can ride
> Through St. Levan's stone,
> The world will be done.

Anxiously do the parishioners scan this stone each Sunday morning as they enter the church. It was on this stone, legend tells us, the Saint used to rest after the fatigue of fishing, and on the same authority we learn that the split in it was made by him with a blow of the fist, and with a view to leaving behind him some abiding memorial of himself. The stone must clearly have been venerated, or the builders of the church would never have neglected such handy material.

In the field adjoining the churchyard on the east is another cross of ruder execution than the other two, but of interest. It is similar on both faces, the crosses cut on each side having an inclination to the right, doubtless in reference to the direction in which Christ's head is traditionally said to have inclined at the Crucifixion.

As in the case of St. Buryan and many other Cornish Saints, little is known of St. Levan, who gives his name to this parish, as well as to the estate of Selena in it, and possibly also to Porthleven. Carew (Survey of Cornwall) calls him St. Siluan, and in the 'Inquisicio Nonarum' of 1340 'Capella Sancti Siluani' is mentioned under Burian. Mr. Lach-Szyrma, in his 'Church History of Cornwall,' suggests that the stone at St. Just (in Penwith), which is generally read 'Silus hic jacet,' refers to this Saint, and, in confirmation of his suggestion, prints the name with a big gap 'Sil . . . s,' which certainly does not exist on the stone itself. The name of the parish is pronounced locally 'Sleven,' and in the valuation of the lands, &c., of Penwith, quoted in a note to the essay 'St. Buryan,' it is called Selevan. Such is all that can be said to be known about St. Levan; whether he was Irish or Armorican is not clear—in *history* he is a name and nothing more, but in *legend* his place is larger than that of most. Walking along the path that leads from the church past Bodellen (where the hut of our Saint once was), and by Rospleth to St. Levan's rocks, whither the Saint was in the habit of going to exercise his skill as a fisherman, you will observe that the grass where his holy feet once

N. E. LICH-GATE AND CROSS

trod is greener and sweeter than any around. One Sunday morning the holy man was walking along this path when one Johanna, who was herself engaged at the time picking herbs in her garden at Rospletha (still called Johanna's garden), sternly rebuked the Saint for fishing on the Sunday (by the way, there is quite a modern ring about this, human nature has not varied much in some 1,300 years). They came to high words (our Saints were always powerful in that line), and St. Levan called Johanna a foolish woman, and prophesied that if any other child was christened by that name in his well she should be even more foolish. Wherefore it is that those who desire to call their children by the name of Johanna wend their way to the neighbouring church of St. Sennen.

Formerly some designs amongst the carving in the church recorded an event in St. Levan's life. Here and there two fishes might be seen on one hook. Seated one day on his favourite rocks he had thrown his hook into the sea, and on drawing it found two chads caught by it. He did not want two fishes, and anxious not to be unfair to either, he threw both back into the water. Three times this happened, and the third time St. Levan concluded that Providence willed he should take both fish home, and he accordingly did so. On reaching his hut he found his sister St. Breaca (some say St. Manacca) awaiting him with two children, whether her own or some one else's does not appear. The fish were cooked, the children ate eagerly, and, neglecting the bones, were both choked. That this legend (which has variants, the best being that which relates the capture and rejection of a single chad which the Saint rejected as not dainty enough) is true is clearly proved by the fact that the chad is still known as the 'Chuck chiel.' The legend of St. Levan's stone in the churchyard we have already referred to.

A little distance from the church, on Porthchapel Point, are the ruins of St. Levan's well, and here formerly is said to have been his hermitage. At Porthcurnow, about a mile from the church, are the ruins of an ancient chapel, one of those interesting little buildings formed of two squares, as at Perran and Madron. It is impossible to say what is the date of these structures, but they were no doubt erected long before the coming of the Normans, and their rectangular form and unbroken sides have had a clearly traceable effect on the traditions of the Cornish church-builders. Like the chapel on Chapel Carn Brea, it was erected in a spot already sacred as a place of burial.

THURSTAN C. PETER.

HYMN OF EXILE

I

Well I know a green hill, well I know a cottage,
  Well I know a window that looks upon the sea;
Young was I and yielded for a mess of pottage,
  Gave for the world what was all the world to me.
Might I now but find them with the West behind them,
  While down the wind the bells of boyhood pealed,
Dim, but not with years now, only dim with tears now,
  Young eyes and old would meet, and both be healed.
*   For it's Home, home, home! far the shadows falling;*
*   Down falls the lark and fails the longest day;*
*   And it's Come, come, come!—kindly voices calling;*
*   Home creeps the child that has been too long at play.*

II

Ah! but void the windows, gone the gentle faces,
  Cross'd are the hands I ne'er shall clasp again;
Father, mother, kindred, laid in quiet places,
  Heed not the hours nor feel the falling rain.
Yet, O hearts immortal! twine the homely portal
  Light the cold hearth with the dandelion blooms;
Though the guest ye prayed for might not be delayed for,
  Love yet abides to bedeck the naked rooms.
*   For it's Home, home, home! faithful tho' they tarried,*
*   Too late across the autumn fields you call:*
*   And it's Come, come, come!—all the harvest carried;*
*   Saved every sheaf, and man the last of all.*

III

Shall I be forgetting, now the twilight gathers,
  Morning in the boy's heart, bird beside the road?
Merciful and mighty, Lord God of my fathers,
  Thanks be to Thee for the hope and help bestowed!
Yet forgive, I pray Thee, that I choose to pay Thee
  Here on the hearth my closing sacrifice;
To Thy ruth commending in the smoke ascending
  The long love, the strong love, that counted not the price.
*   For it's Home, home, home! though the way be weary,*
*   There shines a lamp rememb'ring angels tend:*
*   And it's Come, come, come! Come to me, my deary,*
*   Home to the hearth where the long ways end!*

WHY WAS THE 'MOHEGAN' LOST?

About seven years ago Mr. Thomas Clark, of Truro, tested and mapped the basic rocks of Cornwall, and gave the results in a paper published in the 'Journal of the Royal Institution of Cornwall.' The conclusions arrived at were remarkable, and Mr. Clark expressed the opinion that the subject was 'worthy the attention of the miner, surveyor, and mariner.' Since then he has continued the particular study, and is convinced that his contentions are correct. Generally it is believed there is no other rock in the British Isles whose power over the bar magnet or needle equals that of Compass Rock, on the apex of the Island of Canna, in the Hebrides. But Mr. Clark asserts that from Botallack Mine, near St. Just, and from a quarry near Launceston, he obtained stones whose magnetic power surpasses that of the Canna stone. At present this geologist's opinion of the neighbourhood of the Manacles is interesting particularly. No stone secured from the Menenge district was so strong as the St. Just and Launceston specimens, but Mr. Clark states that all the rocks along the coast from Porthallow to beyond the Lizard are more or less magnetic. Portions of the Manacles did not influence the bar magnet so much as some rocks obtained from the coast near by. In his experiments Mr. Clark used, amongst other things, a bar magnet one foot long, an inch and a quarter deep, and a quarter of an inch thick. When suspended by means of a thread and a tripod, this bar was taken to right angles of its correct bearing by a piece of serpentine from Porthallow, weighing a quarter of a pound. And when a four-pound block of rock from the Blackhead was used, the magnet followed it round and round. In the taking of specimens a curious thing was observed. By the friction of the saw, the magnetic power of the rocks was raised above their normal strength; but tests made after a repose of a day or two showed that there had been a relapse to below the normal strength, while the original magnetic power was again attained during an extended quiescence. Mr. Clark considers that in the case of miles of basic beach and cliffs, where thousands of tons of material of the same nature are brought into motion by a storm, there would be an enormous increase of the magnetic power to which water would be no barrier, being a conductor of magnetism.

STORIES OF CORNISH QUAKERS

By Sir Richard Tangye

At St. Austell the Quakers' Annual Meeting falls in the hay season, and has been held at that time, I believe, uninterruptedly for more than two centuries. The hay season is proverbially wet, and so for generations past the farmers have been warned in rhyme :

'Now varmer, now varmer
Tak care ov your hye,
For 'tes the Quakkers' great mitten to-dye.'

And once, at the same place, when the monthly Advices to the members were being read, it happened that the particular one referring to 'vain sports' was read, whereupon a newly joined member inquired what 'vain sports' were? 'For example,' he asked, 'was kissing mydens [maidens] in the hye [hay] a vain sport?' He did not think it was.

When the Queen visited Falmouth in the 'forties,' the mayor of Truro presented an address to Her Majesty on board the royal yacht, and, on retiring, walked backwards into the sea. On that same occasion the mayor of Falmouth, who was a Quaker, waited upon Her Majesty to present the humble address of the Corporation, but, on arriving, found he had omitted to bring it. Profiting by the sad experience of his Worship of Truro, the Friend, who had conscientious objections to Water Baptism, especially by total immersion, took the liberty of retreating sideways, to the amusement of the Queen and her attendants.

The following couplet about the Quakers used to be very common in my young days, but is now almost forgotten. It was, however, a real terror to my brother and myself after our parents joined the Friends, for as we passed a certain house on our way to school, where lived a shock-headed girl named Jane Kempshorn, she used to come out, pretending to chase us, and crying :

'Lord 'ave marcy 'pon us
Keep the Quakkers from us.'

With some of our schoolfellows, however, the fact of our being Quakers caused us to be looked upon with more respect. I remember one of them telling me his father thought of turning Quaker, *because Quakers had not got to work !*

Here is a story of a member of a highly respected family of Friends at St. Austell. In my youth I was a pupil teacher at a Friends' School in Somersetshire. Every year a public examination of the pupils is held on the school premises, and Friends from the three Western counties attend in considerable numbers. At these meetings all questions affecting the school management are discussed and settled. These discussions are held in the great meeting-house adjoining the school premises, and I shall never forget a debate which once took place there between two sober Friends, named Veale and Pease. The question in dispute was whether the *meat* diet of the scholars was on a sufficiently liberal scale. Friend *Veale* declared that it was not, while Friend *Pease* took the other side, and descanted warmly on the advantages of a *vegetable* diet ! I was the only one who appeared to appreciate the humour of the contest as to the relative merits of Veale and Pease, and got into trouble for giving expression to my feelings of amusement.

CORNISH DIAMONDS

All the crew had been saved, but one poor fellow was brought ashore unconscious. The curate turned to the bystanders.

'How do you usually proceed in the case of one apparently drowned?'

'S'arch his pockets.'

———

Johnny Tregenna was told by the taker of the 'pare' to stay behind and measure the amount of work done, in order to check the capen's measurements.

'Well, Johnny, how much did it come to?'

'A shovel and a shovel-hilt, a swab and a swab stick, two great stones, and my two feet, just azackly.'

———

Time, 1870. New vicar to old parish clerk:

'Look here, Thomas: what was it I heard you saying in the "Te Deum"— "Thou art the *Queen* of Glory"?'

'Iss, be sure.'

'But why?'

'Why, when Queen Victoria come to throne—the dear of her—old Pa'son Kendall he says to me—the dear of 'n— "Thomas," he say, "take the Book and make the necessary alterations." And so I did. Wudn' have us prayin' for Willam, wud a?'

———

'Do you hear anything of what I say, Mrs. Trezona?' shouted an energetic district visitor to a deaf old cottager, after talking an hour.

'Thank 'ee, ma'am, I do hear quite enough for the good of me sawl.'

OF VOLUME I.

INDEX TO VOLUME I.

	PAGE
AD FINEM ....*Riccardo Stephens*	436
ANNALS OF THE SMUGGLERS. Three illustrations. 1 ....*Commander the Hon. H. N. Shore*	111
2 ....*J. B. Cornish*	118
AUSTRALIAN KNIGHTS. Two portraits	239
BACHELOR'S DIARY, A...*H. D. Lowry*	95
BRESSEL THE FISHERMAN..*W. B. Yeats*	461
BURGLARY CLUB, THE...*The Editor*	273
BY PLEASANT STREAMS. 1. Five illustrations......................................*Noss Mayo*	389
2. Three illustrations ....*Lady Onslow*	472
CAWSAND BAY. Three illustrations by R. Morton Nance	127
COLLEGIATE CHURCH OF ST. BURYAN. 1. Five illustrations ....*Thurstan C. Peter*	227
2. Six illustrations ...., ,,	308
COLLINGWOOD ....*Rennell Rodd, C.B., C.M.G.*	110
CORNISH GHOST STORY, A. Four illustrations ....*The Rev. John Ruddle*	283
Its History ....*Alfred Robbins*	289
CORNISH CROSSES, SOME RECENTLY DISCOVERED. Five illustrations ....*Thurstan C. Peter*	74
CORNISH DIAMONDS 78, 160, 240, 320, 400,	486
CORNISH MAIDS, To ....*Riccardo Stephens*	192
CORNUBIENSIBUS ADOPTIVUS ....*Arthur Christopher Benson*	14
COURTNEY, MR. LEONARD ....*Henry W. Lucy*	161
CRYING A NECK ....*The Rev. S. Baring-Gould*	152
DAFFODIL IN CORNWALL, THE. Seven illustrations......................*The Rev. G. H. Engleheart*	321
DOLCOATH, THE GREAT. Nine illustrations ....*Albert Bluett*	168
DUCHY'S HARVEST, THE...*F. G. Aflalo, F.Z.S.*	87
FALMOUTH. Seven illustrations ....*Charles Eyre Pascoe*	210
FIDDLE ROCK, THE ....*Graily Hewitt*	360
FLORA OF A CORNISH CLIFF. Ten illustrations ....*E. Step, F.L.S.*	441
FRUSTRATED ....*Lilian Quiller-Couch*	456
GOLDEN HARBOUR, THE ....*J. H. Pearce*	42
GRACE FOR A CHILD, A. Illustrated by J. D. Mackenzie ....*Robert Herrick*	402
GRAMMER GRACE'S CHEELD..*J. Henry Harris*	202
HEROIC ACTIONS OF LORD EXMOUTH, THE. Five illustrations................*A. H. Norway*	375
HOLIDAY CAMP AT PORT GAVERNE, A. Five illustrations ....*Charles N. Webster*	462
HOME, DEARIE, HOME. Illustrated by R. Morton Nance ....*W. E. Henley*	357

	PAGE
How to Develop Cornwall as a Holiday Resort	70, 157, 232
Hymn of Exile .... The Editor	483
Juggler, The. Five illustrations	230
Luck of Treyolla, The .... H. D. Lowry	333
Lyonesse .... James Dryden Hosken	94
Madame Fanny Moody at Home. Six illustrations .... Laura A. Smith	29
Magpie Jacket, The. Eight illustrations .... E. T. Sachs	298
Manacles, Around the. Twelve illustrations .... Albert Bluett	403
Man's Days .... Eden Phillpotts	41
Merry Ballad of the Cornish Pasty. Three illustrations .... R. Morton Nance	48
'Mohegan,' The, Why Was She Lost?	484
Morwenna of the Shades .... Arnold Lynton	220
Mystery of Joseph Laquedem, The .... The Editor	15
Newlyn Retrospect, A. Eight Illustrations .... Stanhope A. Forbes, A.R.A.	81
Newquay. Seven illustrations .... J. Henwood Thomas	140
Old Man's Corner. With illustrations	317, 394
Owners' Count Step, The .... Herbert Thomas	279
Pair of Hands, A .... The Editor	417
Piskies, The .... The Editor	181
Polly Postes .... The Rev. S. Baring-Gould	182
Pont Eliot. Ten illustrations .... Laura A. Smith	266
Press-Gang, The. Three illustrations by R. Morton Nance	261
Quakers, Stories of Cornish .... Sir Richard Tangye	485
Recollections of a Parish Worker	467
Remember .... Eden Phillpotts	455
Revenge in Arcady .... Fanny Spettigue	130
Romance in Hard Metal: an Interview with Mr. George Tangye. Thirteen illustrations Arthur Lawrence	339
Seven Virgins, The. Three illustrations by R. Morton Nance	438
Sir Henry Irving's Childhood. Six illustrations .... Arthur Brasher	105
St. Clether, The Well-Chapel of. Four illustrations .... The Rev. S. Baring-Gould	449
St. Levan Church. Five illustrations .... Thurstan C. Peter	476
Strong Man, A .... Charles Lee	60
To a Girl in the West .... H. D. Lowry	297
Truro Cathedral. Five illustrations.	
Its History .... Canon Donaldson	1
Its Future .... The Bishop of Truro	12
Two Noble Dames: Margaret Godolphin and Grace Grenville. Two portraits. A. H. Norway	51
Wesleys in Cornwall, Footprints of the. Ten illustrations .... H. Arthur Smith	241
'Western Morning News.' Ten illustrations .... Archibald S. Hurd	426
Wish 'Ee Well .... The Editor	79
Wisht Wood .... Charles Lee	252
Wrestling. Seven illustrations .... W. F. Collier	193

www.ingramcontent.com/pod-product-compliance
Lightning Source LLC
Chambersburg PA
CBHW051201300426
44116CB00006B/392